VALUES, RELIGION, AND CULTURE IN ADOLESCENT DEVELOPMENT

Cultural values and religious beliefs play a substantial role in adolescent development. Developmental scientists have shown increasing interest in how culture and religion are involved in the processes through which adolescents adapt to environments. This volume constitutes a timely and unique addition to the literature on human development from a cultural-contextual perspective. Editors Gisela Trommsdorff and Xinyin Chen present systematic and in-depth discussions of theoretical perspectives, landmark studies, and strategies for further research in the field. The eminent contributors reflect diverse cultural perspectives, transcending the Western emphasis of many previous works. This volume will be attractive to scholars and professionals interested in basic developmental processes, adolescent social psychology, and the sociological and psychological dimensions of religion.

Gisela Trommsdorff is Professor Emeritus for Developmental and Cross-Cultural Psychology at University of Konstanz. She is Research Professor at DIW/GSOEP, Berlin, and President of the German-Japanese Society for Social Sciences. Her main research interests are in intergenerational relations and children's socioemotional development in cultural contexts, including Asia, the United States, and Europe. She has published numerous book chapters and articles in international journals and is coeditor of several books. She has served on several editorial and advisory boards. She is a member of the Academy of Sciences in Erfurt and recipient of the German Federal Cross of Merit, 1st Class.

Xinyin Chen is Professor of Psychology at University of Pennsylvania. He is a Fellow of the American Psychological Association and the Association for Psychological Science and President-elect of the International Society for the Study of Behavioral Development. He is the recipient of a William T. Grant Scholars Award, a Shanghai Eastern Scholars Award, and several other academic awards for his scientific work. His primary research interests are in children's and adolescents' socioemotional functioning from a contextual-developmental perspective. He has published a number of book chapters and articles in major journals such as *Child Development* and *Developmental Psychology*.

THE JACOBS FOUNDATION SERIES ON ADOLESCENCE

Series Editors
Jürgen Baumert
Marta Tienda

The Jacobs Foundation Series on Adolescence presents state-of-the-art research about the myriad factors that contribute to the welfare, social productivity, and social inclusion of current and future generations of young people. Sponsored by the Swiss Jacobs Foundation, the series offers readers cutting-edge applied research about successful youth development, including circumstances that enhance their employability, their respect for and integration with nature and culture, and their future challenges triggered by global economic and technological changes. Contributing authors are internationally known scholars from a variety of disciplines, including developmental and social psychology, clinical psychology, education, economics, communication, sociology, and family studies.

Ann S. Masten, Karmela Liebkind, and Donald J. Hernandez, eds., *Realizing the Potential of Immigrant Youth*

Ingrid Schoon and Rainer K. Silbereisen, eds., *Transitions from School to Work: Globalization, Individualization, and Patterns of Diversity*

Alison Clarke-Stewart and Judy Dunn, eds., *Families Count: Effects on Child and Adolescent Development*

Michael Rutter and Marta Tienda, eds., *Ethnicity and Causal Mechanisms*

P. Lindsay Chase-Lansdale, Kathleen Kiernan, and Ruth J. Friedman, eds., *Human Development across Lives and Generations: The Potential for Change*

Anne-Nelly Perret-Clermont et al., eds., *Joining Society: Social Interaction and Learning in Adolescence and Youth*

Marta Tienda and William Julius Wilson, eds., *Youth in Cities: A Cross-National Perspective*

Roland Vandenberghe and A. Michael Huberman, eds., *Understanding and Preventing Teacher Burnout: A Sourcebook of International Research and Practice*

Ruby Takanishi and David A. Hamburg, eds., *Preparing Adolescents for the Twenty-First Century: Challenges Facing Europe and the United States*

Albert Bandura, ed., *Self-Efficacy in Changing Societies*

Michael Rutter, ed., *Psychosocial Disturbances in Young People: Challenges for Prevention*

Anne C. Petersen and Jeylan T. Mortimer, eds., *Youth Unemployment and Society*

Gisela Trommsdorff and Xinyin Chen, eds., *Values, Religion, and Culture in Adolescent Development*

Values, Religion, and Culture in Adolescent Development

Edited by

Gisela Trommsdorff
University of Konstanz

Xinyin Chen
University of Pennsylvania

CAMBRIDGE
UNIVERSITY PRESS

CAMBRIDGE UNIVERSITY PRESS
Cambridge, New York, Melbourne, Madrid, Cape Town,
Singapore, São Paulo, Delhi, Mexico City

Cambridge University Press
32 Avenue of the Americas, New York, NY 10013-2473, USA

www.cambridge.org
Information on this title: www.cambridge.org/9781107014251

© Cambridge University Press 2012

First published 2012

Printed in the United States of America

A catalog record for this publication is available from the British Library.

Library of Congress Cataloging in Publication data
    Values, religion, and culture in adolescent development / [edited by]
    Gisela Trommsdorff, Xinyin Chen.
       p.   cm. – (The Jacobs Foundation series on adolescence)
    Includes bibliographical references and index.
    ISBN 978-1-107-01425-1
    1. Adolescent psychology.   2. Values,   3. Religion and culture.
    I. Trommsdorff, Gisela.   II. Chen, Xinyin.
    BF724.V35   2013
    155.5′1825–dc23   2012006487

ISBN 978-1-107-01425-1 Hardback

In Memoriam of Professor Fred Rothbaum

Professor Fred Rothbaum (1949–2011) was an innovative scholar,
dedicated researcher, and a kind human being whose legacy will continue
to guide developmental psychology researchers around the world.

Contents

Contributors

Michael Harris Bond, Hong Kong Polytechnic University, China
Michael Harris Bond was born in Canada and educated at the University of Toronto. He received his PhD from Stanford University and postdoctoral at Michigan State University. Bond worked in Japan for three years at Kwansei Gakuin University, developing his skills in doing cross-cultural psychology. Thereafter, he was employed by the Chinese University of Hong Kong, remaining there and practicing social psychology for 35 years, trying to figure out the psychology of the Chinese people. Michael is currently chair professor of psychology in the Department of Applied Social Sciences, Hong Kong Polytechnic University, and looks forward to further intellectual adventures.

Xinyin Chen, University of Pennsylvania, United States
Xinyin Chen is professor of psychology at University of Pennsylvania. He is a Fellow of the American Psychological Association and the Association for Psychological Science and president-elect of the International Society for the Study of Behavioral Development. He is the recipient of a William T. Grant Scholars Award, a Shanghai Eastern Scholars Award, and several other academic awards for his scientific work. His primary research interests are in children's and adolescents' socioemotional functioning from a contextual-developmental perspective. He has published a number of book chapters and articles in major journals such as *Child Development* and *Developmental Psychology*.

Dov Cohen, University of Illinois, United States
Dov Cohen has been on faculty at University of Waterloo (Canada) and University of Illinois, where he is currently a professor of psychology. He is

the coauthor of *Culture of Honor* and coeditor of the *Handbook of Cultural Psychology* and *Culture and Social Behavior*.

Ella Daniel, University of Toronto, Canada
Ella Daniel is currently a postdoctoral Fellow in the Psychology Department at the University of Toronto. Her research focuses on understanding the development of values and identity in adolescence, using approaches from developmental, social, and cross-cultural psychology. Her doctoral dissertation at the Hebrew University of Jerusalem focused on the contextualization of values in relation to developmental stage and migration. She holds a BA in psychology from Ben Gurion University of the Negev, Israel, and an MA in social psychology from the Hebrew University of Jerusalem.

Nancy Eisenberg, Arizona State University, United States
Nancy Eisenberg is regents' professor at Arizona State University. She has published numerous books, chapters, and articles on socioemotional and moral development and is the editor of volume 3 of the *Handbook of Child Psychology*. She is currently the founding editor of the new Society for Research in Child Development journal, *Child Development Perspectives*, and is past editor of *Psychological Bulletin*. She is the 2007 recipient of the Ernest R. Hilgard Award for a Career Contribution to General Psychology, Division 1, American Psychological Association; the 2008 recipient of the International Society for the Study of Behavioral Development Distinguished Scientific Contribution Award; the 2009 recipient of the G. Stanley Hall Award Recipient Award for Distinguished Contribution to Developmental Psychology, Division 7, American Psychological Association; and the 2011 William James Fellow Career Contribution Award from the Association for Psychological Science.

Doran C. French, Purdue University, United States
Doran C. French is professor and department head of the Department of Human Development and Family Studies at Purdue University. He has published articles and chapters on various aspects of child and adolescent peer relationships, including social status, aggression, friendship, and school adjustment. His work on cultural psychology has included research in Indonesia, China, and South Korea. He has recently focused on understanding Islam and the social competence and adjustment of Indonesian adolescents.

Sigal Gabay, Tel Aviv University, Israel
Sigal Gabay is currently an MA student on the clinical psychology track, Psychology Department, Tel Aviv University, Israel. She holds a BA in psychology from the Hebrew University of Jerusalem.

Pehr Granqvist, Stockholm University, Sweden
Pehr Granqvist got his PhD from Uppsala University in 2002. He is currently associate professor in psychology and head of the PhD program in the Psychology Department, Stockholm University. His research has applied attachment theory to religion over the lifespan, including adolescent studies. He is the recipient of two international awards for this research, from the American Psychological Association and the International Association for the Psychology of Religion.

Aisha Griffith, University of Illinois, United States
Aisha Griffith is a doctoral student at University of Illinois, Urbana-Champaign. Her research interests include youth programs for adolescents and the adults who work at these programs.

Jessica Halliday Hardie, Pennsylvania State University, United States
Jessica Halliday Hardie is a NICHD postdoctoral Fellow in Family Demography and Individual Development at Pennsylvania State University. She is interested in how economic and social resources shape pathways through the transition to adulthood, and how this differs by social class, race/ethnicity, and gender. She employs a mixed-methods strategy in order to speak to both the social processes fueling inequality and the size of the population affected.

Lene Arnett Jensen, Clark University, United States
Lene Arnett Jensen is associate professor of psychology and director of the Developmental Psychology Program at Clark University. Dr. Jensen's research addresses cultural identity development in the contexts of migration and global change, immigrants' civic engagement, and how moral reasoning and behavior are culturally and developmentally situated. Her publications include *Immigrant Civic Engagement: New Translations* (2008, with C. A. Flanagan) and *Bridging Cultural and Developmental Psychology: New Syntheses for Theory, Research and Policy* (2012). Dr. Jensen is editor-in-chief of *New Directions for Child and Adolescent Development* (with Reed Larson), on the editorial board of Monographs of the Society for Research in Child Development, and the conference chair of the 2012 Biennial Conference of the Society for Research on Adolescence.

Hyeyoung Kang, Binghamton University, United States
Hyeyoung Kang is an assistant professor of human development at Binghamton University, State University of New York. Her research interests include youth development in diverse contexts, immigrant families and youth, and parent–adolescent relationships.

Ariel Knafo, Hebrew University of Jerusalem, Israel
Ariel Knafo is associate professor of psychology at the Hebrew University of Jerusalem. His research focuses on understanding social development using approaches from developmental, social, and cross-cultural psychology, as well as behavior genetics. His current projects involve understanding how value priorities in adolescence develop and the genetic and environmental contributions to prosociality. He earned his PhD in psychology at the Hebrew University of Jerusalem before postdoctoral fellowships in educational psychology at Ben Gurion University and in behavior genetics at the Institute of Psychiatry, King's College London.

Hans-Joachim Kornadt, University of the Saarland, Germany
Hans-Joachim Kornadt is professor emeritus of educational psychology at the University of the Saarland, Saarbrücken, Germany. He conducted research in Africa and East and South-East Asia and holds several guest professorships in Japan and Indonesia. He was a member of the German National Science Advisory Council, president of the German Psychological Association, and president of the Japanese-German Society for Social Sciences. His research interests include pro- and antisocial motives and socialization in a cross-cultural perspective, and psychological aspects of changes in university and higher education. He has numerous publications about socialization and personality development in different cultures, aggression, and education.

Reed W. Larson, University of Illinois, United States
Reed W. Larson is a professor in the Departments of Human and Community Development, Psychology, and Educational Psychology at the University of Illinois at Urbana-Champaign. His research focuses on the daily developmental experience of adolescents, particularly in the context of youth development programs and families. He is the author of *Divergent Realities: The Emotional Lives of Mothers, Fathers, and Adolescents* (with Maryse Richards) and *Being Adolescent: Conflict and Growth in the Teenage Years* (with Mihaly Csikszentmihalyi). He was recently the chair of the Study Group on Adolescence in the 21st Century, is the editor-in-chief of *New Directions for Child and Adolescent Development* (with Lene Jensen), and was recently the president of the Society for Research on Adolescence.

Liman Man Wai Li, University of Alberta, Canada
Liman Man Wai Li was born in Hong Kong and received her master's degree at the Chinese University. She is now a graduate student in the Psychology Department at the University of Alberta, interested in examining how

cultural/environmental factors interact with individuals' characteristics in predicting individuals' psychological and behavior tendencies.

Junsheng Liu, Shanghai Normal University, China
Junsheng Liu is an associate professor in the Department of Psychology at Shanghai Normal University. He was a visiting scholar at the University of Western Ontario, Canada, and the University of Pennsylvania in 2010 and 2011. Dr. Liu has received a Pujiang Scholars Award, a Chenguang Scholars Award, and several other academic awards. His research focuses on children's and adolescents' social development. He is particularly interested in children's experiences within the peer group. He has conducted several longitudinal projects in China with his international colleagues.

Vivian Miu-Chi Lun, Lingnan University, China
Vivian Miu-Chi Lun was born in Hong Kong and received her education there up to earning her MPhil at the Chinese University. She then undertook her PhD study at the Victoria University of Wellington in New Zealand, where she had much intercultural experience and started thinking of herself as a global citizen. After finishing her PhD, she worked as a part-time lecturer and then later a postdoctoral researcher at the City University of Hong Kong. She is currently working as an assistant professor in the Department of Sociology and Social Policy, Lingnan University, with a goal of exploring further in psychological research.

Sami Mahajna, Beit Berl College, Israel
Sami Mahajna received his PhD in Education and Human Development from the University of Haifa, Israel, in 2007. His dissertation (supervised by Prof. Rachel Seginer) examined the meaning of future orientation for Arab girls in Israel. With a grant he recently received from the Jacobs Foundation, Dr. Mahajna continues his research on adolescent future orientation and examines the developmental aspects of future orientation among Arab girls and boys in Israel. At present he is the chairperson of the Early Childhood program at the Academic Arab Institute for Teacher Education, Beit Berl College, Israel.

Tina Malti, University of Toronto, Canada
Tina Malti, PhD (2003, Developmental Psychology, Max Planck Institute for Human Development and Free University Berlin), is an assistant professor in the Department of Psychology at the University of Toronto. Her research interests are children's and adolescents' moral and social-emotional development, mental health, and developmental intervention to promote social responsibility and well-being.

Boris Mayer, University of Konstanz, Germany
Boris Mayer grew up in southern Germany and received his education in psychology at the University of Konstanz. During his doctoral studies he taught developmental psychology at the same university. His long-standing interest in culture and human development deepened during a research internship in South Korea when he was confronted with a completely different social reality and language. Currently he is a postdoctoral researcher and lecturer of cross-cultural psychology and psychological research methods at the University of Konstanz. His research interests are in adolescent development across cultures as well as in cultural change and globalization. He coedited the book *Psychologie – Kultur – Gesellschaft* [*Psychology – Culture – Society*] and has coauthored several empirical journal articles, published in, among others, the *Journal of Cross-Cultural Psychology*.

Kristina McDonald, University of Alabama, United States
Kristina McDonald received her PhD in developmental psychology from Duke University. She is a research associate at the University of Alabama. Her research interests include peer relationships and social-cognitive processes underlying problematic social behaviors, like aggression.

Ramesh Chandra Mishra, Banaras Hindu University, India
Ramesh Chandra Mishra is professor of psychology at Banaras Hindu University. A D.Phil. from Allahabad University, he has been postdoctoral research Fellow, Shastri research Fellow, and visiting professor at Queen's University, Canada. He has also been a Fellow-in-residence of the Netherlands Institute for Advanced Study in the Humanities and Social Sciences (NIAS), the Netherlands, and a visiting professor at the University of Geneva and Jean Piaget Archives, Switzerland. His principal interest is in cultural influence on human development, and he has contributed numerous research papers and chapters to professional journals and books, both in India and abroad, in the fields of cognition, acculturation, schooling, and cross-cultural studies. He is the coauthor of *Ecology, Acculturation and Psychological Adaptation: A Study of Adivasis in Bihar* (with J. W. Berry and D. Sinha) and *Eco-Cultural Pathways to Geocentric Language and Cognition* (with P. Dasen) and coeditor (with J. W. Berry and R. C. Tripathi) of *Psychology in Human and Social Development: Lessons from Diverse Cultures*.

Bernhard Nauck, Chemnitz University of Technology, Germany
Bernhard Nauck has been the founding chair of sociology at the Chemnitz University of Technology, Germany, since 1992. He received a PhD in 1977 (University of Cologne) and Habilitation in 1983 and 1987 (University of

Bonn and Augsburg). He has been president of the sections for Sociology of Family and Youth and for Migration and Ethnic Minorities in the German Sociological Association and of the Committee on Family Research (RC06) in the International Sociological Association. He is currently the president of the executive committee of GESIS, the German Social Science Infrastructure Services, and P.I. and speaker of PAIRFAM, the German Family Panel. His research interests include family, lifespan, intergenerational relationships, demography, migration, and interethnic relations with an emphasis on cross-cultural comparisons.

Vinai Norasakkunkit, Minnesota State University, United States
Vinai Norasakkunkit received his PhD from University of Massachusetts, Boston, and is associate professor of psychology at Minnesota State University, Mankato. His research interests are in the intersection of cultural psychology and clinical psychology, as well as the psychological consequences of globalization.

Lisa D. Pearce, University of North Carolina at Chapel Hill, United States
Lisa D. Pearce is associate professor of sociology and Carolina population center research Fellow at the University of North Carolina at Chapel Hill. Her research focuses on religion's influence on well-being and family attitudes and behavior in adolescence and young adulthood. She studies these processes in the United States and Nepal using both quantitative and qualitative data. Pearce recently published the book *A Faith of Their Own: Stability and Change in the Religiosity of American Adolescents* with Melinda Lundquist Denton (2011).

Urip Purwono, Universitas Padjadjaran, Indonesia
Urip Purwono received his Drs. in Psychology (Clinical) from Universitas Padjadjaran, Bandung, Indonesia; MS (Education) from Indiana University, Bloomington, Indiana; and MSc and PhD in psychology from the University of Massachusetts at Amherst. His methodological research interests include test theory, test construction, test adaptation, and structural equation modeling. His research also focuses on youth's achievement, values, and religiosity as they are related to the individual's well-being. In addition, he develops educational tests that are widely used in Indonesia.

Vikki Rompala, La Rabida Children's Hospital, Chicago, United States
Vikki Rompala is a licensed clinical social worker. Her clinical, research, and policy experience in child welfare, youth development, and school-based outpatient clinics, hospitals, and in-home services has provides a wider perspective of the overlaps among systems and provides a voice for families and children who are often disenfranchised within these systems.

Fred Rothbaum, Tufts University, United States
Fred Rothbaum was professor and director of graduate studies in the Eliot-Pearson Department of Child Development at Tufts University. He published widely on socialization and cultural processes as they relate to children's perceived control, behavior problems, attachment, and emotion regulation. Dr. Rothbaum also cofounded the Child and Family WebGuide, a Web portal providing research to parents, professionals, and students.

Kenneth H. Rubin, University of Maryland, United States
Kenneth H. Rubin is professor of human development and director of the Center for Children, Relationships, and Culture at the University of Maryland. He received his BA from McGill University (1968) and his MS (1969) and PhD (1971) from the Pennsylvania State University. Ken Rubin is a Fellow of the Canadian and American Psychological Associations and the Association of Psychological Science. In 2008, Rubin received the International Society for the Study of Behavioral Development Award for Distinguished Contributions to the International Advancement of Research and Theory in Behavioral Development, and in 2010 he was awarded the Mentoring Award in Developmental Psychology by the American Psychological Association. He has twice served as associate editor of *Child Development* (1981–1984; 1998–2002) and is currently on several editorial boards. Rubin was president of the International Society for the Study of Behavioral Development from 1998 to 2002; he is currently a member of the Governing Council of the Society for Research in Child Development. During his career, Rubin has published twenty books – including *The Friendship Factor*, which won the Gold Award, National Parenting Publications Awards – and more than 300 peer-reviewed chapters and journal manuscripts on such topics as social competence, social cognition, play, aggression, social withdrawal/behavioral inhibition/shyness, parenting, and children's peer and family relationships. More recently, as director of the International Consortium on the Study of Children, Relationships, and Culture (research sites include Argentina, Australia, Brazil, Canada, China, India, Italy, Korea, Oman, Portugal, and the United States), he and his colleagues have been studying the aforementioned topics from cultural and cross-cultural perspectives. Rubin is currently principal investigator on a project funded by the National Institute of Mental Health entitled "A Multi-Method Early Intervention Program for Socially Reticent, Inhibited Preschoolers" and Co–Principal Investigator on a project funded by the National Institute of Child Health and Human Development entitled "Social Outcomes in Pediatric Traumatic Brain Injury."

Julie A. Sallquist, Arizona State University, United States
Julie A. Sallquist graduated with her PhD in psychology in the area of developmental psychology from Arizona State University in 2009 and is an assistant research professor in the School of Social and Family Dynamics at Arizona State University. Dr. Sallquist's research interests include the socioemotional and cognitive development of young children, the socialization of emotion, and children's peer interactions, with an emphasis on positive affect and adjustment. She also has an interest in cross-cultural research and has been involved in research studies examining Indonesian adolescents' and Ugandan children's socioemotional functioning.

Vassilis Saroglou, University of Louvain, Belgium
Vassilis Saroglou holds a PhD in psychology (University of Louvain) and has studied psychology (MA), religious sciences (MA), and philosophy (BS). He is a professor in the Department of Psychology at the University of Louvain (Belgium) and has been a Fulbright scholar at William and Mary (Virginia), adjunct professor at Arizona State University, and visiting professor at the University of Lille (France). His research has covered many issues in personality, social, cultural, and developmental psychology of religion and led to more than 80 scientific publications. For his research, he received the Early Career Award of the American Psychological Association–Division 36 and the Quinquennial Godin Prize of the International Association for the Psychology of Religion. He currently serves on the editorial boards of the major journals of the field, as an associate editor of the *International Journal for the Psychology of Religion*, and as president of the International Association for the Psychology of Religion.

Shalom H. Schwartz, Hebrew University of Jerusalem, Israel
Shalom H. Schwartz is emeritus professor of psychology at the Hebrew University and scientific supervisor at the International Laboratory of Socio-Cultural Research at the Higher School of Economics, Moscow. He has also taught at the Universities of Wisconsin and Princeton. He is a past president of the International Association for Cross-Cultural Psychology and a Fellow of the American Psychological Association. His individual and culture level value theories have been used in research in more than 75 countries. His current research applies his value theories in the fields of politics, religion, and ethnicity.

Rachel Seginer, University of Haifa, Israel
Rachel Seginer is professor emerita of human development and education in the Faculty of Education, University of Haifa, Israel. Her research and

teaching in developmental psychology has focused on adolescent development in cultural settings examining relationships with parents, siblings, and peers, parents' educational involvement, and future orientation. Her book *Future Orientation: Developmental and Ecological Perspectives* (2009), reviews her work on future orientation, its antecedents and outcomes and integrates research carried out since the 1930s on future orientation and interfacing approaches across the lifespan and divergent cultural settings.

Rivka Shir, Hebrew University of Jerusalem, Israel
Rivka Shir is currently a BA student in psychology in the psychology department, at the Hebrew University of Jerusalem. Her research interests focus on the development of altruism in decision making and on the role of religion with regard to values.

Anja Steinbach, University of Duisburg-Essen, Germany
Anja Steinbach is professor of sociology at the University of Duisburg-Essen; she received her PhD in 2003 and Habilitation in 2010 (Chemnitz University of Technology). She has been lecturer, senior researcher, and manager of PAIRFAM, the German Family Panel, at Chemnitz University of Technology. She currently serves as president of the section for Sociology of Family in the German Sociological Association. Her research focus is on step-families, division of household labor, intergenerational relationships, and migrant families.

Gisela Trommsdorff, University of Konstanz, Germany
Gisela Trommsdorff is professor emeritus for developmental and cross-cultural psychology at the University of Konstanz. She is research professor at DIW/GSOEP, Berlin, and president of the German-Japanese Society for Social Sciences. Her main research interests are in intergenerational relations and children's socioemotional development in cultural contexts, including Asia, the United States, and Europe. She has published numerous book chapters and articles in international journals and is coeditor of several books. She has served on several editorial and advisory boards. She is member of the Academy of Sciences in Erfurt and recipient of the German Federal Cross of Merit, 1st Class.

Yukiko Uchida, Kyoto University, Japan
Yukiko Uchida received her PhD from Kyoto University in 2003. She is associate professor in the Kokoro Research Center, Kyoto University. She has investigated how culture shapes emotional experiences and social relationships, as well as happiness and subjective well-being across cultures.

Contributors

xxiii

Li Wang, Peking University, China

Li Wang is an associate professor in the Psychology Department, Peking University. Her research focuses on children's social emotion and emotion regulation and their role in social, school, and psychological adjustment from a contextual-developmental perspective. She has conducted, in collaboration with her international colleagues, a series of longitudinal projects on Chinese and Western children's social emotion development. She is also interested in how schools, families, and peers influence the development of social functioning in early childhood. She has published in many journals such as *Child Development*, *International Journal of Behavioral Development*, and *Pediatrics*.

Yan Z. Wang, Endicott College, United States

Yan Z. Wang is assistant professor at Endicott College. Dr. Wang has published on methodological issues in cultural studies, dinnertime family interactions, and immigrant parenting.

Ran Zilber, Tel Aviv University, Israel

Ran Zilber is currently an MA student on the clinical psychology track, Psychology Department, Tel Aviv University. He holds a BA in psychology from the Hebrew University of Jerusalem.

Preface

The focus of this volume is the development of adolescents' values and religiosity in cultural context. Values are a major motivational and normative basis for the development of individual identity, belief systems, and behaviors. Moreover, values serve to guide social processes in interpersonal interactions. Similarly, religious beliefs and practices play a significant role in adolescent social behaviors, relationships, and adjustment. Adolescents' values and religiosity are typically related to cultural norms and models. Cultural factors affect what specific values and religious beliefs are endorsed by adolescents in the society and how value and religious systems direct their beliefs, decision making, and actions during their development.

However, research on adolescents' values and religiosity has unfortunately been conducted primarily in Western societies, and the role of the cultural context has received relatively little attention in both theoretical and empirical approaches. As a result, our understanding of adolescents' values and religious functioning has been largely limited to Western, particularly North American, cultures.

Over the past few decades, interest in the role of culture in value and religious development in adolescence has burgeoned and has expanded exponentially in many regions of the world, particularly Asia, Europe, the Middle East, and South America. A number of research programs have developed in different cultural contexts; the findings so far are inconsistent. In this volume, we intend to address the questions of whether and how adolescent values and religious beliefs and behaviors may vary in their prevalence, interpretations, causes, and consequences across cultures. For example, across cultures, adolescents may differ in their perceived importance of values such as personal achievement and group well-being. There are also substantial cultural variations in religious orientation, beliefs, practices, and involvement. Relatedly, cultural values guide the interpretation of specific values, religious beliefs, and behaviors and thus impart psychological "meanings" related to a worldview. Consequently, the developmental processes and patterns of values and religion may differ from one culture to another.

In preparation for this volume, the editors organized an international and interdisciplinary conference in 2010 at the Marbach Castle, supported by the Jacobs Foundation. At the conference, 25 scholars from Europe, the United States, Israel, Canada, China, Palestine, Japan, Indonesia, and India presented their studies and, together with 10 junior researchers, discussed issues related to values and religion in youth development. The conference cut across several areas of psychology, sociology, and religious studies. This book is largely a product of the conference, although the chapters in the book do not simply summarize the conference presentations and discussions. The book builds on intensive discussions and further research following the conference. The authors of each chapter attempt to provide a novel and broad perspective on culture, values, and religion in youth development, and to integrate theoretical approaches and empirical findings on a particular topic.

The chapters in this volume are concerned with various issues in the field, such as the impact of social changes and cultural conditions on values and religious orientations and practices, culturally prescribed socialization processes in value and religious development, the cultural interpretations of adolescents' religious experience and expression, and adaptive and maladaptive values and religious activities from a cultural perspective. The authors have incorporated into their discussions findings from research programs that have used multiple methodologies, including both qualitative (e.g., interviewing) and quantitative (e.g., large-scale surveys, standardized questionnaires) approaches, and adolescents in cultures from East to West and from South to North (Asia, the Middle East, Eastern Europe, and ethnic groups in the United States, and Western and Eastern Europe). The authors also pay attention to various religious and nonreligious groups (e.g., Christian, Jewish, Muslim, Buddhist, and Hindu for religious groups).

This volume consists of 18 chapters in 4 parts. It is unique in that it focuses on social and cultural contexts, includes perspectives from multidisciplinary backgrounds, and presents recent research findings based on diverse methodologies. Most chapters are organized according to theoretical issues with an in-depth discussion of related empirical findings concerning basic developmental processes, culture, social values, and religion. The volume is of interest not only to social and behavioral scientists who study adolescent development, but also to sociologists, economists, and political scientists. This volume is also useful to educators and practitioners (e.g., counseling and clinical psychologists, social workers) who provide services to youth, particularly with diverse cultural backgrounds.

To conclude, values and religion as part of cultural context obviously play a substantial role in adolescent development. As most societies in today's world are undergoing rapid changes, how values, religious beliefs, and culture affect social competence, attitudes, and behaviors of adolescents in their adaptation to the new environment is an important issue for developmental scientists. Our goal in putting together this volume is to provide a forum for systematic and in-depth discussions of theoretical perspectives, research findings, existing problems in the research, and strategies to solve the problems in this area. We hope these discussions will be conducive to a better understanding of adolescent development in a changing context and further exploration of the involvement of contextual factors in development in the future.

Acknowledgments

This volume could not be produced without the substantial contribution of the authors and the support of many individuals. Therefore, we are indebted to all who contributed to this book.

We are particularly grateful to Simon Sommer, who was responsible for coordinating the conference. He always provided helpful advice in solving problems in the preparation and organization of the conference. The editors also owe special thanks to the Advisory Board of the Jacobs Foundation for their trust and support.

The volume also benefited from other participants in the conference who did not author a chapter in this volume but who contributed to the discussion at the conference. We want to express our gratitude to Jeanette Ziehm for her careful secretarial support, her continuous highly responsible assistance throughout all the stages of the production of this volume, and her patience and efficiency in managing unexpected work loads. Finally, we want to thank Holly Bunje for her language editing of three contributions, and the staff of Cambridge University Press for their work in producing this volume.

Part One

THEORETICAL PERSPECTIVES ON VALUES,
RELIGION, AND ADOLESCENT DEVELOPMENT
IN CULTURAL CONTEXT

1 Cultural Perspectives on Values and Religion in Adolescent Development

A Conceptual Overview and Synthesis

Gisela Trommsdorff

Abstract

This chapter discusses why research on adolescent development will benefit from a focus on values and religion using a culture-sensitive approach. In the first part, the relations among culture, values, and religion in adolescent development are briefly summarized. The second part deals with the topic of adolescent values, and the third part addresses religion and religiosity. Each part discusses relevant research from a multidisciplinary perspective and highlights major issues, results, and gaps in sociological and psychological research. Finally, the theoretical and empirical contributions of this volume are discussed, and suggestions are made for future research in order to achieve a better understanding of adolescent development in a changing cultural context.

Can a cultural perspective on adolescent values and religion contribute to a better understanding of the dynamics of adolescent development? Adolescents experience major biological, psychological, and social transitions that may be characterized as relatively universal developmental challenges (Graber & Brooks-Gunn, 1996). However, research has primarily focused on European-American adolescents, disregarding the cultural context of development. This is surprising given that Bronfenbrenner (1979) introduced an ecological perspective into developmental psychology more than three decades ago. Even globalization and growing awareness of the cultural and socioeconomic diversity of adolescent environments have rarely resulted in empirical research (Steinberg & Morris, 2001). Only recently were some culture-informed edited volumes (e.g., Arnett, 2012; Brown, Larson, & Saraswathi, 2002) and theoretically based culture-sensitive reviews (Arnett, 2011) on adolescent development published.

What can a culture-sensitive approach to adolescent development contribute? First, it may help clarify questions about how values and religion impact adolescent development. Values and religion are assumed to be important in adolescent development as part of the formation of a meaningful view of the self and the world (Rothbaum & Wang, 2010; Trommsdorff, 2012). The construction of self- and world-views is often motivated by identity development, one of the main developmental tasks in adolescence (Erikson, 1968). Identity has been seen as providing a sense of coherence and continuity in one's life, thereby reducing uncertainty and confusion in understanding oneself, one's relation to others, and the world. However, it is not clear which factors contribute to the processes and outcomes of identity development. For example, an extension of the social and cultural boundaries and contexts because of an increasing globalization has given rise to multiple choices in identity development (Azmitia, Syed, & Radmacher, 2008).

The present volume attempts to clarify the role of culture, values, and religion as the assumed major factors in adolescent development. These factors are seen here as part of interrelated meaning systems influencing self- and world-views. They are also seen as part of social institutions and personal (e.g., peer, parent–child) relationships representing distant and proximal contexts for adolescents' development. A number of open issues have to be dealt with to achieve a better understanding of how adolescent development is related to the cultural context, values, and religion, and how these affect the development of adolescents' self- and world-views, goals, behavior, everyday practices, and social adjustment.

In this overview, I begin with a brief outline of the main issues in past research on adolescent development in cultural context. This is followed by sections on values and youth and on religion and youth, both from a culture-informed perspective. These two sections note open questions from past research and highlight insights from this volume regarding the interrelations of culture, values, and religion in adolescent development. As a whole, this volume is organized around four major issues in research on adolescent development, each of which is affected by the multiple interrelations of culture, values, and religion: (1) theoretical perspectives, (2) universal and culture-specific functions of values and religion in adolescent development, (3) adolescent adjustment in times of social change, and (4) socialization processes of values and religion in adolescent development.

Culture, Values, and Religion in Adolescent Development

What do we know about adolescent development cross-culturally in a globalizing world where different values and religions prevail?

Developmental science assumes basic processes of development ranging from biological, psychological, and social functions to societal, ecological, cultural, and historical levels (e.g., Lerner, Lewin-Bizan, & Warren, 2011). Adolescent development is a period in the lifespan that includes systematic successive changes in the person, based on changes at the biological, psychological, social, and cultural levels, with nature and nurture interacting in the dynamics of development. The dynamic systems approach to adolescent development (Kunnen, 2012) attempts to provide explanations for stability and change based on nonlinear interaction processes. Normative and history-graded factors are especially relevant in adolescence and early adulthood (Baltes & Brim, 1980). These factors are regarded here as part of individual-context relations, assuming that their influence is modified by cultural phenomena and individual agency in development. This assumption has recently stimulated some culture-informed research (see Arnett, 2006, 2011, 2012; Brown et al., 2002), but many questions still remain unanswered. Therefore, a main purpose of this volume is to clarify whether and in which aspects adolescent development is similar or different in varying parts of the world, and what role values and religion play in adolescent development in different cultural contexts.

Our interest in cultural perspectives on values and religion in adolescent development is informed by ecological theorizing (Bronfenbrenner, 1979), questions regarding interactions between person and context ("goodness of fit"), and the assumption of adolescents as agents of their development. From an ecological perspective, values and religion constitute developmental contexts where family, peers, and school play important roles in adolescents' socialization in the respective culture. The goal of the culture-informed ecological approach is to take into account cross-cultural and intracultural differences in adolescent development while also analyzing universal processes. However, research to date has largely neglected the role of culture with respect to the function of values and religion in adolescent development. Therefore, the purpose of this chapter is to provide an overview of the relevant literature, note unanswered questions, and describe the contributions of chapters in this volume, all of which highlight the importance of cultural variables for values and religion in adolescents' development.

Cultural variables have been related to various macrolevel variables such as aspects of socioeconomic status (e.g., economic growth, educational level, urbanization, etc.), and to the individual-level variables of value orientation and religiosity. Both levels of cultural variables are relevant for developmental processes and outcomes. "Culture" has been conceptualized in different ways in past research. Sociologists have described culture with collective and individual representations (Durkheim, 1981) or as "norm-cycles" in line with an "objective" culture (Elder-Vass, 2010). Anthropologists have described cultures with respect to rituals, myths, symbols (Jahoda, 2007), cultural practices (Cole & Packer, 2011), or *"Gemeinschaft"–"Gesellschaft"* (Greenfield, 2010). Psychologists have used the concepts of cultural dimensions (e.g., individualism, collectivism; Hofstede, 1980; Triandis, 1995), tight and loose cultures (Gelfand et al., 2011), shared meaning systems (Bruner, 1990), cultural tasks (Kitayama & Imada, 2010), or cultural models of agency (e.g., independence, interdependence) describing how specific beliefs, values, and practices vary across nations (Markus & Kitayama, 1991). Here, I perceive culture as a complex, major developmental context offering specific *cultural models of agency*, which imply certain self- and world-views (Rothbaum & Wang, 2010; Trommsdorff, 2012). These cultural models of agency influence further developmental contexts on different levels of socialization, such as at the macrolevel of economic, educational, and religious institutions and the microlevel of the family.

Developmental contexts can undergo processes of *historical* and *social change*. Adolescents in many parts of the world experience sociopolitical, economic, and cultural changes that have an impact on their lives (e.g., regarding family, employment, technology, mobility, health). Several reviews on adolescent development have shown that the experience of transitions and changes does not necessarily result in problematic or difficult development (e.g., Coleman, 2011; Steinberg, 1999). Empirical research has dealt with questions of whether certain political and socioeconomic changes include risks and chances and how these impact adolescent development (e.g., Chen, 2012; Chen & French, 2008; Elder & Shanahan, 2006; Kagitcibasi, 2006, 2007; Trommsdorff, 2009b). However, several questions remain, some of which are dealt with in this volume by focusing on different cultures, values, and religious orientations. For example, issues during times of social change are examined by discussing the impact of values for adjustment (see Norasakkunkit & Uchida, Chapter 9 in this volume, for Japanese youth; Chen, Wang, & Liu, Chapter 10 in this volume, for Chinese youth).

An important aspect of adolescents' development is related to *values* in the cultural context. Adolescents undergo processes of identity development that reflect on cultural and individual values and beliefs as part of one's relation to the world. During this developmental period of constructing self- and world-views (see Kornadt, Chapter 2 in this volume; Rothbaum, Wang, & Cohen, Chapter 3 in this volume), adolescents are determining which values to adopt to guide their own individual development, including goal setting, decision making, and behavior (e.g., Alsaker & Kroger, 2006). Because there is little research on the role of cultural factors in the development of values, related questions – including questions of cultural fit (as a condition for positive development) and processes in the socialization and transmission of values among peers or from parents to their adolescent children – are addressed in all sections of this volume.

Assuming that the development of adolescents' values is related to more general cultural value orientations, questions also arise as to whether and in which way values are related to *religion* and individual religiosity, and whether religion and religiosity have a specific function in adolescent development. In past research, the relations between values and religion have seldom been studied systematically. Researchers have usually investigated values and religion in relative isolation. Exceptions are Rokeach (1969) and a meta-analysis by Saroglou, Delpierre, and Dernelle (2004).

Past neglect of this issue may be owing to a relative lack of psychological research on the role of religiosity and religion in adolescent development (Roelkepartain, King, Wagener, & Benson, 2005). Recently, questions that have been of specific interest include whether the often-assumed increase in secularization, the rise of religious fundamentalism, and the development of new forms of spirituality are relevant to positive youth development (King & Roeser, 2009). For a fruitful study of these questions, researchers must take into account both cultural variables and the effect these variables may have on adolescents' developmental pathways.

Therefore, the present volume attempts to address the relations between culture, religion, and values in adolescent development. These issues are discussed with respect to theoretical approaches and empirical studies focusing on socialization conditions for developmental outcomes such as adolescent adjustment. For example, Kornadt (Chapter 2) discusses theoretical questions on the roles of culture, values, and religion in adolescent development from historical, motivation-psychological, and cultural perspectives. Rothbaum, Wang, and Cohen (Chapter 3) provide a theoretical framework assuming cultural differences in the development and quality of self-awareness related to differences in spirituality. Saroglou (Chapter 17) integrates empirical findings into a theoretical approach on the psychological functions of religiosity as an individual difference dimension, pointing out the different impact of religion on personal stability as compared to personal growth. This approach is related to questions on developmental outcomes and conditions. Other chapter topics include the role of culture, values, and religion in adjustment of Indian (Mishra, Chapter 18) and Indonesian Muslim youth (French, Eisenberg, Purwono, & Sallquist, Chapter 6), as well as the role of religion and culture in life-satisfaction (Bond, Lun, & Li, Chapter 5), in future orientation of Israeli Palestinian girls (Seginer & Mahajna, Chapter 11), in career orientation of U.S. girls (Pearce & Hardie, Chapter 12), and in romantic relationships of Israeli and German adolescents (Nauck & Steinbach, Chapter 13). Several authors deal with the socialization and developmental conditions for the role of culture, religion, and values in adolescent development. For example, Granqvist discusses preconditions and implications of attachment in the development of adolescents' self- and world-views. Socialization in the family in different cultures is discussed by several authors (e.g., Knafo, Daniel, Gabay, Zilber, & Shir, Chapter 16; Mayer & Trommsdorff, Chapter 15; Rubin, Malti, & McDonald, Chapter 8), as are the effects of culture and socialization in the peer group (Chen et al., Chapter 10; French et al., Chapter 6; Larson, Jensen, Kang, Griffith, & Rompala, Chapter 7). Cultural socialization in different educational institutions is discussed by Mishra for Indian youth (Chapter 18).

To summarize, the work in this volume assumes that cultural models of agency give meaning to values and religion and also influence their role in adolescent development. However, studies on the nature, correlates, and function of adolescents' values and religious orientations in cultural contexts are rare in developmental research. Therefore, selected major theoretical and empirical contributions to this topic, open questions, and insights from chapters of this volume are summarized in the following overviews on values and religion.

Values and Youth from a Culture-Informed Perspective

Theoretical and Empirical Approaches to Values

From a social sciences and psychological perspective, values are embedded in culture: they impact the societal institutions and they structure, motivate, and give meaning to individual behavior and social interactions. The meaning of certain values is influenced by the self- and world-view transmitted in a certain culture. For example, the values of freedom, honor, and justice have different meanings in different cultural contexts. In line with Schwartz (1992), values are defined here as desirable, transsituationally enduring goals that vary in importance and serve as guiding principles in people's lives. The internalization of cultural values constitutes an important developmental task for adolescents in all cultures.

Sociological Approaches. Weber (1988) and Parsons (1951), the founding fathers of value research in sociology, distinguished between individual values (motivational aspects) and group values (normative aspects; Parsons & Shils, 1951). Interestingly, although this differentiation is difficult to assess empirically, it still guides most research on values. More recently, theories on modernization and secularization have shifted the perspective in value research, focusing on questions of stability and changes in values.

Early value research assumed that the cultural context is interwoven with values, norms, and meaning. An example is the famous Values Project by Kluckhohn and Strodtbeck (1961), which was influenced by sociologists (e.g., Talcott Parsons), social psychologists (George Homans), and anthropologists (John and Beatrice Whiting), among others. This Values Project was a starting point for several studies to focus on value orientations as a means to differentiate cultural dimensions. However, according to D'Andrade (2008), the study of cultural values was left without an organizing framework. In his recent study on value orientations in three societies, D'Andrade (2008) dealt with institutionalized values, personal values, and the degree of fit between both, thus relating issues from sociological and psychological value research in his anthropological approach on personal and cultural values. Across societies, he did not see many differences in personal values due to universal needs and motives; however, differences in institutionalized values were great. The antecedents of values are seen in the cultural heritage of ideas, in institutions (norms, roles), and in individual feelings and motives. Accordingly, some values may be stable while other values may change.

The influential sociological theory on value change by Ronald Inglehart (1977, 1997, 2007) assumes that values change from materialism (traditional values) to post-materialism in industrializing countries. Traditional "materialist" values are seen in the need for security, achievement, and discipline; modern "post-materialist" values include the need for self-realization, participation, and environmental concerns (Inglehart & Baker, 2000). Three basic assumptions underlie Inglehart's theory on the "silent revolution": (1) the socialization thesis, which assumes a lifelong stability of values that are formed in early childhood; (2) the thesis of a generation-specific value change, which contrasts to the life-cycle assumption and to the assumption of period effects (historical events such as the postwar period or reunification of Germany); and (3) the basic-need thesis, which refers to Maslow's (1943) assumption of a hierarchy of material and nonmaterial needs. Adolescent development is of special importance to Inglehart because he believes that changes in adolescents' values can drive societal value changes.

Inglehart's (1977, 1997, 2007) assumptions on long-term effects of socialization experiences in childhood and adolescence, on the validity of Maslow's theory on a hierarchy of needs, and on the effects of modernization as typical for industrial societies has been criticized on theoretical and empirical grounds. Related discussions have stimulated an extensive research program in social and political science based on national comparisons of value change, partly modifying Inglehart's original theory (Inglehart & Welzel, 2005). The Eurobarometer, the European Values Study (EVS), the World Values Survey (WVS), and other sources of data were coordinated for the European Social Survey (ESS; e.g., Inglehart, Basañez, & Moreno, 1998; Jowell, Kaase, Fitzgerald, & Eva, 2007). These comparative studies have challenged the assumption that secularization is increasing while the value of religiosity is declining (e.g., Pettersson, 2007).

Another major topic in the discussions on value change is whether an individualization of family values has taken place. In their study on two decades of value change in Europe and the United States (based on the European Values Study), Scott and Braun (2006) concluded that the individualization thesis is overstated because considerable diversity in family values across Western countries can be observed. This result is in line with research on the similarities and differences of family values of adolescents across Western and Asian societies, and across "modern" versus traditional countries (Mayer & Trommsdorff, 2010; Chapter 15 in this volume). Furthermore, cross-cultural studies on value change have shown that value changes do not follow the same patterns; for example, "traditional" and "modern" values can coexist (e.g., Chen, 2012; Kagitsibasi, 2006, 2007; Trommsdorff, 2007; Trommsdorff, Cole, & Heikamp, in press; Trommsdorff, Suzuki, & Sasaki, 1987).

Chapters in this volume focusing on family-related values in different cultures present results that underline the impact of religious belief in the specific cultural context. These results specify the interrelations among culture, values, and religion regarding family values (e.g., Mayer & Trommsdorff, Chapter 15; Nauck & Steinbach, Chapter 13; Seginer & Mahajna, Chapter 11).

In general, the assessment of values and value change has to differentiate between the cultural/societal and the individual levels. More specifically, questions regarding the stability and change of values and the different phenomena of value change over the lifespan and across situations remain to be discussed. Most important, the confounding effects of time period, cohort, and aging have to be disentangled. This brings us to *psychological approaches.*

Psychological Approaches. Values have long been a topic in psychology beginning with the work of Wilhelm Wundt (1926), the founding father of experimental psychology, who attempted to study the sociocultural basis of psychological phenomena as part of his *Völkerpsychologie*. One of the earliest examples of an empirically oriented approach was that of Allport and Vernon (1931) influenced by Spranger's (1921) "Lebensformen." An influential approach to the study of values was initiated by Milton Rokeach (1973) on the basis of his widely used Rokeach Value Survey (RVS), which, however, did not follow a consistent theoretical model. His view on values as guiding principles in people's behavior (Rokeach, 1973) is generally in line with Schwartz (1992).

Schwartz's complex theoretical model allows researchers to study values on both the cultural and individual levels, including individual differences in value priorities and their effects on attitudes and behavior. His theory on the structure of human values refers to culture-specific and universal aspects. A central assumption of Schwartz's theory of basic individual values is that the array of values represents a circular continuum of motivations. Partitioning the continuum into 10 discrete values or into broader or more finely tuned value constructs depends on how one's preference discriminates among motivations. The underlying structure of the relations among the 10 value types has been validated in more than 50 countries (e.g., Schwartz, 2006), supporting the assumption of a universal structure of human values. The study by Bilsky, Janik, and Schwartz (2011) based on the European Social Survey supported the circular structure across and within countries across time. Results also showed less deviation from the structure in more developed countries (with larger contrast between protection and growth values). Recently, Schwartz and Vecchione (2011, June) presented a revised theory allowing for greater predictive and interpretive power by partitioning the value continuum into 19 distinct values (which can be combined to recapture the original 10 or the 4 higher-order values). In a study of 73 countries, the dimensions suggested by Inglehart and by Schwartz are shown to be overlapping (Schwartz, 2006). These results support the idea of national cultures without neglecting intracultural variations.

However, several questions remain to be answered, such as whether and when a universal motivational structure of relations among values of adolescents from different cultures and age groups emerges, and whether there are differences in the impact of values on social behavior. In this volume, Schwartz discusses additional refined questions. His contribution is based on the analyses of representative national samples from 30 countries, including different religious groups and different developmental stages (mid- and late adolescence), taking into account the motivational structure of values and value priorities, and the impact of religion and religiosity on value priorities and attitudes toward family, prosocial behavior, and acceptance of the law. The implications of his study are manifold, suggesting the need for more research on the role of parents and the agency of adolescents (e.g., rejecting or accepting parents' values) in their value development.

From a different theoretical perspective, Hofstede (1980, 2001), a pioneer in the study of cultural dimensions of values, proposed a culture-level approach; his focus is on national-level patterns of values. Many studies have used his concept of individualism/collectivism as a personality variable and for predicting behavior (for features distinguishing individualists from collectivists on the individual level, see Triandis, 1995). However, the assumption that individualism/collectivism are two poles of one dimension is not supported empirically, as Oyserman, Coon, and Kemmelmeier (2002) showed in their extensive meta-analysis. Another problem is that the individual level and the cultural level have often been confused in past research. It is necessary to ask how individual and cultural value orientations are interrelated, and how the individual and cultural levels of values can be disentangled (for overviews, see Davidov, Schmidt, & Billiet, 2011; Smith & Schwartz, 1997; van de Vijver, Hemert, & Poortinga, 2008; for an example of an empirical cross-cultural study on values of adolescents regarding their future and the family, see Mayer & Trommsdorff, 2010).

The question of whether values can predict behavior has been dealt with in various studies, which, however, have mostly ignored the role of cultural variables. A cultural focus for the prediction of behavior is suggested by Schwartz's value theory and also by the social axioms theory that draws on expectancy-value theory to predict behavior (e.g., Bond, Leung, Au, Tong, & Chemonges-Nielson, 2004). There is considerable empirical evidence on the motivational and behavioral qualities of values based on the Schwartz Value Theory. According to Schwartz (2006), values represent priorities in life and serve a motivational function. Self-reported value priorities are related to certain personality variables and reported (or observed) behaviors such as prosocial, antisocial, environmental, political, consumer, and intellectual behaviors (see Bardi & Schwartz, 2003, for a review). However, research on individual and cultural/structural aspects regarding the value-behavior relationship is still rare (for exceptions, see Schwartz, 1996; Schwartz & Sagi, 2000; Schwartz, Chapter 4 in this volume).

Development of Adolescents' Value Orientations
Only a few culture-informed studies on adolescents' development of values are available. Therefore, this volume attempts to contribute to this open

issue. Adolescence has been recognized as a crucial period for value development. In the literature, it is widely assumed that a certain level of abstract thinking, brain maturation, and identity formation is a precondition for adolescents' value development (cf. Nurmi, 1998; Schwarz, 2007). Erikson's (1968) view of the process of identity formation has been further elaborated by Marcia (1966; for a meta-analysis of studies on identity status change, see Kroger, Martinussen, & Marcia, 2010). Recent discussions by Azmitia et al. (2008) on identity, including the individual and social self, link the development of a personal identity and a social identity, opening the perspective for interdisciplinary approaches on adolescent development (Phinney, 2008). This recent issue may stimulate a culture-informed approach as suggested in the present volume.

Several value-related studies on adolescent development have dealt with adolescents' self-concept (e.g., a longitudinal study by Alsaker & Olweus, 1992), life goals (e.g., Grob, 1998; Nurmi, 1998), or future orientation (Steinberg et al., 2009; for an extensive overview, see Seginer, 2009). However, culture and religion have rarely been taken into account in these studies. Therefore, the present volume addresses this gap and includes chapters that address the often missing link between specific aspects of self and culture. Rothbaum, Wang, and Cohen (Chapter 3) discuss the increasing self-awareness in adolescence and explain cultural differences in key concepts of self-awareness, related to the vantage point of awareness, the conception of self, and the nature of self-evaluation. The authors further discuss the function of these aspects of self-awareness in cultural differences in spirituality. Two other chapters discuss the relation between future orientation (occupational aspirations) and religious socialization (e.g., Seginer and Mahajna [Chapter 11] for Israeli Palestinian girls; Pearce and Hardie [Chapter 12] for girls from the United States).

Research on values leads to the further question of the relations between values and behavior. Findings of relations between prosocial values, moral development, and prosocial behavior such as civic engagement or political activity (e.g., Flanagan, 2004) have stimulated questions regarding the context in which such values and behaviors develop. In this volume, Rubin, Malti, and McDonald (Chapter 8) investigate personal relationships and moral development in relation to the development of civic competence. Larson, Jensen, Kang, Griffith, and Rompala (Chapter 7) examine peer processes associated with the development of prosocial values and how they are shaped by culture. The authors base their discussion on ("youth-centered") programs including ethnically diverse youth. These chapters are of special interest for better understanding the role of values in positive youth development.

Although there is much evidence for the validity of Schwartz's (1992) theory regarding the universal structure of values for college students, the question arises as to whether a universal value structure also occurs for younger age groups or at an earlier developmental age. So far, only a few studies on the actual *development* of adolescents' values have been carried out. In 2004, Bubeck and Bilsky showed that for a large sample of German children and adolescents (aged 10–17 years), the value structure of both the younger and older youths was similar and in line with Schwartz's conceptualization of 10 basic values (see also Boehnke & Welzel, 2006). In this volume, Schwartz (Chapter 4) extends this issue and investigates whether his value theory is also applicable to adolescents of different developmental ages and from different religions and cultures.

However, these studies do not deal with questions of developmental processes of values. Therefore, a developmental and culture-sensitive approach is needed for further clarification. A promising approach is the theoretical model by Markus and Kitayama (1991), who discuss the impact of cultural values on the independent and interdependent self. The authors conceive of self-construals as reflecting basic cultural models and individual value orientations. In line with this view, Rothbaum, Pott, Azuma, Miyake, and Weisz (2000) showed that adolescent development, including values and beliefs, follows a developmental path that is organized according to the respective cultural model (e.g. "path of symbiotic harmony and path of generative tension"). Accordingly, the cultural models of independence and interdependence can be assumed to structure the value development of adolescents, affecting the developmental task of individuation and the related values of autonomy and relatedness in culture-specific ways. However, the values of autonomy and relatedness (1) have a differing importance and meaning; (2) are related to each other differently in Western versus Asian cultures; and (3) influence the social, emotional, and cognitive development of adolescents, including their value orientations (for a culture-informed overview, see Rothbaum & Trommsdorff, 2007; Trommsdorff, 2007; Trommsdorff & Rothbaum, 2008).

Research on adolescents' cultural value development is an important step forward. However, open questions remain to be answered, such as how the *socialization* and *transmission* of values in the cultural context occurs. Socialization and the transmission of value orientations are influenced by parents, peers, and other agents in interaction with the adolescents, while child-rearing practices and parent–child relationships are influential mechanisms in the transmission process. According to the model by Grusec and Goodnow (1994), children's accuracy of perception and their acceptance of parental values accounts for parent–child value congruence. These factors relate to the quality of the relationship between the parent and child (for culture-specific patterns of bidirectionality, see Trommsdorff, 2007; Trommsdorff & Kornadt, 2003), interparental value agreement, and the general value orientation in the respective culture, all of which are important factors for the transmission of values (Knafo & Schwartz, 2009; Trommsdorff, 2006, 2009a).

However, this model needs further specifications regarding the negotiation, transmission, and modification across generations. These issues are addressed in this volume by Knafo, Daniel, Gabay, Zilber, and Shir (Chapter 16) who demonstrate how religion affects the intergenerational continuity of values in different cultural groups. This chapter underlines the interrelations between culture, religion, and values in adolescent development.

Considerable research into parent–child similarity was stimulated by the assumption that similarity is an indicator of parents' successful influence over and socialization of adolescents. However, congruence of values between parents and children can indicate various phenomena beyond successful unidirectional transmission of values. Congruence may depend on the content of the value; for example, congruence is usually higher for religious than for nonreligious values (Miller & Glass, 1989). Other sources of parent–child congruence in values beside the unidirectional influence of parents include children's impact on their parents' values, genetically based factors (shared temperament), and/or environmental conditions such as high normativity of certain values affecting the socialization process and reinforcing parents' and children's values (Albert, 2007; Albert, Trommsdorff, & Sabatier, 2011; Boehnke, Hadjar, & Baier, 2009; Friedlmeier & Trommsdorff, 2011; Knafo et al., Chapter 16 in this volume; Knafo & Schwartz, 2009; Trommsdorff, 2009a). Value congruence between parents and children is related to the issue of the effects of normativity of values, which is discussed in several chapters of this volume. Further, Norasakkunkit and Uchida (Chapter 9) describe how adolescents' low preference for dominant cultural values of interdependence may be related to their social withdrawal. This is an especially relevant issue in times of social change.

In a *changing environment*, or for migrant youth, the transmission of values is even more difficult to measure and explain. When values in the learning environment of school do not coincide with peer values and values in the family, the adolescent has to cope with conflicting expectations and special problems of identity achievement (e.g., Knafo, Assor, Schwartz, & David, 2009). This problem is discussed by Knafo et al., Chapter 16 in this volume. Furthermore, the *zeitgeist*, the dominant mainstream belief of the majority of a society, influences value congruence, as Boehnke et al. (2009) have shown. Immigrants who are acculturating within a new cultural environment prefer "in-group-serving" types of values across generations (Kornadt, Chapter 2 in this volume; Phalet & Schönpflug, 2001). Collectivistic groups prefer higher authoritarianism while endorsing warm relationships that promote the transmission of values more easily (Rudy & Grusec, 2001).

Of special importance is the study of value similarities in multigeneration families and related analyses of *historical and developmental changes in the transmission of values* (Bengtson, 1975, Silverstein, Gans, Lowenstein, Giarrusso, & Bengtson, 2010). For this research, a family design is necessary, which is only rarely used for empirical studies. Exceptions include studies on self-reports of values and life goals of three family generations (for one culture, see Grob, Weisheit, & Gomez, 2009). The recent Value of Children research has initiated cross-cultural comparisons based on two- and three-generation family designs to study changes in value orientations regarding the family and children (e.g., Albert, 2007; Albert et al., 2011; Mayer, Trommsdorff, Kagitcibasi, & Mishra, in press; Nauck, 2009, 2010; Trommsdorff, 2009a; Trommsdorff, Mayer, & Albert, 2004).

This research on specific individual value orientations and behavior in relation to national levels of cultural values and socioeconomic development has been initiated by Trommsdorff and Nauck (2005, 2006, 2010), building on the previous Value of Children (VOC) studies by Arnold et al. (1975), Hoffman and Hoffman (1973), and Kagitcibasi (1973). This theoretically and methodologically revised VOC research program is investigating the relations between aspects of culture (e.g., social structure, urbanization), individual value orientations, and behavior (fertility and child-rearing goals and practices) in three generations, taking into account sociocultural changes. These studies also demonstrate the function of the value of children and family for fertility behavior, providing cultural, structural, and psychological explanations (Nauck, 2010; Trommsdorff & Nauck, 2005, 2010). This research attempts to integrate the individual and cultural levels for the study of values and behavior in a cross-cultural and multigenerational design. Cultural conditions and changing socialization contexts for the development of adolescents' values have been shown to be of special importance. Mayer and Trommsdorff (Chapter 15) discuss some of these issues, focusing on family values in times of social change.

To date, only a few studies have taken into account sociocultural changes as a changing context for adolescent development. In an extensive analysis, the Study Group on Adolescence in the 21st Century chaired by Reed Larson and colleagues examined the expected societal and developmental trends in the next few decades including regional studies on the transformation from childhood to adulthood (Brown et al., 2002; Larson, Wilson, Brown, Furstenberg, & Verma, 2002). The authors note various ongoing changes in the proximate and distal contexts of adolescents' daily lives that point to new developmental tasks for adolescents worldwide. However, adolescents' development of values in rapidly changing sociocultural contexts is only rarely studied (e.g., Silbereisen & Chen, 2010; Trommsdorff, 1992, 2000).

The issues of value change in adolescent development under conditions of major social and economic changes and related questions are discussed in this volume by several authors. For example, Chen, Wang, and Liu (Chapter 10) focus on changing values and behavior regarding individuality and group orientation of urban and rural Chinese adolescents who live in very different socioeconomic and cultural contexts. In their discussion on Japanese youth, Norasakkunkit and Uchida (Chapter 9) address the problem of youth having withdrawn from participating in the society due to Japan's transition into a postindustrial economy. The authors show that high- as compared to low-risk adolescents prefer less interdependent values, thus departing from the predominant cultural value of interdependence in Japan. This result adds to the general goal of this volume to clarify effects of culture on adolescent development.

Anthropological, sociological, and psychological research on values all indicate that individual values are embedded in the broader sociocultural context and differ in content and relative importance. However, more research is needed to bridge the cultural and individual levels of values and to clarify the conditions for the transmission and stability of values and their association with behavior.

Religion and Youth from a Culture-Informed Perspective

Developmental theories suggest that adolescence is a period in human development when religion and religiosity may become important. It is unclear, however, whether and how adolescents' religiosity, and more specifically, its developmental conditions and outcomes, may differ across various cultural contexts. Before I discuss these developmental questions, I present a short overview on sociological studies.

Theoretical and Empirical Approaches to Religion and Culture
Sociological Studies. Whereas religion has only recently been "discovered" as an understudied psychological phenomenon, religion has been a major topic of interest in social and political science since Durkheim (1975a, b) and Max Weber (1958) (e.g., Berger, 1999; Berger, Davie, & Fokas, 2008; Casanova, 1994; Davie, 1999; Huntington, 1996; Lenski, 1961).

Since Weber's studies on the emergence of the Protestant ethic and the related stimulation of capitalism in Europe, accompanied by a process of disenchantment, several sociological studies have dealt with the "secularization thesis," assuming that advanced modernity weakens religion. In contrast, Daniel Bell (1977) observed a "return of the sacred" in the 1970s in the United States. Other studies also report an emergence of religious movements; a transformation to popular religious orientations (e.g., the Pope as a star of the mass media); and individualized, private forms of religion, including spiritualism (e.g., Woodhead, 2008). These phenomena can be seen as "religious experimentation," stimulating a hybrid religiosity as a form of religious popular culture (Turner, 2011). According to Turner, major issues for understanding religion in modern societies are related to globalization. Fundamentalism and religious violence are two examples.

The secularization thesis is still a debated topic (e.g., Halman & Pettersson, 2006), in part due to the different definitions of religion and secularization, which have often been criticized for having a Eurocentric bias (e.g., a monotheistic approach to religion). Studies on secularization and religion have also been criticized on account of their methodological shortcomings (e.g., indicators of religiosity). Sociologists of religion have distinguished between beliefs, practices, and affiliation. Religious practices such as church attendance may have another meaning than subjective religious beliefs and spirituality. Therefore, conceptual clarification is needed, and methods for measurement should be refined. The assumption of "religious decline" can hardly be tested empirically when the underlying concept refers to different phenomena.

Religion and religiosity have been conceived of as a system of beliefs and practices surrounding faith in the divine (Sasaki, Kim, & Xu, 2011). *Religion* is related to organizational–institutional aspects, and *religiosity* is related to personal and psychological aspects of religious beliefs. As an example, Europeans are less inclined to go to church or to rely on church leaders than are many Americans; however, this does not necessarily indicate a decline in religious beliefs (Halman & Pettersson, 2006). Research by Davie (2002) based on data from the European Values Study shows a mismatch between religious practices and belief. The Church has lost its influence but religious beliefs persist and have become increasingly personal, particularly among young people. Accordingly, the reported differences between Europe and the United States regarding changes in religiosity (Berger et al., 2008; Esmer & Pettersson, 2007; Norris & Inglehart, 2004) need to be discussed from a methodologically sound and culture-informed perspective.

In general, it has been observed that religion becomes less related to institutions and instead more related to individual taste and private life in Western countries. Large-scale comparative studies report a more complex picture on the "religious decline," distinguishing among various nations (e.g., Höllinger & Haller, 2009). Accordingly, the secularization thesis has to be revised by taking into account cultural and psychological factors. Also, these studies did not specifically focus on adolescents.

Psychological Studies. Wilhelm Wundt (1926) was one of the first scientists in the psychology of religion to elaborate on the psychological, cultural, and anthropological foundations of religion, highlighting these relations in one of the 20 volumes of his *Völkerpsychologie*. Different theoretical approaches have followed, such as the phenomenological approach of William James (1985; religion as useful hypothesis), Sigmund Freud's theories on religion (1961; religion as solid illusion), attachment theory (God as attachment figure), and humanistic psychology (for a review on the psychology of religion, see Paloutzian & Park, 2005; Wulff, 1991). The study of religion has recently been the subject of new interest in psychological research (e.g., Emmons & Paloutzian, 2003; Hinde, 1999; Hood, Spilka, Hunsberger, & Gorsuch, 1996; Paloutzian & Park, 2005; Pargament, 2002; Saroglou, 2011). Among other approaches, evolutionary (Atran, 2002, 2007), neuroscientific (Kapogiannis et al., 2009), and cultural psychological perspectives (Belzen, 2010) have been suggested. This diversity may provide good arguments for bridging different disciplines in the psychology of religion.

Recent studies in the psychology of religion have focused on the individual level of religiosity (including emotions, cognitions, and behavior) as a subjective experience (Emmons, Barrett, & Schnitker, 2008) and have examined religion as an individual and a collective "meaning system" (Silberman, 2005). Some approaches view religion as unique because it provides people with ultimate meaning in life (Emmons, 1999; Emmons et al., 2008; Pargament, 2002), whereas others regard religion as a cultural artifact (Belzen, 2010), as a cultural byproduct among the various aspects of cultural activity, or as an output of cognitive systems that do not exclusively apply to religion but are shaped by the history of human evolution (Boyer & Bergstrom, 2008; Hinde, 1999). The relation between religion and cultural context is therefore seen as bidirectional in the present volume: the cultural context shapes religion, and religion contributes to cultural and individual differences via processes of socialization and development.

Recently, the construct of *spirituality* has been discussed as being distinct from religiosity and as related to psychological growth (Boyatzis, 2005). Whereas religiosity encompasses the institutional aspects of religious beliefs, spirituality encompasses the personal and transcendent aspects (Barry, Nelson, Davarya, & Urry, 2010). Warren, Lerner, and Phelps (2011) view adolescents' spirituality as promoting actions that transcend self-interest and focus on the benefit to others and to society. This is in line with the theory on positive youth development and spirituality by Lerner, Roeser, and Phelps (2008). From a culture-sensitive approach, Hill and Pargament (2003) argue that religion and spirituality cannot be separated in some cultures. Verma and Maria (2006) note: "Spiritual experiences during adolescence are, therefore, not only closely tied to cultural notions of adolescence, childhood, selfhood, and personhood. They are also closely linked to notions about the nature of relations one has with others in one's social world, as well as the emotions one invests in these relationships" (p. 133f).

This debated issue is dealt with in some chapters of this volume: For example, French, Eisenberg, Purwono, and Sallquist (Chapter 6) have studied religiosity–spirituality as one combined latent construct, and Saroglou (Chapter 17) points out that although religiosity and spirituality partly overlap, they should be studied as separate phenomena.

In his overview on religion/religiosity, Saroglou (2011) distinguishes between four basic psychological dimensions: beliefs (in truth), rituals/emotions, moral rules, and affiliation (community/group). Both values and religion can be seen as based on universal human motives. However, the manifestation of these motives may differ among cultures, and also differ for values and for religion.

Of special interest is the question of *which conditions* may contribute to religiosity. In their cross-cultural study, Diener, Tay, and Myers (2011) show that nations with difficult life conditions (e.g., low economic development) score higher in religiosity. Here the question arises as to whether results are the same for the macro- and individual levels of life conditions. In their study on patterns of religiosity in 27 Christian societies around the world, Höllinger and Haller (2009) report a negative correlation between the Human Development Index and the level of religiousness of the population of the respective countries. This relation on the macrolevel differs from the individual level because it does not hold for the relation between individual (e.g., economic) life conditions and religiosity. In the same line of reasoning, the study by Hayward and Kemmelmeier (2011) using cross-national panel data on religiosity and economic attitudes shows stronger associations of Protestantism with respect to indicators of cultural Protestantism as compared to individual Protestant religiosity. This study, as well as chapters in this volume (e.g., Bond, Lun, & Li [Chapter 5]; Mayer & Trommsdorff [Chapter 15]; Schwartz [Chapter 4]), underscore the need for multilevel modeling in this research area.

Another main issue is the *function of religion*. A functional approach has been suggested from evolution theoretical perspectives indicating that religion has contributed to the development of mankind and cultures (e.g., Atran & Norenzayan, 2004; Boyer & Bergstrom, 2008; Wilson, 2003). More specifically, psychological researchers have studied the function of religion for individuals and groups for interpersonal behavior, assuming that religiosity is related to cooperation and prosocial behavior (Bremmer, Koole, & Bushman, 2011; Henrich et al., 2010; Norenzayan & Sheriff, 2008). Religious beliefs may encourage virtues such as prosocial behavior and positive psychological states such as hope, which, in turn, may impact mental health and life-satisfaction (Loewenthal, 2007). Further functions of religions may include satisfying basic needs (e.g., for security, self-regulation, autonomy, and connectedness; Baumeister, Bauer, & Lloyd, 2010; Saroglou, 2011), providing resilience (Pargament & Cummings, 2010), and increasing life-satisfaction (Myers, 2008; Pollner, 1989). However, empirical results on these assumed functions of religiosity are not consistent.

Recently, and in contrast to views on religion as beneficial, some authors have seen religion as a risk factor, undermining health and well-being and inducing conflict (Raiya, Pargament, & Magyar-Russell, 2010). Religion may stimulate adolescents to engage in risk-taking behavior, violence, and self-sacrifice. Pargament (2002) contends that religion is a unique force that may play a beneficial role but also can be a source of distress. Culture and individual values may influence the way religion is manifested in behavior and adolescent development.

The often-assumed simplistic relationship between religiosity and life-satisfaction is actually quite complex. Multiple factors may mediate and moderate the links between religion and well-being (or health). For example, Galen and Kloet (2011) have reported a reverse u-shaped curve for adult samples in the United States, showing that both people who are confidently religious and those who are atheists report higher well-being than do people with low certainty of their belief or nonbelief in God. Furthermore, in contexts with difficult life conditions, religiosity is highly related to subjective well-being (Diener et al., 2011). These studies underline the role of context in the function of religiosity. In a study on Japanese individuals, Jagodzinski (2011) reports a low level of influence of religion on life-satisfaction due to a general low individual sense of autonomy and control. This result is in line with the finding by Sasaki and Kim (2010) on the impact of religion on secondary control and social affiliation in the United States and Korea. In Asian communities, as compared to European-American communities, social affiliation and belonging are more highly valued than is personal agency; therefore, religion seems to fulfill a different function in both cultures – either promoting affiliation or fostering a sense of control.

The recent cross-cultural study by Sasaki et al. (2011) demonstrates a three-way interaction of genes, culture, and religiosity predicting well-being, thus underscoring the multilevel relationships between biological factors, culture, religiosity, and well-being. Sasaki et al. (2011) have examined how culture (value of social affiliation) and biology (oxytocin receptor gene) may interact in their impact on this association in Korean and European-American samples. This line of research may provide a better understanding of the harmful or beneficial effects of religion for well-being. "Religious factors can affect mental health, sometimes for the good, sometimes not, and some of these effects vary with the cultural context" (Loewenthal, 2007, p. 140).

It is assumed here that the complexity of this issue cannot be reduced when ignoring cultural factors and developmental processes. Accordingly, more research is needed on the culture-specific effects of religion because cultural factors may limit or support religious influence. In addition to independent influences of contexts, one also has to understand how contexts combine and interact (Huston & Bentley, 2010). Therefore, this volume deals with much-neglected questions regarding the psychological and sociological aspects of religion in adolescent development taking into account cultural context.

Religiosity in Adolescence. Before Erikson (1968) had published his theory on identity development, empirical studies on the issue of religiosity in adolescence were rare. As previously mentioned, individuals undergo significant changes in physical (e.g., brain maturation), cognitive, and psychosocial development during adolescence, which stimulate the search for self definition, identity, and religious orientations. The field of sociology has recognized adolescence as a crucial period for religious and spiritual development as well (Desmond, Morgan, & Kikuchi, 2010; Smith & Lundquist Denton, 2005).

A major shortcoming of empirical studies on adolescence and religion is that these studies have usually been carried out in Western countries and have been based on descriptive, nonrepresentative data. A few studies on youth and religion in Germany have provided empirical results on the religious orientations of adolescents, including new forms of spirituality such as youth sects, New Age, and Occultism, and the special situation of youth and religion in the former German Democratic Republic (GDR) (Barz, 1992; Hurrelmann, Albert, & TNS Infratest Sozialforschung, 2006). Representative data on this topic can be retrieved at the German Socio-Economic Panel Study (GSOEP), the ALLBUS, or from the reports by the The Allensbacher Institute for Public Opinion Research (Bundesministerium für Familie, Senioren, Frauen und Jugend, 2005). These studies show a great variety of forms of religiosity, even as traditional formal institutions and church attendance have become less prominent.

Overviews on youth and religion in the United States have shown that the majority of adolescents report following the teachings of their religion (King & Boyatzis, 2004). However, no simple generalizations are possible, as shown by Smith and Lundquist Denton (2005) in their extensive, nationwide representative, and both quantitative and qualitative study on the religious and spiritual lives of American teenagers. This "National Study on Youth and Religion" (NSYR) is a unique research project, combining survey and interview methods. The authors demonstrate considerable variance in U.S. teenagers' religious and spiritual practices and experiences. For example, race, gender, and socioeconomic status are important predictors of teenage religiosity. Regarding the developmental conditions of religiosity, the authors show that parents play an important role in their children's religious commitments. Also, social locations, key social relationships, and organizations influence the religiosity of American teenagers. This study gives a detailed picture on the religious and spiritual lives of American youth. Whereas religious beliefs of American emerging adults seem to increase, religious practices decline (see Barry et al., 2010, for a summary).

A major gap in the study of adolescents' religiosity is the lack of research contextualizing the findings based on U.S. college students. Only recently has religiosity in adolescent development become a topic in sociological and psychological research, as a result of ongoing globalization, including immigration and religious pluralism. This has given rise to questions of whether and how culture and changing contexts affect adolescents' religious development (e.g., Casanova, 2007).

However, comparative research that provides theory-based representative cross-national studies on culture, values, and religiosity of adolescents is rare. Therefore, a major goal of this volume is to fill this gap. Culture-sensitive theorizing is needed to discuss the developmental conditions and the functions of religiosity in adolescents. One focus is on the *developmental conditions*; another focus is on the *developmental outcomes* and *functions* of religiosity.

Developmental Conditions for Religiosity. The focus on *developmental conditions* and descriptions of the religious and spiritual development of adolescents points to the specific developmental tasks that adolescents face during this period of crucial developmental transition between childhood and adulthood. As previously indicated, a foremost task during this period is identity development (Alsaker & Kroger, 2006; Erikson, 1968; Marcia, 1993), including religious and spiritual issues (Elkind, 1999; Waterman, 1985). Adolescents' identity development is related to social development (Erikson, 1968). Social relationships, in turn, are the context for experiencing religious and spiritual beliefs and practices (Barry et al., 2010). From a culture-informed perspective, and in contrast to Western societies, in some traditional cultures, the transition to adolescence is embedded in religious rituals and does not necessarily imply insecurity or a difficult search for identity (Schwartz, 2007).

Several theoretical approaches to the development of religiosity have not yet been integrated. According to Oser, Scarlett, and Bucher (2006), three main paradigms have dominated explanations of religious development: (1) the person maturing, (2) the person coping (functional approach), and (3) the person perfecting. Levesque (2002) summarizes three theoretical approaches for religious development: (1) daily activities such as prayer, (2) the process of meaning-making, and (3) the role of the context (mainly parents). A closer look at the literature shows that several paradigms are still competing, including the organismic or cognitive–structural paradigm, basing on stage theories by Kohlberg (1981), Piaget (1928), and Werner (1948); the cognitive developmental approach (Harris, 2000) and the related cognitive anthropological approach (Johnson & Boyatzis, 2006); the affective sensitive stage approach (Good & Willoughby, 2008), which is partly related to the approach on the achievement of identity by Erikson (1968) and Marcia (1993); and the person-context-interaction approach (developmental systems paradigm) by Lerner (2002), which has been expanded in a theoretical framework on positive youth development and spirituality (Lerner et al., 2008).

However, all these approaches neglect the role of culture and values in adolescent religious development; this volume attempts to fill the gap. For example, Kornadt (Chapter 2) discusses the culture-specific role of adolescents from a historical and psychological perspective, clarifying the motivational components in the development of religiosity. Rothbaum et al. (Chapter 3) elaborate culture-specific aspects of the development of self-awareness in relation to religiosity. The authors perceive of spirituality as coping with existential concerns engendered by self-awareness and perceived threats to the self.

Socialization Conditions. In terms of socialization conditions for religious development, parents are the primary socializing agents, although other adults, peers, media, and institutions serve as socializing agents as well (for an overview regarding the socialization of emerging adults, see Barry et al., 2010). There is substantial empirical evidence that the quality of a youth's relationship with his or her parents predicts the effectiveness of parental religious socialization (Ream & Savin-Williams, 2003). This finding is in line with studies that indicate a correlation between adolescents' secure attachment and their similarity to their parents' religiosity (for an overview, see Granqvist, Chapter 14 in in this volume). However, the cultural context has to be taken into account as well because basic factors in socialization conditions are cultural variables (Whiting & Whiting, 1975), including self- and world-views and religious beliefs (Trommsdorff, 2012). In his classical anthropological cross-cultural study on the associations between socialization practices and religious beliefs, Lambert (1992) used ethnographic material from 62 traditional cultures. He showed that in these cultures, a general belief in the relative malevolence (in contrast to benevolence) of supernatural beings (gods or spirits) was related to painful and strict socialization procedures by socialization agents: children experienced early, harsh discipline and were rewarded for self-reliance and independence. In contrast, in cultures where a belief in benevolent gods was institutionalized, children experienced less punishment and less rigid training; they were socialized for a more supportive world. This study underlines the impact of culture-specific world-views on socialization practices.

Socialization experiences in the family have been reported as the most powerful factor influencing religious development in industrialized countries (Boyatzis, Dollahite, & Marks, 2006). Pankhurst and Houseknecht (2000) argue that the relationship between family and religiosity has been neglected in past research and assert the importance of family influence on religious development in times of social change. In contrast, Desmond et al. (2010) have demonstrated in their representative longitudinal study on American youth (National Youth Survey) that family structure may only influence religious service attendance and not affect private religious beliefs. Taking into account the role of the cultural context, Kelley and De Graaf (1997) showed that the impact of parents' religiosity is moderated by the national religious context. This is an important result in line with conclusions from some chapters in this volume (e.g., Mayer & Trommsdorff, Chapter 15).

In their longitudinal study of intergenerational transmission of religion, Bengtson, Copen, Putney, and Silverstein (2008) demonstrated that grandparents and parents are independent and joint agents of religious socialization. Knafo et al. (Chapter 16 in this volume) show that direct influence occurs through parental values and practices. The mother influences adolescents' religious development most strongly, followed by the church, the father, and friends (Hunsberger, 1995; Hunsberger & Brown, 1984). Family values (Sabatier, Mayer, Friedlmeier, Lubiewska, & Trommsdorff, 2011) and, moreover, the parent–child relationship have been identified both as direct influences and as mediating factors in the development of adolescents' religiosity (Granqvist, 2002; Granqvist & Dickie, 2006).

Results from chapters in this volume are in line with this conclusion. For example, Granqvist (Chapter 14) has shown that the quality of parent–child relationships is related to adolescents' secure or insecure attachment patterns, which in turn may influence one's relation to God or the divine as an attachment figure (see also Kirkpatrick, 1995). This idea has been further elaborated by Rothbaum et al. (Chapter 3) in their theoretical approach on self-awareness and religiosity.

An important theoretical and empirical question that remains open is: can religiosity be seen as a specific value system that is transmitted through socialization processes in the family and other contexts, similarly to other values, or is religiosity a unique phenomenon that only partly resembles or overlaps with values? In the latter case, different processes of socialization and transmission may be relevant. Therefore, a question for further research is whether the theoretical and empirical approaches to the transmission of values (see Schönpflug, 2009) are applicable to the transmission and the development of religiosity as well. Most research on the religiosity of adolescents is not based on longitudinal data, and thus lacks empirical evidence on the transmission process. Reported similarities between parents and their adolescent children are not necessarily a valid indicator of "successful" socialization processes, as studies on parent–child value congruence have shown (see Knafo et al., Chapter 16 in this volume; Trommsdorff, 2009a).

Culture-informed empirical approaches to the socialization conditions of religiosity are rare. An exception is the research by the Study Group on

Adolescence in the 21st Century, chaired by Reed Larson and colleagues (Brown et al., 2002; Larson et al., 2002). In addition, few studies have investigated the socialization of religiosity in minority groups and migrant youth. Here, the question of transmission of religiosity in a changing cultural context is of special interest. Phinney (2008) argues that little attention has been given to actual interactions in the family, and further stresses that both acculturative and developmental changes should be taken into account.

Accordingly, there is a need for culture-informed research on the socialization of religion that focuses both on the study of religious beliefs and practices in different cultures and on their specific impact on adolescent religious development. Therefore, the present volume attempts to address these questions. For example, Granqvist (Chapter 14) elaborates on socialization conditions for religiosity in adolescent development in an attachment theoretical framework. Socialization in the family is discussed by several authors referring to different cultural contexts (e.g., Knafo et al. [Chapter 16]; Mayer & Trommsdorff [Chapter 15]; Rubin et al. [Chapter 8]). Since the family is only one among many agents of socialization, Mayer and Trommsdorff (Chapter 15) discuss the question of normativity of religiosity as a cultural factor (in addition to economic development and cultural values) influencing adolescents' religious development. Further, several chapters provide culturally sensitive accounts of socialization in the peer group (Chen et al. [Chapter 10]; French et al. [Chapter 6]; Larson, Jensen, Kang, Griffith, & Rompala [Chapter 7]); and Mishra (Chapter 18) describes Indian youths' socialization in school, taking into account the cultural context and the related traditional Hindu values.

Religiosity and Developmental Outcomes. Researchers have also focused on the development of religiosity by studying its psychological processes and developmental outcomes. For example, the relation between religiosity and moral development has been of interest in some research. According to Kohlberg (1981), moral development occurs rather independently from religious development, but religious structures support morality. In contrast, Nunner-Winkler (1995) concluded that religious orientation and moral commitment are not necessarily related to each other. Whereas these studies have been carried out in Western societies, Bucher, Oser, and Reich (2007) discussed the applicability of their method (based on Kohlberg's dilemma situations) to Buddhist, Hindu, and African children and adolescents and reported a trend of age-related development in moral judgments. However, in this study, behavioral indicators for religiosity and relations to values and behavior were largely missing.

Cultural psychological studies focusing on associations between adolescents' religious orientation and behavior-relevant values such as the value of children and the family provide more specific information (e.g., Brisset, Sabatier, & Trommsdorff, 2008, July; Mayer & Trommsdorff, Chapter 15 in this volume; Sabatier et al., 2011). In highly religious populations where traditional family structures are still prevalent, like in Israel, the value of children is very high due to religious reasons. Thus, religious orientations may influence fertility decisions, which in turn have sociodemographic implications in certain cultures (Suckow, 2005). Pearce and Thornton (2007) explored the relations between religion and various family ideologies, underlining the role of religion for family values, desirable family behaviors, and career planning in early adulthood.

Religiosity is often assumed to be related to positive developmental outcomes such as prosocial development. Relations between spirituality, religion, and positive developmental outcomes such as civic engagement have been discussed by Lerner et al. (2008) and, more recently, by Warren et al. (2011). The search for identity may motivate adolescents to make valued contributions to self, family, and civil society (Warren et al., 2011). Empirical studies on adolescents' involvement in religious institutions have shown positive associations with community service (Youniss, McLellan, & Yates, 1999), self-regulation (McCullough & Willoughby, 2009), health outcomes (Miller & Thoresen, 2003; Plante & Sherman, 2001), and healthy lifestyles (Powell, Shahabi, & Thorensen, 2003). In line with these studies, Johnson (2008) discussed the association between religion and positive development. He suggested that religion may increase well-being, meaning in life, and educational attainment thus contributing to capacities which help individuals' positive development. Other empirical results on the relationship between adolescents' life-satisfaction and religiosity are inconsistent and point to the importance of cultural aspects (e.g., Sabatier et al., 2011; Sasaki et al., 2011). A major flaw in these studies is the neglect of cultural variables and the neglect of longitudinal studies examining causal relations between religiosity and positive development. A very rare exception is the study by Eisenberg et al. (2011) investigating the trajectories of religious coping from adolescence into early adulthood. The authors could show for an Italian Catholic sample that adolescents high in stable religious coping showed more prosocial behavior at three ages as compared to adolescents who were undergoing changes in their religious coping.

To summarize, whether or not adolescents' religiosity is related to positive developmental outcomes remains a debated issue (Pargament, 2002). Empirical findings to date cannot be generalized because cultural factors and values have been neglected. Therefore, several chapters in this volume discuss whether and how religious beliefs are associated with positive youth development taking into account the cultural context.

Several authors of this volume (e.g., Bond et al.; Granquist; Kornadt; Rothbaum et al.) call attention to the function of religiosity in fulfilling basic human needs (e.g., for security, belonging). However, under certain conditions, religiosity may result in distress and antisocial behavior as Kornadt (Chapter 2) argues. In line with attachment theory, Granqvist (Chapter 14) shows that religiosity may also be related to insecure attachment and negative developmental outcomes. A possibly positive developmental outcome may be seen in the culture-specific associations between religiosity and future orientations for Israeli Palestinian Muslim girls (see Seginer & Mahajna, Chapter 11). However, a somewhat different view is suggested by Pearce and Hardie (Chapter 12) regarding the gender-specific career expectations for religious female adolescents from the United States.

Saroglou (Chapter 17) discusses whether religiosity can predict positive developmental outcomes from an individual difference perspective, thus arriving at different implications of religiosity for personality stability versus personal growth. Consequently, he discusses the possibly adaptive function of religious doubt in adolescence.

French et al. (Chapter 6) report positive outcomes (e.g., adjustment and social competence) of religiosity for Indonesian Muslim adolescents in West Java, a highly homogenous culture. This result was expected because of parents' authoritative parenting style and adolescents' involvement with religious peers.

The chapter by Bond, Lun, and Li (Chapter 5) is a valuable example of how to identify conditions for positive and negative functions of religiosity in different cultures. The authors related macro- and microlevels in order to examine the associations between religiosity and well-being and happiness. Taking into account sociocultural factors, the authors analyzed data from the World Values Survey to explore the impact of the national context on the strength of the relations between both personality (values) and social factors (religious engagement) and life-satisfaction. Different results for life-satisfaction occurred depending on the (national or individual) level of analyses. These results underline the role of normativity (social support) in religious values and practices for positive developmental outcomes such as life-satisfaction.

Conclusions

The chapters of this volume clearly show that culture, values, and religion have significant impacts on youth development. These studies therefore have several implications for a developmental approach to adolescence. Although values and religiosity are relevant factors in youth development, the respective developmental conditions and functions differ depending on the cultural context. In addition to universal structures and functions of values and religion, certain culture-specificities (e.g., socioeconomic factors, cultural models of agency) have been observed. On the one hand, universalities in value dimensions and religious orientations have been empirically demonstrated in cross-cultural comparisons. On the other hand, cultural differences in the dimensions and functions of value orientations and religiosity have been reported. How values and religiosity are related to developmental outcomes depend on the cultural context.

An issue for future research is to analyze the role of biological factors and their assumed interactions with the functions of values and religiosity in the given cultural context. However, this topic was beyond the scope of the present volume.

Further research is also needed on the role of values and religion for adolescent development across cultures in changing societies. This volume has contributed to a better understanding of the culture-specific transmission processes of values and religiosity and their effects on adolescents' development. However, more longitudinal studies are needed. Respective studies should try to bridge the developmental and the ecological, culture-informed perspectives by also taking into account changing socioeconomic contexts. However, methodological shortcomings have to be dealt with first. For example, the conceptualization and measurement of values and religiosity still pose several problems related to issues of the validity of indicators (which may depend on the cultural context and the developmental time), issues of dimensions (the ranking-rating controversy), verbal and behavioral methods, and ethnocentric measurement (e.g., Jagodzinski, 2004 for values; Saroglou, 2011 for religiosity). Furthermore, a solid methodological basis such as the multilevel method is necessary to disentangle cultural and individual values (van de Vijver et al., 2008). As this volume makes clear, this is a necessary methodology because phenomena on the cultural level cannot necessarily be observed on the individual level (e.g., see Bond et al. [Chapter 5] and Mayer & Trommsdorff [Chapter 15] in this volume). A major gap is the lack of longitudinal data and the scarcity of culture-informed approaches.

The development of values and religiosity is an important issue because values and religion can shape cultural and societal conditions whereas the function of values and religion for individual behavior is simultaneously influenced by cultural factors. Here, questions regarding the relations between cultural models of agency, values, and religion arise. These phenomena may partly overlap but differ in their impact on individual development. Their overlap may consist of providing a self- and world-view based on a meaning system including goals and control beliefs necessary for adolescent development. Although Johnson, Hill, and Cohen (2011) have suggested conceiving of culture and religion as world-views, our suggestion here is to go a step further by understanding all three phenomena – cultural models of agency, values, and religion – as interrelated *self- and world-views* that influence adolescent development (Trommsdorff, 2012). This approach could provide a fruitful theoretical basis for future research in this area, as has been elaborated in this volume, because it takes into account the cultural context of values and religion in adolescent development.

In this volume, Kornadt (Chapter 2) discusses religion as a world-view guiding the development of adolescents' values, identity, and behavior. He suggests a historical and motivational approach to religiosity, assuming basic needs for security and belonging. In Chapter 2, he also describes relations between values and religion in different cultural contexts, which may induce pro- and antisocial behavior. Rothbaum et al. (Chapter 3) focus on implications in the increasing development of self-awareness, and the cultural differences in the key components. The authors conceive of spirituality as a way of coping with existential concerns. More specifically, Granqvist (Chapter 14) discusses the religious development of adolescents and their respective self- and world-views in an attachment theoretical framework, referring to the socialization conditions and functions of secure and insecure attachment. Accordingly, a major theoretical contribution of this volume is its focus on cultural values and religiosity in the development and function of self- and world-views.

Further, ongoing globalization, including immigration and religious pluralism (Casanova, 2007), gives rise to questions of whether and how this societal change affects adolescents' development. These questions have been dealt with in this volume (e.g., by Chen et al. [Chapter 10]; Knafo et al. [Chapter 16]; Larson et al. [Chapter 7]; Nauck & Steinbach [Chapter 13]; Norasakkunkit & Uchida [Chapter 9]; Pearce & Hardie [Chapter 12]; Saroglou [Chapter 17]; Seginer & Mahajna [Chapter 11]) and have stimulated areas for future research.

In addition, the social and psychological conditions for nonreligiosity (see Atran & Norenzayan, 2004) and for conversion to new religious movements (Streib, Hood, Keller, Csöff, & Silver, 2009 view conversion as "deconversion") need more clarification, as the chapters by Knafo et al. (Chapter 16) and Saroglou (Chapter 17) indicate. Studies on the conditions for religious fundamentalism in adolescence also need more clarification as Chapter 2 by Kornadt points out. How do fundamentalist movements succeed in attracting certain youth? Can the criterion of fundamentalism, which Herriot (2009) views as being in opposition to modernity, be generally regarded as a motivating force?

To summarize, several questions arise from the past studies on adolescence, values, and religion that need to be discussed from both developmental and culture-informed perspectives, thus overcoming the dominant Western individualistic focus. More exchange between sociological, anthropological, and psychological approaches will be fruitful for addressing the open questions that this volume shows to be relevant. These questions concern relations between values and religiosity and their respective changes during development, the conditions and functions of values and religiosity for both positive and negative developmental outcomes, and the role of cultural factors in these processes. This volume addresses several major gaps in the literature and contributes to a clarification of some of these questions by dealing with cultural, social, and psychological aspects of adolescent development focusing on mutual relations between religiosity and value orientations of youth from a cross-cultural perspective. We thereby emphasize the need to build a theoretical framework on adolescent development that bridges approaches in social science and culture-sensitive developmental psychology.

Acknowledgments

This research was supported by a grant from the German Research Foundation (DFG GZ, TR 169/14–2) as part of the project "Developmental Conditions of Intentionality and its Limits" and as part of the Interdisciplinary Research Center "Limits of Intentionality" at the University of Konstanz. I thank Boris Mayer for his comments to an earlier version of this chapter, Jeanette Ziehm for editing the references, and Holly Bunje for language editing.

REFERENCES

Albert, I. (2007). *Intergenerationale Transmission von Werten in Deutschland und Frankreich* [Intergenerational transmission of values in Germany and France]. Lengerich, Germany: Pabst Science.
Albert, I., Trommsdorff, G., & Sabatier, C. (2011). Patterns of relationship regulation: German and French adolescents' perceptions with regard to their mothers. *Family Science, 2*, 58–67.

Allport, G. W., & Vernon, P. E. (1931). *A study of values.* Boston, MA: Houghton Mifflin.

Alsaker, F. D., & Kroger, J. (2006). Self and identity. In S. Jackson & L. Goossens (Eds.), *Handbook of adolescent development: European perspectives* (pp. 90–117). Hove: Psychology Press.

Alsaker, F. D., & Olweus, D. (1992). Stability of global self-evaluations in early adolescence: A cohort longitudinal study. *Journal of Research on Adolescence,* **2,** 123–145.

Arnett, J. J. (2006). *Emerging adulthood. The winding road from the late teens through the twenties.* Oxford: Oxford University Press.

(2011). Bridging cultural and developmental psychology: New syntheses in theory, research, and policy. In L. A. Jensen (Ed.), *Emerging adulthood(s): The cultural psychology of a new life stage* (pp. 255–275). New York: Oxford University Press.

(Ed.). (2012). *Adolescent psychology around the world.* New York: Psychology Press.

Arnold, F., Bulatao, R. A., Buripakdi, C., Chung, B. J., Fawcett, J. T., Iritani, T., ... Wu, T. S. (1975). *The value of children: A cross-national study. Vol. 1. Introduction and comparative analysis.* Honolulu: East-West Population Institute.

Atran, S. (Ed.). (2002). *In gods we trust. The evolutionary landscape of religion.* Oxford: Oxford University Press.

Atran, S. (2007). The nature of belief. *Science,* **317,** 456.

Atran, S., & Norenzayan, A. (2004). Why minds create gods: Devotion, deception, death, and arational decision making. *Behavioral and Brain Sciences,* **27,** 713–770.

Azmitia, M., Syed, M., & Radmacher, K. (2008). On the intersection of personal and social identities: Introduction and evidence from a longitudinal study of emerging adults. *New Directions for Child & Adolescent Development,* **120,** 1–16.

Baltes, P. B., & Brim, O. G. (Eds.). (1980). *Life-span development and behavior.* Hillsdale, NJ: Lawrence Erlbaum Associates.

Bardi, A., & Schwartz, S. H. (2003). Values and behavior: Strength and structure of relations. *Personality and Social Psychological Bulletin,* **29,** 1207–1220.

Barry, C. M., Nelson, L., Davarya, S., & Urry, S. (2010). Religiosity and spirituality during the transition to adulthood. *International Journal of Behavioral Development,* **34,** 311–324.

Barz, H. (Ed.). (1992). *Religion ohne Institutionen? Eine Bilanz der sozialwissenschaftlichen Jugendforschung. Teil 1 des Forschungsbericht "Jugend und Religion" im Auftrag der Arbeitsgemeinschaft der Evangelischen Jugend in der Bundesrepublik Deutschland (aej)* [Religion without institutions? A balance of the social science youth research. First part of the research report "youth and religion" on behalf of the Arbeitsgemeinschaft der Evangelischen Jugend in der Bundesrepublik Deutschland]. Opladen: Leske + Budrich.

Baumeister, R. F., Bauer, I. M., & Lloyd, S. A. (2010). Choice, free will, and religion. *Psychology of Religion and Spirituality,* **2,** 67–82.

Bell, D. (1977). The return of the sacred? The argument of the future of religion. *British Journal of Sociology,* **28,** 419–451.

Belzen, J. A. (2010). *Towards cultural psychology of religion: Principles, approaches, applications.* New York: Springer Science + Business Media.

Bengtson, V. L. (1975). Generation and family effects in value socialization. *American Sociological Review,* **40,** 358–371.

Bengtson, V. L., Copen, C. E., Putney, N. M., & Silverstein, M. (2008). Religion and intergenerational transmission over time. In K. W. Schaie & R. P. Abeles (Eds.), *Social structures and aging individuals: Continuing challenges* (pp. 305–333). New York: Springer.

Berger, P., Davie, G., & Fokas, E. (2008). *Religious America, secular Europe? A theme and variations.* Aldershot: Ashgate.

Berger, P. L. (Ed.). (1999). *The desecularization of the world: Resurgent religion and world politics.* Grand Rapids, MI: Eerdmans.

Bilsky, W., Janik, M., & Schwartz, S. H. (2011). The structural organization of human values – Evidence from three rounds of the European Social Survey (ESS). *Journal of Cross-Cultural Psychology, 42*, 759–776.

Boehnke, K., Hadjar, A., & Baier, D. (2009). Value transmission and zeitgeist revisited. In U. Schönpflug (Ed.), *Cultural transmission. Psychological, developmental, social, and methodological aspects.* New York: Cambridge University Press.

Boehnke, K., & Welzel, C. (2006). Wertetransmission und Wertewandel: Eine explorative Drei-Generationen-Studie [Value transmission and value change: An exploratory three-generation study]. *Zeitschrift für Soziologie der Erziehung und Sozialisation, 26*, 341–360.

Bond, M. H., Leung, K., Au, A., Tong, K. K., & Chemonges-Nielson, Z. (2004). Combining social axioms with values in predicting social behaviors. *European Journal of Personality, 18*, 177–191.

Boyatzis, C. J. (2005). Religious and spiritual development in childhood. In R. F. Paloutzian & C. L. Park (Eds.), *Handbook of the psychology of religion and spirituality* (pp. 123–143). New York: The Guilford Press.

Boyatzis, C. J., Dollahite, D. C., & Marks, L. D. (2006). The family as a context for religious and spiritual development in children and youth. In E. C. Roehlkepartain, P. E. King, L. Wagener, & P. L. Benson (Eds.), *The handbook of spiritual development in childhood and adolescence* (pp. 297–309). Thousand Oaks, CA: Sage.

Boyer, P., & Bergstrom, B. (2008). Evolutionary perspectives on religion. *Annual Review of Anthropology, 37*, 111–130.

Bremmer, R. H., Koole, S. L., & Bushman, B. J. (2011). "Pray for those who mistreat you": Effects of prayer on anger and aggression. *Personality and Social Psychological Bulletin, 37*, 830–837.

Brisset, C., Sabatier, C., & Trommsdorff, G. (2008, July). Values, family relationships, and religiosity in two European countries: France and Germany. In G. Trommsdorff & C. Kagitcibasi (Chairs), *Cultural patterns of family relationships and value orientations.* Symposium conducted at the 19th International Congress of Psychology (ICP), Berlin, Germany.

Bronfenbrenner, U. (1979). *The ecology of human development: Experiments by nature and design.* Cambridge, MA: Harvard University Press.

Brown, B. B., Larson, R. W., & Saraswathi, T. S. (Eds.). (2002). *The world's youth: Adolescence in eight regions of the globe.* New York: Cambridge University Press.

Bruner, J. S. (1990). *Acts of meaning.* Cambridge, MA: Harvard University Press.

Bubeck, M., & Bilsky, W. (2004). Value structure at an early age. *Swiss Journal of Psychology, 63*, 31–41.

Bucher, A. A., Oser, F., & Reich, K. H. (2007). Religiosität und Spiritualität im Kulturvergleich [Religiosity and spirituality in cross-cultural comparison]. In G. Trommsdorff & H.-J. Kornadt (Eds.), *Enzyklopädie der Psychologie: Themenbereich C. Theorie und*

Forschung: Serie VII. Kulturvergleichende Psychologie: Band 1: Theorien und Methoden der kulturvergleichenden Psychologie (pp. 677–702). Göttingen, Germany: Hogrefe.

Bundesministerium für Familie, Senioren, Frauen und Jugend (2005). *12. Kinder und Jugendbericht* [12th report of children and adolescents]. Berlin: Bundesministerium für Familie, Senioren, Frauen und Jugend.

Casanova, J. (1994). *Public religions in the modern world.* Chicago: University of Chicago Press.

(2007). Immigration and the new religious pluralism: A European Union/United States comparison. In T. Banchoff (Ed.), *Democracy and the new religious pluralism* (pp. 59–83). Oxford: Oxford University Press.

Chen, X. (2012). Culture, peer interaction, and socioemotional development. *Child Development Perspectives,* 6, 27–34. Retrieved from http://onlinelibrary.wiley.com/doi/10.1111/j.1750–8606.2011.00187.x/pdf

Chen, X., & French, D. C. (2008). Children's social competence in cultural context. *Annual Review of Psychology,* 59, 591–616.

Cole, M., & Packer, M. (2011). Culture in development. In M. H. Bornstein & M. E. Lamb (Eds.), *Developmental science: An advanced textbook* (6th ed., pp. 51–108). New York: Psychology Press.

Coleman, J. C. (2011). *The nature of adolescence* (4th ed.). New York: Psychology Press.

D'Andrade, R. (2008). *A study of personal and cultural values. American, Japanese, and Vietnamese.* New York: Palgrave Macmillan.

Davidov, E., Schmidt, P., & Billiet, J. (Eds.). (2011). *Cross-cultural analysis: Methods and applications.* New York: Routledge.

Davie, G. (1999). Europe: The exception that proves the rule? In P. L. Berger (Ed.), *The desecularization of the world: Resurgent religion and world politics* (pp. 65–84). Grand Rapids, MI: Eerdmans.

(2002). *Europe: The exceptional case. Parameters of faith in the modern world.* London: Darton, Longman and Todd Ltd.

Desmond, S. A., Morgan, K. H., & Kikuchi, G. (2010). Religious development: How (and why) does religiosity change from adolescence to young adulthood? *Sociological Perspectives,* 53, 247–270.

Diener, E., Tay, L., & Myers, D. G. (2011). The religion paradox: If religion makes people happy, why are so many dropping out? *Journal of Personality and Social Psychology,* 101, 1278–1290.

Durkheim, E. (1975a). *Religion in sociological perspective: Essays in the empirical study of religion.* Belmont, CA: Wadsworth.

(1975b). *On religion.* London: Routledge & Paul.

(1981). *Die elementaren Formen des religiösen Lebens* [The elementary forms of religious life]. Frankfurt am Main: Suhrkamp.

Eisenberg, N., Castellani, V., Panerai, L., Eggum, N. D., Cohen, A. B., Pastorelli, C., & Caprara, G. V. (2011). Trajectories of religious coping from adolescence into early adulthood: Their form and relations to externalizing problems and prosocial behavior. *Journal of Personality,* 79, 841–873.

Elder, G. H., & Shanahan, M. J. (2006). The life course and human development. In R. M. Lerner (Ed.), *Theoretical models of human development* (6 ed., Vol. 1: *The handbook of child psychology,* pp. 665–715). New York: Wiley.

Elder-Vass, D. (2010). The emergence of culture. *Kölner Zeitschrift für Soziologie und Sozialpsychologie,* 50, 351–363.

Elkind, D. (1999). Religious development in adolescence. *Journal of Adolescence*, **22**, 291–295.

Emmons, R. A. (1999). *The psychology of ultimate concerns: Motivation and spirituality in personality*. New York: Guilford.

Emmons, R. A., Barrett, J. L., & Schnitker, S. A. (2008). Personality and the capacity for religious and spiritual experience. In O. P. John, R. W. Robins, & L. A. Pervin (Eds.), *Handbook of personality: Theory and research* (pp. 634–653). New York: Guilford.

Emmons, R. A., & Paloutzian, R. F. (2003). The psychology of religion. *Annual Review of Psychology*, **54**, 377–402.

Erikson, E. H. (1968). *Identity: Youth and crisis*: New York: Norton.

Esmer, Y., & Pettersson, T. (Eds.). (2007). *Measuring and mapping cultures: 25 years of comparative value surveys* (Vol. 104). Leiden, The Netherlands: Brill.

Flanagan, C. A. (2004). Volunteerism, leadership, political socialization, and civic engagement. In R. M. Lerner & L. Steinberg (Eds.), *Handbook of adolescent psychology* (pp. 721–746). New York: Wiley.

Freud, S. (1961). *The future of an illusion*. New York: Norton.

Friedlmeier, M., & Trommsdorff, G. (2011). Are mother–child similarities in value orientations related to mothers' parenting? A comparative study of American and Romanian families with adolescents. *The European Journal of Developmental Psychology*, **8**, 661–680.

Galen, L. W., & Kloet, J. D. (2011). Mental well-being in the religious and the non-religious: Evidence for a curvilinear relationship. *Mental Health, Religion, and Culture*, **14**, 673–689.

Gelfand, M. J., Raver, J. L., Nishii, L., Leslie, L. A., Lun, J, Lim, B. C., … Yamaguchi, S. (2011). Differences between tight and loose cultures: A 33–nation study. *Science*, **332**, 1100–1104.

Good, M., & Willoughby, T. (2008). Adolescence as a sensitive period for spiritual development. *Child Development Perspectives*, **2**, 32–37.

Graber, J. A., & Brooks-Gunn, J. (1996). Transitions and turning points: Navigating the passage from childhood through adolescence. *Developmental Psychology*, **32**, 768–776.

Granqvist, P. (2002). Attachment and religiosity in adolescence: Cross-sectional and longitudinal evaluations. *Personality and Social Psychological Bulletin*, **28**, 260–270.

Granqvist, P., & Dickie, J. (2006). Attachment and spiritual development in childhood and adolescence. In E. C. Roehlkepartain, P. E. King, L. Wagener, & P. Benson (Eds.), *The handbook of spiritual development in childhood and adolescence* (pp. 197–210). Thousand Oaks, CA: Sage.

Greenfield, P. M. (2010). Particular forms of independence and interdependence are adapted to particular kinds of sociodemographic environment: Commentary on "Independence and interdependence in children's developmental experiences." *Child Development Perspectives*, **4**, 37–39.

Grob, A. (1998). Adolescents' subjective well-being in fourteen cultural contexts. In J. E. Nurmi (Ed.), *Adolescents, cultures and conflicts – Growing up in contemporary Europe. European advances in adolescent research* (pp. 199–224). New York: Garland.

Grob, A., Weisheit, W., & Gomez, V. (2009). The intergenerational transmission of xenophobia and rightism in East Germany. In U. Schönpflug (Ed.), *Cultural transmission.*

Psychological, developmental, social, and methodological aspects (pp. 338–369). New York: Cambridge University Press.

Grusec, J. E., & Goodnow, J. J. (1994). Impact of parental discipline methods on the child's internalization of values: A reconceptualization of current points of view. *Developmental Psychology, 30*, 4–19.

Halman, L., & Pettersson, T. (2006). A decline of religious values? In P. Ester, M. Braun, & P. Mohler (Eds.), *Globalization, value change and generation* (pp. 31–60). Leiden, The Netherlands: Brill.

Harris, P. L. (2000). On not falling down to earth. Children's metaphysical questions. In K. S. Rosengren, C. N. Johnson, & P. L. Harris (Eds.), *Imagining the impossible. Magical, scientific and religious thinking in children* (pp. 157–178). Cambridge, MA: Cambridge University Press.

Hayward, R. D., & Kemmelmeier, M. (2011). Weber revisited: A cross-national analysis of religiosity, religious culture, and economic attitudes. *Journal of Cross-Cultural Psychology, 42*, 1406–1420.

Henrich, J., Ensminger, J., McElreath, R., Barr, A., Barrett, C., Bolyanatz, A., ... Ziker, J. (2010). Markets, religion, community size, and the evolution of fairness and punishment. *Science, 327*, 1480–1484.

Herriot, P. (2009). *Religious fundamentalism. Global, local and personal.* New York: Routledge.

Hill, P. C., & Pargament, K. I. (2003). Advances in the conceptualization and measurement of religion and spirituality: Implications for physical and mental health research. *American Psychologist, 58*, 64–74.

Hinde, R. A. (1999). *Why gods persist: A scientific approach to religion.* London: Routledge.

Hoffman, L. W., & Hoffman, M. L. (1973). The value of children to parents. In J. T. Fawcett (Ed.), *Psychological perspectives on population* (pp. 19–76). New York: Basic Books.

Hofstede, G. H. (1980). *Culture's consequences: International differences in work–related values.* Los Angeles, CA: Sage.

(2001). *Culture's consequences: Comparing values, behaviors, institutions and organizations across nations* (2nd ed.). Thousand Oaks, CA: Sage.

Höllinger, F., & Haller, M. (2009). Decline or persistence of religion? Trends in religiosity among Christian societies around the world. In M. Haller, R. Jowell, & T. W. Smith (Eds.), *The international social survey programme, 1984–2009. Charting the globe* (pp. 281–301). London: Routledge.

Hood, R. W. J., Spilka, B., Hunsberger, B., & Gorsuch, R. (1996). Religious socialization and thought in adolescence and young adulthood. In R. W. J. Hood, B. Spilka, B. Hunsberger, & R. Gorsuch (Eds.), *The psychology of religion. An empirical approach* (pp. 72–110). New York: Guilford.

Hunsberger, B. (1995). Religion and prejudice: The role of religious fundamentalism, quest, and right–wing authoritarianism. *Journal of Social Issues, 51*, 113–129.

Hunsberger, B., & Brown, L. B. (1984). Religious socialization, apostasy, and the impact of family background. *Journal for the Scientific Study of Religion, 23*, 239–251.

Huntington, S. P. (Ed.). (1996). *The clash of civilizations and the remaking of world order.* New York: Simon and Schuster.

Hurrelmann, K., Albert, M., & TNS Infratest Sozialforschung (2006). *15. Shell-Jugendstudie: Jugend 2006. Eine pragmatische Generation unter Druck* [15th Shell-youth study: Youth 2006. A pragmatic generation under pressure]. Frankfurt: Fischer-Taschenbuch-Verlag.

Huston, A. C., & Bentley, A. C. (2010). Human development in societal context. *Annual Review of Psychology*, **61**, 411–437.

Inglehart, R. (1977). *The silent revolution: Changing values and political styles among Western publics*. Princeton, NJ: Princeton University Press.

    (1997). *Modernization and postmodernization: Cultural, economic and political change in 43 societies*. Princeton, NJ: Princeton University Press.

    (2007). Mapping global values. In Y. Esmer & T. Pettersson (Eds.), *Measuring and mapping cultures: 25 years of comparative value surveys* (pp. 11–32). Leiden, The Netherlands: Brill.

Inglehart, R., & Baker, W. E. (2000). Modernization, cultural change, and the persistence of traditional values. *American Sociological Review*, **65**, 19–51.

Inglehart, R., Basañez, M., & Moreno, A. (1998). *Human values and beliefs – A cross-cultural sourcebook: Political, religious, sexual, and economic norms in 43 societies. Findings from the 1990–1993 World Values Survey*. Ann Arbor: University of Michigan Press.

Inglehart, R., & Welzel, C. (Eds.). (2005). *Modernization, cultural change and democracy*. New York: Cambridge University Press.

Jagodzinski, W. (2004). Methodological problems of value research. In H. Vinken, J. Soeters, & P. Ester (Eds.), *Comparing cultures. Dimensions of culture in a comparative perspective* (pp. 97–121). Leiden, The Netherlands: Brill.

    (2011). Autonomy, religiosity and national identification as determinants of life satisfaction: A theoretical and empirical model and its application to Japan. *Contemporary Japan*, **23**, 93–127.

Jahoda, G. (2007). Kulturkonzepte im Wandel [Changing conceptions of culture]. In G. Trommsdorff & H.-J. Kornadt (Eds.), *Enzyklopädie der Psychologie: Themenbereich C. Theorie und Forschung: Serie VII. Kulturvergleichende Psychologie: Band 1. Theorien und Methoden in der kulturvergleichenden und kulturpsychologischen Forschung* (pp. 3–24). Göttingen, Germany: Hogrefe.

James, W. (1985). *The varieties of religious experience*. Cambridge, MA: Harvard University Press.

Johnson, B. R. (2008). A tale of two religious effects: Evidence for the protective and prosocial impact of organic religion. In K. Kovner Kline (Ed.), *Authoritative communities: The scientific case for nurturing the whole child* (pp. 187–225). New York: Springer.

Johnson, C. N., & Boyatzis, C. J. (2006). Cognitive–cultural foundations of spiritual development. In E. C. Roehlkepartain, P. Ebstyne King, L. Wagener, & P. Benson (Eds.), *The handbook of spiritual development in childhood and adolescence* (pp. 211–223). Thousand Oaks, CA: Sage.

Johnson, K. A., Hill, E. D., & Cohen, A. B. (2011). Integrating the study of culture and religion: Toward a psychology of worldview. *Social and Personality Psychology Compass*, **5**, 137–152.

Jowell, R., Kaase, M., Fitzgerald, R., & Eva, G. (2007). The European Social Survey as a measurement model. In R. Jowell, C. Roberts, R. Fitzgerald, & G. Eva (Eds.),

Measuring attitudes cross-nationally: Lessons from the European Social Survey (pp. 1–31). Los Angeles, CA: Sage.

Kagitcibasi, C. (1973). Psychological aspects of modernization in Turkey. *Journal of Cross Cultural Psychology, 4*, 157–174.

(2006). Theoretical perspectives on family change. In J. Georgas, J. W. Berry, F. J. R. van de Vijver, C. Kagitcibasi, & Y. H. Poortinga (Eds.), *Families across cultures: A 30-nation psychological study* (pp. 72–89). New York: Cambridge University Press.

(2007). *Family, self, and human development across cultures: Theory and applications* (2nd ed.). Hillsdale, NJ: Erlbaum.

Kapogiannis, D., Barbey, A. K., Su, M., Zamboni, G., Krueger, F., & Grafman, J. (2009). Cognitive and neural foundations of religious belief. *PNAS Proceedings of the National Academy of Sciences of the United States of America, 106*, 4876–4881.

Kelley, J., & De Graaf, N. D. (1997). National context, parental socialization, and religious belief: Results from 15 nations. *American Sociological Review, 62*, 639–659.

King, P. E., & Boyatzis, C. J. (2004). Exploring adolescent spiritual and religious development: Current and future theoretical and empirical perspectives. *Applied Developmental Science, 8*, 2–6.

King, P. E., & Roeser, R. W. (2009). Religion and spirituality in adolescent development. In R. M. Lerner & L. Steinberg (Eds.), *Handbook of adolescent psychology, Vol 1: Individual bases of adolescent development* (pp. 435–478). Hoboken, NJ: Wiley.

Kirkpatrick, L. A. (1995). Attachment theory and religious experience. In I. R. W. Hood (Ed.), *Handbook of religious experience* (pp. 446–475). Birmingham, AL: Religious Education Press.

Kitayama, S., & Imada, T. (2010). Implicit independence and interdependence: A cultural task analysis. In B. Mesquita, L. F. Barrett, & E. R. Smith (Eds.), *The mind in context.* (pp. 174–200). New York: Guilford.

Kluckhohn, C. K., & Strodtbeck, F. L. (1961). *Variations in value orientations.* Evanston, IL: Row, Peterson and Company.

Knafo, A., Assor, A., Schwartz, S. H., & David, L. (2009). Culture, migration, and family value socialization: A theoretical model and empirical investigation with Russian immigrant youth in Israel. In U. Schönpflug (Ed.), *Cultural transmission. Psychological, developmental, social, and methodological aspects* (pp. 269–296). New York: Cambridge University Press.

Knafo, A., & Schwartz, S. H. (2009). Accounting for parent–child value congruence: Theoretical considerations and empirical evidence. In U. Schönpflug (Ed.), *Cultural transmission. Psychological, developmental, social, and methodological aspects* (pp. 240–268). New York: Cambridge University Press.

Kohlberg, L. (1981). *Essays on moral development: Vol 1. The philosophy of moral development.* San Francisco, CA: Harper & Row.

Kroger, J., Martinussen, M., & Marcia, J. E. (2010). Identity status change during adolescence and young adulthood: A meta-analysis. *Journal of Adolescence, 33*, 683–698.

Kunnen, S. (2012). Introduction. In S. Kunnen (Ed.), *A dynamic systems approach to adolescent development* (pp. 1–2). New York: Psychology Press.

Lambert, W. W. (1992). Cultural background to aggression: Correlates and consequences of benevolent and malevolent gods and spirits. In A. Fraczek & H. Zumkley (Eds.), *Socialization and aggression* (pp. 217–230). Berlin: Springer.

Larson, R. W., Wilson, S., Brown, B. B., Furstenberg, F. F., Jr., & Verma, S. (2002). Changes in adolescents' interpersonal experiences: Are they being prepared for adult relationships in the twenty-first century? *Journal of Research on Adolescence*, 12, 31–68.

Lenski, G. (1961). *The religious factor: A sociological study of religion's impact on politics, economics, and family life*. Garden City, NY: Doubleday.

Lerner, R. (2002). *Concepts and theories of human development* (3rd ed.). Mahwah, NJ: Erlbaum.

Lerner, R. M., Lewin-Bizan, S., & Warren, A. E. A. (2011). Concepts and theories of human development. In M. H. Bornstein & M. E. Lamb (Eds.), *Cognitive development: An advanced textbook* (pp. 19–65). New York: Psychology Press.

Lerner, R. M., Roeser, R. W., & Phelps, E. (Eds.). (2008). *Positive youth development and spirituality: From theory to research*. West Conshohocken, PA: Templeton Foundation Press.

Levesque, R. R. (2002). *Not by faith alone: Religion, law, and adolescence*. New York: New York University Press.

Loewenthal, K. (2007). *Religion, culture and mental health*. New York: Cambridge University Press.

Marcia, J. E. (1966). Development and validation of ego–identity status. *Journal of Personality & Social Psychology*, 3, 551–558.

(1993). The ego identity status approach to ego identity. In J. E. Marcia, A. S. Waterman, D. R. Matteson, S. L. Archer, & J. L. Orlofsky (Eds.), *Ego identity: A handbook for psychosocial research* (pp. 3–21). New York: Springer.

Markus, H. R., & Kitayama, S. (1991). Culture and the self: Implications for cognition, emotion, and motivation. *Psychological Review*, 98, 224–253.

Maslow, A. H. (1943). A theory of human motivation. *Psychological Review*, 50, 370–396.

Mayer, B., & Trommsdorff, G. (2010). Adolescents' value of children and their intentions to have children: A cross-cultural and multilevel analysis. *Journal of Cross-Cultural Psychology*, 41, 671–689.

Mayer, B., Trommsdorff, G., Kagitcibasi, C., & Mishra, R. (in press). Family value patterns of independence/interdependence and their intergenerational similarity in Germany, Turkey, and India. *Family Science*. doi: 10.1080/19424620.2011.671503

McCullough, M. E., & Willoughby, B. L. B. (2009). Religion, self–regulation, and self–control: Associations, explanations, and implications. *Psychological Bulletin*, 135, 69–93.

Miller, R. B., & Glass, J. (1989). Parent–child attitude similarity across the life course. *Journal of Marriage and the Family*, 51, 991–997.

Miller, W. R., & Thoresen, C. E. (2003). Spirituality, religion, and health: An emerging research field. *American Psychologist*, 58, 24–35.

Myers, D. G. (2008). Religion and human flourishing. In M. Eid & R. J. Larsen (Eds.), *The science of subjective well–being* (pp. 323–346). New York: Guilford.

Nauck, B. (2009). Intergenerational transmission, social capital, and interethnic contact in immigrant families. In U. Schönpflug (Ed.), *Cultural transmission. Psychological, developmental, social, and methodological aspects* (pp. 161–184). New York: Cambridge University Press.

(2010). Intergenerational relationships and female inheritance expectations: Comparative results from eight societies in Asia, Europe, and North America. *Journal of Cross-Cultural Psychology*, 41, 690–705.

Norenzayan, A., & Shariff, A. F. (2008). The origin and evolution of religious prosociality. *Science*, 322, 58–62.

Norris, P., & Inglehart, R. (2004). Measuring secularization. In P. Norris & R. Inglehart (Eds.), *Sacred and secular – Religion and politics worldwide* (pp. 33–52). New York: Cambridge University Press.

Nunner-Winkler, G. (1995). Moralentwicklung im Kindesalter. Zur Frage nach dem Verhältnis von Moral und Religion [Moral development in childhood. The question of the relationship of moral and religion]. In E. Gross (Ed.), *Der Kinderglaube. Perspektiven aus der Forschung für die Praxis* (pp. 47–64). Donauwörth, Germany: Auer.

Nurmi, J. E. (1998). *Adolescents, cultures and conflicts – Growing up in contemporary Europe. European advances in adolescent research.* New York: Garland.

Oser, F. K., Scarlett, W. G., & Bucher, A. (2006). Religious and spiritual development throughout the life span. In R. M. Lerner & W. Damon (Eds.), *Handbook of child psychology (6th ed.): Vol. 1, Theoretical models of human development.* (pp. 942–998). Hoboken, NJ: Wiley.

Oyserman, D., Coon, H. M., & Kemmelmeier, M. (2002). Rethinking individualism and collectivism: Evaluation of theoretical assumptions and meta–analyses. *Psychological Bulletin*, 128, 3–72.

Paloutzian, R. F., & Park, C. L. (Eds.). (2005). *Handbook of the psychology of religion and spirituality.* New York: Guilford.

Pankhurst, J. G., & Houseknecht, S. K. (2000). Introduction: The religion–family linkage and social change – a neglected area of study. In S. K. Houseknecht & J. G. Pankhurst (Eds.), *Family, religion, and social change in diverse societies* (pp. 1–40). Oxford: Oxford University Press.

Pargament, K. I. (2002). Is religion nothing but …? Explaining religion versus explaining religion away. *Psychological Inquiry*, 13, 239–244.

Pargament, K. I., & Cummings, J. (2010). Anchored by faith: Religion as a resilience factor. In J. W. Reich, A. J. Zautra, & J. Hall (Eds.), *Handbook of adult resilience* (pp. 193–210). New York: Guilford.

Parsons, T. (1951). *The social system.* London: Routledge & Paul.

Parsons, T., & Shils, E. A. (Eds.). (1951). *Toward a general theory of action.* Cambridge, MA: Harvard University Press.

Pearce, L. D., & Thornton, A. (2007). Religious identity and family ideologies in the transition to adulthood. *Journal of Marriage and the Family*, 69, 1227–1243.

Pettersson, T. (2007). Religion in contemporary society: Eroded human well–being, supported by cultural diversity. In Y. Esmer & T. Pettersson (Eds.), *Measuring and mapping cultures: 25 years of comparative value surveys* (pp. 127–153). Leiden, The Netherlands: Brill.

Phalet, K., & Schönpflug, U. (2001). Intergenerational transmission in Turkish immigrant families: Parental collectivism, achievement values and gender differences. *Journal of Comparative Family Studies*, 32, 489–504.

Phinney, J. S. (2008). Bridging identities and disciplines: Advances and challenges in understanding multiple identities. In M. Azmitia, M. Syed, & K. Radmacher (Eds.),

The intersections of personal and social identities. New Directions for Child and Adolescent Development, **120**, 97–109.

Piaget, J. (1928). Immanence et transcendence [Immanence and transcendence]. In J. Piaget & J. de la Harpe (Eds.), *Deux types d'attitude religieuse: Immanence et transcendence* (Editions de l'Association Chretienne d'Etudiants de Suisse Romande, Depot ed., pp. 5–40). Geneva: Labor.

Plante, T. G., & Sherman, A. (Eds.). (2001). *Faith and health: Psychological perspectives.* New York: Guilford.

Pollner, M. (1989). Divine relations, social relations, and well–being. *Journal of Health and Social Behavior*, **30**, 92–104.

Powell, L. H., Shahabi, L., & Thorensen, C. E. (2003). Religion and spirituality: Linkages to physical health. *American Psychologist*, **58**, 36–52.

Raiya, H., Pargament, K. I., & Magyar-Russell, G. (2010). When religion goes awry: Religious risk factors for poorer health and well–being. In P. J. Verhagen, H. M. van Praag, J. López-Ibor Jr., L. Cox, & D. Moussaoui (Eds.), *Religion and psychiatry: Beyond boundaries* (pp. 389–411). New York: Wiley–Blackwell.

Ream, G. L., & Savin-Williams, R. C. (2003). Religious development in adolescence. In G. R. Adams & M. D. Berzonsky (Eds.), *Blackwell handbook of adolescence.* (pp. 51–59). Malden, MA: Blackwell Publishing.

Roelkepartain, E. C., King, P. E., Wagener, L., & Benson, P. L. (Eds.). (2005). *The handbook of spiritual development in childhood and adolescence.* Thousand Oaks, CA: Sage.

Rokeach, M. (1969). Value systems and religion. *Review of Religious Research*, **22**, 2–23.

(1973). *The nature of human values.* New York: Free Press.

Rothbaum, F., Pott, M., Azuma, H., Miyake, K., & Weisz, J. (2000). The development of close relationships in Japan and the United States: Paths of symbiotic harmony and generative tension. *Child Development*, **71**, 1121–1142.

Rothbaum, F., & Trommsdorff, G. (2007). Do roots and wings oppose or complement one another? The socialization of autonomy and relatedness in cultural context. In J. E. Grusec & P. Hastings (Eds.), *The handbook of socialization* (pp. 461–489). New York: Guilford.

Rothbaum, F., & Wang, Y. Z. (2010). Fostering the child's malleable views of the self and the world: Caregiving practices in East Asian and European-American communities. In B. Mayer & H.-J. Kornadt (Eds.), *Psychologie – Kultur – Gesellschaft* (pp. 101–120). Wiesbaden: VS Verlag.

Rudy, D., & Grusec, J. E. (2001). Correlates of authoritarian parenting in individualist and collectivist cultures and implications for understanding the transmission of values. *Journal of Cross-Cultural Psychology*, **32**, 202–212.

Sabatier, C., Mayer, B., Friedlmeier, M., Lubiewska, K., & Trommsdorff, G. (2011). Religiosity, family orientation, and life satisfaction of adolescents in four countries. *Journal of Cross-Cultural Psychology*, **42**, 1375–1393.

Saroglou, V. (2011). Believing, bonding, behaving, and belonging: The big four religious dimensions and cultural variation. *Journal of Cross-Cultural Psychology*, **42**, 1320–1340.

Saroglou, V., Delpierre, V., & Dernelle, R. (2004). Values and religiosity: A meta-analysis of studies using Schwartz's model. *Personality and Individual Differences*, **37**, 721–734.

Sasaki, J. Y., & Kim, H. S. (2010). At the intersection of culture and religion: A cultural analysis of religion's implications for secondary control and social affiliation. *Journal of Personality and Social Psychology, 101,* 401–414.

Sasaki, J. Y., Kim, H. S., & Xu, J. (2011). Religion and well-being: The moderating role of culture and the oxytocin receptor (OXTR) gene. *Journal of Cross-Cultural Psychology, 42,* 1394–1405.

Schönpflug, U. (Ed.). (2009). *Cultural transmission. Psychological, developmental, social, and methodological aspects.* New York: Cambridge University Press.

Schwartz, S. H. (Ed.). (1992). *Universals in the content and structure of values: Theoretical advances and empirical tests in 20 countries.* San Diego, CA: Academic Press.

(1996). *Value priorities and behavior: Applying a theory of integrated value systems.* Hillsdale, NJ: Erlbaum.

Schwartz, S. H. (2006). A theory of cultural value orientations: Explication and applications. *Comparative Sociology, 5,* 137–182.

(2007). Cultural and individual value correlates of capitalism: A comparative analysis. *Psychological Inquiry, 18,* 52–57.

Schwartz, S. H., & Sagi, G. (2000). Value consensus and importance: A cross-national study. *Journal of Cross Cultural Psychology, 31,* 465–497.

Schwartz, S. H., & Vecchione, M. (2011, June). A revised theory and new instrument to measure basic individual values. In S. H. Schwartz (Chair), *A refined theory of human values: What, how, and why?* Symposium conducted at the Regional Meeting of the International Association of Cross-Cultural Psychology (IACCP), Istanbul, Turkey.

Schwarz, B. (2007). Jugend im Kulturvergleich [Adolescence in cross-cultural comparison]. In G. Trommsdorff & H.-J. Kornadt (Eds.), *Enzyklopädie der Psychologie: Serie VII, Band 2. Kulturvergleichende Psychologie: Kulturelle Determinanten des Erlebens und Verhaltens* (pp. 599–641). Göttingen, Germany: Hogrefe.

Scott, J., & Braun, M. (2006). Individualization of family values? In P. Ester, M. Braun, & P. Mohler (Eds.), *Globalization, value change, and generations.* (pp. 61–88). Leiden, The Netherlands: Brill.

Seginer, R. (2009). *Future orientation: Developmental and ecological perspectives.* New York: Springer Science + Business Media.

Silbereisen, R. K., & Chen, X. (Eds.). (2010). *Social change and human development: Concepts and results.* London: Sage.

Silberman, I. (2005). Religion as a meaning system: Implications for the new millennium. *Journal of Social Issues, 61,* 641–663.

Silverstein, M., Gans, D., Lowenstein, A., Giarrusso, R., & Bengtson, V. L. (2010). Older parent–child relationships in six developed nations: Comparisons at the intersection of affection and conflict. *Journal of Marriage and Family, 72,* 1006–1021.

Smith, C., & Lundquist Denton, M. (2005). *Soul searching. The religious and spiritual lives of American teenagers.* Oxford: University Press.

Smith, P. B., & Schwartz, S. H. (1997). Values. In J. W. Berry, M. H. Segall, & C. Kagitcibasi (Eds.), *Handbook of cross-cultural psychology. Social behavior and applications* (Vol. 3, pp. 77–118). Needham Heights, MA: Allyn & Bacon.

Spranger, E. (1921). *Lebensformen. Geisteswissenschaftliche Psychologie und Ethik der Persönlichkeit* [Life forms. Humanistic psychology and ethic of personality]. Halle, Germany: Max Niemeyer.

Steinberg, L. D. (1999). *Adolescence (5th ed.)*. New York: McGraw–Hill.

Steinberg, L., Graham, S., O'Brien, L., Woolard, J., Cauffman, E., & Banich, M. (2009). Age differences in future orientation and delay discounting. *Child Development*, **80**, 28–44.

Steinberg, L., & Morris, A. S. (2001). Adolescent development. *Annual Review of Psychology*, **52**, 83–110.

Streib, H., Hood, R. W., Keller, B., Csöff, R. M., & Silver, C. F. (2009). *Deconversion: Qualitative and quantitative results from cross-cultural research in Germany and the United States of America*. Göttingen, Germany: Vandenhoeck & Ruprecht.

Suckow, J. (2005). The value of children among Jews and Muslims in Israel: Methods and results from the VOC–field study. In G. Trommsdorff & B. Nauck (Eds.), *The value of children in cross-cultural perspective. Case studies from eight societies* (pp. 121–143). Lengerich, Germany: Pabst Science.

Triandis, H. C. (1995). *Individualism & collectivism*. Boulder, CO: Westview Press.

Trommsdorff, G. (1992). Values and social orientations of Japanese youth in intercultural comparison. In S. Formanek & S. Linhart (Eds.), *Japanese biographies: Life histories, life cycles, life stages* (pp. 57–81). Vienna: Verlag der Österreichischen Akademie der Wissenschaften.

(2000). Effects of social change on individual development: The role of social and personal factors and the timing of events. In L. Crocket & R. K. Silbereisen (Eds.), *Negotiating adolescence in times of social change* (pp. 58–68). Cambridge: Cambridge University Press.

(2006). Parent–child relations over the life-span. A cross-cultural perspective. In K. H. Rubin & O. B. Chung (Eds.), *Parenting beliefs, behaviors, and parent–child relations. A cross-cultural perspective.* (pp. 143–183). New York: Psychology Press.

(2007). Entwicklung im kulturellen Kontext [Development in cultural context]. In G. Trommsdorff & H.-J. Kornadt (Eds.), *Enzyklopädie der Psychologie: Themenbereich C Theorie und Forschung, Serie VII Kulturvergleichende Psychologie. Band 2: Kulturelle Determinanten des Erlebens und Verhaltens* (pp. 435–519). Göttingen, Germany: Hogrefe.

(2009a). Intergenerational relations and cultural transmission. In U. Schönpflug (Ed.), *Cultural transmission. Psychological, developmental, social, and methodological aspects* (pp. 126–160). New York: Cambridge University Press.

(2009b). A social change and a human development perspective on the value of children. In S. Bekman & A. Aksu-Koc (Eds.), *Perspectives on human development, family and culture* (pp. 86–107). Cambridge: Cambridge University Press.

(2012). Development of agentic regulation in cultural context: The role of self and world views. *Child Development Perspectives*, **6**, 19–26.

Trommsdorff, G., Cole, P. M., & Heikamp, T. (in press). Cultural variations in mothers' intuitive theories: A preliminary report on interviewing mothers of five nations about their socialization of children's emotions. *Global Studies of Childhood*.

Trommsdorff, G., & Kornadt, H.-J. (2003). Parent–child relations in cross-cultural perspective. In L. Kuczynski (Ed.), *Handbook of dynamics in parent–child relations* (pp. 271–306). Thousand Oaks, CA: Sage.

Trommsdorff, G., Mayer, B., & Albert, I. (2004). Dimensions of culture in intra-cultural comparisons: Individualism/collectivism and family-related values in three generations. In H. Vinken, J. Soeters, & P. Ester (Eds.), *Comparing cultures: Dimensions of culture in a comparative perspective* (pp. 157–184). Leiden, The Netherlands: Brill.

Trommsdorff, G., & Nauck, B. (Eds.). (2005). *The value of children in cross-cultural perspective. Case studies from eight societies.* Lengerich, Germany: Pabst Science.

Trommsdorff, G., & Nauck, B. (2006). Demographic changes and parent–child relationships. *Parenting: Science and Practice,* **6,** 343–360.

Trommsdorff, G., & Nauck, B. (Eds.). (2010). The value of children: Overview and progress and recent contributions [Special section]. *Journal of Cross-Cultural Psychology,* **41.**

Trommsdorff, G., & Rothbaum, F. (2008). Development of emotion regulation in cultural context. In S. Ismer, S. Jung, S. Kronast, C. von Scheve, & M. Vandekerckhove (Eds.), *Regulating emotions: Social necessity and biological inheritance* (pp. 85–120). New York: Blackwell.

Trommsdorff, G., Suzuki, T., & Sasaki, M. (1987). Soziale Ungleichheiten in Japan und der Bundesrepublik Deutschland [Social disparities in Japan and Germany]. *Kölner Zeitschrift für Soziologie und Sozialpsychologie,* **39,** 496–515.

Turner, B. S. (2011). *Religion and modern society: Citizenship, secularisation and the state.* Cambridge: Cambridge University Press.

van de Vijver, F. J. R., Hemert, D. A., & Poortinga, Y. H. (Eds.). (2008). *Multilevel analysis of individuals and culture.* New York: Erlbaum.

Verma, S., & Maria, M. S. (2006). The changing global context of adolescent spirituality. In E. C. Roehlkepartain, P. Ebstyne King, L. Wagener, & P. L. Benson (Eds.), *The handbook of spiritual development in childhood and adolescence* (pp. 124–136). London: Sage.

Warren, A. E. A., Lerner, R. M., & Phelps, E. (2011). Research perspectives and future possibilities in the study of thriving and spirituality: A view of the issues. In A. E. A. Warren, R. M. Lerner, & E. Phelps (Eds.), *Thriving and spirituality among youth: Research perspectives and future possibilities* (pp. 1–18). Hoboken, NJ: Wiley.

Waterman, A. S. (1985). Identity in the context of adolescent psychology. *New Directions for Child Development,* **30,** 305–324.

Weber, M. (1958). *The protestant ethic and the spirit of capitalism.* New York: Scribner.

(1988). *Gesammelte Aufsätze zur Religionssoziologie* [Collected articles about sociology of religion] (9th ed.). Tübingen, Germany: Mohr.

Werner, H. (1948). *Comparative psychology of mental development.* Oxford: Follett.

Whiting, B. B., & Whiting, J. W. M. (1975). *Children of six cultures: A psycho–cultural analysis.* Cambridge, MA: Harvard University Press.

Wilson, D. S. (2003). *Darwin's cathedral: Evolution, religion, and the nature of society.* Chicago: University of Chicago Press.

Woodhead, L. (2008). Gendering secularisation theory. *Social Compass,* **55,** 187–193.

Wulff, D. (1991). *Psychology of religion: Classic and contemporary views.* New York: Wiley & Sons.

Wundt, W. (1926). *Völkerpsychologie: Eine Untersuchung der Entwicklungsgesetze von Sprache, Mythus und Sitte* [Ethnopsychology: An investigation of the developmental laws of speech, myth, and convention]. Leipzig: Alfred Kröner Verlag.

Youniss, J., McLellan, J.A., & Yates, M. (1999). Religion, community service, and identity in American youth. *Journal of Adolescence,* **22,** 243–253.

2 Psychological Functions of Religion in Youth – A Historical and Cultural Perspective

Hans-Joachim Kornadt

Abstract

Psychological functions of religion in youth are discussed from a motivational and anthropological approach including a historical and cultural perspective. The role of religious beliefs in ancient, medieval, and traditional societies are described, referring to some possible origins in the evolution of such beliefs. These origins are seen in the belief in an invisible "other" (or spiritual) world, motivated to make sense of otherwise incomprehensible events. This is assumed to have strong psychological effects on the formation of religion in mankind, on the development of religious practices, and the role and importance of shamans and priests. The psychological functions of religion in adolescents' development by initiation rites, and in modern societies with focus on natural sciences and a secularization of the worldview are discussed. There are a great variety of beliefs and strong differences in the importance of religion in different cultures. The importance and power of religion differ, ranging from fundamentalism to secularization. The importance of these differences for emergent adults are considered. Religiosity may foster identity development, civic engagement, prosocial activities, and life satisfaction. However, it can also promote other less desirable behaviors in youth like intolerance and aggressiveness against unbelievers. Both the cultural context and individual motivations are shown to affect religious development and personality development in adolescence in various ways.

In this chapter, I discuss religion and the power of religious belief from a psychological perspective and describe the effects of belief in God and an "other" spirit world. First, I discuss the stabilizing role of religion for societies and for the power of priests and shamans. Second, I describe the ambiguous importance of religion and the power of belief for the development and value orientation of youth.

Role of Religious Belief in Ancient, Medieval, and Traditional Societies

Historical View on the Development of Religion. Wilhelm Wundt, the founder of cultural psychology, held that the beginning of religion dates back to the early development of mankind, based on archaeological and ethnological findings (Wundt, 1926). Early prehistoric people had to survive in a dangerous world with only a limited understanding of nature and the events around them. They were certainly aware of some immediate cause-and-effect relationships of their own actions like throwing stones or angering another person by injuring him or her, but dramatic events like lightning, illness, or death were incomprehensible, causing permanent uncertainty. They needed to make sense of the world around them. With the universal human tendency to engage in causal attributions (Heider, 1958) they assumed the existence of an invisible world with powerful spirits behind those events. They believed in the permanent influence of those spirits on everyday life. In the case of a geocentric worldview, humans may be conceived of as part of the environment (e.g., Mishra & Dasen, 2005) and, when combined with strong emotional responses like anxiety, that belief can strengthen to become absolutely convincing.

Even much later, in the Neolithic period, an example of the origin of such a belief can be found: In the *Rigveda*, the oldest Indian religious text, whose content is about 4000 years old. The Rigveda describes *Agni*, who was worshipped as the God of fire and believed to be born out of a stone. Sparks, the source of fire, can come from flint stones. This illustrates how such a belief can develop from the interpretation of natural phenomena (Maier, 2008). Those events were incomprehensible and therefore mysterious. In the Palaeolithic period it was therefore not unreasonable to assume the existence of an invisible other world with secret powerful spirits to be feared, admired, and worshipped. Because people had only limited knowledge, they likely conceived the spirits to be like themselves and ascribed them good and bad tempers and intentions. Thus, it would be logical to try to appease the spirits with prayers or offerings or by worshipping them, often at places believed to be their home, like big trees, rocks, or springs (Bellah, 1970). Later in the Palaeolithic era, the *Homo neanderthalensis* seem to have believed in a life after death: they buried their deceased with funerary goods, perhaps to make the deceased comfortable in the other world (Clark, 1962).

Some gifted members of the group became middlemen for the invisible world and its spirits. They became *priests* or and sometimes *shamans*. They interpreted natural phenomena as signs of the spirits and the spirits' demands, using oracles and *omina*. They told how the spirits should be appeased by rituals, offerings, and worshipping (Wahle, 1973). In this stage of development, worshipping and offerings were presented in order to receive the god's benevolence. Thus, offerings and praying had the character of *do ut des*: it was a pragmatic action, like exchanging presents with neighbors to establish a friendly relationship or to make peace with enemies or rivals.

The nature of worship as a "deal" between men and spirits changed fundamentally when divine demands were no longer seen as directed to the benefit of the gods, but to *fellow men*. People had developed – based on the theory of mind – the ability to understand others' intentions and wishes, which led to them experiencing others' needs and emotions as well. This empathy became a central component of religious beliefs, at least for one's own religious group. This was, for instance, expressed by King Musili of the Hittites in the 14th century before Christ. He declared that an oracle had disclosed that the misfortunes their people had suffered over the last 20 years were the divine punishment for a crime among humans (Maier, 2008). This indicates the belief that a god is demanding moral conduct between men – not just toward the god alone – and that disobeying this demand is a sin, which will be severely punished by invisible powers or gods. In the Bible, the same is described as a consequence of "eating from the tree of knowledge," and "recognizing one another" became the precondition of sin. Religious moral demands became the basis for guilt and the fear of being severely punished, possibly with eternal punishment after death.

Religion in Ancient Elaborated Cultures. In historical times, many differentiated cultures emerged, such as in Egypt, Sumer, Assyr, and China. Various elaborate belief systems developed with differing views of the relationship between the real, visible world and the "other" world, sometimes differentiated as Heaven and the Underworld. Gods were assumed to have a special interest in humans and special temples were built and rituals developed for their worship. Elaborate religious systems became the basic ideology and distinguishing characteristic of cultures and the most important order in establishing, and unifying, a society. Sometimes the king was the highest priest and a theocracy was developed; religion and the tribe or the state were unified. Even details like what to eat, what to wear, and when to pray were prescribed. Nonbelievers were not tolerated and were sometimes seen as enemies and prosecuted.

Men strived to gain the gods' benevolence, and sometimes attempted to come as close as possible to the divine powers by meditation or ecstasy.

Various mystery cults developed (Kloft, 2010), such as the Osiris cult in ancient Egypt and later in Rome, the Demeter cult in ancient Greece, and the Persian Mithras cult, which later in Roman times even spread through Western Europe.

In many of these cultures, the priest held high status and a great deal of power as the interpreter of the meaning and wishes of the gods. Priests could order special offerings, which in some cultures even included human sacrifices. The Celtic Druids in Ireland offered human sacrifices until the third century after Christ (Cunliffe, 1993; Demandt, 2005).

Religion and Shamanism in Traditional Cultures. In more traditional, indigenous cultures, religious belief and the imagined "other world" are usually less elaborate. This is the case in Haiti, for instance, with believers in voodoo, and was true in Indonesia until the 20th century with the Batak (Sumatra) and Dayaks (Sulawesi) and is the case with the Sundanese and even the Balinese today. Moral demands here also have a metaphysical importance. In these primarily subsistence economies, every culture developed its own rules and rights. Each member of the tribe or group obeyed the customs (*Adat*) of worshipping or offerings. These religious beliefs had a stabilizing function for the social structure, distinguishing each particular tribe from others. The belief in the other world was in a way simpler, but the mysticism associated with the other world was stronger, endowing the shamans with a great deal of magical power.

Shamanism was an early development in human prehistory, dating back at least to the Paleolithic era (approximately 200,000 years ago). Scenes of shamanistic séance, as they appear today in North-Asiatic tribes, have existed at least since the young Paleolithic period (approximately 14,000 years ago): in the Lascaux cave (Dordogne, southern France), a man is depicted lying on the ground as if in a trance, wearing a mask of a bird head; a bird on a stick is thought to symbolize his soul on the way to the other world (Müller, 2006). Shamanism existed in most ancient hunting and fishing cultures, spreading from Feuerland through all North-Eurasian hunting and fishing cultures until reaching Tibet, Japan, Indonesia, and the Australian Aborigines (Müller, 2006). Fertility in humans and nature and success in hunting were people's primary interests, and shamans played an important role in mitigating concerns: both areas were believed to depend on the good or evil will of supernatural powers, and the shamans had the ability to communicate with those powers (Winstedt, 1982). The basis of those beliefs and therefore, the power of the shamans was based on the cosmologic dualism between the visible world and the other, supernatural invisible world with its mighty spirits. Shamanism is therefore also a particularly impressive example for the power of belief in the other world. Shamans were like priests – the middlemen between the present and the other world, men and spirits, the living and the ancestors.

The central concept in Shamanism is the belief in the soul. The *vital soul* enables the body to live. Decline of vitality was interpreted as weakness of the vital soul, caused for example, by an enemy's sorcery or contact with the "radiation" of another strange soul. A *free soul* can leave the body for a limited time: if the shaman is in a trance, his or her soul can get in contact with spirits of the other world, and return with knowledge (e.g., how to heal a sick person, who told the truth, or what the best time is for harvesting, hunting, or warfare). For any human, when a dramatic event occurs – such as a sudden, severe shock or a serious argument – the soul becomes severely disturbed and can even temporarily leave the body, causing serious sickness or even death (Winstedt, 1982). All these phenomena demonstrate the strong power of belief. Bad events were mostly interpreted as being caused by one's own mistakes or wrongdoings.

Religion and Adolescent Development in Traditional Societies. Youth in ancient, medieval, and traditional societies grew up without many puberty problems, embedded in their culture with its material and spiritual world, which were structured on religious belief. They grew up in close, intimate contact with others of various ages: with siblings, parents, and many other adults together in an extended group. They had to take on duties and learn the skills and attitudes needed to survive in the adult world as early as possible. They learned how to master useful tasks according to their age and thereby developed self-confidence and their own identity as members of their culture. With puberty, they were seen as adults and expected to assume all duties, tasks, and rights of an adult. The social organization, its rules, values, and skills needed were taken for granted, as self-understanding (Brown, Larson, & Saraswathi, 2002).

Of course, the average life expectancy in these cultures was quite short, not much more than 30 years of age. In the early European middle ages (11–15th centuries), for instance, after a period of strict training, young men were knighted at about 14 years of age, and were then seen as adults and allowed to marry.

In many traditional cultures, adolescents went through formalized rites of passage. They have been and still are different in different cultures. These rites of passage are always aimed at supporting integration into the world of adults and preserving cultural traditions. In many cultures, elaborate initiation rituals are established. Boys and girls are often first isolated and then undergo initiation procedures that are sometimes very stressful and anxiety inducing. Adolescents may have to endure painful procedures like circumcision, teeth cutting (e.g., formerly in Bali), or tattooing, among others. Only when they have passed these rites will they be accepted in the world of the adults, and told the duties and rules of adulthood. Mythical traditions, beliefs, and fears, and, in some cases, secret customs and holy stories of their origin or holy places are entrusted to the newly recognized adults. The passage through frightening situations and the successful coping with such tasks enforces cultural ties and the social structure. The experience of these traumatic initiation rites also reinforces the belief in the other world and the belief in the power of shamans or magicians (Winstedt, 1982).

Psychological Aspects of Religious Belief. From a psychological point of view, it is necessary to understand the immense convincing power that a religious belief in another world and its spirits can have. An example comes from ancient Greece: their gods could intervene in human fate, and they disclosed their intervention through, for example, the oracle in Delphi, where the gods were worshipped. In some cultures, however, there is a complete penetration of the other world into what we understand to be the real world, so that every step and every action might somehow be under the possible influence of spirits, or permanently observed or governed by God. This is the case with some indigenous cultures, such as the former Batak cultures, which viewed spirits as mostly evil and dangerous; this is similar today in Thai and Balinese cultures as well. Their spirits are rather hostile but can be calmed by rituals and offerings. In Bali, temples are everywhere, both tiny and big, and the gods receive offerings every day (Kornadt, 2011). In some religious systems, there is no distinction between this world and the other world: there is only one universe (e.g., in some forms of Buddhism [*Sankya*]). There is no real distinction between the invisible world and our existence in everyday life, everything is complexly connected (Dalai Lama, 2005).

Importantly, if such a belief is established, it is immune against rational arguments. Being convinced about the existence of an invisible other world with secret powers beyond understanding or about immediate divine revelation is a matter of faith and thus cannot be disproven. According to some beliefs, the real world is the other world, whereas our "real world" is seen as a kind of shadow, or as reflecting a small portion of the universe.

Summary
There are three points to underline: first, the idea of an invisible other world exists more or less in all cultures. This is sometimes a special sphere distinct from our real, visible world. Sometimes, there is no real distinction: the spirits of the other world are present everywhere and the real world is only a part of the whole unknown universe, or a transition to the invisible world. Second, belief in the other world can be an extreme power. With the Batak of northern Sumatra, the shaman, or *Datu*, could in former days be the master of life and death. A man who violated a taboo or was condemned by the Datu to face an ordeal could die within a few days, even though he was physically untouched. It was the effect of a shock owing to guilt, or to anxiety of severe punishment in the other world (Kornadt, 2011; Winkler, 1925; M. Yamaluddin, personal communication, March, 1985). Third, any belief referring to the invisible other world is immune against logical arguments. The details of such a belief are seen as higher wisdom and therefore irrefutable. The power of belief is strikingly formulated by the German writer Wilhelm Busch (1954): "*Nur was wir glauben, wissen wir gewiss*" (Only what we believe do we know with certainty).

Psychological Functions of Religion for Adolescents' Development in Modern Societies

Religion in Modern Societies
In the second part, I describe the ambiguous role of religion for the development and value orientation of youth in modern societies. The function of religion has changed since modernization in most societies. Therefore, the importance of religion to youth and emerging adults has also changed, namely transforming into a private matter (Hölliger & Haller, 2009; Sinabell, 2009). In postmodern, industrialized societies, the pervasive power of religion with its function of providing common norms and social cohesion has mostly vanished (Sinabell, 2009). In our Western societies, we are used to seeing our world and the universe today as it is conceptualized by natural sciences. In Western Europe, the idea of an invisible other world, commandments by God, and an afterlife have mostly lost their convincing power. Also, the concept of sin has lost its metaphysical meaning. Laws are manmade by political negotiation, variables, and are different in each state. Violating moral rules is not much more than breaking an ordinary law (Sinabell, 2009).

The shift in religious beliefs occurring in Europe is remarkable because it differs so greatly from religiosity in medieval times. People at that time believed in the afterlife, and earthly life was seen as a passage toward the last judgment, leading either into paradise or to eternal damnation. Christians who did not accept parts of the official faith were prosecuted (e.g., Albigenser; Jan Huss), others were burned as witches. In famous European paintings of the 15th and 16th centuries, those beliefs are convincingly depicted.

Today in some art circles, it has become even fashionable to trivialize Christian symbols like the Holy Communion or the crucifix as a joke. In Germany, there is scarcely any protest against such Christian sacrilege, although the same is not true for acts of Islamic heresy (Huber, 2010).

However the importance of religion varies considerably between cultures: the importance of Christianity varies between West and East Europe, Russia, and the United States. In Germany, 33 percent claim to be without any religious association (Gasper, 2009). In the United States, in contrast, intensive religious life exists in numerous communities, and 80 percent of students report to believe in God (Higher Education Research Institute, 2003; Smith & Lundquist Denton, 2005). Within these communities, there is a great variety of beliefs: even members of the Evangelical Alliance, which have similar positions regarding the creation and rejection of evolutionary theory can have opposite positions in other important aspects. All of these mostly protestant communities descend from the early European immigrants who left their homes to practice their individual interpretations of Christianity (Gasper, 2009).Within Islam there is splitting between the Sunnis and the Shiites, and differences exist as well between the orthodox Wahhabites (in Saudi Arabia) and more moderate forms of Islam (in Tunisia, hitherto Indonesia).

Religion and Adolescent Development

Youth in modern societies face difficulties growing up and becoming well-integrated and productive members of their societies because of many reasons (see Arnett, 2000, 2007). An important factor is the prolonged emerging adulthood (Arnett, 2000), during which adolescents do not have the social roles and obligations of adulthood. Instead, adolescents spend many years on training and education, often until age 25 or older. Some individuals are students even until 30 years of age. This tendency is increasing in Germany: in 1999, one-third of adults between 20 and 24 years of age were students or trainees, whereas in 2009, already nearly one-half were (Kary, 2011, March). During this developmental stage, adolescents experience greater instability and are searching for identity (Elkind, 1999; Roeser, Lerner, & Phelps, 2008). Without responsible duties it becomes difficult to establish self-confidence and a self-identity (Arnett, 2007; Eccles, 2007). For the formation of self-image and personal and social identity, this is a crucial developmental period, and it is a sensitive time for religiosity (Barry, Nelson, Davarya, & Urry, 2010; Good & Willoughby, 2008). Especially in Western European societies, adult life has become very diverse, embracing a wide variety of lifestyles (Côté, 2009; Gagné, 2011; Patterson & Hastings 2007; Spilka, Hood, Hunsberger, & Gorsuch, 2003). The media has a diverse and important influence. In one's professional life, there is decreasing stability. For youth, it is therefore difficult to develop an image of what kind of a person they want to be in the future (see Seginer, 2008, 2009, for future orientation and identity development of adolescents). Adolescents have difficulty fulfilling their basic needs for autonomy and relatedness in different cultural contexts (Rothbaum & Trommsdorff, 2007) and in a permanently changing environment (Mayer & Trommsdorff, Chapter 15 in this volume).

In this circumstance, the timing of puberty becomes relevant. Whereas puberty coincided with the transition to adulthood in the past, that is no longer the case today. During puberty, physiological hormonal changes are accompanied by psychological effects that often result in higher emotional liability (Arnett, 2000, 2007) and excitability, combined with a need for higher physical activity (Steinberg, 2005), especially in males because of an increase of testosterone (Henning & Netter, 2005). In behavior, this is expressed through sensation seeking and an increased tendency toward aggressive behavior (Rosenblitt, Soler, Johnson, & Quadagno, 2001). In some traditional cultures, these tendencies have been channeled through initiation rites, sometimes by headhunting – the practice of taking and preserving a person's head after killing them (Cunliffe, 1993; Hoskins, 1989). The Christian equivalent is confirmation in Catholicism and Protestantism, but confirmation takes place between 12 and 15 years of age and, as a result, is no longer associated with a transition to adulthood.

It is not surprising that more or less isolated youth cultures (Bukowski, Brendgen, & Vitaro, 2007) have developed, separate from adult life with its duties and regularities (Süss, 2009). During emerging adulthood (Arnett, 2000), youth have a great deal of time to explore their personal identity. Some experiment with various identities (Baer, 2009), sometimes reinventing themselves to match the prevailing norm of their special social circle (Baier, Pfeiffer, Simonson, & Rabold, 2009; Farin, 2010). They experiment with premarital sex, drugs, alcohol, and other risky behaviors. Some come even in serious conflicts (Arnett, 2007): contest binge drinking is on the rise. In Germany, for example, the number of youths between ages 10 and 19 who were hospitalized with severe alcohol intoxication increased by 178 percent (to 26,428 youth) between 2000 and 2009 (Statistisches Bundesamt,

2011). I assume that religion is mostly of no relevance here, in contrast to consumption (Deutsch & Theodorou, 2010).

Other adolescents seek an orderly life regulated by rules and moral principles and long for a relatively stable and reliable social surrounding. These youth tend to join sports or other clubs, such as emergency service or voluntary fire brigade or church choir. A sense of belonging is important in adolescence, and these activities can provide the desired social contact and embeddedness (Bukowski et al., 2007).

Here the question arises, can *religion* be a stabilizing factor for personality development? An understanding and supporting person – for instance, a teacher or a priest – can guide the way to religious belief. In particular, insecurely attached youths can develop a real belief in and a strong attachment to a transcendental God, who is permanently watching and protecting them (Birgegard & Granqvist, 2004; Emmons & Paloutzian, 2003; Granqvist, 1998, 2002; Kirkpatrick & Shaver, 1990). The rules and norms for moral conduct that are an integral part of religion, together with mutual reinforcement and encouragement, can give individuals enormous inner security, self-control and stability (McCullough & Willoughby, 2009; Saroglou, Chapter 17 in this volume; Trommsdorff, 2012); this can give pride in having escaped temptation. This sense of security and stability is independent of the kind of religion.

For individuals who are actively religious, religion has an important influence on their behavior and development. Many empirical studies have shown that, in general, religious adolescents have more and better social relationships, engage in fewer risky behaviors, are more civically engaged, and report themselves to be happier and healthier than nonreligious adolescents (Bond, Lun, & Li, Chapter 5 in this volume; Emmons & Paloutzian, 2003; King & Furrow, 2004; Lerner, Roeser, & Phelps, 2008; Sherrod & Spiewak, 2008; Steenwyk, Atkins, Bedics, & Whitley, 2010; Urry & Poey, 2008). However, the exact meaning of being "religious" is unclear. The studies mostly use external indicators for religiousness, with statements such as "being a member of a church or a religious community," "going to church every Sunday," or "I believe in God." It turns out, however, that strong religiosity can also have negative consequences, for example, less openness and less critical thinking (Mayer & Trommsdorff, Chapter 15 in this volume; Pargamont, 2002; Saroglou, Chapter 17 in this volume).

Answers reported in an anonymous questionnaire cannot definitively speak to the psychological content of being religious or believing in God. In a 2005 study by Smith and Lundquist Denton for example, the authors described the prevailing religious worldviews among adolescents in the United States in terms of Moralistic Therapeutic Deism (MTD). They suggested that the MTD "worldview among American adolescents is deism because the sacred idea is that a deity, an ultimate being called God (or Allah or Yahweh) created the universe, ordered it with divine moral laws, and watches over human life on earth ... God wants them to be happy ... by obeying moral laws ... good people go to Heaven when they die" (Smith & Lundquist Denton, 2005, p. 163). It is a distant God, who is only selectively invoked to take care of certain needs.

Most studies on religion and youth have been conducted in the United States. The studies have primarily focused on whether religion promotes well-being, better health, or civic engagement. This question is relevant because there is a rising concern in the United States that young people might be "more self-obsessed than ever before" (Dingfelder, 2011, p. 64).

In one such study, Barry and Nelson (2005) compared 445 students from three different universities – a private Catholic university, a large Mormon university, and a large public university – investigating the relationship between the role religion has played in students' lives and students' reported readiness for adulthood. The authors assumed that students selecting these universities subscribed to the universities' values and religious culture and accepted their rules of conduct. The Mormon university requested that students sign a strict honor code (which stipulated rules for dress, grooming, substance use, and sexual behavior); the students at the Catholic university had to sign an academic honor code, but personal conduct was stipulated only by student conduct guidelines; in the public university, an academic honor code existed, but no personal code. Students completed a questionnaire that asked questions both about religion (e.g., the importance of their religious beliefs and whether they believed in God) and about reaching adulthood (e.g., to what extent they had reached independence and norm compliance). As expected, the Mormon students rated themselves higher on all criteria for adulthood.

Yet again, the meaning of religion in psychological terms of the subjective content of belief and its emotional importance is unclear. Successful personality development and social behavior can also be promoted by many other kinds of social support, such as being well embedded in a secular youth club with positive social values. However, there are other phenomena that provide information about the importance and effect of religious belief for personality development.

Sects and Adolescent Development

Sects (small groups split from the regular church or belief) have developed in most world religions. However, in Islam, any deviation from official

Islamic belief is severely punished, sometimes by death. Within the context of this chapter, sects of interest are those that explicitly aim to further a more intensive spiritual life and connection to God or to the universe according to unlimited consciousness (e.g., "Brahma," like in the Hindu Marga Sect). Within the Christian world, there are many different forms, often in explicit contrast to the mainstream religion.

Sects are often founded by a charismatic leader, who may claim to possess a new revelation or the ultimate truth, or claim that he or she can provide a close relationship to God. These assertions can be attractive to believing youth, who may feel disoriented in their everyday world and long to feel close to God. The sect imparts the conviction of being chosen, offers meaning to their lives, and safety in the community (Sinabell, 2009). For some youth, this belief can stabilize their personality development. However, we can also sometimes see negative sides of the power of religious belief.

One characteristic of sects known as "youth cults" is a high conformity within the sect and isolation from the outer world. The experience of being in close proximity to God is sometimes enhanced by intensive meditation and yoga, psychedelic drugs, other "mind expanding" psychological techniques, or by sexual attachment to the leader ("liberated sexuality"). Critics describe these means as brainwashing (Valentin & Gasper, 2009).

In the case of strong internal pressure for conformity and isolation from the outside world, a mindset can develop that is characterized by a rigid one-sided orientation to God and redemption in the afterlife, thereby neglecting the "real" world. Under external pressure, the internal group cohesion becomes tightened and accepting orders by the leader becomes unavoidable. Those conditions have led to some dramatic and destructive events: for example in Jonestown in Guyana, over 900 members of the Peoples Temple cult died in 1978, mostly by suicide at the behest of cult leader Jim Jones (Lademann-Priemer, 2009).

Muslim Youth in Germany

Islam provides another example of the role and power of religious belief. About four million Muslims live in Germany; most of them are from Turkey (sometimes from remote areas in Anatolia) or Arab countries. About 1.8 million Muslims are under 25 years of age. Among those Muslim youth, a special youth culture ("Pop–Islam") has developed that has many different forms of behavior and values. For these adolescents, Islamic belief, being a member of German society, and the modern lifestyle, can all become part of their identity ("hybrid identity"; Nordbruch, 2010, p. 34). Some adolescents, however, even when they are raised by parents with moderate religious beliefs, develop an identity as *true Muslims*, in opposition to their parents.

Radical Islamic preachers are active in several mosques in Germany and especially on the Internet. They preach hatred against the "decadent Western Christian world," reject every modern interpretation of the Koran, and advertise for the Jihad. Some even propagate the Sharia and the rule that one should behead an apostate and stone an unfaithful wife. Under these conditions, it is an interesting question as to how young Muslims develop their identity: on the one hand, they may be influenced by radical preachers, and on the other hand, they must meet the challenge of integrating into the German secular majority culture in order to earn a living. Not all Muslim adolescents develop the hybrid identity.

Studies by Holtz and Wagner (2010, September) and Holtz, Wagner, and Sartawi (2011) provide some empirical data regarding this question. Holtz and Wagner (2010, September) analyzed over 6,500 Internet postings by young Muslims between 2008 and 2009. As expected, they found a great variety of topics discussed in these forums, reflecting all aspects of daily life. However, the authors also identified a particular kind of religious fundamentalism – a strong rigid belief – that was mostly aimed at fighting against secularity (viewed as dominated by the simple dichotomy between "good" and "evil") and referring to divine authority (as found in the Koran). The need for a militant Jihad was approved, but suicide assassins and terror against civilian persons were heatedly discussed. Religious fundamentalism as a political instrument was well accepted and the creation of a new identity as true Muslims in contrast to a secular identity was promoted. In addition, modern, rather secular Muslims were declared to be unbelievers (*takfir, Kuffar*).

Holtz et al. (2011) analyzed 966 Internet postings in 45 threads on the topic of the Swiss minaret ban in 2009. This study revealed two primary groups of Muslims with opposite positions: one group was fundamentalist and reactivist (in the *Ahlu Sunnah* discussion board), and the other was a moderate and rather secular group (in the *Vaybee* board). According to the study authors, the fundamentalists "argue from the position of a 'total Moslem identity'" (p. 17). They reject the "domination of Western politics, economy and cultural products." They are against building mosques in Europe "as long as the Western world is at war with Islam ... the time for building will come when Islam has finally won" (p. 13). Their personal identity has changed very little, and thus differs a great deal from their Western host culture. Their strong, rigid faith will make living in Western society more difficult, and they perhaps will become targets for stereotyping and rejection. This, and their orthodox Islamic faith, will pose severe difficulties for their personality development and future development in Western society.

The secular participants in the *Vaybee* board also "identify with their original nation" (Holtz et al., 2011) and do not really belong to the group with the hybrid identity (p. 17). They accept living in a foreign country, and their primary aims are economic success and to take advantage of learning opportunities. Those who support the construction of minarets show a stronger identification with Germany, but they fear right-wing extremism as well as orthodox Islamism. This, and their moderate Islamic faith, will make their further development in Germany easier.

The difference between the two groups was also expressed in the prevalence of mentioning certain topics: typical Islamist terms like *Sharia*, *Kuffar*, and *Jihad*, as well as the simplifying alternative of *good* versus *evil* – indicating little critical thinking – appeared frequently on the *Ahlu Sunnah* discussion board but rarely if at all on the *Vaybee* board. The topics within the *Vaybee* discussions often focused on identity and integration into German culture, probably indicating a successful personality development.

Islam in German Youth

In Germany, some adolescents are disappointed by the perceived decadence of society. They are not well integrated and therefore, often don't have conventional friends (see Bukowski et al., 2007). Some of these adolescents are attracted to Islam, especially by the idea of living according to strict rules (e.g., fasting, no premarital sex) and allowing their religion to penetrate their everyday life. In particular for adolescents who are not well integrated in society or do not have much hope for a better future (such as those who did not finish school), the strict regulations may provide a sense of security and purpose. Even the radical principles of the *salafistic* preachers do not seem to be a deterrent.

Under these conditions, some young Germans have converted to Islam and become strong believers. Again, negative consequences of the power of belief become obvious: some have even joined militant groups fighting in Afghanistan with the Taliban, others have remained in Germany but turned into terrorists. Individuals in the "Sauerland group," for example, prepared bombs to be exploded in the railway that only by chance failed. In March 2011, a young man raised in Germany by a moderate Islamic family was influenced by radical Islamic preachers and Internet films after failing in school. He became radical, convinced of the necessity to fight for Islam, and killed two American soldiers in Frankfurt. The motivations of this adolescent and other youths are certainly complex, likely a result of an amalgam with social problems. Nevertheless, the power of a belief in God and the other world is certainly part of their motive.

Fundamentalistic Faith in Muslim Arab Youth

The link between radical acts and the power of religious belief is more clearly drawn when examining young suicide assassins: they certainly are motivated by an extremely strong belief in the afterlife. Suicide assassins are mostly young Arab boys, although sometimes girls as well, who have grown up under desperate conditions. Some are in the third or fourth generation of refugees from Palestine, and have grown up in the restricted surroundings of a refugee camp. Some have little knowledge of the outside world, others are well educated. Most of them have grown up without hope for a change in their situation. The social and economic situation in Palestine, Jordan, and Syria is desolate: one half of the population is younger than 25 years of age and there is no hope for an economic improvement in the near future. Other youth were educated in one of *medresses* in Pakistan (Ladurner, 2008). All were under the influence of radical teachers, who can be extremely influential (King & Roeser, 2009) and who preach hatred against infidels and the immoral Western world, which allegedly attempts to destroy Islam and is responsible for their misfortune and misery. The immediate symbol of the aggressiveness of Western society is Israel, the hated enemy. Therefore, aggression is justified as defense as mentioned in the Koran (i.e., fighters for Islam are rewarded in Paradise). The young boys or girls learn to devote their life to God as is demanded by the Koran and some of the *Hadiths* (e.g., Ahmad al–Qadi, 1977/2006). They often live in a group with "sacred values" (Ginges & Atran, 2011) and have developed a collective identity. They, and sometimes their families, can feel a strong conformity pressure in their group (Atran, 2010) to fight against the decadent enemy – the infidels – and for Islam. They are taught that after dying while fighting for Islam, they can immediately enter Paradise where the *Huries* are waiting (Ahmad al–Qadi, 1977/2006, 45, 46, pp. 183–185). Along with the social pressure, the belief in Allah and the promise of Paradise is so strong for some youth (Sagemann, 2008) that they are willing to sacrifice their lives by committing a suicide attack. They often prepare for the reception in Paradise by settling their debts, praying, fasting, washing, cutting their hair, and using new or clean underwear (R. Seginer, personal communication, July 2011). For those who are willing to die as strong believers and warriors for the true belief, entering Paradise is a temptation and a realistic expectation.

Here we see the danger of a strong power of a religious belief: we have to assume a closed mindedness – with all attention focused primarily on the afterlife – where interests in real life are nearly unimportant. This is comparable to what an elder Christian monk after a long life in the monastery said facing an ossuary: "For those who consider themselves already dead to the world and are living for God, leaving this world is easy" (Father Markarios, in Draper, 2009, p. 148). And to die as a young martyr is also easy, like a redemption.

Conclusion

Belief in a caring God can provide adolescents with support and stability and further their positive development. However, although fundamentalist beliefs can be accepted in orthodox cultures, these beliefs can lead to serious difficulties in secular societies. This underlines the importance of cultural fit in development. Further research is needed on the psychological functions of spiritual practices (e.g., prayer and meditation) and the development of religious belief and its consequences for personality development.

Acknowledgments

I thank Rachel Seginer and Holly Bunje for their valuable comments and I thank Jeanette Ziehm for assistance in editing the manuscript.

REFERENCES

Ahmad al-Qadi, I. A. R. (1981/2006). *Das Totenbuch des Islam / Islamic book of the dead.* (S. Makowski & S. Schuhmacher, Transl.). Frankfurt: S. Fischer (Original work published 1977).

Arnett, J. J. (2000). Emerging adulthood: A theory of development from the late teens through the twenties. *American Psychologist, 55,* 469–480.

  (2007). Emerging adulthood: What is it, and what is it good for? *Child Development Perspectives, 1,* 68–73.

Atran, S. (2010). *Talking to the enemy: Faith, brotherhood, and the (un)making of terrorists.* New York: Harper Collins.

Baer, H. (2009). Jugendreligionen [Religious youth]. In J. Sinabell, H. Baer, H. Gasper, & J. Müller (Eds.), *Lexikon neureligiöser Bewegungen, esoterischer Gruppen und alternativer Lebenshilfen* (pp. 108–110). Freiburg: Herder.

Baier, D., Pfeiffer, C., Simonson, J., & Rabold, S. (2009). *Jugendliche in Deutschland als Opfer und Täter von Gewalt* [Youth in Germany as delinquents and victims of violence]. Hannover: Kriminologisches Forschungsinstitut Niedersachsen.

Barry, C. M., & Nelson, L. J. (2005). The role of religion in the transition to adulthood for young emerging adults. *Journal of Youth and Adolescence, 34,* 245–255.

Barry, C. M., Nelson, L., Davarya, S., & Urry, S. (2010). Religiosity and spirituality during the transition to adulthood. *International Journal of Behavioral Development*, 34, 311–324.

Bellah, R. (1970). *Beyond belief*. New York: Harper & Row.

Birgegard, A., & Granqvist, P. (2004). The correspondence between attachment to parents and God: Three experiments using subliminal separation cues. *Personality and Social Psychology Bulletin*, 30, 1122–1135.

Brown, B. B., Larson, R. W., & Saraswathi, T. S. (2002). *The world's youth: Adolescence in 8 regions of the globe*. New York: Cambridge University Press.

Bukowski, W. M., Brendgen, M., & Vitaro, F. (2007). Peers and socialization: Effects on externalizing and internalizing problems. In J. E. Grusec & P. D. Hastings (Eds.), *Handbook of socialization: Theory and research* (pp. 355–381). New York: Guilford Press.

Busch, W. (1954). *Nur was wir glauben, wissen wir gewiss. Der Lebensweg des lachenden Weisen* [Only what we believe do we know with certainty. The life of the smiling sage]. Berlin: Evangelische Verlagsanstalt.

Clark, G. (1962). *World prehistory. An outline*. London, UK: Cambridge University Press.

Côté, J. E. (2009). Identity formation and self-development in adolescence. In R. M. Lerner & L. Steinberg (Eds.), *Handbook of adolescent psychology, Vol 1: Individual bases of adolescent development (3rd ed.)* (pp. 266–304). Hoboken, NJ: John Wiley & Sons.

Cunliffe, B. W. (1993). *The Celtic world*. New York: St. Martin's Press.

Dalai Lama (2005). *Die Welt in einem einzigen Atom: Meine Reise durch Wissenschaft und Buddhismus* [The world in a single atom: My journey through science and Buddhism]. Berlin: Theseus.

Demandt, A. (2005). *Die Kelten* [The Celts]. München: Beck.

Deutsch, N. L., & Theodorou, E. (2010). Aspiring, consuming, becoming: Youth identity in a culture of consumption. *Youth and Society*, 42, 224–254.

Dingfelder, S. F. (2011). Reflecting on narcissism: Are young people more self-obsessed than ever before? *Monitor on Psychology*, 42, 64–66. Retrieved from: http://www.apa.org/monitor/2011/02/narcissism.aspx

Draper, R. (2009). The holy peninsula of Mount Athos. *National Geographic*, 216, 134–149.

Eccles, J. S. (2007). Families, schools, and developing achievement-related motivations and engagement. In J. E. Grusec & P. Hastings (Eds.), *Handbook of socialization: Theory and research* (pp. 665–691). New York: Guilford.

Elkind, D. (1999). Religious development in adolescence. *Journal of Adolescence*, 22, 291–295.

Emmons, R. A., & Paloutzian, R. F. (2003). The psychology of religion. *Annual Review of Psychology*, 54, 377–402.

Farin, K. (2010). Jugendkulturen heute [Youth cultures today]. *Politik und Zeitgeschichte*, 27, 3–8.

Gagné, I. (2011). Spiritual safety nets and networked faith: The "liquidity" of family and work under late modernity. *Contemporary Japan*, 23, 71–92.

Gasper, H. (2009). Das Christentum und seine Ränder. [Christianity and its borders]. In H. Gasper, H. Baer, J. Sinabell, & J. Müller (Eds.). *Lexikon christlicher Kirchen und Sondergemeinschaften* (pp. 9–34). Freiburg: Herder.

Ginges, J., & Atran, S. (2011). The challenge of violent extremism. *American Psychologist*, 66, 507–519.

Good, M., & Willoughby, T. (2008). Adolescence as a sensitive period for spiritual development. *Child Development Perspectives*, 2, 32–37.

Granqvist, P. (1998). Religiousness and perceived childhood attachment: On the question of compensation or correspondence. *Journal for the Scientific Study of Religion*, 37, 350–367.

(2002). Attachment and religiosity in adolescence: Cross-sectional and longitudinal evaluations. *Personality and Social Psychology Bulletin*, 28, 260–270.

Heider, F. (1958). *The psychology of interpersonal relations*. Oxford, UK: Wiley.

Henning, J., & Netter, P. (Eds.). (2005). *Biopsychologische Grundlagen der Persönlichkeit* [Biopsychological fundamentals of personality]. München: Elsevier.

Higher Education Research Institute (2003). *The spiritual life of college students: A national study of college students' search for meaning and purpose.* Los Angeles: University of California Graduate School of Education and Information Studies. Retrieved from http://spirituality.ucla.edu/docs/reports/Spiritual_Life_College_Students_Full_Report.pdf

Hölliger, F., & Haller, M. (2009). Decline or persistence of religion? In M. Haller, R. Jowell, & T. W. Smith (Eds.) *The international social survey program, 1984–2009.* London: Routledge.

Holtz, P., & Wagner, W. (2010, September). *Religiöser Fundamentalismus 2.0: Ergebnisse einer Analyse von über 6500 Postings in neun vorwiegend von jungen Muslimen genutzten deutschsprachigen Internetforen* [Religious fundamentalism 2.0: Results of an analysis of more than 6500 postings in nine German Internet forums, which are mainly used by young Muslims]. Paper presented at the 47th Congress of the Deutschen Gesellschaft für Psychologie (DGP's), Bremen, Germany.

Holtz. P., Wagner, W., & Sartawi, M. (2011). *Discrimination and minority identities: Fundamentalist and secular Muslims facing the Swiss minaret ban.* Manuscript submitted for publication.

Hoskins, J. A. (1989). On losing and getting a head: Warfare, exchange, and alliance in a changing Sumba, 1888–1988. *American Ethnologist*, 16, 419–440.

Huber, W. (2010). Das Abendmahl als Lachnummer [The Holy Communion as joke]. *Die Zeit*, 48. Retrieved from: http://www.zeit.de/2010/48/Sakrileg–Oper

Kary, J. (2011, March). Mehr Studienanfänger in Ingenieurswissenschaften / Immer längere Ausbildungszeiten [More freshmen for engineering science / Increasing duration of education]. *Markt und Mittelstand*. Retrieved from: http://www.marktundmittelstand.de/portal/strategie-personal/2078/mehr-studienanfaenger-in-ingenieurswissenschaften-immer-laengere-ausbildungszeiten/

King, P. D., & Roeser, R. W. (2009). Religion and spirituality in adolescent development. In R. M. Lerner & L. Steinberg (Eds.), *Handbook of adolescent psychology* (3rd ed., pp. 435–478). Hoboken, NJ: Wiley.

King, P. E., & Furrow, J. L. (2004). Religion as a source for positive youth development: Religion, social capital, and moral outcomes. *Developmental Psychology*, 40, 703–713.

Kirkpatrick, L. A., & Shaver, P. R. (1990). Attachment theory and religion: Childhood attachments, religious beliefs, and conversion. *Journal for the Scientific Study of Religion*, 29, 315–334.

Kloft, H. (2010). *Mysterienkulte der Antike: Götter, Menschen, Rituale* [Mystery cults of the ancient world: Gods, men, rituals]. München: Beck.

Kornadt, H.-J. (2011). *Aggression: Die Rolle der Erziehung in Europa und Ostasien* [Aggression: The role of child rearing in Europe and East Asia]. Wiesbaden: VS Verlag.

Lademann-Priemer, G. (2009). Eltern-und Betroffenen-Initiativen. [Initiatives of parents and persons concerned]. In J. Sinabell, H. Baer, H. Gasper, & J. Müller (Eds.), *Lexikon neureligiöser Bewegungen, esoterischer Gruppen und alternativer Lebenshilfen* (pp. 53–55). Freiburg: Herder.

Ladurner, U. (2008). *Bitte informieren Sie Allah! Terrornetzwerk Pakistan.* [Please inform Allah! Terror network Pakistan]. München: Herbig.

Lerner, R. M., Roeser, R. W., & Phelps, E., (Eds.). (2008). *Positive youth development and spirituality.* West Conshohocken, PA: Templeton.

Maier, B. (2008). *Sternstunden der Religionen. Von Augustinus bis Zarathustra* [Great moments of religion. From Augustine to Zarathustra]. München: Beck.

McCullough, M. E., & Willoughby, B. L. B. (2009). Religion, self-regulation, and self-control: Associations, explanations, and implications. *Psychological Bulletin, 135,* 69–93.

Mishra, R. C., & Dasen, P. R. (2005). Spatial language and cognitive development in India: Urban/rural comparison. In W. Friedlmeier, P. Chakkarath, & B. Schwarz (Eds.), *Culture and human development* (pp. 31–51). New York: Psychology Press.

Müller, K. E. (2006). *Schamanismus: Heiler, Geister, Rituale* [Shamanism: Healers, spirits, rituals]. München: Beck.

Nordbruch, G. (2010). Islamische Jugendkulturen in Deutschland [Islamic youth cultures in Germany]. *Politik und Zeitgeschichte, 27,* 34–38.

Pargament, K. I. (2002). The bitter and the sweet: An evaluation of the costs and benefits of religiousness. *Psychological Inquiry, 13,* 168–181.

Patterson, C. J., & Hastings, P. D. (2007). Socialization in the context of family diversity. In J. E. Grusec & P. D. Hastings (Eds.), *Handbook of socialization: Theory and research* (pp. 328–351). New York: Guilford.

Roeser, R., Lerner, R., & Phelps, E. (Eds.). (2008). *On the study of spirituality and development during adolescence.* West Conshohocken, PA: Templeton.

Rosenblitt, J. C., Soler, H., Johnson, S. E., & Quadagno, D. M. (2001). Sensation seeking and hormones in men and women: Exploring the link. *Hormones and Behavior, 40,* 396–402.

Rothbaum, F., & Trommsdorff, G. (2007). Do roots and wings oppose or complement one another? The socialization of autonomy and relatedness in cultural context. In J. E. Grusec & P. Hastings (Eds.), *The handbook of socialization* (pp. 461–489). New York: Guilford.

Sagemann, M. (2008). *Leaderless Jihad: Terror-networks in the twenty-first century.* Philadelphia: University of Pennsylvania Press.

Seginer, R. (2008). Future orientation in times of thread and challenge: How resilient adolescents construct their future. *International Journal of Behavioral Development, 32,* 272–282.

(2009). *Future orientation. Developmental and ecological perspectives.* New York: Springer.

Sherrod, L. R., & Spiewak, G. (2008). Assessing spiritual development in relation to civic and moral development during adolescence. In R. Roeser, R. Lerner, & E. Phelps (Eds.), *On the study of spirituality and development during adolescence* (pp. 322–338). West Conshohocken, PA: Templeton.

Sinabell, J. (2009). Wandel und Bedeutung von Religion – über die Zunahme der Zahl religiöser Gruppen und den Verlust ihres gesellschaftlichen Einflusses [Change and meaning of religion – About the increase of religious groups and the loss of their societal influence]. In J. Sinabell, H. Baer, H. Gasper, & J. Müller (Eds.), *Lexikon neureligiöser Bewegungen, esoterischer Gruppen und alternativer Lebenshilfen* (pp. 9–26). Freiburg: Herder.

Smith, C., & Lundquist Denton, M. (2005). *Soul searching: The religious and spiritual lives of American teenagers.* New York: Oxford University Press.

Spilka, B., Hood, I. R. W., Hunsberger, B., & Gorsuch, R. (2003). Religious socialization and thought in adolescence and young adulthood. In B. Spilka, I. R. W. Hood, B. Hunsberger, & R. Gorsuch (Eds.), *The psychology of religion* (pp. 106–147). New York: Guilford.

Statistisches Bundesamt (2011). Diagnose Alkoholmissbrauch: 2,8% mehr junge Krankenhauspatienten im Jahr 2009 [Diagnosis alcohol abuse: About 2.8% more young hospital patients in 2009]. Pressemitteilung, 39. Retrieved from: http://www. destatis.de/jetspeed/portal/cms/Sites/destatis/Internet/DE/Presse/pm/2011/01/P D11__039__231,templateId=renderPrint.psml

Steenwyk, S. A. M., Atkins, D. C., Bedics, J. D., & Whitley, B. E., Jr. (2010). Images of God as they relate to life satisfaction and hopelessness. *International Journal for the Psychology of Religion,* **20,** 85–96.

Steinberg, L. (2005). Cognitive and affective development in adolescence. *Trends in cognitive sciences,* **9,** 69–74.

Süss, J. (2009). Kinder Gottes/die Familie [Children of God/the family]. In J. Sinabell, H. Baer, H. Gasper, & J. Müller (Eds.), *Lexikon neureligiöser Bewegungen, esoterischer Gruppen und alternativer Lebenshilfen* (pp. 115–116). Freiburg: Herder.

Trommsdorff, G. (2012). Development of agentic regulation in cultural context: The role of self and world views. *Child Development Perspectives,* **6,** 19–26.

Urry, H. L., & Poey, A. P. (2008). How religious/spiritual practices contribute to well-being. In R. M. Lerner, R. W. Roeser, & E. Phelbs (Eds.), *Positive youth development and spirituality* (pp. 145–163). West Conshohocken, PA: Templeton.

Valentin, F., & Gasper, H. (2009). Sekten [Sects]. In J. Gasper, H. Baer, J. Sinabell, & J. Müller (Eds.), *Lexikon Christlicher Kirchen und Sondergemeinschaften* (pp. 207–212). Freiburg: Herder.

Wahle, E. (1973). *Ur- und Frühgeschichte im mitteleuropäischen Raum* [Prehistory and ancient history in central Europe]. München: Deutscher Taschenbuch Verlag.

Winkler, J. (1925). *Die Toba-Batak auf Sumatra in gesunden und kranken Tagen* [The Toba-Batak in Sumatra in healthy and sick days]. Stuttgart: Belfer.

Winstedt, R. (1982). *The Malay magician.* Oxford: Oxford University Press.

Wundt, W. (1926). *Völkerpsychologie. Eine Untersuchung der Entwicklungsgesetze von Sprache, Mythus und Sitte. Band 4: Mythus und Religion* [Ethnopsychology. A study of the developmental rules of language, myth, and convention. Edition 4: Myth and religion]. Leipzig: Kröner Verlag.

3 Cultural Differences in Self-Awareness in Adolescence Pathways to Spiritual Awareness

Fred Rothbaum, Yan Z. Wang, and Dov Cohen

Abstract

Self-awareness increases dramatically for adolescents worldwide. We seek to understand how cultural differences in self-awareness may contribute to cultural differences in spiritual awareness among adolescents. The focus is on comparisons between European-Americans and East Asians. There is little research on cultural differences in self-awareness, despite substantial evidence of cultural differences in its key components: (1) the vantage point of awareness – whether it is a first person perspective, from the inside-out (European-Americans) or a third person perspective, from the outside-in (East Asians); (2) the conception of self and of standards – whether self is seen as relatively independent and standards are based on personal desires and ideals (European-Americans) or self is seen as interdependent and standards are based on social obligations and norms (East Asians); and (3) the nature of self-evaluation – whether it is focused on enhancing esteem (European-Americans) or maintaining face (East Asians). We suggest that self-awareness may activate mortality salience and thereby may elicit cultural worldviews. Cultural differences in self-awareness leads to different spiritualities that present different "worldview" defenses against the existential concerns engendered by the interaction of self-awareness and mortality salience. Salvation through prayer and through good deeds, and approval from a loving God, common in Christianity, alleviate European-Americans' mortality concerns. By contrast, meditation, self change, and unity with the universe, common in Buddhism, alleviate East Asians' mortality concerns.

We begin with two quotes. The first is from Herman Hesse's (2008) powerful and lyrical novel *Siddhartha*. The novel concerns a young man's search for self-discovery in the time of the Buddha. Prior to the Buddha's enlightenment, his name was Siddhartha:

Slower, he walked along in his thoughts and asked himself: "But what is this, what you have sought to learn from teachings and from teachers, and what they, who have taught you much, were still unable to teach you?" And he found: "It was the self, the purpose and essence of which I sought to learn. It was the self I wanted to free myself from, which I sought to overcome. But I was not able to overcome it, could only deceive it, could only flee from it, only hide from it. Truly, no thing in this world has kept my thoughts thus busy, as this my very own self, this mystery of me being alive, of me being one and being separated and isolated from all others, of me being Siddhartha!" ("Awakening," para. 3)

Siddhartha's awareness of the self and his desire to overcome that awareness is, we suggest, a first step in his journey to spirituality. This notion is clearly and succinctly captured by Ho and Ho (2007) in their very thoughtful review of the literature on spirituality: "Awareness of one's existence does not qualify as an essential aspect of spirituality; awareness of that awareness does. A spiritual person is aware of not only his existence, but also aware that he is aware of it; he is, furthermore, capable of contemplating the frightful consequences of losing his self awareness or even his being" (p. 69).

Building on these ideas, we claim that the common denominator of diverse forms of spirituality is awareness of a higher order existence that is rooted in self-consciousness and is liberated from secular concerns. According to Hart & Goldenberg (2007, p.104), "societies in the east and west have made sense of humans' self conscious nature in ways that trivialize the body and glorify the spiritual self. All spiritual systems of belief focus on a nonmaterial realm that is essentially infinite and eternal."

Spiritual awareness is poorly understood in part because the research that helps clarify it is located in relatively segregated literatures. The questions raised in this chapter are alternately developmental, cultural, and social psychological in nature and almost always spiritual: (1) Why does spirituality increase markedly in adolescence? (2) Why are there cultural differences in spirituality? and (3) Why does mortality salience lead to increases in spirituality?

Echoing Ho and Ho (2007), we suggest that the answers to these three questions center on self-awareness. To support this claim, we review evidence that: (1) self-awareness increases dramatically for adolescents worldwide, (2) cultural differences in spirituality – between Christians' focus on God's approval of self on one hand and Buddhists' focus on transcending self (embracing non-self) on the other hand – reflect differences in self-awareness, and (3) mortality salience leads to spiritual awareness because it leads to changes in the nature of self-awareness.

The chapter is divided into five sections: First, we examine basic experimental research on self-awareness, almost all of which was conducted by Western investigators. Second, we examine the development of self-awareness, focusing on three aspects. Third, we consider cultural differences in those three aspects of self-awareness, as well as cultural differences in the broader construct. Fourth, we consider how self-awareness fosters mortality salience, and how mortality salience strengthens worldviews, especially spiritual ones. Fifth and finally, we draw from the above research to explain how cultural differences in spiritual awareness, as seen in Christianity and Buddhism, reflect cultural differences in self-awareness.

Experimental Studies of Self-Awareness

There are over 100 studies indicating that, following failure, people who are made self-aware are more likely to *compare their behavior to standards*, and to experience a variety of negative consequences of those comparisons, particularly negative emotion and negative self-evaluations. As a result, people seek ways to avoid self-awareness and/or its negative consequences (Duval & Silvia, 2002), especially when social rejection is possible (Twenge, Catanese, & Baumeister, 2003). Failure is a critical factor in these studies – following success, people who are made self-aware experience it is as positive (because they have exceeded standards) and seek to maintain self-awareness rather than to escape it (Duval & Wicklund, 1972). The self-awareness research is much more concerned with failure than success because self-awareness is usually triggered by disruptions in the ongoing flow of behavior and disruptions are more commonly associated with failure. Self-awareness is typically induced by situating people in front of a mirror, instructing them to write about themselves, or arranging for them to be observed by an audience (Duval & Silvia, 2002; Wiekens & Stapel, 2010).

Because self-awareness following failure is aversive, various strategies are adopted to lessen it. These strategies involve avoiding the source of self-awareness (e.g., others' gaze or reminders of the self) and distracting attention away from the self (e.g., through sensation seeking or de-individuation – focusing attention on mindless activities and decreasing attention to distinctive aspects of self) (Rothbaum et al., 1982). Other strategies are aimed at lessening self-awareness's aversive consequences, particularly the low self-evaluations that follow from self-awareness. For example, following self-awareness, people derogate the unattainable goal (Brehm, Wright, Solomon, Silka, & Greenberg, 1983), they pursue substitute goals that they are better able to attain (Wicklund & Gollwitzer, 1982), and they attribute negative outcomes to external forces and attribute positive outcomes to the self (Duval & Silvia, 2002). These strategies are especially common when improvement in performance is unlikely, a circumstance that sustains self-awareness and its negative effects.

Not all strategies are equal in their ability to alleviate negative self-evaluations. Findings from diverse literatures including coping (Creswell, Lam, Stanton, Taylor, Bower, & Sherman, 2007; Wachholtz & Pearce, 2009), positive psychology (Fredrickson, 2004), terror management theory (Dechesne et al., 2003; Schimel, Landau, & Hayes, 2008), the self (Baumeister, 1987, 2010; Leary, Adams, & Tate, 2006), and mindfulness (Brown & Ryan, 2003; Walach, Buchheld, Buttenmüller, Kleinknecht, & Schmidt, 2006) indicate that spirituality provides a particularly effective avenue for preserving and protecting self-evaluations. The effectiveness of spirituality is partly because of its affirmation of the self and partly because of its redirection of attention away from self-awareness and self-judgment and toward awareness of others, compassion, and non-judgment.

Although research on self-awareness has overwhelmingly been conducted by Western investigators and with Western samples, there is reason to believe that similar phenomena pertain to East Asians. They, too, respond to awareness of their failures with decreased self-evaluations and with efforts to elevate their evaluations, although the nature of their efforts differs. Rather than seeking positive self-evaluations "candidly," publicly, and for purposes of self-advancement, they are more likely to seek positive self-evaluations "tactically," privately, and for purposes of self-protection (Sedikides & Gregg, 2008; see also Heine & Hamamura, 2007). According to Heine (2001), East Asians are more likely to seek self-improvement whereas European-Americans are more likely to seek self-enhancement. Although the nature of self-evaluation striving varies in important ways across community, our point is that all people seek to bolster evaluations of self when made aware of their failure to achieve standards (Heine, Takemoto, Moskalenko, Lasaleta, & Henrich, 2008; Kim, 2009; Lalwani, Shrum, & Chiu, 2009).

Development of Self-Awareness

Self-awareness is a process that evolves throughout childhood (Damon & Hart, 1982). It begins with recognition of the physical self in infancy and progresses to a "theory of mind" in early childhood. Theory of mind refers to children's understanding of their own and other individuals' mental states. It involves the ability to consider the perspective of others and to make judgments from that perspective even when it differs from one's own perspective. There is considerable cross-cultural synchrony in the developmental sequence, if not the exact age, at which children gain facility with various theory of mind tasks such as those involving awareness that the self can hold false beliefs (Callaghan et al., 2005; Liu, Wellman, Tardif, & Sabbagh, 2008; Sabbagh, Xu, Carlson, Moses, & Lee, 2006).

Children's knowledge about mental representations continues to increase during middle childhood (Hughes & Leekam, 2004). Developments relevant to self-awareness include understanding second-order beliefs (e.g., John thinks that Mary thinks that…"; Perner & Wimmer, 1985); the role of pre-existing biases and expectations in influencing decisions (Carpendale & Chandler, 1996; Chandler, Sokol, & Hallett, 2001; Pillow & Henrichon, 1996); deception (Happé, 1994); and mixed and ambivalent emotions (Harris, Johnson, Hutton, Andrews, & Cooke, 1989). Particularly relevant to spiritual awareness is the finding that prior to age eight, children do not understand that prayer is often in response to negative emotions and that praying can improve emotions (Bamford & Lagattuta, 2010).

According to Flavell (1999), there is a marked increase during adolescence in the ability to see the self and others as actively interpreting rather than as passively responding to the environment. Adolescents realize that divergent, even conflicting, intentions and views about the self arise because people are multidimensional and context-dependent (Oosterwegel & Oppenheimer, 2002; Proulx & Chandler, 2009). Adolescents' increases in perspective taking and in understanding of mind (Epley, Keysar, Van Boven, & Gilovich, 2004; Guroglu, van den Bos, & Crone, 2009; see also research on "mind mindedness," Demers, Bernier, Tarabulsy, & Provost, 2010; Meins et al., 2003) may reflect growth in brain regions that are implicated in social cognition (Choudhury, Blakemore, & Charman, 2006). Increased perspective taking from ages 8–36, evidenced by the ability to rapidly switch between a first and third person perspective, has been linked to the development of brain regions presumed to control that ability (Choudhury et al., 2006).

Perhaps the crowning achievement of adolescent cognitive development is the ability to habitually think about thought – to regularly take one's own thought as an object of reflection (Elkind, 1985; Inhelder & Piaget, 1958). This achievement, which is elaborated throughout adolescence (Bacow, Pincus, Ehrenreich, & Brody, 2009; Enright, Shukla, & Lapsley, 1980; Sauter, Heyne, Blote, van Widenfelt, & Westenberg, 2010), makes possible the "awareness of the awareness of one's existence" emphasized by Ho and Ho (2007, p. 69). There are several components to this achievement, including: (1) recognition of the distinction between psychological-mental aspects of self and physical-observable aspects; (2) understanding of self's agency to monitor and manipulate experience; (3) awareness of limitations in the knowability of self, including awareness of the unconscious; and (4) concern with coherence between aspects of self – for example, between present and past, between public and private, and between morality and desires (Broughton, 1978; Choudhury et al., 2006; Damon & Hart, 1982; Mazor & Enright, 1988; Selman, 1980).

Field studies of trick-or-treaters' behavior during Halloween demonstrate the age related nature of self-awareness (Beaman, Klentz, Diener, & Svanum, 1979). Self-awareness induced by the presence of a mirror placed behind a candy bowl decreased cheating behavior for children who had been individuated by asking them their name and address, but did not affect the behavior of children left anonymous. These effects were clearly demonstrated for adolescents, but were not evident in children five to eight years old. The authors conclude, "by ages 9–12, self awareness has an effect in reducing transgressions, and by 13 and above self awareness substantially reduces antinormative behaviour" (p. 1842). Although we are not aware of a similar study in other cultures, recent neuroimaging research demonstrates that activity in brain regions associated with self-processing, including the medial prefrontal cortex, changes between early adolescence and adulthood. These studies indicate that neurocognitive development might contribute to increases in adolescent self-consciousness (Dosch, Loenneker, Bucher, Martin, & Klaver, 2010; Sebastian, Burnett, & Blakemore, 2008). At the same time, there is evidence that culture can influence how the self is construed on a neural level. For example, for East Asians as compared to European-Americans, thoughts of an intimate other are more likely to activate brain areas associated with self-awareness (Heatherton, 2011)

Developments in children's self-awareness, particularly in their understanding of mind, result from both brain maturation, such as developments in neurological functioning responsible for executive functioning, and social conditions (Liu et al., 2008). In communities where perspective taking is more emphasized and practiced, such as China, adolescents and adults may engage in more pervasive and effortless perspective taking (Wu & Keysar, 2007). The ability to be self-aware makes self-awareness possible but does not determine its incidence or form. To better understand the latter issues, we turn next to research on cultural differences.

Culture and Self-Awareness

Culture and the Elements of Self-Awareness

Although adolescents in all communities become self-aware, what self-awareness means to them is not the same. We examine three closely inter-related aspects of self awareness – the vantage point of awareness, the conception of self, and the nature of self-evaluation – and developmental and cultural differences in each.

First, there are differences in perspective. The self can be viewed from the vantage point of a generalized other or from one's own vantage point (Cohen, Hoshino-Browne, & Leung, 2007). In general, East Asians more often take a generalized other's perspective and view themselves as would a third party, whereas European-Americans more often take their own naïve perspective on the world. The greater adoption of a generalized other's perspective by East Asians than European-Americans is seen in their greater focus on obligations, social roles, self-effacement, and group control, and their lesser emphasis on individual choice, personal preferences, self-enhancement, and personal control. The greater adoption of one's own personal perspective by European-Americans explains the opposite pattern. Because of East Asians' greater emphasis on a generalized other's perspective, there is more socialization pressure to adopt that perspective earlier in childhood. Findings indicate that East Asian, as compared to U.S. children, take a generalized other's perspective at an earlier age, and more effortlessly, than children in the United States (Cohen et al., 2007; Epley et al., 2004). Chinese as compared to U.S. adults show greater awareness of others' perspective, presumably reflecting exposure to cultural beliefs and practices that promote other-orientation and that provide the tools necessary to automatically interpret actions from the perspective of others (Wu & Keysar, 2007).

Second, there are differences in conceptions of self and the standards that define the self. The self can be construed as independent or interdependent and can be compared to self's own standards or to others' standards (Markus & Kitayama, 1991). East Asians more often view themselves as interdependent and compare themselves to others' standards and obligations, whereas European-Americans more often view themselves as independent and compare themselves to their own desires, standards, and personal ideals. Because adults in East Asian and other collectivistic communities are more focused on, and place greater value on, social obligations than personal preferences and personally-endorsed standards, they socialize their children to do the same, beginning at young ages (Greenfield,

Keller, Fuligni, & Maynard, 2003; Rothbaum, Pott, Azuma, Miyake, & Weisz, 2000). In European-American communities, early childhood is seen as a time to cultivate personal preferences and self-distinctiveness. In East Asian and other collectivistic communities, there is much less emphasis on these early expressions of individualism. Instead, there is relatively greater emphasis on fostering young children's adherence to role expectations, social norms, and authority (Greenfield et al., 2003; Rothbaum et al., 2000; Rothbaum & Trommsdorff, 2007).

Third, there are differences in evaluation. Self-evaluation can take the form of face, which is conferred by others (I am what you think I am) and is reciprocal – others' obligation to confer face to self relates to self's obligation to confer face to others. Alternately, self-evaluation can take the form of self-esteem, which is conferred by self (I am what I think I am, not what you think I am) and is one-way – conferring esteem to self does not require conferring esteem to others (Heine, 2001; Kim & Cohen, 2010).

East Asians are more concerned with face and European-Americans are more concerned with self-esteem. There is greater emphasis on, elaboration of, and earlier use of face concepts in Chinese children (Wu, 2009) and on self-esteem in U.S. children (Miller et al., 2001). Chinese children are aware at an earlier age than U.S. children that people sometimes present misleading information about themselves (Heyman, Fu, & Lee, 2007). In European-American communities, caregivers emphasize the importance of fostering children's positive view of themselves, and they seek to instill such views through the use of praise. In East Asian and other collectivistic communities, there is much less emphasis on developing a positive self-evaluation (Rothbaum et al., 2000). Indeed, too positive a view of self is discouraged and self-criticism is valued at least as much as caregivers' praise (Kitayama, Markus, Matsumoto, & Norasakkunkit, 1997; Miller, Sandel, Liang, & Fung, 2001; Miller, Wang, Sandel, & Chao, 2002; Wang, Wiley, & Chiu, 2008). Modesty and humility are more likely to foster a concern with face than are pride and self-confidence (Kitayama et al., 1997).

Differences in evaluation relate to the differences in perspective and conception of self. In a self-focused condition, the more people have an independent conception of self, the greater their self-deceptive enhancement, which relates to self-esteem concerns. In the same (self-focused) condition, the more people have an interdependent conception of self, the greater their impression management, which relates to face concerns (Lalwani & Shavitt, 2009).

Cultural differences in perspective, in conception of self and self's standards, and in evaluation, which are fostered in early childhood, become greater as children mature. By adolescence there are well-established cultural differences in all three aspects of self-awareness. That is, self's viewpoint, self's conceptions, and evaluation of self are very different for adolescents and adults in East Asian as compared to European-American communities (Chiu, Gelfand, Yamagishi, Shteynberg, & Wan, 2010; Kitayama & Imada, 2010;).

Culture and Effects of Self-Awareness
Surprisingly, there is very little research directly addressing cultural differences in self-awareness. Even the research cited in the last section is not focused on the larger phenomenon of self-awareness; it only examines aspects of the larger phenomenon. Self-awareness comes in two forms – public and private. *Private* self-awareness refers to what I think about myself and is induced by manipulations such as mirrors or autobiographical descriptions. *Public* self-awareness refers to what others think about me and is induced by manipulations such as the presence of an audience (Baumeister, 2010; Froming, Walker, & Lopyan, 1982; Pham, Goukens, Lehmann, & Stuart, 2010; Wiekens & Stapel, 2010).

There are a few recent, landmark demonstrations of cultural differences in self-awareness. In one, Heine et al. (2008) used a mirror to increase self-awareness. Prior research indicates that self-awareness manipulations involving mirrors induce at least as much private as public self-awareness (Froming et al., 1982; Pham et al., 2010; Scheier & Carver, 1980; Shavitt, Swann, Lowrey, & Wanke, 1992). In private self-awareness, the eyes of the self are on the self. Heine et al.'s mirror manipulation led Americans to become more socially conforming – self-critical and unlikely to cheat – consequences similar to those reported in earlier studies. On the other hand, increasing self-awareness via the mirror had no effect on Japanese. Assuming that the mirror induced primarily private (versus public) self-awareness, Japanese may not have been influenced by the mirror because any increased *private* self-awareness is of less relevance to them. Just the opposite is true of Americans – they are highly influenced by private self-awareness because of their concern with self-esteem. Private self-awareness is not the default state for Americans, but the effects of inducing private self-awareness are likely to be much greater for them than for Japanese (Lalwani et al., 2009).

Also relevant to self-awareness is research by Kitayama, Snibbe, Markus, and Suzuki (2004) in which participants were situated in front of a set of schematic faces – pictures of people looking back at them. The presence as compared to the absence of schematic faces primed differences in awareness that the eyes of others are on the self, that is, face concerns. This increase in *public* self-awareness (how others see me) led Japanese to demonstrate greater concern about the consistency of their attitudes and behaviors (e.g., to demonstrate greater dissonance reduction effects). However, an increase in public self-awareness had no such effect on European-Americans and, in a more recent study, it had the opposite effect on them (Imada & Kitayama, 2010). European-Americans justified their choices less when the eyes of schematic others were on them than when others' eyes were not on them, presumably because they felt constrained by others and did not seek to defend choices they made under external pressure. They are more invested in choices they see as free and as springing from the authentic self.

Similar cultural differences were observed when the social eyes priming method was used to examine how hard people work (Na & Kitayama, 2010). Task performance was much better when the task had been chosen in the absence of the social eyes priming than in the presence of such priming for European-Americans, but the pattern was reversed for Asians (i.e., Koreans) and Asian-Americans, suggesting that Americans work harder on a task that is chosen in private, but Asians work harder on a task that is chosen in public or, at least, when public self-awareness is raised. Because participants were seemingly not conscious of the social eyes priming manipulation, these effects are most likely caused by unconscious processes (Imada & Kitayama, 2010).

It is important to note that Americans justify choices more than the Japanese when others are not made salient (Kitayama et al., 2004). Several studies indicate that Americans are especially invested in choices they make in private (Patall, Cooper, & Robinson, 2008; Savani, Markus, Naidu, Kumar, & Berlia, 2010). Findings from these studies as well as from the studies by Kitayama, Heine, and their colleagues are consistent with our interpretation that private, as compared to public, self-awareness may be of greater concern to, and have greater effects on, European-Americans than East Asians.

Related findings are reported in the literature on public versus private "self-consciousness" – a close cousin of self-awareness (Lalwani et al., 2009). Collectivists, such as Japanese, are high on impression management, which is consistent with their face concerns. Collectivists' efforts to mold others' impressions of themselves are linked to their public self-consciousness. By contrast, individualists, such as Americans, are relatively low on impression management and high on self-deceptive enhancement, which is consistent with self-esteem concerns. When they are high in private self-consciousness, people have greater awareness of themselves and real-istic understandings of their skills and capabilities, and are less prone to self-deceptive enhancement (Lalwani et al., 2009). These findings, as well as those previously reported, suggest that a) the form of self-awareness that most influences East Asians' behavior is predominantly public in nature and levels of public self-awareness tends to be chronically high for them (as compared to levels found in other cultures); and b) the form of self-aware-ness that most influences European-Americans' behavior is predominantly private in nature and levels of private self-awareness tend *not* to be chroni-cally high for them.

From Self-Awareness to Spiritual Worldviews: The Role of Mortality Salience

Self-awareness is closely related to mortality salience (Silvia & Duval, 2001). Mortality is salient when people are acutely aware – consciously or unconsciously – of the inevitability and finality of death. Mortality salience is typically induced by explicitly or implicitly bringing to mind participants' death-relevant thoughts, for example, by writing about death or embedding death-related words in a cover task (Pyszczynski, Abdollahi, Solomon, Greenberg, Cohen, & Weise, 2006). According to terror management theory, cultural worldviews, and particularly spiritual worldviews, serve as a buffer against the anxiety that results from aware-ness of human mortality (Greenberg, Pyszczynski, & Solomon, 1986; Solomon, Greenberg, & Pyszczynski, 1991). The theory maintains that protection from anxiety requires that one achieve a sense of value or self-esteem within the cultural context. Security derives from a belief in the validity of the cultural worldview and its standards, which transcend the individual's lifetime, as well as from a belief that one is meeting or exceed-ing those standards.

Mortality salience is rooted in self-awareness. "It is the uniquely human capacity to be self aware ... that reveals to us our vulnerability and mortal-ity – to know that we exist is to know that one day we will not exist" (Arndt, Greenberg, Simon, Pyszczynski, & Solomon, 1998, p. 1216). Self-awareness manipulations such as situating people in front of a mirror or having them write about themselves lead to increased mortality salience (Silvia, 2001). Stated simply, "Self awareness alone can induce mortality salience" (p. 73).[1] To the extent that self-awareness induces mortality salience, it also induces defenses against the anxiety that accompanies mortality salience – that is, it induces cultural worldviews and particularly spiritual worldviews (Jonas

& Fischer, 2006; Koole & Van den Berg, 2004; Silvia, 2001; Solomon et al., 1991; Vail et al., 2010).

The above findings indicate that self-awareness can, but does not always, elicit cultural worldviews. The pathway from self-awareness to cultural worldviews is moderated by mortality salience (Mandel & Smeesters, 2008). Worded otherwise, people are likely to come to embrace cultural worldviews as a response to being self-aware and having their own mortality highly salient to them. Both conditions (self-awareness and mortality salience) are likely when people are exposed to events that disrupt the ongoing flow of behavior (prompting comparison to standards) and that threaten one's way of life – a serious illness or injury, a significant loss, failure, or rejection, or events that threaten to undermine deeply held beliefs or values.

Spiritual and religious beliefs are frequently relied upon worldviews, especially when mortality is salient (Greenberg et al., 1990; Vail et al., 2010). Spiritual worldviews are particularly well suited to mitigate death anxiety because they are all encompassing, rely on concepts that are not easily disconfirmed, and promise literal immortality (Vail et al., 2010). Spiritual worldviews provide an antidote to concerns about self's non-existence by preserving "life in a symbolic and indirect manner" (Pyszczynski, Greenberg, & Solomon, 1999, p. 838). A belief in larger forces that are eternal, that transcend the self, and to which self is connected, serves to (a) extend the meaning of one's existence and (b) extend one's personal existence (e.g., through one's immortal soul, in Christianity). In addition to promising an afterlife and supernatural agency, Christian spiritual worldviews typically entail belief in human ascension from nature, and spiritual distinctions between mind and body (Vail et al., 2010). There are hundreds of studies supporting the thesis that reminders of death increase people's advocacy of worldviews that reinforce their sense of themselves as worthy members of a meaningful universe, rather than as mere animals fated only for obliteration (Greenberg, Sullivan, Kosloff, & Solomon, 2006).

Whereas spiritual and other cultural worldviews are most often sought under threat, terror management theory explicitly claims that worldviews are pursued even when threats are not salient. Worldviews provide a general reservoir of protection against chronic anxiety associated with ongoing awareness of the inevitability of death. "Even when people are not consciously thinking about death and external events are not drawing attention back to this problem, the pursuit of self-esteem and faith in one's worldview are ongoing endeavors that function to protect them from implicit knowledge of their ultimate fate" (Pyszczynski, Greenberg, Solomon, Arndt, & Schimel, 2004, p. 437). People's knowledge of their existence, and of their ultimate fate, is owing to their self-awareness. Ultimately, then, it is self-awareness that underlies motivation for spiritual worldviews.

Culture and Spiritual Worldviews

Several studies indicate that the effects of mortality salience on cultural worldviews are manifested by East Asians as well as by European-Americans: following threats to mortality, East Asians uphold cultural worldviews and the standards associated with them because those worldviews, and fulfillment of their standards, increase self-esteem and thereby defend against death anxiety (e.g., Heine, Hahihara, & Niiya, 2002; Kashima, Halloran, Yuki, & Kashima, 2004; Tam, Chiu, & Lau, 2007; Wakimoto, 2006). One meta-analysis supports this conclusion (Burke, Martens, & Faucher, 2010) whereas another meta-analysis, relying mainly on unpublished studies, does not (Yen & Cheng, 2010).

The inconsistent findings may be because of cultural differences in the relationship between affirming worldviews and self-esteem. For European-Americans, affirming worldviews in the face of death anxiety serves to increase self-esteem. For East Asians, however, affirming worldviews in the face of death anxiety has very different effects, including self-effacement (Wakimoto, 2006), acceptance of fate (Yen & Cheng, 2010), and positive in-group evaluations as opposed to self-evaluations (Tam et al., 2007; Wakimoto, 2006). Across diverse cultures, affirming worldviews reduces anxiety associated with mortality salience by increasing self's security, but the nature of self's security differs. Differences in security (e.g., increased self-esteem versus maintaining face) that follow from affirming worldviews are likely to reflect differences in the worldviews themselves (e.g., emphasizing individualism and free choice versus collectivism and resignation to fate) (Yen & Cheng, 2010).

European-American and East Asian Spiritual Worldviews

Christianity is the major spiritual worldview in many European-American communities, and Buddhism is the major spiritual worldview in many East Asian communities (United States Department of State, 2004). A consideration of differences between these spiritual worldviews paves the way for a deeper understanding of how they parallel differences in self-awareness.

First, however, we wish to highlight fundamental similarities between diverse spiritual worldviews, including Buddhism and Christianity. Both traditions entail a belief in an existence after death and a higher being (Buddha and Jesus/God) who points the way toward transcendence and salvation. Both traditions value reflection/contemplation (meditation and prayer) and good/virtuous action. The principles of goodness and virtue in both traditions involve reciprocity, justice, charity, consideration, love of others (Ekman, Davidson, Ricard, & Wallace, 2005; Haidt, 2006; Smith, 1991; Tsai, Miao, & Seppala, 2007), and gratitude (McCullough, Emmons, & Tseng, 2002). Both traditions preach the importance of self-control and responsible action, and prescribe exercises for pursuing them (McCullough & Willoughby, 2009; Rachlin, 2000; see also similarities noted by Tsai et al., 2007). Because spiritual worldviews serve as a defense against mortality salience and because concerns about mortality are similar across culture, it is not surprising that there are cross-cultural similarities in spiritual worldviews.

The differences between Christian and Buddhist spiritual worldviews are also fundamental. Perhaps the major difference is that anxiety about death leads Christians to seek approval of and alignment with God, whereas anxiety about death leads Buddhists to seek a state of non-self and oneness with the universe. A related difference is that Jesus/God is an omnipotent deity whereas Buddha is not a deity. Buddhist sects differ in whether or not they recognize deities, but none recognize a single, omnipotent deity. Another major difference is that Christianity is about reaching heaven in the afterlife through faith and good deeds, whereas Buddhism is about ending suffering (the endless cycle of re-birth) and achieving enlightenment on earth through contemplating the nature of reality.

From Spiritual Worldviews to Spiritual Awareness

People adopt the spiritual worldviews prevalent in their community because of their exposure to those worldviews, often from an early age, and because of the unity with others that endorsing those worldviews provides. In this section we suggest that the kinds of spiritual worldviews to which individuals are receptive, and which best serve to buffer mortality concerns, are those that are congruent with the type of self-awareness prevalent in the culture.

We distinguish between spiritual worldviews, a focus of terror management theory, and spiritual awareness, our focus in this chapter. We view spiritual awareness as lying at the heart of spiritual worldviews – that is, spiritual awareness is the irreducible core of spiritual worldviews. Spiritual worldviews, which are the subject of prolific tomes, involve issues of creation, the

Table 3.1. Aspects of Self- and Spiritual Awareness among European-Americans and East Asians

	Aspect of Self-Awareness	Self-Awareness	Spiritual Awareness
European-American Self-Awareness (Private Self-Awareness)	Perspective	Self's own private, first-person perspective	The perspective of an all-powerful God
	Conception of Self	An independent self – a self that exists apart from its context and is judged on the basis of its own standards	A self that is aligned with God
	Evaluation	High or low self-esteem	Approval of the self (by God)
East Asian Self-Awareness (Public Self-Awareness)	Perspective	Generalized other, public, third-person perspective	Common humanity perspective
	Conception of Self	An interdependent self that is embedded in relationships and is judged on the basis of others' standards	Non-self – self that is fully integrated with others
	Evaluation	Face or lack of face	Compassion (not judging) of self and others

meaning of life, the afterlife, divinity, salvation, compassion, higher forms of morality, justice, and love. By contrast, spiritual awareness is a more delimited phenomenon, involving only those elements that define self-awareness: a perspective, a conception of self and standards, and an evaluation of the self. Spiritual awareness differs from self-awareness in that all three of these elements are transcendent – operating in relation to the spiritual world rather than the secular one. For parallels between self and spiritual awareness among both European-Americans and East Asians, see Table 3.1.

Despite these parallels, we suspect that spiritual awareness is a later developing phenomenon than self-awareness. Because self-awareness is a necessary but not a sufficient ingredient of spiritual awareness, not all adolescents who become highly self-aware become highly spiritually aware. Whereas self-awareness is typically triggered by failures and other adverse events, spiritual awareness is triggered primarily by events that make mortality salient. People who are adept at suppressing concerns about mortality are unlikely to develop spiritual awareness. Because people are highly motivated to suppress thoughts about salient negative events, especially negative events pertaining to the self (Newman, Duff, & Baumeister, 1997; Wenzlaff & Wegner, 2000), mortality salience, and the spiritual awareness to which it gives rise, are not frequent experiences for many individuals. This is especially the case for most youth whose exposure to death is infrequent and thus more easily suppressed.

As noted earlier, one of the most common ways of overcoming the adverse effects of death anxiety, and obviating the need for worldview defenses, is by bolstering self-evaluations (or in-group evaluations). High levels of self- (and in-group) esteem reduce the likelihood that manipulations of mortality salience will trigger worldview defenses (Pyszczynski et al., 2004). When self- or in-group esteem is high, spiritual awareness is less necessary to defend against threats to mortality. The converse is also true: people high in spiritual awareness are cognizant of forces much larger than themselves and they have less need for self-esteem as a defense against mortality (Dechesne et al., 2003).

Spiritual Awareness and Self-Awareness in Different Cultures

Judaic-Christian awareness, the dominant form of spiritual awareness among European-Americans, centers on seeking unity with an omnipotent being. This form of spiritual awareness arises from changes along the dimensions of perspective, conception of self, and evaluation – the same three dimensions that define self-awareness (Lillard et al., 1998). The three changes are:

- a shift from one's own perspective (European-Americans' most common perspective) to God's perspective. Importantly, this shift is from a first person perspective to a third person perspective. That is, the spiritual awareness of European-Americans in some respects resembles the self-awareness (i.e., perspective taking) of East Asians more than it resembles European-Americans' customary self-awareness (perspective taking).
- a shift from an independent conception of self to a conceptualization of self as aligned with a single, personal, all-powerful God. There is a corresponding shift from pursuing one's own desires or one's personal ideals to pursuing God's standards. Unlike Buddha, God is the primary cause of everything (the creator of the universe), which makes alignment with him all the more attractive, because it enhances the agency of the aligned self.
- a decreased concern with self-esteem (European-Americans' most common form of self-evaluation) and greater concern with God's approval and love. God's judgment determines one's fate in the afterlife. Approval is gained through faith (particularly in Protestantism) and good deeds – i.e., performing God's work. Positive judgment leads to eternal existence

with God in Heaven. Further, as compared to Buddhism, Christianity places relatively greater emphasis on high intensity positive emotions, such as ecstasy and rapture, in addition to feelings of peace and contentment (Tsai et al., 2007).

Buddhist awareness, the dominant form of spiritual awareness among East Asians, centers on acceptance of non-self and merging with the universe. This form of spiritual awareness arises from changes along the same three dimensions of perspective, conceptions of self and standards, and evaluation.

– a shift from an interdependent perspective (the most common perspective of East Asians) to a greater awareness of common humanity. This shift is from a conventional third person perspective to a higher order perspective in which self's and others' perspectives are integrated. An integration of perspectives results from the dissolution of the boundary between self and other.
– a reconceptualization of the notion of interdependence from a sense of unity with one's in-group to a sense of deep personal connection with others. This deep form of connection is characterized by a full embracing of the thoughts, feelings, and goals of others, merging with the broader context, and letting go of the illusion of self-hood (that there is a self separate from everything else). In Buddhism there is no single God. Rather, divinity is to be found in all things through alignment with a unitary life force. The emphasis on a common humanity and de-emphasis on the distinction between self and other, or us and them, reflects the shift away from a secular notion of collectivism.
– a decreased concern with face (East Asians' most common form of self-evaluation) and greater concern with accepting (not judging) and experiencing compassion for self and others, and gaining enlightenment. Enlightenment is gained through mindful meditation. Acceptance is contrasted with the perpetual pursuit of desires which are unfulfillable – a pursuit that leads to suffering. Acceptance leads to calmness (Tsai et al., 2007) and an end of suffering. In contrast to Christianity, there is no hell, but negative karma prolongs *samsara* (the cycle of birth and re-birth) and prevents attainment of nirvana.

On the Relationship between Self-Awareness and Spiritual Awareness

Despite evidence that spiritual awareness is predicated on self-awareness, the relation between the two is likely to be complex. When self-awareness gives rise to spiritual awareness, there is a corresponding decrease in secular/non-spiritual self-awareness' presence in consciousness. This process might be likened to other dynamic processes, such as cognitive dissonance. Conflicting cognitions lead to uncomfortable feelings of dissonance; this discomfort motivates people to change their cognitions, which in turn lessens the dissonance. Similarly, the discomfort of self-awareness motivates spiritual awareness, which in turn displaces the self-awareness and negative emotion that gave rise to it (Leary et al., 2006; also Arndt et al., 1998).

Throughout this chapter we have emphasized the aversiveness of self-awareness and how it gives rise to defenses such as spiritual awareness. A seemingly related process, referred to as compensation, is described by attachment researchers. When the individual determines that an attachment figure is not available or responsive, s/he increases behavior that is intended to restore adequate proximity and safety. In situations where the primary attachment figure is persistently unavailable, "the behavior can become directed towards some substitute object" (Bowlby, 1969, p. 313). Research by attachment theorists indicates that God can serve as the substitute attachment object. Loss of and separation from an attachment figure and traumatic events, as well as insecure relationships with caregivers, are likely to foster turning to God (Granqvist, Mikulincer, & Shaver, 2010). A meta-analysis including over 1,500 participants provided substantial support for the compensation hypothesis (Granqvist & Kirkpatrick, 2004).

Similarly, we are suggesting that aversive forms of self-awareness, a hallmark of which is negative evaluation of the self (low self-esteem), may prompt individuals to flee the discomfort of self-awareness in search of comforts they might find in spiritual awareness. Although we emphasize different precursors than do attachment theorists, the precursors are related: negative evaluations ("negative working models") of the self are closely linked to insecure attachment to others (Mikulincer, 1998; Roberts, Gotlib, & Kassel, 1996).

Attachment researchers contrast the compensation hypothesis with the correspondence hypothesis. According to the latter, individual differences in religious or spiritual beliefs correspond to individual differences in attachment relationships with caregivers. Individuals secure in relationships with caregivers develop secure relationships with God and those insecure in relationships with caregivers develop insecure relationships with God. As indicated above, there is overall a correlation between insecure attachment to caregivers and religiosity. However – consistent with the correspondence hypothesis – individuals who were securely attached to parents who were highly religious also became highly religious themselves (Granqvist, 2002;

Granqvist & Hagekull, 1999; Granqvist et al., 2010; Kirkpatrick & Shaver, 1990; Reinert & Edwards, 2009). Similarly, we suggest a correspondence effect whereby security in self-awareness, owing to high levels of self-esteem, gives rise to security in spiritual awareness. The latter is likely to be manifested as confidence in a safe spiritual base to which the individual can return if spiritual exploration leads to feelings of danger – for example, fears of mortality or punishment.

Following the reasoning of attachment theorists, we are suggesting that spiritual awareness can serve as a defense against self-awareness (the compensation dynamic) as well as a mirror of self-awareness (the correspondence dynamic). Self-awareness is often triggered by failure and leads to unfavorable comparisons to self's standards (I am not doing as well as I should) and to negative emotion. In those cases, self-awareness can motivate people to compensate for their negative feelings, and spiritual awareness can serve as a defense against perceived vulnerability, inadequacy and, ultimately, mortality. Spiritual awareness provides "relief" either in the form of alignment with an omnipotent God or "no self" – a merging of self with the cosmos, thereby taking the "bite" out of self-awareness or lessening its presence in self's consciousness.

In cases of correspondence, by contrast, negative self-awareness motivates people to adopt a negative model of spiritual awareness: "a view of God as remote and inaccessible" or a fear that one might easily fall out of God's favor (Granqvist et al., 2010, p.54). People's relationships with God and the afterlife are not necessarily benign. In the Judeo-Christian tradition, God accepts and forgives, but also judges and punishes. We must account for our sins and we might have a blissful afterlife – or we might be punished and sent to hell. Correspondence also occurs in cases of positive self-awareness. When people feel comfortable in a state of self-awareness, they are likely to develop a corresponding (positive) spiritual awareness. In these cases, spiritual awareness provides an other-worldly frontier that one feels safe to explore, just as a positive view of the self as worthy of protection and care provides the safety to explore the secular world (Bowlby, 1969). Spiritual awareness can be uplifting, allowing people to align with forces greater than the self or with humanity generally, and to move away from earthly concerns and toward ultimate concerns and things that matter most.

It is also possible that spiritual awareness feeds back to influence self-awareness. According to attachment theorists, spirituality as compensation might set in motion an "earned security" process for individuals who are initially insecure with respect to attachment. As noted by Granqvist et al. (2010), "it is even possible that a process of positive change in working models (especially in the model of self) of relatively insecure individuals might be initiated by experiencing God's love and forgiveness" (p. 54).

Research is needed to clarify the relationship between self-awareness and spiritual awareness. We need to assess the relationship between levels of spiritual awareness and levels of self-awareness as enduring characteristics of individuals and as responses to stressors. Although the evidence indicates that self-awareness is a fundamental precondition of spiritual awareness, and that the two forms of awareness are related in important ways, we know very little about their co-occurrence at any point in time, in specific situations, and over development.

Summary

Cultural differences in self-awareness lay the foundation for differences in spiritual awareness. Among Westerners, the shift is from one's own first person perspective to the perspective of an all-powerful God, from an independent sense of self to a self aligned with God, and from a concern with self-esteem to a concern with God's approval. Among Easterners, in contrast, the shift is from a secular, collectivistic worldview to a worldview emphasizing a common humanity, from an interdependent sense of self to a nonself, and from a concern with maintaining face to a concern with compassion and not judging self or others.

Increased spiritual awareness requires three elements:

- First, it requires cognitive changes in adolescence, leading to increased self-awareness. The nature of self-awareness in different cultures depends on the perspective, conception of self, and form of evaluation that is prevalent in the culture.
- Second, it requires high levels of mortality salience, which result from threats to self and to self-awareness. Adolescents do not just fear death of the body, but also loss of consciousness. The ways in which adolescents negotiate mortality salience differs across cultures largely because of cultural differences in self-awareness.
- Third, spiritual awareness requires spiritual worldviews, which are prevalent in each culture and which become more accessible under conditions of mortality salience.

Differences between European-Americans' Christian spiritual awareness and East Asians' Buddhist spiritual awareness reflect culturally specific solutions to universal existential problems engendered by the interaction of self-awareness and mortality salience.

NOTES

1. Opposite dynamics have also been found – inducing mortality salience (e.g., subliminally presenting words about death) leads to increased concerns about self-awareness, as indicated by efforts to decrease self-awareness (Arndt et al., 1998).

REFERENCES

Arndt, J., Greenberg, J., Simon, L., Pyszczynski, T., & Solomon, S. (1998). Terror management and self-awareness: Evidence that mortality salience provokes avoidance of the self-focus state. *Personality and Social Psychology Bulletin*, **24**, 1216–1227.

Bacow, T. L., Pincus, D. B., Ehrenreich, J. T., & Brody, L. R. (2009). The metacognitions questionnaire for children: Development and validation in a clinical sample of children and adolescents with anxiety disorders. *Journal of Anxiety Disorders*, **23**, 727–736.

Bamford, C., & Lagattuta, K. H. (2010). A new look at children's understanding of mind and emotion: The case of prayer. *Developmental Psychology*, **46**, 78–92.

Bargh, J. A. (2004). Bypassing the will: Towards demystifying the nonconscious control of social behavior. In R. R. Hassin, J. S. Uleman, & J.A. Bargh (Eds.), *The new unconscious* (pp. 37–60). New York: Oxford University Press.

Baumeister, R. F. (1987). How the self became a problem: A psychological review of historical research. *Journal of Personality and Social Psychology*, **52**, 163–176.

(2010). The self. In R. F. Baumeister & E. J. Finkel (Eds.), *Advanced social psychology: The state of the science* (pp. 139–176). New York: Oxford University Press.

Beaman, A. L., Klentz, B., Diener, E., & Svanum, S. (1979). Self-awareness and transgression in children: Two field studies. *Journal of Personality and Social Psychology*, **37**, 835–846.

Bowlby, J. (1969). *Attachment and loss: Vol. 1. Attachment* (2nd ed.). New York: Basic Books.

Brehm, J. W., Wright, R. A., Solomon, S., Silka, K., & Greenberg, J. (1983). Perceived difficulty, energization, and the magnitude of good valence. *Journal of Experimental Social Psychology*, **19**, 21–48.

Broughton, J. (1978). Development of concepts of self, mind, reality, and knowledge. In W. Damon (Ed.), *Social cognition: New directions for child development. Vol. 1* (pp. 75–100). San Francisco, CA: Jossey-Bass.

Brown, K. W., & Ryan, R. M. (2003). The benefits of being present: Mindfulness and its role in psychological well-being. *Journal of Personality and Social Psychology*, **84**, 822–848.

Burke, B. L., Martens, A., & Faucher, E. H. (2010). Two decades of terror management theory: A meta-analysis of mortality salience research. *Personality & Social Psychology Review*, **14**, 155–195.

Callaghan, T. C., Rochat, P., Lillard, A., Claux, M. L., Odden, H., Itakura, S., … Singh, S. (2005). Synchrony in the onset of mental-state reasoning. *Psychological Science*, **16**, 378–384.

Carpendale, J. I., & Chandler, M. J. (1996). On the distinction between false belief understanding and subscribing to an interpretive theory of mind. *Child Development*, **67**, 1686–1706.

Chandler, M. J., Sokol, B. W., & Hallett, D. (2001). Moral responsibility and the interpretative turn: Children's changing conceptions of truth and rightness. In B. F. Malle, L. J. Moses, & D. A. Baldwin (Eds.), *Intentions and intentionality: Foundations of social cognition* (pp. 345–366). Cambridge, MA: MIT Press.

Chiu, C. Y., Gelfand, M. J., Yamagishi, T., Shteynberg, G., & Wan, C. (2010). Intersubjective culture: The role of intersubjective perceptions in cross-cultural research. *Perspectives on Psychological Science, 5*, 482–493.

Choudhury, S., Blakemore, S. J., & Charman, T. (2006). Social cognitive development during adolescence. *Social Cognitive and Affective Neuroscience, 1*, 165–174.

Cohen, D., Hoshino-Browne, E., & Leung, A. (2007). Culture and the structure of personal experience: Insider and outsider phenomonologies of the self and social world. In M. Zanna (Ed.), *Advances in experimental social psychology, 39* (pp. 1–67). San Diego, CA: Academic Press.

Creswell, J. D., Lam, S., Stanton, A. L., Taylor, S. E., Bower, J. E., & Sherman, D. K. (2007). Does self-affirmation, cognitive processing, or discovery of meaning explain cancer-related health benefits of expressive writing? *Personality and Social Psychology Bulletin, 33*, 238–250.

Damon, W., & Hart, D. (1982). The development of self understanding from infancy through adolescence. *Child Development, 53*, 841–864.

Dechesne, M., Pyszczynski, T., Arndt, J., Ransom, S., Sheldon, K. M., van Knippenberg, A., & Jannsen, J. (2003). Literal and symbolic immortality: The effect of evidence of literal immortality on self-esteem striving in response to mortality salience. *Journal of Personality and Social Psychology, 84*, 722–737.

Demers, I., Bernier, A., Tarabulsy, G., & Provost, M. (2010). Maternal and child characteristics as antecedents of maternal mind-mindedness. *Infant Mental Health Journal, 31*, 94–112.

Dosch, M., Loenneker, T., Bucher, K., Martin, E., & Klaver, P. (2010). Learning to appreciate others: Neural development of cognitive perspective taking. *Neuroimage, 50*, 837–846.

Duval, T. S., & Silvia, P. J. (2002). Self-awareness, probability of improvement, and the self-serving bias. *Journal of Personality and Social Psychology, 82*, 49–61.

Duval, T. S., & Wicklund, R. A. (1972). *A theory of objective self-awareness.* New York: Academic Press.

Ekman, P., Davidson, R. J., Ricard, M., & Wallace, B. A. (2005). Buddhist and psychological perspectives on emotions and well being. *Current Directions in Psychological Science, 14*, 59–63.

Elkind, D. (1985). Egocentrism redux. *Developmental Review, 5*, 218–226.

Enright, R. D., Shukla, D. G., & Lapsley, D. K. (1980). Adolescent egocentrism-sociocentrism and self-consciousness. *Journal of Youth and Adolescence, 9*, 101–115.

Epley, N., Keysar, B., Van Boven, L., & Gilovich, T. (2004). Perspective taking as egocentric anchoring and adjustment. *Journal of Personality and Social Psychology, 87*, 327–339.

Flavell, J. H. (1999). Cognitive development: Children's knowledge about the mind. *Annual Review of Psychology, 50*, 21–45.

Fredrickson, B. L. (2004). Gratitude, like other positive emotions, broadens and builds. In R. A. Emmons & M. E. McCullough (Eds.), *The psychology of gratitude* (pp. 145–166). New York: Oxford University Press.

Froming, W. J., Walker, G. R., & Lopyan, K. J. (1982). Public and private self-awareness: When personal attitudes conflict with societal expectations. *Journal of Experimental Social Psychology*, **18**, 476–487.

Goukens, C., Dewitte, S., & Warlop, L. (2009). Me, myself, and my choices: The influence of private self-awareness on choice. *Journal of Marketing Research*, **46**, 682–692.

Granqvist, P. (1998). Religiousness and perceived childhood attachment: On the question of compensation or correspondence. *Journal for the Scientific Study of Religion*, **37**, 350–367.

(2002). Attachment and religiosity in adolescence: Cross-sectional and longitudinal evaluations. *Personality and Social Psychology Bulletin*, **28**, 260–270.

Granqvist, P., & Hagekull, B. (1999). Religiousness and perceived childhood attachment: Profiling socialized correspondence and emotional compensation. *Journal for the Scientific Study of Religion*, **38**, 254–273.

Granqvist, P., & Kirkpatrick, L. A. (2004). Religious conversion and perceived childhood attachment: A meta-analysis. *International Journal for the Psychology of Religion*, **14**, 223–250.

Granqvist, P., Mikulincer, M., & Shaver, P. R. (2010). Religion as attachment: Normative processes and individual differences. *Personality and Social Psychology Review*, **14**, 49–59.

Greenberg, J., Pyszczynski, T., & Solomon, S. (1986). The causes and consequences of the need for self-esteem: A terror management theory. In R. F. Baumeister (Ed.), *Public self and private self* (pp. 189–212). New York: Springer-Verlag.

Greenberg, J., Pyszczynski, T., Solomon, S., Rosenblatt, A., Veeder, M., Kirkland, S., & Lyon, D. (1990). Evidence for terror management theory II: The effects of mortality salience on reactions to those who threaten or bolster the cultural worldview. *Journal of Personality and Social Psychology*, **58**, 308–318.

Greenberg, J., Sullivan, D., Kosloff, S., & Solomon, S. (2006). Souls do not live by cognitive inclinations alone, but by the desire to exist beyond death as well. *Behavioral and Brain Sciences*, **29**, 474–475.

Greenfield, P. M., Keller, H., Fuligni, A., & Maynard, A. (2003). Cultural pathways through universal development. *Annual Review of Psychology*, **54**, 461–490.

Guroglu B., van den Bos, W., & Crone, E. A. (2009). Fairness considerations: Increasing understanding of intentionality in adolescence. *Journal of Experimental Child Psychology*, **104**, 398–409.

Haidt, J. (2006). *The happiness hypothesis: Finding modern truth in ancient wisdom*. New York: Basic Books.

Happé, F. G. E. (1994). An advanced test of theory of mind: Understanding of story characters' thoughts and feelings by able autistic, mentally handicapped, and normal children and adults. *Journal of Autism and Developmental Disorders*, **24**, 129–154.

Harris, P. L., Johnson, C. N., Hutton, D., Andrews, G., & Cooke, T. (1989). Young children's theory of mind and emotion. *Cognition and Emotion*, **3**, 379–400.

Hart, J., & Goldenberg, J. L. (2007). A terror management perspective on spirituality and the problem of the body. In A. Tomer, G. T. Eliason, & P. T. P. Wong (Eds.), *Existential and spiritual issues in death attitudes* (pp. 91–114). Mahwah, NJ: Erlbaum.

Heatherton, T. F. (2011). Neuroscience of self and self-regulation. *Annual Review of Psychology*, **62**, 363–390.

Heine, S. J. (2001). Self as a product of culture: An examination of East Asian and North American selves. *Journal of Personality, 69*, 881–906.

Heine, S. J., & Hamamura, T. (2007). In search of East Asian self-enhancement. *Personality and Social Psychology Review, 11*, 4–27.

Heine, S. J., Harihara, M., & Niiya, Y. (2002). Terror management in Japan. *Asian Journal of Social Psychology, 5*, 187–196.

Heine, S. J., Takemoto, T., Moskalenko, S., Lasaleta, J., & Henrich, J. (2008). Mirrors in the head: Cultural variation in objective self-awareness. *Personality and Social Psychology Bulletin, 34*, 879–887.

Hesse, H. (2008). *Siddhartha (EBook)*. Retrieved from http://www.gutenberg.org/files/2500/2500-h/2500-h.htm

Heyman, G. D., Fu, G., & Lee, K. (2007). Evaluating claims people make about themselves: The development of skepticism. *Child Development, 78*, 367–375.

Ho, D., & Ho, R. (2007). Measuring spirituality and spiritual emptiness: Toward ecumenicity and transcultural applicability. *Review of General Psychology, 11*, 62–74.

Hughes, C., & Leekam, S. (2004). What are the links between theory of mind and social relations? Review, reflections and new directions for studies of typical and atypical development. *Social Development, 13*, 598–619.

Imada, T., & Kitayama, S. (2010). Social eyes and choice justification: Culture and dissonance revisited. *Social Cognition, 28*, 589–608.

Inhelder, B., & Piaget, J. (1958). *The growth of logical thinking from childhood to adolescence*. New York: Basic Books.

Jonas, E., & Fischer, P. (2006). Terror management and religion: Evidence that intrinsic religiousness mitigates worldview defense following mortality salience. *Journal of Personality and Social Psychology, 91*, 553–567.

Kashima, E. S., Halloran, M., Yuki, M., & Kashima, Y. (2004). The effects of personal and collective mortality salience on individualism: Comparing Australians and Japanese with higher and lower self-esteem. *Journal of Experiment Social Psychology, 40*, 384–392.

Kim, H. S. (2009). Express your social self: Cultural differences in choice of brand-name versus generic products. *Personality and Social Psychology Bulletin, 35*, 1555–1566.

Kim, Y. H., & Cohen, D. (2010). The jury and abjury of my peers: The self in face and dignity cultures. *Journal of Personality and Social Psychology, 98*, 904–916.

Kirkpatrick, L. A., & Shaver, P. R. (1990). Attachment theory and religion: Childhood attachments, religious beliefs, and conversion. *Journal for the Scientific Study of Religion, 29*, 315–334.

Kitayama, S., & Imada, T. (2010). Implicit independence and interdependence. In B. Mesquita, L. Feldman Barret, & E. Smith (Eds.), *The mind in context* (pp. 174–200). New York: Guildford.

Kitayama, S., Markus, H. R., Matsumoto, H., & Norasakkunkit, V. (1997). Individual and collective processes in the construction of the self: Self-enhancement in the United States and self-criticism in Japan. *Journal of Personality and Social Psychology, 72*, 1245–1267.

Kitayama, S., Snibbe, A. C., Markus, H. R., & Suzuki, T. (2004). Is there any "free" choice? Self and dissonance in two cultures. *Psychological Science, 15*, 527–533.

Koole, S. L., & Van den Berg, A. E. (2004). Paradise lost and reclaimed: An existential motives analysis of human-nature relations. In J. Greenberg, S. L. Koole, & T. Pyszczinsky (Eds.), *Handbook of experimental existential psychology* (pp. 86–103). New York: Guildford.

Lalwani, A. K., & Shavitt, S. (2009). The "me" I claim to be: Cultural self-construal elicits self-presentational goal pursuit. *Journal of Personality and Social Psychology*, 97, 88–102.

Lalwani, A. K., Shrum, L. J., & Chiu, C. Y. (2009). Motivated response style: The role of cultural values, regulatory focus, and self-consciousness in socially desirable responding. *Journal of Personality and Social Psychology*, 96, 870–882.

Leary, M. R., Adams, C. E., & Tate, E. B. (2006). Hypo-egoic self-regulation: Exercising self-control by diminishing the influence of the self. *Journal of Personality*, 74, 1803–1831.

Lillard, A. S. (1998). Ethnopsychologies: Cultural variations in theories of mind. *Psychological Bulletin*, 123, 3–32.

Liu, D., Wellman, H. M., Tardif, T., & Sabbagh, M. A. (2008). Theory of mind development in Chinese children: A meta-analysis of false belief understanding across cultures and languages. *Developmental Psychology*, 44, 523–531.

Mandel, N., & Smeesters, D. (2008). The sweet escape: The effects of mortality salience on consumption quantities for low and high self-esteem consumers. *Journal of Consumer Research*, 35, 309–323.

Markus, H., & Kitayama, S. (1991). Culture and the self: Implications for cognition, emotion, and motivation. *Psychological Review*, 98, 224–253.

Mazor, A., & Enright, R. D. (1988). The development of the individuation process from a social-cognitive perspective. *Journal of Adolescence*, 11, 29–47.

McCullough, M. E., Emmons, R. A., & Tsang, J. (2002). The grateful disposition: A conceptual and empirical topography. *Journal of Personality and Social Psychology*, 82, 112–127.

McCullough, M. E., & Willoughby, B. L. B. (2009). Religion, self control, and self-regulation: Associations, explanations, and implications. *Psychological Bulletin*, 135, 69–93.

Meins, E., Fernyhough, C., Wainwright, R., Clark-Carter, D., Gupta, M. D., Fradley, E., ... Tuckey, M. (2003). Pathways to understanding mind: Construct validity and predictive validity of maternal mind-mindedness. *Child Development*, 74, 1194–1211.

Mikulincer, M. (1998). Attachment working models and the sense of trust: An exploration of interaction goals and affect regulation. *Journal of Personality and Social Psychology*, 74, 1209–1224.

Miller, J. G. (1994). Cultural diversity in the morality of caring: Individually oriented versus duty-based interpersonal codes. *Cross-Cultural Research*, 28, 3–39.

Miller, P. J., Sandel, T. L., Liang, C. H., & Fung, H. (2001). Narrating transgressions in Longwood: The discourses, meanings, and paradoxes of an American socializing practice. *Ethos*, 29, 159–186.

Miller, P. J., Wang, S., Sandel, T., & Cho, G. E. (2002). Self-esteem as folk theory: A comparison of European American and Taiwanese mothers' beliefs. In C. S. Tamis-LeMonda & R. Harwood (Eds.), *Special issue of parenting: Science & practice: Parental ethnotheories: Cultural practices and normative development*, 2, 209–239.

Na, J., & Kitayama, S. (2010). *Motivational effects of choice in East and West: The moderating role of social eyes priming.* Unpublished manuscript, University of Michigan, Ann Arbor.

Newman, L. S., Duff, K. J., & Baumeister, R. F. (1997). A new look at defensive projection: Thought suppression, accessibility, and biased person perception. *Journal of Personality and Social Psychology, 72,* 980–1001.

Oosterwegel, A., & Oppenheimer, L. (2002). Jumping to awareness of conflict between self representations and its relation to psychological well-being. *International Journal of Behavioral Development, 26,* 548–555.

Patall, E. A., Cooper, H., & Robinson, J. C. (2008). The effects of choice on intrinsic motivation and related outcomes: A meta-analysis of research findings. *Psychological Bulletin, 134,* 270–300.

Perner, J., & Wimmer, H. (1985). "John thinks that Mary thinks that..." Attribution of second-order beliefs by 5–10 year old children. *Journal of Experimental Child Psychology, 39,* 437–471.

Pham, M. T., Goukens, C., Lehmann, D. R., & Stuart, J. A. (2010). Shaping customer satisfaction through self-awareness cues. *Journal of Marketing Research, 47,* 920–932.

Pillow, B. H., & Henrichon, A. J. (1996). There's more to the picture than meets the eye: Young children's difficulty understanding biased interpretation. *Child Development, 67,* 803–819.

Proulx, T., & Chandler, M. J. (2009). Jekyll and Hyde and me: Age-graded differences in conceptions of self-unity. *Human Development, 52,* 261–286.

Pyszczynski, T., Abdollahi, A., Solomon, S., Greenberg, J., Cohen, F., & Weise, D. (2006). Mortality salience, martyrdom, and military might: The great Satan versus the axis of evil. *Personality and Social Psychology Bulletin, 32,* 525–537.

Pyszczynski, T., Greenberg, J., & Solomon, S. (1999). A dual-process model of defense against conscious and unconscious death-related thoughts: An extension of terror management theory. *Psychological Review, 106,* 835–845.

Pyszczynski, T., Greenberg, J., Solomon, S., Arndt, J., & Schimel, J. (2004). Why do people need self-esteem? A theoretical and empirical review. *Psychological Bulletin, 130,* 435–468.

Pyszczynski, T., Greenberg, J., Solomon, S., & Hamilton, J. (1990). A terror management analysis of self-awareness and anxiety: The hierarchy of terror. *Anxiety Research, 2,* 177–195.

Rachlin, H. (2000). *The science of self-control.* Cambridge, MA: Harvard University Press.

Reinert, D., & Edwards, C. (2009). Attachment theory, childhood mistreatment, and religiosity. *Psychology of Religion and Spirituality, 1,* 25–34.

Roberts, J. E., Kassel, J. D., & Gotlib, I. H. (1996). Adult attachment security and symptoms of depression: The mediating role of dysfunctional attitudes and low self-esteem. *Journal of Personality and Social Psychology, 70,* 310–320.

Rothbaum, F., Pott, M., Azuma, H., Myake, K., & Weisz, J. (2000). The development of close relationships in Japan and the United States: Paths of symbiotic harmony and generative tension. *Child Development, 71,* 1121–1142.

Rothbaum, F., & Trommsdorff, G. (2007). Do roots and wings complement or oppose one another? The socialization of relatedness and autonomy in cultural context. In

J. E. Grusec & P. D. Hastings (Eds.), *Handbook of socialization: Theory and research* (pp. 461–489). New York: Guilford.

Rothbaum, F., Weisz, J., & Snyder, S. S. (1982). Changing the world and changing the self: A two-process model of perceived control. *Journal of Personality and Social Psychology, 42,* 5–37.

Sabbagh, M. A., Xu, F., Carlson, S. M., Moses, L. J., & Lee, K. (2006). The development of executive functioning and theory of mind: A comparison of Chinese and U.S. preschoolers. *Psychological Science, 17,* 74–81.

Sauter, F. M., Heyne, D., Blote, A. W., van Widenfelt, B. M., & Westenberg, P. M. (2010). Assessing therapy-relevant cognitive capacities in young people: Development and psychometric properties of the self-reflection and insight scale for youth. *Behavioral and Cognitive Psychotherapy, 38,* 303–317.

Savani, K., Markus, H. R., Naidu, N. V. R., Kumar, S., & Berlia, N. (2010). What counts as a choice? U.S. Americans are more likely than Indians to construe actions as choices. *Psychological Science, 21,* 391–398.

Scheier, M. F., & Carver, C. S. (1980). Private and public self-attention, resistance to change, and dissonance reduction. *Journal of Personality and Social Psychology, 39,* 514–521.

Schimel, J., Landau, M., & Hayes, J. (2008). Self-esteem: A human solution to the problem of death. *Social and Personality Psychology Compass, 2,* 1218–1234.

Sebastian C., Burnett S., & Blakemore, S. J. (2008). Development of the self-concept during adolescence. *Trends in Cognitive Science, 12,* 441–446.

Sedikides, C., & Gregg, A. P. (2008). Self-enhancement: Food for thought. *Perspectives on Psychological Science, 3,* 102–116.

Selman, R. L. (1980). *The growth of interpersonal understanding: Development and clinical analyses.* New York: Academic Press.

Shavitt, S., Swann, S., Lowrey, T. M., & Wanke, M. (1992). The interaction of endorser attractiveness and involvement in persuasion depends on the goal that guides message processing. *Journal of Consumer Psychology, 3,* 137–162.

Silvia, P. J. (2001). Nothing or the opposite: Intersecting terror management and objective self-awareness. *European Journal of Personality, 15,* 73–82.

Silvia, P. J., & Duval, T. S. (2001). Objective self-awareness theory: Recent progress and enduring problems. *Personality and Social Psychology Review, 5,* 230–241.

Silvia, P. J., & Phillips, A. G. (2011). Evaluating self-reflection and insight as self-conscious traits. *Personality and Individual Differences, 50,* 234–237.

Smith, H. (1991). *The world's religions.* New York: HarperCollins.

Solomon, S., Greenberg, J., & Pyszczynski, T. (1991). A terror management theory of social behavior: The psychological foundation of self-esteem and cultural worldviews. In M. P. Zanna (Ed.), *Advances in experimental social psychology. Vol. 24* (pp. 93–159). San Diego, CA: Academic Press.

Tam, K. P., Chiu, C. Y., & Lau, I. Y. M. (2007). Terror management among Chinese: Worldview defense and intergroup bias in resource allocation. *Asian Journal of Social Psychology, 10,* 93–102.

Taylor, S. E., Sherman, D. K., Kim, H. S., Jarcho, J., Takagi, K., & Dunagan, M. S. (2004). Culture and social support: Who seeks it and why? *Journal of Personality and Social Psychology, 87,* 354–362.

Tsai, J. L., Miao, F. F., & Seppala, E. (2007). Good feelings in Christianity and Buddhism: Religious differences in ideal affect. *Personality and Social Psychology Bulletin, 33*, 409–421.

Twenge, J. M., Catanese, K. R., & Baumeister, R. F. (2003). Social exclusion and the deconstructed state: Time perception, meaninglessness, lethargy, lack of emotion, and self awareness. *Journal of Personality and Social Psychology, 85*, 409–423.

United States Department of State, Bureau of Democracy, Human Rights, and Labor (2004). *International Religious Freedom Report.* Retrieved from http://www.state.gov/g/drl/rls/irf/2004/c12779.htm.

Vail, K. E., Rothschild, Z. K., Weise, D. R., Solomon, S., Pyszczynski, T., & Greenberg, J. (2010). A terror management analysis of the psychological functions of religion. *Personality and Social Psychology Review, 14*, 84–94.

Wachholtz, A. B., & Pearce, M. J. (2009). Does spirituality as a coping mechanism help or hinder coping with chronic pain? *Current Pain and Headache Reports, 13*, 127–132.

Wakimoto, R. (2006). Mortality salience effects on modesty and relative self-effacement. *Asian Journal of Social Psychology, 9*, 176–183.

Walach, H., Buchheld, N., Buttenmüller, V., Kleinknecht, N., & Schmidt, S. (2006). Measuring mindfulness – the Freiburg Mindfulness Inventory (FMI). *Personality and Individual Differences, 40*, 1543–1555.

Wang Y. Z., Wiley, A. R., & Chiu, C. Y. (2008). Independence-supportive praise versus independence-promoting praise. *International Journal of Behavioral Development, 32*, 13–20.

Wenzlaff, R. M., & Wegner, D. M. (2000). Thought suppression. *Annual Review of Psychology, 51*, 59–91.

Wicklund, R. A., & Gollwitzer, P. M. (1982). *Symbolic self-completion.* Hillsdale, NJ: Erlbaum.

Wiekens, C. J., & Stapel, D. A. (2010). Self-awareness and saliency of social versus individualistic behavioral standards. *Social Psychology, 41*, 10–19.

Wu, S., & Keysar, B. (2007). Cultural effects on perspective taking. *Psychological Science, 18*, 600–606.

Wu, X. (2009). The dynamics of Chinese face mechanisms and classroom behaviour: A case study. *Evaluation & Research in Education, 22*, 87–105.

Yen, C. L., & Cheng, C. P. (2010). Terror management among Taiwanese: Worldview defense or resigning to fate? *Asian Journal of Social Psychology, 13*, 185–194.

Part Two

UNIVERSAL AND CULTURE-SPECIFIC
FUNCTIONS OF ADOLESCENT VALUES AND
RELIGION

4 Values and Religion in Adolescent Development
Cross-National and Comparative Evidence

Shalom H. Schwartz

Abstract

This chapter briefly reviews the nature of ten basic values recognized in cultures around the world that influence attitudes and behavior in all societies. Using data on Protestant, Roman Catholic, Muslim, Eastern Orthodox, Jewish, and no religion samples of adolescents and adults from representative national samples from 30 countries, it addresses questions important for understanding the development of adolescents' values and the relations of their values to religion. Research reveals that, by mid-adolescence, the dynamic structure of conflicts and compatibilities that gives coherence to adult value systems has already developed. Moreover, this holds in all six religion groups. Thus, the structure of relations among the ten basic values is largely a function of universal developmental processes rather than of socialization into particular religions. Adolescents understand and organize the ten basic values in ways similar to adults, but their value priorities differ from those of adults. Adolescents accord substantially less importance than adults do to all of the other-oriented values. They are less concerned than adults with promoting the welfare of members of their in-group (benevolence) and of the wider society (universalism) and with avoiding change or uncertainty (security, conformity, and tradition). On the other hand, adolescents give higher priority than adults to self-enhancing values (achievement and power) and to values that encourage the pursuit of excitement (stimulation) and pleasure (hedonism). Values that emphasize autonomy (self-direction) peak in late-adolescence and remain very important until the mid-30s before declining thereafter. The chapter discusses aspects of development and socialization that can account for these near universal trends and for small changes in value priorities that occur between mid- and late-adolescence. Do more and less religious adolescents differ in their value priorities? The chapter reports that, strikingly, very similar patterns emerge regardless of religion. Religiosity relates most positively to tradition values, positively to conformity values, negatively to self-direction, stimulation, and power values, and most negatively to hedonism and stimulation values. These findings suggest that differences in religiosity among adolescents are largely a product of adolescents' choices about how religious they should be based on their individual value priorities. Socialization and teaching within particular religions plays a smaller role. We consider values and religiosity to be important because we assume that they influence significant attitudes and behavior. The chapter examines how adolescents' basic values and/or their religiosity influence the centrality of family in their lives, the importance of helping needy people, and the importance of always obeying the law. Analyses reveal that adolescents' individual value priorities have a much stronger influence on these attitudes than their degree of religiosity does. Finally, the chapter examines processes of value acquisition that affect parent–adolescent value similarity, using data from Israeli adolescents. It notes that what may appear to be parental value transmission actually involves active value acquisition by adolescents. Exposure to parents' social circles and parental warmth and responsiveness increase value similarity by contributing to accurate perception of parents' socialization values and/or acceptance of these values, whereas autocratic and indifferent parenting and love withdrawal undermine similarity in Western cultures.

Adolescence is a critical period in the development of our basic values. Our system of value priorities crystallizes during this period. By basic values, I refer to our beliefs about how important or desirable such abstract goals as wisdom, security, equality, wealth, freedom, obedience, and pleasure are to us as guiding principles in life (Schwartz, 1992; cf. Rokeach, 1973). Values are important because they motivate our behavior (what we do), justify our past behavior (why we did it), direct our attention (what we notice), and serve as standards for evaluating people and events (who and what we like or dislike) (Schwartz, 2006). As standards, basic values underlie our attitudes. Many believe that religion plays an important role in the development of values (e.g., Baker, 2005, Weber, 1905/1958). This chapter focuses on relations between basic values and religion in adolescence.

The chapter briefly reviews the nature of basic values and their near universal structure. Using data from representative national samples from 30 countries, it addresses five questions concerned with adolescents' values and religion that have concerned researchers:[1]

(1) A near universal structure of relations among different values that reflects the motivations they express characterizes adults around the world. Has this motivational *structure* of relations among values emerged yet by mid- or by late-adolescence?
(2) Do adolescents who are members of the different major Western religious groups (Roman Catholics, Protestants, Eastern Orthodox,

Muslims, Jews, and no religion) differ in the motivational structure of their values?

(3) What patterns of development can we discern in value *priorities* as youth move from mid- to late-adolescence and then to adulthood?

(4) Do more and less religious adolescents have different value priorities, and does the association between religiosity and values depend upon the religion to which they adhere?

(5) How, if at all, do adolescents' basic values and/or their religiosity influence three significant attitudes: the centrality of family in their lives, the importance of helping needy people, and the importance of always obeying the law?

Finally, the chapter discusses processes of value acquisition that affect parent–adolescent value similarity and parenting variables that influence these processes.

The Nature of Basic Values and their Structure

Basic values are beliefs about what is important and desirable. Whenever a person expresses, pursues, or defends one of his or her values, positive or negative feelings are aroused. The Schwartz (1992) value theory identifies ten basic values that derive from universal requirements of human existence. Listed next are the ten values, each defined by the distinct motivational goals it expresses.

Power: social status and prestige, control, or dominance over people and resources

Achievement: personal success through demonstrating competence according to social standards

Hedonism: pleasure and sensuous gratification for oneself

Stimulation: excitement, novelty, and challenge in life

Self-direction: independent thought and action – choosing, creating, exploring

Universalism: understanding, appreciation, tolerance, and protection for the welfare of all people and for nature

Benevolence: preservation and enhancement of the welfare of people with whom one is in frequent personal contact

Tradition: respect, commitment, and acceptance of the customs and ideas that traditional culture or religion provide the self

Conformity: restraint of actions, inclinations, and impulses likely to upset or harm others and violate social expectations or norms

Security: safety, harmony, and stability of society, of relationships, and of self

The theory further specifies a structure of dynamic relations among the ten values. Figure 4.1 depicts this structure as a circular motivational continuum reflecting the conflict and compatibility among values. The closer any two values around the circle, the more compatible their motivations. The same action or attitude usually expresses or promotes both values. The more distant any two values around the circle, the more conflicting their motivations. Any action or attitude that expresses or promotes one value is likely to oppose or undermine attaining the other value. The circular motivational continuum describes relations among all values as an integrated structure. It implies that any behavior or attitude that is congruent with one basic value (e.g., controlling others' decisions – power) should also be congruent with its adjacent values (security and achievement). Moreover, the behavior or attitude should conflict with the opposing values across from it in the circle (universalism, benevolence, and self-direction). Thus, the whole integrated structure of values relates systematically to other variables.

As Figure 4.1 shows, the ten values are organized along two bipolar dimensions: (1) self-enhancement values (power, achievement) that encourage and legitimize the pursuit of self-interest are opposed to self-transcendence values (universalism, benevolence) that emphasize concern for the welfare of others, and (2) openness values (self-direction, stimulation) that favor change, encourage the pursuit of new ideas and experiences, are opposed to conservation values (security, tradition, conformity) that emphasize maintaining the status quo and avoiding threat. Hedonism values share elements of both openness and self-enhancement values, so hedonism is located between the two sets of values.

The circular structure of values also reflects another dynamic organizing principle (Schwartz, 2006). The values in the bottom half of the circle (Figure 4.1) are based in the need to avoid, control, and protect oneself against anxiety and threat. The values on the bottom right emphasize avoiding conflict, uncertainty, and change by submitting to others' expectations and passively accepting the status quo. The values on the bottom left emphasize overcoming possible sources of anxiety by gaining dominance over people and resources or by gaining others' admiration for one's achievements. In contrast, values in the top half of the circle are relatively anxiety free; they express motivations for growth and self-expansion. The values on the top right emphasize promoting the welfare of others. Those on the top left emphasize autonomous self-expression. Research with adults in over 70 countries supports the motivationally distinct content of these ten values. It also confirms the near universal structure of relations of conflict

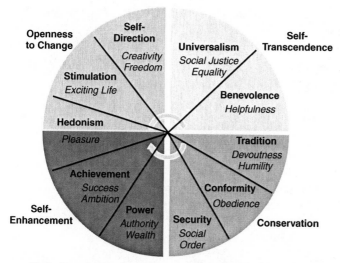

Circle Organized by Motivational Congruence and Opposition

Figure 4.1. Ten motivationally distinct values and their circular motivational structure.

and compatibility among the ten values (Schwartz, 1992, 2006; Schwartz & Boehnke, 2004).

Data and Measurement

The European Social Survey gathered data from representative national samples in 30 countries in its first three rounds (2002–2003, 2004–2005, 2006–2007).[2] Respondents from Eastern and Western Europe plus Turkey and Israel completed face-to-face interviews. The samples included 4,962 mid-adolescents (age 15–17), 6,940 late adolescents (18–21), and 90,563 adults (22+). Respondents were asked: "Do you belong to a particular religion or denomination?" This chapter examines values and religion among six groups: Roman Catholics (38,498), Protestants (16,958), Eastern Orthodox (8,128), Muslims (3,467), Jews (1,570), and those who reported that they belong to no religion (42,409).

Respondents completed a short version of the Portrait Values Questionnaire (PVQ; Schwartz, 2003; Schwartz et al., 2001) specially designed for the European Social Survey. This version included verbal portraits of 21 different people, gender-matched with the respondent. Each portrait described a person's goals, aspirations, or wishes that point implicitly to the importance of a value. For example, "Thinking up new ideas and being creative is important to her. She likes to do things in her own original way" describes a person for whom self-direction values are important. "It is important to him to be rich. He wants to have a lot of money and expensive things" describes a person who cherishes power values. We inferred respondents' own values from their self-reported similarity to people described implicitly in terms of particular values.

For each portrait, respondents answered: "How much like you is this person?" Six labeled responses ranged from "not like me at all (1)" to "very much like me (6)." The score for the importance of each value is the mean response to the items that measure it. Two portraits operationalized each value, with three for universalism because of its very broad content. To eliminate individual differences in use of the response scale, each person's responses were centered on his or her own mean.

The Motivational Structure of Values among Adolescents

I first examine whether the motivational structure of relations among the ten values that is typically found among adults has already emerged by mid- or by late-adolescence. To answer this question, I used multi-dimensional scaling. This scaling technique starts with the matrix of intercorrelations among the 21 value items. It represents each item as a point in a two-dimensional space. The distances between the points reflect the correlations between the items. Items that operationalize the same value (e.g., stimulation) should correlate highly positively and they should have low or negative correlations with items that operationalize opposing values (e.g., security and conformity). Therefore, the items that operationalize each basic value should be close to each other in the space and they should be distant from the group of items that operationalize the opposing values. If this is the case, it will be possible to partition the space into ten distinct regions, each containing the items that represent one of the ten values.

Figure 4.2 presents the empirical map of relations among the 21 value items from the ESS in the full sample of 11,902 adolescents; it shows that eight of the ten values can be discriminated clearly by partitioning the space. The items that measure hedonism and stimulation are intermixed in a way that makes it impossible to split them into separate regions. Comparing Figure 4.2 to Figure 4.1, we see that hedonism and stimulation are adjacent in the circle. That means that their motivations are quite similar. Perhaps the two values have not yet been discriminated by adolescents.

Because values form a motivational continuum, meanings of items near the boundaries of adjacent values inevitably overlap somewhat. Consequently, value items from adjacent values also intermix sometimes,

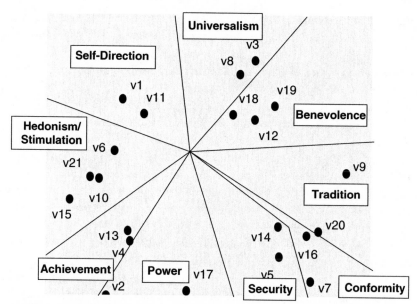

Figure 4.2. Value structure based on 11,902 adolescents (multidimensional scaling).

rather than emerging in clearly distinct regions. Item 19, protecting the environment, emerges in the universalism region for adults but in the adjacent benevolence region for adolescents. This suggests a slight difference in the meaning of this value. Its location with benevolence, a value concerned with the welfare of close others, suggests that adolescents see protecting the environment as a more personal concern than adults do. This generational difference may reflect the much greater emphasis on preserving the environment in the socialization and education of children as compared to their parents.

From Figure 4.2 we can conclude that, when we take mid- and late adolescents together, the significant distinctions among the basic values found among adults are indeed already present. Moreover, separate multi-dimensional scaling analyses of the value items in the mid- and late adolescent samples yield virtually identical projections. In sum, on average, adolescents apparently develop an understanding of the ten basic values by age 15, and they already make the distinctions among the values that they will continue to make in adulthood.

Do adolescents recognize the same conflicts and compatibilities among the basic values that adults do? That is, is the circular motivational structure, with the same opposed and compatible values, already present among adolescents? Comparing Figure 4.2 to Figure 4.1, we see that adolescents, like adults, organize their values into the opposing types of self-transcendence versus self-enhancement values and of openness to change versus conservation values. Moreover, the order of the basic values around the circle is the same as that typically found among adults. This also holds true in separate analyses of the data for the mid- and late adolescents. Thus, by mid-adolescence, the dynamic structure of conflicts and compatibilities that comprise adult value systems has already developed.

Melech (2001) found that a sample of Israeli 12-year-olds exhibited a less refined structure that distinguished only the broad oppositions between self-transcendence and self-enhancement and between openness to change and conservation values. This suggests that the more fined-tuned structure of basic values may develop gradually between ages 12 and 15. However, research using instruments more suited to children suggests that it may begin to develop earlier. Using a picture-based value survey, Döring, et al. (2010) found that 9–10-year-old German children already discriminated among the ten values and ordered them in the same motivational circle as adults. Moreover, a study of German twins aged 7–11 that used a simplified version of the PVQ to measure eight values (Knafo & Spinath, 2011) found that these eight values were discriminated.

These findings fit the developmental view that children in late childhood and early adolescence begin to organize the concrete, observable elements of their world into trait categories when they describe themselves and other persons (Harter, 1999). They act like "intuitive moralists" (Thompson, Meyer, & McGinley, 2006) who hold a basic conception of desirable goals that are stable over time (Harter, 1999). Such emerging basic conceptions fit my definition of values. Apparently, early adolescents not only form these conceptions but they organize them into reasonably coherent systems.

What about the effect of religion on the motivational structure of adolescents' values? Do adolescents from different religious groups organize their value systems into ten values that reflect the same relations of compatibility and conflict? Separate analyses within each religious group suggest that they do. In the Protestant, Roman Catholic, and Muslim adolescent samples, the results were the same as in Figure 4.2, with hedonism and stimulation intermixed. In the Eastern Orthodox, Jewish, and no religion samples, all ten basic values were discriminated and ordered around the circle as among adults (i.e., as in Figure 4.1).

Taken together, this set of analyses implies that the structure of relations among the ten basic values is largely a function of universal developmental processes. Socialization into particular religions with their unique value priorities does not appear to affect the way adolescents distinguish among values and organize them into a coherent system. This does not mean that social experience has no influence on the emergence of the value structure. The structure reflects the conflicts people experience when they must choose between mutually opposed goals (Schwartz, 2006). Such conflicts arise in the everyday experience of children, adolescents, and adults in all human groups. They help to shape the structure of values.

The observed similarity of the value structure across groups makes it legitimate to compare the values of these groups. It allows us to assume that the meanings of the ten values are reasonably similar for adolescents and adults and for adolescents from different religious groups. This is critical when we look at similarities and differences in value *priorities*.

Development and Change in Value Priorities
We next examine patterns of development in value priorities as youth move from mid- to late-adolescence and then to adulthood. Consider first the other-oriented values, security, conformity, tradition, benevolence, and universalism. Figure 4.3 reveals that adolescents attribute substantially less importance than adults do to every one of these other-oriented values. Adolescents are much less concerned than adults are about promoting the welfare both of members of their in-group (benevolence) and of the wider society (universalism). Moreover, it is much less important to them to preserve the status quo and to avoid change or uncertainty (security, conformity, and tradition).

Several factors may explain these differences between adolescents and adults (Arnett, 2000; Elliott & Feldman, 1990; Lerner & Steinberg, 2009). These include: (1) adolescents have less responsibility for maintaining the major groups of which they are part (e.g., families) and caring for the welfare of others, (2) they are less committed to the established ways of doing things, (3) they are more invested in establishing their independent identities and in trying out new roles, and (4) they have greater freedom from social constraints and physical limitations.

Comparing mid-adolescents to late adolescents, they do not differ in the importance they attribute to security and conformity values. However, tradition, benevolence, and universalism values are slightly stronger among late adolescents. The change in benevolence may reflect increasing commitments among late adolescents to intimate relationships of their own choosing (e.g., Collins, Welsh, & Furman, 2009). The change in universalism values may derive from increasing awareness of human interdependence through greater exposure to different groups and to events in the

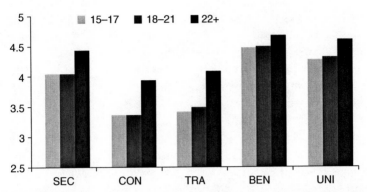

Figure 4.3. Adolescents' and adults' priorities for other-oriented values compared. *Note:* SEC = security, CON = conformity, TRA = tradition, BEN = benevolence, UNI = universalism

wider society (Schwartz & Bardi, 2001). The change in tradition occurred only among Protestant adolescents, for unclear reasons. The other-oriented values became increasingly important with age from adolescence across each succeeding adult cohort until at least age 75 (except for universalism that levels off after age 50). For security and conformity values, however, this trend begins only after adolescence.

Now consider the self-oriented values: self-direction, stimulation, hedonism, achievement, and power. Figure 4.4 reveals that adolescents attribute substantially more importance than adults do to all of them except self-direction. Not surprisingly, stimulation and hedonism show the biggest differences. These values express adolescents' greater pursuit of excitement and pleasure as they explore and experiment, still relatively free of the social role constraints and physical limitations of adulthood (Lerner & Steinberg, 2009). Adolescents also give higher priority than adults do to the self-enhancing values of achievement and power. This may reflect their pursuit of social acceptance and success as part of their emerging identities (Jarvinen & Nichols, 1996). After adolescence, all four of these values show decreased importance in each adult age cohort until at least age 75. This decrease is already underway between mid- and late-adolescence for stimulation, hedonism, and achievement values.

Self-direction values follow a somewhat different trajectory. These values express the importance of autonomy of thought and action, of independence in making decisions. They are at the peak of importance in late-adolescence and remain very important until the mid-30s. During this period, individuals establish and consolidate their distinct identities in the world of work

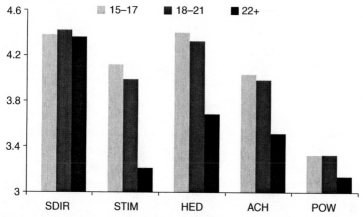

Figure 4.4. Adolescents' and adults' priorities for self-oriented values compared. *Note:* SDIR = self-direction, STIM = stimulation, HED = hedonism, ACH = achievement, POW = power

and intimate relations, separate from their family of origin (Côté, 2009). Thereafter, like the other self-oriented values, self-direction is less important with each succeeding adult age cohort.

Value Priorities and Religiosity

We have seen that adolescents have different value priorities than adults. However, do more and less religious adolescents differ in their value priorities? Consider two ways in which values and religiosity may become associated (Schwartz & Huismans, 1995). First, religious socialization, both formal (e.g., schooling, preaching) and informal (e.g., youth groups, family practices), might inculcate values. The values of more and less religious adolescents may differ because they are exposed to different degrees of religious socialization. Moreover, religions may emphasize somewhat different values in socialization (e.g., benevolence more or universalism more; self-direction more or conformity more). If so, the value differences between more and less religious adolescents produced by religious socialization should vary across religions.

A second way in which values and religiosity may become associated focuses on adolescents' active choices rather than on how they are socialized. Adolescents may choose how religious to be, depending on the values that are important to them. For example, adolescents who value hedonism may choose to be less religious because religions generally oppose hedonistic pleasure seeking. Adolescents who value conformity may choose to be more religious because they are comfortable conforming to socially approved expectations that religions provide. Of course, most adolescents are born into and exposed to a particular religion. In this view, however, how important religion becomes in their lives depends on the extent to which the religion facilitates or interferes with the pursuit of their important values.

According to the religious socialization process, the experiences tied to belonging to a religious group influence the value priorities of adolescents: causality flows from religion to personal value priorities. According to the process of choosing how religious to be based on personal values, the adolescents' own value priorities influence their degree of religiosity: causality flows from personal value priorities to religiosity. Of course, both processes may operate.

To examine relations of value priorities to religiosity, I adopted an index of religiosity demonstrated to have a similar meaning across the ESS samples (Billiet & Meuleman, 2007). The index included three items[3]: (1) "How religious are you (11 pt. scale)?" (2) "How often do you attend religious services apart from special occasions (7 pt. scale)?" and (3) "How often do you pray apart from at services (7 pt. scale)?" Table 4.1 displays the correlations between values and religiosity in each religious group, controlling gender and age.

Note first that, for every religious group, religiosity relates most positively to tradition values and most negatively to hedonism or stimulation values. In every religious group, religiosity also relates positively to conformity values and negatively to self-direction, stimulation, and power values. Thus, the more religious an adolescent, the less importance he or she attributes to openness values, regardless of the religion to which he or she belongs. Moreover, the more religious an adolescent, the more importance he or she attributes to conservation values, regardless of religion (excepting security among Jews).

The similarity of this pattern of correlations between values and religiosity across different religions is more compatible with the process of value-based choice of level of religiosity than with the process of religious socialization. Adolescents for whom it is especially important to pursue their own ideas and lifestyles (openness values) are likely to find religion constraining and therefore less attractive. Adolescents who strongly value meeting social expectations and preserving the status quo (conservation values) are more comfortable adopting the relatively conservative ideas and lifestyles promulgated by religions. They are therefore more attracted to religion and become more religious.

Table 4.1. Correlations of Religiosity with Values among Adolescents in Five Religious Groups, Controlling Gender and Age

	Average Five Religious Groups	Roman Catholics (3,339)	Protes-tants (1,033)	Eastern Orthodox (584)	Jews (412)	Muslims (572)
Security	.03	.09**	.06	.04	−.07	.03
Conformity	.11	.16**	.15**	.12**	.03	.08
Tradition	.31	.21**	.28**	.25**	.57**	.19**
Benevolence	.05	−.06**	.07*	.16**	.10*	.00
Universalism	.03	.01	−.16**	.14**	−.15**	.01
Self-direction	−.11	−.08**	−.04	−.22**	−.14*	−.06
Stimulation	−.10	−.07**	−.19**	−.03	−.14**	−.06
Hedonism	−.18	−.27**	−.25**	−.19**	−.03	−.15**
Achievement	−.08	.01	−.11	−.10*	−.17**	−.02
Power	−.11	−.05**	−.16**	−.20**	−.12*	−.01
Mn Religiosity (0–7)		3.79	3.44	3.88	3.59	3.96
Standard Deviation		.71	.69	.61	.91	.69

Note: The average correlations are calculated giving equal weight to each religious group. Mean religiosity is controlled for age and gender.
** $p<.01$, 2-tailed; *$p<.05$, 2-tailed

Central to the doctrines and teaching of all religions is an emphasis on benevolence (concern for the welfare of close others). Most religions also emphasize universalism (concern for the weak and vulnerable in society). If religion influences the values of adolescents, one might therefore expect these two values to be among the most positively correlated with religiosity. The quite modest correlations of religiosity with benevolence and universalism values cast doubt on the impact of religion as a force for value socialization.

However, Table 4.1 also provides some evidence for religious socialization. In several instances, the magnitude of the religiosity value correlations for the same value varies substantially across religions. Nontrivial correlation differences between religions are .38 for tradition, .31 for universalism, .18 for self-direction, and .18 for achievement. These correlation differences between religions may reflect doctrinal emphases (encouraging or discouraging autonomous thinking) and/or the social organization of the religions (e.g., activity directed more to the religious in-group or to the wider community). Religious socialization may express these doctrinal and organizational differences between religions that thereby influence the associations of religiosity with values. However, these differences may also make various religions more or less attractive to adolescents depending on their values, thereby affecting their implicit choices to be religious.

The bottom part of Table 4.1 reports the means and standard deviations for the religious groups on the religiosity index, controlled for age and gender. An analysis of covariance reveals that self-reported religiosity scores of Muslim and Eastern Orthodox adolescents do not differ. However, both have significantly higher scores than the other groups. Each of the other groups differs significantly from those with lower scores. Not surprisingly, adolescents who indicated no religious affiliation had a substantially lower score (2.76, SD = .49). The variance of religiosity is especially large among Jewish adolescents. This reflects the fact that being Jewish is both an ethnic and religious identity. One can be a secular as well as a religious Jew. High variances of both traditional values and of religiosity account for the extremely strong correlation between them among Jewish adolescents. A detailed analysis of the observed differences on religiosity between religions is beyond the scope of this chapter.

Influences of Adolescents' Values and Religiosity on Significant Attitudes

The main reason for considering values or religiosity to be important is that we assume they influence people's significant attitudes and behaviors. I therefore examine next how adolescents' basic values and/or their religiosity influence three significant attitudes that were measured in the European Social Survey.

Centrality of the Family in Adolescents' Lives. Presumably, religion strengthens family ties (e.g., Bahr & Chadwick, 1985; Sherkat & Ellison, 1999). We might therefore expect the family to be more central in the lives of more religious adolescents. Several values are also likely to promote centrality of the family. Conservation values, which emphasize maintaining a stable environment (security), keeping family customs (tradition), and avoiding conflict in close relationships (conformity), can find expression and fulfillment in the family. Among the self-transcendence values, benevolence, which emphasizes concern for the welfare of in-group (i.e., family) members, should also be conducive to retaining strong family ties. However, universalism values may be unrelated to family centrality because they focus on the welfare of those in the wider society. Individuals for whom power values are important are likely to break away from the family because they are concerned with promoting their self-interests even at the expense of others.

To examine whether adolescents' values affect the centrality of family in their lives, I regressed responses to the question, "How important is the family in your life?" on the six basic values that are potentially most relevant to social behavior and on gender and age (Table 4.2, column 1). To assess whether adolescents' religiosity adds to or even replaces the influence of values on family centrality, I added religiosity in a second regression model (Table 4.2, column 2). Security values promoted family centrality most strongly and power values reduced it most (Table 4.2, column 1). Benevolence, conformity, and tradition values were also conducive to family centrality, as expected. Girls consider the family more central, but age – in the 15 to 21-year-old range – has no effect. Religiosity added only .7 percent to the variance explained (column 2), replacing tradition values as a significant predictor. In sum, basic values, particularly security, predicted the centrality of family for adolescents more than their religiosity did.

Citizenship: Supporting Those Who Are Worse Off. Virtually all religions call upon their members to support those worse off than they are. Do adolescents who are more religious respond to this call more than less religious adolescents do? Does religiosity play a larger or smaller role than basic values in the endorsement of this call? The most relevant basic values are universalism that should promote concern for the weak in society and power that should inhibit sacrificing own interests to support others. Respondents were asked, "To be a good citizen, how important is it to support those who are worse off?" Columns 3 and 4 of Table 4.2 show the results of regressing responses to this question on values and religiosity.

Universalism and benevolence values contributed most positively to support for those who are worse off, tradition values also contributed positively, and power values fostered opposition to endorsing this view. Girls and younger adolescents viewed supporting others who are worse off as more important. Together, the values, age, and gender explained 10.1 percent of the variance in responses. Adding religiosity as a predictor (Table 4.2, column 4) increased the variance explained to 11.4 percent. Adding religiosity reduced the contribution of tradition values to insignificance, reflecting the correlation of religiosity with this basic value. Although religiosity explained an additional 1.3 percent of the variance in the attitude toward supporting the less well off, its contribution was less than that of both universalism and benevolence values. The analysis suggests that adolescents' basic values have a stronger impact on their stance toward this social behavior than their religiosity does.

Table 4.2. Regressions of Three Significant Attitudes on Religiosity Age, Gender, and Relevant Basic Values among Adolescents (Betas)

	1	2	3	4	5	6
Predictor Variables	Centrality of Family in Life	Centrality of Family in Life	Supporting Those Who are Worse Off	Supporting Those Who are Worse Off	Always Obey Laws/ Regulations	Always Obey Laws/ Regulations
Age	−.03	−.03	−.06**	−.06**	−.08**	−.07**
Gender	.08**	.06**	−.05*	.04*	.05**	.04*
Security Values	.14**	.14**	.03	.02	.17**	.16**
Power Values	−.10**	−.09**	−.08**	−.08**	−.09**	−.08**
Benevolence Values	.05**	.05**	.14**	.14**	.01	.01
Conformity Values	.05**	.05**	−.04	−.04*	.29**	.28**
Universalism Values	−.01	−.01	.16**	.16**	.01	.01
Tradition Values	.06**	.03	.07**	.03	−.01	−.04*
Religiosity		.09**		.13**		.10**
p value<	.001	.001	.001	.001	.001	.001
Adjusted R²	.060	.067	.101	.114	.150	.159
Observations	3834	3834	3802	3802	3806	3806

**p<.001, *p<.01, 2-tailed

Citizenship: Always Obeying Laws and Regulations. Key functions of religion are to anchor the most important norms of society and to promote codes of conduct that foster cooperation and cohesion among societal members (e.g., Durkheim, 1954/1912; Hamilton, 2001). One might therefore expect adolescents who are more religious to think it is more important to be law-abiding citizens. Valuing conformity and security should also increase adolescents' commitment to being law-abiding citizens. How well do adolescents' religiosity and values explain this attitude? Responses to the question, "To be a good citizen, how important is it always to obey laws and regulations?" provide an answer.

Columns 5 and 6 of Table 4.2 report results of regressing responses to this question on values and religiosity. Values, age, and gender accounted for 15.0 percent of the variance in this attitude (column 5). Security and conformity values promoted commitment to abiding by the law whereas power values undermined this commitment. Adding religiosity as a predictor (column 6) increased the variance explained only minimally (.9 percent).

Religiosity predicted less than security and conformity values. Interestingly, with religiosity included, tradition values negatively affect commitment to obeying the law. This negative beta must capture effects of a component of tradition values not shared with security and conservation values and with religiosity. That unique component might express a motivation to preserve traditions that reject the current social order, a phenomenon found among radical groups (e.g., Gallagher, 1997).

Parental Value Transmission of Values and Adolescent Value Development

Parents care greatly about influencing their children's values, although their success is often quite minimal (e.g., Homer, 1993; Knafo & Schwartz, 2001). Through which processes do parents influence their children's values? Which processes lead to more or less similarity (congruence) between parents' and adolescents' value priorities? Building on a model proposed by Grusec and Goodnow (1994), Knafo and Schwartz (2008) specify two preconditions for parent–adolescent value congruence. First, adolescents must perceive their parents' values accurately. Second, adolescents must accept those values, adopting them as their own. If adolescents perceive their parents' values accurately and accept them as well, value congruence should be substantial. However, if they misperceive their parent's values or reject those values, congruence is likely to be low. In this analysis, adolescents are hardly passive recipients of value transmission. Instead, they participate actively in determining their parents' influence on their values.

Accuracy and Acceptance as Mediators. A study of 591 Israeli Jewish families illustrates the effects of accuracy of perception and acceptance of perceived parental values as mediators of adolescent–parent value congruence (Knafo & Schwartz, 2008). Adolescents (mean age 17.1, $SD = .7$) responded twice to the PVQ items. The first time, the standard PVQ was used to infer their own values. The second time, some 20 minutes later, a modified PVQ asked how they thought their father/mother would want them to respond to each item. We used this response to infer the values that adolescents thought their parents wanted to transmit (i.e., perceived parental socialization values). Parents reported their own socialization values by completing the PVQ as they would want their son/daughter to respond to it.

From these three value measures, we derived indexes of accuracy, acceptance, and congruence for each of the ten values. To simplify, I average findings across the four combinations of mother/father X daughter/son dyads. Adolescent–parent value similarity was greatest for tradition values. Value congruence was also relatively high for power values. Value dissimilarity was greatest for hedonism values. Adolescents' values correlated approximately .81 with their parents' socialization values for tradition, .44 for power values, but less than .28 for hedonism, benevolence, universalism, and achievement values.

Did adolescents' accuracy and/or acceptance of parental values account for the levels of value similarity? For most values, both accuracy in perceiving the values parents sought to transmit and acceptance of those values contributed to adolescent–parent value congruence. Indeed, the combination of accuracy and acceptance largely, although not completely, explained the level of congruence. Across the ten values and four dyad combinations, accuracy had a somewhat stronger impact on congruence than acceptance did.

Two interesting variations merit comment. The relatively high congruence for power values was due to an especially high level of acceptance. Adolescents adopted the same orientation to controlling people and resources they perceived their parents expressed through power values. Regarding conformity, sons (but not daughters) tended both to misperceive their parents' conformity values and to reject the conformity values they perceived. Thus, sons rebelled against their parents' normative expectations, and their rebellion blinded them to the degree of conformity their parents actually expected of them.

Exposure to Parental Social Circles. Although both accuracy and acceptance contributed to the very high congruence of tradition values, substantial variance in the congruence of tradition values was still unexplained. This implies that there were other sources of parent–adolescent congruence as well. One important source was parents' influence upon the environment to which their adolescent children are exposed. This is particularly true in the domain of religion. Parents may choose whether or not to send their children to religious schools (especially in Israel where there is a state religious system) and youth groups. Parents typically bring their children together with the children of the families similar to their own with which they share religious outlooks. If adolescents acquire tradition values in such school and peer environments, their tradition values are likely to become more similar to those of their parents. This may explain the quite consistent finding that congruence for values related to religion is usually higher than for other values (Kalish & Johnson, 1972; Miller & Glass, 1989).

Exposure to the social circles parents choose, circles which endorse values similar to those of their parents, can also increase the *accuracy* of adolescents' perception of their parents' values. If the values of their parents' social circles are distinct from those prevalent in society, these values will be salient to the adolescents. This helps them to perceive the importance of these values to their parents accurately. In support of this idea, we found that accuracy was higher for values that were associated with parents' religiosity, age, education level, and ethnicity. Endorsement of these values was distinctive of the social circles of which their parents were a part.

Exposure to the social circles their parents choose can also increase *acceptance* of parental values. Endorsement of their parents' values by other members of these social circles gives greater legitimacy to these values, making them more attractive. Supporting this idea, we found that acceptance, like accuracy, was also higher for values associated with the parental characteristics that affect participation in distinctive social circles – religiosity, age, education level, and ethnicity.

We did not study parental influence on adolescents' religious belief and observance. Research suggests that it is quite strong (e.g., summary in Hood, Hill, & Spilka, 2009). The mechanism of parental control over adolescents' social circles that applies to value acquisition explains much of parental influence on religiosity as well.

Types of Values. Adolescents are more likely to accept some types of perceived parental values than others. They tend to view values that deal mainly with personal issues as outside their parents' legitimate regulation (Smetana, 2000). Hedonism, stimulation, self-direction, and achievement values deal with personal issues because their consequences essentially affect only the actor, not others (Schwartz, 1992). In contrast, adolescents tend to think it is more legitimate for parents to pressure them with regard to moral values, those that affect others' welfare (benevolence, universalism, and power), and values concerned with social conventions and safety (conformity, tradition, and security). We found that adolescents accepted their parents' perceived moral and conventional socialization values more than they accepted their values concerned with personal issues. Conformity values, the value most in contention as adolescents seek to establish their independence, were the exception, with low adolescent acceptance.

Parenting Styles. I next examine how parenting styles affect parent–adolescent value congruence through their effects on accuracy and acceptance. Combinations of the two dimensions of warmth (responsiveness) and demandingness (control) form the parenting styles most frequently discussed in the literature (Darling & Steinberg, 1993). Authoritative parents are high on both warmth and demandingness. They try to consider the child's point of view in setting standards, explain what they demand, and are willing to negotiate. Indulgent parents are high on warmth but low on demandingness. Autocratic (authoritarian) parents are high on demandingness and low on warmth. Unlike authoritative parents, they impose their standards on the child and do not negotiate. Indifferent (permissive-neglectful) parents are low on both demandingness and warmth. The following analyses of the effects of parenting styles are based on the same sample discussed above (Knafo & Schwartz, 2003, 2005). Parental warmth and demandingness were measured as perceived by adolescents.

The only parenting styles that correlated significantly with parent–adolescent value congruence were those that affected both accuracy and acceptance of perceived parental values. Indulgent and authoritative parenting were not related to congruence. Both correlated positively with acceptance but not with accuracy. The warmth aspect of these two parenting styles may have motivated adolescents to accept their parents' values. Yet indulgent parents may not articulate their values clearly enough to enable adolescents to perceive them accurately. The index of authoritative parenting was particularly weak. This may account for why, despite the fact that authoritative parents make clear demands and explain them, this parenting style did not affect accuracy of perception.

The warmth (responsiveness) aspect of parenting was measured as a latent variable based on seven items (Knafo & Schwartz, 2003). Warmth correlated positively with accuracy, with acceptance, and with congruence. Adolescents are likely to find interacting with warm, responsive parents both comfortable and unthreatening and therefore, spend more time with their parents. They would therefore have more opportunity to see and hear what their parents value and, being less anxious, be able to better understand the values their parents express. Warmth might also increase their identification with their parents and motivate adolescents to accept their parents' values.

Both autocratic and indifferent parenting correlated negatively with accuracy, with acceptance, and with congruence. In Western cultures, autocratic parenting is accompanied by anger, coercion, and humiliation of children (Rudy & Grusec, 2001). This is likely to reduce adolescents' desire to spend time with their parents, to interfere with their ability to understand the values their parents express, and to undermine their motivation to accept whatever values they do perceive. Indifferent parenting provides no clear expectations or standards from which to infer parental values accurately.

Moreover, when parental warmth is absent, adolescents are less likely to be motivated to accept the parental values they do perceive.

Love withdrawal is a specific parenting technique that also relates to parent–adolescent value congruence. Parents who use love withdrawal condition their affection on their child's compliance with their demands. Western adolescents dislike this parenting behavior (Siegal & Barclay, 1985). It produces anxiety and guilt in children and leads them to avoid their parents (Maccoby & Martin, 1983). Not surprisingly, love withdrawal correlated negatively with accuracy, with acceptance, and with congruence (Knafo & Schwartz, 2003, 2005). The negative emotional responses it elicits may interfere with adolescents' understanding of their parents' messages, cause them to attend less to these messages and avoid their parents' presence, and undermine their motivation to accept their parents' values.

Conclusion

Examination of the structure of values among adolescents from 30 countries revealed that the near universal motivational structure of relations among different values is already present by mid-adolescence. Adolescents experience the same conflicts and compatibilities among their values that adults do. This pattern emerges even before adolescence. Socialization into particular religions with their unique value priorities does not appear to affect the basic values adolescents distinguish or the way they organize these values into a coherent system. Separate analyses of Roman Catholic, Protestant, Eastern Orthodox, Muslim, Jewish, and non-religious adolescents yielded virtually the same motivational structure of values.

Adolescents attribute substantially less importance than adults do to all the other-oriented values: benevolence, universalism, security, conformity, and tradition. They attribute substantially more importance than adults do to four self-oriented values – hedonism, stimulation, achievement, and power – but differ little in self-direction. Physical development and identity construction processes, together with social structural constraints and opportunities, explain the adolescent–adult value differences. Between mid- and late-adolescence, only small, but meaningful, changes occur in value priorities.

Regardless of their religion, adolescents who are more religious give higher priority to tradition and conformity values and lower priority to hedonism, self-direction, stimulation, and power values than less religious adolescents do. Religiosity relates only weakly to benevolence and universalism values, despite the centrality of these values in religious doctrines.

The findings suggest that how religious adolescents are depends more on their own value-based choice than on religious socialization. Adolescents' value priorities have greater influence than their religiosity on the centrality of the family in their lives and on how important they think it is to help the needy and always to obey the law.

What may appear to be parental value transmission actually involves active value acquisition by adolescents. Parent–adolescent value similarity depends on accurate perception of parents' socialization values and acceptance of these values. Various parenting factors influence value similarity by affecting accuracy and acceptance. Exposure to parents' social circles and parental warmth and responsiveness increase similarity. Autocratic and indifferent parenting and love withdrawal undermine similarity in Western cultures.

Overall, what does this chapter and my other research suggest about the joint roles of values and religiosity in adolescence? Adolescents actively participate in acquiring their value priorities rather than passively internalizing them. Adolescents from different national and religious cultures express their basic motivations through the same set of near universal values. Although they are born into a particular religion (or none), how religious adolescents are depends mainly on choices they make based on their personal values. Among adolescents (as among adults), religiosity expresses conservation and openness values. However, these are not the main values that provide autonomous motivation for positive social behavior. Rather, universalism and benevolence values promote such behavior and power opposes it. Religion typically adds to this motivation primarily through encouraging conformity to social expectations.

There are, of course, types of religion and religious people that give priority to a different set of values. The examination of relations between values and religion presented here points to many questions for future research. I conclude by mentioning only a few. (1) Do the associations between religiosity and value priorities described here hold for all types of religions? What of nonestablished religions, non-monotheistic religions, religions that focus on universalistic social action or that emphasize individual spirituality? (2) Are there really differences between religions in the value priorities of their adherents? Observed value differences are heavily confounded with demographic differences between religious groups and with the cultural, social, economic, political, and historical characteristics of the countries in which different religions are concentrated. Can impacts of religion per se be isolated from those of these confounds? (3) Does the impact on social behavior and attitudes of religiosity as compared with basic values vary across religions? The current study found relatively weak impacts of religiosity versus values, but it did not separate religious groups. (4) In studying these three questions and others, do we expect different findings for adolescents and adults?

NOTES

1. See, for example: Beech & Schoeppe (1974); Bilsky, Döring, Niemann, Rose, Schmitz, Aryus, Drögekamp, & Sinderman, (in press); Boekaerts, de Koning, & Vedder (2006); Bubeck & Bilsky (2004); Daniel, Benish-Weisman, Knafo, & Boehnke (in press); Grusec & Kuczynski (1997); Harter (1999); Keats (1986); Knafo & Schwartz (2004); Roccas (2005); Saroglou & Muñoz-García (2008); Saroglou, Pichon, Trompette, Verschueren, & Dernelle (2005); Thompson, Meyer, & McGinley (2006).
2. Data downloaded on April 20, 2008 from http://ess.nsd.uib.no/streamer/? m o d u l e = d o w n l o a d & y e a r = - 1 & c o u n t r y = & d o w n l o a d = \ Cumulative+Data\01%23ESS1–3+-+Cumulative+data+file%2C+edition+1.0\.\ ESS1–3e01.spss.zip. R Jowell and the Central Coordinating Team, European Social Survey 2002/2003: Technical Report, London: Centre for Comparative Social Surveys, City University (2003).
3. The coefficients in the index showed partial scalar invariance across all ESS countries except Turkey. I use the Turkish coefficients Billiet and Meuleman provided for the Muslim sample. Correlations are comparable across the five religious groups, but caution should be exercised in drawing conclusions about mean differences.

REFERENCES

Arnett, J. J. (2000). Emerging adulthood: A theory of development from the late teens through the twenties. *American Psychologist*, 55, 469–480.
Bahr, H. M., & Chadwick, B. A. (1985). Religion and family in Middletown, USA. *Journal of Marriage and Family*, 47, 407–414.
Baker, W. E. (2005). *America's crisis of values*. Princeton, NJ: Princeton University Press.
Beech, R. P., & Schoeppe, A. (1974). Development of value systems in adolescents. *Developmental Psychology*, 10, 656–664.
Billiet, J., & Meuleman, B. (2007, October). Religious diversity in Europe and its relation to social attitudes and value orientations. Paper delivered at the European Social Survey conference on Citizenship and Cultural Identities in the EU, Istanbul: Turkey.
Bilsky, W., Döring, A. K., Niemann, F., Rose, I., Schmitz, J., Aryus, K., … Sinderman, J. (in press). Investigating children's value structures – Testing and expanding the limits. *Journal of Cross-Cultural Psychology*.
Boekaerts, M., de Koning, E., & Vedder, P. (2006). Goal-directed behavior and contextual factors in the classroom: An innovative approach to the study of multiple goals. *Educational Psychologist*, 41, 33–51.
Bubeck, M., & Bilsky, W. (2004). Value structure at an early age. *Swiss Journal of Psychology*, 63, 31–41.

Collins, W. A., Welsh, D. P., & Furman, W. (2009). Adolescent romantic relationships. *Annual Review of Psychology*, **60**, 631–652.

Côté, J. E. (2009). Identity formation and self-development in adolescence. In R. Lerner & L. Steinberg (Eds.), *Handbook of adolescent psychology. Volume 1: Individual bases of adolescent development* (pp. 266–304). Hoboken, NJ: John Wiley and Sons.

Daniel, E., Benish-Weisman, M., Knafo, A., & Boehnke, K. (in press). Personal and culture-dependent values as part of immigrant adolescent identity. In R. K. Silbereisen & Y. Shavit (Eds.), *Living together apart: Migrants in Israel and Germany*.

Darling, N., & Steinberg, L. (1993). Parenting style as context: An integrative model. *Psychological Bulletin*, **113**, 487–496.

Döring, A. K., Blauensteiner, A., Aryus, K., Drögekamp, L., & Bilsky, W. (2010). Assessing values at an early age: The picture-based value survey for children (PBVS–C). *Journal of Personality Assessment*, **92**, 439–448.

Durkheim, E. (1954/1912). *The elementary forms of religious life*. J. W. Swain (trans.) Glencoe, IL: Free Press.

Elliott, G. R., & Feldman, S. S. (1990). Capturing the adolescent experience. In S. S. Feldman & G. R. Elliott (Eds.), *At the threshold: The developing adolescent* (pp. 1–14). Cambridge, MA: Harvard University Press.

Gallagher, E. V. (1997). God and country: Revolution as a religious imperative on the radical right. *Terrorism and Political Violence*, **9**, 63–79.

Grusec, J. E., & Goodnow, J. J. (1994). Impact of parental discipline methods on the child's internalization of values: A reconceptualization of current points of view. *Developmental Psychology*, **30**, 4–19.

Grusec, J. E., & Kuczynski, L. (1997). *Parenting and children's internalization of values*. New York: Wiley.

Hamilton, M. (2001). *The sociology of religion: Theoretical and comparative perspectives*. London: Routledge.

Harter, S. (1999). The normative development of self-representations during adolescence. In S. Harter (Ed.), *The construction of the self: A developmental perspective*. New York: Guilford.

Homer, P. M. (1993). Transmission of human values: A cross-cultural investigation of generational and reciprocal influence effects. *Genetic, Social, and General Psychology Monographs*, **119**, 343–367.

Hood, R. W. Jr., Hill, P. C., & Spilka, B. (2009). *The psychology of religion: An empirical approach, 4th Ed*. New York: Guilford Press.

Jarvinen, D. W., & Nichols, J. G. (1996). Adolescents' social goals, beliefs about the causes of social success, and satisfaction in peer relations. *Developmental Psychology*, **32**, 435–441.

Kalish, R. A., & Johnson, A. I. (1972). Value similarities and differences in three generations of women. *Journal of Marriage and the Family*, **34**, 49–54.

Keats, D. M. (1986). A cross-cultural model for the development of values. *Australian Journal of Psychology*, **38**, 297–308.

Knafo, A., & Schwartz, S. H. (2001). Value socialization in families of Israeli-born and Soviet-born adolescents in Israel. *Journal of Cross-Cultural Psychology*, **32**, 213–228.

Knafo, A., & Schwartz, S. H. (2003). Parenting and adolescents' accuracy in perceiving parental values. *Child Development*, **73**, 595–611.

Knafo, A., & Schwartz, S. H. (2004). Identity formation and parent–child value congruence in adolescence. *British Journal of Developmental Psychology*, **22**, 439–458.

Knafo, A., & Schwartz, S. H. (2008). Accounting for parent–child value congruence: Theoretical considerations and empirical evidence. In U. Schönpflug (Ed.), *Perspectives on cultural transmission* (pp. 240–268). New York: Cambridge University Press.

Knafo, A., & Spinath, F. M. (2011). Genetic and environmental influences on girls' and boys' gender-typed and gender-neutral values. *Developmental Psychology*, **47**, 726–731.

Lerner, R. M., & Steinberg, L. (Eds.). (2009). *Handbook of adolescent psychology, 3rd Ed., Volume 1: Individual bases of adolescent development*. Hoboken, NJ: Wiley.

Maccoby, E. E., & Martin, J. A. (1983). Socialization in the context of the family: Parent-child interaction. In P. H. Mussen (Series Ed.) & E. M. Hetherington (Vol. Ed.), *Handbook of child psychology: Vol. 4. Socialization, personality, and social development* (pp. 1–102). New York: Wiley.

Melech, G. (2001). *Value Development in Adolescence* [in Hebrew]. Unpublished doctoral dissertation. The Hebrew University of Jerusalem.

Miller, R. B., & Glass, J. (1989). Parent-child similarity across the life course. *Journal of Marriage and the Family*, **51**, 991–997.

Roccas, S. (2005). Religion and value systems. *Journal of Social Issues*, **61**, 747–59.

Rokeach, M. (1973). *The nature of human values*. New York: Free Press.

Rudy, D., & Grusec, J. E. (2001). Correlates of authoritarian parenting in individualist and collectivist cultures and implications for understanding the transmission of values. *Journal of Cross-Cultural Psychology*, **32**, 202–212.

Saroglou, V., & Muñoz-García, A. (2008). Individual differences in religion and spirituality: An issue of personality traits and/or values. *Journal for the Scientific Study of Religion*, **47**, 83–101.

Saroglou, V., Pichon, I., Trompette, L., Verschueren, M., & Dernelle, R. (2005). Prosocial behavior and religion: New evidence based on projective measures and peer ratings. *Journal for the Scientific Study of Religion*, **44**, 323–48.

Schwartz, S. H. (1992). Universals in the content and structure of values: Theoretical advances and empirical tests in 20 countries. *Advances in Experimental Social Psychology*, **25**, 1–65.

(2003). A proposal for measuring value orientations across nations. Chapter 7 in the Questionnaire Development Package of the European Social Survey. Website: http://www.europeansocialsurvey.org/index.php?option=com_docman&task=doc_view&gid=126&Itemid=80.

(2006). A theory of cultural value orientations: Explication and applications. *Comparative Sociology*, **5**, 136–182.

Schwartz, S. H., & Bardi, A. (2001). Value hierarchies across cultures: Taking a similarities perspective. *Journal of Cross-Cultural Psychology*, **32**, 268–290.

Schwartz, S. H., & Boehnke, K. (2004). Evaluating the structure of human values with confirmatory factor analysis. *Journal of Research in Personality*, **38**, 230–255.

Schwartz, S. H., & Huismans, S. (1995). Value priorities and religiosity in four Western religions. *Social Psychology Quarterly*, **58**, 88–107.

Schwartz, S. H., Melech, G., Lehmann, A., Burgess, S., & Harris, M. (2001). Extending the cross-cultural validity of the theory of basic human values with a different method of measurement. *Journal of Cross-Cultural Psychology*, **32**, 519–542.

Sherkat, D. E., & Ellison, C. G. (1999). Recent developments and current controversies in the sociology of religion. *Annual Review of Sociology*, **25**, 363–394.

Siegal, M., & Barclay, M. S. (1985). Children's evaluations of fathers' socialization behavior. *Developmental Psychology*, **21**, 1090–1096.

Smetana, J. G. (2000). Middle class African American adolescents' and parents' conceptions of parental authority and parenting practices: A longitudinal investigation. *Child Development*, **71**, 1682–1686.

Thompson, R. A., Meyer, S., & McGinley, M. (2006). Understanding values in relationships: The development of conscience. In M. Killen & J. G. Smetana (Eds.), *Handbook of moral development* (pp. 267–297). Mahwah, NJ: Lawrence Erlbaum.

Weber, M. (1905/1958). *The Protestant ethic and the spirit of capitalism.* New York: Scribner's.

5 Religion and Life Satisfaction of Young Persons around the World

Personal Values and Societal Context

Michael Harris Bond, Vivian Miu-Chi Lun, and Liman Man Wai Li

Abstract

Current satisfaction with life may be taken as a positive achievement for youth, and considered a prophylactic against antisocial and self-destructive behavior. The roles of a youth's values and religious engagement in the achievement of satisfaction with life were explored in this study, using the most recent data from the World Values Survey (WVS). Multinational in provenance, the WVS affords the opportunity for researchers to explore the impact of national context on the strength of the linkages from personality factors (such as values) and social factors (such as religious engagement) to life satisfaction, thereby providing assurance of the universality or cultural groundedness of the psychological phenomenon in question.

In this study, we examined the moderating roles of three societal factors: human development, government restriction on religion, and social hostility toward religion. We found that, at the national level, the reported life satisfaction of youth was positively related to the level of development of a society; at the individual level, it was negatively linked to their level of secularism in value, but positively to their level of social-religious engagement. The negative role of secularism did not vary across nations, but the positive effect of social-religious engagement on satisfaction with life was found to vary as a function of the level of religious restriction in a society. Specifically, the effect of social-religious engagement on life satisfaction among youth was enhanced under the societal conditions of lower government restriction and higher social hostility toward religion.

Together, these findings suggested that apart from general socioeconomic development of a society, religious values and practices are also important predictors of life satisfaction among youth; however, the impact of social-religious practices appears to be susceptible to the influence of restriction on religion imposed by a society on its members. We interpret these outcomes in terms of youth's apparently universal search for meaning and the social support for religious belief provided by shared worship and societal structures that enhance or restrain the plausibility of religious belief in a secular world (Berger, 1969).

How do personal characteristics and social practices contribute toward a youth's satisfaction with his or her life? How are these contributions affected by institutional practices of the society in which that youth is living? This paper attempts to address these questions for a youth's religiousness, and will test its ideas empirically by using the relevant data provided by the World Values Survey (WVS), suggesting how this source of worldwide data may be used to assess further speculations. In this way, we will be able to address the universality or cultural groundedness of the individual psychological phenomena being examined, an opportunity that is only available with multinational studies.

As such, this paper is an initial response to Eccles, Templeton, Barber, and Stone's (2003) call for more research on the crucial transition period of youth, as they confront the expanding options available to them in contemporary societies. They point out that the search for, and establishment of, meaning and purpose in life are two crucial axes of adolescent development. In discussing the personal and social assets linked to positive adolescent and adult well-being, Eccles and Gootman (2002) include "a coherent and positive personal and social identity," "spirituality and/or a sense of purpose in life," and "a strong moral character" (p. 66) in their listing. In describing the available research around their list of such assets, however, Eccles et al. (2003) hasten to point out that,

"Far fewer studies have investigated the relation of such moral and value-based characteristics as prosocial values, spirituality, moral character, personal responsibility, a sense that one is making a meaningful contribution, to one's community, and personal identity with other indicators of adolescent and adult well-being" (p. 399).

In light of this lacuna in our literature, we undertook the current study to explore the more specific roles of youth values and religious engagement in their current levels of life satisfaction. To do so, we exploited the data available from the latest wave of the World Values Survey, as its multicultural sweep allowed for the examination of moderating influences from national context on the individual processes being assessed in contemporary youth. Any conclusions concerning the universality of these putatively general processes can thus stand on firmer ground.

Satisfaction with Life as Desirable Personal Outcome

We take current assessments of young persons' satisfaction with life as our outcome of interest. There is a plethora of research on life satisfaction, with a recent journal, *The Journal of Happiness Studies*, dedicated to the understanding of life satisfaction and its associated determinants and consequences. As higher levels of life satisfaction are associated with lower levels of depression, suicidal thoughts, anomie, and delinquent behavior, it has become a topic of much governmental concern, with different nations developing measurement tools to monitor changing levels of its citizens' contentment with their current life experience (Kleiner, 2010). There is even a movement to include some measure of life satisfaction within national development in a United Nations-sponsored human development index (Diener & Tov, 2012).

There is considerable variation in life satisfaction across the citizens of many nations (Inglehart & Klingemann, 2000; Li & Bond, 2010; Morrison, Tay, & Diener, 2010; Veenhoven, 2005). A basic political goal of responsible governmental systems, as opposed to failed states preoccupied with internal stability, is to enhance their citizens' satisfaction with life by creating and maintaining societal institutions that address the full range of human needs. In crafting these initiatives, governmental and civic agencies put youth front and center, as they constitute future social capital whose integration into the social system will ensure its flourishing survival.

Individual Characteristics Predicting Satisfaction with Life. Recent research from a study involving 3,000 American twins has indicated that a considerable amount of our life satisfaction is genetically determined (Lykken & Telegen, 1996). However, which features of genetically determined individual characteristics are associated with life satisfaction? A host of such constructs has previously been explored, including dimensions of the Big-Five personality (see e.g., Kwan, Bond, & Singelis, 1997) and psychosocial needs (Diener & Tay, 2012). In addition to genetically determined features of individual characteristics, other components have been linked to life satisfaction, including values (e.g., Sagiv & Schwartz, 2000) and beliefs regarding the world (Lai, Bond, & Hui, 2007).

The Psychology of Religion

There is a lively empirical discourse on the psychology of religion. Surveying this literature, Saucier and Skrzypińska (2006) conclude that, "Beliefs about religious or spiritual phenomena have important effects on human behavior and functioning" (p. 1257). They list the following functions served by religious–spiritual concerns:

They can provide one with a cognitive map of the world that makes it meaningful. Such worldview beliefs can fill many functions. They provide a paradigm for, among other things, how the universe began, what the purpose of life is, and how to understand injustice and death (Argyle & Beit-Hallahmi, 1975); they may provide a buffer against mortality-based anxiety, enhancing a sense of safety and security (Greenberg, Pyszczynski, & Solomon, 1986), and they may satisfy needs for a purpose in life, anchoring a sense of what is right and wrong (Baumeister, 1991). Moreover, such beliefs connect people, enabling the sharing of a system of values and rules that is obligatory for a social group (Kuczkowski, 1993), values and rules that may be a prime guiding force for actual behavior (Mądrzycki, 1996) (pp. 1257–1258).

Given this broad and fundamental range of human concerns addressed by religious and spiritual phenomena, one would expect that measures of a person's religiousness or spirituality would connect to important life outcomes. Saucier and Skrzypińska (2006) summarize the available findings thus: "Religiousness appears to have some positive effects on health and longevity (Kozielecki, 1991; Powell, Shahabi, & Thoresen, 2003). These include protective effects with respect to alcohol/drug abuse (Miller, 1998). Nonetheless, there may be negative effects as well as positive ones (Koenig, 1997)" (p. 1258).

This is an ambivalent conclusion. In a recent (and rare) cross-national study on religiousness and well-being, Diener, Tay, and Myers (2010) suggest one reason for this inconclusiveness – they have shown that more religious persons are happier than less religious persons, but only in more religious nations. This finding suggests a context dependency to the role of religion in life satisfaction, making it difficult to draw conclusions from the bulk of previous research on this topic, most of which is monocultural in provenance.

As opposed to religiosity, spirituality, at least as measured by claiming that one has a purpose in life, is connected to measures of well-being (e.g., Shek, 1993) and helps buffer the impact of dysfunctional parenting on children's satisfaction with life (Shek, 1999). There are, of course, other ways to conceptualize spirituality, and these conceptualizations with their attendant operationalisms may relate differently to positive life outcomes, perhaps even predicting negative outcomes in certain contexts.

Measuring "Religiousness". One plausible reason for the ambiguity surrounding the positivity or negativity of outcomes predicted by "religiousness" may lie in the plethora of definitions and measurements that have been developed by those studying the psychology of religion. Shek (2010) reports thus:

Based on content analyses of 31 definitions of religiousness and 40 definitions of spirituality, Scott (1997) reported that the conceptions [of both types of definitions] were distributed over nine content areas, with no definition containing most of the conceptions in different domains. These content areas include: 1) experiences related to connectedness or relationship; 2) processes contributing to a higher level of connectedness; 3) reactions to sacred and secular things; 4) beliefs or thoughts; 5) traditional institutional structures; 6) pleasurable existence; 7) beliefs in a sacred or higher being; 8) personal transcendence; and 9) existential issues and concerns (p. 343, brackets added).

Each of these nine categories has inspired the creation of associated measures to assess the strength of that aspect of religious orientation in individuals. Correlating such scores with various outcome measures is bound to yield various conclusions regarding the positive, neutral, or negative consequences of spiritual orientations.

Adding to the confusion is the possible impact of national–cultural context on any of the reported findings on the psychology of religion – the same process could show different strengths, or even reversals, in different national–cultural groups (see e.g., Li & Bond, 2010). Multinational studies thus become necessary to ascertain the universality or cultural groundedness to the functioning of religious phenomena in young people. The cultural context surrounding religious enactments by youth probably makes a difference in how "religiousness" is conceptualized among the young people.

Distinguishing Spirituality and Religiosity. A further complicating factor is the distinction between spirituality and religiosity in conceptualizations of a person's religiousness. Saucier and Skrzypińska (2006) describe this shared territory and its borderlines in these terms:

Argyle and Beit-Hallahmi (1975) defined religion as "a system of beliefs in a divine or superhuman power, and practices of worship or other rituals directed towards such a power" (p. 1). The emphasis on worship and rituals implies community activity that binds or ties people together. Indeed the word religion comes from Latin *religio*, derived from *ligo*, meaning "to tie or bind" ... Definitions of spirituality usually put more emphasis on the individual and on his or her subjective experience ... Shafranske and Gorsuch (1984) defined spirituality broadly as "a transcendent dimension within human experience

... discovered in moments in which the individual questions the meaning of personal existence and attempts to place the self within a broader ontological context" (p. 231). Vaughan (1991) provided a useful, more specific, definition: "a subjective experience of the sacred" (p. 105) (p. 1257–1258).

This distinction between religiosity and spirituality is maintained in a person's self-perceptions and his or her perception of others: lexical measures of related terms reveal that Americans use two distinct and orthogonal dimensions or factors in perceiving any person's "religiousness"; namely, tradition-oriented religiousness (TR) and subjective spirituality (SS) (Saucier and Skrzypińska, 2006). These two axes of perceiving religiousness find their parallels in the personality literature:

...MacDonald (2000) ... sought to identify the common dimensions in 11 prominent measures of religious and spiritual constructs. He found five factors: Religiousness, Cognitive Orientation Towards Spirituality (COTS), Experiential/ Phenomenological (E/P), Paranormal Beliefs, and Existential Well-Being. A higher-order factor analysis found two factors. One was labeled Cognitive and Behavioral Orientation Towards Spirituality and included Religiousness and COTS. The other factor was labeled Non-Ordinary Experiences and Beliefs; capturing distinctions in previous measures of mysticism, it included E/P and Paranormal Beliefs. Existential Well-Being, whose content overlaps with Emotional Stability versus Neuroticism, did not have appreciable loadings on either higher-order factor. These two higher-order factors appear to correspond to TR and SS (Saucier & Skrzypińska, 2006, p. 1261).

This two-dimensional distinction has been found in other attempts to make sense of the literature in the psychology of religion, for example, Emmons (1999), and so appears robust and of probable importance for personal functioning.

In the present study, we attempt to extract a parallel distinction from the measures of religiousness that we have identified in the World Values Survey. We regard its measure of social-religious engagement as an interpersonal process reflecting tradition-oriented religiousness (TR) and its value measure of traditionalism-secularism as an individual characteristic reflecting subjective spirituality (SS). We propose that each measure of a person's religiousness, the interpersonal and the personal, may respectively contribute toward his or her satisfaction with life.

The Role of "Religiousness" in Enhancing Satisfaction with Life
There is thus a clear empirical distinction in both conceptualizations and measures between spirituality and religiosity, with the former generally

referring to the domain of internal, subjective experiences and the latter referring to the domain of activity and practice associated with specific religious communities. This distinction suggests that the individual satisfaction derived from one's religiousness may arise from each of these two sources – the personal or subjective and the interpersonal or social. Measures of relevant constructs from each of these two sources may then each contribute toward the life satisfaction derived from one's religiousness. For present purposes, we will then focus on secularism in personal values as a representative of the personal domain; social-religious engagement, as a representative of the interpersonal domain.

Values and Life Satisfaction. Despite the importance of values as a marker of national–cultural differences (e.g., Schwartz, 1994), there are few studies attempting to link values with life satisfaction. Of these occasional studies, most are monocultural (e.g., Bergin, Stinchfield, Gaskin, Masters, & Sullivan, 1988) and a few bicultural (e.g., Sagiv & Schwartz, 2000). A variety of value instruments is used in these studies, and the type of participants varies, so it is difficult to draw reliable conclusions out of this meager yield from the literature.

Recently, however, Li and Bond (2010) conducted a multicultural study on the relationship between secularism in values and life satisfaction. Using the World Values Survey, they were able to assess this linkage across representative populations drawn from a total of 75 nations over the first four waves of the WVS (1984–2004). This wide demographic, temporal and national–cultural coverage lends considerable confidence to their conclusion about the role of values, namely, "Secularism (in personal values) was found to predict life satisfaction scores [negatively] at a small but statistically very significant level in persons from all nations participating in all four waves of the World Values Survey" (p. 443).

In the interests of cross-study consistency and in light of the multicultural and representative reach of the WVS, we will extend the study of secularism in personal values and life satisfaction using the fifth wave of the WVS (2005), focusing upon its sampling of youth across the nations and reporting results using the measures provided in this survey instrument.

Religious Engagement and Life Satisfaction. Participation in religious gatherings, rituals, and ceremonies (including group prayer and fasting) is a component of social life for many people of different traditions of faith and spiritual communities. As Li and Bond (2010) maintained, "This religious belonging provides opportunity for spiritual experience (Schwenka,

2000), social support, and a cognitive framework for responding to existential questions (Ellison, 1991)" (p. 445). Berger (1967, chapter 6) has likewise argued that shared religious activities conducted with other coreligionists within an institutional framework provides a "plausibility structure" for vulnerable religious belief, sustaining the participants' sense that their faith is vital, viable, timeless, and true – buttressing belief against the corrosive influence of secularism. Coreligionists help confirm belief and sustain commitment. Those who participate in such religious activities should thus show higher satisfaction with their current life than those who do not receive such ongoing social confirmation.

Societal Factors as Moderators of Individual Processes Leading to Life Satisfaction

Most previous work on cross-national psychology has focused on documenting mean differences in the level of a particular psychological construct across equivalent populations of respondents. The resulting differences in "citizen scores" so produced are then related to features of the national or societal system in which citizens are socialized (see e.g., Bond, 1988, on values; Leung & Bond, 2004, on social axioms). This approach potentiates the development of theories about how national culture operates to strengthen psychological dispositions in its members, an effect termed the "positioning effect of culture" (Leung & Bond, 1989).

An emerging approach to conceptualizing culture's role is more social-psychological – it explores the *linkage* between *psychological* constructs, investigating how a personal or social-psychological variable may relate to any outcome of interest, including religiosity. So, for example, Fu et al. (2004) explored the link between reward for application (an individual belief characteristic) and judgments regarding the efficacy of using assertive tactics of influence in an organization (a social-psychological outcome). It was found that the relationship between individual beliefs and preferences for different influence strategies was moderated by national cultural values such as uncertainty avoidance and in-group collectivism. This finding exemplifies how the characteristics of a cultural context may affect individual psychological processes.

Such studies of cultural influences on psychological processes may be bicultural (e.g., Bond & Forgas, 1984) or multicultural, as in Fu et al. (2004). In either case, what sometimes results from such research is the discovery that a respondent's national culture modifies the *linkage* between the predictor variable and the outcome of interest. In these cases, what emerges is an interaction between a higher-level variable, like national culture, and an individual-level process. National culture is thereby shown to vary the impact of a predictor variable, making it either more or less important in generating an outcome of interest. Such findings demonstrate what might be termed the "induction effect of culture" or the "moderation effect of culture" (Bond & van de Vijver, 2011).

Bicultural research may demonstrate such interactions between national culture and individual process by showing a significant interaction effect between culture and an individual predictor on the outcome of interest (see e.g., Kam & Bond, 2008, on the impact of face loss on relationship harmony in American and Hong Kong cultures). Multicultural research with fewer than 10 or so cultural groups cannot, however, provide internal evidence regarding what feature of the national culture relates to, or is responsible for, that difference in impact; such evidence can only come from multicultural studies with a minimum of 10 or more constituent groups – be they classrooms, organizations, districts, or nations – to ensure sufficient statistical power for the test of higher-level effects (see Hofmann, 1997).

With an extensive sampling of national cultures, features of the national system may then be correlated with the size of the impact exercised by the predictor variable on the outcome (see e.g., Matsumoto et al., 2008). These features may be derived from "hard" data; for example, human rights observance or economic growth over a given time period. Alternatively, they may be derived from "soft" data; that is, citizen scores on theoretically relevant psychological variables, like the value of traditionalism or the self-construal of allocentrism (interdependence). In either case, larger multicultural studies provide us with more reliable conclusions of *how* and possibly *why* culture exercises its impact on social-psychological processes. Bond (2009) has termed such demanding and complex research "Einsteinian," as it allows us to build sophisticated, complex, measurement-based models to explain culture's influence on psychological process.

Level of Societal Development. Contemporary societal development is regarded as inducing a pervasive secular press on the worldviews of its members:

By secularization, we mean the process by which sectors of society and culture are removed from the domination of religious institutions and symbols ... it affects the totality of cultural life and ideation, and may be observed in the decline of religious contents in the arts, in philosophy, in literature, and most important of all, in the rise of science as an autonomous, thoroughly secular perspective on the world. (Berger, 1967, p. 107)

In consequence, one should expect that a more modernized nation would provide a cultural context that moderates the connection between individual secularism and life satisfaction. Accordingly, Li and Bond (2010) found that a nation's Human Development Index (HDI), as an index of societal development, interacted with the psychological link between secularism and life satisfaction in each of the waves of the World Values Survey, although the strength of that interaction varied across the four waves in which the survey was conducted. We will again examine the possible moderating role of HDI for youth on the links between their secularism in value, social-religious engagement and satisfaction with life.

Institutional Restriction on Religious Practice. Another potential influence of national culture on the link between social-religious engagement and life satisfaction derives from the strength of a society's institutional restrictions on religious practice. Such restrictiveness would make the enactment of any religious observance counter-normative when compared to societies where freedom of religious practice was guaranteed in the national constitution and supported by its legal system. In such societies, an adherent is free to believe and practice whatever religion he or she may choose because institutional pressure to be nonreligious or to embrace the state religion is lacking. In such religiously freer nations, we anticipate that the link between types of religious practice and life satisfaction would be stronger, since there is no ambivalence generated by societal opposition toward one's religious engagement.

Social Hostility toward Religious Groups. The same reasoning applies to social systems where violence is enacted toward religious groups, either because they endorse a religious worldview against a state-mandated secular ideology, like communism, or because they fail to embrace the state-sponsored or majority religion. We expect that the link between social-religious practice and life satisfaction would be weaker in such types of national context since an adherent's practice would draw negative social consequences for his or her well-being regardless of solace and social support provided by fellow adherents.

An Empirical Demonstration
We tested the aforementioned hypotheses using the Wave 5 data of the World Value Survey (WVS 2005–2008). Our focus was to understand the effect of religious values and practices on the satisfaction with life among youth, so only the data provided by young people between 15 and 24 years

old were selected for analysis. Due to missing data on some or all of the questionnaire items of current interest, only 9,618 young people (51.8 percent female) from 43 countries were included in the final analysis.

As for personal values, a person high in traditionalism endorsed authority, the importance of God, and national pride more, but endorsed the post-materialistic values of self-expression and independence, as well as autonomy, less; the opposite would be true for a person high in secularism. A person's level of social-religious engagement was captured by the question, "Apart from weddings, funerals and christenings, about how often do you attend religious services these days?" This item was used as a measure of the level of social-religious involvement of the participants. To assess their level of life satisfaction, participants answered the question, "All things considered, how satisfied are you with your life as a whole these days?" using a 10-point rating scale.

Social Indicators

The Human Development Index (HDI) was used as our measure of the national context for human development. The HDI was devised by the United Nations Development Program (UNDP) as part of the Human Development Report. The index includes equally weighted measures of life expectancy, educational development, and GDP to indicate a country's level of development. HDI ranges between 0 and 1, with a higher value indicating a higher level of development in a society. The index in 2007 (UNDP, 2009) was used to match the WVS Wave 5 data used in the present research.

The Government Restriction Index (GRI) and Social Hostilities Index (SHI) were the two other measures of the national context for religious practice. The Pew Forum on Religion and Public Life is a project involving the collation of information pertinent to religious practices in different societies around the world (Pew Forum on Religion and Public Life, 2009). According to the report of the Pew Forum on Religion and Public Life regarding global restrictions surrounding religion, government actions and hostility toward religious groups are the two main ways in which religion is restricted in a society. The measure of government restriction in a society was created through identifying: "(1) constitutional restrictions or restrictions based in national law or policy; (2) restrictions imposed by government officials at any level, whether codified in law or not; (3) use of force or coercion against religious groups by government agencies or their representatives; and (4) government favoritism toward particular religious groups" (Pew Forum on Religion and Public Life, 2009, p. 31).

The measure of societal hostilities toward religions was captured by identifying: "(1) crimes or malicious acts motivated by religious hatred or bias;
(2) public religious tensions that lead to violence; and (3) religion-related
terrorism and war" (Pew Forum on Religion and Public Life, 2009, p. 31).
Multiple indicators, based on data drawn between mid-2006 and mid-2008,
were used to enhance the accuracy of both indexes. The information sources
involve 16 frequently cited reports, including the U.N. Special Rapporteur
on Freedom of Religion or Belief reports, the Human Rights Watch topical
reports, and the Council of the European Union's annual report on human
rights, which documented religion-related government restrictions and
social hostilities in different societies. Both indexes have a possible range
of score between 0 and 10, with 10 indicated the highest level of religion-
related government restriction or societal hostilities in a society.

Descriptive Statistics. Fisher-z transformations were applied to the correlation matrixes among the individual-level variables in each country,
and the transformed correlation matrixes were averaged to provide an
overall correlation among the individual-level variables. The correlation
between secularism and social-religious engagement was negative. Life
satisfaction was correlated with secularism and social-religious engagement across nations, but the exact relationships between satisfaction with
life and the proposed predictors were examined together with the other
relevant societal variables in the Hierarchical Linear Modeling (HLM)
analysis (reported later in this chapter) for more country-sensitive
interpretation.

Table 5.1 shows the correlation among the three social indicators and
the citizen mean scores of life satisfaction, secularism, and social-religious engagement. Interestingly, the nation-level correlation between life
satisfaction and secularism was positive, whereas the correlation at the
individual level was negative. A similar pattern of reversal was observed
for the country-level correlations between life satisfaction and social-
religious engagement, where the correlation was in an opposite direction
to that at the individual level. These results provide an opportunity to
commit the ecological fallacy whereby one incorrectly infers individual-level patterns from the country-level patterns; individual-level and
country-level findings require different interpretations (Leung & Bond,
2007).

Considering the social indicators, both GRI and SHI were found to be
negatively related to citizen ratings on life satisfaction. Consistent with the
findings based on the previous four waves of WVS data (Li & Bond, 2010),

Table 5.1 Correlation among the Country-Level Variables

	1	2	3	4	5
1. Life Satisfaction (citizen mean)	–				
2. Secularism (citizen mean)	.26	–			
3. Social-Religious Engagement (citizen mean)	–.41**	–.74**	–		
4. GRI	–.32*	–.27	.16	–	
5. SHI	–.26	–.26	.24	.72**	–
6. HDI	.69**	.65**	–.71**	–.17	–.14

Note: $**p < .01$; $*p < .05$; N = 43.

the correlation between HDI and life satisfaction was significantly positive at the country level.

Effects of Individual Characteristics and Cultural Contexts on Life Satisfaction. Hierarchical Linear Modeling (HLM; Bryk & Raudenbush, 1992; Raudenbush & Bryk, 2002) was used to examine the relationships between life satisfaction and the other individual-level predictors, and how these correlations at the psychological level would be influenced by the social indicators.

Consistent with the findings in some of the waves of the WVS in the Li and Bond (2010) study, secularism was a significant negative predictor of life satisfaction; that is, a person endorsing a higher level of secular values reported a lower level of life satisfaction. Social-religious engagement also significantly predicted life satisfaction, but positively. Except for the interaction between secularism and social-religious engagement (see Figure 5.1), all the other interaction terms at the individual level were statistically not significant.

Among the three social indicators, only HDI was significant in predicting life satisfaction, showing that the relative development of a society contributed to an individual's satisfaction with life, a finding consistent with a host of related national-level research (see e.g., Inglehart & Klingemann, 2000).

Gender did not show any effect on individual life satisfaction, alone or in interaction with other individual-level variables. The interaction between gender and HDI was statistically significant, however; in societies with higher levels of development, the level of life satisfaction of males was slightly higher than that of females but in societies with lower levels of development, males showed a lower level of life satisfaction than their female counterparts.

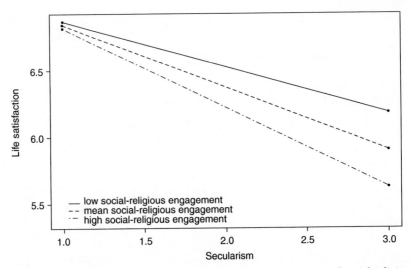

Figure 5.1. Visual depiction of the interaction between secularism and social-religious engagement on predicting life satisfaction.

The relationship between secularism and life satisfaction was not moderated by any of the proposed social indicators. However, cross-level interaction effects were observed in the relationship between social-religious engagement and life satisfaction. Specifically, both GRI and SHI moderated the relationship between social-religious engagement and life satisfaction, albeit in different directions. Figures 5.2 and 5.3, again produced by the HLM software, depict these interactions. Although GRI and SHI are both indicators of obstacles to unfettered religious practice in a society, hostilities directed toward religious groups in the society strengthened the beneficial effect of social-religious engagement on life satisfaction.[1] As expected, however, higher levels of governmental restriction on religion appeared to be detrimental to the relationship between social-religious engagement and life satisfaction.

These findings indicate that different sources of restrictive forces surrounding religious involvement in a society function differently to affect how social-religious engagement predicts a person's satisfaction with life. Paradoxically, the more proximal contextual factor of hostility strengthened the link between social-religious practice and life satisfaction; the more distal contextual factor of governmental restrictions weakened that same link.

Values, Social-Religious Engagement and the Life Satisfaction of Youth. Results at the individual level of analysis in this empirical study show

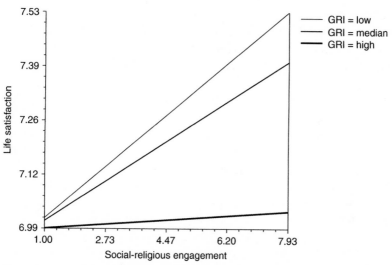

Figure 5.2. Visual depiction of the interaction between GRI and social-religious engagement in predicting life satisfaction.

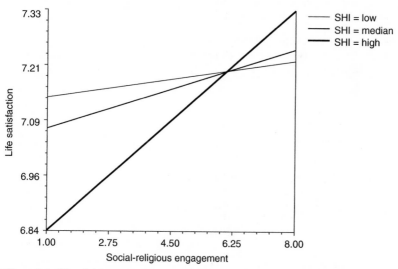

Figure 5.3. Visual depiction of the interaction between SHI and social-religious engagement in predicting life satisfaction.

that lower secularism, higher traditionalism, and higher social-religious engagement each lead to greater life satisfaction for contemporary youth; they are additive in their impact. The interaction between these personal and social components of religiousness simply indicates that the effect of traditionalism-secularism is more marked for those higher in social-religious engagement. This enhancement effect is evident in Figure 5.1.

Social-religious engagement in turn is responsive to features of the national context inimical to religious practice: the interaction between GRI and social-religious engagement is negative as expected, whereas that between SHI and social-religious engagement is positive. In other words, the lower the level of governmental restriction, the greater the positive impact of social-religious engagement on life satisfaction. The higher the level of societal hostility against religion, the greater the impact of social-religious engagement on youth's satisfaction with life. Under no national conditions inimical to religion, however, did higher social-religious engagement fail to predict higher life satisfaction; rather, under certain national conditions, this connection between social-religious engagement and life satisfaction was stronger. The generality of the positive effect for social-religious engagement is clear when examining Figures 5.2 and 5.3.

Although of tangential interest in this study, the country-level effects found in this research bear notice: as in much previous work (e.g., Inglehart & Klingemann, 2000), HDI, like other indexes of national development, is positively related to its citizens' levels of life satisfaction. National development does not interact with the individual-level variables of traditionalism-secularism as it did in Li and Bond (2010) or with social-religious engagement; all the effects of the previously noted individual variables can be obtained regardless of a nation's level of development. Given the larger number of nations involved in the present study, we can generalize these findings with greater confidence.

The Bigger Picture: Secularism and Life Satisfaction

Why should a personal valuation of traditionalism, as compared to its opposite, secularism, be associated with greater life satisfaction? First, we should note that this relationship is not always positive across all the waves of the World Values Survey (Li & Bond, 2010), at least not for fully representative samples, so this is not a transhistorical, trans-generational relationship. Whether these effects are confined to contemporary youth could be assessed with further research, inspired by the present demonstration.

Second, we should also note that secularism is not a strong predictor of life satisfaction, with the overall correlation accounting for less than 1 percent of the variance between these two variables. This is an increase in predictable variance, however, that should be integrated into our existing knowledge of the host of other personality factors influencing the life satisfaction of youth.

Third, we should note that the negative relationship between secularism and life satisfaction for youth occurs regardless of any other personal or societal conditions. Perhaps it is a "contemporary universal" for youth; indeed, for any generational cohort. Future research, inspired by this demonstration, could assess the generalizability of this finding.

This consistent, negative relationship between secularism and life satisfaction may be re-construed as a consistent, positive relationship between traditionalism and life satisfaction. Traditionalism in values, as operationally described in this study, involves the endorsement of a belief in God, the value of obedience, respect for authority, national pride, and security as opposed to the more secular emphases on self-determination, independence, self-expression, and quality of life. So, the traditionalism associated with life satisfaction for these contemporary youth has a deferential, submissive quality, embracing religious and other sources of authority. The hunger for stability and security provided by these bulwarks of support during a searching stage of life (e.g., Erikson, 1964, on the developmental challenge of identity versus role confusion or Eccles et al., 2003, on the importance of meaning in life), and amid the welter of possible alternatives supported by their less authoritative peers, may be decisive in promoting some degree of life satisfaction for these young persons.

Berger (1967) has written persuasively of the human need for structure, providing an endorsable meaning and sense of resolution to the uncertainties of our "throwness" into the world. The religious dimension to this resolution adds the element of transcendence to the struggle for meaning and purpose, providing perspective and detachment from pressing worldly alternatives for a youth's decision regarding how to live. The religious component to some youth's traditionalism may add to their sense of satisfaction already sustained by sources of authority in this world.

Such confirmation may be less important for other persons at different stages of the life cycle. It will be recalled that the occasional reversals of the positive relationship between traditionalism and life satisfaction in Li and Bond (2010) was found in representative samples of the population age groups, and then only for nations high in HDI. Given our present results for Wave 5, we expect that a reanalysis of youth alone in Waves 1–4 would reveal the pattern of results observed here, namely (for youth), secularism in values is always associated with lower level of life satisfaction regardless of their nation's HDI.

The Bigger Picture: Social-Religious Engagement and Life Satisfaction

Youth's involvement in religious activities is consistently associated with greater life satisfaction. Given that this effect generalizes across the 43 nations of Wave 5, we may confidently claim that the social support provided by any type of religious community is associated with greater life satisfaction for youth. This life satisfaction may, of course, arise from our human desire for association; thus, any social practices for youth would connect to greater life satisfaction. We believe, however, that it is the confirmation of the youth's particular religious solution to the quest for meaning that drives this happy outcome.

It will be recalled that the strength of the positive connection between traditionalism and life satisfaction increases when the individual involves himself or herself in religious activities. That is, traditional youth are especially responsive to the satisfaction-promoting effect of social-religious engagement; secular youth also show higher levels of life satisfaction the more they are involved with social-religious activities, but the effect of engagement is stronger for those youth high in traditionalism of values. This strengthening suggests that those who already endorse a religious worldview are especially responsive to the satisfying confirmation that coreligionists can supply.

The Bigger Picture: Impact of Youth's National Context

As Berger (1969, chapter 6) suggested, social confirmation of one's tenuous religious commitment should be especially welcome in a secularizing world with the wide array of alternative lifestyles and worldviews available. Their ubiquity makes religious, and hence other-worldly, views of reality less tenable. A religious support group becomes especially important in sustaining religious belief in contemporary youth. Given this historical context, "Only in a counter-community of considerable strength does cognitive deviance have a chance to maintain itself" (p. 32). Youth are thus happier the more they engage in religious activities with supportive coreligionists.

Contrary to Berger's speculation, however, is the fact that the comfort provided by social-religious engagement is now stronger in highly developed societies than in less developed societies – regardless of a nation's HDI, it is religiously engaged youth who are happier. The social confirmation provided by religious engagement is satisfying at this developmental stage. Again, future research, inspired by this demonstration, could assess the generalizability of this finding across the life course.

However, certain other societal contexts support and sustain the strength of the connection between social-religious engagement and life satisfaction. Li and Bond (2010) have argued that the strengthening between a psychological input, like secularism of values for example, and life satisfaction is a consequence of the stronger sense of worldview confirmation provided in these contexts. So, in less developed societies, they showed that traditionalism was more strongly connected to life satisfaction because the plausibility structures for a traditional worldview are more ubiquitous in less modernized societies; uncertainty is thus less frequently provoked, and citizens endorsing traditional values are sustained by these structures; they are more satisfied with their lives.

We believe that the same confirmation dynamic arises for the positive relationship between a youth's social-religious engagement and his or her life satisfaction. As shown in the present research, this social-psychological process is strengthened in societies where there are either higher levels of hostility directed toward religious groups or lower levels of governmental restriction on religion. So, certain features of the national context matter; there are undoubtedly other features of the national context moderating this relationship.

It is compatible with our hypothetical "plausibility structures" that, in societies with lower governmental restrictions on religions, the relationship between religious engagement and life satisfaction should be stronger – there is no direct institutional challenge to one's religious practices. However, why should the link between social-religious engagement and life satisfaction be *strengthened* in societies where there is active hostility against religious groups? Surely, this active aggression against religious groups undercuts the plausibility of one's religious belief.

Instead, societal hostility enhances the level of life satisfaction that results from social-religious engagement. So, societal opposition to religion, more directly and interpersonally expressed, is different in its social-psychological impact than is resistance at the national–institutional level. We speculate that the dynamics of group cohesion change when out-group hostility is perceived to operate. First, less committed religious group members will reduce their social-religious engagement. For those who remain, and as research on realistic group conflict has shown, in-group cohesion will be enhanced under conditions of hostility practiced against the in-group by various out-groups (Levine & Campbell, 1972). Ironically, the hostility leveled by out-group persons may act as a confirmation of in-group members' beliefs.

This enhancement may be more apparent than real in a societal context characterized by such hostility because some in-group members will abandon their social-religious engagement under conditions of active hostility being practiced against their group by out-groups. So, only more highly committed in-group members remain to participate in the threatened group (Hogg, Adelman, & Blagg, 2010). These more religiously committed individuals then derive satisfaction from participating in a religious group that practices under the specter of religious hostility. This winnowing effect would not occur in societies marked by less hostility, so that the linkage between social-religious engagement and life satisfaction is somewhat weaker in such societies.

Conclusion

Current satisfaction with life may be taken as a positive outcome for youth to have achieved and may be considered a prophylactic against antisocial and self-destructive behaviors. The roles of a youth's values and religious practice in the achievement of such a crucial outcome were explored in this study, using the most recent data from the World Values Survey. As it is multinational in provenance, the WVS enables researchers to explore the impact of national–societal context on the strength of the linkages between individual characteristics (such as one's basic value orientations) and interpersonal dynamics (such as social-religious engagement) on a youth's current satisfaction with life, thereby providing some empirical assurance of the universality or cultural groundedness of the psychological processes in question.

In this paper, we examined the moderating roles of three national–societal factors – a nation's level of human development (HDI), its social hostility toward religion, and its government's restriction on religion – on these individual processes. Both a youth's traditionalism and social-religious engagement associated positively and separately to his or her life satisfaction, an outcome arising from youths' need for a structured, transcendent, and socially supported worldview. The positive effect of traditionalism (the opposite of secularism) was consistent across nations, but the positive effect of social-religious engagement on satisfaction with life was found to be qualified as a function of the two types of religious restriction in a society. Specifically, the link between social-religious engagement and life satisfaction among youth was enhanced under the societal conditions of lower government restriction and of higher social hostility. Thus, a youth's religious values and social practices are important predictors of his or her life satisfaction, but the impact of religious practice appears to be susceptible to the institutional and social support accorded to one's religion in his or her nation. They were strengthened in those societies where institutional restrictions were lower and hostility toward religions greater, both enhancements arising, we believe, because the plausibility of the youth's religious belief is enhanced under such societal conditions generating social support for one's worldview.

These findings were discussed in terms of youths' search for spiritual meaning and their need for social support in this quest.

NOTES

1. Given that GRI and SHI are highly positively correlated with each other, we were aware of the possibility that suppressor effect may be the alternative explanation to the opposite signs of their respective interactions with social-religious engagement. To examine this possibility, additional HLM analyses were conducted with these two indices separated. In the model with GRI and HDI as level-2 predictors, it was found that the interaction between GRI and social-religious engagement was still negative though non-significant, $b = -0.01$, $p = .14$. In the model with SHI and HDI as level-2 predictors, the interaction between SHI and social-religious engagement remained positive but became statistically non-significant, $b = 0.001$, $p = .81$. Therefore, the opposite signs of the two interaction terms may not be accounted for by statistical artifact.

REFERENCES

Berger, P. L. (1967). *The sacred canopy: Elements of a sociological theory of religion.* Garden City, NY: Anchor.

(1969). *A rumour of angels: Modern society and the rediscovery of the supernatural.* Harmondsworth, UK: Penguin.

Bergin, A. E., Stinchfield, R. D., Gaskin, T. A., Masters, K. S., & Sullivan, C. E. (1988). Religious life-styles and mental health: An exploratory study. *Journal of Counseling Psychology, 35*(1), 91–98.

Bond, M. H. (1988). Finding universal dimensions of individual variation in multi-cultural studies of value. *Journal of Personality and Social Psychology, 55*, 1009–1015.

(2009). Circumnavigating the psychological globe: From yin and yang to starry, starry night. In S. Bekman & A. Aksu-Koc (Eds.), *Perspectives on human development, family, and culture* (pp. 31–49). Cambridge: Cambridge University Press.

Bond, M. H., & Forgas, J. (1984). Linking person perception to behavior intention across cultures: The role of cultural collectivism. *Journal of Cross-Cultural Psychology, 15*, 337–352.

Bond, M. H., & Van de Vijver, F. J. R. (2011). Making scientific sense of cultural differences in psychological outcomes: Unpacking the *magnum mysterium*. In D. Matsumoto & F. J. R. van de Vijver (Eds.), *Cross-cultural research methods in psychology* (pp. 75–100). New York: Cambridge University Press.

Bryk, A. S., & Raudenbush, S. W. (1992). *Hierarchical linear models for social and behavioural research: Applications and data analysis methods.* Newbury Park, CA: Sage Publications.

Diener, E., & Tay, L. (2010). *Needs and subjective well-being around the world.* Paper under revision for *Journal of Personality and Social Psychology.*

Diener, E., Tay, L., & Myers, D. (2010). *Religiosity and subjective well-being across the world and the USA*. Paper in revision.

Diener, E., & Tov, W. (2012). National accounts of well-being. In K. C. Land, A. C. Michalos, & M. J. Sirgy (Eds.), *Handbook of social indicators and quality of life research* (pp. 137–157). New York: Springer.

Eccles, J., & Gootman, J. A. (2002). *Community programs to promote youth development.* Washington, DC: The National Academies Press.

Eccles, J., Templeton, J., Barber, B., & Stone, M. (2003). Adolescence and emerging adulthood: The critical passage ways to adulthood. In M. H. Bornstein, L. Davidson, C. L. M. Keyes, & K. A. Moore (Eds.), *Well-being: Positive development across the life course* (pp. 383–406). Mahwah, NJ: Erlbaum.

Emmons, R. A. (1999). Religion in the psychology of personality: An introduction. *Journal of Personality,* **67**, 873–888.

Erikson, E. (1964). *Childhood and society.* New York: Norton.

Fu, P. P., Kennedy, J., Tata, J., Yukl, G., Bond, M. H., Peng, T. K. … Cheosakul, A. (2004). The impact of societal cultural values and individual social beliefs on the perceived effectiveness of managerial influence strategies: A meso approach. *Journal of International Business Studies,* **35**, 284–305.

Hofmann, D. A. (1997). An overview of the logic and rationale of hierarchical linear models. *Journal of Management,* **23** (6), 723–744.

Hogg, M. A., Adelman, J. R., & Blagg, R. D. (2010). Religion in the face of uncertainty: An uncertainty-identity theory account of religiousness. *Personality and Social Psychology Review,* **14**, 72–83.

Inglehart, R., & Klingemann, H. D. (2000). Genes, culture, democracy, and happiness. In E. Diener & E. M. Suh (Eds.), *Culture and subjective well-being* (pp. 165–183). Cambridge, MA: MIT Press.

Kam, C. C. S., & Bond, M. H. (2008). The role of emotions and behavioral responses in mediating the impact of face loss on relationship deterioration: Are Chinese more face-sensitive than Americans? *Asian Journal of Social Psychology,* **11**, 175–184.

Kleiner, K. (2010). Is life getting better? Moving beyond economic measures of well-being. *U of T Magazine,* Winter, 29–32.

Kwan, V. S. Y., Bond, M. H., & Singelis, T. M. (1997). Pancultural explanations for life satisfaction: Adding relationship harmony to self-esteem. *Journal of Personality and Social Psychology,* **73**, 1038–1051.

Lai, J. H. W., Bond, M. H., & Hui, N. H. H. (2007). The role of social axioms in predicting life satisfaction: A longitudinal study in Hong Kong. *Journal of Happiness Studies,* **8**, 517–535.

Leung, K., & Bond, M. H. (1989). On the empirical identification of dimensions for cross-cultural comparisons. *Journal of Cross-Cultural Psychology,* **20**, 133–152.

(2004). Social axioms: A model for social beliefs in multicultural perspective. *Advances in Experimental Social Psychology,* Vol. 36, 119–197. San Diego, CA: Elsevier Academic Press.

(2007). Psycho-logic and eco-logic: Insights from social axiom dimensions. In F. van de Vijver, D. van Hemert, & Y. P. Poortinga (Eds.), *Individuals and cultures in multilevel analysis* (pp. 199–221). Mahwah, NJ: Lawrence Erlbaum Associates.

Levine, R. V., & Campbell, D. T. (1972). *Ethnocentrism: Theories of conflict, ethnic attitudes and group behavior.* New York: Wiley.

Li, L. M. W., & Bond, M. H. (2010). Does individual secularism promote life satisfaction? The moderating role of societal development. *Social Indicators Research, 99*, 443–453.

Lykken, D., & Tellegen, A. (1996). Happiness is a stochastic phenomenon. *Psychological Science, 7*, 186–189.

Matsumoto, D., Yoo, S. H., Nakagawa, S., Alexandre, J., Altarriba, J., Anguas-Wong, A. M., & Zengeya, A. (2008). Culture, emotion regulation, and adjustment. *Journal of Personality and Social Psychology, 94*, 925–937.

Morrison, M., Tay, L., & Diener, E. (2010). *Subjective well-being and national satisfaction: Findings from a worldwide survey.* Manuscript submitted for publication.

Pew Forum on Religion and Public Life (2009). *Global Restrictions on Religion.* Retrieved August 24, 2010 from http://pewforum.org/uploadedFiles/Topics/Issues/Government/restrictions-fullreport.pdf

Raudenbush, S. W., & Bryk, A. S. (2002). *Hierarchical linear models: Applications and data analysis methods* (2nd ed.). Newbury Park, CA: Sage.

Sagiv, L., & Schwartz, S. H. (2000). Value priorities and subjective well-being: Direct relations and congruity effects. *European Journal of Social Psychology, 30*, 177–198.

Saucier, G., & Skrzypińska, K. (2006). Spiritual but not religious? Evidence for two independent dispositions. *Journal of Personality, 74*, 1257–1292.

Schwartz, S. H. (1994). Beyond individualism and collectivism: New cultural dimensions of values. In U. Kim, H. C. Triandis, Ç. Kağıtçıbaşı, S. C. Choi, & G. Yoon (Eds.), *Individualism and collectivism: Theory, method and applications* (pp. 85–119). Thousand Oaks, CA: Sage.

Shek, D. T. L. (1993). Meaning in life and psychological well-being in Chinese college students. *The International Forum for Logotherapy, 16*, 35–42.

(1999). Parenting characteristics and adolescent psychological well-being: A longitudinal study in a Chinese context. *Genetic, Social and General Psychology Monographs, 125*, 27–44.

(2010). The spirituality of the Chinese people: A critical review. In M. H. Bond (Ed.), *The Oxford handbook of Chinese psychology* (pp. 343–366). Oxford: Oxford University Press.

UNDP (2009). *Human Development Report.* Retrieved August 24, 2010 from http://hdr.undp.org/en/media/HDR_2009_EN_Complete.pdf

Veenhoven, R. (2005). If life getting better? How long and happily do people live in modern society? *European Psychologist, 10*, 330–343.

6   Indonesian Muslim Adolescents and the Ecology of Religion

Doran C. French, Nancy Eisenberg, Urip Purwono, and
Julie A. Sallquist

Abstract

In this chapter, we provide an overview of our studies that have explored
the relations between Indonesian Muslim adolescents' religiosity and spirituality with their social competence and their relationships with peers and
parents. We first reviewed our findings that individual differences in adolescent religiosity and spirituality (SR) was associated with multiple aspects of
competence including positive associations with peer acceptance, prosocial
behavior, regulation, self-esteem, and academic achievement and negative
associations with externalizing behavior, loneliness, and aggression. We then
reviewed studies suggesting that religious adolescents tended to develop
friendships with others of similar religiosity. These associations predicted
that adolescents who were friends with highly religious peers increased
their religiosity over time. Finally, we looked at the interconnection between
parent–adolescent relations and adolescent SR and adjustment. Parental
warmth moderated the relation between parent religiosity and adolescent
SR, and SR mediated the relation between parental warmth, parental religiosity, and adolescent prosocial behavior. These results are consistent with our
view that in this highly religious community, religion is strongly associated
with multiple aspects of adolescents' lives. Second, we argue that adolescent
religiosity must necessarily be understood within a relationship context, an
idea that is consistent with an ecological perspective on child and adolescent
religiousness.

There has been increased interest in understanding the connections
between adolescents' religiousness and other aspects of their development (Oser, Scarkett, & Bucher, 2006). Despite the need to expand the
scope of research on youths' religiosity across countries and religions,
almost all research on child and adolescent development and religion

has been conducted in Western countries with Christian populations (Roehlkepartain, Benson, King, & Wagener, 2006). The paucity of research on Islam and adolescent development is particularly problematic given the current world instability associated with the rise of radical Islamic groups and the need to understand youth development within mainstream Muslim communities.

In this chapter, we explore the connection of Indonesian adolescents' religiosity and spirituality with their social competence and their relationships with peers and parents. Throughout our discussion, we consider two underlying themes. The first is the view articulated in the classic work of Clifford Geertz (1973) that in some highly religious communities, religion and culture are strongly interconnected such that it is difficult to separate meaning systems and practices associated with each. Religion is an underexplored component of cultural meaning systems (Tarakeshwar, Stanton, & Pargament, 2003), one that may be particularly important for understanding adolescent religiousness, social competence, and parenting within the Muslim communities of West Java. The relevance of Geertz's interpretations to our work is understandable given that his ideas on the interconnection between religion and culture were in part developed based on his study of Muslim communities in Central Java. Our second theme is that adolescent religiosity must necessarily be understood within a relationship context, an idea that is consistent with an ecological perspective on child and adolescent religiousness (Regnerus, Smith, & Smith, 2004). We suggest that our understanding of adolescent religiousness is enhanced by considering how religion is connected to adolescents' daily life and ongoing patterns of behavior. It is particularly important to understand how religion impacts relationships with peers, parents, and others. We will expand on each of these themes in the following sections.

Current researchers of adolescent religion distinguish between spirituality and religiosity (Dowling, Gestsdottir, Anderson, von Eye, Almerigi, & Lerner, 2004; Hill & Pargament, 2003; Roehlkepartain et al., 2006). *Spirituality* refers to the personal beliefs and practices (e.g., meditation and prayer) that may be unconnected to an organized religion. *Religiosity* involves adherence to the practices of a particular religious community. Although there is some evidence of the independence of these two constructs among U.S. youth (Dowling et al., 2004), we expected the overlap would be substantial among Indonesian youths given suggestions that people's religiosity and spirituality are likely to be highly associated in cultures that are very religious and within which there is uniformity of religious affiliation (French, Eisenberg, Vaughan, Purwono, & Suryanti, 2008; Rich & Cinamon, 2007).

Indonesia
Indonesia is the fourth most populous country and is the home of the largest Muslim population. The participants in the studies reviewed in this chapter attended public schools in Bandung, a city of approximately two million inhabitants in West Java. This region is considered one of the most strongly religious in Indonesia (Bianchi, 2004; Glicken, 1987) and the form of Islam typically practiced here is similar to that practiced elsewhere in its focus on the textual foundations of the Koran and its emphasis on the five pillars of Islam (i.e., testimony of faith, performance of the five daily prayers, fasting during Ramadan, almsgiving, and making the Hajj pilgrimage to Mecca) (Gade & Feener, 2004). The government is a democracy within which six religions are officially recognized. Religious affiliation appears on official identification cards and religion is a required subject in both public and private schools. Although there have been some calls to incorporate Sharia "Islamic law" into the judicial code (Bianchi, 2004), there is little public support for this (Davis & Robinson, 2006). In the year 2000 World Values Survey of 18- to 24-year-old youth, 100 percent of the Indonesian sample indicated that religion was very important in their daily life (Lippman & Keith, 2006), providing further evidence of the importance of religion in this country.

The context within which religion is experienced by adolescents in our sample differs in numerous ways from that typically experienced by youths in North America and Europe. Adolescents in our sample attended schools where almost all students, as well as most of their teachers, were Muslim. Furthermore, Islam in Indonesia is interwoven with culture and tied into collectivist patterns of behavior (Cohen, Hall, Koenig, & Meador, 2005; Snibbe & Markus, 2002), and the distinction between secular and religious worlds is diminished and religion permeates daily life. Religious practice is often observable as classmates are aware of mosque attendance, adherence to prayer requirements, and compliance with fasting.

We expected that religion would be connected with many aspects of the social life of Indonesian adolescents. This hypothesis is based on the salience of religion in the lives of West Javanese adolescents, the interconnection between religious and cultural values and world views, and the extent to which adolescents interact with peers and adults who are observant Muslims. In the following sections, we review our past research that assessed the relation between religion and social competence, peer relationship, and parent and adolescent relationships.

Our Samples

The studies that we describe in this chapter came from two longitudinal studies, both of which were completed with Muslim students from public schools in Bandung, West Java as participants. Using Sample 1, we assessed the relations between religion and social competence and religion and parent–adolescent relationships. Sample 2 focused specifically on the religion and peer relationships.

Sample 1 came from a study designed to assess relationships between Christian and Muslim adolescents (Eisenberg, Sallquist, French, Purwono, Suryanti, & Pidada, 2009). As described by Sallquist, Eisenberg, French, Purwono, and Suryanti (2010), data were obtained at four different points in time. After an initial screening (T1), a sample (T2) of 1,254 seventh grade students, 285 adolescents, including 205 Muslim youth ($M = 13.47$ years), were assessed and extensive information was obtained from parents, adolescents, teachers, and peers. Approximately five months later at T3 ($M = 13.88$ years), data were obtained from 183 eighth grade Muslim youth. Finally at T4, approximately one year later, 300 Muslim ninth grade adolescents ($M = 14.91$ years) were assessed. This sample included 136 adolescents who had participated in earlier assessments and 164 who were newly recruited from the classrooms of prior participants. All of the participants were Muslim, but varied in the consistency of their participation in expected religious practices.

At T2, 19.1 percent were classified as very consistent, 65.0 percent consistent, 13.7 percent inconsistent and 1.1 percent nonpracticing. The majority of participants in the T2 sample were in the middle class, with 2 percent lower, 20 percent lower middle, 32 percent middle, 43 percent upper middle, and 2 percent upper SES levels. There were 46 percent of mothers and 64 percent of fathers who reported having some college education. The studies that we describe in the following sections used data from different time periods, a necessity because different measures were administered at each assessment period.

Sample 2 (French, Purwono, & Triwahyuni, 2011) included 1,010 Muslim adolescents in the eighth ($M = 13.37$ years) and tenth ($M = 15.36$) grades. One year later, we sought to recruit those participants who remained in their sample school, yielding a Y2 sample of 889 adolescents. Within the Y1 population, 1.85 percent reported always performing both the required and recommended practices, 51.51 percent reported always performing required practices, and 51.51 percent reported intermittent performance of required practices; there were no adolescents in this sample who were nonpracticing. The majority of participants were from middle-class families, an assertion supported by the finding that 46 percent of mothers and 56 percent of fathers had some post high school education, 40 percent of mothers and 36 percent of fathers had a high school education, and 11 percent of mothers and 6 percent of fathers had a junior high school education.

Islam and the Social Competence of Indonesian Adolescents. Our work was guided by the expectation that adolescents' spirituality and religiosity would be associated with multiple aspects of social competence, a hypothesis based on extensive prior research conducted with U.S. Christian youth (King & Roeser, 2009; Oser et al., 2006; Thomas & Carver, 1990). Specifically, religiousness in U.S. youth has been associated with academic success (Elder & Conger, 2000; Regnerus, 2000; Smith & Denton, 2005), prosocial behavior and volunteerism (Donahue & Benson, 1995), and in some populations, enhanced self-esteem (Elder & Conger, 2000). Religiousness has also been associated with reduced externalizing and delinquent behavior (Benda & Corwyn, 1997; Blakeney & Blakeney, 2006; Elder & Conger, 2000; Elifson, Peterson, & Hadaway, 1983) and internalizing behavior (Smith & Denton, 2005).

French, Eisenberg, Vaughan, Purwono, and Suryanti (2008) and Sallquist et al. (2010) assessed Indonesian Muslim parents' and adolescents' ratings of spirituality using items from the Daily Spiritual Experience Scale (Underwood & Teresi, 2002) and measured religiosity by assessing the parent and adolescent reports of the consistency with which participants practiced behaviors expected of Muslim youth in Indonesia (e.g., fasting during Ramadan, reading the Koran, attending the Mosque, and performing the five daily prayers). Parent and adolescent ratings of religiosity and spirituality were loaded onto a spirituality–religiosity (SR) latent construct. This strategy of obtaining information from multiple informants was used when possible throughout our studies to address the considerable problems associated with the exclusive use of self-report data (Patterson, Reid, & Dishion, 1992).

Our first set of analyses (French et al., 2008) used data from T2 and T3 of Study 1. Because of the short time period between the two data collection occasions and the fact that different measures came from each assessment period, we did not assess longitudinal changes in these analyses. In Figure 6.1 are the results from a structural equation modeling (SEM) analysis demonstrating negative relations between SR and both internalizing and externalizing behavior and the positive association with self-esteem. The externalizing variable was indicated by teachers' and parents' ratings of externalizing and parents' and children's ratings of minor deviant

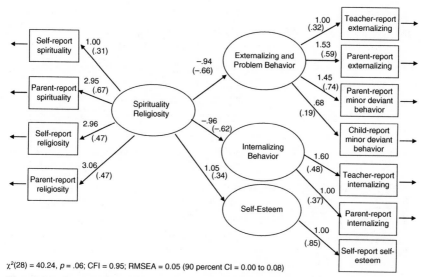

$\chi^2(28) = 40.24$, $p = .06$; CFI = 0.95; RMSEA = 0.05 (90 percent CI = 0.00 to 0.08)

Figure 6.1. Structural equation model of religiosity and adjustment.
Note: Unstandardized loadings are reported. Completely standardized loadings are reported in parentheses. Solid lines represent paths that are significant at $p < .05$. Long dashed lines represent marginal paths, $p < .10$. The initial model did not include the correlated errors; however, this model did not fit. In response to the modification indexes, correlations between errors were added to the model.

behavior whereas the internalizing latent variable was indicated by teachers' and parents' reports of internalizing. Self-esteem was indicated by the children's completion of the general self-worth scale of the Harter (1988) Self-Perception Profile for Adolescents. Other SEM analyses (see French et al., 2008) indicated that SR was positively associated with prosocial behavior, peer group status, academic achievement, and regulation. In sum, these findings provide consistent support for the hypothesis that Indonesian Muslim adolescents' SR is associated with multiple aspects of competence.

Using data from the T4 follow-up, Sallquist et al. (2010) found a decline in mean levels of SR from eighth to ninth grade, a finding consistent with similar declines reported for Christian adolescents in the United States (King & Roeser, 2009). Further, eighth grade SR was positively associated with ninth grade teacher-rated socially appropriate behavior whereas it was negatively associated with self-reports of loneliness. Changes in SR were marginally associated with increased prosocial behavior and significantly associated with socially appropriate behavior. Increases in SR were also associated with decreased loneliness. Changes in SR, however, did not predict decreases in either internalizing or externalizing behavior over time, suggesting that more complex casual models connecting SR with adolescent adjustment may be required. In later sections of this chapter, we expand upon this theme by exploring the possibility that adolescents' interpersonal relationships contribute to these pathways.

These two studies suggest that adolescent SR is associated with multiple aspects of competence within this culture. We hypothesize that one explanation for these relations is that culture and religion are intertwined and together provide systems of meanings and values (Geertz, 1973). Standards of competence are likely grounded within these systems (Ogbu, 1981) such that individuals strive to meet these standards and others consider those who do so as successful. The ability to develop relationships with others is a central component of competence and we argue that within this culture, religion is also a salient aspect of adolescents' relationships with both parents and peers.

Religion and Parent and Adolescent Relationships. Dating from the classic work of Geertz (1961), most of the research on parent–child relationships of Muslim populations in Java has been conducted by anthropologists. Farver and Wimbarti (1995) suggested that Indonesian child rearing typically emphasizes emotional control and the development of harmonious interpersonal relationships. Javanese and Sundanese parents (the two largest ethnic groups in Indonesia) have been described as being highly indulgent, particularly with young children, and as rarely using physical punishment (Zevalkink & Riksen-Walraven, 2001). Older children and adolescents are expected to comply with parental requests (Sarwono, 2005) and failure to do so has historically been considered a violation of the moral order (Keeler, 1987; Mulder, 1992). This may be changing, however, as parents in Indonesia, particularly those exposed to Western influences, have developed more equalitarian methods of relating to their children (Mulder, 1996).

We expected that Indonesian Muslim adolescents' relationships with their parents would be interconnected with religion given the arguments presented previously regarding the pervasiveness of religion within this culture, the extent to which religion is interconnected with cultural norms and values, and the importance of religion in daily life. We also expected parenting to be associated with religion because of the strong focus within Islam on parenting (Holdon & Vittrup, 2010). Based on her anthropological studies in Indonesia, Glicken (1987) suggested that the strong hierarchical positioning of parents and the expectations that parents must be unquestionably obeyed have their foundations in Islam, an idea that is consistent with suggestions that relationships between Indonesian parents and adolescents incorporate religious aspects.

Based on research conducted with the United States, we expected that adolescents' religiousness would be associated with parents' religiousness (Boyatzis, Dollahite, & Marks, 2006; Ozorak, 1989), and that parental religiousness would be associated with warm relationships between parents and their adolescent children (Gunnoe, Hetherington, & Reiss, 1999; Schottenbauer, Spernak, & Hellstrom, 2007). We also expected that parents would be more likely to transmit religious beliefs to their adolescent children if parent–adolescent relationships were warm and accepting. This later hypothesis is based on Bao, Whitbeck, Hoyt, and Conger's (1999) findings from the study of U.S. rural families that perceived parental acceptance moderated the relation between parents' and adolescents' religiosity, an effect that was particularly strong for the relation between mothers and their sons. Further evidence that family environment is associated with children's adoption of religious views came from Myers (1996) who analyzed telephone survey data comparing the religiosity of parents with that of their offspring 12 years later. He found that reported parental happiness was directly related to the religiosity of their children. Parental happiness also interacted with parental religiosity to predict the religiosity of their children more than a decade later, suggesting that a warm family environment facilitated the transmission of religiosity from parents to children. Consistent with this hypothesis were the findings of Okagaki and Bevis (1999) that the relation between parents' and their daughters' religious beliefs, as reported by college students, were mediated by perceptions of parent–child warmth and those of Granqvist (2002) that secure parent–child relationships mediated the relation between Swedish parents' and adolescents' religiousness.

We used data from the T4 assessment of Sample 1 (French, Eisenberg, Purwono, & Sallquist, 2011) to assess how parent religiosity and parent–adolescent warmth contributed to the prediction of adolescent SR. SR (as described in the prior section) was indicated by both parents' and adolescents' reports of religiosity and spirituality, and parent–adolescent warmth was defined by parents' ratings of warmth and adolescents' ratings of affection received from mother and from father. As expected, there was a significant pathway from parent religiosity to adolescents' SR and a significant pathway from parents' religiosity to parent–adolescent warmth. There was also a significant pathway from parent–adolescent warmth to SR. Most importantly, we found that parent–adolescent warmth moderated the relation between parent religiosity and adolescent SR. In other words, the relation between parents' and adolescents' SR was partially explained by the extent to which they had a warm relationship. These findings add to those of Bao et al. (1999), Myers (1996), Okagaki and Bevis (1999), and Granqvist (1998; 2002) that warm and positive parent–child relationships moderate the relation between parents' and adolescents' religiousness.

We also explored how parental religiosity, parent–adolescent warmth, and adolescents' SR combine to predict multiple aspects of competence. As reported in the previous section, we found (using information from T2, T3, and T4 of the Sample 1 data) that adolescents' SR was associated with multiple aspects of competence, including low levels of externalizing and internalizing behavior, high self-esteem, and prosocial behavior. Thus, in addition to exploring the extent that parental religiosity, parent–adolescent warmth, and SR directly predicated aspects of social competence, we were curious about the possibility that SR might mediate some of these relations. Consistent with our hypotheses, we found that the associations between parental warmth and a prosocial latent variable were mediated by ado- lescent SR. In other words, the associations between parent–adolescent warmth and these multiple aspects of competence were explained by the level of the adolescents' SR.

Evidence that parental warmth moderates the relation between parent religiosity and adolescent SR in conjunction with the finding that adolescent SR mediates the relation between parent religiosity and parental warmth and adolescent prosocial behavior provides evidence in support of our posi- tion that religion plays an important role in the relation between parent– adolescent relationships and adjustment. We argue that these findings are consistent with suggestions that parenting is embedded within the cultural context and that cultural meaning systems are integral to understand the relationships between children and parents (Bornstein & Lansford, 2010; Harkness & Super, 1995). We suspect that within this collectivist and highly religious culture, the behaviors of parents and children are strongly influ- enced by the religion that permeates daily life and is interconnected with cultural meaning systems. In the next section, we review evidence that reli- gion in this culture is also connected with adolescents' relationships with peers.

Peers and Religion. There is evidence from studies in the United States that peer relationships are relevant to understanding adolescents' religiosity (Regnerus, Smith, & Smith, 2004; Schwartz, Bukowski, & Aoki, 2006) and may help explain mechanisms by which religiosity and social competence are connected (Wallace & Williams, 1997). In this section we review our research on Indonesian adolescents that pertains to these hypotheses.

Researchers of peer influence have focused on two synergistic processes, both of which are relevant to understanding the impact of peers on religion (Prinstein & Dodge 2008). First, youths tend to most often develop friendships and other associations with others who are similar to themselves. This process, labeled homophily, has been demonstrated with respect to antisocial behavior (Cairns, Cairns, Neckerman, Gest, & Gariépy, 1988), internalizing behavior (Hogue & Steinberg 1995), and academic achievement (Cook, Deng, & Morgano, 2007). There is some evidence that a similar process occurs in U.S. adolescents with respect to religiosity such that adolescents tend to associate with others with similar levels of religiosity (Smith & Denton 2005). The second process is that peers influence each other in ways that may lead them to change their behavior, thus leading them to become increasingly prosocial, antisocial, or academically successful over time (Prinstein & Dodge 2008). Similar process may occur with religiosity. Regnerus et al. (2004) found that the adolescents' church attendance was predicted by the church attendance of their friends one year previously. These results add to those of others (King, Furrow, & Roth, 2002; Schwartz et al., 2006) that adolescents' religiosity is associated with the religiosity of their friends. Adolescents who have religious friends also appear to exhibit less problematic behavior as illustrated by the findings of Burkett and Warren (1987) that religiosity appears to influence marijuana use indirectly through involvement with peers who abstain from such use and Simons, Simons, and Conger's (2004) observations that children's religiosity was negatively associated with involvement with deviant peers, a pathway that accounted for the lower delinquency of religious children.

Friends and the Religiosity of Muslim Indonesian Adolescents. Here we report on analyses from the Sample 2 longitudinal investigation (French, Purwono, & Triwahyuni, 2011) that assessed the similarity between the religiosity of adolescents and their friends, and the possible effects that friendships and network associations with religious peers might have on both religiosity and the exhibition of antisocial behavior. All of the students in the sample were practicing Muslims, although they differed in the consistency with which they practiced the required and recommended religious behaviors.

The first question was the extent to which adolescents developed friendships and network associations with peers similar to themselves in religiosity. Friendships were defined by mutual nominations. In contrast to friendships that are defined by shared affinities, network associations are defined by shared engagement in activities; thus, participants and their classmates were asked to identify those individuals who tend to spend time together. These reports were used to identify membership in social networks using the Social Cognitive Mapping method (SCM version 4.0). Participants self-reported their religiosity using a measure within which they reported their consistency of exhibiting both required (e.g., performing the five daily prayers) and recommended (e.g., performing additional prayers) practices. Adolescents were similar to their friends in their levels of religiosity, an effect that did not differ significantly by sex. Boys and girls were also similar to their network associates in their religiosity, but this similarity was larger for boys than for girls.

It is possible that the similarity between the religiosity of adolescents and their friends and network associates in their levels of religiosity could arise spuriously to the extent that religiosity is correlated with other qualities that underlie friendship and network associations. To address this question, we used a path model in which we simultaneously evaluated the similarity between adolescents and their friends on religiosity, academic achievement, antisocial behavior, and popularity. Adolescents were similar to their friends on all four qualities. Thus, the similarity between adolescents and their friends on religiosity existed despite simultaneously controlling for these other variables, an effect that also emerged when adolescents were compared with network associates on these same qualities.

We then explored the relation of friends' religiosity to adolescents' religiosity one year later. For these analyses, adolescents were categorized as being either consistent in their religiosity (i.e., regularly performing all required behaviors) or inconsistent in their religiosity. For those adolescents who were inconsistent in the first year of the study, high religiosity of their friends was associated with them becoming more consistent the next year. Similarly, for those adolescents who were consistent in their religiosity during the first year, friendships with religious peers were associated with the maintenance of this level of religiosity in the next year.

One possible explanation for these results is that adolescents discuss their religious views with friends and that they are influenced by these discussions. Some support for this view is provided by Chaudhury and Miller's (2008) finding from a qualitative study of Bangladeshi American Muslim adolescents of the importance of peer interactions in the formation of religious identities. Furthermore, it is possible that adolescents influence each other to perform or not perform religiously required behaviors. For example, adolescents' attendance at the Mosque might be in part attributable to their friends' attendance. It is also likely that adolescents who are inclined to either increase or decrease their levels of religiosity might befriend others who support these changes.

We then looked at the relation between having religious friends and network associates and the exhibition of antisocial behavior using data from the first year of Sample 2. We found that for boys, having both religious friends and religious network associates added to self-religiosity in predicting desistance from antisocial behavior. For girls, these effects were much weaker, with only marginal effects for the relation between self- and network members' religiosity.

The results of the analyses above add to findings from the studies of U.S. adolescents that relationships with religious peers are associated with reduced antisocial behavior. Perhaps as suggested by Stark (1996), religious adolescents contemplating deviant behavior might discuss the extent to which their behavior is consistent with religious values with their friends and network associates. Second, because religious adolescents exhibit lower levels of deviancy than nonreligious adolescents, interactions with religious peers are likely to be associated with reduced facilitation of antisocial behavior. Consistent with this hypothesis, Simons et al. (2004) found that child religiosity was negatively associated with involvement with deviant peers. Third, it is likely that religious youths engage in activities that contribute to reduced antisocial behavior as well as put them in proximity to peers with shared interests that they are likely to befriend. In the United States, religiously devoted youth tend to participate in organized clubs and activities (Smith & Denton, 2005) and engagement in such activities undoubtedly increases their exposure to other religious youth and may increase their prosocial behavior and decrease their involvement in unsupervised activity (Eccles, Barber, Stone, & Hunt, 2003). It is reasonable to suppose that a similar process might occur in Indonesian adolescents, but this has not been studied.

The results from these two studies provide evidence that peers tend to associate both in friendships and networks with others of similar religiosity and suggest that these associations may impact adolescents' religiosity and their exhibition of antisocial behavior. These conclusions must be offered tentatively, given our inability to test causality using our correlational methodology. Nevertheless, such causal pathways are reasonable given other findings of the extensivity of peer influence (Prinstein & Dodge, 2008), and may be extremely important in explaining mechanisms by which individuals' religious beliefs translate into exhibited behavior (Wallace & Williams, 1997). These findings further provide support for a central thesis of this chapter, that is, that the religion of Indonesian youths is reflected in daily activities and is connected to their social relationships.

Conclusions

We argue that in the highly religious culture of West Java, religion is inter-connected with worldviews, values, and relationships. Although we believe that similar processes occur within other religions and in other areas of the world, we urge caution in generalizing our results obtained from the study of Indonesian Muslim youth in West Java. We are uncertain whether our results would also be seen in Muslim youth in other countries. The cultural context within which Islam exists in Indonesia is substantially different than that which exists in many other regions and further research is needed to explore how adolescents in these countries experience religion.

Likely even more extreme is the contrast between the context within which youths in this study and those in many Western cultures experience religiosity. All of the adolescents in these studies were Muslim and nearly all exhibited moderate to high levels of religiosity. They attended schools and lived in communities where most of the persons with whom they interacted were also Muslim. Furthermore, as noted throughout this chapter, Islam in Indonesia is interwoven with culture and tied to collectivist patterns of behavior (Cohen et al., 2005; Snibbe & Markus, 2002). The strong distinc-tions that are made between the religious and secular worlds are less pro-nounced in West Java than they are in many Western countries.

Nevertheless, there are grounds to believe that religion is also inter-connected with social competence and relationships for youths in North America and Europe, although perhaps not to the same extent as for Indonesian youth. As reviewed in earlier sections of this chapter, studies of North American youths have revealed that religion is related to multiple aspects of social competence, interconnected with parenting, and associ-ated with peer relationships.

In our research, the religious involvement of Muslim children and ado-lescents has been consistently associated with positive outcomes such as social competence and warm parent–child relationships. It is apparent, however, that this is not always the case in Indonesia or in other parts of the world (Kimball, 2002). Boyatzis et al. (2006) notes that religiousness in some U. S. families is associated with bigotry and abusive parenting. In Indonesia and elsewhere, terrorist acts have been committed with religion as a stated justification. In our work, however, we have seen no evidence that religious involvement is associated with negative outcomes although we are cognizant of the possibility that this might be the case for some outcomes, under select circumstances, in some populations, and for some individuals.

Findings that religion is interconnected with relationships as well as activities and daily life point to the usefulness of adopting an ecological approach to understanding religion in the lives of adolescents (King & Roeser, 2009). Within this perspective, adolescents' religiosity occurs within a context that includes individuals, organizations, activity structures, and cultural practices, values, and meaning systems. We suggest that such a perspective is important not only for understanding the place of religion in the lives of Indonesian Muslim youths, but also for understanding youths from other regions and from different religions. It is particularly important to understand how religion connects with relationships as well as aspects of adolescent development such as identity and self-esteem. Our study of influence of Islam within the lives of Indonesian Muslim youth, however, provides an illustration of the value of using an ecological perspective to understand adolescent religion.

REFERENCES

Bao, W. N., Whitbeck, L. B., Hoyt, D. R., & Conger, R. D. (1999). Perceived parental acceptance as a moderator of religious transmission among adolescent boys and girls. *Journal of Marriage and the Family,* **61**, 362–374.

Benda, B. B., & Corwyn, R. F. (1997). Religion and delinquency: The relationship after considering family and peer influences. *Journal for the Scientific Study of Religion,* **36**, 81–92.

Bianchi, R. R. (2004). *Guests of God: Pilgrimage and politics in the Islamic world.* New York: Oxford University Press.

Blakeney, R. F., & Blakeney, C. D. (2006). Delinquency: A quest for moral and spiritual integrity. In E. C. Roehlkepartain, P. L. Benson, P. E. King, & L. M. Wagener (Eds.), *The handbook of spiritual development in childhood and adolescence* (pp. 371–383). Thousand Oaks, CA: Sage.

Bornstein, M. C., & Lansford, J. E. (2010). Parenting. In M. Bornstein (Ed.), *Handbook of cultural developmental science* (pp. 259–277). New York: Psychology Press.

Boyatzis, C. J., Dollahite, D. C., & Marks, L. D. (2006). The family as a context for religious and spiritual development in children and youth. In E. C. Roehlkepartain, P. L. Benson, P. E. King, & L. M. Wagener (Eds.), *The handbook of spiritual development in childhood and adolescence* (pp. 297–309). Thousand Oaks, CA: Sage.

Burkett, S. R., & Warren, B. O. (1987). Religiosity, peer associations, and adolescent marijuana use: A panel study of underlying causal structures. *Criminology,* **25**, 109–131.

Cairns, R. B., Cairns, B. D., Neckerman, H. J., Gest, S. L. L., & Gariépy, J. L. (1988). Social networks and aggressive behavior: Peer support or peer rejection? *Developmental Psychology,* **24**, 815–823.

Chaudhury, S. R., & Miller, L. (2008). Religious identity formation among Bangladeshi American Muslim adolescents. *Journal of Adolescent Research*, **23**, 383–410.

Cohen, A. B., Hall, D. E., Koenig, H. G., & Meador, K. G. (2005). Social versus individual motivation: Implications for normative definitions of religious orientation. *Personality and Social Psychology Review*, **9**, 48–61.

Cook, T. D., Deng, Y., & Morgano, E. (2007). Friendship influences during early adolescence: The special role of friends' grade point average. *Journal of Research on Adolescence*, **17**, 325–356.

Davis, N. J., & Robinson, R. V. (2006). The egalitarian face of Islamic orthodoxy: Support for Islamic law and economic justice in seven Muslim-majority nations. *American Sociological Review*, **71**, 167–190.

Donahue, M. J., & Benson, P. L. (1995). Religion and the well-being of adolescents. *Journal of Social Issues*, **51**, 145–160.

Dowling, E. M., Gestsdottir, S., Anderson, P. M., von Eye, A., Almerigi, J., & Lerner, R. M. (2004). Structural relations among spirituality, religiosity, and thriving in adolescence. *Applied Developmental Science*, **8**, 7–16.

Eccles, J. S., Barber, B., Stone, M., & Hunt, J. (2003). Extracurricular activities and adolescent development. *Journal of Social Issues*, **59**, 865–889. doi:10.1046/j.0022–4537.2003.00095.x.

Eisenberg, N., Sallquist, J., French, D. C., Purwono, U., Suryanti, T., & Pidada, S. (2009). The relations of majority-minority group status and having an other-religion friend to Indonesian youths' socioemotional functioning. *Developmental Psychology*, **45**, 248–259.

Elder, G. H., & Conger, R. D. (2000). *Children of the land: Adversity and success in rural America*. Chicago: University of Chicago Press.

Elifson, K. W., Petersen, D. M., & Hadaway, C. K. (1983). Religion and delinquency: A contextual analysis. *Criminology*, **21**, 505–527.

Farver, J. M., & Wimbarti, S. (1995). Indonesian children's play with their mothers and older siblings. *Child Development*, **66**, 1493–1503.

French, D. C., Eisenberg, N., Vaughan, J., Purwono, U., & Suryanti, T. A. (2008). Religious involvement and social competence and adjustment of Indonesian Muslim adolescents. *Developmental Psychology*, **44**, 597–611.

French, D. C., Purwono, U., & Triwahyuni, A. (2011). Friendship and religiosity of Indonesian Muslim adolescents. *Journal of Youth and Adolescence*, **40**, 1623–1633. doi: 10.1007/s10964–011–9645–7.

Gade, A., & Feener, R. M. (2004). Muslim thought and practice in contemporary Indonesia. In R. M. Feener (Ed.), *Islam in world cultures: Comparative perspectives* (pp. 183–215). Santa Barbara, CA: ABC-CLIO.

Geertz, C. (1973). *The interpretations of cultures*. New York: Basic Books.

Geertz, H. (1961). *The Javanese family; a study of kinship and socialization*. New York: Free Press of Glencoe.

Glicken, J. (1987). Sundanese Islam and the value of hormot: Control, obedience, and socialization in West Java. In R. S. Kipp & S. Rogers (Eds.), *Indonesian religions in transitions* (pp. 238–252). Tucson: University of Arizona Press.

Granqvist, P. (1998). Religiousness and perceived childhood attachment: On the question of compensation or correspondence. *Journal for the Scientific Study of Religion*, **37**, 350–367.

(2002). Attachment and religiosity in adolescence: Cross-sectional and longitudinal evaluations. *Personality and Social Psychology Bulletin*, **28**, 260–270. Doi:10.1177/0146167202282011.

Gunnoe, M. L., Hetherington, E. M., & Reiss, D. (1999). Parental religiosity, parenting style, and adolescent social responsibility. *Journal of Early Adolescence*, **19**, 199–225.

Harkness, S., & Super, C. M. (1995). Culture and parenting. In M. C. Bornstein (Ed.), *Handbook of parenting* (Vol. 2): *Biology and ecology of parenting* (pp. 211–234).

Harter, S. (1988). *Self-perception profile for adolescents*. Denver, CO: University of Denver Press.

Hill, P. C., & Pargament, K. I. (2003). Advances in the conceptualization and measurement of religion and spirituality: Implications for physical and mental health. *American Psychologist*, **58**, 64–74.

Hogue, A., & Steinberg, L. (1995). Homophily of internalized distress in adolescent peer groups. *Developmental Psychology*, **31**, 897–906.

Holdon, G., & Vittrup, B. (2010). Religion. In M. H. Bornstein (Ed.), *Handbook of cultural developmental science* (pp. 279–295). New York: Psychology Press.

Keeler, W. (1987). *Javanese shadows, Javanese selves*. Princeton, NJ : Princeton University Press.

Kimball, C. (2002). *When religion becomes evil*. San Francisco, CA: Harper and Row.

King, P. E., Furrow, J. L., & Roth, N. (2002). The influence of families and peers on adolescent religiousness. *Journal of Psychology and Christianity*, **231**, 109–120.

King, P. E., & Roeser, R. W. (2009). Religion and spirituality in adolescent development. In R. M. Lerner & L. Steinberg (Eds.), *Handbook of adolescent psychology, 3rd Edition* (pp. 435–478). Hoboken, NJ: Wiley & Sons.

Lippman, L. H., & Keith, J. D. (2006). The demographics of spirituality among youth: International perspectives. In E. C. Roehlkepartain, P. L. Benson, P. E. King, & L. M. Wagener (Eds.), *The handbook of spiritual development in childhood and adolescence* (pp. 109–123). Thousand Oaks, CA: Sage.

Mulder, N. (1992). *Individual and society in Java: A cultural analysis*. Yogyakarta, Indonesia: Gadjah Mada University Press.

(1996). *Inside Indonesian Society: Cultural change in Indonesia*. Amsterdam: Pepin Press.

Myers, S. M. (1996). An interactive model of religiosity inheritance: The importance of family context. *American Sociological Review*, **61**, 858–866.

Ogbu, J. (1981). Origins of human competence: A cultural- ecological perspective. *Child Development*, **52**, 413–429.

Okagaki, L., & Bevis, C. (1999). Transmission of religious values: Relations between parents' and daughters' beliefs. *Journal of Genetic Psychology*, **160**, 303–318.

Oser, F. K., Scarkett, W. G., & Bucher, A. (2006). Religious and spiritual development throughout the life span. In W. Damon & R. M. Lerner (Eds.), *Handbook of child psychology: Vol. 1. Theoretical models of human development* (6th ed., pp. 942–998). New York: Wiley.

Ozorak, E. W. (1989). Social and cognitive influence on the development of religious beliefs and commitment in adolescence. *Journal for the Scientific Study of Religion*, **28**, 448–463.

Patterson, G. R., Reid, J. B., & Dishion, T. J. (1992). *Antisocial boys*. Eugene, OR: Castalia.

Prinstein, M. J., &. Dodge, K. A. (Eds.). (2008). *Understanding peer influence in children and adolescents.* New York: Guilford.

Regnerus, M. D. (2000). Shaping schooling success: Religious socialization and educational outcomes in metropolitan public schools. *Journal for the Scientific Study of Religion, 39,* 363–370.

Regnerus, M. D., Smith, C., & Smith, B. (2004). Social context in the development of adolescent religiosity. *Applied Developmental Science, 8,* 27–38.

Rich, Y., & Cinamon, R. G. (2007). Conceptions of spirituality among Israeli Arab and Jewish late adolescents. *Journal of Humanistic Psychology, 47,* 7–29.

Roehlkepartain, E. C., Benson, P. L., King, P. E., & Wagener, L. M. (2006). Spiritual development in childhood and adolescence: Moving to the scientific mainstream. In E. C. Roehlkepartain, P. L. Benson, P. E. King, & L. M. Wagener (Eds.), *The handbook of spiritual development in childhood and adolescence* (pp. 1–15). Thousand Oaks, CA: Sage.

Sallquist, J., Eisenberg, N., French, D. C., Purwono, U., & Suryanti, T. A. (2010). Indonesian adolescents' spiritual and religious experiences and their longitudinal relations with socioemotional functioning. *Developmental Psychology, 46*(3), 699–716. doi:10.1037/a0018879

Sarwono, S. W. (2005). Families in Indonesia. In J. L. Roopnarine & U. P. Gielen (Eds.), *Families in global perspective* (pp. 104–119). Boston: Allyn & Bacon.

Schottenbauer, M. A., Spernak, S. M., & Hellstrom, I. (2007). Relationship between family religious behaviors and child well-being among third-grade children. *Mental Health, Religion, & Culture, 10,* 191–198.

Schwartz, K. D., Bukowski, W. M., & Aoki, W. T. (2006). Mentors, friends, and gurus: Peer and non-parent influences on spiritual development. In E. C. Roehlkepartain, P. L. Benson, P. E. King, & L. M. Wagener (Eds.), *The handbook of spiritual development in childhood and adolescence* (pp. 109–123). Thousand Oaks, CA: Sage.

Simons, L. G., Simons, R. L., & Conger, R. D. (2004). Identifying the mechanisms whereby family religiosity influences the probability of adolescent antisocial behavior. *Journal of Comparative Family Studies, 35*(4), 547–563.

Smith, C., & Denton, M. L. (2005). *Soul searching: The religious and spiritual lives of American teenagers.* Oxford: Oxford University Press.

Snibbe, A. C., & Markus, H. R. (2002). The psychology of religion and the religion of psychology. *Psychological Inquiry, 13,* 229–234.

Stark, R. (1996). Religion as context: Hellfire and delinquency one more time. *Sociology of Religion, 57,* 163–173.

Tarakeshwar, N., Stanton, J., & Pargament, K. (2003). Religion: An overlooked dimension of cross-cultural psychology. *Journal of Cross-Cultural Psychology, 34,* 377–394. doi:10.1177/0022022103034004001

Thomas, D. L., & Carver, C. (1990). Religion and adolescent social competence. In T. P. Gullotta & R. Montemayor (Eds.), *Developing competence in adolescence: Advances in adolescent development* (pp. 195–219). Newbury Park, CA: Sage.

Underwood, L. G., & Teresi, J. A. (2002). The daily spiritual experience scale: Development, theoretical description, reliability, exploratory factor analysis, and preliminary construct validity using health related data. *Annals of Behavioral Medicine, 24,* 22–33.

Wallace, J. M., & Williams, D. R. (1997). Religion and adolescent health-compromising behavior. In J. Schulenberg, J. Maggs, & K. Hurrelmann (Eds.), *Health risks and developmental transitions during adolescence* (pp. 444–468). New York: Cambridge University Press.

Zevalkink, J., & Riksen-Walraven, J. M. (2001). Parenting in Indonesia: Inter- and intra-cultural differences in mother's interactions with their young children. *International Journal of Behavioral Development*, **25**, 167–175.

7 Peer Groups as a Crucible of Positive Value Development in a Global World

Reed W. Larson, Lene Arnett Jensen, Hyeyoung Kang, Aisha Griffith, and Vikki Rompala

Abstract

Globalization is increasing the challenges adolescents face in developing coherent prosocial values. In many societies, traditional systems of value transmission are eroding and youth are exposed to more diverse reference groups and cultural belief systems. This chapter examines the developmental processes through which youth *work together with peers* to formulate values in the face of these challenges. We focus on organized youth programs as a valuable arena to understand and support these processes. Using qualitative longitudinal data from 11 culturally diverse, high quality programs, we identified two interlinked peer processes of value work. The first process entailed youth *actively opening themselves up* to moral realities beyond their own. This occurred through listening, "talking out," and coming to empathize with the personal experiences of others. The second process involved *collective analysis*. Youth discussed each other's stories; they compared, challenged, and critiqued the basis for different value positions.

Piaget theorized that youth develop moral principles through interactions with peers. This chapter provides grounded theory on how similar processes function in a global world. Under favorable conditions, peers play powerful roles assisting youth's efforts to synthesize hybrid value perspectives. They pool their collective experiences to analyze and wrestle with the vexing value issues of a pluralistic world. The chapter concludes with a review of how similar and differing processes of value development may be enacted across global cultural contexts.

Globalization is increasing the challenges that adolescents face in developing values. In many societies, adult authority and traditional systems for transmitting values are diminishing (Friedman, 2000; Schlegel, 2011) and youth are confronted with more diverse value positions. Furthermore, migration and urbanization place large numbers of youth in multicultural communities in which they encounter different value systems on a daily basis (Tienda & Wilson, 2002). A young person, for example, may experience traditional Muslim, Hindu, or Christian values at home, secular values at school, and materialistic values in the media.

How do youth form prosocial values in the face of this diversity? Much has been written about how the global confluence of diverse groups creates stress and alienation (Berry, 1997; Chao & Otsuki-Clutter, 2011). In this chapter we examine conscious *constructive processes* through which youth facing this challenge are able to develop positive, prosocial values.[1] Theories often describe adolescent value development as a solitary Eriksonian undertaking. In contrast, we identify processes within peer groups through which constructive value work is accomplished. To do this, we are going to focus on peer interactions within organized youth programs (such as arts, technology, civic, and faith-based programs and youth organizations), a setting that provides a rich laboratory for observing positive developmental processes, including value development (Larson, 2000, 2011). Hosang (2008) suggests that programs can provide "structured strategic spaces" in which youth "can make sense of the vexing and contradictory forces that shape their lives" (p.16).

Why focus on peer processes? Given the erosion of traditional authority, peers often fill the vacuum as a major arena in which youth shape their values. We know peers can be powerful (Chen, 2011). Volumes of research show how they can have negative influences. Processes of imitation, peer pressure, and "deviance training" can increase teenagers' prejudicial (Gaertner & Dovidio, 2000; Gonzales & Cauce, 1995) and antisocial behaviors (Dodge, Lansford, & Dishion, 2006). Yet the positive role that peers can play in adolescent development is often underestimated (Allen & Antonishak, 2008; Newman & Newman, 2001). Research shows that the majority of peer influence is toward prosocial values (Brown, 2004) and that peer interactions can enhance learning through processes of reciprocal scaffolding and co-construction (Rogoff, 1998). In this chapter we advance the theory that – under the right conditions – peer processes can be a powerful vehicle for value development in a global world.

Piaget (1965) provided preliminary theory on constructive peer processes associated with value development. He posited that the experience of equality and reciprocity in peer relationships creates conditions in which moral values and principles "impose" themselves on older children's and adolescents' reasoning. In an expansive passage, he argued that relations of reciprocity with peers "will suppress egocentrism and suggest to the intellectual and moral consciousness norms capable of purifying the contents of the common laws themselves" (p. 395). Interactions with equals, Piaget argued, can make moral codes logically self-evident and compelling. Piaget's conception of these processes, we now realize, was the product of Western culture, indeed an optimistic enlightenment strain within that culture. Young people's moral development involves more than logical principles. It involves cultivation of moral reasoning adapted to the nuances of situations, contexts, and cultural meaning systems (Jensen, 2008).

We begin this chapter by providing groundwork for thinking about adolescents' task of value development within a world of diverse values. Next, we discuss what is known about the conditions needed for positive value development and examine organized youth programs as an institutional context that can provide these conditions. In the heart of the chapter we then describe three peer processes that our research suggests can be vehicles of prosocial value development. We employ a case study of one American youth program to illustrate how youth can work together to actively co-construct prosocial values adapted to a heterogeneous society. In the final section, we then broaden the discussion to consider how these processes might vary across societal and cultural contexts.

The Challenges Adolescents Face and the New Skills They Bring to the Table

Adolescence is a key time for youth to begin to inhabit value systems. Research shows it is a time of flux when values are changing and becoming internalized (Eisenberg, Fabes, & Spinrad, 2006; Jensen, 2008). Traditional societies have long recognized this and held adolescent rites of passage aimed at passing on value systems to youth (Gilmore, 1990). It is notable that youth typically participate in these rites as members of a peer group.

Challenges to Value Development in Heterogeneous Societies

In a global world, however, taking ownership of a system of values has become a more difficult task, one that requires more deliberate agency from youth. Children may be raised within parents' value system, yet (especially as they move into adolescence) they are exposed to multiple moral codes (Jensen, 2011). These codes can involve fundamentally different assumptions, world views, and degrees of priority given to self, community, and a deity (Jensen, 2008). Youth may face the challenge of reconciling their parents' conceptions of right and wrong with alternative moral codes. They may face daily situations that pit different value systems and moral priorities against each other: loyalty to clan, sacred traditions, individualism; also different notions of when and how respect for others is expressed. For youth from immigrant families and minority groups, the challenges may include dealing with people and images that denigrate one's own value system, practices, and identity (Berry, 1997; Halverson, 2009). Whether a youth is part of a stigmatized or privileged group, prosocial value development requires dealing with the injustice of cross-group misunderstanding and mistreatment.

The stakes are high. Some youth fail to formulate a consistent set of values. At the psychological level, this confluence of cultures can result in cultural dislocation (Berry, 1997; Giddens, 2000) and identity confusion (Jensen, Arnett, & McKenzie, 2011). At the societal level, it can feed intergroup conflict and lead to a citizenry that is uncommitted to and disengaged from civic participation (Huntington, 2004).

Value development entails the task of understanding how different codes apply to self and others across daily situations. Youth must begin to sort out how different moral arguments translate to variegated cultural contexts. How do you act in a situation when your parents' values dictate a different response than the moral codes in force with peers, at school, or in a work context? How do you "do to others as you would have them do to you" when the others have been shaped by different life experiences – or when they disrespect your values?

These are complex questions. In order to comfortably inhabit prosocial values, adolescents must figure out how to act in contexts where multiple mentalities and value systems are at play.

The New Cognitive Skills of Adolescence

Although the task is formidable, adolescents become capable of developing new *metacognitive skills* for doing this value work. They become able to reason about complex systems. These include systems of abstract principles (including value systems) (Fischer & Bidell, 2006; Kuhn, 2009). They also include "messy" human systems; for example, the diverse untidy dynamics of psychological processes and social transactions. These new skills include those for thinking about *interactions between* different kinds of systems (Fischer & Bidell, 2006), such as interactions between two moral codes – or between the principles of a moral code and the real-world dynamics of human relationships. Adolescents start to be able to compare, construct, analyze, and apply arguments across diverse systems. Given the right experiences, they become able to think systematically about arguments that begin from different premises (Kuhn, 2009).

For the task of prosocial development in a heterogeneous world, a key is adolescents' expanding potentials for perspective taking: for understanding other people's subjective points of view. With the right experiences, they can learn to better imagine and predict the thoughts, feelings, and actions of others (Selman, 2003), including others from different backgrounds (Killen, Lee-Kim, McGlothlin, & Stangor, 2002; Quintana, 1998). Adolescents also develop the capacity for biographical reasoning. They become able to think about how the experiences in people's lives have influenced them: why they act as they do (Chandler, Lalonde, Sokol, & Hallett, 2003; Habermas, 2011). Along with this, adolescents gain the potential to recognize the systematic fallacies and biases in *their own* thought processes and learn to counter-act them (Watkins, Larson, & Sullivan, 2007). Although adolescents are at a novice level, these new and more advanced capabilities allow them to progressively understand others as moral beings, reacting to situations in intentional, predictable ways.

These diverse skills – it must be emphasized – are potentials. They can-not be expected to develop and become elaborated automatically. To learn to apply them to complex daily contexts requires work. It should also be emphasized that these skills are acquired over time through many small steps. There is a broad consensus in developmental psychology that "what develops" in social-cognitive development is not so much formal logical operations (as envisioned by Piaget) but a *constructed web*. As articulated by Fischer and Bidell (2006), young people accumulate "strands" of knowl-edge, insights, arguments, elements of skills, and so forth and they con-nect them together: "a given strand may be tenuous at first" but with added experience, "it becomes a stable part of the web" (p. 319).

This metaphor of a web is better fitted to the requirements young peo-ple face in understanding messy human systems in which behavior is con-textual, contingent, and multilayered. Although not nearly as elegant as Piaget's formal structures, this conception of development as a process of constructing webs will be helpful when we consider how youth figure out different value codes – and how to apply them across the nuances of daily situations.

The Task of Value Development

Of course, value development is not entirely a deliberate cognitive pro-cess. Moral thought and behavior are also influenced by basic human needs and emotions (although they, too, can be developed). First, neurological mechanisms, such as those for attachment and empathy, are believed to exert an influence toward the development of prosocial behavior and values (Eisenberg et al., 2006; Laursen & Hartup, 2002). Humans are social creatures, programmed to help each other – at least within their circle of kith and kin. However, there are other basic dispositions that can compete with prosocial behavior, such as emotional systems that serve self-preservation. It is argued that extending prosocial behavior beyond one's immediate family and community may necessitate overriding one's basic evolutionary dispositions toward in-group favoritism (Templeton & Eccles, 2008).

The task of positive value development involves nurturing prosocial dispositions while balancing needs of the self in accordance with cultural codes. To become a contributing member of society requires the work of training oneself *when* to feel anger, contempt, pity, and benevolence – and when to suppress inappropriate expressions of these feelings. This is hardly a new insight: 2500 years ago, Confucius described moral development as involving a process of refining moral emotions and sensibilities. David Hume said similar things from a Western cultural perspective. In a multicultural world this may involve cultivating hybrid moral sensibilities that incorporate multiple value traditions.

This difficult value work is not easily done alone. Youniss (2009) argues that it is more likely to happen within the context of institutions and through interpersonal interaction. Youth programs are institutions that generally see value development as one of their goals; and they see peer interactions as a mechanism for cultivating it.

Organized Youth Programs as a Peer Arena for Value Development

The young women in SisterHood,[2] a consciousness raising program, were struggling with the challenges of fitting into a world of diverse values. SisterHood is in a Chicago neighborhood that has been an entry point for generations of immigrant groups. About half the young women's families were from West African nations and they experienced challenges reconciling their parents' values with values they experienced in other parts of their lives. One youth, Bernita, said her Nigerian mother kept telling her, "You're not an American girl. You remember that. You don't act like an American girl." The other youth were African American, and they also faced intergenerational tensions. The mother of one expected her to adhere to strict Mormon values. Some SisterHood youth acceded to parents' values; some resisted. Many were attracted to materialistic or street values; some were experimenting with sexuality. All experienced the challenges of growing up as a black woman in America.

We use Sisterhood to provide a close-up view of one ethnically diverse peer group's processes in addressing the challenges of value development. It is, of course, only one group of youth within one program; and these youth were coming of age within a particular cultural context: an individualistic society that places a high emphasis on individual agency (Markus & Kitayama, 2003). However, it is illustrative of other American programs we have studied and we will give central attention to issues of cultural context in our final section.

Youth Programs and Value Development

As is true of many organized programs, value development was part of Sisterhood's mission. In the United States, most youth programs identify prosocial value development as one of their goals (Roth & Brooks-Gunn, 2003). This mission of encouraging positive value development appears to be present in programs across nations, although differences occur in programs' philosophies for achieving it and the cultural code of values that programs aim to cultivate (e.g., Alvarez, 1994; Haedicke & Nelhaus, 2001; Patel, 2007).

Research confirms that youth programs, indeed, can positively impact values. Longitudinal and experimental studies in the United States show significant effects of programs on prosocial behavior (Durlak, Weissberg, & Pachan, 2010; Mahoney, Vandell, Simpkins, & Zarrett, 2009). In two surveys, American teens reported substantially *higher* rates of experiences that promote prosocial value development in organized programs than in school classes. These experiences included learning to help others, stand up for what is right, compromise, and appreciate people from different ethnic backgrounds (Hansen, Larson, & Dworkin, 2003; Larson, Hansen, & Moneta, 2006). Although less complete, survey and qualitative data from other countries provides evidence of similar effects of programs on prosocial values (Alvarez, 1994; Johnson, Johnson-Pynn, & Pynn, 2007).

In our longitudinal qualitative study of SisterHood and 10 other high quality arts, technology, and leadership programs, we observed these changes over time.[3] First, across programs, many youth described a shift in their value orientation from "I" toward "we." They reported becoming less self-focused, learning to give more attention to other people's needs and the common good. Jackie, a 14-year-old, reported that a year before joining SisterHood she had been engaged in antisocial activities: "getting into fights and getting into gangs … I really didn't care about people. I had no remorse." However, she said that SisterHood, "surely did help me, because ... this year, I think about people's feelings more, and how I would feel if that was me." Her fighting had diminished and she was no longer involved in gangs. This value shift from I toward we has been found in other research on youth programs as one from "atomism to collective agency" (Kirshner, 2009) and "island to archipelago" (Deutsch, 2007).

Second, many youth in our programs reported learning to better understand and appreciate the value codes of others. They described learning to examine assumptions of different value systems, sort out moral arguments, and develop moral sensibilities that took this diversity into account. For example, a young woman at Youth Action explained, "Now I see different races and I try to talk to them and try to be as friendly as I [would] be to my own race" (Watkins et al., 2007). A number of youth also said the programs broadened their sense of responsibility to the wider society – they developed civic and social justice values (Dawes & Larson, 2011). Latisha at SisterHood said: "Being in that program makes you want to better yourself and the community around you." They widened their circle of empathic and moral concern (cf. Templeton & Eccles, 2008).

Conditions for Value Development

How do these value changes occur? Before describing the change processes, it is important to discuss what is known about the contextual preconditions for these processes. Research (mostly in the United States) indicates that positive development is most likely in settings that have specific features. These include supportive relationships and positive social norms; they also include youth feeling safe, feeling they belong, and having an active role in what happens in the setting (Durlak et al., 2010; Eccles & Gootman, 2002).

A more focused body of research shows specific features associated with reduction in prejudice toward and acceptance of outsiders (i.e., expanded moral inclusivity). Consistent findings across nations indicate that this value change is most likely when youth interact with members of diverse groups under conditions of equality, cooperation, and common purpose; also when adults in the setting support this change (Pettigrew, 1998).

SisterHood as a Setting for Youth Development

The adult leaders of SisterHood, Lynn and Janet, wanted to create similar conditions for facilitating youth's development of prosocial values. They also were acutely aware of the challenges these young women faced in a value-heterogeneous and sometimes hostile society. Therefore, they placed a high priority on helping members become independent critical thinkers who were prepared to act on their beliefs. To achieve this goal, they felt that the conditions within the group and the process of value development had to come at least partly from the youth.

To this end, at the start of the year, Lynn and Janet asked one of the returning members to lead a discussion to set the rules the youth wanted to follow. Youth started with humorous suggestions: "no fighting; no biting." Then they came up with a good American list: listening without interrupting, being nonjudgmental, offering experience not advice, sharing decision making, upholding honesty and confidentiality. The youth and leaders reminded each other of these rules over subsequent sessions, sometimes challenging members who violated them. Over time, these rules became internalized as group norms. They became part of a *group culture* that created conditions of equality, cooperation, and common purpose (see also Larson, 2007).

Research on group dynamics indicates that a crucial step in formation of a well-functioning group is development of mutual trust (Wheelan, Davidson, & Tilin, 2003). At SisterHood these rules – this internalized culture – became the foundation for this trust. Mutual trust in groups creates a feeling of interpersonal safety, which allows people to take risks and break out of their egocentric shell (Hollingshead et al., 2005). Midway through the year, Chantel reported: "We're like this big group of goofy people that like to be around each other. We give each other space and we respect each other's ideas." K'sea said of her peers, "like they understand you and you understand them." We found that a similar shared culture and mutual trust developed, in differing degrees, across other programs we studied.

Research on group dynamics identifies another feature of groups that may facilitate the difficult work of developing values and learning to apply them to complex contexts. They can provide beneficial conditions for collaborative information processing (Hinsz, Tindale, & Vollrath, 1997). When there is mutual trust, working groups develop collective memory. They become better at retrieving past information than when individuals are alone. Such groups are also more reliable and consistent than individuals in how they process information. As a result, they are often found to be better at formulating solutions to problems. Knowledge, thinking, and critical judgment are pooled.

In the programs we studied, youth pooled not only their memories but their newly developing metacognitive skills. They used these skills to work together on the difficult tasks of value development in a complicated world.

Constructive Processes of Value Work

Each weekly two-hour session at SisterHood was focused on a challenging topic: reproductive rights, discrimination, fathers, lying, anger, and dealing with stress, among others. Our observer described how youth freely shared intimate experiences and feelings. They also expressed sharp differences, for example, on gay-lesbian relationships, sex for pleasure, and the demeaning stereotypes that the African Americans held of Africans. Youth sometimes stood up, gesticulating to express their views. Yet these conversations readily shifted from serious discussion to humor, and then back again. Youth described their processes of value development within this give and take.

We chose SisterHood as a central illustration because it was (with one exception that we mention later, Faith in Motion) the program in which youth's work was most directly focused on values. However, we saw similar value development in the other programs as youth worked on arts and leadership projects, and we will include some examples. We will also introduce observations from Erica Halverson's (2009) analysis of a set of theater programs in which the youth were engaged in constructive value work.

Across these programs we identified three interrelated processes through which youth described prosocial value change: opening themselves up, collective analysis, and enactment.

Opening Themselves Up: Constructing the Moral Realities of Others

The process of "opening up" enables adolescents to discover new moral realities beyond their own. At SisterHood, this occurred through an active process of listening, understanding, and coming to empathize with the personal experiences of others. Chantel, an African American, described how her moral perspective was changed by taking in the African youth's family stories. She made it sound clandestine: "You don't know what people do behind closed doors. You can only find that out if they are willing to tell you. So discussing all of that kind of opens you up." She reported opening herself up to people from different cultures and nationalities: "to everybody else that you're not used to being around." Across programs, youth described how hearing and discussing other's experiences in a safe and trusting context allowed them to overcome stereotypes and discover the humanity of others. Straight youth described coming to understand the subjective worlds of GLBT youth, farm kids to the experiences of "punks," and youth from different religions and social classes to those of each other (Larson et al., 2004; Watkins et al., 2007). Through listening and actively piecing together the narrative strands of others' lives, these individuals and their experiences became vivid, authentic, and morally significant.

This discovery process, we believe, was aided by the youth's new meta-cognitive skills, including those for perspective taking and biographical reasoning. Opening oneself up is a constructive process. These new potentials enable teens to perform abstract mental operations to understand how others' lives shape who they are now (Habermas, 2011). Chantel described coming to understand how past experiences shaped what the African youth thought and felt. Youth used their new skills for biographical reasoning to understand how formative experiences, parents, and culture influence each other's moral beliefs and actions. These metacognitive skills helped them expand their circle of moral inclusivity.

However, this was not just a dry cognitive process. It often involved emotion, including empathizing with others' experiences of pain and hardship. Baumeister, Vohs, DeWall, and Zhang (2007) describe how emotions can serve an important developmental function by directing attention to the causes of the emotion and then stimulating analyses that influence future emotion and behavior. Chernise recounted exactly this process at SisterHood. The interviewer asked her to explain what accounted for the greater sense of civic responsibility she developed in the program. Chernise then described their experience watching videos in which people had been treated unfairly – in one case, news footage from an incident in which white vigilantes dragged an African American man to death behind a pickup truck. These experiences she said, "make us upset; we cry and we cry as a group." The group then discussed the roots of what they felt; in this case, the pernicious prejudice against people of African descent in the United States. Chernise said these emotions and the subsequent discussions made her want to speak up in the future when she witnessed acts of racism. She was developing moral emotional sensibilities.

Youth often drew on their own experiences as a tool for these empathic processes. Anthropologist Ronato Rosaldo (1989) describes how empathy with someone from a different culture is catalyzed by discovery of comparable emotional experiences. Donato at Youth Action reported this empathetic breakthrough in listening and talking with GLBT youth. He discovered how similar their experiences of prejudice were to his as a Mexican American. This discovery, he said, made him stop making gay jokes and start challenging peers who did. Other youth described these breakthroughs in hearing about the humiliation, anger, absurdity, and joys people experienced in different life situations (Watkins et al., 2007). They discovered that these "others" are not just objective abstractions; they are living, breathing, feeling human beings. Their values and actions had been wrought by powerful experiences, deserving of moral respect.

Collective Analysis
The process of active opening up included more than individual epiphanies. It involved deliberative processes of collective analysis. Youth discussed each other's stories, asked questions, compared, challenged, and critiqued the basis for different value positions. Chernise summarized the deliberative process the group used at SisterHood to discuss powerful issues like the video in which the man was dragged to death:

We just speak on it and try to come up with different solutions … We talk about it and ask questions like, "Why does this happen?" … We just go around the group, one by one and we say our different opinions and then like, if we want, to further someone else's opinion to our opinion, or ask questions why we feel this way.

Youth drew conclusions by evaluating and building on the pool of information and arguments offered by the group. In interviews, they attributed their value changes to comparing value positions, defending their opinions, "talking it out," and combining their different perspectives.

A frequent topic of youth's collective deliberations at SisterHood was their parents and their parents' traditional values. K'sea, whose parents came from Ghana, said of her father: "I kind of see him as an individual who is stuck on traditions and the whole Ghana tradition and a lot of stuff like that. But other people telling me about their experiences with their fathers made me appreciate what he does."

By comparing her experiences with others' (including joking about their parents' strange ways), K'sea said she came to have a more accepting understanding of her father and his firmly held values. Similarly, in her first interview, Bernita expressed dissonance because her mother (from Cameroon) "doesn't want anything to do with America." Later, however, she described coming to understand and become more accepting of her mother's values and worldview, partly because she was able to hear insider reports on American parents. She explained: "People got to see how my mom was, and I got to see how – to compare." Just as youth came to see diverse peers as moral entities, they came to see parents through deliberative analysis. They opened their value frameworks to encompass wider perspectives.

Again we suggest that the new cognitive skills of adolescence are at work. These youth appeared to be using their new skills to examine the assumptions behind value positions, analyze the parents' value systems, and modify their own value constructions to be more inclusive.

Perhaps the most challenging value work is dealing with people's negative views of one's own group (Phinney & Kohatsu, 1997). We have already discussed how youth at SisterHood talked through their reactions to a horrifying video of an African American being dragged to death. In research on youth theater programs, Halverson (2009) describes a more structured deliberative process of value work through which youth from marginalized groups addressed these issues. This process began with each youth bringing in an autobiographical or other story related to a focal topic youth had selected. Focal topics included immigration, racial discrimination, and being gay in America. The youth then identified and analyzed the underlying elements of episodes that cut across their separate stories, including both positive experiences (the strengths of immigrant families) and negative experiences (episodes that typify prejudices or how their group is perceived by the majority of society). In the next step, the youth selected, reshaped, and fused these stories into a collective script that, for example, addressed the challenges faced by immigrant Mexican youth in the United States. These scripts often contained *counter-narratives* in which patterns of prejudice were exposed and that positioned the youth as moral agents. This deliberative process, Halverson reports, allows youth to critique different value positions, including negative representations of themselves. It also allows them to recast these representations in the final script in ways that articulate values. As in the programs we studied, emotions contributed to this deliberative process, and were shaped by it.

These collective analyses had some resemblance to the collective peer processes that Piaget described. However, in addition to logic, youth were employing cultural reasoning that considered value positions in relationship to multiple moral codes. Often youth's analyses led them to syntheses of parents' and others' values. Youth were constructing hybrid moral sensibilities.

Enactment

The first two peer processes in the youth's value work involved thinking and feeling. The third process entailed enactment of values in a social arena. This is an important step. To be meaningful, values have to survive the test of being operationalized in real-life contexts. Indeed, research shows that values are as likely to *follow from actions* as they are to produce actions (Allen & Antonishak, 2008). Our data suggested the two worked together: that youth refined values through practice.

One way youth did this was through addressing real-world dilemmas. Members of SisterHood confronted one of these dilemmas when several members had not sold the group's agreed-upon quota of candy for their fundraiser. This was hard because it was a breach of trust within the group. (In one case, a girl sold her quota but her parents had found the money and used it to buy food.) After much deliberation, they decided they had to be firm and stick to their initial decision to exclude people from their final retreat if they had not done their part. Cassandra said they had learned how important it is to talk directly to the people involved, rather than ignoring the problem or using it as an excuse to not do their own part. Real-life situations like this required youth to learn the pragmatics of applying values to complex contexts.

Youth also reported value development from sticking up for their values and beliefs. Jade at SisterHood described the youth's interactions in the program "as a test for the real world." It was a chance to practice and learn how to deal with people of different races and religions. Quite a number of youth in the activism programs we studied described learning to "speak up" for their values; for example, learning to stand up against bigotry with peers (Watkins et al., 2007) or to lobby public officials for a cause they believed in (Larson & Angus, 2011). This process of standing up for values was also important in the theater and film programs described by Halverson (2009). By enacting stories that identified injustices and expressed their values, youth were articulating their beliefs to an audience.

Enactment moves one from possessing abstract values to taking stances as a moral actor. Youth learned to express and manage their values in the face of disagreement and stigmatization.

Co-constructing Values in a Heterogeneous World

Peers, we have argued, can provide a powerful crucible for youth's work of constructing positive values in a world of diverse value systems. When conditions are right, peers can work effectively together to sort through arguments, emotions, moral priorities, and prejudices – and develop prosocial values applied to the complex situations of daily life.

In this final section, we first review the peer-driven processes that we described and ask how they might be similar or different across cultural contexts that have different norms for peer behavior. Second, we consider the role of institutions, such as youth programs, in facilitating peer value work: how might the processes and their outcomes vary as a function of different institutional philosophies and staff practices?

The Power of Peers and How It Might Vary across Cultures

Researchers examining how peers contribute to adolescent value change have typically looked for simple mechanisms – imitation, conformity, modeling – *unidirectional* influences from peers to youth.[4] Yet peer influence, Brown, Bakken, Ameringer, and Mahon (2008) argue, almost always entails transactional processes; multiple processes often operate simultaneously.

Our analyses – based primarily on American programs – suggest how peer groups can employ such transactional processes for constructive value development. Youth mobilize their new capacities for perspective taking to expand their understanding of and empathy for people different from themselves. They draw on their new metacognitive skills to compare, contrast, and challenge. They try out values on each other. Over time, we suggest, these iterative transactions build "constructive webs" of integrated and operative values adapted to the situations of their lives.

These co-creative peer processes, we argue, are especially suited to the challenges of coming of age in a heterogeneous world. Decades of research has shown that the work done by effective small groups entail broadband, eclectic processes (Magen & Mangiardi, 2005). In our view, this eclecticism is exactly what makes them valuable in a complex world. Peer processing helped youth to do *cross-paradigm work*. In our examples, youth listened to and opened themselves up to emotionally charged stories from unfamiliar frameworks. They allowed each other to hold and express different value positions. They pooled their collective experiences to analyze the diverse situational, biographical, and cultural contexts of value issues. They worked separately (parallel processing) and together to wrestle with the vexing contradictions of a complex society.

However, how prevalent are these constructive peer processes beyond the limited set of the mostly American contexts we have considered? At a general level, we can point to numerous examples of co-constructive peer value work across the world, including outside adult-structured institutions. One can think of the many virtual peer groups flourishing on social networking sites that, at least in some instances, allow youth to do positive value work (e.g., Tynes, 2007). As we were finishing this article in early 2011, youth in Egypt, Tunisia, Bahrain, and other Middle Eastern countries used social media for collective information-sharing, analysis, and planning to coordinate political protest. Other examples of these co-constructive processes include young people's development of local genres of hip-hop music as vehicles to explore values (Mitchell, 2001) and their development of faith communities that help them navigate between a religious heritage and contemporary life (Freeman, 2009).[5]

It is essential, however, to consider cultural and other factors that might alter, facilitate, or inhibit these constructive peer dynamics. These factors include differences in the normative structure of peer groups (e.g., how equal vs. hierarchical relationships are) and the normative functions of such group – what youth expect to happen in peer interactions. Let us speculate on how these might influence the three constructive processes we identified.

Opening Themselves Up. We first observed a process through which youth actively listened to and opened themselves up to differing moral realities. Might this process be different (or less frequent) in cultures in which norms for peer relationships differ? American peer norms encourage individual initiative, imaginative activities, and self-expression – types of behavior that might be necessary to this process. Yet Chen, Chung, and Hsiao (2009) cite findings suggesting that these three types of behavior are less normative among peers in Latin America, Africa, and East Asia than in North America. They suggest that in China, for example, the cultural emphasis on social harmony, modesty, and self-control discourages individual expression. Such factors might well inhibit the sharing of personal feelings and stories that appeared to be integral to the processes at SisterHood.[6] Chen (2011), however, also finds that the norms for peer relationships in China are changing in ways that reward self-assertion and self-expression, which leads to many provocative questions.

Collective Analysis. We also found that constructive processes at SisterHood and other American programs included comparing, talking out, and analyzing topics (such as the different values of their parents). Research shows that peer norms in East Asian cultures place a high emphasis on prosocial cooperative behavior (Chen et al., 2009). This suggests the hypothesis that, under the right conditions, Asian youth might be *more* capable than American youth of working together on this type of analytic value work.

Enactment. Third, we observed a process in which youth developed values by trying them out with each other and sometimes with people outside the program. Cultural differences in social initiative and self-expression might influence whether and how this process might play out across contexts. Cultures may also differ in the opportunities and encouragement they provide for youth to try out new value positions, especially with adults.

This discussion is highly speculative. Research is needed and we should be prepared to be surprised. There may be *entirely different processes* – as well as outcomes – in different cultural contexts as a product of differing norms for peer interactions, as well as social conditions that influence peer inter- actions (e.g., a history of conflict between ethnic groups). Nevertheless, the potential power of peers as a catalyst of positive value development should not be ignored.

The Role of Institutional Philosophies and Professional Practices

We cannot close without questioning how the peer processes described here were shaped within an institutional context – youth programs. This brings in another level of analysis at which culture matters. Most youth programs have a deliberate mission of influencing young people's values, but they dif- fer widely, between and within nations, in the approaches they use; many see their mission as inculcating a fixed set of cultural values (Alvarez, 1994). It is important to consider how these different approaches are related to value processes and outcomes, including how well they prepare youth for a heterogeneous global world. These are applied questions, but also questions that need the critical eye of theorists and researchers.

The processes of value co-construction that we described at SisterHood and other American programs were embedded within a philosophy of "youth-led" programming (Larson, Walker, & Pearce, 2005). This philos- ophy stresses giving youth agency, choice, and "voice" – both as individu- als and as a group. In a Western context, it is rooted in cultural beliefs (a la Montessori, Dewey, Piaget, etc.) that educators should support young people as the producers of their own development. To be clear, this does not mean that program leaders abdicate authority. Instead, they lead from behind. At Sisterhood, Lynn and Janet helped youth formulate their own rules, which facilitated youth's formation of mutual trust and other critical conditions for constructive work. They also primed youth's value work by showing films and arranging field trips that challenged youth. Lynn and Janet wanted them to experience ownership of the discussions that fol- lowed, so they often stood back. Yet, as described by Bernita, "They take the lead at the right time, like when the group needs that kind of authority to get them going or stay on track or topic." By leading from behind, these and other leaders helped create conditions for – and keep youth engaged in – the processes of active listening, analysis, and enactment.

A youth-led philosophy is not unique to Western cultures or nations. It can be found in youth programs across the world, and is acknowledged by the United Nations (Alvarez, 1994; Lansdown, 2001). One prominent exam- ple is peace education programs, which have a youth-led philosophy cou- pled with a focus on the type of value work we have described (Ardizzone,

2002). These have often been developed locally in response to conflicts between groups (e.g., in Israel/Palestine, Latin America, Sierre Leone, and South Africa), with the goal of cultivating mutual understanding among youth. Like at SisterHood, the adult advisors of these programs support honest and open communication between youth. Youth work together to share personal experiences, raise difficult value issues (e.g., injustice and oppression), and analyze assumptions and fears (Norman, 2009).

However, a youth-led program philosophy is hardly universal. Many programs across nations are adult-structured and adult-led (Alvarez, 1994). We are aware of no global survey of youth programs, but it is likely that this philosophy is more frequent in cultural contexts where the norms for youth–educator relationships emphasize interpersonal hierarchy and respect for elders (Saraswathi, Mistry, & Dutta, 2011; Serpell & Hatano, 1997). Different processes of peer value work can be expected under this philosophy.

Within our study of American programs, there was one program, "Faith in Motion," that provides an illustration of the peer processes under a more adult-led approach. The leaders were deliberate in inculcating prosocial, evangelical Christian values. They often led activities from the front of the room, and peer dynamics among the mixed-race youth were directed in ways that reinforced adult-prescribed values, religious submission, and collective harmony. For example, rather than encouraging youth to analyze racial prejudice, they told youth that they were "all equal under God" and that the ethnic/racial differences between them did not matter. Activities were structured to encourage cooperation among all, and from our vantage point, appeared to be quite successful in cultivating positive peer interactions and prosocial values.

Yet adult-led philosophies are typically justified as providing youth a secure grounding in an existing value system. It is important to ask whether (and how) this approach can be formulated to help young people learn to adapt on their own as they encounter new and diverse value systems. We argue that peer processes that are youth-led (while being adult-guided) may be better suited to the cross-paradigm value work required to understand, critique, and develop moral sensibilities for this diversity.

The options, of course, are never so simple as one approach versus another. There are many permutations to program philosophy, and many possible adaptations to differing cultural contexts, groups of youth, and goals. Johnson et al. (2007) describe a rapidly growing environmental youth activism program in China that combines traditional Chinese Buddhist and Taoist notions of oneness and selflessness, with an emphasis on social justice and an operational philosophy that is more democratic and youth-led than the traditional Chinese leadership style. Of course, programs may also differ in the importance they give to different value priorities (e.g., to self, community, and deity).

Further inquiry is needed on how these and other variations in institutional approaches shape peer processes of value development. Piaget's optimism that peer interactions inevitably lead to the development of prosocial values is unwarranted. There is strong consistent evidence that, even within organized programs, certain groups of adolescent peers teach each other antisocial rather than prosocial behavior (Dodge et al., 2006; Stattin, Kerr, Mahoney, Persson, & Magnusson, 2005). Evidence also suggests that well-meaning programs aimed at bridging large divides between youth from hostile groups (such as between Israeli and Palestinian youth) can fail to do so (Hammack, 2006). Research can help identify practices that are effective in facilitating constructive peer value work with different groups of youth and under a range of different program and cultural conditions. There is a wide world of variations in positive peer developmental processes to be explored.

Acknowledgments

We would like to give special thanks to the youth and program staff who shared their experiences with us, especially those in SisterHood. We are also indebted to Kevin Thomas, Andrew Tonachel, and many others. Finally, we thank the William T. Grant Foundation for their generous funding of this research.

NOTES

1. We recognize that the meaning of terms like positive, prosocial, and even development can vary across (and even within) cultures (Jensen, 2011), but we hope our text adequately reflects this possibility without our taking pains to make it a major focus.
2. All names of programs, youth, and leaders are pseudonyms.
3. In each of the 11 programs, we followed a sample of 8–12 youth (total 108) over two to nine months of program activity (a total of 712 interviews). We also conducted site observations and interviews with program leaders. The majority of the programs were urban. Two-thirds of the youth were from non-European ethnic groups, and approximately a quarter were from immigrant families (see Larson & Angus, 2011).
4. This search for simple causes, Brown et al. (2008) suggest, is because the statistical techniques available to quantitative researchers constrain them from testing more complex bilateral relationships.
5. These illustrations, of course, do not address the unanswered question of how frequent different co-constructive processes are across nations or in peer interactions within or outside of adult-structured institutions.

6. It is also worth noting that the peer group has a less prominent place in the lives of Asian than North American youth. Less time is spent with peers (Larson & Verma, 1999) and they are found to be less dependent on peers for self-validation (Chen et al., 2009). Thus, they may be less motivated to turn to peers for value work.

REFERENCES

Allen, K., & Antonishak, J. (2008). Adolescent peer influence: Beyond the dark side. In M. J. Prinstein & K. A. Dodge (Eds.), *Understanding peer influence in children and adolescents* (pp. 141–160). New York: Guilford.

Alvarez, B. (1994). Assessing youth programs: An international perspective. *Comparative Education Review*, **38**, 253–266.

Ardizzone, L. (2002). Towards global understanding: The transformative role of peace education. *Current Issues in Comparative Education*, **4**, 16–25.

Baumeister, R., Vohs, J., DeWall, C., & Zhang, L. (2007). How emotion shapes behavior: Feedback, anticipation, and reflection, rather than direct causation. *Personality and Social Psychology Review*, **11**, 167–203.

Berry, J. (1997). Immigration, acculturation, and adaptation. *International Journal of Applied Psychology*, **46**, 5–34.

Brown, B. B. (2004). Adolescents' relationships with peers. In R. M. Lerner & L. Steinberg (Eds.), *Handbook of adolescent psychology* (2nd ed.) (pp. 363–394). Hoboken, NJ: Wiley.

Brown, B. B., Bakken, J., Ameringer, S., & Mahon, S. (2008). A comprehensive conceptualization of the peer influence process in adolescence. In M. J. Prinstein & K. A. Dodge (Eds.), *Understanding peer influence in children and adolescents* (pp. 17–44). New York: Guilford.

Chandler, M. J., Lalonde, C. E., Sokol, B. W., & Hallett, D. (2003). Personal persistence, identity development, and suicide. In W. F. Overton (Ed.), *Monographs of the Society for Research in Child Development*, Serial no. 273, **68** (2).

Chao, R. K., & Otsuki-Clutter, M. (2011). Racial and ethnic differences: Sociocultural and contextual explanations. *Journal of Research on Adolescence*, **21**, 47–60.

Chen, X. (2011). Culture, peer relationships, and human development. In L. A. Jensen (Ed.), *Bridging cultural and developmental approaches to psychology: New syntheses in theory, research, and policy* (pp. 92–112). Oxford: Oxford University Press.

Chen, X., Chung, J., & Hsiao, C. (2009). Peer interactions and relationships from a cross-cultural perspective. In K. H. Rubin, W. Bukowski, & B. Laursen (Eds.), *Handbook of peer interactions, relationships, and groups* (pp. 432–451). New York: Guilford.

Dawes, N. P., & Larson, R. W. (2011). How youth get engaged: Grounded-theory research on motivational development in organized youth programs. *Developmental Psychology*, **47**(1), 259–269.

Deutsch, N. (2007). From island to archipelago: Narratives of relatedness in an urban youth organization. In R. Josselson, A. Lieblich, & D. P. McAdams (Eds.), *The meeting of others: Narrative studies of relationships*. Washington, DC: American Psychological Association.

Dodge, K., Dishion, T., & Landsford, J. (Eds.). (2006). *Deviant peer influences in programs for youth: Problems and solutions*. New York: Guilford.

Durlak, J. A., Weissberg, R. P., & Pachan, M. (2010). A meta-analysis of after-school pro-grams that seek to promote personal and social skills in children and adolescents. *American Journal of Community Psychology, 45*, 294–309.

Eccles, J. S., & Gootman, J. A. (Eds.). (2002). *Community programs to promote youth development: Committee on community-level programs for youth.* Washington, DC: National Academy Press.

Eisenberg, N., Fabes, R., & Spinrad, T. (2006). Prosocial development. In W. Damon & R. M. Lerner (Eds.), *Handbook of child psychology* (6th ed.) (Vol. 3, pp. 646–718). Hoboken, NJ: Wiley & Sons.

Fischer, K. W., & Bidell, T. R. (2006). Dynamic development of action and thought. In W. Damon & R. M. Lerner (Eds.), *Handbook of child psychology* (6th ed.) (Vol. 3, pp. 313–399). Hoboken, NJ: Wiley.

Freeman, S. G. (2009, August 22). Young Sikhs find a way to express faith with a mix of tradition and modernity. *New York Times*, A15.

Frey, L., & Sunwolf (2005). The symbolic-interpretive perspective of group life. In M. S. Poole & A. B. Hollingshead (Eds.), *Theories of small groups: Interdisciplinary perspectives* (pp. 185–239). Thousand Oaks, CA: Sage.

Friedman, T. L. (2000). *The Lexus and the olive tree: Understanding globalization.* New York : Anchor.

Gaertner, S. L., & Dovidio, J. F. (2000). *Reducing intergroup bias: The common ingroup identity model.* Philadelphia: Psychology Press.

Giddens, A. (2000). *The consequences of modernity.* Cambridge, UK: Polity Press.

Gilmore, D. D. (1990). *Manhood in the making: Cultural concepts of masculinity.* New Haven, CT: Yale University Press.

Gonzales, N. A., & Cauce, A. M. (1995). Ethnic identity and multicultural competence: Dilemmas and challenges for minority youth. In W. Hawley & A. Jackson (Eds.), *Toward a common destiny: Improving race and ethnic relations in America* (pp. 131–162). San Francisco, CA: Jossey-Bass.

Habermas, T. (Ed.). (2011). The development of autobiographical reasoning in adolescence and beyond. *New Directions for Child and Adolescent Development, 131*, 1–17.

Haedicke, S., & Nellhaus, T. (Eds.). (2001). *Performing democracy: International perspectives on urban community-based performance.* Ann Arbor: The University of Michigan Press.

Halverson, E. (2009). Artistic production processes as venues for positive youth development. *Revista Interuniversitaria de Formacion del Profesorado (Interuniversity Journal of Teacher Education), 23*(3), 181–202.

Hammack, P. L. (2006). Identity, conflict and coexistence: Life stories of Israeli and Palestinian adolescents. *Journal of Adolescent Research, 21*, 323–369.

Hansen, D., Larson, R., & Dworkin, J. (2003).What adolescents learn in organized youth activities: A survey of self-reported developmental experiences. *Journal of Research on Adolescence, 13*, 25–56.

Hinsz, V., Tindale, R., & Vollrath, D. (1997). The emerging conceptualization of groups as information processors. *Psychological Bulletin, 121*, 43–64.

Hollingshead, A. B., Wittenbaum, G., Paulus, P., Hirokawa, R., Ancona, D., Peterson, R., … Yoon, K. (2005). A look at groups from the functional perspective. In M. S. Poole & A. B. Hollingshead (Eds.), *Theories of small groups: Interdisciplinary perspectives* (pp. 21–62). Thousand Oaks, CA: Sage.

Hosang, D. (2008). Beyond policy: Ideology, race and the reimagining of youth. In S. Pedro, J. Ginwright, & N. Cammarota (Eds.), *Beyond resistance! Youth activism and community change: New democratic possibilities for practice and policy for America's youth* (pp. 3–20). London: Routledge.

Huntington, S. P. (2004). *Who are we? The challenges to America's national identity.* New York: Simon & Schuster.

Jensen, L. A. (2008). Through two lenses: A cultural-developmental approach to moral psychology. *Developmental Review, 28*, 289–315.

(2011). The cultural-developmental theory of moral psychology: A new synthesis. In L. A. Jensen (Ed.), *Bridging cultural and developmental psychology: New syntheses in theory, research and policy* (pp. 3–25). New York: Oxford University Press.

Jensen, L. A., Arnett, J. J., & McKenzie, J. (2011). Globalization and cultural identity developments in adolescence and emerging adulthood. In S. J. Schwartz, K. Luyckx, & V. L. Vignoles (Eds.), *Handbook of identity theory and research* (pp. 285–301). New York: Springer Publishing Company.

Johnson, L. R., Johnson-Pynn, J. S., & Pynn, T. M. (2007). Youth civic engagement in China: Results from a program promoting environmental activism. *Journal of Adolescent Research, 22*, 355–386.

Killen, M., Lee-Kim, J., McGlothlin, H., & Stangor, C. (2002). How children and adolescents evaluate gender and racial exclusion. *Monographs of the Society for Research in Child Development, 67*, 120–129.

Kirshner, B. (2009). "Power in numbers": Youth organizing as a context for exploring civic identity. *Journal of Research on Adolescence, 19*, 414–440.

Kuhn, D. (2009). Adolescent thinking. In R. M. Lerner & L. Steinberg (Eds.), *Handbook of adolescent psychology* (3rd ed.) (Vol. 1, pp. 152–186). Hoboken, NJ: Wiley.

Lansdown, G. (2001). *Promoting children's participation in democratic decision-making.* Florence, Italy: Innocenti Research Center, UNICEF.

Larson, R. W. (2000). Toward a psychology of positive youth development. *American Psychologist, 55*, 170–183.

(2007). From "I" to "We": Development of the capacity for teamwork in youth programs. In R. Silbereisen & R. Lerner (Eds.), *Approaches to positive youth development* (pp. 277–292). Thousand Oaks, CA: Sage.

Larson, R. W. (2011), Positive development in a disorderly world. *Journal of Research on Adolescence, 21*, 317–334.

Larson, R. W., & Angus, R. M. (2011). Adolescents' development of skills for agency in youth programs: Learning to think strategically. *Child Development, 82*, 277–294.

Larson, R., Hansen, D., & Moneta, G. (2006). Differing profiles of developmental experiences across types of organized youth activities. *Developmental Psychology, 42* (5), 849–863.

Larson, R., Jarrett, R., Hansen, D., Pearce, N., Sullivan, P., Walker, K. … Wood, D. (2004). Organized youth activities as contexts of positive development. In P. Linley & S. Joseph (Eds.), *Positive psychology in practice* (pp. 540–560). New York: Wiley.

Larson, R. W., & Verma, S. (1999). How children and adolescents around the world spend time: Work, play, and developmental opportunities. *Psychological Bulletin, 125*, 701–736.

Larson, R. W., Walker, K., & Pearce, N. (2005). Youth-driven and adult-driven youth development programs: Contrasting models of youth-adult relationships. *Journal of Community Psychology, 33*, 57–74.

Laursen, B., & Hartup, W. H. (2002). The origins of reciprocity and social exchange in friendships. *New Directions in child and adolescent development: Social exchange in development*, **95**, 27–40.

Magen, R. H., & Mangiardi, E. (2005). Groups and individual change. In S. Wheelan (Ed.), *Handbook of group research and practice* (pp. 351–361). Thousand Oaks, CA: Sage.

Mahoney, J. L., Vandell, D. L., Simpkins, S., & Zarrett, N. (2009). Adolescent out-of-school activities. In R. M. Lerner & L. Steinberg (Eds.), *Handbook of adolescent psychology* (3rd ed.) (Vol. 2, pp. 228–267). Hoboken, NJ: Wiley.

Markus, H. R., & Kitayama, S. (2003). Models of agency: Sociocultural diversity in the construction of action. *Nebraska Symposium on Motivation*, **49**, 1–57.

Mitchell, T. (Ed.). (2001). *Global noise: Rap and hip-hop outside the USA*. Middletown, CT: Wesleyan University Press.

Newman, B., & Newman, P. (2001). Group identity and alienation: Giving the we it's due. *Journal of Youth and Adolescence*, **30**, 515–538.

Norman, J. M. (2009). Creative activism: Youth media in Palestine. *Middle East Journal of Culture and Communication*, **2**, 252–274.

Patel, E. (2007). *Acts of faith: The story of an American Muslim, the struggle for the soul of a generation*. Boston: Beacon Press.

Pettigrew, T. (1998). Intergroup contact theory. *American Review of Psychology*, **49**, 65–85.

Phinney, J. S., & Kohatsu, E. L. (1997). Ethnic and racial identity development and mental health. In J. Schulenberg, J. Moggs, & K. Hurrelman (Eds.), *Health risks and developmental transitions in adolescence* (pp. 420–443). New York: Cambridge University Press.

Piaget, J. (1965). *The moral judgment of the child* (T. A. Brown & C. E. Kaegi, Trans.) Palo Alto, CA: Annual Reviews.

Quintana, S. M. (1998). Children's developmental understanding of ethnicity and race. *Applied and Preventive Psychology*, **7**, 27–45.

Rogoff, B. (1998). Cognition as a collaborative process. In W. Damon, D. Kuhn, & R. Siegler (Eds.), *Handbook of child psychology* (5th ed.) (Vol. 2, pp. 679–744). New York: Wiley.

Rosaldo, R. (1989). *Culture and truth: The remaking of social analysis*. Boston: Beacon Press.

Roth, J., & Brooks-Gunn, J. (2003). Youth development programs: Risk, prevention and policy. *Journal of Adolescent Health*, **32**, 170–182.

Saraswathi, T. S., Mistry, J., & Dutta, R. (2011). Reconceptualizing lifespan development through a Hindu perspective. In L. A. Jensen (Ed.), *Bridging cultural and developmental approaches to psychology: New syntheses in theory, research, and policy* (pp. 276–302). Oxford: Oxford University Press.

Schlegal, A. (2011). Adolescent ties to adult communities: The intersection of culture and development. In L. A. Jensen (Ed.), *Bridging cultural and developmental approaches to psychology: New syntheses in theory, research, and policy* (pp. 138–160). Oxford: Oxford University Press.

Selman, R. L. (2003). *The promotion of social awareness: Powerful lessons from the partnership of developmental theory and classroom practice*. New York: Russell Sage Foundation.

Serpell, R., & Hatano, G. (1997). Education, schooling, and literacy. In J. W. Berry, P. R. Dasen, & T. S. Saraswathi (Eds.), *Handbook of cross-cultural psychology: Basic processes and human development* (2nd ed.) (pp. 339–376). Boston: Allyn & Bacon.

Stattin, H., Kerr, M., Mahoney, J., Persson, A., & Magnusson, D. (2005). Explaining why a leisure context is bad for some girls and not for others. In J. Mahoney, R. Larson, & J. Eccles (Eds.), *Organized activities as contexts of development* (pp. 211–234). Mahwah, NJ: Lawrence Erlbaum Associates.

Templeton, J., & Eccles, J. (2008). Spirituality, "Expanding circle morality," and positive youth development. In R. M. Lerner, R. W. Roeser, & E. Phelps (Eds.), *Positive youth development and spirituality: From theory to research* (pp. 197–209). West Conshohocken, PA: Templeton Foundation Press.

Tienda, M., & Wilson, W. (2002). *Youth in cities: A cross-national perspective.* Cambridge: Cambridge University Press.

Tynes, B. (2007). Internet safety gone wild? Sacrificing the educational and psychosocial benefits of online social environments. *Journal of Adolescent Research, 22,* 575–584.

Watkins, N., Larson, R., & Sullivan, P. (2007). Learning to bridge difference: Community youth programs as contexts for developing multicultural competencies. *American Behavioral Scientist, 51,* 380–402.

Wheelan, S. A., Davidson, B., & Tilin, F. (2003). Group development across time: Reality or illusion? *Small Group Research, 34,* 223–245.

Youniss, J. (2009). When morality meets politics in development. *Journal of Moral Education, 38,* 129–144.

8 Civic Development in Relational Perspective

Kenneth H. Rubin, Tina Malti, and Kristina McDonald

Abstract

Civic competence has been posited as an important outcome of productive adolescent development. This chapter introduces a relational model of civic competence, including factors that may lead some individuals onto pathways to the development of civically competent behavior. More specifically, the model describes the significance of relationship quality with parents, peers, and friends as well as socially competent (or incompetent) behaviors in the development of civic competence. The model suggests social relationships as a significant antecedent to civic competence and as a buffer for risks associated with disengagement. Because this model focuses on relationship quality, it is evident that it is embedded in cultural practices and values. Inevitably, the role of relationships and social competence on civic competence outcomes also varies as a function of who the child, the parents, and the friends are. Finally, we propose that adolescents' positive experiences with friends and parents may encourage the development of civic competence even for individuals who were initially aggressive or anxiously withdrawn as children.

Civic competence, reflecting the acquisition of cognitions and behaviors that allow citizens to discuss and collaborate to promote interests within a framework of democratic principles (Youniss et al., 2002), has been posited as a significant outcome of productive adolescent development. In an increasingly diversified world, the acquisition of social responsibility, tolerance, and civic engagement represents a significant step in the securing of social integration and democratic values (Larson, Brown, & Mortimer, 2002). Part of the "decentering process" during the transition from adolescence to young adulthood is learning to understand how the self fits into and can make constructive contributions to the community-at-large (Schulenberg, Sameroff, & Ciccchetti, 2004).

The primary purpose of this chapter is to present a conceptual model that describes factors that may lead some individuals onto pathways to the development of civically competent behavior. Surprisingly, there have been few *longitudinal* studies of the relational and developmental precursors of civic competence in emerging adulthood. The extant longitudinal research has focused primarily on the sorts of early activity involvement that may predict subsequent civic engagement (e.g., Gardner, Roth, & Brooks-Gunn, 2008; Hart, Donnelly, Youniss, & Atkins, 2007). Few researchers have focused on the potential significance of interpersonal relationships (e.g., parent–child relationships, friendships, peer acceptance/exclusion/victimization), and both socially skilled (e.g., prosocial behavior, leadership), and unskilled behaviors (e.g., aggression, social withdrawal). In one exception, Obradović and Masten (2007) recently reported that variability in adolescent social competence (as indicated by the extent to which the adolescent seemed to have a positive and active social life, was socially accepted, and had qualitatively rich friendships) predicted civic engagement in early adulthood, above and beyond the effects of earlier activity involvement. However, Obradović and Masten did not compare behavioral and relational indicators of social competence in the prediction of later civic competence. Our present work addresses this research question; we compared the relative influences of social competence and indicators of relationship quality with parents and friends in the prediction of later civic engagement.

In the present chapter, we present a model that suggests that civic competence may be explained, in part, by child and adolescent social competence (or incompetence) and the quality of relationships with parents, peers, and friends. The conceptual model examines both direct and indirect associations of competence and parent and peer relationship to later civic engagement. Because this model focuses on relationship quality, it is clear that it is embedded in cultural practices and values. We also suggest that adolescent relationships may moderate the influences of behavioral competence on later civic competence. We propose that positive experiences with friends and parents in adolescence may encourage civic engagement even for individuals who were initially aggressive or anxiously withdrawn as children.

Clearly, civic competence is a significant outcome in the lives of young adults. And yet, there has not been a longitudinal study in which researchers have examined the independent contributions of behavioral competence and how relationships with parents and peers predict the prevalence,

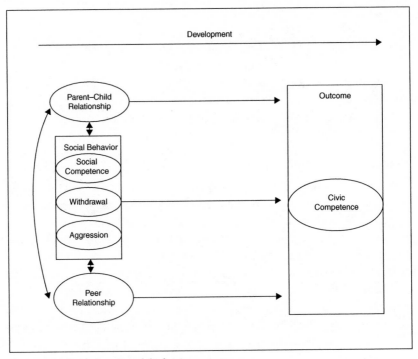

Figure 8.1. A relational model of civic competence.

breadth, and quality of civic competence in early adulthood. We have initiated such a study and describe some initial findings in this chapter. In our investigation, we examine these associations longitudinally by following a sample of individuals through middle school and high school. The conceptual model guiding this project is found in Figure 8.1 and is discussed, in detail, below.

A Relational Model of Civic Competence

Young people who successfully transition into adulthood are those who demonstrate social responsibility and who are capable of practicing civic engagement (Flanagan & Gallay, 1995; Havighurst, 1972). Recently, scholars have raised the question as to whether adolescents' *interpersonal* experiences provide them with the social resources and competencies required to succeed and develop civic competence (Larson, Wilson, Brown, Furstenberg, & Verma, 2002). This question underpins the conceptual model presented herein and initial findings of a study we describe in this chapter.

Social-Constructivist Models of Moral Development in Cultural Context

Social-constructivist models of moral and civic development have empha-sized the role of culture and social interactions in the genesis of inter-individual differences in moral and civic development, such as social responsibility and civic engagement. The culture in which a child grows up has specific social expectations and norms for social interactions within relationships (Chen, 2011; Rubin, Oh, Menzer, & Ellison, 2011). Children and adolescents also construct meaning for interpersonal moral situations through their experiences in close relationships (Keller, 2004).

For example, cross-cultural research indicates that people in collectivist cultures find that meeting interpersonal and social responsibilities to fam-ily and friends is personally satisfying. In contrast, people in individualistic cultures treat such responsibilities as obligations (see Malti & Keller, 2010). Benevolence and concern for the well-being of other members of the com-munity are central moral values in the Confucian tradition (Bond, 1996).

These values influence social interactions, and social interactions serve as mediators of how cultural values influence children's and adolescents' moral and civic development. Likewise, it has been argued that societal eth-ics regarding social responsibility play a role in how much adolescents are bound to their larger communities. For example, research indicates that adolescents in stable democratic versus declining socialist societies in cen-tral Eastern Europe differ in their values and political theories (Flanagan, 2000). From a constructivist perspective then, culturally guided values and social interaction processes affect the adolescent's construction of moral norms involving civic responsibility (Malti & Keller, 2010; see Lerner, 2004). Research also indicates that participation in civic activities promotes a moral-civic identity (Yates & Youniss, 1996).

Psychosocial Theory

Psychosocial theorists (Erikson, 1968) have long stressed the significance of relational antecedents for the development of civic competence. It has been posited that, particularly in adolescence and emerging adulthood, social relationships serve as the experiential backgrounds for the growth of civic competence. Thus, for example, the emergence of personal iden-tity and related motivational orientations toward social justice and care are thought to develop, in part, as a function of interpersonal experiences in close, supportive social relationships. Psychosocial theory also argues that the processes, skills, knowledge, and social support that make competence possible in the major tasks of one developmental period serve to build the foundation for adaptation in subsequent periods of development (Erikson, 1968).

Relatedly, from the perspective of developmental science, competence in salient domains of one developmental period may predict subsequent competence in newly emerging domains, thereby reflecting heterotypic continuity (Roisman, Masten, Coatsworth, & Tellegen, 2004). Initial support for these psychosocially derived contentions derives from research demonstrating that resilience and well-being in emerging adulthood is a function of previous success across developmental tasks in the domains of citizenship, work, and romantic involvement (Schulenberg et al., 2004).

Relationship Theories

Perhaps of equal or greater relevance are the premises drawn from social relationship theories. These theories make significant contributions to understanding the development, over the long term, of civic competence and engagement. Attachment theorists (Bowlby, 1969), for example, have suggested that the development of secure relationships with primary caregivers enable (and predict) the development, not only of social competence and a positive sense of self, but also of qualitatively rich extra-familial relationships. It has been suggested that the development of an "internal working model" (IWM), which allows for the internalization of security and trust within familial and extra-familial relationships (Mikulincer & Shaver, 2005), may provide the basis for a willingness to act prosocially and generously on the behalf of others (Hastings, Utendale, & Sullivan, 2007). In sum, children's relationships and social experiences with others may well influence, both directly and indirectly, the development of civic competence in adolescence and early adulthood. The processes by which this may occur are described in the section on Hinde's perspective.

Hinde's Perspective

We frame our research within the interpersonal, theoretical framework offered by Hinde (e.g., 1979). Hinde has suggested that social development can best be understood by distinguishing among the contributing characteristics of (1) the individual, (2) the interactions between individuals, and (3) the relationships formed and maintained by individuals, in part as a function of their individual characteristics and the nature of their social interactions. Individuals bring to social exchanges fairly stable orientations and a repertoire of skills for perspective taking and thinking about the self in relation to others. These social cognitions about such matters as societal issues and solving interpersonal dilemmas are believed to predict the ways in which individuals interact in the company of others. Importantly, individuals' *interactions* with others vary in form and function in response to fluctuations in the parameters of the social situation, such as the partner's characteristics, overtures, and responses. Interactions can be simply categorized as involving movements toward (e.g., prosocial, friendly initiations and responses), against (e.g., agonistic initiations and responses), or away (e.g., withdrawal) from others (Rubin, Bukowski, & Parker, 2006). Finally, *relationships* involve a succession of interactions between two individuals known to each other. The nature and course of each interaction is influenced by the history of past interactions between the individuals as well as by their expectations for interactions in the future.

Hinde's (1979) conceptual orientation may allow for the simultaneous investigation of individual, interactional, and relational antecedents of civic competence. Relational antecedents have largely been ignored in the study of civic competence. Few, if any, researchers have examined individual differences in the early adolescent precursors of civic competence. Thus, our research is among the first longitudinal examinations to simultaneously examine the individual, interactional, and relational predictors of civic competence. In this chapter, we examine individual and relationship factors that may lay the basis for and help predict the subsequent development of civic competence.

Parent–child Relationships and the Development of Civic Competence

The Secure Attachment Relationship. A basic assumption of attachment theory is that the child's relationships with primary caregivers provide models for all relationships to follow, including friend and romantic relationships (Furman & Collins, 2009). Secure relationships with parents during childhood and early adolescence is associated with increased empathy and emotion regulation skills, which shape interactions and relationships with others in adolescence and adulthood (Furman & Collins, 2009). From this perspective, a foundation of emotional and behavioral interdependence in early life lays the basis for the development of social competence, self-assuredness, and the development of supportive extra-familial relationships.

The putative, proximal causes of the development of a secure attachment relationship are the expressions of parental support, responsivity, warmth, and sensitivity. The sensitive and responsive parent recognizes the child's emotional signals, considers the child's perspective, and responds promptly and appropriately to the child's needs. In turn, the child develops a belief system that incorporates the parent as someone who can be relied on for protection, nurturance, comfort, and security; a sense of trust in relationships results from the secure child–parent bond. Furthermore, the child forms a belief that the self is competent and worthy of positive responses from others.

The process by which a secure attachment relationship is thought to result in the development of social competence and positive relationships with peers may be described briefly as follows. The internal working model (IWM) of the securely attached young child allows him or her to feel secure, confident, and self-assured when introduced to novel settings; this sense of felt security fosters the child's active exploration of the social environment (Sroufe, 1983). In turn, exploration of the social milieu leads to peer interaction and play. Peer interactions and play allow children to experience the interpersonal exchange of ideas, perspectives, roles, and actions. From such social interchanges, children develop social competence, mature ways of thinking about the social world, and positive peer relationships (see Rubin et al., 2006a for a review).

Research also indicates that securely attached elementary and middle schoolers are more socially competent, are better able to make and keep friends and to experience qualitatively rich and supportive friendships (e.g., Booth-LaForce, Rubin, Rose-Krasnor, & Burgess, 2004). With this in mind, secure attachment, perhaps through facilitating a "mutual responsive orientation," may enhance the demonstration of prosocial acts and the internalization of parental values (Rose-Krasnor & Denham, 2009). It may well be that young adolescents who have experienced positive, supportive, and secure relationships with parents and peers would be inclined to consider the well-being of others and participate in activities that would enable others in their social communities to benefit from their own good deeds.

Relatedly, developmental models of social responsibility and morality propose that a sense of social responsibility is rooted in the formation of close relationships to significant others, such as parents (Smetana, 1997). As noted above, supportive, secure parent–child relationships reinforce the demonstration of supportive, prosocial behaviors in extra-familial relationships and with others in general (Kochanska & Murray, 2000). This process may promote later trust in one's own moral judgments and foster principled moral reasoning (Arsenio & Gold, 2006), compassion, altruism, tolerance, and empathy (Mikulincer & Shaver, 2005).

Social Competence, Social Relationships, and the Development of Civic Competence

Social competence has been defined as the ability to achieve personal goals in social interaction while simultaneously maintaining positive relationships with others over time and across settings (Rose-Krasnor, 1997).

This definition includes both positive, prosocial, and socially acceptable behavior, but also the absence of unfriendly and agonistic behavior (for a review, see Rubin et al., 2006a). Civic competence frequently appears to be an extension of such social competencies as empathy, prosocial behavior, the ability to take alternate perspectives, solve interpersonal problems, and commitment to moral norms, the latter frequently leading to civic engagement and courage (Flanagan & Faison, 2001).

From the review of the extant literature offered above, it seems clear that the quality of the parent–child relationship is associated with, and predictive of the ways in which children and adolescents behave in their social worlds and the prevalence and quality of their close, dyadic relationships (e.g., friendship). Insofar as child and adolescent social behavior is concerned, we have noted that individuals with secure parent–child attachment relationships, whose parents are supportive and appropriately controlling, are likely to demonstrate the ability to: 1) take the perspectives of others, 2) think confidently and positively about the self, 3) be motivated to follow rules of fairness and justice, and 4) resolve interpersonal conflicts constructively. These competencies, when "translated" into the expression of social behavior, allow the expression of sociable, prosocial behaviors that promote co-constructive peer interaction (Malti & Noam, 2009). In turn, this constellation of competencies and behaviors are posited to contribute to adaptive development and civic competence (e.g., Keller, 2004; Malti, Gummerum, Keller, & Buchmann, 2009).

Secure, competent adolescents are accepted by the peer group and are viewed positively as prospective friendship partners (Rubin et al., 2006a). Furthermore, their friendships tend to be with others much like them (Rubin, Lynch, Coplan, Rose-Krasnor, & Booth, 1994) and the quality of their friendships tend to be supportive, appropriately intimate, constructive and helpful, and trusting. The friendships of socially competent children and adolescents become increasingly conceptualized in terms of commitment and reciprocity. From learning about the provisions of friendship (e.g., trust, support, helpfulness, partnership), and from experiencing close affective ties to others outside the family circle, socially competent children, through the mutually reciprocal experience of reliable alliances and support, develop the motivation to act fairly and prosocially in one's community (Keller & Edelstein, 1993). This reflects Aristotle's notion that "the *polis* is a network of friends bound together by a mutual pursuit of a common good" (Flanagan & Faison, 2001, p. 7). Indeed, recent research indicates that friendship quality may positively affect moral reasoning and moral motivations, a correlate of civic competence (Malti & Buchmann,

2010; McDonald, Malti, Killen, & Rubin, personal correspondence), supporting our hypothesis that social competence and the experience of rich, supportive friendships contribute to the development of later civic competence. Also, high quality friendships may, in part, make up for poor quality relationships with parents: high quality friendships may buffer children who have less secure or supportive relationships with parents (e.g., Rubin et al., 2004).

Although researchers have reported relations between attachment, morality, and behaviors in adolescence and young adulthood (Bradford, Vaughn, & Barber, 2008; van Ijzendoorn, 1997), there have been few, if any, longitudinal studies of the relations between the quality of close relationships with parents and peers, social competence, and civic competence. Taken together, our perspective suggests that social competence may mediate the relation between earlier parent–child relations and later civic engagement. Alternatively, social competence and civic engagement may only be associated because quality parent–child relationships and friendships are a common precursor for both. Moreover, extant studies have not examined how quality relationships may interact with social competence to predict civic competence. In our model, which examines social competence and relationships as separate predictors of competence, we can examine these different hypotheses.

Thus, in our research, we have begun to address some of these questions, including: (1) Does the quality of relationships with parents and friends in late childhood/early adolescence predict civic competence in later adolescence? (2) Does late childhood/early adolescent social competence predict civic competence in later adolescence? (3) Is this latter association moderated, in part, by the quality of relationships that young adolescents have with friends? In the present chapter we examine two of these questions: how behavioral competence (as indexed by prosocial behavior) and quality relationships with parents and friends directly and indirectly predict civic competence in late adolescence.

Preliminary Results on Civic Development and Social Relationships

Our data derives from an ongoing longitudinal study, in which social relationships (i.e., friendships and parent–child relationships) and social competencies were examined longitudinally. Four cohorts of young adolescents participated in the study. The sample was followed from the first year of middle school (6th grade; Time 1) to the final year of middle school (8th grade; Time 2). Additionally, data from two cohorts of 12th graders was included in the present analysis ($N = 167$; Time 3). The sample attended middle schools in middle- to upper-middle class neighborhoods in the suburbs of Washington, DC. Approximately, 62 percent of adolescents' mothers and 65.3 percent of their fathers had a university degree.

A larger sample of 1,461 6th graders participated in grade-wide sociometric and behavioral nomination assessments. Participants completed surveys in group testing sessions (at lunch or in gym). Then a subsample of targeted participants was invited to complete additional questionnaires during a laboratory visit in the spring of their 6th grade year. For 8th and 12th grade assessments, participants completed questionnaires on a computer, via an online survey tool, or by paper and pencil questionnaires sent home.

Civic competence was measured in 12th grade (Time 3) by civic activity engagement and meaningfulness of civic engagement. Participants completed The Leisure Activities Questionnaire (LAQ; based on Passmore & French, 2001), which in part assesses the nature, frequency, and enjoyment of community service activities, as indexes of civic activity engagement. Adolescents were asked to report their most frequent community service activities, indicate the frequency of participation, and rate their enjoyment of the activity. Participants were asked to provide up to three activities, which were coded into two categories: civic and non-civic. Activities were judged as *civic* if they were community, service-oriented or politically-oriented (e.g., canned food drive, soup kitchen, volunteering at a hospital). A sum score of civic activities was created and used as an indicator of "civic engagement."

In addition, for the 12th grade assessments, young adults were asked to rate how meaningful and important community service activities were to them. Perceived meaningfulness of community service activities was assessed by four items (e.g., "How much are community service activities an important part of who you are?"). A sum score was created (Cronbach's $\alpha = .90$) and labeled "meaningfulness of civic engagement."

The Network of Relationships Inventory Questionnaire (NRI; Furman & Buhrmester, 1985) was completed at T1 by participants and assessed provisions of close relationships with mothers and fathers. The NRI comprises 10 conceptually distinct subscales that load onto two factors (e.g., Furman, 1996): (1) support (affection, admiration, instrumental aid, companionship, intimacy, nurturance, and reliable alliance) and (2) negativity (antagonism and conflict). Perceptions of maternal and paternal support were combined, and a mean score for parental support at T1 ($M = 4.04$, $SD = 0.54$; Cronbach's $\alpha = .69$) was created.

Additionally, participants completed the Friendship Quality Questionnaire (FQQ) at T1. The FQQ comprises six subscales (i.e., companionship, validation and caring, help and guidance, intimate disclosure, lack of conflict and betrayal, conflict resolution) that together can be combined as an index of friendship quality ($M = 3.94$, $SD = 0.62$; Cronbach's $\alpha = .82$).

The *Extended Class Play* (ECP; e.g., Rubin et al., 2006b) was administered at T1 and T2. Adolescents nominated up to three classmates who would best fit a variety of behavioral descriptors. For this chapter, we focus on prosocial behavior, comprised of six items that assessed kind, helpful, and cooperative behaviors (e.g., "helps others," "polite," and "trustworthy;" T1 $\alpha = .88$; T2 $\alpha = .82$).

The majority of adolescents in 12th grade were involved in at least one civic activity regularly ($M = 1.98$, $SD = 0.89$), and, on average, participants attached high value to civic engagement ($M = 2.60$, $SD = 0.96$). The correlations between the civic competence variables with the social relationship and social competence variables are displayed in Table 8.1. As can be seen, civic engagement in 12th grade was positively associated with prosocial behavior in 6th and 8th grades. Perceived meaningfulness of civic engagement was positively associated with parent–child relationships and friendship relationships in 6th grade.

To test our relational model of civic competence, we next investigated the hypothesis that civic engagement and civic valuation in 12th grade were related to earlier parent–child and friendship relationships and prosocial behavior. Separate path analyses were completed for civic engagement in 12th grade and the meaningfulness of civic engagement in 12th grade. As independent variables, we used parental and friendship support in 6th grade as well as prosocial behavior in both 6th and 8th grade. The analyses for the present study were conducted using AMOS 6.0 and full maximum likelihood estimation of missing data. Model fit was evaluated using the Comparative Fit Index (CFI); CFIs greater than .90 indicate good model fit. Parameter estimates are given in parentheses and refer to standardized estimates.

The model of civic engagement provided a good fit to the data, CFI = .97. Civic engagement was marginally predicted by parental support in 6th grade (.14, $p < .10$). Additionally, prosocial behavior in 6th grade and friendship support in 6th grade predicted prosocial behavior in 8th grade (.78, $p < .001$; .09, $p < .05$). However, there was no direct relation between prosocial behavior and civic engagement.

Table 8.1 Correlations between Civic Competence Variables with Social Relationships and Social Competence Variables

Variable	Civic Competence	
Variable	Civic Engagement in 12th grade	Meaningfulness of Civic Engagement in 12th grade
Parent–child relationship 6th grade	.14	.20*
Friendship relationship 6th grade	.07	.20*
Prosocial behavior 6th grade	.15*	.07
Prosocial behavior 8th grade	.17*	.06

Note: CE = Civic engagement.
* $p < .05$.

The model on perceived meaningfulness of civic engagement also provided a good fit to the data, CFI = .98. Perceived meaningfulness of civic engagement was predicted by parental support in 6th grade (.22, $p < .01$) and marginally by friendship support in 6th grade (.14, $p < .10$). There was no direct relation between prosocial behavior and perceived meaningfulness of civic engagement. Again, prosocial behavior in 6th grade predicted prosocial behavior in 8th grade (.78, $p < .001$; see Figure 8.2).

Summary and Future Directions

The goal of this chapter was to describe a relational model of civic competence that links social relationships and social competence development to civic competence outcomes in adolescence and young adulthood. Because civic competence and social responsibility have been posited as significant positive outcomes in the lives of adolescents and young adults, we have argued that longitudinal studies on the social competence and relationship antecedents of civic competence have great potential to contribute to our understanding of how early precursors of civic competence develop. In addition to our conceptual model, we provided some initial findings to test longitudinal associations between social relationships, prosocial behaviors, and civic competence outcomes.

Together, the results of our preliminary analyses suggest that civic competence in late adolescence is directly related to earlier parent–child relationship quality. Although, 12th grade civic engagement was correlated with prosocial behavior in 6th and 8th grade, the path model did not indicate any significant direct relationships between prosocial behavior and civic engagement. Perhaps this is because of the direct associations of civic

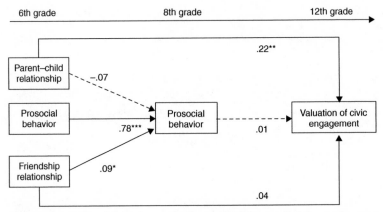

Figure 8.2. Path model of perceived meaningfulness of civic engagement, social relationships, and social competence (prosocial behavior). Bolded solid lines represent significant paths. Solid lines represent marginally significant paths at p < .10.
* p < .05. ** p < .01. *** p < .001.

engagement with parent–child relationship quality in early adolescence. Together, these preliminary results suggest that civic competence in late adolescence is predicted by the quality of earlier relationships with parents. Further, any associations between prosocial behavior and later civic competence may be explained by their common relationship with quality parent–child relationships.

We should note that these preliminary analyses were powered at low levels, and that when a larger longitudinal sample is analyzed, direct relations between prosocial behavior and civic competence may be significant. However, it is clear that the direct associations between parent–child relationships and civic competence are larger in size than those between prosocial behavior and civic competence, suggesting at the least, that prosocial behavior may only be a partial mediator of the link between parent–child relationships and civic engagement.

Our findings suggest that an interpersonal theoretical framework (Hinde, 1979) is well suited to understand how civic competence develops as a function of the nature of social relationships with significant others. We have emphasized that this interpersonal framework is embedded in the cultural constraints and opportunities in which relationships are inevitably immersed (see Rubin et al., 2011). This finding is also in line with research on the role of family socialization and youth responsibility (Pancer & Pratt, 1999), as well as the role of peers and friendship relationships on civic competence development (Wray-Lake, Syvertsen, & Flanagan, 2010). Taken together, the findings reflect the assumption that there is correspondence between a young person's civic competence and those of parents and peers (McLellan & Youniss, 2003).

Our analyses revealed no direct influence of friendship relationship quality on civic outcomes. It is likely, however, that the association between friendship quality and civic engagement varies as a function of who the friend is. Thus, further empirical analyses are needed to control for who the friend is and his/her behavioral characteristics to disentangle if and how friendship may, in addition to indirect paths, also directly contribute to civic engagement.

In future analyses, we will also investigate how and whether indicators of social incompetence (i.e., aggression, anxious withdrawal) are predictive of later civic competence. Aggressive children and adolescents are largely rejected by their peers (Miller-Johnson, Coie, Maumary-Gremaud, & Bierman, 2002). However, they may be friends with other aggressive children and these friendships may contribute to future maladjustment (Adams, Bukowski, & Bagwell, 2005). The friendships of aggressive children differ from those of nonaggressive children. In particular, investigators have shown that aggressive children are more likely to engage in "deviant" talk than nonaggressive children, which in turn, reinforces their aggressive and delinquent behavioral patterns (Poulin, Dishion, & Haas, 1999). Moreover, the friendships of aggressive children have been characterized by high levels of aggression within the friendship and lower levels of intimacy (Brendgen, Vitaro, Turgeon, & Poulin, 2002).

Despite these differences in whom they befriend and the nature of their relationships, there is some evidence suggesting that aggressive children's friendships can function protectively, in much the same way as those of nonaggressive children. For instance, Poulin and colleagues (Poulin et al., 1999) found that boys who were highly delinquent at age 13–14 *and* who had a friendship that was *low* in friendship quality were those whose delinquent behaviors increased over time. A *high* quality friendship protected highly delinquent boys from increasing delinquent behavior, regardless of the degree to which their friends were also delinquent. Thus, examinations of how aggressive behavior and relationships with parents and friends directly predict and interact in their predictions of later civic competence (and incompetence) are warranted in future studies.

Additionally, anxious withdrawn children and adolescents are largely rejected by their peers (e.g., Valdivia, Schneider, Chavez, & Chen, 2005) and have difficulty forming large numbers of friendships (Pedersen, Vitaro, Barker, & Borge, 2007). Nevertheless, like aggressive children, they are known to have friendships with others much like them (Rubin et al.,

2006a). Moreover, the friendships of socially withdrawn children have been characterized by low levels of conversation, fun, helpfulness, and intimacy (Rubin et al., 2006b). At this time, virtually nothing is known about the possible roles of anxious withdrawn children's friendships in the extent to which they are civically engaged. We also suggest that anxious withdrawal, in conjunction with indicators of relationship quality, also be investigated as a predictor of later civic competence.

Future analyses should also test our theoretical hypothesis that relationships might buffer shy, withdrawn, and aggressive children and young adolescents and help them to subsequently become civically engaged. Supportive relationships with parents and friends may buffer the relation between social withdrawal or aggression and subsequent maladaptive outcomes and help children and young adolescents at risk for maladaptation overcome these behavioral problems and meaningfully engage in the community. A compensatory model, in which youth with developmental problems can overcome these by experiencing supportive and caring relationships with peers and parents, offers promising ground for interventionists. Future studies are needed to further investigate if and how civic competence is shaped by the interaction between social relationships and individual behavioral characteristics.

It is also important to consider our proposed relational model of civic competence in different cultural contexts in future research. Our initial investigations of this model are limited to a Western cultural context, and care should be taken when generalizing to other populations. Further, just as definitions of social competence may vary cross-culturally (Rose-Krasnor, 1997) the definitions of civic competence or civic engagement may differ cross-culturally. Culturally sensitive investigations of this topic should first make an effort to identify those behaviors and attitudes that may define civic competence within the cultural group being examined.

However, we do expect that many of the hypotheses proposed in the relational model of civic competence would hold for other cultural groups: the implications of close relationships, especially with parents, for social and emotional adjustment may be similar cross-culturally (Khaleque & Rohner, 2002). In fact, it is likely that the role of close relationships with parents and friends and the role of social competence in predicting later civic competence would be similar in most, if not all, Western cultures and in many Eastern cultures as well. For example, Rohner (1986) has suggested that parental warmth may have cross-culturally universal significance for child development. In support of this hypothesis, parental warmth has been found to be predictive of concurrent and later social, emotional, and academic competence in both Western and Eastern cultures (e.g., Khaleque & Rohner, 2002; see Rubin et al., 2011). Further, although relationships with caregivers are affected by cultural-specific norms and thus may vary in the qualities of a typical parent–child relationship, the significance of the parent–child (or caregiver–child) relationship for later social and emotional competence is undeniable (van IJzendoorn & Sagi-Schwartz, 2008). Based on this literature, it is likely that caregiver–child relationships will have consequences for later civic competence for most cultural groups.

In summary, this chapter has provided a first attempt to develop and test a relational model of civic competence. This model posits social relationships as a significant antecedent and a buffer of individual behavioral risk or support of individual social competence, respectively, in the development of civic competence. Future longitudinal studies are needed to test and validate the model's assumption empirically. It has also become clear that the role of relationships and social competence development on civic competence outcomes varies as a function of who the child, the parents, and the friends are. Thus, an analysis of moderating variables is needed to clarify if and how individual characteristics interact with social relationships and conjointly contribute to civic competence development in adolescence and young adulthood. Likewise, future analyses may investigate the impact of culture as a broader social context in which social relationships are embedded and their influence on later civic competence.

REFERENCES

Adams, R. E., Bukowski, W. M., & Bagwell, C. L. (2005). Stability of aggression during early adolescence as moderated by reciprocated friendship status and friend's aggression. *International Journal of Behavioral Development, 29,* 139–145.

Arsenio, W. F., & Gold, J. (2006). The effects of social injustice and inequality on children's moral judgments and behavior: Towards a theoretical model. *Cognitive Development, 21,* 388–400.

Bond, M. H. (Ed.). (1996). *The Handbook of Chinese psychology.* Hong Kong: Oxford University Press.

Booth-LaForce, C., Rubin, K. H., Rose-Krasnor, L., & Burgess, K. B. (2004). Attachment and friendship predictors of psychosocial functioning in middle childhood, and the mediating roles of social support and self-worth. In K. A. Kerns & R. A. Richardson (Eds.), *Attachment in middle childhood* (pp. 161–188). New York: Guilford.

Bowlby, J. (1969). *Attachment and loss: Vol. I. Attachment.* New York: Basic Books.

Bradford, K., Vaughn, L. B., & Barber, B. K. (2008). When there is conflict: Interparental conflict, parent–child conflict, and youth problem behaviors. *Journal of Family Issues, 29,* 780–805.

Brendgen, M., Vitaro, F., Turgeon, L., & Poulin, F. (2002). Assessing aggressive and depressed children's social relations with classmates and friends: A matter of perspective. *Journal of Abnormal Child Psychology*, 30, 609–624.

Chen, X. (2011). Culture, social interaction, and socioemotional functioning: A contextual-developmental perspective. In X. Chen & K. H. Rubin (Eds.), *Socioemotional development in cultural context* (pp. 29–52). New York: Guilford.

Dodge, K. A., Coie, J. D., & Lynam, D. (2006). Aggression and antisocial behavior in youth. In N. Eisenberg, W. Damon, & R. M. Lerner (Eds.), *Handbook of child psychology: Vol. 3, Social, emotional, and personality development* (pp. 719–788). Hoboken, NJ: John Wiley & Sons Inc.

Erikson, E. H. (1968). *Identity: youth and crisis*. Oxford: Norton & Co.

Flanagan, C. A. (2000). Social change and the 'social contract' in adolescent development. In L. J. Crockett & R. K. Silbereisen (Eds.), *Negotiating adolescence in times of social change* (pp. 191–198). New York: Cambridge University Press.

Flanagan, C. A., & Faison, N. (2001). Youth civic development: Implications of research for social policy and programs. *Social Policy Report*, Vol. XV (1). Ann Arbor, MI: Society for Research in Child Development.

Flanagan, C. A., & Gallay, L. S. (1995). Reframing the meaning of "political" in research with adolescents. *Perspectives on Political Science*, 24, 34–41.

Furman, W. (1996). The measurement of children and adolescent's perceptions of friendships: Conceptual and methodological issues. In W. M. Bukowski, A. F. Newcomb, & W. W. Hartup (Eds.), *The company they keep: Friendships in childhood and adolescence* (pp. 41–65). Cambridge, MA: Cambridge University Press.

Furman, W., & Buhrmester, D. (1985). Children's perceptions of the personal relationships in their social networks. *Developmental Psychology*, 21, 1016–1024.

Furman, W., & Collins, W. A. (2009). Adolescent romantic relationships and experiences. In K. H. Rubin, W. Bukowski, & B. Laursen (Eds.), *Handbook of peer interactions, relationships, and groups* (pp. 341–360). New York: Guilford.

Gardner, M., Roth, J., & Brooks-Gunn, J. (2008). Adolescents' participation in organized activities and developmental success 2 and 8 years after high school: Do sponsorship, duration, and intensity matter? *Developmental Psychology*, 44, 814–830.

Hart, D., Donnelly, T. M., Youniss, J., & Atkins, R. (2007). High school community service as a predictor of adult voting and volunteering. *American Educational Research Journal*, 44, 197–219.

Hastings, P. D., Utendale, W. T., & Sullivan, C. (2007). The socialization of prosocial development. In J. E. Grusec & P. D. Hastings (Eds.), *Handbook of socialization: Theory and research* (pp. 638–664). New York: Guilford.

Havighurst, R. J. (1972). *Development tasks and education*. New York: McKay.

Hinde, R. A. (1979). *Towards understanding relationships*. London: Academic Press.

Keller, M. (2004). Self in relationship. In D. K. Lapsley & D. Narvaez (Eds.), *Moral development, self, and identity* (pp. 267–298). Mahwah, NJ: Lawrence Erlbaum Associates.

Keller, M., & Edelstein, W. (1993). The development of the moral self from childhood to adolescence. In G. G. Noam, T. E. Wren, G. Nunner-Winkler, & W. Edelstein (Eds.), *The moral self* (pp. 310–336). Cambridge, MA: The MIT Press.

Khaleque, A., & Rohner, R. P. (2002). Perceived parental acceptance-rejection and psychological adjustment: A meta- analysis of cross-cultural and intracultural studies. *Journal of Marriage and Family*, 64, 54–64.

Kochanska, G., & Murray, K. T. (2000). Mother-child mutually responsive orientation and conscience development: From toddler to early school age. *Child Development*, **71**, 417–431.

Larson, R., Brown, B. B., & Mortimer, J. (Eds.). (2002). Adolescents' Preparation for the Future: Perils and Promise [special issue]. *Journal of Research on Adolescence*, **12**, 1–166.

Larson, R. W., Wilson, S., Brown, B. B., Furstenberg, F. F. Jr., & Verma, S. (2002). Changes in adolescents' interpersonal experiences: Are they being prepared for adult relationships in the twenty-first century? *Journal of Research on Adolescence*, **12**, 31–68.

Lerner, R. M. (2004). *Liberty: Thriving and civic engagement among America's youth*. Thousand Oaks, CA: Sage Publications.

Malti, T., & Buchmann, M. (2010). Socialization and individual antecedents of adolescents' and young adults' moral motivation. *Journal of Youth and Adolescence*, **39**, 138–149.

Malti, T., Gummerum, M., Keller, M., & Buchmann, M. (2009). Children's moral motivation, sympathy, and prosocial behavior. *Child Development*, **80**, 442–460.

Malti, T., & Keller, M. (2010). Development of moral emotions in cultural context. In W. Arsenio & E. Lemerise (Eds.), *Emotions, aggression, and morality in children: Bridging development and psychopathology* (pp. 177–198). Washington: American Psychological Association.

Malti, T., & Noam, G. G. (2009). A developmental approach to the prevention of adolescents' aggressive behavior and the promotion of resilience. *European Journal of Developmental Science*, **3**, 235–246.

McLellan, J. A., & Youniss, J. (2003). Two systems of youth service: Determinants of voluntary and required youth community service. *Journal of Youth and Adolescence*, **32**, 47–58.

Mikulincer, M., & Shaver, P. R. (2005). Attachment theory and emotions in close relationships: Exploring the attachment-related dynamics of emotional reactions to relational events. *Personal Relationships*, **12**, 149–168.

Miller-Johnson, S., Coie, J. D., Maumary-Gremaud, A., Bierman, K., & Conduct Problems Prevention Research Group (2002). Peer rejection and aggression and early starter models of conduct disorder. *Journal of Abnormal Child Psychology*, **30**, 217–230.

Obradovic, J., & Masten, A. S. (2007). Developmental antecedents of young adult civic engagement. *Applied Developmental Science*, **11**, 2–19.

Olweus, D. (1993). *Bullying at school: What we know and what we can do*. Cambridge, MA: Blackwell.

Pancer, S. M., & Pratt, M. W. (1999). Social and family determinants of community service involvement in Canadian youth. In M. Yates & J. Youniss (Eds.), *Community service and civic engagement in youth: International perspectives* (pp. 32–55). Cambridge: Cambridge University Press.

Passmore, A., & French, D. (2001). Development and administration of a measure to assess adolescents' participation in leisure activities. *Adolescence*, **36**, 67–75.

Pedersen, S., Vitaro, F., Barker, E. D., & Borge, A. I. H. (2007). The timing of middle-childhood peer rejection and friendship: Linking early behavior to early adolescent adjustment. *Child Development*, **78**, 1037–1051.

Poulin, F., Dishion, T. J., & Haas, E. (1999). The peer influence paradox: Friendship quality and deviancy training within male adolescent friendships. *Merrill-Palmer Quarterly*, **45**, 42–61.

Rohner, R. P. (1986). *The warmth dimension: Foundations of parental acceptance-rejection theory*. Beverly Hills, CA: Sage Publications.

Roisman, G. I., Masten, A. S., Coatsworth, J. D., & Tellegen, A. (2004). Salient and emerging developmental tasks in the transition to adulthood. *Child Development*, **75**, 123–133.

Rose-Krasnor, L. (1997). The nature of social competence: A theoretical review. *Social Development*, **6**, 111–135.

Rose-Krasnor, L., & Denham, S. (2009). Socio-emotional competence in early childhood. In K. H. Rubin, W. Bukowski, & B. Laursen (Eds.), *The handbook of peer interactions, relationships, and groups* (pp. 162–179). New York: Guilford.

Rubin, K. H., Bukowski, W. M., & Parker, J. G. (2006a). Peer interactions, relationships, and groups. In N. Eisenberg, W. Damon, R. M. Lerner (Eds.), *Handbook of child psychology: Vol. 3, Social, emotional, and personality development* (pp. 571–645). Hoboken, NJ: John Wiley & Sons Inc.

Rubin, K. H., Coplan, R. J., & Bowker, J. (2009). Social withdrawal and shyness in childhood and adolescence. *Annual Review of Psychology*, **60**, 141–171.

Rubin, K. H., Dwyer, K. M., Booth-LaForce, C., Kim, A. H., Burgess, K. B., & Rose-Krasnor, L. (2004). Attachment, friendship, and psychosocial functioning in early adolescence. *The Journal of Early Adolescence*, **24**, 326–356.

Rubin, K. H., Lynch, D., Coplan, R., Rose-Krasnor, L., & Booth, C. L. (1994). "Birds of a feather … :" Behavioral concordances and preferential personal attraction in children. *Child Development*, **65**, 1778–1785.

Rubin, K. H., Oh, W., Menzer, M., & Ellison, K. (2011). Dyadic relationships from a cross-cultural perspective: Parent-child relationships and friendship. In X. Chen & K. H. Rubin (Eds.), *Socioemotional development in cultural context* (pp. 208–236). New York: Guilford.

Rubin, K. H., Wojslawowicz, J. C., Rose-Krasnor, L., Booth-LaForce, C., & Burgess, K. B. (2006b). The best friendships of shy/withdrawn children: Prevalence, stability, and relationship quality. *Journal of Abnormal Child Psychology*, **34**, 143–157.

Schulenberg, J. E., Sameroff, A. J., & Cicchetti, D. (2004). The transition to adulthood as a critical juncture in the course of psychopathology and mental health. *Development and Psychopathology*, **16**, 799–806.

Smetana, J. G. (1997). Parenting and the development of social knowledge reconceptualized: A social domain analysis. In J. E. Grusec & L. Kuczynski (Eds.), *Parenting and children's internalization of values: A handbook of contemporary theory* (pp. 162–192). Hoboken, NJ: John Wiley & Sons Inc.

Sroufe, L. A. (1983). Infant–caregiver attachment and patterns of adaptation in preschool: The roots of mal-adaptation and competence. In M. Perlmutter (Ed.), *Minnesota Symposia in Child Psychology* (Vol. 16, pp. 41–83). Hillsdale, NJ: Erlbaum.

Stouthamer-Loeber, M., Wei, E., Loeber, R., & Masten, A. S. (2004). Desistance from persistent serious delinquency in the transition to adulthood. *Development and Psychopathology*, **16**, 897–918.

Valdivia, I. A., Schneider, B. H., Chavez, K. L., & Chen, X. (2005). Social withdrawal and maladjustment in a very group-oriented society. *International Journal of Behavioral Development, 29*, 219–228.

van IJzendoorn, M. H. (1997). Attachment, emergent morality, and aggression: Toward a developmental socioemotional model of antisocial behaviour. *International Journal of Behavioral Development, 21*, 703–727.

van IJzendoorn, M. H., & Sagi-Schwartz, A. (2008). Cross-cultural patterns of attachment: Universal and contextual dimensions. In J. Cassidy & P. R. Shaver (Eds.), *Handbook of attachment. Theory, research, and clinical applications* (2nd ed., pp. 880–905). New York: Guilford.

Wray-Lake, L., Syvertsen, A. K., & Flanagan, C. A. (2010, March). *A multidimensional, longitudinal approach to understanding adolescents' values of social responsibility.* Paper presented at the Society for Research on Adolescence meeting, Philadelphia, PA.

Yates, M., & Youniss, J. (1996). Community service and political-moral identity in adolescents. *Journal of Research on Adolescence, 6*, 271–284.

Youniss, J., Bales, S., Christmas-Best, V., Diversi, M., McLaughlin, M., & Silbereisen, R. (2002). Youth civic engagement in the twenty-first century. *Journal of Research on Adolescence, 12*, 121–148.

Part Three

IMPACT OF VALUES AND RELIGION ON
ADOLESCENT ADJUSTMENT IN TIMES OF
SOCIAL CHANGE

9 Marginalized Japanese Youth in Post-industrial Japan

Motivational Patterns, Self-Perceptions, and the Structural Foundations of Shifting Values

Vinai Norasakkunkit and Yukiko Uchida

Abstract

There is an increasing population of youth in Japan who are being pushed to the periphery of Japanese society. These include the *NEETs* (Not in Employment Education or Training), the *Freeters* (low-skill workers in highly insecure jobs), and the *hikikomori* (social isolates). We argue that Japanese youth marginalization has resulted, in large part, from economic and social structural changes in post-industrial Japan. We further argue that any discussion of values and motivational processes of youth should be examined within the context of the cultural and societal forces that are marginalizing many of them. In doing so, we compare at-risk youth with mainstream youth on independence and interdependence, post-materialist attitudes, and motivational styles. Additionally, we discuss the role that religion has played on helping youth transition into adulthood in the past versus in the present. Finally, we conclude the chapter by discussing the youth volunteer movement in the wake of the March 11, 2011 earthquake and what that might represent for the values and future of Japanese youth.

Background on Japanese Values and Japanese Youth Problems

Markus and Kitayama's (1991) classic theory of independent self-construal in the West and interdependent self-construal in the East has served as a parsimonious model for describing, explaining, and predicting cultural differences in various mental operations between East and West, thereby helping to make psychological theories more relevant to realms outside the Western model of self. Markus and Kitayama's cultural self-construal model was primarily derived from studies in the United States and Japan with the idea that these two cultures serve as useful approximations for psychological realities in Western cultures and Eastern cultures, respectively.

Recently, however, some researchers have questioned whether Japanese and Westerners are really all that different. Specifically, on an attitudinal level, Japanese youth and American youth endorse about the same level of individualistic tendencies and the Japanese are not necessarily more interdependent than their Western counterparts (see Oyserman, Coon, & Kemmelmier, 2002). Indeed, in an attempt to move from an industrialized society to a post-industrialized society, Japanese institutions have recently been encouraging the expression of individuality and downplaying the image of collective operation (Matsumoto, 2002). However, whereas these trends are more easily captured by self-reported attitude measures of cultural values, they are still likely to be congruent with traditional values when cultural values are measured at the implicit or automatic level(Uchida, 2002; Uchida, Park, & Kitayama, 2008). In fact, in a recent study, when Japanese youth were primed to increase attitude levels related to interdependence, they resisted the manipulation and responded in the opposite direction by decreasing levels of self-reported interdependence, whereas independent priming worked in the expected direction by increasing levels of self-reported independence (Norasakkunkit, 2007). This may suggest that Japanese youth today are consciously trying to resist the idea that they are predominantly interdependent, even though interdependent tendencies still show up reliably on a plethora of studies that examine Japanese youth responses at the level of automatic psychological processes (e.g., Kitayama, Mesquita, & Karasawa, 2006; Masuda & Nisbett, 2001; Uchida, 2002; Uchida, Park, & Kitayama, 2008). Thus, the stability of psychological processes oriented toward interdependence among Japanese may suggest that the resistance to interdependence may only be manifesting at a somewhat superficial level or is overstated by the volatility of self-reported values.

On the other hand, there is an easily identifiable and growing population of Japanese teens and young adults, cutting across all social classes, who are living lifestyles that deviate significantly from interdependent norms predominant in Japanese society. Indeed, many of them can be described as cultural dropouts. In addition to the two-thirds of the so-called *Freeters* who do irregular, nonstandard work and have virtually no prospects of eventually securing a full-time job (Statistics Bureau, 2011), there is an estimated 640,000 *NEETs* (Cabinet Office, Government of Japan, 2009), which stands for *Not in Employment, Education, or Training*, a term originally coined by the British government to describe British youth who were temporarily not participating in society (DfEE, 2001). There is also an estimated 700,000 *hikikomori* or social isolates (Cabinet Office, Government of Japan, 2009) who withdraw into their own bedrooms from six months to decades at a time without necessarily suffering from any individual psychopathology (Koyama et al., 2010; Saito, 1998). Finally, birth and marriage rates are declining (Statistics Bureau, 2011) and suicide rates are high: the second highest among the G-8 nations after Russia and the leading cause of death among youth below 30 years of age (The Cabinet Office, 2007). Japan faces a situation where a growing number of Japanese youth are deviating from the normative path to adulthood and success.

On the one hand, these disturbing trends among many Japanese youth have received much attention from clinical psychologists and government agencies as issues of individual adjustment problems that require individual rehabilitation and/or therapy (e.g., Sakai, Horikawa, Nonaka, Matsumoto, & Hirakawa, 2011). On the other hand, there are those who see these trends as a "psychopathology of motivation" (e.g., Koyama et al., 2010) or as the moral failure of young people living in an affluent society (e.g., Yamada, 1999). In this chapter, we attempt to understand these trends in the context of the sociocultural and multi-layered structural forces (global, cultural, societal, institutional, and religious) in which they are occurring and therefore see them as potentially being, in large part, consequences of such forces and even as symptoms of a society in transition or a society with core institutions attempting to resist an inevitable transition. This approach to understanding youth psychology is similar to Bronfenbrenner's (1979) Ecological Systems Theory of human development in which the many layers of society and environment have to be considered in the study of child development. Indeed, in a rapidly changing world of globalization, it is essential that any discussion of values and motivational processes of young people be examined within such a context, especially if the society in question is in the midst of transitioning, either smoothly or turbulently, from an economically affluent industrialized society into a post-industrialized society where the young become increasingly concerned with post-materialist values that lead them to seek out meaning and self-fulfillment rather than primarily security and stability (Arnett, 2004; Inglehart, 2008; Trommsdorff, Chapter 1 in this volume).

Caught between Culture and Society

There is a growing historical trend toward valuing inner happiness over working hard for their in-group among today's Japanese youth (Mainichi

Japan, 2010). Indeed, many Japanese youth report future goals that do not include becoming a leader or overachieving in their careers but rather having more leisure time (Zielenziger, in press). The idea that Japanese youth are starting to place greater value on their inner happiness is consistent with Inglehart's (1977) contention that as industrialized societies accumulate wealth to the point where the basic needs of most members of the society are met for a prolonged period of time, individual values, especially among the youth, will begin to switch from materialist values (emphasizing economic and physical security) to post-materialist values (emphasizing meaning and self-expression).

Inglehart (1977) argues that the switch in values from materialist to post-materialist among the youth can occur even as the values of older generations remain unaffected by the economic affluence of society. Inglehart further argues that under these circumstances, it should not be surprising that an intergenerational gap, and even an intergenerational conflict, could ensue. However, in Western societies, the youth who are in conflict with the older generation will express their grievances through rebellion and protest, as was seen during the Vietnam era in the United States.

What is different about Japan is that despite the two-decade long economic stagnation, structural changes in the labor markets, and the importance of fresh ideas, innovation, creativity, flexibility, openness, trust, and calculated risks in sustaining a healthy post-industrial economy, a rigid seniority system within corporate structures and government bureaucracy is still very much in place (Sato, 2010). Consequently, young Japanese people continue to be disempowered from having much of a voice in reshaping core institutions or playing an active role in the economic futures of their society. To make matters worse, economic opportunities in the form of long-term employment, are still largely preserved for middle-aged male workers. Many young job seekers have to take on a series of part-time or temporary jobs with little prospects for upward mobility, as is the case for most *Freeters* (Genda, 2005; Kosugi, 2008). Even in such precarious positions, it is in the interest of the youth to remain in the labor market as it becomes substantially more challenging to reenter the Japanese workforce should there be any gaps in their employment histories. The tendency for youth to fall into such disempowered positions suggests that, as one analyst has put it, "Japan is a country run by old men, for old men" (Lehmann, 2002). This is especially true at a time when the geriatric population is growing whereas the youth population is shrinking.

Thus, it is not surprising that within the protected bubble of their unreformed lifetime employment system, the senior elites continue to propagate traditional cultural expectations for Japanese youth to follow the idealized life course: transition from full-time students to full-time employees in a large company by the time they graduate from secondary or tertiary school. Those who deviate from this "legitimate" path to security and success, or happen to miss the very narrow window of opportunity to transition from school to full-time work before graduation, are relegated to the periphery of society and regarded as second-class citizens with few prospects of ever entering a long-term employment system. The problem, of course, is that the well-oiled system that once helped to smoothly transition youth from one stable social location or *ba* (i.e., the school) to the next stable social location or *ba* (i.e., the long-term employment system) during the economic bubble years of the 1970s and 1980s is no longer in place for many of today's younger generation.

This is especially true for those attempting to transition from high school to work (Brinton, 2011). However, it is also true for an increasing population of university graduates who can now obtain higher education degrees, no matter how poor their secondary school performance was, as a result of the large number of private colleges and universities viciously competing to recruit from a rapidly shrinking youth population. Given the easy access to higher education today, employers are much more cautious about recruiting university graduates, who they perceive as being products of a system that promotes "credential inflation," unless they are coming from the most elite of higher educational institutions (Kariya, 2011).

For those who are fortunate enough to make it into the protected bubble of the long-term employment system, interdependent norms and expectations prevail, with its accompanying benefits for security, assurances, sense of belonging, and structural supports. Those outside the bubble are left to fend for themselves without a secure social location in which to belong, or else they take refuge within their homes and families as *NEETs* and *hikikomori*. Even when youth do enter the full-time employment system, many face adverse circumstances that make it unpleasant for them to remain in their place of employment for a prolonged period of time, let alone for a lifetime. In interviewing such youth and their corporate elders, Mathews (2004) found that many of the young employees in large corporations are criticized by their corporate elders as being "self-absorbed," having "no guts," "really being unable to think," and "lacking in common sense" (p. 124). The young employees, in turn, complain that despite all the superficial attempts to liberalize corporate practices and structures, "not much ever changes" (p. 124). Furthermore, they also felt that there was no way they could express their discontent within the company. Having said that, it is probably the case that the younger generation is simply not as motivated to work as hard as their predecessors who were strongly driven by the desire to improve their own standards of living while building up their own nation from the ruins of World War II to become a global economic powerhouse by the end of the twentieth century.

Mathews (2004) argues that whereas criticisms from the older generation to the younger generation are likely to occur in every generation and that every younger generation will grow older only to similarly criticize the next younger generation (see also Trzesniewski & Donnellan, 2010), he also argues that young Japanese today may never be like their elders because many young employees intend to eventually leave their companies, even though doing so would likely result in a decline in salary and status. Mathews thus concluded that many of the young employees' discontent with their companies outweighed the financial loss and insecurities they may experience in leaving their companies. This willingness to put self-fulfillment over security also speaks to the emergence of post-materialist values of Japanese youth today.

Thus, even when the select few (mostly males) make it into the long-term employment system, their potential for leaving their companies may be associated with less secure prospects than their predecessors were able to take for granted. Because Japanese society continues to operate under a breadwinner ideology, the lowered prospects for economic security among young Japanese males today means that Japanese women would be less interested in marrying them or wanting to start families with them. Indeed, the lowered status of men in such a breadwinner system is arguably responsible for the dangerously low marriage and birth rates among young adults in Japan (Brinton, 2011).

In sum, the scholarly work of researchers like Brinton (2011), Genda (2005), Kariya (2011), and Kosugi (2008) have revealed that the increasing population of *Freeters*, *NEETs*, and *hikokomori* in modern Japan stem from young people being trapped between cultural expectations and the reality of a society in which the institutional means for supporting those expectations are hardly in place anymore. Yet, no obvious alternative path to achieving full status in society seems to exist other than to follow the ethos of the post-war manufacturing economy where self-sacrifice and constant calibration of the self to social expectations are to be made for one's company and for national economic growth. Post-materialist values have little room to be realized and actualized in this type of social reality. It should therefore come as no surprise that the youth of today's Japan are becoming increasingly demotivated to conform to interdependent norms. At the same time, however, they may also be feeling lost about how to fend for themselves in a post-industrialized world fraught with uncertainties when all their parents and teachers did for them was to aspire for them to enter the security of the protected bubble, albeit a shrinking one, of the long-term employment system. Nor did their parents and teachers seem to consider what would happen to them if they failed. Ultimately, this is, in large part, how Japan created its own lost generation in the 21st century (Zielenziger, 2006).

The Role of Religion and the Lack Thereof

According to Zielenziger (2006), when the IMF (International Monetary Fund) crisis hit South Korea in 1998, largely as a result of rigid hierarchy, nepotism, corporate corruption, and a lack of transparency taking its toll on the national economy, citizens and political leaders had to make a choice between accumulating more national debt as the status quo was maintained or making major structural and ideological adjustments at the national level. Quite boldly, the government decided to implement the latter option very quickly, in part, by galvanizing as many of its citizens to sell as much of the personal gold they owned as possible to prop up the value of their currency. The government did this, in part, by working with Korean churches and appealing to their citizens' calling to serve their own country, even as they were asked to prepare for social turmoil in the process. Fortunately, this bold move paid off! Over 1.5 million citizens donated what amounted to over one billion dollars' worth of gold. Within a few months of the crisis, a new democratically elected president implemented structural and legal reforms that encouraged greater consumerism, allowing failing companies to fail, making it easier for employers to lay off redundant workers, and flattening the hierarchical structure of the employment system. Consequently, within four years of the crisis, South Korea paid off all of its IMF obligations.

Despite being a secularist American Jew himself, Zielenziger (2006) argues that Christianity, especially Protestantism, which has now gained a strong foothold in South Korea, played a major role in affording the type of agency and new value system that it took to adapt to an era of uncertainty and to make bold moves on the part of the government, organizations, and individual citizens. Specifically, the culturally embedded Korean churches, Zielenziger argues, "coached" the Korean people to embrace building trust among strangers, forming new social networks, accepting universal ethics, and harboring a healthy attitude toward reasonable risk-taking (for more on the psychological influences of the Protestant ethic, see also Giorgi &

Marsh, 1990; McClelland, 1961; Quinn & Crocker, 1999; Sanchez-Burks, 2002; Weber, 1904/1930). These institutional and structural reforms also prevented many Korean youth from falling through the cracks of a hierarchical autocratic system that would have narrowed the opportunities for them to gain full status in their own societies.

In contrast, monotheistic Abrahamic religions like Judaism, Christianity, and Islam were sufficiently muted throughout Japanese history to prevent them from gaining a strong foothold and thereby threatening the authority of warrior autocrats such as the Shogun during the Edo period or the deity status of the emperor during the Meiji and the former half of the Showa eras, for example. Moreover, the facts that the Japanese culture is steeped deeply in a system based on social assurances rather than on social trust (Yamagishi, 1999) and employs a habit of relying on avoidance strategies rather than promotion strategies (Hamamura, Meijer, Heine, Kamaya, & Hori, 2009) make it all the more difficult to expect the same kind of transformative leaps that took place in South Korea to also occur in Japan.

Of course, there is an indigenous religion in Japan, called *Shintoism*, which translates to the "Way of the God." Shintoism is not quite an organized religion but a somewhat disorganized system of folklore, history, and mythology. Therefore, it can be practiced quite flexibly with no absolute dogma and can serve various purposes, including war memorials, harvests, romance, individual success, and so forth. If Shintoism played a role in youth inclusion, it did so in pre-war Japan when individuals lived primarily in agricultural communities. According to nationally renowned religious philosopher and folklore scholar, Toji Kamata (2000), in such communities, there was a need to initiate adolescents into the adult world and so Shintoism was used to devise coming-of-age rituals in which adolescents had to go through an ordeal before being recognized by the village elders as full status adult members of the community.

Kamata (2000) argues that the initiating of youth into the adult world in these village communities served to reify the feeling in young adults that they were recognized as meaningful members of society who were needed and valued by other adults. However, during the post-war period, many village communities were dismantled for the sake of rapid urbanization. As a result, local coming-of-age rituals were replaced by a national holiday in which youth, in the year that they turn twenty years old, attend a sanitized coming-of-age ceremony called *seijinshiki* or literally, "Coming of Age Ceremony" where they are simply "declared" adults and given money from the government without having to go through any kind of ordeal or initiation process. Kamata is critical of this ceremony, as it fails to trigger a true paradigm shift for the youth to conceive of himself/herself as an adult who is truly included in the adult world; it does not provide a sense of being taken seriously, a sense of meaning and purpose, or a sense of needing and being needed by others. Although declaring a 20-year-old an adult may seem somewhat premature given that today's youth need more time to prepare themselves for the adult world than was true in the past (see Arnett, 2004), it is unlikely that the ceremony itself would be any more effective in instilling a sense of belonging to the adult world had the official age of adulthood been pushed up by a few years or more.

Given the lack of some kind of initiation process, especially in a hierarchical social structure, the youth are more likely to remain disjointed from a society where the cost of societal structural changes are unevenly distributed across generations. Indeed, Kamata (personal communication) points out that there are plenty of themes embedded in the Japanese pop culture about how the youth in Japan are yearning to be included and needed. This theme is quite apparent, for example, in popular Japanese science-fiction animation stories such as *Gundam* and *Evangelion* where the most talented pilots of war machine robots are adolescents who the elders have to constantly rely on. One can also interpret these portrayals of youth in fantasy stories as projections of youth who want to assert their centrality to society.

Although it is probably true that voluntary religious organization can easily create opportunities for youth to be initiated into the adult world, the Japanese are often described as having *shuukyo arerugee* (an allergy to religion). In post-war Japan, various "New Religion" movements started to erupt throughout the country to address issues and concerns of living in an era of rapid development, including poverty, disease, and even self-discovery. In 1995, however, all the New Religion momentum came to a screeching halt when the infamous *Aum Shinrikyou* cult, in an attempt to implement their apocalyptic plans, dispersed sarin gas in a Tokyo subway, killing 12 people, seriously injuring 54, and affecting some 980 more.

According to Kamata (personal communication), the national suspicion toward religion grew exponentially after the Tokyo sarin gas attack, especially among the young, and there was no turning back for them. However, the Japanese tended to target their suspicions on religious dogma rather than all things supernatural. In fact, the Japanese people still remain highly spiritual to this day, especially in their receptivity to supernatural beliefs such as "power spots" (places where people can go to collect positive mystical energy), astrology, haunted houses, and a variety of other superstitions. In other words, innocuous supernatural beliefs, devoid of any kind of dogmatic spiritual messages, continue to be tolerated in the mainstream and have, in fact, captivated the Japanese imagination, as is reflected in much of Japanese pop culture (e.g., anime, J-horror, morning fortune-telling shows, etc.).

In the interest of not leaving out the other historically influential religion in Japan, Buddhism, it is worth mentioning that Zen Buddhism has very much influenced the Japanese post-war ethic of hard work and self-sacrifice. Zielenziger (2006) discusses how Buddhist doctrines, as reinterpreted by the seventieth century scholar Baigan Ishida, saw hard labor as an expression not of self or even selflessness but of self-denial. Zielenziger argues that the meticulous attention to detail that Japanese show in their craftsmanship, such as in the fine artwork inside a kimono sleeve, pays homage to this ideal because it is the labor itself, not efficiency, that matters. This kind of work ethic and self-denial is not appealing to the increasing population of marginalized Japanese youth who are probably more concerned with not having enough outlets in society to express their post-materialist values and need for self-fulfillment. Any religion that interferes with self-fulfillment for youth who are beginning to embrace post-materialistic values will tend to become less popular among them (Schwartz, Chapter 4 in this volume). Therefore, it should come as no surprise that the explicit practice of Zen Buddhism has been phasing out for some time in modern Japan (Kamata, personal communication).

Given the peripheral role that religion plays in Japanese society, religion is unlikely to facilitate the kind of agency and value system that can help transform Japanese institutional and social structures to the benefit of Japanese youth any time soon. Instead, Japan will just have to find another path to reinvent itself on its own terms, no matter how arduous and time-consuming that process is. In the meantime, however, youth marginalization in Japan, such as *NEET* and *hikikomori*, is likely to persist. The psychological consequences and implications of youth marginalization is what we turn to next.

Deviation from Interdependence in Values and Motivation

Traditionally, most cross-cultural psychological studies have relied on examining segments of the population that represent the center of a given society; namely, middle class and occupationally functional individuals. Relying on this segment of the population, whether the sample is young or old, may necessarily create a tendency to endorse an entity view of culture rather than a dynamic view of culture, especially if the center of society represents the relatively stable aspects of society. If this is the case, it is more likely that those who are most affected by economic structural change because of globalization processes are segments of the population that flow from the center of society to the fringes of society at increasing rates. As these individuals move from the center of society to the periphery of society, they may no longer be under the pressure to internalize the dominant psychological tendencies of their society and may be able to maintain more "atypical" psychological tendencies, whether they were prone to those tendencies to begin with or whether they adopted them as a consequence of moving to alternative spaces in their societies.

We have taken the approach of comparing young people who are likely to remain in the center of society with those who are *NEET* or who are at risk of becoming *NEET*. We believe that the differences between these two groups' values and motivational processes represent changing trends in society owing to the multi-layered structural forces in society that are pushing many young people to the periphery. Moreover, it should come as no surprise that in any society undergoing post-industrialization, there will be economic instability. Furthermore, it is the youth who are going to be affected most by this economic instability, usually by experiencing the most insecurity in the labor markets (OECD stat, 2009). Thus, the strategy of comparing youth who are *NEETs* and *hikokomori* or at risk of becoming *NEET* versus youth not at risk seemed to be a valid cross-sectional strategy for capturing shifting values and motivational processes among youth in a society that is presumably in the midst of shifting to a new institutional equilibrium because of economic structural changes.

Comparing Self-Relevant Values

To measure values, Uchida and Norasakkunkit (2011) distributed survey packets to: (1) *NEETs* in a nationwide online survey targeted at those who are not employed and are not seeking employment, (2) recovering *hikikomori* clients through a non-profit organization (NPO) that reaches out to them, (3) Kyoto University students, an elite group of students who are likely to thrive in the mainstream of Japanese society, and (4) North American university students. The North American sample was included to compare *NEET* tendencies across cultures. We also included a *NEET* Risk Factor Scale we developed that required individuals to evaluate themselves on actual attitudes that *NEETs* and *hikokomori* harbor, according to the literature. After validating the scale on these known groups, we then used the scores on this scale to divide the Kyoto University students into a high risk group and a low-to-moderate risk group (henceforth referred to as low risk group) according to a cut-off score.

Uchida and Norasakkunkit (2011) also measured self-reported values congruent with independence and interdependence with the Singelis (1994) Self-Construal Scale and implicit values related to independence and interdependence with the Self-Construal Implicit Association Test (Self-Construal IAT; Uchida, Park, & Kitayama, 2008), although for pragmatic reasons, the Self-Construal IAT was not included in the nationwide online survey for non-*hikikomori NEETs*.

The findings confirmed that: (1) *NEET* tendencies are more likely to be found in the Japanese population relative to the North American population; (2) *NEETs*, *hikikomori*, and high risk students in Japan were also found, as expected, to deviate from interdependent values (i.e., scored lower on interdependence), both at the self-report and implicit levels, relative to low risk students; (3) surprisingly, it was also found that *NEETs* and *hikikomoris* also scored lower on independent self-construal relative to students, although there was no difference between high risk students and low risk students in levels of independent self-construal.

Comparing Motivational Tendencies

The Japanese idea of persistence is believed to be the key to achieving great success through the focus of group harmony (Wagatsuma, 1983). Given that the phenomena of *NEETs* and *hikikomori* have also been understood as a "psychopathology of motivation" (Koyama et al., 2010), it was also important to go beyond a self-report study to compare this kind of motivation between high risk students and low risk students at the behavioral level. To do this, Norasakkunkit and Uchida (2011) examined the conditions in which high risk students and low risk students would persist on a challenging task by replicating the procedure used by Heine and colleagues (2001) who showed that mainstream Japanese persisted longer on a similar follow-up challenging task after they had failed at an initial challenging task, compared to after they had succeeded at that initial task. In contrast, this pattern was reversed for North Americans. Presumably, this was because of the emphasis on constant improvement through the responsiveness to negative feedback over the emphasis on self-enhancement through responsiveness to positive feedback as the more adaptive motivational style in Japan's mainstream, interdependent cultural system (Fiske, Kitayama, Markus, & Nisbett, 1998). Indeed, persistence and determination, referred to in daily life as *gambari* or *gambaru*, is often the hallmark of Japanese motivation to try to work hard and meet others' expectations.

High Risk versus Low Risk Youth. Norasakkunkit and Uchida (2011) were able to replicate the prototypical Japanese persistence pattern produced in Heine and colleagues' (2001) study among the low risk students. However, among the high risk students, the pattern was reversed, as was expected. This finding suggests that high risk students exhibited a persistence style that deviated from that which would be considered adaptive in an interdependent cultural system. Although the persistence style of high risk students appeared to resemble that of the North American students found in Heine and colleagues' study, a closer look at the association between *NEET* tendencies and persistence levels, through simple slope analyses, suggested that whereas *NEET* tendencies were indeed associated with being *demotivated* by failure, *NEET* tendencies were not necessarily associated with being more motivated by success.

Changing Motivation across Generations. The combination of high risk students being lower on interdependent values and their tendency to deviate from a persistence style oriented toward interdependence may suggest a general refusal to conform to interdependent norms and expectations among high risk students, *NEET*s, and *hikikomori*s. However, in order to suggest that distancing oneself from interdependent norms and expectations may be a trend among Japanese youth today, such a trend has to be observable among youth who are also not necessarily at risk of being marginalized in Japanese society, even if such trends are subtle.

Fortunately, because both sets of Japanese data from Heine and colleague (2001) and Norasakkunkit and Uchida (2011) came from undergraduate students at the same university under the exact same experimental conditions exactly 10 years apart, it was also fruitful to compare the two samples on overall persistence, regardless of feedback condition, to look for historical trends associated with a decreased level of persistence.

When the data was examined in this way, it was indeed confirmed that there was a generation main effect that suggested that the low risk and high risk students were more similar to each other and therefore different from the students from 10 years ago. Specifically, the students from 10 years ago were willing to persist and persevere for a significantly longer period of time than the high risk *and* low risk students of today under the same experimental conditions, whereas the difference in persistence time between the high risk students and low risk students of today was not statistically significant (see Figure 9.1).

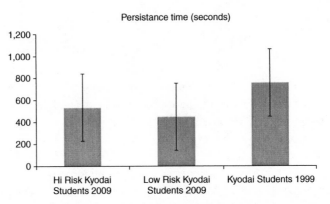

Figure 9.1. Overall persistence time: Kyoto University (Kyodai) students in 2009 versus 1999.

Post-materialist Values

At face value, it is tempting to simply suggest that the lifestyles chosen by *Freeters* and *NEETs* represent youth's post-materialist values and rebellion against what they perceive to be outmoded values embodied in society's expectation for them to conform to the "legitimate" path to responsible and respectable Japanese adulthood. Although there is no doubt that some youth have chosen to lead a lifestyle of a *NEET* for those reasons, and indeed, such explanations were quite popular in the 1990s (e.g., see Yamada, 1999), we tend to agree with Brinton (2011), Genda (2005), and Zielenziger (2006) that the problems of *Freeters*, *NEETs*, and *hikikomori* are largely a function of changing societal structures that are pushing young Japanese people to the periphery of society.

Therefore, to look for signs of post-materialist values, it is more appropriate to directly measure attitudes and choices that are in the control of the individual. One way is to look at attitudes toward competition, presumably because competition is a value that tends to promote materialist interests but detracts from post-material pursuits, unless the society is deeply entrenched in the Protestant ethic like the United States where attitudes toward competition tends to remain quite favorable (see Hayward & Kemmelmeier, 2007; Weber, 1904/1930). Thus, if some segment of marginalized Japanese youth (i.e., *NEETs* and *hikikomori*) represent individuals who are most affected by structural changes in society, it seemed reasonable to compare Kyoto University students with *NEETs/hikikomori* on attitudes toward competition to see if there is a trend toward moving away from competition as a necessary virtue for society.

In Uchida and Norasakkunkit's (2011) previously discussed study comparing values between students and marginalized youth, five items measuring attitudes toward competition were also included in the survey packet. These items were: (1) "I grew up in a competitive environment," (2) "I don't want to work in a competitive environment," (3) "Competition does not do anyone any good," (4) "Competition brings progress to society," and (5) "There are many competitive people around me." Because this set of items was not cohesive enough to collectively measure attitudes toward competition, levels of agreement on a 5-point Likert scale were compared separately for each item.

There was no group difference on items 1 and 5, which suggests that both samples were equally exposed to the idea of competition. However, marginalized youth scored significantly: (1) higher in their desire *not* to work in a competitive environment; (2) higher in the belief that competition does *not* do anyone any good, and (3) lower in their belief that competition brings progress to society. These findings suggest Japanese youth may be moving away from seeing competition as a necessary virtue for society.

What about Japanese youth who are not as affected by society's structural changes? One way to investigate this question is to examine the choices that youth make for their academic majors. Students, parents, and even professors have ideas for what majors are more practical than others (Moore, 2009). Thus, if economic and physical security take precedence over self-expression and self-fulfillment, then students should choose "practical" majors with presumably a higher pay-off in the job market, such as business, engineering, computer science, math, and natural science. On the other hand, if self-expression and self-fulfillment take precedence over economic and physical security, then students may choose "less practical" majors (e.g., art, humanities, and social sciences). The choice for practical majors should be especially compelling when the cost of a university education is very high, which is usually the case for any student studying abroad for their college degrees. Given this logic, we decided to examine some archival data on international students in the United States to compare students from more interdependently-oriented societies.

If it is the case that there is a growing trend among Japanese youth who are embracing post-materialist values, then there should be more Japanese students than students from other interdependently-oriented societies who choose less practical majors. We therefore examined archived data from the Institute of International Education (Chow & Bhuandari, 2011) and looked at the break down by majors of students coming only from Asian countries among the 25 top countries that send their students to the United States for higher education (see Table 9.1). The first column

Table 9.1. Breakdown by Nationality and Major of International Students in the United States

Rank	Place of Origin	Business/ Management (%)	Engineering (%)	Physical/Life Sciences (%)	Math/Computer Science (%)	Social Sciences (%)	Intensive English (%)	Fine/Applied Arts (%)	Health Professions (%)	Education (%)	Humanities (%)	Undeclared (%)	Other* (%)	"Practical" Majors (combined first four columns) (%)	"Less Practical" Majors (combined remaining columns, excluding undeclared majors (%)
1	China	24.30	20.20	12.60	10.70	6.70	4.90	2.80	2.10	1.90	1.10	2.60	10.10	67.80	29.60
2	India	15.30	38.80	10.20	19.80	3.00	0.20	1.40	4.90	0.70	0.60	0.90	4.20	84.10	15.00
3	South Korea	17.00	12.60	7.60	5.20	10.00	4.90	10.80	5.10	3.90	4.70	4.10	14.10	42.40	53.50
5	Taiwan	25.50	16.60	9.40	5.80	7.10	4.60	7.70	4.00	5.80	1.90	1.80	9.80»	57.30	40.90
6	Japan	20.90	4.40	5.70	2.90	13.20	11.30	8.80	3.20	3.40	4.40	4.80	17.00	33.90	61.30
7	Saudi Arabia	22.10	24.00	4.10	9.60	2.50	21.40	1.20	4.20	2.00	0.80	2.80	5.30	59.80	37.40
9	Vietnam	39.70	10.80	6.80	9.40	3.40	6.30	2.60	5.50	1.60	1.20	3.50	9.20	66.70	29.80
10	Turkey	18.60%	23.30%	7.90%	10.00%	12.60%	4.70%	3.60%	1.10%	3.70%	0.60%	2.20%	9.70%	59.80%	38.00%
11	Nepal	26.20%	13.80%	15.80%	11.70%	6.00%	0.20%	1.40%	9.20%	0.80%	1.90%	1.80%	11.20%	67.50%	30.70%
15	Thailand	26.60%	18.80%	7.10%	8.30%	7.00%	4.40%	3.70%	4.40%	3.10%	1.70%	2.30%	12.60%	60.80%	36.90%
16	Hong Kong	31.90%	9.40%	7.40%	4.90%	13.80%	2.10%	6.10%	2.30%	1.20%	2.40%	5.70%	12.80%	53.60%	40.70%
18	Indonesia	36.70%	18.80%	5.30%	6.30%	6.30%	6.20%	5.80%	3.50%	2.50%	1.80%	2.00%	10.70%	67.10%	36.80%
21	Malaysia	21.50%	28.40%	10.50%	6.00%	8.00%	0.70%	3.10%	3.90%	3.00%	1.40%	4.30%	9.20%	66.40%	29.30%
23	Pakistan	24.50%	23.20%	6.10%	10.70%	9.50%	0.90%	2.50%	5.10%	2.70%	1.90%	3.30%	960%	64.50%	32.20%

* Includes primarily agriculture, communications, law, general studies, and multi-interdisciplinary studies.
Note: Data from the Open Doors Report on International Educational Exchange, retrieved May 12, 2011 from http://www.iie.org/opendoors.

ranks the countries according to the number of international students sent from those countries. Japan is ranked sixth. The top row displays the various majors in order of popularity from left to right. Not surprisingly, the top four majors among international students are the practical majors, followed by the less practical majors. For each country, we summed the percentages of the first four columns (starting with Business/Management and ending with Math/Computer Science) to calculate the aggregate percentage of students from that country who selected a practical major. The cells for the remaining columns, excluding undeclared category, was summed for each country to compute the aggregate percentages of students from each country who selected the less practical major. As expected, Japan ranked at the bottom of the Asian countries in the selection of practical majors and at the top of the Asian countries in the selection of less practical majors. Incidentally, the ranking did not change for Japan whether or not African countries were also included in the list and whether or not the "other" majors category was included in the computations of aggregate percentages.

These findings suggest that Japanese international students, despite the high cost of studying in the United States as international students, were more willing to select majors based on their own preferences and self-fulfillment rather than based on a commonly perceived economic pay-off for selecting the practical majors. This is an indication that there is a growing trend among Japanese youth to embrace post-materialistic values in their choices. This trend is probably not unique to Japan. As other interdependently-oriented societies begin to enter the post-industrial phase of their society, the youth in those societies will likely make similar choices that Japanese youth are making now. Indeed, there is some evidence of such shifting values among Chinese adolescents in China today as well (see Chen, Wang, & Liu, Chapter 10 in this volume).

Taken together, the findings discussed above suggest that marginalized Japanese youth such as *Freeters*, *NEETs*, and *hikikomori* may represent an extreme version of a growing trend among today's Japanese youth to deviate, to some degree, from interdependent values and from interdependently-oriented motivational processes. At the same time, Japanese youth are more often embracing a greater desire for individual self-fulfillment and self-expression. Although such trends should be expected in any interdependently-oriented society undergoing a transition to a post-industrial economy, what is unique about Japan is the manifestation of these trends as chronic and targeted marginalization of youth.

Volunteerism and its Lessons for Japanese Youth Values

On March 11, 2011, a devastating earthquake (magnitude 9 on the Richter scale) shook northeast Japan and was followed by catastrophic tsunami waves of up to about 130 feet that killed over 15,000 residents in the region. Additionally, 8,500 citizens were declared missing and presumed dead, over 5,000 people injured, and millions either lost their homes or suffered significant damages to their homes. To make matters worse, the tsunami struck a number of nuclear power plants in Fukushima prefecture and triggered a nuclear disaster rated at the same level of disaster as the Chernobyl nuclear power plant meltdown.

In a government sponsored nationwide survey with a sample size of over 10,700 individuals ages 20 to 39, Uchida, Takahashi, and Kawahara (2011) found that 68 percent of their sample reported having their values significantly impacted as a direct result of the earthquake. In addition to reporting that they were significantly disturbed by the disaster, they indicated that they reported having reevaluated what they appreciated in their lives. For 90 percent of them, the value they placed on their social connectedness with others increased the most. The other value that increased was the value to work. These people reported that the earthquake increased their own motivation to work harder. The only exception to these trends were those who tended to score high on *NEET* tendencies according to the Uchida and Norasakkunkit (2011) *NEET* Risk Factor Scale. For these people, there was a tendency not to think or be affected, either positively or negatively, by the disaster. This unfortunate finding speaks to the chronic demotivated states of many *NEET*s and *hikikomori*s, suggesting that they are probably in a state of disillusionment and emotional numbness (see also Kameda & Inukai, under review).

For the youth who were impacted by the disaster, many of them fulfilled their need for social connectedness and hard work by volunteering in the disaster areas. Just as they did in the 1995 Kobe earthquake in Western Japan, which killed close to 6,500 individuals and left 300,000 individuals homeless, the world watched in dumbfounded admiration as ordinary citizens maintained social order and reached out to support one another (see Hunter, 2011).

Among the first to volunteer was the Japanese youth. High schools, universities, and aid agencies such as Youth for 3.11 (http://youthfor311.jimdo. com/) helped to inspire and organize students and working and nonworking young adults (*The Japan Times* Online, March 27, 2011). The volunteer organizations helped to communicate to youth what the victims needed.

In Japan, student volunteering is undervalued by employers and university admissions offices, and unlike other countries, Japan does not have an infrastructure of religious organizations promoting the idea of volunteering as a moral virtue. Yet, even during the 1995 Kobe earthquake, approximately 620,000 youth volunteers stepped up during the first month of the disaster (Sankei News, 2011). Prior to 1995, the concept of volunteerism hardly existed in Japan because the Social Service Law had put charity and philanthropy under the strict control of the state. Thus, 1995 came to be known as "Year One of Volunteerism" in Japan (Tatsuki, 2000). In 2011, the number of youth volunteers during the first month of the disaster was approximately 104,000 (Sankei News, 2011). Although this number is about one-sixth of that in the 1995 Kobe earthquake, probably because of fear of exposure to radiation emanating from the Fukushima nuclear power plants, the volunteers of 2011 were more organized this time, in part, because of Japanese social network websites like Mixi that was used to communicate with fellow volunteers in the affected regions to streamline the recovery effort.

Given the lack of material incentive, why are so many Japanese youth drawn to volunteering, especially in times of national crisis? Testimonials from the volunteers suggest that when local and national governments are insufficient, the opportunity for youth to help shape the future of the country opens up. Volunteering is also an opportunity for youth to feel more connected with others.

When John Burnett (2011), a reporter for National Public Radio, interviewed youth volunteers in northeastern Japan, he was met with the following responses. "I thought it would be cool, because we're all Japanese, that's why I came," said a 25-year-old art student. Futoshi Sato, a resident of the port city of Sendai said, "Here in Miyagi prefecture, people used Mixi to ask the victims who live in the tsunami-hit cities of Ishinomaki and Kesennuma how people could help them and what they needed and they told us how they wanted us to help."

Laura Gottesdiener (2011), a reporter for *Huffington Post*, recorded similar testimonials. Akiko Karako, a university student volunteer from Tokyo said, "Students are enthusiastically trying to organize volunteer groups and build connections between places and organizations, and those are things worth respecting from the adults' viewpoint." Also, when Kentaro Watari, one of the organizers of Youth for 3.11, was asked why a group of university student volunteers from Tokyo at the scene of devastation was crying, he said, "...because they've never been [in] such a good team...Youth for 3.11's number one vision is to do the best we can for the relief victims, but our secondary mission is to create a student movement that will change volunteering and youth in Japan. Our generation has been hated on by a lot of society, and I think that after the earthquake students have woken up and realized there's more to life, that we can make a big difference."

Volunteering also came up when we visited a youth support agency that helped us obtain data from recovering *hikikomori* clients for our studies previously discussed (Norasakkunkit & Uchida, 2011; Uchida & Norasakkunkit, 2010; Uchida et al., 2010). In a meeting for the parents of *hikikomori*, one fully recovered *hikikomori* came up front to talk about his experience. When he was asked what experience most impacted him during his recovery, he talked about his volunteering experience. "I didn't feel any pressure. Yet, when I volunteered, I felt that people were appreciative of me. I felt needed," he said. "I think that's when I started to feel good about working."

Although it is too soon to tell how volunteering will be shaped by the crisis currently unfolding in Japan, we believe that one of the important lessons that can be learned from the impact of the March 11, 2011 natural disaster and from youth volunteers in Japan is that many Japanese youth are not seeking to be left alone by the older generation. Instead, the values that changed the most as a result of the disaster and their motivations to volunteer suggest that they seek connection from a position of mutual respect, self-fulfillment, and even mutual sacrifice, not from a position of low status, self-denial, and disempowerment. Although Western pop culture has no doubt influenced the values of Japanese youth, it is unlikely that Japanese youth want to fully embrace American-style rugged individualism with its emphasis on self-reliance and independence. Rather, they appear to be seeking a more compassionate and egalitarian kind of interdependence where the self also has some room to be expressed and where their post-materialist values can have a place to live and breathe. If the youth of Japan are allowed to negotiate a role in shaping such a future, the pervasiveness of youth problems such as NEETs, *hikikomori*s, and teenage suicide may finally be a thing of the past.

REFERENCES

Arnett, J. J. (2004). *Emerging adulthood: The winding road from the late teens through the twenties.* Oxford: Oxford University Press.

Brinton, M. (2011). *Lost in transition: Youth, work, and instability in postindustrial Japan.* New York: Cambridge University Press.

Bronfenbrenner, U. (1979). *The ecology of human development. Experiments by nature and design.* Cambridge, MA: Harvard University Press.

Burnett, J. (2011, April 12). *Japanese youth step up in earthquake aftermath.* Retrieved May 30, 2011, from http://www.npr.org/2011/04/12/135348165/japanese-youth-step-up-in-earthquake-aftermath.

Cabinet Office, Government of Japan (2009). *Hikikomori ni kansuru jittai chosa [An investigation of the nature of hikikomori].* Retrieved from http://www8.cao.go.jp/youth/kenkyu/hikikomori/pdf_index.html.

Chow, P., & Bhandari, R. (2011). *Open doors 2011 report on International Educational Exchange.* New York: Institute of International Education. Retrieved May 12, 2011 from http://www.iie.org/opendoors.

DfEE (2001). Transforming youth work. Department for Education and Employment [in the UK].

Fiske, A. P., Kitayama, S., Markus, H. R., & Nisbett, R. E. (1998). The cultural matrix of social psychology. In D. Gilbert, S. Fiske, & G. Linzey (Eds.), *Handbook of social psychology* (pp. 915–981). Boston: McGraw-Hill.

Genda, Y. (2005). *A nagging sense of job insecurity: The new reality facing Japanese youth.* Tokyo: International House of Japan, Inc.

Giorgi, L., & Marsh, C. (1990). The Protestant work ethic as a cultural phenomenon. *European Journal of Social Psychology,* **20,** 499–517.

Gottesdiener, L. (2011, April 7). Japan's youth build generations' identity in time of crisis. Retrieved May 30, 2011, from http://www.huffingtonpost.com/2011/04/07/japan-earthquake-tsunami-youth_n_846178.html.

Hamamura, T., Meijer, Z., Heine, S. J., Kamaya, K., & Hori, I. (2009) Approach-avoidance motivations and information processing: A cross-cultural analysis. *Personality and Social Psychology Bulletin,* **35,** 454–462.

Hayward, R. D., & Kemmelmeier, M. (2007). How competition is viewed across cultures: A test of four theories. *Cross-Cultural Research,* **41,** 364–395.

Heine, S. J., Kitayama, S., Lehman, D. R., Takata, T., Ide, E., Leung, C., & Matsumoto, H. (2001). Divergent consequences of success and failure in Japan and North America. An investigation of self-improving motivations and malleable selves. *Journal of Personality and Social Psychology,* **81,** 599–615.

Hunter, M. (2011, March 12). *Orderly disaster reaction in line with deep cultural roots.* Retrieved May 30, 2011, from http://news.blogs.cnn.com/2011/03/12/orderly-disaster-reaction-in-line-with-deep-cultural-roots/.

Inglehart, R. (1977). *The silent revolution: Changing values and political styles among Western publics.* Princeton, NJ: Princeton University Press.

(2008). Changing values among Western publics from 1970 to 2006. *West European Politics,* **31,** 130–146.

Kamata, T. (2000). *Ethos of edge (Oudouron vol.3): Edge no shisou waraberon: Initiation naki jidai wo ikinukutameni* [The guide to survive the modern era without an initiation process]. Tokyo: Shinyousha.

Kameda, T., & Inukai, K. (under review). Emotional functioning, socio-economic uncertainty, and cultural pathology: An investigation of the impact of SES on momentary and elicited emotion.

Kariya, T. (2011). Credential inflation and employment in 'universal' higher education: Enrollment, expansion and (in)equity via privatisation in Japan. *Journal of Education and Work,* **24** (1–2), 69–94.

Kitayama, S., Mesquita, B., & Karasawa, M. (2006). Cultural affordances and emotional experience: Socially engaging and disengaging emotions in Japan and the United States. *Journal of Personality and Social Psychology*, **91**(5), 890–903.

Kosugi, R. (2008). *Escape from work: Freelancing youth and challenge to corporate Japan*. Melbourne: Trans Pacific Press.

Koyama, A., Miyake, Y., Kawakami, N., Tsuchiya, M., Tachimori, H., & Takeshima, T. (2010). Lifetime prevalence, psychiatric comorbidity and demographic correlates of "hikikomori" in a community population in Japan. *Psychiatry Research*, **176**, 69–74.

Lehman, J. P. (2002, April 22). *Gerontocracy and its perks sap resources*. Retrieved May 22, 2011, from http://search.japantimes.co.jp/cgi-bin/eo20020422jl.html.

Mainichi News (2010, April 27). *More Japanese children lack motivation, value inner happiness*. Retrieved May 20, 2010 from http://mdn.mainichi.jp/features/news/20100426p2a00m0na006000c.html.

Markus, H. R., & Kitayama, S. (1991). Culture and the self: Implications for cognition, emotion, and motivation. *Psychological Review*, **98**(2), 224–253. doi:10.1037/0033-295X.98.2.224

Masuda, T., & Nisbett, R. E. (2001). Attending holistically vs. analytically: Comparing the context sensitivity of Japanese and Americans. *Journal of Personality and Social Psychology*, **81**, 922–934.

Mathews, G. (2004). Seeking a career, finding a job: How young people enter and resist the Japanese world of work. In G. Mathews & B. White (Eds.), *Japan's changing generations* (pp. 69–93). New York: Guilford Press.

Matsumoto, D. (2002). *The new Japan: Debunking seven cultural stereotypes*. Yarmouth, ME: Intercultural Press.

McClelland, D. (1961). *The achieving society*. Princeton, NJ: Van Nostrand.

Moore, J. C. (2009, July 28). *Students giving up dream majors for practical pick*. Retrieved May 12, 2011, from http://www.vcstar.com/news/2009/jul/28/local-students-forgo-dream-majors-in-hopes-of-a/.

Norasakkunkit, V. (2007, July). *Pictorial versus verbal priming: Standardizing an experimental priming procedure in the United States and Japan*. Paper presented at the 7th Biennial Conference of the Asian Association of Social Psychology, Kota Kinabalu, Malaysia.

Norasakkunkit, V., & Uchida, Y. (2011). Psychological consequences of post-industrial anomie on self and motivation among Japanese youth. *Journal of Social Issues*, **67**(4), 774–786.

OECD Stat (2009). *Country statistical profiles*. Retrieved from http://stats.oecd.org/Index.aspx?DataSetCode=CSP2009.

Oyserman, D., Coon, H. M., & Kemmelmeier, M. (2002). Rethinking individualism and collectivism: Evaluation of theoretical assumptions and meta-analyses. *Psychological Bulletin*, **128**(1), 3–72.

Quinn, D. M., & Crocker, J. (1999). When ideology hurts: Effects of feeling fat and the Protestant ethic on the psychological well-being of women. *Journal of Personality and Social Psychology*, **77**, 402–414.

Saito, T. (1998). *Shakaiteki hikikomori: Owaranai shishunki* [Social withdrawal: Unending adolescence]. Tokyo: PHP Shuppan.

Sakai, M., Horikawa, H., Nonaka, S., Matsumoto, M., & Hirakawa, S. (2011). Research report on the nature of *hikikomori*. Proceedings of the KHJ Parents' Association Meeting.

Sanchez-Burks, J. (2002). Protestant relational ideology and (in) attention to relational cues in work settings. *Journal of Personality and Social Psychology, 83*, 919–929.

Sankei News (2011, April 26). *The number of volunteers at the disaster site sharply decrease compared with the Hanshin Great Earthquake*. Retrieved May 30, 2011 from http://sankei.jp.msn.com/life/news/110426/trd11042607400003-n1.htm.

Sato, Y. (2010). *Japan's traditional seniority system fading as new disparities emerge*. Retrieved May 30, 2011, from http://www.fgl.tohoku.ac.jp/rsch/05/tpc01.shtml.

Singelis, T. M. (1994). The measurement of independent and interdependent self-construals. *Personality and Social Psychology Bulletin, 20*(5), 580–591.

Statistics Bureau (2011). *Labor force survey (long term time series data)*. Tokyo: Ministry of Internal Affairs and Communications, the Government of Japan. URL: http://www.estat.go.jp/SG1/estat/List.do?bid=000001007702&cycode=0 (accessed May 5, 2011).

Tatsuki, S. (2000). The Kobe earthquake and the renaissance of volunteerism in Japan. *Journal of Kwansei Gakuin University Department of Sociology Studies, 87*, 185–196.

The Japan Times Online (2011, March 27). *The young volunteers*. Retrieved May 30, 2011 from http://search.japantimes.co.jp/cgi-bin/ed20110327a2.html.

Trzesniewski, K. H., & Donnellan, M. B. (2010). Rethinking "Generation Me": A study of cohort effects from 1976–2006. *Perspective in Psychological Science, 5*(1), 58–75.

Uchida, Y. (2002). *Culture and implicit self-construals*. Paper presented at the International Symposium on the Socio-Cultural Foundations of Cognition, Kyoto University, Kyoto, Japan.

Uchida, Y., & Norasakkunkit, V. (2011). *Hikikomori/NEET keikou to taijinkankei no kentou* [The *NEET* Risk Factor Scale and special considerations to interpersonal factors]. Manuscript in prep.

Uchida, Y., Norasakkunkit, V., Kishimoto, S., Fujiwara, M., Kondo, M., & Morisaki, S. (December 18, 2010). *Seinenki no shakaiteki tekiyou: hikikomori/NEET no bunkashinrigakuteki kentou* [The social adaptation of youth: Considerations from a cultural psychological perspective]. The Kokoro Research Center Convention on Research Findings (2010). Kokoro Research Center, Kyoto University, Kyoto, Japan.

Uchida, Y., Park, J., & Kitayama, S. (2008, February). *Explicit and implicit social orientations: Independence and interdependence in Japan and the U.S.* Paper presented at the 9th Annual Conference of the Society of Personality and Social Psychology, Albuquerque, New Mexico.

Uchida, Y., Takahashi, Y., & Kawahara, K. (2011). Higashi nihon daishinsai chokugo no jakunen sou no seikatsu koudo oyobi koufukudo ni kansuru eikyou [The immediate effects of the great earthquake of eastern Japan on the lifestyle and happiness of youth]. *Working paper of the Economic and Social Research Institute*. Cabinet Office of the Japanese Government.

Wagatsuma, H. (1983). *Encyclopedia of Japan 3*. Tokyo: Kodansha.

Weber, M. (1904/1930). *The protestant ethic and the spirit of capitalism*. New York: The Citadel Press.

Yamada, M. (1999). *Parasaito shinguru no jidai* [The age of parasite singles]. Tokyo: Chikuma Shobo.

Yamagishi, T. (1999). Trust and social intelligence. *Genetics*, **11**, 158–165. (In Japanese)

Zielenziger, M. (2006). *Shutting out the sun: How Japan created its own lost generation.* New York: Nan A. Talese.

(in press). In T. Kawai & Y. Uchida (Eds.). *Hikikomori-ko.* Kyoto: Sogensha.

10 Adolescent Cultural Values and Adjustment in the Changing Chinese Society

Xinyin Chen, Li Wang, and Junsheng Liu

Abstract

Over the past two decades, China has been changing dramatically toward a market-oriented society, particularly in urban areas, which may undermine the traditional cultural and religious systems. Individualistic ideologies and values are required for adjustment and success in the new competitive environment and are increasingly appreciated by individuals, especially in the young generations. This chapter focuses on cultural values and their relations with adjustment in Chinese youth from urban, rural, and rural-to-urban migrant backgrounds. There is emerging evidence suggesting differences between the urban and rural adolescents in their cultural values. Whereas group orientation and social connectedness continue to be valued among rural and urban adolescents, urban adolescents are more likely than their rural counterparts to appreciate and approve the expression of personal distinctiveness and develop a "unitary and stable" self that is separate from social context. Moreover, among urban, but not rural or migrant, adolescents, values of uniqueness have become important for the development of social status in the peer group and school achievement. As a future direction, it will be interesting to explore how adolescents in China integrate diverse values in their adaptation to the changing sociocultural context.

How macro-level societal changes affect the socioemotional and cognitive functioning of children and adolescents is an important issue in developmental science (Bronfenbrenner & Morris, 2006; Elder & Shanahan, 2006; Silbereisen, 2005). Research findings have indicated considerable implications of social, economic, and cultural changes for human development during modernization in traditionally rural societies (e.g., Kagitcibasi & Ataca, 2005) and in the Great Depression in the 1930s in the United States

(Elder 1974). Recent studies (e.g., Silbereisen, 2005) have also revealed that sociopolitical changes in Eastern European nations after the fall of the Berlin Wall have pervasive effects on the relationships, behaviors, and life adjustment of youth.

Researchers who study social change and human development are often interested in individual cultural values (e.g., Silbereisen, 2005). Value systems are highly susceptible to the influence of environmental change and, at the same time, serve as a guideline for interpersonal interaction and individual functioning. Kagitcibasi and Ataca (2005), for example, found that the cultural values of Turkish parents changed over the past three decades as a result of the transformation of the society. Turkish parents in 2003, particularly in high socioeconomic status urban families, valued autonomy and independence more than those in 1975. The urbanization and socioeconomic development were associated with a decline in material dependence within the family and an increase in positive attitudes toward children's independent and exploratory behaviors. Similar findings concerning changes in cultural values of independence and individuality have been reported in other societies such as Maya communities in Mexico and Guatemala (e.g., Greenfield, Maynard, & Childs, 2000) and Germany (Eickhorst, Lamm, Borke, & Keller, 2008; Keller & Lamm, 2005).

The Economic Reform, Social Change, Regional Differences, and Internal Migration in China

China has been a primarily agrarian society for thousands of years, with most people living under adverse conditions during most periods of its history. The economy was poor in the nineteenth and the most of the twentieth centuries. After the Communists took power in 1949, the government installed a centrally planned economy, which eventually resulted in a drop in living standards. Since the early 1980s, China has carried out a large-scale economic reform, moving toward a market-oriented society. The main goal of the reform is to transform the planned economy dominated by state-owned enterprises to one that is increasingly market-oriented and inclusive of state and private enterprises. The initial phase of the reform was the "internal vitalization" in rural areas and the "open-the-door" movement in some southern regions. The reform was expanded to cities and other parts of the country in the early 1990s. The rapid expansion of the market systems to various sectors has led to major changes in economic and social structures in the country. Consequently, there are substantial increases in individual and family income and its variation, massive movement of the population, decline in the government control of social welfare and protection, and rapid rise in unemployment and competition (e.g., Chen & Chen, 2010; Zhang, 2000).

The economy in China is currently one of the largest in the world and growing at the rate of approximately 10 percent a year. According to the National Bureau of Statistics of China (Bulletin, 2010), in comparison to the 1949 annual per capita income of 100 and 50 Yuan for urban and rural areas, respectively, the annual per capita income was 10,493 and 17,175 Yuan (approx. US$1,312 and $2,450) for urban residents and 3,255 and 5,153 Yuan (approx. US$406 and $736) for rural residents in 2005 and 2009, respectively. A major feature of the economic reform is to break the "iron rice bowl" in jobs with guaranteed security and steady income and benefits in the traditional command economy. According to Zheng and Yang (2009), private enterprises have continuously increased in number at the rate of more than 30 percent since 1992 and contributed to one-third of GDP and four-fifths of new employment in recent years. As a result, many people choose, or are forced, to "jump into the sea" by entering self-employment or private sectors where they face a higher risk in job security and greater work autonomy.

As an important aspect of social change, Western technologies have been imported into the country along with efficient management in economy, which has gradually affected social, educational, and other daily life activities of Chinese people. High-technology products such as computer, Internet, and electronics such as cell phones/mobile devices, digital cameras and camcorders are now popular in cities and towns in China. In Beijing, for example, over 70 percent of families possess a computer, and most people report that they use the Internet to obtain information, chat, play games, read news, and receive and sending emails (Yi & Yu, 2003). Although the exposure to high technology is a common experience of adults and adolescents in many other contemporary societies, this experience is related to the "open-the-door" policy in China, which may have particular implications for the development of Chinese adolescents.

There are substantial regional, particularly urban and rural, differences in social and economic developments within China. The massive social and economic reform such as the opening of stock markets in China has been largely limited to urban centers and cities, although the reform started in rural areas in the early 1980s. Families in rural China have lived mostly agricultural lives, and rural adolescents, accounting for approximately 60 percent of the adolescents in the country, do not have as much exposure as their urban counterparts to the influence of the dramatic social transformation (Huang & Du, 2007; Li, 2006). China's policies and development strategies have created huge gaps between rural and urban populations in many aspects of life including health care conditions, educational opportunities, and income levels (Yang & Zhou, 1999). Rural population is generally at a disadvantage in these aspects.

A significant phenomenon related to urban-rural differences in China is internal migration. Since the early 1990s, the Chinese government has relaxed the enforcement of migration restriction and allowed cities to absorb surplus rural labor. As a result, millions of rural people have moved to cities to seek opportunities. With relatively limited education, most rural-to-urban migrants become unskilled workers in the city in such sectors as manual labor (e.g., manufacturing, cleaning streets, transporting goods), construction, and commerce (e.g., street peddlers, small vendors). Many rural migrant workers have brought their families including children to the cities. In 2005, approximately 20 million school-age rural children lived in cities with their parents (Nielsen, Nyland, Nyland, Smyth, & Zhang, 2005). Rural migrant families often stay in the city for years while maintaining links to their villages of origin (e.g., Wang, 2004). Under the *hukou* system of household registration, migrant children do not have an urban registration and thus do not have the same privileges as urban children. Many rural children are unable to enter public city schools because of various obstacles such as extra fees they have to pay. To address the problem, the municipal government and the migrant community within major cities such as Beijing and Shanghai have set up migrant children schools.

Cultural and Religious Backgrounds and Changes of Values

Traditional Chinese society is relatively homogenous in its cultural background, with Confucianism serving as a predominant ideological guideline for social activities. Confucius (551–479 B.C.) believed that, to achieve and maintain social order, it is important to establish a set of moral and social standards to guide interpersonal interactions and individual behaviors in daily life. The highest social-moral standards in the Confucian system include 仁 or *ren* (benevolence, humanity), 义 or *yi* (righteousness), 礼 or *li* (propriety, proper conduct), 智 or *zhi* (wisdom and knowledge), and 信 or *xin* (trustworthiness). To reach these standards, individuals in different roles should follow specific social rules such as 孝 or *Xiao* (filial piety) that stipulates that children must pledge obedience and reverence to parents. Confucianism provides a hierarchical, holistic cultural framework that emphasizes the control of individual desires and behaviors for the well-being of the collective; the expression of individual needs or striving for autonomous behaviors is considered socially unacceptable. Confucian principles concerning individual behaviors and relationships have been adopted by most rulers of the country in its history and have had a remarkable influence on socialization and human development in China.

Taoism is another indigenous belief and religious system in China that has significantly influenced the values of the Chinese people. Similar to Confucianism, Taoism emphasizes connections among different external and internal conditions of human functioning from a holistic perspective. According to Taoist philosophy, human beings live between heaven and earth (i.e., macrocosm) and comprise a miniature universe within themselves (i.e., microcosm). Maintaining harmony between the macrocosms and the microcosms is critical to healthy individual development. Unlike Confucianism, Taoism advocates extremely passive attitudes and behaviors in daily life activities to pursue internal peace and well-being. It is believed that pursuing external material possessions leads to desires and confusions, which cause internal emotional disturbances. Softness, tenderness, and weakness are the desirable attributes of life, whereas firmness, strength, and stiffness are undesirable concomitants of death. Human beings should remain flexible and take "no action" in dealing with challenges and adversities (Wang, 2006). Another major difference between Confucianism and Taoism is that whereas the former is largely a philosophical system, the latter is a mixture of philosophy and religion. Like many religions, religious Taoism includes a variety of practices. There are Taoist temples, monasteries, priests, rituals, and a number of gods and goddesses for believers to worship. Taoist beliefs are reflected in many aspects of the lives of Chinese people such as politics, medicine, calligraphy, and poetry. Taoist believers in China often engage in activities such as physical cultivation (e.g., Tai Chi exercise) and contemplation that are developed based on Taoist beliefs.

It is important to note that Chinese society is not homogeneous in beliefs and values concerning human behavior and development, despite the dominance of Confucianism and popularity of Taoism in the traditional Chinese culture. Although Confucian values generally emphasize the suppression and restraint of personal desires for social harmony, for example, some Confucian scholars such as Mencius discussed the role of individual active attitudes in self-cultivation and character development (Yu, 2004). Within the holistic and naturalistic framework, Taoism advocates avoiding and resisting social constraints including the influence of social-moral standards and group norms and the control of the authority. The primary proponents of Taoism, Laotze and Zhuangtze, endorsed the rebellion of social and political order of the society and even encouraged the pursuit of personal freedom, although the notion of individuality in Taoism has not been generally recognized in Chinese culture (Yu, 2004). This may be illustrated in Zhuangtze's teaching, "Going back and forth between heaven and earth and moving freely around the world without being hindered by others are called 'du you' (keeping something to self, uniqueness). A person with the quality of 'du you' is a noble person." (Zhuangtze, 2006; p. 99).

Moreover, the Chinese society has been changing since early in the last century when Western ideologies were introduced into the country (Yu, 2004). This change has accelerated over the past three decades as a result of the economic reform in China. Many traditional Chinese cultural values are incompatible with the requirements of the market-oriented society that emphasizes individual initiative, active exploration, and competitiveness. To function adequately and obtain success in the new environment, individuals need to learn skills that help them behave in an independent and assertive manner (Chen & Chen, 2010). In a recent study, Liu et al. (2005) found in an observational study of parent–child interactions that Canadian parents had relatively higher scores on the encouragement of autonomy/individuality whereas Chinese parents had relatively higher scores on encouragement of connectedness. However, within the Chinese sample, there was a substantial individual variability on both autonomy- and connectedness-oriented parenting behaviors. Indeed, like Canadian parents, Chinese parents had higher scores on encouragement of autonomy than on encouragement of connectedness. In both Chinese and Canadian samples, parental encouragement of autonomy was associated with child autonomous behavior whereas parental connectedness was associated with child connectedness and affiliative behavior.

Of particular relevance to adolescent development are the significant changes in educational policies and practices in Chinese schools. As required in the "Outline of the educational reform" established by the Ministry of Education of (Yu, 2002), many schools have expanded the goals of education to include helping children develop social and behavioral qualities that are required for adaptation in the competitive society. Whereas academic achievement continues to be emphasized, children are also encouraged to develop social skills such as expression of personal opinions, self-direction and self-confidence, which have traditionally been neglected in Chinese culture (Yu, 2002). A variety of strategies (e.g., encouraging students to engage in public debate and to plan and organize their own extracurricular activities) has been used to facilitate the development of these skills. The emphasis on individuality and self-expression in education and other social activities, particularly in urban schools, is likely to have implications for the development of values in Chinese adolescents.

Zhang and Zhao (2006) conducted a study in an urban area of China to compare the values of high school students and their parents. A large random sample of students in several high schools and their parents completed a self-report questionnaire assessing values in multiple domains such as family responsibility, independence, equality, personal privacy, interpersonal relationships, pursuit of modern lifestyle, maintenance of tradition, learning, and self-orientation. The results indicated that students were more likely than parents to value self-orientation, independence, personal privacy, social interaction, and interpersonal equality. In contrast, parents were more likely than students to endorse values of family responsibility, harmoneous family atmosphere, knowledge, and tradition. These results indicate different values of two generations of people in China, although various factors such as age and role of parent versus child may be related to the differences in values.

The implications of social change may be illustrated by different perceptions and evaluations of shy, wary, and restrained behavior in urban Chinese children and adolescents at different historical times (Chen & Chen, 2010; Hart et al., 2000). Despite its potential detrimental effects on self-expression and active social participation, shy and restrained behavior has been traditionally valued and encouraged in China because it is believed to indicate social maturity and understanding (Chen, Rubin, & Li, 1995). However, this behavior is viewed by adolescents in urban areas as increasingly maladaptive and deviant; it is associated with more negative social evaluations and has become a more undesirable characteristic in social and psychological adjustment in recent years. Specifically, Chen, Cen, Li, and He (2005) explored how shyness was associated with peer attitudes in three cohorts (1990, 1998, and 2002) in Shanghai, China. Whereas people in the early 1990s experienced relatively limited influence from the comprehensive reform and people in early 2000s were socialized in an increased self-oriented cultural context, the 1998 cohort represented an intermediate phase in which individuals might have mixed socialization experiences. The study revealed significant cross-cohort differences in the relations between shyness and social attitudes and reactions. Whereas shyness was positively associated with peer acceptance and leadership in the 1990 cohort, it was positively associated with peer rejection and negative self-feelings such as loneliness and depression in the 2002 cohort. The patterns of the relations between shyness and peer evaluations and adjustment variables were nonsignificant or mixed in the 1998 cohort. The results showed that by the early part of the twenty-first century as cities in China became more deeply immersed in a market economy, shy children, unlike their counterparts in the early 1990s, were perceived as incompetent and problematic and thus rejected by peers and displayed adjustment problems. Similar results were reported in samples of high school students in China (Liu, Chen, Li, & French, in press).

It has been argued that whereas individuality and independence are increasingly valued, group orientation and social connectedness may not necessarily be discouraged or weakened in China (Yang, 1986). According to this argument, during the transition to modernization, some traditional values, especially those with vigorous cultural roots, may be maintained and manifested in the social lives of Chinese people. As a core aspect of Confucian holistic philosophy and contemporary collectivistic ideologies, group orientation is likely to display its robustness in the context of social change and continue to affect social interaction and individual functioning in Chinese adults and children (Oyserman Coon, & Kemmelmeier, 2002; Triandis, 1995).

Cultural Values of Urban, Rural, and Migrant Adolescents
Traditional Chinese values such as group harmony and self-control are more highly emphasized in interpersonal interaction in rural than urban areas of China (Fuligni & Zhang, 2004; Shen, 2006; Sun, 2006). For example, parents in rural families are more likely than parents in urban families to maintain socialization goals and use childrearing practices that are consistent with the traditional beliefs such as filial piety and self-sacrifice for the family (e.g., China Youth & Children Research Center, 2007; Shen, 2006). Corresponding to the urban-rural variation in socialization expectations and practices, urban and rural adolescents have been found to differ in their values and attitudes with regard to group and individual interests (e.g., Sun, 2006). In general, relative to their urban counterparts, rural youth are more concerned about group or collective well-being, display greater social responsibility, and are less likely to pursue individual interests (Guo, Yao, & Yang, 2005).

We recently conducted a study of cultural values and adjustment in Chinese youth of different backgrounds. In the study, we focused on two main categories of values, individuality and social affiliation. Individuality, including personal assertiveness and uniqueness, is concerned with the expression of one's views and behavioral styles and the display of distinctiveness of oneself from others. In contrast, social affiliation, including group orientation and interpersonal connectedness, mainly taps into a sense of belonging and fitting in and intertwining with social context.

In the study, we collected data on cultural values through self-reports from urban ($n = 1097$), rural ($n = 569$), and migrant ($n = 296$) children and adolescents in grades four to six, aged 10 and 12 years, in China. The participants in the urban and migrant groups were students in city schools and rural migrant children schools in Beijing. The migrant children schools were set up by the Beijing government in the communities of the rural migrant families. Students in these schools came to Beijing from different provinces of the country. The participants in the rural group were students in schools in a Northern region near Beijing. Four major domains of cultural values, individual assertiveness (e.g., "I like to express my own opinions," "I rely on myself most of time, rarely rely on others"), uniqueness (e.g., "I enjoy being unique and different from others in many respects," "I like to behave in my own way"), group orientation (e.g., "It is important to me to respect decisions made by the group," "I will sacrifice my self-interest for the benefit of the group I am in"), and social connectedness (e.g., "It is important to get along with others," "To me, pleasure is spending time with others") were assessed, using a measure adapted from Singelis (1994).

The means and standard deviations for boys and girls in each group are presented in Table 10.1. The results first indicated that urban students had higher scores than rural students on uniqueness. Displaying personal unique and distinct characteristics and behaviors is clearly incompatible with the collectivistic orientation and has been traditionally discouraged in Chinese society. As urban China becomes increasingly market-oriented, modernized, and Westernized, however, children and adolescents start to appreciate the values of personal uniqueness and attempt to behave in a distinct manner.

Relative to urban and rural students, migrant students had lower scores on all cultural values. The lower scores on group orientation and social connectedness might be because of the fact that migrant students did not form stable peer groups and social relationships because their families tended to move frequently from one place to another. On the other hand, their rural background and experiences of difficulties such as prejudice and discrimination of urban residents related to their undesirable status (e.g., Sun, 2006; Zhan, Sun, & Dong, 2005) might make migrant students anxious about displaying self-directive and unique behaviors. It has been argued (e.g., Berry, Phinney, Sam, & Vedder, 2006) that migrants are likely to experience various acculturation processes including maintaining values of origin, acquiescing to requirements in the new environment, and integrating diverse values. The results from our study suggest that mixed backgrounds of migrant students in China may lead to a lack of endorsement of either

Table 10.1. Means and Standard Deviations of Values in Urban, Rural, and Migrant Groups

	Urban			Rural			Migrant		
	Boys	Girls	Total	Boys	Girls	Total	Boys	Girls	Total
	n=544	n=553	n=1097	n=296	n=273	n=569	n=168	n=127	n=295
Individual	3.87	3.84	3.86	3.75	3.83	3.79	3.34	3.43	3.38
assertiveness	(.89)	(.76)	(.83)	(.77)	(.78)	(.77)	(.77)	(.78)	(.78)
Uniqueness	3.91	3.99	3.95	3.55	3.48	3.52	3.20	3.33	3.24
	(.83)	(.69)	(.76)	(.78)	(.79)	(.78)	(.80)	(.76)	(.78)
Group	4.05	4.17	4.11	3.90	4.06	3.98	3.64	3.87	3.74
orientation	(.83)	(.67)	(.75)	(.80)	(.71)	(.76)	(.85)	(.75)	(.82)
Social	3.96	3.93	3.96	3.92	3.90	3.91	3.55	3.64	3.59
connectedness	(.82)	(.77)	(.80)	(.87)	(.77)	(.82)	(.87)	(.80)	(.84)

Note: SDs are in parentheses under M scores.

traditional group-oriented values or urban individualistic values. It will be an interesting question whether migrant adolescents gradually accept values of individual assertiveness and uniqueness as they become more acculturated in the urban environment.

Cultural Values and Adjustment among Urban, Rural, and Migrant Adolescents

Do cultural values mean anything in adolescent social, school, and psychological adjustment? Are they associated with social relationships, behaviors, school performance, and psychological well-being in adolescents? These are interesting and important questions for developmental researchers, but unfortunately, have been largely neglected in empirical research. According to the pluralist perspective (Garcia Coll et al., 1996; Hong, Morris, Chiu, & Benet-Martinez, 2000; Zhou, 1997), different beliefs and values may serve different, perhaps complementary, functions in human development. For example, whereas individuality may be conducive to the acquisition of social status and school achievement (achieving personal goals in social and academic areas), group orientation may play a greater role in establishing social support systems and positive social relationship, which in turn may help psycho-emotional adjustment.

The functional significance of cultural values may also depend on specific context. For example, values of initiative-taking, independence, and self-expression may be particularly beneficial for adolescents to acquire leadership, social status, and achievement in urban Chinese schools where students are encouraged to engage in self-directed and exploratory activities. The emphasis of self-direction and exploration in school activities may create a favorable atmosphere for students to develop self-confidence and to display sociable assertive behavior and for students who display this behavior to acquire social status and success in school performance. On the other hand, in rural areas where group harmony and interdependence are strongly encouraged, adolescents with individualistic values may experience more difficulties in social interaction; as a result, these adolescents may feel frustrated and develop negative attitudes toward others and self. In contrast, adolescents who hold group-oriented values may follow the social expectations, obtain social approval, or function well psychologically.

In the "Cultural values and adjustment in Chinese youth" project, we examined relations between the four values and social, school, and psychological adjustment. In addition to the information on cultural values, we collected data on individual adjustment from multiple sources. Specifically, we administered to the participants a peer assessment measure of social behaviors and a sociometric nomination measure. The peer-assessments of social behaviors provided information on individual sociability (e.g., "makes new friends easily," "helps others when they need it," "polite") and aggression (e.g., "gets into a lot of fights," "picks on other kids"). The measure of positive and negative sociometric nominations ("Tell us the classmates you most like to be with/you would rather not be with") provided information on peer acceptance and peer rejection, which formed an index of peer preference indicating how the participant was liked by others in the class. We also asked the participants to complete a loneliness measure (e.g., "I feel lonely," "I have nobody to talk to"). Teachers completed a rating scale for each participant concerning his/her school-related competence (e.g., "participates in class discussion," "copes well with failure"). Finally, data concerning academic achievement in Chinese language and mathematics was obtained from school records.

As shown in Table 10.2, the results indicated that individual assertiveness was positively associated with sociability, teacher-rated competence, and academic achievement in both urban and rural groups. Assertiveness was also positively associated with aggression and negatively associated with loneliness in all three groups. Uniqueness was positively associated with peer preference and academic achievement in the urban group, but

Table 10.2. Effects of Values in Predicting Adjustment Variables in Urban, Rural, and Migrant Groups Adjustment Variable

Values	Urban	Rural	Migrant
Peer preference			
Assertiveness	.04 (.08)	−.01 (.11)	−.11 (.12)
Uniqueness	.18 (.08)*	.10 (.09)	−.14 (.11)
Group orientation	−.05 (.09)	.25 (.10)*	.25 (.13)*
Social connectedness	.25 (.08)**	.10 (.10)	.23 (.12)
Sociability			
Assertiveness	.35 (.05)***	.22 (.07)***	.14 (.09)
Uniqueness	.00 (.05)	.09 (.06)	−.04 (.08)
Group orientation	−.06 (.05)	.11 (.07)	.08 (.09)
Social connectedness	−.01 (.05)	−.06 (.06)	.22 (.08)**
Aggression			
Assertiveness	.11 (.05)*	.15 (.07)*	.23 (.09)**
Uniqueness	−.04 (.05)	−.07 (.06)	.07 (.08)
Group orientation	−.06 (.05)	−.12 (.07)	−.07 (.09)
Social connectedness	−.06 (.05)	−.06 (.06)	−.12 (.08)
Teacher-rated competence			
Assertiveness	.23 (.05)***	.20 (.07)**	.07 (.09)
Uniqueness	−.02 (.05)	−.03 (.06)	−.06 (.08)
Group orientation	.00 (.05)	.09 (.07)	.33 (.09)***
Social connectedness	.00 (.05)	.04 (.07)	−.02 (.08)
Academic achievement			
Assertiveness	.12 (.05)**	.22 (.08)**	.06 (.09)
Uniqueness	.13 (.05)**	.06 (.06)	−.11 (.08)
Group orientation	−.02 (.05)	.19 (.07)**	.21 (.09)*
Social connectedness	.05 (.05)	−.04 (.07)	−.02 (.08)
Loneliness			
Assertiveness	−.22 (.03)***	−.26 (.05)***	−.19 (.06)***
Uniqueness	−.02 (.03)	.10 (.04)**	.14 (.05)**
Group orientation	−.07 (.04)	−.10 (.04)*	−.09 (.06)
Social connectedness	−.15 (.03)***	−.13 (.04)**	−.18 (.06)**

Note: SEs are in parentheses after the coefficients.

not in the other two groups. Uniqueness was also positively associated with loneliness in rural and migrant groups. In contrast, group orientation was positively associated with peer preferences and academic achievement in rural and migrant groups, but not in the urban group. Finally, social connectedness was positively associated with peer preference in urban students and negatively associated with loneliness in all groups.

The associations of individual assertiveness with both sociability and aggression are rather interesting. The results suggest that regardless of the background, adolescents who are socially competent and aggressive in China are more likely than others to value assertiveness. These results are consistent with the argument that sociability and aggression are both based on a high level of social initiative or a tendency to actively participate in social interaction (Chen & French, 2008). To display either sociable or aggressive behavior in social situations, adolescents need to be confident and motivated to interact with others. Values of assertiveness may be conducive to the development of self-confidence and social interest. The differences between social competence and aggression may be derived from different levels of self-control, the ability to modulate social initiative or assertiveness. Whereas social assertiveness based on a high level of self-control may lead to socially competent behavior, the combination of high assertiveness and low self-control constitutes a basis for the development of aggressive-disruptive behavior (Chen & French, 2008).

Values of uniqueness and group orientation appeared to be particularly useful in characterizing the differences between the urban and rural students; uniqueness positively predicted peer preference and academic achievement in urban students, and group orientation positively predicted these variables in rural students. More strikingly, uniqueness positively predicted feelings of loneliness in rural students. The results clearly showed that values of uniqueness and group orientation have different meanings in adolescent social and psychological adjustment in urban and rural regions. Unique personal characteristics and distinct behavioral styles not only are more appreciated but also play a more important role in shaping social relationships and school performance in urban youth. However, striving for uniqueness may not fit with the social expectations of conformity, unity, and obedience that are traditionally valued in rural Chinese society (Chen, 2010). Thus, it is not surprising that adolescents in rural areas who value uniqueness tend to feel lonely and socially dissatisfied. Consistent with these arguments, rural adolescents who value group orientation appear to have advantage in obtaining peer support and achieving school success.

The relations between values and adjustment in migrant students were largely similar to those in rural students. Like their rural counterparts, for example, migrant students who valued uniqueness tended to report higher loneliness than others. Therefore, although migrant students did not endorse either traditional group-oriented values or urban individualistic values, the functional meanings of these values in social, school, and psychological adjustment remained virtually the same as those in the rural group. This may be because the migrant sample was selected from the migrant children's school where almost all students came from rural areas of the country. These students were raised and socialized mainly in the country-side. Because of their temporary residence in the city, migrant students often think of themselves more as members of their hometown than as a part of the urban population (Sun, 2006; Zhan et al., 2005). The extensive early experience, continuous influence of the family and the community, and frequent contact with relatives and peers in the village (e.g., stay in the hometown for several months each year when the school is closed in the summer and in the spring holidays) are likely to help rural migrant students to form a climate in the school in which traditional group-oriented values are emphasized and used to guide social interactions.

General Issues and Future Directions

The development of individuality and social affiliation is a major task of children and adolescents in most societies (e.g., Chen & French, 2008). Young people need to establish a sense of self as an individual and, at the same time, connect with others. Moreover, it has been increasingly recognized that individuality and social relationships are two important aspects of the integrated self system, which may be associated with various developmental outcomes (e.g., Kagitcibasi & Ataca, 2005; Tamis-LeMond et al., 2008). It is a common belief that Chinese culture, particularly Confucianism, emphasizes interdependence among individuals and group orientation (Triandis, 1995). Accordingly, the primary goal of socialization in Chinese society is to help children and adolescents develop attributes that are conducive to the formation and maintenance of positive interpersonal relationships and group harmony (Chen, 2010; Ho, 1986; Oyserman et al., 2002). In contrast, individual autonomy or independence is not highly valued or appreciated because it may not bear much relevance to group functioning (Greenfield, Suzuki, & Rothstein-Fisch, 2006). The expression of personal needs or striving for individual autonomy and distinctiveness, especially when it threatens the group well-being, is often viewed as anti-collective and thus unacceptable (Greenfield et al., 2006).

As China is changing toward a market-oriented society and as Western ideologies are introduced into the country along with high-technologies, traditional Chinese cultural values become weaker because they are incompatible with the requirements of the new competitive environment. In contrast, individualistic values such as initiative-taking, active exploration, and self-expression are more important for achieving success in the society. Cumulative research evidence has supported this argument, particularly about the enhanced awareness of individuality and its significance for adjustment. The differences between the urban and rural groups on uniqueness in the "Cultural values and adjustment in Chinese youth" project suggest that urban adolescents in China have started to appreciate and approve the expression of personal distinctiveness and develop a "unitary and stable" self that is separate from social context (Markus & Kitayama, 1991). Moreover, among urban (but not rural or migrant) adolescents, values of uniqueness contribute to the development of social status in the peer group and school achievement.

On the other hand, the results from the "Cultural values and adjustment in Chinese youth" project suggest that, although individual assertiveness and uniqueness may be increasingly valued, group orientation and social connectedness are not necessarily weakened in China, even in urban adolescents. As indicated by Yang (1986), group harmony and social affiliation represent the core of Confucian value system, which has played a crucial role in shaping the attitudes and behaviors of Chinese people for thousands of years and thus is likely robust in spite of social change. It is also plausible that traditional and new values serve different functions in adolescent lives. For example, whereas individuality helps adolescents achieve personal goals in social and academic areas, group orientation and social connectedness may help them develop support systems, which in turn may enhance psychological well-being. Adjustment in the new challenging environment is likely to be stressful and results in negative emotions such as frustration and distress in Chinese adolescents. Group affiliation may be a protective factor that buffers against maladaptive emotional development. The results from our project appear to be consistent with this argument; students who endorsed group orientation and social connectedness were likely to be accepted by peers and reported low loneliness in urban, rural, as well as migrant groups.

In this chapter, we focus on traditional values of group affiliation and relatively new Western values of individuality in adolescents of different backgrounds. There are many other values such as family responsibility, self-control, and emotion expression that are associated with social and psychological adjustment of adolescents in different contexts. In the future, researchers need to explore these values and their functional meanings in China. It should also be noted that cultural exchanges and interactions may lead to the merging and co-existence of diverse value systems (Kagitcibasi & Ataca, 2005; Tamis-LeMond et al., 2008). The integration of diverse values may be particularly beneficial for the development of social competence because maintaining a balance between pursuing own ends and establishing group harmony is important for social interaction. It will be interesting to investigate how adolescents develop their social competence in the culturally integrated and sophisticated settings.

REFERENCES

Berry, J. W., Phinney, J. S., Sam, D. L., & Vedder, P. (2006). *Immigrant youth in cultural transition: Acculturation, identity, and adaptation across national contexts.* Mahwah, NJ: Erlbaum.

Bronfenbrenner, U., & Morris, P. A. (2006). The bioecological model of human development. In W. Damon (Series Ed.) & R. M. Lerner (Vol. Ed.), *Handbook of child psychology: Vol 1. Theoretical models of human development* (pp. 793–828). New York: Wiley.

Bulletin of China's Economic and Social Development in 2009 (2010, February, 25). Xin Hua She, Beijing.

Chen, X. (2010). Socioemotional development in Chinese children. In M. H. Bond (Ed.), *Handbook of Chinese psychology* (pp. 37–52). Oxford: Oxford University Press.

Chen, X., Cen, G., Li, D., & He, Y. (2005). Social functioning and adjustment in Chinese children: The imprint of historical time. *Child Development, 76*, 182–195.

Chen, X., & Chen, H. (2010). Children's social functioning and adjustment in the changing Chinese society. In R. K. Silbereisen & X. Chen (Eds.), *Social change and human development: Concepts and results* (pp. 209–226). London: Sage.

Chen, X., & French, D. (2008). Children's social competence in cultural context. *Annual Review of Psychology, 59*, 591–616.

Chen, X., Rubin, K. H., & Li, Z. (1995). Social functioning and adjustment in Chinese children: A longitudinal study. *Developmental Psychology, 31*, 531–539.

China Youth & Children Research Center (2007). A study of adaption of children of migrant workers to the urban life. *Reports of the China Youth & Children Research Center*, November 16. http://www.cycs.org/Article.asp?Category=1&Column=130 &ID=5809

Eickhorst, A., Lamm, B., Borke, J., & Keller, H. (2008). Fatherhood in different decades: Interactions between German fathers and their infants in 1977 and 2001. *European Journal of Developmental Psychology, 5*, 92–107.

Elder, G. H. Jr. (1974). *Children of the Great Depression.* Chicago: University of Chicago Press.

Elder, G. H. Jr., & Shanahan, M. J. (2006). The life course and human development. In W. Damon (Series Ed.) & R. M. Lerner (Vol. Ed.), *Handbook of child psychology: Vol 1. Theoretical models of human development* (pp. 665–715). New York: Wiley.

Fuligni, A. J., & Zhang, W. X. (2004). Attitudes toward family obligation among adolescents in contemporary urban and rural China. *Child Development, 74*, 180–192.

Garcia Coll, C., Crnic, K., Lamberty, G., Wasik, B. H., Jenkins, R., Garcia, H. V., & McAdoo, H. P. (1996). An integrative model for the study of development competencies in minority children. *Child Development, 67*, 1891–1914.

Greenfield, P. M., Maynard, A. E., & Childs, C. P. (2000). History, culture, learning and development. *Cross-Cultural Research, 34*, 351–374.

Greenfield, P. M., Suzuki, L. K., & Rothstein-Fisch, C. (2006). Cultural pathways through human development. In K. A. Renninger & I. E. Sigel (Eds.), *Handbook of child psychology: Vol. 4. Child psychology in practice* (pp. 655–699). New York: Wiley.

Guo, L., Yao, Y., & Yang, B. (2005). Adaptation of migrant children to the city: A case study at a migrant children school in Beijing. *Youth Study, 3*, 22–31.

Hart, C. H., Yang, C., Nelson, L. J., Robinson, C. C., Olson, J. A., Nelson, D. A. ... Wu, P. (2000). Peer acceptance in early childhood and subtypes of socially withdrawn behaviour in China, Russia and the United States. *International Journal of Behavioral Development*, **24**, 73–81.

Ho, D. Y. F. (1986). Chinese pattern of socialization: A critical review. In M. H. Bond (Ed.), *The psychology of the Chinese people* (pp. 1–37). New York: Oxford University Press.

Hong, Y. Y., Morris, M. W., Chiu, C. Y., & Benet-Martinez, V. (2000). Multicultural minds: A dynamic constructivist approach to culture and cognition. *American Psychologist*, **55**, 709–720.

Huang, A., & Du, X. (2007). Comparative analysis of urban-rural differences of family education in China. *Journal of Yibin University*, **1**, 107–110.

Kagitcibasi, C., & Ataca, B. (2005). Value of children and family change: A three-decade portrait from Turkey. *Applied Psychology: An International Review*, **54**, 317–337.

Keller, H., & Lamm, B. (2005). Parenting as the expression of sociohistorical time: The case of German individualisation. *International Journal of Behavioral Development*, **29**, 238–246.

Li, L. (2006). A study of home education styles in rural areas. *Research on Continuing Education*, **2**, 95–97.

Liu, J., Chen, X., Li, D., & French, D. (in press). Shyness-sensitivity, aggression, and adjustment in urban Chinese adolescents at different historical times. *Journal of Research on Adolescence*.

Liu, M., Chen, X., Rubin, K. H., Zheng, S., Cui, L., Li, D. ... Wang, L. (2005). Autonomy-vs. connectedness-oriented parenting behaviors in Chinese and Canadian mothers. *International Journal of Behavioral Development*, **29**, 489–495.

Markus, H., & Kitayama, S. (1991). Culture and the self: Implications for cognition, emotion, and motivation. *Psychological Review*, **98**, 224–253.

Nielsen, I., Nyland, B., Nyland, C., Smith, R., & Zhang, M. (2006). Determinants of school attendance among migrant children: Survey evidence from China's Jiangsu province. *Pacific Economic Review*, **11**, 461–476.

Oyserman, D., Coon, H. M., & Kemmelmeier, M. (2002). Rethinking individualism and collectivism: Evaluation of theoretical assumptions and meta-analyses. *Psychological Bulletin*, **128**, 3–72.

Shen, R. (2006). Problems and solutions for child education for migrant rural worker families. *Journal of China Agricultural University (Social Science Edition)*, **64**, 96–100.

Silbereisen, R. K. (2005). Social change and human development: Experiences from German unification. *International Journal of Behavioral Development*, **29**, 2–13.

Singelis, T. M. (1994). The measurement of independent and interdependent self-construals. *Personality and Social Psychology Bulletin*, **20**, 580–591.

Sun, H. (2006). About the social adaptation of children of migrant workers in the city. *Reports of the China Youth & Children Research Center*, December 2. http://www.cycrc.org/cnarticle_detail.asp?id=1421

Tamis-LeMonda, C. S., Way, N., Hughes, D., Yoshikawa, H., Kalman, R. K., & Niwa, E. (2008). Parents' goals for children: The dynamic co-existence of collectivism and individualism in cultures and individuals. *Social Development*, **17**, 183–209.

Triandis, H. C. (1995). *Individualism and collectivism*. Boulder, CO: Westview Press.

Wang, B. (2006). *The philosophy of Zhuangzi*. Beiijng: Peking University Press.

Wang, D. (2004). A survey of educational problems among children of migrant workers. *Chinese Population Science, 4*, 58–64.

Yang, D. T., & Zhou, H. (1999). Rural-urban disparity and sectoral labour allocation in China. *The Journal of Development, 35*, 105–133.

Yang, K. S. (1986). Chinese personality and its change. In M. H. Bond (Ed.), *The psychology of the Chinese people* (pp. 106–170). Hong Kong: Oxford University Press.

Yi, X., & Yu, G. (2003). A review on adolescent internet addiction. *China Youth Study, 12*, 60–63.

Yu, R. (2002). On the reform of elementary school education in China. *Educational Exploration, 129*, 56–57.

Yu, Y. S. (2004). *Chinese ideological tradition and its changes in modern times*. Guilin: Guangxi Normal University Press.

Zhan, X., Sun, D., & Dong, Z. (2005). On adolescents' school adjustment in urban and rural China. *Journal of Shangdong Normal University, 203*, 144–147.

Zhang, J., & Zhao, Y. (2006). A study on the difference of values between middle school students and their parents in Chongqing. *Psychological Science, 29*, 1222–1225.

Zhang, W. W. (2000). *Transforming China: Economic reform and its political implications*. New York: St. Martin's Press.

Zheng, H., & Yang, Y. (2009). *Chinese private sector development in the past 30 years: Retrospect and prospect*. Discussion Paper, 45, China Policy Institute, The University of Nottingham, UK.

Zhou, M. (1997). Growing up American: The challenge confronting immigrant children and children of immigrants. *Annual Review of Sociology, 23*, 63–95.

Zhuang, Z. (2006). *A hundred classic works in China: Zhungtze*. Xin Jiang: Yili People's Press.

11 With God's Help

The Future Orientation of Palestinian Girls in Israel
Growing Up Muslim

Rachel Seginer and Sami Mahajna

Abstract

This chapter examines how Sunni Muslim girls in Israel construct their future orientation. Underlying are three basic premises: (1) adolescent future orientation plays a pivotal role in guiding entrance to adulthood, (2) future orientation is shaped by contextual forces including religious–cultural setting and family environment, and (3) religious practices are shaped by local circumstances. The article consists of three parts: (1) the conceptualization of future orientation, (2) the developmental setting of Muslim girls in Israel, and (3) how they construct their future orientation. This part presents a six-step model depicting future orientation, its family antecedents and academic achievement outcomes, and empirical estimates for two pertinent future life domains: higher education and marriage and family. Employing a mixed-method approach, quantitative analyses (Structural Equation Modeling) show a good fit for each of the two empirical models. Yet, higher education has a positive effect and marriage and family has a negative effect on academic achievement. Qualitative analyses of their hopes and fears narratives indicate that these girls resolve the tension between devotion to religious-traditional life via early marriage and aspirations for emancipation via higher education by following three strategies: completing education before getting married, marrying a supportive husband, and harnessing education for the good of the collective.

Our work focuses on Muslim adolescent girls in Israel. Its aim is to examine how these girls construct their future orientation as they grow up in a minority society whose relations with the Israeli Jewish majority are characterized by both inclusion and exclusion. As citizens, they officially bear equal rights, yet in many respects, they are excluded from the Jewish majority society on religious, national, and political grounds. Traditional male dominance makes the life of Muslim women and girls all the more challenging.

The analysis we present here has been instructed by three basic premises. One is that adolescent future orientation plays a pivotal role in guiding entrance to adulthood (Douvan & Adelson, 1966; Erikson, 1968; Lewin, 1939). The second is that development occurs in context, and future orientation – as one developmental process – is shaped by several contextual forces. Of these, here we focus on family environment and the religious–cultural setting. However, whereas family environment dimensions are assessed and included as antecedents in the future orientation model, the religious–cultural setting is limited to one group: Sunni Muslims in Israel. The third premise is that religious tenets affect behavior indirectly via practices derived from those religious tenets. These practices are shaped by local circumstances, and in the specific case studied here, create the unique culture of Sunni Muslims in Israel.

The article consists of three parts. In the first, we introduce future orientation conceptualization and its susceptibility to social and cultural processes. The second relates to the developmental setting of Muslim girls in Israel. Here we focus on three sociocultural processes particularly relevant to their development: (1) the religious, cultural, and political forces affecting the everyday life of the Muslim community in Israel; (2) the debate about and multiple interpretations of women's rights in Islam and its expression in the Muslim scene in Israel; and (3) family environment particularly relevant to the construction of future orientation: adolescent–parent relationships and parental beliefs as perceived and reported by adolescents.

In the third part we examine how Muslim girls in Israel construct their transition to adulthood. Toward this end, we present a multiple-step model depicting future orientation, its family antecedents, and academic achievement outcomes. In light of earlier findings (Seginer, 1988; Seginer & Mahajna, 2004) showing the concern of Muslim girls in Israel about higher education and marriage and family, we test the model on these domains and include academic achievement as an outcome variable.

Future Orientation

Future orientation is an umbrella concept defined differently by various future-thinking researchers. Assuming that time perspective is not independent of its content (Nuttin and Lens, 1985) our analyses have taken

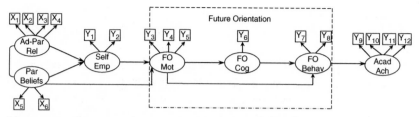

Figure 11.1. The six-step future orientation theoretical model.
Ad-Par Rel = Perceived adolescent–parent relationship, Par Beliefs = Perceived parental beliefs, Self Emp = Self empowerment, FO Mot = Future orientation motivational component, FO Cog = Future orientation cognitive representation component, FO Behav. = Future orientation behavioral component, Acad. Ach. = academic achievement, X_1 = Mother autonomy granting, X_2 = Mother acceptance, X_3 = Father autonomy granting, X_4 = Father acceptance, X_5 = Mother's beliefs re: higher education/early marriage, X_6 = Father's beliefs re: higher education/ early marriage, Y_1 = Self empowerment re: education, Y_2 = Self empowerment re: the materialization of hopes, Y_3 = Value, Y_4 = Expectance, Y_5 = Internal control, Y_6 = My future higher education/marriage and family, Y_7 = Exploration, Y_8 = Commitment, Y_9 = Final grade Arabic, Y_{10} = Final grade Hebrew, Y_{11} = Final grade English, Y_{12} = Final grade mathematics.

the thematic approach to future orientation. Starting with a unidimensional approach that focused on cognitive representation (Seginer, 1988; Trommsdorff, 1986) we – like Nurmi (1991) – developed a multivariate model (Seginer, 2009). This model applies to different life domains and consists of the following three components.

The Future Orientation Three Component Model. The model was developed in response to questions about the psychological forces that prompt representation of future images (antecedents) and the behavioral processes it induces (outcomes). Consequently, the model consists of motivational, cognitive representation, and behavioral components – each indicated by two or three variables – and the relations between them. Given that motivational forces prompt both cognitive representation and behavioral engagement, they are directly linked to both (Figure 11.1, box).

The Motivational Component. Drawing on the value-expectance motivation theory (Atkinson, 1964; Eccles & Wigfield, 2002) and earlier future orientation research (Nuttin & Lens, 1985; Trommsdorff, 1983), this component is indicated by three variables: the *value* of prospective life domains, *expectance* (i.e., subjective probability) of materialization of hopes and plans and its affective tone, and a sense of *internal control* attributing responsibility for the materialization of prospective hopes and plans to the self.

The Cognitive Representation Component. This component draws on two assumptions: (1) future images have both approach and avoidance aspects as reflected in hopes and fears, respectively, and (2) assessed by how often individuals think about each.

The Behavioral Component. This component is indicated by two variables: exploration and commitment. Exploration pertains to behaviors such as advice seeking and information gathering regarding future options, whereas commitment relates to the decision to pursue one option. Their theoretical underpinnings draw on the work of Lewin and Erikson. The purpose of exploration is to examine future options and the extent to which they fit personal abilities and values, social expectations, and environmental circumstances (Lewin, 1939). Commitment results in "a sense of knowing where one is going" (Erikson, 1968, p. 165). Both add to the instrumentality of future orientation for the achievement of future goals.

Future Life Domains. Earlier research (Seginer, 2008) has shown that adolescents across different sociocultural settings include in their future life space three core domains: higher education, work and career (instrumental domains), and marriage and family (relational domain). As indicated earlier, we will analyze two life domains in this study: higher education and marriage and family. Underlying it is the importance Muslim girls in Israel have been giving to higher education ("education is a weapon in women's hands," Seginer & Mahajna, 2003, 2004) and the pressure for arranged early marriage (in 2008, the median age of marriage for Muslim girls in Israel was 20.3 and the average age 21.3; Israel Central Bureau of Statistics, 2010).

Given the importance of context for the study of developmental issues (Bronfenbrenner, 1979), the empirical analyses of the future orientation model follow the description of Israeli Muslim cultural–religious setting and its meaning for adolescent girls.

The Developmental Setting of Muslim Girls in Israel

This section consists of three parts. The first two describe two aspects of the macrosystem: the world of Muslims in Israel, and growing up a Muslim woman. The third part focuses on the microsystem as it applies to family environment.

The World of Muslims in Israel: An Intricate Setting

As previously noted, a basic premise of our work has been that whereas religion is a potent marker (Paloutzian & Park, 2005), its effect is entwined with that of culture, politics, socio-economic status, and language, and shaped by local circumstances. Three issues are particularly relevant here. One is that for Arabs in Israel – 83 percent of them Sunni Muslims – ethnicity, culture, and religion are so closely interwoven that recent comprehensive analyses of the Arab society in Israel (Manna, 2008; Muhammad, 2005; Rekhess & Rodntzki, 2009) and Arab women in Israel (Azaiza, Abu-Baker, Hertz-Lazarowitz, & Ghanem, 2009) do not include a section on religion.

The second issue relates to the status of Arabs in Israel as an oppressed minority despite holding Israeli citizenship. As a result of the 1947–1948 Jewish-Arab war and the establishment of the State of Israel, they lost their religious leadership and their land, and many became refugees in their own country. Following the 1967 war, as contact with the West Bank and Gaza Strip Palestinians resumed and disillusionment of emerging secular leadership grew stronger; religious participation – particularly in response to subsequent military or political crises (Rekhess, 2000) – has been on the rise.

This is indicated by growth in the construction of mosques, opening of religious schools, and adoption of Islamic dress for women. Although statistical data on religiosity among Arabs in Israel is not available, a rough estimate can be drawn from a recent Israel Central Statistics Bureau report (2011) that among non-Jews in Israel (68 percent of whom are Muslims), only 15 percent of women and 27 percent of men age 20+ described themselves as nonreligious.

The third issue pertains to the web of contradicting conditions that characterize the life of Arabs in Israel. Although their rights as citizens are curbed, public investment in their communities is lower, and their sense of being discriminated against persists (Smooha, 2009), their standard of living, level of education, and occupational opportunities continuously improve (Israel Central Statistics Bureau, 2010). Consequently, both parents and adolescents aspire for adolescents' higher education and professional careers (Khattab, 2003). Underlying it are three motives: (1) obtain a higher standard of living and integrate into the Israeli society, (2) attain alternative capital to replace family land lost during the 1948 war (Seginer & Vermulst, 2002), and (3) use education and a subsequent career as a source of personal strength, family pride (Gregg, 2005), and national parity.

Growing Up a Muslim Woman in Israel

Understanding the status of Sunni Muslim women in Israel and the prospects of girls growing up in this society calls for the examination of two issues: the debate about women in the Islam, and the reality of Muslim women in Israel.

The Debate about Women in the Islam. Like holy writings of other religions, the Qur'an is rich with ideas, represents multiple views, and is open to interpretation. What is true of its entirety is particularly relevant to women in the Qur'an (Ahmed, 1992). Moreover, as noted by Pickthall (1999), although the Qur'an mentions the name of only one woman, many of its verses are devoted to women, including their behavior, relations with men, and the way they dress. The main debate is whether the Qur'an teaches equality of the sexes indicated by verses that give equal standing to men and women (Jones, 2007, 33: 35) or male dominance, indicated by verses in which men are described as controlling women (Jones, 2007, 4:34).

According to Ahmed (1992), Muhammad's teachings advocated both. However, the Abbasid Caliphate of Iraq (750–1258) chose to ignore the equality teachings and inculcated its subjects with male dominance principles. The power given to patriarchs created a misogynist society that survived the Caliphate and continues to shape relationships between women and men in the family, the workplace, and the political system. This interpretation survived not because it represented a more authentic version of Muhammad's teachings but because it was initiated by the politically dominant (Ahmed, 1992).

The Reality of Muslim Women in Israel. Presumably, the situation in Israel should have been different. Three reasons account for this assumption. The first is based on Israeli legislation on compulsory education and women's status. *Compulsory education* was introduced in 1953 and presently applies to all children age 5 (kindergarten) to 18 (high school graduation). By requiring parents to send their daughters (not only their sons) to school, legislation created a new prospect for women. However, the greater earning potential of adolescent boys reversed the trend. At present, school drop out is higher among boys and more girls than boys graduate from high school with a matriculation certificate (54 percent vs. 35 percent of the cohort for boys) (Israel Central Statistics Bureau, 2011). Concerning *women's status*, Israeli law prohibits polygamy, minor marriage (the official marriage age for women is 17), and unilateral divorce. In addition, the Women's Equal Rights Law grants women equal guardianship over their children. Nonetheless, to avoid open conflict with the Shari'a (Islam religious law) and introduce a gradual reform, the state allows for concessions with the Muslim law (Peled, 2001).

The second reason is that the ethnic labor market in occupations such as teaching, health services, and municipal services offers women jobs in which they do not compete with the Jewish majority (Khattab, 2003), thereby granting them greater employment openings. The third reason is that opportunities for higher education create another avenue for professional jobs, and in principle also enable participation in the political system. The trend that starts in high school continues in college and has a direct bearing on women's participation in the workforce.

Eight years after high school graduation, 30 percent of the women but only 19 percent of the men earned a university degree. However, overall, fewer Arab and Jewish women than Arab and Jewish men hold a paid job (21 percent and 60 percent of Arab women and men and 58 percent and 62 percent of Jewish women and men, respectively). Among women with 16+ years of education, the workforce gap narrows: 74 percent of Arab women (compared to 79 percent of Jewish women) hold a paid job (Israel Central Statistics Bureau, 2011).

However, the benefits of education and career are double-edged. As in other Muslim societies in the Middle East, educated women's paid jobs contribute to the family's standard of living but do not improve their status. Instead, men use it to substantiate patriarchal family patterns that lead to women's frustration and sense of powerlessness, which at times also affects their health and obstructs political participation (Azaiza et al., 2009). Moreover, the burden of carrying out two jobs – at home and in the job market – with no help from husbands has led women to quit paid jobs (Abu-Baker, 2003).

Family Environment
Underlying our conceptualization of family environment are two assumptions: (1) that adolescents' outcomes are affected mainly by how adolescents *experience* family environment (*perceived* family environment), and (2) that given its multidimensionality, the family environment in this analysis consists of *adolescent–parent relationships* as one dimension relevant for a wide range of adolescent development outcomes and *parents' beliefs regarding adolescent girls' roles* as a dimension specifically relevant to future orientation. Together, these two dimensions address the relational–emotional (adolescent–parent relationships) and the cognitive–ideational (parental beliefs) aspects of home environment.

Adolescent–Parent Relationships. Underlying the sustained importance of parents for their adolescent children is the universal psychological need for relatedness. This has been substantiated by research indicating that adolescents regard parents as a primary source of closeness and support (Laursen & Collins, 2009), and that perceived parental acceptance, autonomy granting, and strict (vs. lax) behavioral control explain a range of adolescent developmental outcomes across age and culturally diverse groups (Barber, Stolz, & Olson, 2005). Their inclusion in the model draws on the relevance of each to adolescents' future orientation and is supported by earlier findings (Seginer, Vermulst, & Shoyer., 2004).

Briefly, autonomy granting conveys a sense of parental confidence in their adolescent children's ability to explore new roles and tasks, parental warmth and support indicate a safe base to which adolescents can return after exploring new options, and behavioral control (limit setting) guides adolescents to stay within normative boundaries. Nonetheless, our analyses for both Israeli Jews (Seginer et al., 2004) and Arabs in Israel (Seginer, 2009) resulted in a two-variable construct. For both Jewish and Arab adolescents in Israel, the indicators are perceived granted autonomy and parental acceptance.

Parental Beliefs. Parental beliefs pertain to the ideas and subjective knowledge individuals hold, specifically applying to their role as parents. Like all other beliefs, they draw on social models and personal experiences as filtered through cultural lenses (Goodnow & Collins, 1990). Their content – communicated in family discourse and via parental behaviors – pertains to a wide range of issues regarding the nature of children in general and of parents' individual children, child rearing practices, and the values underlying them.

As noted earlier, in this analysis we focus on beliefs about young women's roles vis-à-vis higher education and early marriage. Underlying these beliefs is the tension between entering the traditional role of wife and mother at an early age and the pursuit of equal opportunities for education and occupation (Mahajna, 2007; Seginer & Mahajna, 2004). Because beliefs reflect cultural models and because collectivistic societies expect a greater sense of commitment to the in-group, we assume parental beliefs about young women's roles are of particular relevance to Muslim girls.

How Muslim Girls in Israel Construct Transition to Adulthood

Given that for adolescents, adulthood belongs in the future, we employ our future orientation model to answer this question. A basic premise underlying this model has been that each of its three components plays a part in constructing the future. Specifically, it involves pondering the value of each future life domain, the probability and controllability of fulfilling their hopes (the motivational component), considering the future via hopes and fears (the cognitive component), weighing options and focusing on one (the behavioral component). To examine future orientation in context and indicate its consequences for adolescents' functioning, we developed an extended model of future orientation that includes both family antecedents and academic achievement outcomes, as described in the next section.

The Future Orientation Extended Model

The extended model consists of six steps: family environment, self-representation, the motivational, cognitive, and behavioral components of future orientation, and academic achievement (Figure 11.1). Underlying the extended model are three considerations: the importance of the family during adolescence, the role of the self in linking interpersonal relationship and human functioning, and the effect of future orientation on behavior. The paths between the future orientation components are explained in the section on future orientation; therefore, in this section, we focus on the direct and indirect paths between family environment and future orientation via self-representation, and the path between future orientation and academic achievement.

The Paths between Family Environment and Future Orientation. Underlying these paths are three notions. One relates to the importance of family environment to adolescents' future orientation, as previously discussed. The second draws on family environment as consisting of relational–emotional (adolescent–parent relationships) and cognitive (parental beliefs) aspects. The third pertains to self-representations as consciously experienced and self-reported by the individual, and the role of the self in processing incoming information and prompting a wide range of behaviors (Harter, 1999).

Given the importance of the evaluative aspect of the self (James, 1890/1950) and drawing on Muslim girls' narratives in which they emphasize self-reliance (Mahajna & Seginer, 2004), Mahajna (2007) focused on self-empowerment. Based on the role of the self as processer of incoming information, we postulated that the path between each of the two aspects of family environment – i.e., adolescent–parent relationships and parental beliefs – is indirect and goes via self-empowerment. However, earlier findings (Seginer & Mahajna, 2004; Seginer, 2009) showing that parental beliefs are directly linked to future orientation led us to also postulate a direct parental beliefs–future orientation path.

Future Orientation and Academic Achievement. The link between future orientation and academic achievement draws on research about the instrumentality of present behavior for materializing future goals. This research – emanating from different psychological traditions and using different terminologies – has taken two directions. One examines the extent to which individuals are cognizant of the future goals–present behavior contingency. Research on *considering future consequences* of present behavior (Joireman, Anderson, & Strathman, 2003) or *perceived instrumentality* of present behavior for the materialization of future goals (Husman & Lens, 1999; Nuttin & Lens, 1985) addresses this issue. The second direction focuses on behaviors relevant to the materialization of future goals, such as task-specific *self regulating* strategies (Oyserman, Bybee, & Terry, 2006) and domain-specific behaviors of exploration and commitment.

Domain Specificity. Although the model is *generic* and fits data about various future life domains, we propose that the path between future orientation and academic achievement is positive for higher education and negative for marriage and family. Underlying it is the different meaning of the two domains and the girls' awareness that academic achievement is instrumental for higher education admission but of no avail for early marriage. To illustrate, "…I am getting married this summer, so why should I worry about education?" (Seginer & Mahajna, 2011).

Empirical Estimates. To empirically estimate this model we collected data from 617 11th grade girls (Mahajna, 2007) who attended the Arab educational system in Israel and participated in the matriculation program. A year later (at the end of 12th grade), girls successfully passing the state-administered examinations would be granted a State of Israel matriculation certificate (a necessary but not sufficient condition for admission to colleges and universities). Our participants grew up in rural Israel, in large families (mean number of children = 6.46 SD = 2.40) and relatively low education parents (M = 9.87 years for mothers and 10.89 years for fathers, with SDs of 3.13 and 3.28 for mothers and fathers, respectively). Whereas all fathers were wage earners, only 30 percent of the mothers held a paid job. Given their level of education, only 15 percent of fathers and 4 percent of mothers held professional jobs. Data about family environment, self-empowerment, and future orientation were collected by self-report native language

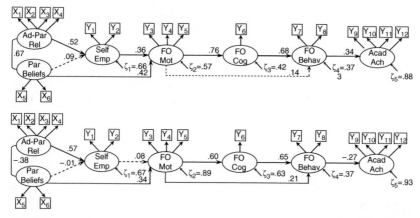

Figure 11.2 Empirical estimate of the six-step future orientation model: (a) The higher education domain N = 617, CFI = .963 RMSEA = .045; (b) The marriage and family domain. N = 617, CFI = .944 RMSEA = .055.

(Arabic) questionnaires, and academic achievement by end-of-year school reports of final grades in four core subjects: Arabic, Hebrew, English, and mathematics.

Specifically, perceived family environment was assessed using the Mother-Father questionnaire as a measure of perceived adolescent–parent relationships (Epstein, 1983; Seginer, 1998; Seginer, Shoyer, Hossessi, & Tannous, 2007) and by the perceived parental beliefs questionnaire pertaining to parents' beliefs about girls' higher education and early marriage (Mahajna, 2007). Self-empowerment was assessed by a scale developed by Mahajna (2007), and future orientation by an Arabic version (Mahajna, 2000, 2007) of the future orientation battery (Seginer, 2009, Seginer et al., 2004). All scales had adequate internal consistency coefficients, ranging from α = .62 (a 3-item scale) to α = .90 (a 5-item scale).

Employing structural equation modeling (SEM, Amos 17), the model was tested once for the *higher education* domain and once for the *marriage and family* domain. Figures 11.2a and 11.2b show the relations between the latent variables (parameters are standardized regression weights) and the goodness of fit of each model; the factor loadings of the manifest (empirical) variables on respective latent variables are all significant and range from .40 to .95.

Examination of the relations between the latent variables points to four findings worth noting here. (1) Perceived adolescent–parent relationships is positively related to perceived parental beliefs favoring *higher education* and negatively related to perceived parental beliefs favoring *early marriage*. (2) Regardless of their content, for both empirical models, the perceived parental beliefs–self-empowerment path is nonsignificant. Thus, it is perceived relationship and not perceived ideas that affect the girls' sense of self-empowerment. (3) The path from self-empowerment to the motivational component is positive and significant for the *higher education* but not for the *marriage and family* domain. Two conclusions follow. One, motivation for *higher education* draws on the girls' intrapersonal forces indicated by sense of self-empowerment as well as on perceived parental beliefs about higher education. Conversely, motivation for *marriage and family* is affected only by the cognitive–ideational aspect of family environment instantiated by perceived parental beliefs regarding early marriage. Second, self-representation indicated by self-empowerment may not be a generalized mediator; instead, it is especially relevant for mediating relational–emotional aspects of reality.

(4) The behavioral component–academic achievement path is positive for the *higher education* domain and negative for the *marriage and family* domain. The meaning of the difference between these paths goes beyond their different signs. The positive link between the behavioral component of the *higher education* is in line with theory and earlier findings about Israeli Muslim and secular Jewish girls and boys, and ultraorthodox Jewish girls (Seginer, 2009). Conversely, as also reported in other studies (Seginer, 2009), the negative path between the behavioral component of *marriage and family* and academic achievement is unique to Muslim girls; it is nonsignificant for Israeli Muslim boys and Jewish secular girls and boys, and positive for Jewish ultraorthodox girls (Seginer, 2009). Underlying it are two opposite considerations: one of girls presently giving priority to education and high academic achievement over early marriage, and the other of girls engaged to be married and who therefore view education as unimportant.

In sum, in constructing their future, Muslim girls in Israel both resemble and differ from other adolescent groups. Similar to other groups (such as Muslim boys and Jewish girls and boys), their future orientation plays a pivotal role in linking family environment and academic achievement, perceived adolescent–parent relationship is directly related to the self, and *higher education* (an instrumental domain) has a positive effect on academic achievement.

Differences pertain mostly to the *marriage and family* domain. Specifically, its motivational component is affected only by parental beliefs (not by the self) and academic achievement is negatively linked to future orientation. Of special interest is the link with academic achievement. Whereas for Muslim boys and secular Jewish girls and boys this link is nonsignificant (indicating they regard academic achievement as irrelevant to marriage and family), Jewish ultraorthodox girls consider it relevant (as indicated by the positive link): they regard it as facilitating their role in providing income and being good mothers (Seginer, Shoyer, & Dekel, 2011).

Navigating toward the Future in Context: Entwining Education and Family. As noted earlier, Muslim girls in Israel grow up in an intricate religious-cultural-political reality. We would like to argue that its relevance to their future orientation, its family and self antecedents, and academic achievement outcomes is enhanced because of the keen awareness Muslim girls in Israel have of their reality. Thus, one girl described their situation as emanating from growing up in "… a country that does not exactly provide equal opportunities, which adds to the unique difficulties of young Arab women." These difficulties emanate from community and family pressure toward early marriage and the girls' struggle to enter higher education. In the girl's voice:

I hope public opinion about women and girls will change one day, so that girls will not be engaged to be married while still in junior high school.[1]

I know girls face big challenges in our society. Many people, especially those in their immediate environment try to stand in their way [to pursue education]. I worry about them but will not give in.

As we interpret these findings, two processes become clear and both draw on Muslim male dominance. One recognizes the importance of *self-empowerment* for pursuing the nontraditional path of higher education, and the second relies on *parental beliefs* about early marriage for pursuing the religion-instructed path of early marriage and family. In a society strongly encouraging early marriage for women and expressing ambivalence toward higher education (considered positive because education is good for child rearing and may also give better job opportunities; negative because it may mean being away from home, seeking independence, and interfering with early marriage), a future orientation emphasizing higher education must rely on the girls' inner strength and self-determination (self-empowerment).

The relevance of self-reliance to girls' academic achievement has been indicated by an earlier study of Israeli Muslim 8th graders (Seginer & Vermulst, 2002). The study reports that girls' academic achievement is directly affected by educational aspirations, whereas boys' academic achievement is directly and negatively affected by parental demands. Thus, as early as 8th grade for Muslim girls in Israel, academic achievement does not draw on parental guidance but rather on their own.

Moreover, our findings have shown that whereas in all other groups examined by us, the motivational component of the instrumental domains (higher education, work and career) as well as the relational domain (marriage and family) is affected by a sense of self-worth (Seginer, 2009; Seginer et al., 2004), for Muslim girls, the motivational component of the marriage and family domain is linked only to traditional Muslim parental beliefs that instruct early marriage for women. Underlying it is the Muslim patriarchal family system (Booth, 2002) whereby through marriage, male dominance is transmitted from father and other family males to husband.

However, as noted in earlier analyses of Muslim girls' future orientation (Seginer, 2005; Seginer & Mahajna, 2004), the pursuit of higher education rarely involves an open questioning of religious practices or paternal authority. Instead, Muslim girls seek ways to intertwine emancipation (via education) and tradition (via accepting arranged marriage). Their hopes and fears narratives reveal three such ways. One is *sequential pursuit* of education and marriage: the preferred order is education first followed by marriage. Consider the following excerpts from our study interviews:

"Regarding marriage, I think a girl should get married only after completing her education. I hope God will help with my education and my marriage. I am not against being engaged after I complete my matriculation examinations. As long as my fiancé will agree that I continue my education and that our wedding will not take place immediately."

However, girls for whom marriage has been arranged before high school graduation find comfort in hopes to resume education, "later on."

In the future I would like to continue my education and I will insist on it. At the end of the school year I am getting married. I hope my family life will be good and successful and my husband will support and encourage me to continue my education.

I wish I could graduate from high school, study Psychology and only then think about marriage. But the circumstances in which I live force me to get married now after I graduate from 11th grade. I fear I will regret I left school although it is not my fault. But I think that later on I will go back to school.

A second way is *hoping for a supportive husband*. This is the most common and least efficacious consolation girls develop for themselves: "I hope to be fortunate and be engaged to a person who is understanding, open, and respects the woman, and will agree to share responsibility for our home and children. I hope he will support me so I can continue my education and not be a stumbling block against my dream for higher education." Another states, "I hope to God to send me a man who encourages women's education. I do not think I have a hope which is more important than this one."

The third way is harnessing education for *the good of her family and community*:

"I want to be a devoted wife. Therefore, I need to have education so that I can be a devoted wife" and "My hopes are to continue my education, be an excellent medical doctor, get married, be an exemplary wife and contribute to our society."

Will an Entwined Future be Materialized?

This study as the one by Pearce and Hardie (Chapter 12 in this volume) shows that across different cultural settings and when using different research question, religion has a considerable impact on how girls chart their future. Whether or not Muslim girls in Israel will be successful in meeting the challenges emanating from being a devoted Muslim and a dutiful wife without giving up higher education and career is not clear. On the one hand, as Islamization grows stronger in the majority of Middle East societies, the tension between it and democracy grows stronger and has a direct bearing on women (Rizzo, Meyer, & Ali, 2002). On the other hand, recent data (Israel Central Statistics Bureau, 2011) showing rise in the number of Muslim girls in Israel who graduate from high school and college suggest education is becoming more accessible to them. Underlying this trend are multiple psychological and social processes that future research needs to examine. One relates to recent "Muslim ethicist" religiosity that endorses the personal achievement of young *men* as a source of family pride (Gregg, 2005), raising the question whether it will also become acceptable for women. The other pertains to their families and community. Specifically, the questions remain as to whether women's emancipation via higher education and career will indeed be endorsed by the cohort of men to whom they will be married, and if the image of the ideal husband who supports women's education will indeed become true.

Acknowledgment

The authors wish to acknowledge the help of Sandra Zukerman in data analysis and of Shirli Shoyer in the production of this manuscript.

NOTES

1. All quotes of girls' narratives were jointly translated and back-translated by both authors. Mahajna is native speaker of Arabic and Seginer is responsible for the English.

REFERENCES

Abu-Baker, K. (2003). "Career woman" or "working woman"? Change versus stability for young Palestinian women in Israel. *Journal of Israeli History*, **21**, (1–2), 85–109.

Ahmed, L. (1992). *Women and gender in Islam: Historical roots of modern debate*. New Haven, CT: Yale University Press.

Atkinson, J. W. (1964). *An introduction to motivation*. Princeton, NJ: Van Nostrand.

Azaiza, F., Abu-Baker, K., Hertz-Lazarowitz, R., & Ghanem, A. (2009). Introduction. In F. Azaiza, K. Abu-Baker, R. Hertz-Lazarowitz, & A. Ghanem (Eds.), *Arab women in Israel: Current status and future trends* (pp. 5–16). Tel Aviv: Ramot. (Hebrew)

Barber, B., Stolz, H., Olson, J. O., Collins, A., & Burchinal, M. (2005). Parental support, psychological control, and behavioral control: Assessing relevance across time, culture, and method. *Monographs of the Society for Research in Child Development*, **70**, 1–137. doi: 10.1111/j.1540–5834.2005.00365.x

Booth, M. (2002). Arab adolescents facing the future: Enduring ideals and pressures to change. In B. B. Brown, R. W. Larson, & T. S. Saraswathi (Eds.), *The world's youth: Adolescence in eight regions of the globe* (pp. 207–242). New York: Cambridge University Press.

Bronfenbrenner, U. (1979). *The ecology of human development: Experiments by nature and design*. Cambridge, MA: Harvard University Press.

Douvan, E., & Adelson, J. (1966). *The adolescent experience*. New York: Wiley

Eccles, J. S., & Wigfield, A. (2002). Motivation, beliefs, and goals. *Annual Review of Psychology*, **53**, 109–132. doi: 10.1146/annurev.psych.53.100901.135153

Epstein, S. (1983). *Scoring and interpretation of the mother-father-peer scale*. Unpublished manuscript, University of Massachusetts.

Erikson, E. H. (1968). *Identity, youth and crisis*. New York: Norton.

Goodnow, J. J., & Collins, W. A. (1990). *Development according to parents*. Hillsdale, NJ: Erlbaum.

Gregg, G. S. (2005). *The Middle East: A cultural psychology*. New York: Oxford University Press.

Harter, S. (1999). *The construction of the self*. New York: Guilford.

Husman, J., & Lens, W. (1999). The role of the future in student motivation. *Educational Psychologist*, **34**, 113–125. doi: 10.1207/s15326985ep3402_4

Israel Central Statistical Bureau (2010). *Israel Statistical Yearbook*. Jerusalem: Central Bureau of Statistics.

(2011). *Women and men*. Jerusalem: Central Bureau of Statistics. (Hebrew)

James, W. (1890/1950). *The principles of psychology*. New York: Dover Publications.

Joireman, J., Anderson, J., & Strathman, A. (2003). The aggression paradox: Understanding links among aggression, sensation seeking, and the consideration of future consequences. *Journal of Personality and Social Psychology*, **84**, 1287–1302. doi: 10.1037/0022–3514.84.6.1287

Jones, A. (2007). *The Qur'an translation into English*. Cambridge: Gibbs Memorial Trust.

Khattab, N. (2003). Segregation, ethnic labor market and the occupational expectations of Palestinian students in Israel. *British journal of sociology*, **54**, 259–285. doi: 10.1080/0007131032000080230

Laursen, B., & Collins, W. A. (2009). Parent–child relationships during adolescence. In R. M. Lerner & L. Steinberg (Eds.), *Handbook of adolescent psychology* (3rd Ed., Vol. 2, pp 3–42). Hoboken, NJ: Wiley.

Lewin, K. (1939). Field theory and experiment in social psychology. *American Journal of Sociology*, 44, 868–896. doi: 10.1086/218177

Mahajna, S. (2007). *Future orientation: Its nature and meaning among girls from different Israeli Arab settings.* Unpublished doctoral dissertation, University of Haifa, Israel.

Manna, A. (2008). *Arab society in Israel.* Jerusalem: The Van Leer Jerusalem Institute. (Hebrew)

Muhammad, A. E. (2005). *Palestinians in Israel: Socio-economic survey.* Shefa-Amr, Israel: The Galilee Society.

Nurmi, J. E. (1991). How do adolescents see their future? A review of the development of future orientation and planning. *Developmental Review*, 11, 1–59. doi: 10.1016/0273-2297(91)90002-6

Nuttin, J., & Lens, W. (1985). *Future time perspective and motivation: Theory and research method.* Location: Erlbaum.

Oyserman, D., Bybee, D., & Terry, K. (2006). Possible selves and academic outcomes: How and when possible selves impel action. *Journal of Personality and Social Psychology*, 91, 188–204. doi: 10.1037/0022-3514.91.1.188

Paloutzian, R. F., & Park, C. L. (2005). Integrative themes in the current science of the psychology of religion. In R. F. Paloutzian & C. L. Park (Eds.), *Handbook of the psychology of religion and spirituality* (pp. 3–20). New York: Guilford.

Peled, A. R. (2001). *Debating Islam in the Jewish state.* Albany: State University of New York Press.

Pickthall, M. (1999). The Quran: Differing interpretation of the divine word. In R. Roded (Ed.), *Women in the Middle East* (pp. 27–31). New York: I. B. Tauris.

Rekhess, E. (2000). The Islamic movement in Israel. In R. Gabizon & D. Hacker (Eds.), *The Jewish-Arab rift in Israel* (pp. 271–296). Jerusalem: The Israel Democracy Institute.

Rekhess, E., & Rodnitzki, A. (2009). *Information manual on the Arab society in Israel.* Neve Ilan, Israel: The Abraham Fund Initiatives. (Hebrew)

Rizzo, H., Meyer, K., & Ali, Y (2002). Women's political rights: Islam, status and networks in Kuwait. *Sociology*, 36, 639–662. doi: 10.1177/0038038502036003008

Seginer, R. (1988). Social milieu and future orientation: The case of kibbutz vs. urban adolescents. *International Journal of Behavioral Development*, 11, 247–273.

(1998). Adolescents' perception of relationships with older sibling in the context of other close relationships. *Journal of Research on Adolescence*, 8, 287–308. 10.1207/s15327795jra0803_1

(2005). Adolescent future orientation: Intergenerational transmission and intertwining tactics in cultural and family settings. In W. Friedlemeier, P. Chakkarath, & B. Schwarz (Eds.), *Culture and human development: The importance of cross-cultural research for the social sciences* (pp. 231–251). New York: Psychology Press.

(2008). Future orientation in times of threat and challenge: How resilient adolescents construct their future. *International Journal of Behavioral Development*, 32, 272–282. doi: 10.1177/0165025408090970

(2009). *Future orientation: Developmental and ecological perspectives.* New York: Springer.

Seginer, R., & Mahajna, S. (2004). How the future orientation of traditional Israeli Palestinian girls link beliefs about women's roles and academic achievement. *Psychology of Women Quarterly*, **28**, 122–135. doi: 10.1111/j.1471–6402.2004.00129.x

(2012). How future orientation links parenting and academic achievement: Gender differences among Muslim adolescents. Manuscript submitted for publication.

Seginer, R., Shoyer, S., & Dekel, S. (2011). Future orientation in context: The case of Jewish ultra-orthodox and secular girls. In preparation.

Seginer, R., Shoyer, S., Hossessi, R., & Tannous, H. (2007). Adolescent family and peer relationships: Does culture matter? In R. W. Larson & L. A. Jensen (Series Eds.), *New Directions for Child and Adolescent Development* (No. 116). B. B. Brown & N. S. Mounts (Vol. Eds.), *Linking parents and family to adolescent peer relations: Ethnic and cultural considerations* (pp. 83–99). San Francisco: Jossey Bass.

Seginer, R., & Vermulst, A. (2002). Family environment, educational aspirations, and academic achievement in two cultural settings. *Journal of Cross-Cultural Psychology*, **33**, 540–558. doi: 10.1177/00220022102238268

Seginer, R., Vermulst, A., & Shoyer, S. (2004). The indirect link between perceived parenting and adolescent future orientation: A multiple-step analysis. *International Journal of Behavioral Development*, **28**, 365–378. doi: 10.1080/01650250444000081

Smooha, S. (2009). *The 2008 Index of Arab-Jewish Relations in Israel 2008*. Haifa, Israel: The Jewish-Arab Center, the University of Haifa (Hebrew).

Trommsdorff, G. (1983). Future orientation and socialization. *International Journal of Psychology*, **18**, 381–406. doi: 10.1080/00207598308247489

(1986). Future time orientation and its relevance for development as action. In R. K. Silbereisen, K. Eyferth, & G. Rudinger (Eds.), *Development as action in context: Problem behavior and normal youth development* (pp. 121–136). New York: Springer-Verlag.

12 Religion's Role in the Development of Girls' Occupational Aspirations

Lisa D. Pearce and Jessica Halliday Hardie

Abstract

In this chapter we explore the influence of religion on female adolescents through the use of both nationally representative, longitudinal survey data and semi-structured, in-person interviews from the National Study of Youth and Religion. Our results suggest that growing up in a religious family, especially those involved in religious institutions, may result in an increased identification with femininity and a heightened emphasis on care, leading to preference for more female-dominated jobs like teaching, nursing, and other medical assistant type work. Adolescent girls (ages 16–21) express a preference for these careers over business, science, or other male-dominated (and more highly paid) professions while directly referring to a personal desire for an altruistic, rewarding, and "family friendly" career track. These gendered career aspirations sort girls into limited career tracks early in their educational lives and often well before family formation processes begin, likely contributing to continued gender inequality in educational and career attainment. Although occupational aspirations are thought to be primarily products of social class and ability, we argue that cultural forces such as religion provide a system of meaning and values that shape how girls imagine their futures.

When adolescents imagine their future selves, they are setting goals that will influence their current behavior (Oyserman & James, 2009). They are defining the potential they see in themselves. Although adolescent career or occupational aspirations are not perfectly correlated with eventual achievement, there is a sizeable association (Campbell, 1983; Eccles, Vida, & Barber, 2004; Schoon, 2001; Sewell, Haller, & Portes, 1969). Further, although the gap is shrinking, girls tend to have less prestigious occupational aspirations than boys, and this likely contributes to continued gender inequality in occupational prestige and earnings (Correll, 2001; Lips, 2004; Mahaffy & Ward, 2002; Marini & Greenberger, 1978; Nash, 1979). Specifically, largely owing to forces of gender socialization, girls tend to imagine themselves attaining jobs that women more typically hold (e.g., teacher, nurse, waitress, etc.) (Frome, et al., 2006; Murrell, Frieze, & Frost, 1991; Shu & Marini, 1998). These female-dominated occupations are less prestigious and pay less than male-dominated jobs with similar educational or experience prerequisites (Glick, 1991; Yoder, 1994). It is therefore important to understand the social forces shaping girls' occupational aspirations, especially the level of female presence in the occupations to which they aspire.

Prior studies of youth occupational aspirations have primarily focused on social class and intergenerational processes to explain differences in aspirations that ultimately influence social mobility and the reproduction of inequality (Massey, Gebhardt, & Garnefski, 2008). Few studies have addressed the role of cultural factors, such as religion, that may shape the goals to which youth and especially young girls aspire. Yet religious involvement in the United States has been found to increase social capital and encourage prosocial and achievement-oriented behavior in youth (Muller & Ellison, 2001). At the same time, many American religious institutions send overt messages to girls about the value of motherhood and family life (Denton, 2004; Fan & Marini, 2000). In this chapter, we explore how values encouraged through religious participation and internalization shape girls' occupational aspirations. We use nationally representative, longitudinal survey data and semi-structured, in-person interviews from the National Study of Youth and Religion (Smith & Denton, 2005) to show how parent religiosity and youth religious affiliation and religiosity are related to girls' aspirations.

Possible Selves, Possible Careers

"Possible selves" are visions of oneself at a future point in time or the "future-oriented aspects of self-concept" (Oyserman & James, 2009). Adolescence is a time in which youth are especially focused on developing their possible selves in terms of education, occupation, and future family life (Massey et al., 2008). How one imagines his/her future in terms of education, career, or family life depends on the other two types of possible selves. Research suggests that girls consider future family desires even more than boys when setting educational and career goals (Eccles, 1994; Nurmi, 1994). They may therefore select occupations that appear family friendly or are similar to jobs held by mothers they know. Their personal value orientations may also influence their occupational aspirations. Research shows that in general, young women attach greater value to intrinsic, altruistic, and social rewards from their work than young men and this shows in the types of jobs to which they aspire (Marini, et al., 1996; Weisgram, Bigler, & Liben, 2010).

Prior studies have identified several correlates of the occupational aspirations of adolescent girls. First, as adolescents age, they mature cognitively and begin to more seriously consider their occupational goals (Nurmi, 1994). Second, the family context greatly shapes the type of career to which a girl aspires. Living with two parents increases the financial and emotional support available to girls as they develop their aspirations (Teachman & Paasch, 1998). However, the more siblings one has, the further the resources are stretched, so it is likely that girls from larger families temper their aspirations. Also, the more education one's mother and/or father have attained, the more prestigious is the occupation to which a girl aspires (Glick & White, 2003; Hitlin, 2006; Shu & Marini, 2008). Family income signals resources, and is likely to increase a girl's confidence in being able to accomplish her goals (Massey et al., 2008). Finally, aspirations are often shaped by one's assessment of their abilities and dedication. This is reflected through evidence that an adolescent's GPA is related to her aspirations (Davis & Pearce, 2007).

What is conspicuously missing from research on the development of girls' occupational aspirations is the role of cultural institutions such as religion that cultivate values that influence aspirations. Culture is an important context in which the development of aspirations occurs (Seginer 2003), so studies often evaluate whether there are racial/ethnic differences in prestige of occupational aspirations after socioeconomic factors are controlled, but evidence is weak for any such differences in the United States (Chang, et al., 2006; Phinney, Baumann, & Blanton, 2001). Culture expressed through the tenets of a religious congregation, however, may influence adolescents' aspirations. Seginer (2003) reports that Israeli Jewish (kibbutz and urban), Arab, and Druze adolescents have unique future orientations, specifically, some think more prospectively than others. To further explore the role of cultural factors in shaping occupational aspirations in adolescence, we focus on religion and the aspiration to a more female-dominated occupation among girls.

Religion and Possible Careers

There is a great deal of research and attention to the relationship between one's religious background and educational aspirations and achievement or economic well-being as adults. However, far less attention has been paid to religion's role in the forming of occupational aspirations, a key mechanism linking educational aspirations and attainment to eventual occupational prestige and achievement. Therefore, as we theorize the possible influence that religious affiliation, parent religiosity, and youth religiosity might have on the careers to which an adolescent girl aspires, we draw on the literature relating religion to educational and occupational outcomes.

Religious Affiliation

The religious tradition, group, or denomination with which an individual affiliates is largely representative of the types of religious beliefs and ideologies to which she is most exposed (Mishra, Chapter 18 in this volume). When it comes to adolescents, they often carry the same religious affiliation as their parents, but as they develop autonomy, they may switch or drop religious affiliations altogether (Pearce & Denton, 2011). In recent research, the religious groups that have been shown to be most different in terms of educational and occupational aspirations and achievement are conservative Protestants, sometimes referred to as Evangelical or Fundamentalist[1] Protestants. This is argued to be especially relevant for girls because conservative Protestant leaders, writings, and adherents are more likely to idealize a breadwinner-housewife model of marriage such that men work outside the home and women specialize in managing the home and caring for children (Denton, 2004; Pearce & Thornton, 2007). It is not that education and labor force participation are completely discouraged, but home- and family-based labor is prioritized over breadwinning activities. Given that less importance is placed on women's occupational achievement, and that gendered socialization is a powerful force among this group, it is likely that conservative Protestant girls will be especially likely to aspire to more female-dominated occupations.

Public Religiosity

Another dimension of religiosity is public practice or attending religious services. Most religions promote family life (childbearing and child rearing) and, to some degree, most religious institutions socialize adherents to the notion that these are primarily women's responsibilities (Edgell, 2006; Seginer and Mahajna, Chapter 11 in this volume). Therefore, the time that parents and children spend in religious institutions is likely to cultivate values that gender the worlds of family and work (Glass & Kanellakos, 2006). Parents' attendance will reinforce these values about the gendered nature of work and family life that they will then demonstrate for their children.

Adolescent girls' exposure to religious services and coreligionists will be a source of socialization for the notion that women should specialize in caring for family members (Glass & Jacobs, 2005). It is often assumed that if they do work, they should choose careers that are typically held by women. Many of the male-dominated professional occupations have reputations as demanding personal or family sacrifice and punishing those who take time out of the labor force for such reasons as maternity leave (Ridgeway, 2002).

Private Religiosity

Yet another dimension of religiosity is the private or personal dimension. It may be the importance one places on religion, the time one spends praying alone, the reading of sacred scripture, or other private practices. This is a unique aspect of religiosity because it does not involve social interaction. It represents the degree to which someone internalizes religiosity as part of his or her identity. Again, because religions are often pro-family, especially for women, the internalization and valuing of these messages reinforced by one's own personal reliance on religious faith could mean that when parents find religion to be an important aspect of their identity, they are more encouraging of their daughters choosing a more female-dominated career. Girls themselves who find religion to be a very important part of their lives might prioritize their future family plans over investments in education and career achievement that are likely to lead to more prestigious occupations more commonly held by men (Glass & Jacobs, 2005; Glass & Kanellakos, 2006).

Linking Religion to Girls' Possible Careers

Our goal in this chapter is to understand the ways religion shapes girls' occupational aspirations. Prior research has found that holding values for altruism and family tend to motivate interest in female-dominated occupations (Marini, et al., 1996; Weisgram, et al., 2010), occupational aspirations predict attainment (Campbell, 1983; Eccles, et al., 2004; Schoon, 2001; Sewell, et al., 1969), and that female-dominated occupations typically offer less pay and prestige than male-dominated occupations at equivalent levels of education (Glick, 1991; Yoder, 1994). Religion is expected to play a role in this process by influencing girls' occupational values and aspirations (Trommsdorff, Chapter 1 in this volume). Girls who are affiliated with more conservative Protestant denominations, for instance, may be more likely to aspire to female-dominated occupations because of the messages about gender and family these congregations promote (Mayer and Trommsdorff,

Chapter 15 in this volume). Similarly, girls who attend religious services more frequently will receive these messages on a more consistent basis, and therefore are likely to aspire to more female-dominated occupations. Personal religiosity is also expected to play a role, as girls who internalize these religious messages and values express them in their daydreams about the future. Finally, young women's gender role attitudes and family plans may be mechanisms through which religious affiliation, religiosity, and attendance influence occupational aspirations.

To examine the role of religion in girls' occupational aspirations, our study employs quantitative survey data and qualitative interview data from the National Study of Youth and Religion (NSYR) to examine whether and how religion shapes girls' occupational aspirations. In the next section, we describe our survey data and findings. Following this, we describe our analytic design and data for the qualitative portion of the study and discuss our findings.

National Study of Youth and Religion

The NSYR is a nationally representative survey of youth, designed to provide information regarding the religious beliefs and practices of teenagers in the United States. The first wave of this study was conducted in 2002 and 2003 with a sample of 3,290 teenagers between the ages of 13 and 17 and their parents. In 2005, nearly 80 percent of these participants were reinterviewed. For our analysis of girls' occupational aspirations, we include only female respondents who participated in Waves 1 and 2, for a sample size of 1,039. Our aim in using this data was to understand the role religious affiliation, religious attendance, religiosity, and gender role attitudes played in predicting teenage girls' occupational aspirations.

In the NSYR survey, respondents were asked, "What job or occupation do you think you will have when you are thirty-five years old?" Responses were transformed into the percent of job holders who were women using published data available through the U.S. Bureau of Labor Statistics (U.S. Bureau of Labor Statistics [BLS], 2006). For example, the occupational aspiration "lawyer" was recoded into a value of 30.2, because 30.2 percent of lawyers were female in 2005. This is a measure of the current "female-ness" of a given occupation's population. Those with a percentage higher than 50 are more female-dominated, and those with a percentage lower than 50 are more male-dominated occupations. Figure 12.1 shows the distribution of this variable for all female NSYR survey respondents. The mean is 59 percent female, and we have highlighted where a few occupations fall on the continuum.

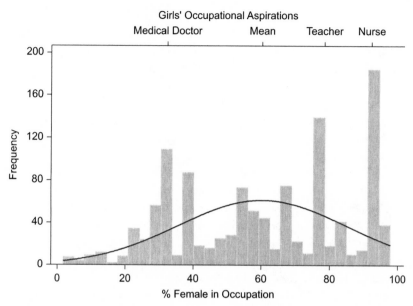

Figure 12.1. Distribution of percent-female in the occupations to which NSYR female survey respondents aspire.

Participants' reports of their religious affiliations, beliefs, and practices show a generally high level of membership in Protestant religions and high public and private religiosity among parents and children. Our measure of religious affiliation[2] was created by the youth respondent's report of the "religious tradition, denomination, or church" with which they identified most closely. Evangelical Protestants comprised 32 percent of our samples, compared to 12 percent Mainline Protestant, 11 percent African American Protestant, 26 percent Catholic, 3 percent Mormon, 2 percent Jewish, 5 percent other religion, and 6 percent unaffiliated. Our parent religious service attendance indicates how often the responding parent had attended religious services in the previous 12 months from never (0) to more than once a week (6). On average, parents reported attending church slightly more than 2–3 times a month, but less than once a week. Youth were asked the same question about religious service attendance that parents received, and reported similar levels of attendance. Our measure of parental importance of religion comes from parents being asked, "How important is your religious faith in providing guidance in your own day-to-day living: Extremely Important (coded 6), Very, Fairly, Somewhat, Not very, or Not Important at all (coded 1)?" Parents reported an average response of 5, equivalent to "very important." Teens' private religiosity is a scaled measure of the sum of all standardized measures of the following variables: wear religious jewelry, fast as part of a religious ritual, listen to religious music, try to practice weekly day of rest, read religious/spiritual books, pray by yourself alone, read from the Bible alone, importance of faith in shaping daily life, and importance of faith in shaping decisions.

We also include measures of young women's gender role attitudes and family plans to test whether any of these factors act as mechanisms for the influence of religion on occupational aspirations. Responses were asked if they "Strongly Agree (5), Agree (4), Disagree (2), or Strongly Disagree (1)" that "A working mother can establish as warm and secure a relationship with her children as a mother who does not work" and "It is better if a man makes money and a woman takes care of home and family." Undecided responses were coded 3. We also use measures of ideal age at marriage (What do you think is the ideal age to get married?) and fertility intentions (In total, how many children do you intend to have?).

Finally, we incorporate a standard set of control variables to account for youth and family characteristics at Wave 1 that are likely related to both religious characteristics and occupational aspirations. We use self-reports of age and race/ethnicity from Wave 1 (2002). Family socioeconomic status is controlled for through measures of parents' education and household income. Income was grouped into categories of less than 150 percent of the poverty line, 150 to 250 percent of the poverty line, 250 percent to four times the poverty line, and over four times the poverty line.[3] We also include a variable for missing income. Family structure is measured using a measure of the number of children living in the same household as the focal child and a dichotomous indicator of whether the youth lived with his or her married (biological or adoptive) parents. GPA was measured categorically and converted into approximate numeric values to match a 0–4.0 scale from "Fs" to "As."

Survey Findings

Table 12.1 displays results from an ordinary least squares regression analysis of how parent and youth religious characteristics shape subsequent occupational aspirations through a set of attitudes and controlling for a set of standard sociodemographic characteristics. We find that affiliation is unrelated to occupational aspirations, except among Jewish respondents. On average, Jewish girls aspire to occupations that are 11 percent lower on the continuum of percent female than the average occupational aspiration

Table 12.1. Coefficients of Ordinary Least Squares Regression of Percent-Female of Occupational Aspiration on Religious Characteristics, Demographics, Family Background, and Attitudes

	Coefficients	T-ratios
Teen's religious affiliation[e]		
Evangelical Protestant	1.92	0.87
Mainline Protestant	4.82	1.77
African American Protestant	−0.18	0.05
Jewish	−11.30*	1.98
Mormon	5.35	1.02
Other religious affiliation	−3.01	0.78
No religious affiliation	2.78	0.84
Parent religious service attendance	0.31	0.61
Parent importance of faith	2.33**	3.08
Teen religious service attendance	1.02*	2.07
Teen private religiosity	−0.07	0.38
Agreement with: "A working mother can have a warm and loving relationship with children."	−1.33*	1.67
Agreement with: "Better if a man earns money and woman takes care of home and family."	1.86**	2.73
Ideal age of marriage	−0.51*	2.02
Number of children teen wishes to have	1.90**	2.90
Parent education[c]		
Some college	0.30	0.15
Received BA/BS	−3.99	1.54
Graduate/professional schooling	−1.96	0.67
Unknown	−2.16	0.52
Family income[d]		
150% to 250% of poverty line	−2.83	1.19
250% to 400% of poverty line	−3.15	1.21
Over 400% of poverty line	−4.00	1.31
Income missing	−1.74	0.44
Grade point average	−4.94***	3.72
Constant	82.84***	8.94
N	1039	
adj. R^2	0.078	

* $p < 0.05$, ** $p < 0.01$, *** $p < 0.001$; one-tailed tests
[a] Reference category is "Age 13"
[b] Reference category is "White"
[c] Reference category is "High school graduate"
[d] Reference category is "Less than 150% of poverty line"
[e] Reference category is "Catholic"

of Catholic girls. In analyses not shown here, we ran models using other religious groups as the reference group, and Jewish girls' aspirations were different than all other religious groups, but no other differences between other religious groups were statistically significant. In a full regression model including parent and child measures of religiosity, the daughter's public practice of religiosity is the more significant type of religiosity. The more often a girl attends religious services herself, the more female-dominated occupation she prefers. Of course, parent and child religious importance and parent religious service attendance are correlated with the daughter's attendance level, so in a sense, the various dimensions of religiosity are working through the daughter's attendance. On average, a one unit increase in religious service attendance is associated with a 1 percent increase in the percent female for her occupational aspiration. Girls' own importance of faith does not seem related to the type of occupational aspiration they hold, even when this is the only measure of religiosity in the model (results not shown).

Our findings suggest that attitudes toward family life are mechanisms through which religion influences girls' occupational aspirations. Girls who disagree that a working mother can establish a warm and loving relationship with her children, agree that men should be responsible for breadwinning and women should take care of the home, those who desire to marry earlier, and those who desire more children have occupational aspirations that are significantly more female-dominated than their counterparts. In the progression of models not presented here, the addition of each additional attitude about family life shrinks the size of the coefficients for parent importance of religiosity and youth religious service attendance. These dimensions of religiosity still remain statistically significant, suggesting they have their own independent relationship with occupational aspirations, but part of those relationships are explained by more religious girls, with more religious parents having ideas about women investing more heavily in housework, childcare, childbearing, and marrying earlier.

To get an overall sense of how related religiosity is to girls' occupational aspirations, we prepared predicted probabilities for three different types of youth and have displayed these in Figure 12.2. Girls with lower attendance and importance of faith average occupational aspirations at about the level of 58 percent female, which are jobs like being an editor, a bartender, or a real estate broker. At the other end, girls with high religious involvement and importance of faith average occupational aspirations that are about 72 percent female, like waitresses, insurance underwriters, and cardiovascular technicians.

Low Religious Attendance & Faith	Mean Religious Attendance & Faith	High Religious Attendance & Faith
57.8 % Female	60.8% Female	71.9% Female
(E.g., Editor, bartender, real estate broker)	(E.g., Food preparation worker, retail sales, public relations)	(E.g., Waitress, insurance underwriter, cardiovascular technician)

Figure 12.2. Predicted percent-female in occupation to which a female respondent aspires at low, mean, and high levels of youth religiosity.

The descriptive and statistical analyses presented here offer a snapshot of the relationships between religious experiences and beliefs, attitudes and family plans, and occupational aspirations for girls. Next, we turn to qualitative data from semi-structured interviews for more evidence regarding how religion may shape aspirations. First, we describe our sample and methods and then we report our findings.

Semi-structured Interview Data

To further explore the relationship between religiosity and occupational aspirations in a more inductive manner, we draw on qualitative data collected through an approach called Systematic Anomalous Case Analysis (Pearce, 2002) in which a regression model is used to produce anomalous cases and a set of non-anomalous comparison cases that can be reinterviewed in a more open-ended format so that additional themes that will help explain the development of occupational aspirations can emerge.

In this case, we took the regression model presented here (Table 12.1) and ran regression diagnostics to obtain values for residuals, leverage scores, Cooks Distance, and DFFITS. These values indicate how well or not well individual cases fit along a regression line and how much influence a case has on regression results. For example, if a participant's survey responses predict that she should hold an aspiration for a job that is about 80 percent female, but her reported aspiration is 20 percent female, she would be considered an outlying case. Using our diagnostic values, we created a list of all girls in our sample between the ages of 16–18 who were outliers. From that list we randomly selected 11 cases. Next we picked 11 non-anomalous cases who best matched our 11 anomalous cases on age, race, occupational aspiration, religiosity, and GPA. Of the 22 eligible cases, eight were interviewed, two refused to participate, and twelve were unreachable because of moves (and family members refusing to share new contact information) or no one answering the phone. In total, five anomalous cases and three comparison cases were interviewed in eight different states.

Each interview started with a pile sort activity. Participants were handed a pile of cards that each listed an occupation.[4] The first sorting activity was very open. Participants were asked to sort the cards into any piles that made sense to them. The rule was just that every card had to go in a pile, and there had to be more than one pile. If they had not done so in the initial activity, they were then asked to sort the cards into "jobs they desired" and "jobs they did not desire." Next they were asked to sort the cards into "jobs suited for women" and "jobs suited for men." Following each sorting activity, the participants were asked to discuss why certain cards ended up in the piles that they did. These sorting activities gave us data on how the participants saw various occupations, and served as a very nice ice breaker to get them talking. The rest of the interview was about their lives and operated by providing an open-ended life history calendar that interviewer or participant could write on to map out key aspects of their lives, including their aspirations and religious lives over time. All participants consented to have the interviews audio recorded, and the recordings were subsequently transcribed into typed transcripts stripped of all identifiers. Both authors and two graduate student research assistants have been involved in the inductive coding and discussion of emerging themes from the transcripts.

Interview Findings

Gender Identity

The most striking theme emerging from our interviews was the extent to which girls expressed their career aspirations as an extension of how feminine (or masculine) they viewed themselves or even how feminine (or not) others viewed them. Mandy, a young girl who aspires to be a pilot and police officer, demonstrates this theme well. Mandy, a 17-year-old living in a working class neighborhood in the Midwest, was tall, thin, and blond, wearing jeans, a white blouse, tennis shoes, and a turquoise necklace. She wore little make-up and carried an army green canvas purse. At the time of the 2005 NSYR survey, Mandy said she hoped to be a pilot when she was 35 years old, an occupation in which 95 percent of employees are male. Mandy likely registered as an anomalous case because her mother finds religion to be extremely important, Mandy attended religious services at least three times a month, and Mandy reported the ideal age at marriage to be 20 years old (all characteristics related to aspiring to more female-dominated jobs); however, Mandy aspires to a very male-dominated occupation.

At the time of the interview, Mandy was still hoping to be a pilot at the encouragement of her father who takes her to a small airport for free plane rides and bought her private lessons for her last birthday. She also considered becoming a police officer at the encouragement of her grandfather, or a realtor based on discussions with one of her parents' friends. During the pile sort activity, Mandy placed the "pilot" and "police officer" cards in the "best suited for men" pile. The interviewer asked, "So, the two jobs that you are most interested in ended up in the male pile. That's interesting. Have you thought about that before?" Mandy replied, "Yeah, how I like, how everybody sees me as just one of the guys." The interviewer follows up on this theme later and Mandy says,

I would always, like girls would sit on the side and watch the guys play basketball, but I'd be the one that would kind of like go and play, and I'd try to beat 'em you know. And try to show them that I was just another one of the guys, or maybe even better. And my boyfriend kind of finds that threatening because he knows this summer I'm probably gonna, because I'm living in a new neighborhood, and there's like a park right down the street from me. So I told him I was interested in trying to get to know people again. And he's like, "So you're gonna try to get to know guys?" He's always saying, "You're always trying to be just another one of the guys." And, my friends are saying that too, because they're not like big into sports.

A few times in the interview, Mandy talks about relating better to her father than her mother. Mandy's father is not as religiously active as her mother who insists Mandy attend church, and she reports sharing her father's skepticism of organized religion. When describing what jobs do not appeal to her, Mandy clearly states multiple times that she does not like children as a condition that ruled her out for typically female-dominated jobs such as teaching. She also makes a point of saying it's her boyfriend that remembers the day they started dating, not her, that he's "clingy" and he wants to move in together soon and get married some day, but she would rather have her independence. She says people tell her she gets along well with her boyfriend because he is more feminine and she is more masculine. She describes herself as a unique girl, because she likes to "push the limits" of what a girl is expected to do.

Other girls who are anomalous cases described themselves as possessing stereotypically female characteristics. Caitlin is endlessly teased for being overweight, unattractive, and unable to read at grade level. She lives in a small town and attends a small public high school where she says all the female teachers grew up and were cheerleaders in that same town. She feels that she has nothing in common with them and that they are mean to her. Although her lower GPA and desire for seven children predict that she would be more likely to aspire toward a female-dominated occupation, Caitlin wants to do something in the field of agriculture, working with farmers, generally a more male-dominated field. Although Caitlin does not directly discuss feeling like "one of the guys" as Mandy does, a similar theme of not fitting the expectations of what a girl in her community is like may contribute to her thinking about her future, or her possible careers in terms of something that bends gender norms as well.

Frome and colleagues (2006) find that girls who aspire to male-dominated jobs often adjust their aspirations to more female-typical occupations later in adolescence. This was particularly true of girls who placed less value on physical science and expressed a desire for family friendly work, suggesting that girls tend to align their aspirations with what society expects of women. What some of our anomalous cases suggest is that girls who already identify as different from the average girl, like Mandy and Caitlin, may be more comfortable retaining aspirations for occupations not typically held by women.

Religion is a cultural force often implicated as a social institution that reinforces patriarchal aspects of society, such as promoting ideas of men being the heads of households, the breadwinner-housewife model of family organization, and glorifying women's femininity (Edgell, 2006; Glass & Jacobs, 2005). Lower levels of religious exposure and participation as is the case for Caitlin, and limited internalization as is the case for Mandy, leave more opportunity for girls to imagine themselves working in jobs that are not as female-dominated. Therefore, it may be that when parents value religion and girls are religiously active, religion serves as a gender socializing force that leads to a preference for more female-dominated occupations. Religion may shape what a girl sees as possible for her, her "possible careers."

Promoting Altruism

We also interviewed girls our regression analysis predicted would aspire to more male-dominated occupations given their GPA and family socio-economic background. For example, Sara, Rachel, and PJ aspired to be a dancer, a surgical nurse, and physical therapist, respectively. None of these girls have particularly religious families, nor are they religiously active, yet they all three share something in common with Anita and Bethany, two girls with religiously active families who aspire to be an elementary school teacher and a physical therapist, respectively. They all place high value on helping and caring for others.

One of us arranged to meet Anita at a local bookstore in a western state, and she arrived 10 minutes early. She came right over and, with a bright, friendly smile, asked, "Are you [Interviewer's name]?" The field notes about the interview mention, "In all my interactions with Anita up until the interview, and during the interview, she was very cheery and friendly, always agreeable, cooperative, and extremely polite. She seemed a bit nervous at first, but was quite willing to answer any question, expanded nicely on her answers, and didn't overtalk." Going through the pile sort activities, there was a great deal of overlap between the pile of jobs she could see herself doing and jobs that she thought were best suited for women. Also, she explained that occupations such as being an artist, a social worker, or a physical therapist are good jobs for women, because women have more compassion than men. In terms of her own aspirations, perfectly matching what she had reported during the NSYR survey, Anita said, "I really, really, really want to be a teacher. I love working with kids." For her senior year high school project, Anita designed a peer counseling program for her school. She clearly values having compassion for others and providing assistance and sees these as especially appropriate values and job characteristics for women. Some of this may have come from her regular involvement in a conservative Protestant church with her family where many of the women are stay-at-home mothers or work as teachers or nurses.

Similar to Anita, Bethany immediately cited her love of helping people in explaining why she had picked certain cards as jobs she would like to have. "Well, with the exception of the lawyer, a lot of these jobs deal with the medical profession. That's something I really am interested in. Just helping people." Also similar to Anita, Bethany is heavily involved in a school club that promotes breaking down cliques and peer pressure at school. It involves a peer counseling component. Bethany lights up when she talks about this club and "being the change" she wants to see at her school.

From these cases and others, we see that when girls embrace the stereo-typically female characteristic of valuing altruism, this shows through in how they evaluate a range of careers and pick one to aspire toward. To the extent that religious institutions promote altruism, this is likely a mechanism for how religion helps shape girls' occupational aspirations.

Final Thoughts

This chapter provides evidence that girls who are not Jewish, and who are religiously active themselves, aspire to more female-dominated occupations. This is after controlling for family socioeconomic differences and girls' scholastic performance. This influence of religion seems to operate through attitudes about women needing to prioritize family care and child rearing over career pursuits that translate to desires for earlier marriage and a larger family size. In addition, it is likely that non-Jewish religious involvement promotes identification with stereotypically female characteristics and imagining a future involving what society defines as more female-typical jobs. Religious institutions especially promote altruism and service, which may make occupations involving care-work (e.g., teaching, nursing, or other medical careers) more desirable. Altogether, these findings suggest that religion can play a key role in shaping the "possible careers" girls imagine for themselves. Although rarely studied before in relation to girls' occupational aspirations, it appears that religion is an important cultural force contributing to the paths girls set out for themselves.

Given findings from the qualitative data presented here on the essential role of gender identity, future work should draw on data that measures aspects of gender identity more richly, especially variance across cultural groups that might explain differences in the types of jobs toward which girls aspire. This would allow for testing of the extent to which gender socialization is a key mechanism for the influence of religion on career aspirations. In addition, ethnographic studies of religious institutions and families or girls' involvement within them will better reveal the practices and messages conveying aspects of gender identity that channel girls' aspirations. This type of work has great potential to contribute to the literature on adolescent aspirations in general.

Girls' occupational aspirations are parts of their "possible selves" (Oyserman & James, 2009). They serve as guides for investment in education and the development of plans for achieving their goals. Although not everyone ends up achieving the specific goals set out in adolescence, they are unlikely to overachieve the level of those goals. Therefore, an essential step in identifying the sources of gender inequality in occupational status is understanding how girls set their aspirations in adolescence. The evidence we present here supports the notion that cultural institutions such as religion, and the values promoted within them, play a role in what girls imagine is possible and preferable. It is not just a girl's family resources and her abilities that inform her future career plans, but the cultural contexts in which she has been socialized about what is preferable for women.

NOTES

1. See Beyerlein (2004) for interesting findings regarding the differences in educational outcomes for Evangelical and Fundamentalist Protestants.
2. We follow Steensland et al. (2000) in constructing these categories, which these authors found useful in identifying distinct religious traditions and predicting religious, political, and social attitudes. We added the Mormon category, given the number of congregants reported in this study and the distinctiveness of their religious traditions.
3. Given that we only had income given in $10,000 categories, we came as close to these figures as possible. The exact groupings were as follows: 0 dollars to 155% of poverty line, 155% to 258% of poverty line, 258% to 413% of poverty line, and over 413% of poverty line.
4. Most occupations on the cards came from a list of the top 20 aspirations for NSYR female respondents, but we also added cards with the specific aspirations of our eight participants if they did not fall on the top 20 list.

REFERENCES

Beyerlein, K. (2004). Specifying the impact of conservative Protestantism on educational attainment. *Journal for the Scientific Study of Religion*, 43(4), 505–518.

Campbell, R. T. (1983). Status attainment research: End of the beginning or beginning of the end? *Sociology of Education*, 56(1), 47–62.

Chang, E. S., Chen, C., Greenberger, E., Dooley, D., & Heckhausen, J. (2006). What do they want in life? The life goals of a multi-ethnic, multi-generational sample of high school seniors. *Journal of Youth and Adolescence*, 35(3), 321–332.

Correll, S. J. (2001). Gender and the career choice process: The role of biased self-assessments. *American Journal of Sociology*, 106(6), 1691–1730.

Davis, S. N., & Pearce, L. D. (2007). Adolescents' work-family gender ideologies and educational expectations. *Sociological Perspectives*, 50(2), 249–271.

Denton, M. L. (2004). Gender and marital decision making: Negotiating religious identity and practice. *Social Forces*, 82(3), 1151–1180.

Eccles, J. S. (1994). Understanding women's educational and occupational choices. *Psychology of Women Quarterly*, 18(4), 585–609.

Eccles, J. S., Vida, M. N., & Barber, B. (2004). The relation of early adolescents' college plans and both academic ability and task-value beliefs to subsequent college enrollment. *The Journal of Early Adolescence*, **24**(1), 63–77.

Edgell, P. (2006). *Religion and family in a changing society*. Princeton University Press Series in Cultural Sociology.

Fan, P., & Marini, M. M. (2000). Influences on gender-role attitudes during the transition to adulthood. *Social Science Research*, **29**(2), 258–283.

Frome, P. M., Alfeld, C. J., Eccles, J. S., & Barber, B. L. (2006). Why don't they want a male-dominated job? An investigation of young women who changed their occupational aspirations. *Educational Research and Evaluation: An International Journal on Theory and Practice*, **12**(4), 359–372.

Glass, J., & Jacobs, J. (2005). Childhood religious conservatism and adult attainment among black and white women. *Social Forces*, **83**, 555–579.

Glass, J., & Kanellakos, L. (2006). Religious conservatism and women's market behavior following marriage and childbirth. *Journal of Marriage and Family*, **68**, 611–629.

Glick, J. E., & White, M. J. (2003). Post-secondary school participation of immigrant and native youth: The role of familial resources and educational expectations. *Social Science Research*, **33**, 272–299.

Glick, P. (1991). Trait-based and sex-based discrimination in occupational prestige, occupational salary, and hiring. *Sex Roles*, **25**(5/6), 351–378.

Hitlin, S. (2006). Parental influences on children's values and aspirations: Bridging two theories of social class and socialization. *Sociological Perspectives*, **49**(1), 25–46.

Lips, H. M. (2004). The gender gap in possible selves: Divergence of academic self-views among high school and university students. *Sex Roles*, **50**(5–6), 357–371.

Mahaffy, K. A., & Ward, S. K. (2002). The gendering of adolescents' childbearing and educational plans: Reciprocal effects and the influence of social context. *Sex Roles*, **46**(11/12), 403–417.

Marini, M. M., Fan, P., Finley, E., & Beutel, A. M. (1996). Gender and job values. *Sociology of Education*, **69**(1), 49–65.

Marini, M. M., & Greenberger, E. (1978). Sex differences in occupational aspirations and expectations. *Work and Occupations*, **5**(2), 147–178.

Massey, E. K., Gebhardt, W. A., & Garnefski, N. (2008). Adolescent goal content and pursuit: A review of the literature from the past 16 years. *Developmental Review*, **28**(4), 421–460.

Muller, C., & Ellison, C. G. (2001). Religious involvement, social capital, and adolescents' academic progress: Evidence from the national education longitudinal study of 1988. *Sociological Focus*, **34**(2), 155–183.

Murrell, A. J., Frieze, I. H., & Frost, J. L. (1991). Aspiring to careers in male-and female-dominated professions: A study of black and white college women. *Psychology of Women Quarterly*, **15**(1), 103–126.

Nash, S. C. (1979). Sex role as a mediator of intellectual functioning. In M. A. Wittig & A. C. Peterson (Eds.), *Sex-related differences in cognitive functioning* (pp. 263–302). New York: Academic Press.

Nurmi, J. E. (1994). The development of future-orientation in a life-span context. In Z. Zaleski (Ed.), *Psychology of future orientation* (pp. 20–616). Lublin, Poland: Wydawnictwo Towarzystwa Naukowego Katolickiego Uniwersytetu Lubelskiego.

Oyserman, D., & James, L. (2009). Possible selves: From content to process. In K. Markman, W. M. P. Klein, & J. A. Suhr (Eds.), *The handbook of imagination and mental stimulation* (pp. 373–394). New York: Psychology Press.

Pearce, L. D. (2002). Integrating survey and ethnographic methods for systematic anomalous case analysis. *Sociological Methodology*, 32(1), 103–132.

Pearce, L. D., & Denton, M. L. (2011). *A faith of their own: Stability and change in the religiosity of American adolescents.* New York: Oxford University Press.

Pearce, L. D., & Thornton, A. (2007). Religious identity and family ideologies in the transition to adulthood. *Journal of Marriage and Family*, 69(5), 1227–1243.

Phinney, J. S., Baumann, K., & Blanton, S. (2001). Life goals and attributions for expected outcomes among adolescents from five ethnic groups. *Hispanic Journal of Behavioral Sciences*, 23(4), 363–377.

Ridgeway, C. L. (2002). Gender, status and leadership. *Journal of Social Issues*, 57(4), 637–655.

Schoon, I. (2001). Teenage job aspirations and career attainment in adulthood: A 17-year follow-up study of teenagers who aspired to become scientists, health professionals and engineers. *International Journal of Behavioral Development*, 25, 124–132.

Seginer, R. (2003). Adolescent future orientation: An integrated cultural and ecological perspective. *Online Readings in Psychology and Culture, Unit 6.* Retrieved from http://scholarworks.gvsu.edu/orpc/vol6/iss1/5

Sewell, W. H., Haller, A. O., & Portes, A. (1969). The educational and early occupational attainment process. *American Sociological Review*, 34(1), 82–92.

Shu, X., & Marini, M. M. (1998). Gender-related change in occupational aspirations. *Sociology of Education*, 71(1), 43–67.

Shu, X., & Marini, M. M. (2008). Coming of age in changing times: Occupational aspirations of American youth in 1966–80. *Research in Social Stratification and Mobility*, 26(1), 29–55.

Smith, C., & Denton, M. L. (2005). *Soul searching: The religious and spiritual lives of American teenagers.* New York: Oxford University Press.

Steensland, B., Park, J. Z., Regnerus, M., Robinson, L. D., Wilcox, W. B., & Woodberry, R. D. (2000). The measure of American religion: Toward improving the state of the art. *Social Forces*, 79(1), 291–318.

Teachman, J. D., & Paasch, K. (1998). The family and educational aspirations. *Journal of Marriage and Family*, 60, 704–714.

U.S. Bureau of Labor Statistics (2006). *Women in the labor force: A databook* (Report 996). Washington, DC: Chao, Elaine L. Retrieved July 5, 2006 from http://www.bls.gov/cps/wlf-databook-2006.pdf.

Weisgram, E. S., Bigler, R. S., & Liben, L. S. (2010). Gender, values, and occupational interests among children, adolescents, and adults. *Child Development*, 81(3), 778–796.

Yoder, J. D. (1994). Looking beyond numbers: The effects of gender status, job prestige and occupational gender-typing on tokenism processes. *Social Psychology Quarterly*, 57(2), 150–159.

13 First Romantic Relationships of Adolescents from Different Religious Groups in Israel and Germany

Bernhard Nauck and Anja Steinbach

Abstract

Based on an extensive literature review on the relationship between religious affiliation, religiosity and engagement in romantic relationships in early adolescence, the chapter deals with first romantic relationships on the basis of survey data of dyads of mothers and their children between 15–17 years of age from Germany and Israel, in which seven culturally different social groups are included, namely native Germans, German repatriates, Turkish immigrants, and Russian Jewish immigrants in Germany, and native Israelis, Russian Jewish immigrants and Israeli Arabs in Israel. Thus, the sample comprises groups of three religions (Christians, Jews, Muslims) and from four regions of origin (Germany, Russia, Turkey, Israel). After an exploration on level differences between these groups with regard to involvement of adolescents in romantic relationships, the subsequent analysis investigates to which extent this involvement is structured by normative beliefs and influenced by intergenerational transmission, the relationship between mothers and adolescents, and experiences, preferences, and competencies of the adolescents.

The establishment of first romantic relationships is one of the central and almost universal developmental tasks of adolescence, in which close asymmetric intergenerational relationships are complemented by close symmetric relationships (usually) to the other sex.[1] In general, the more universal and the more important a developmental tasks for a respective society is, the more likely it is that this developmental task is normatively regulated and subject of social control. Moreover, if a developmental task remains stable in its importance and universality over time, it is also very likely that its normative regulation is deeply rooted in culture and thereby backed by religious beliefs.

Romantic relationships have always been closely related to reproductive behavior, both on the societal level and on the individual level. On the societal level, it refers to the continuity of a sociocultural group based on fertility and of the transmission of culture in general as well as religious beliefs in specific. On the individual level, it refers to the transmission of social status and to the social integration of family and kinship systems. Accordingly, as far as this relationship between romantic relationships and social reproduction is close, it is more than obvious that institutional regulations on the societal level as well as investments in the social control of this developmental task on the side of the parents are a fundamental part of the socialization of the offspring (Knafo et al., 2009; Knafo & Schwartz, 2009; Trommsdorff, 2009). These normative regulations comprise how the establishment of the younger cohorts' relationships are to be located within the life course, which forms of institutionalization they require, and which levels of sexual intensity are considered to be appropriate in these relationships. Thus, first romantic relationships are an issue even in cases where these normative regulations are comparably restrictive and such relationships are not tolerated by the social environment.

At least throughout the last five decades and at least in the affluent welfare societies, the connection between the establishment of first romantic relationships and reproductive behavior has been significantly weakened, based on technological inventions of effective birth control, changes in the standard life course because of earlier puberty, extended phases of education and intergenerational dependence and in the following, the separation of partnership, parenthood, housing, education, and occupation into only loosely connected biographical trajectories. Accordingly, as long as they are based on the *consequences* for the social reproduction, normative regulations of romantic relationships like being with a "wrong" partner or "untimely" have lost much of their legitimation.

The diffusion of knowledge about effective contraceptive methods and about life course scripts, which separate romantic relationships from parenthood, has nowadays reached practically every individual worldwide. However, this knowledge and these scripts may affect individuals in different positions to the ongoing social change and its respective speed and various social settings may result in different reactions to it. The universality of this developmental task and the societal demand for normative regulations and the changing conditions make first romantic relationships an interesting subject for cross-cultural comparisons.

Religious Affiliation, Religiosity and Engagement in Romantic Relationships

Given the importance of first romantic relationships as an individual developmental task and as a social-normative, strongly regulated part of life courses, it is interesting to note, however, that the body of empirical knowledge is extremely scarce regarding the relationship between religious affiliation, religiosity, and the development of romantic relationships in youth and early adolescence. Roehlkepartain et al. (2006: 3) note in their decade review that less than one percent of articles in the leading developmental psychology journals were dedicated to religious or spiritual development of children or adolescents. Although faith development theory claims a developmental coincidence of "sexual changes brought on by adolescence" and "revolutions in cognitive functioning and interpersonal perspective taking" (Fowler & Dell, 2006: 39), mechanisms to interrelate both processes still seem to be lacking, as do assumptions about the interrelation between the *content* of specific belief systems, as provided by the respective religion, the *context* within which these beliefs are transmitted, and the *development* of intimate relationships. With regard to context, Oser, Scarlett and Bucher (2006: 977) state that "family is the most powerful influence on children's religious and spiritual development" and that parents' (and especially mothers') influence in religious behavior is by far more powerful than in other domains of life. They also note that, when treating religiousness as an independent variable, research evidence exists that it has positive effects on well-being and on coping with critical life events (Oser, Scarlett & Bucher, 2006: 982ff.), but provides no results, which may shed light on the relationship between religiosity (in different religious affiliations) and developmental tasks such as entering into intimate relationships.

Results for the newly developed adolescent religious coping scale (Bjorck et al., 2010) provide evidence that religious coping is positively related to emotional functioning and general life satisfaction, even after controlling for relevant factors, and it is accompanied by increased parental support, but "the sample was Christian, and findings cannot be generalized to adolescents from other faith groups" (Bjorck et al., 2010: 357). However, studies by French et al. (2008; Chapter 6 in this volume) on Muslim adolescents in Indonesia point in the same direction. They also find for their Muslim sample that religious involvement is positively related to a set of outcomes, such as peer group status, academic achievement, prosocial behavior and self-esteem. Studies of King and Furrow (2004) as well as Lim and Putnam (2010) have identified an important mediating factor on how religious participation influences moral outcomes. They demonstrate that religious practices may not in themselves increase moral orientation toward altruism, empathy, or life satisfaction but only if they are embedded in supportive and trusting relationships (King & Furrow, 2004: 709). "Religious youths are more likely to interact with, trust, and share similar perspectives with a nonfamilial adult than are those who are only sometimes involved or not at all involved in religious activities" (King & Furrow, 2004: 710), with no differences between the observed ethnic groups and religious affiliations in their U.S. sample of adolescents. More specifically, a study by Bengtson et al. (2009) reveals that not only parents, but also grandparents are important transmitters of religious beliefs, having an independent additive effect to that of parents. Their study also suggests that intergenerational transmission depends largely on the congruence of the transmitted values with the situational societal conditions, suggesting "that when researchers examine the intergenerational transmission of religious beliefs, it is important to also consider the content of those beliefs, in particular their proscriptions and rules for social behavior" (Bengtson et al., 2009: 341).

As differences in religious affiliation in adolescent populations in modern societies are in most cases the result of regional or international migration, a specific context effect on the relationship between religion and involvement in romantic relationships is the belonging to an ethnic and migrant minority, which is typically characterized by higher levels of religiosity within a largely secularized environment. In such a situation, two counteracting forces are to be considered (Nauck, 2001a): On the one hand, increased social contacts to the receiving society (in the kindergarten, at school, in vocational training) may result in higher levels of secularization of the second migrant generation as compared to the (religious) migrants themselves. On the other hand, the minority situation may result in increased intergenerational solidarity and increased efforts of the parental first migrant generation for intergenerational transmission of (religious) values and for social control and surveillance of their offspring, in order to maintain the minority culture over generations. Accordingly, if the first force prevails, assimilation to the secularized context is most likely whereas if the second force prevails, high levels of religiosity may be maintained or even strengthened in the ethnic minority situation.

Studies comparing intergenerational relationships in Turkish migrant families with those of native members of the receiving society Germany and of natives in Turkey show that parents in the migrant families are more likely to perform an authoritarian-controlling parenting style than German or native Turkish families (Nauck, 1989). Moreover, co-orientation and similarities of perceptions and attitudes between generations are higher in migrant families than in native families of the country of origin (Nauck, 1995; 1997). A study with a similar design, comparing the levels of religiosity of adolescents from the society of origin Turkey, Turkish second generation migrants and adolescents from the receiving society Belgium revealed that Belgian adolescents showed lower and declining religiosity with age, whereas Turkish and Turkish Belgian adolescents were more religious regardless of age, but religiosity was even more accentuated in Turkish Belgian adolescents as compared with Turkish adolescents in Turkey (Güngör, Bornstein & Phalet, in press). A complementary study on inter-generational transmission of religious beliefs in Muslim migrant families from Turkey and Morocco in Belgium shows that religious transmission is generally effective for religious identification, beliefs, and practices in both groups, but most effective in the Turkish Belgian groups and when individual orientations toward heritage culture maintenance was high; host culture adoption played a minor role (Güngör, Fleischmann & Phalet, 2011). The study thus confirms findings from Germany on high maintenance of religious orientations in Muslim second generation immigrants (Diehl & König, 2009).

Besides minority membership, the act of migration also has a situational component, as it results in losses in social capital and social integration (Myers, 1999), which may also influence both individual religiosity and the opportunities to engage in romantic relationships. As migration is generally considered to be a stressful event that activates specific coping strategies (Berry, 1997; Nauck, 2008), this may also include religiosity as a source of coping, which may be activated close to the migration event itself but may lose its importance over time, the more the acculturation process has progressed. Migration also shapes and limits the market of available partners for romantic relationships, which, in turn, may have effects on religious orientations. Whereas at the beginning of a migration cycle partners of the same origin (and the same religious affiliation) are scarce and result in high rates of mixed religious partnerships and marriages and hence a lowered religious commitment, opportunities for finding a partner of the same religious affiliation increase in later stages of the migration cycle, which then makes religious commitment a salient signal on the increasing intra-ethnic partnership market (Nauck, 2007a; Baykara-Krumme & Fuß, 2009).

Strong intergenerational transmission of religiously based values may also have an indirect effect on the entry into first romantic relationships in youth and early adolescence. Gans, Silverstein and Lowenstein (2009: 188) have comparatively analyzed the influence of religiosity on intergenerational support for Christian individuals in Europe and for Jews in Israel and are able to verify the same model for the included five societies of Norway, England, Germany, Spain and Israel. They argue that "doctrinal aspects of religion are best summarized by the dictate of the Old Testament to honor one's father and mother, a filial prescription made in various forms by virtually all religions of the world. Individuals who are more involved in practicing religion through both the public sphere (participation in religious services) and the private sphere (family prayers, personal salience of religion) are more likely to be exposed to messages that promote strong family commitment." It is then "likely that religiosity indirectly enhances supportive behavior by strengthening intergenerational cohesion" (Gans, Silverstein & Lowenstein, 2009: 188) and at the same time provides less opportunities and less normative support for engaging in romantic relationships.

In a longitudinal study of white Christian adolescents in the United States, Laflin, Wang, and Barry (2008) found that adolescents with low religious involvement had a more than twice higher likelihood to engage in a sexual relationship within the observed one year. However, this effect was only significant for boys, but not for girls. In their national representative cross-sectional study for the United States, Manlove et al. (2008) were able to identify some mechanisms, which explain the relationship between religiosity and sexual behavior. They found a direct relationship, indicating a lower level of sexual activity for adolescents from religious parental homes, but also two indirect effects: namely, a higher level of social control and surveillance over these adolescents by their parents and less contacts to deviant peer groups. Whereas surveillance was not predictive for girls, it reduced the probability of early sexual activities of boys significantly. Differences between religious affiliations were not included in the analysis of this study.

Empirical evidence on religious affiliation is especially scarce, because most of the studies on adolescent sexual behavior in Western societies tend to lump non-Christian religions together to a residual category ("other"), so that results are generally reported for different Christian confessions only. In their two-decade review, Rostosky et al. (2004: 687) report consistent results from several studies based on different data sources, according to which Catholic and "fundamentalist" Protestant youth are more likely to delay sexual activity than "mainstream" Protestants, but note that the mechanisms behind these results are still unclear, i.e., whether this may be attributed to different contents of the religious message or on different levels of social control. They conclude "that the available evidence supports that religiosity does delay sexual debut. These findings are more frequent and consistent for White females and less so for White males. Relatively few studies have examined this question with adequate samples of racial and ethnic minorities. The few studies that have, however, have found considerable consistency across female adolescents of differing racial or ethnic backgrounds" (Rostosky et al., 2004: 691). They also note as a major deficiency of the current state of research that sexual activity is not contextualized in general strategies of partnership seeking and romantic relationships: "An examination of the influence of religiosity on the initiation, maintenance, and quality of the romantic relationships of adolescents is yet to be undertaken. Although most sexual decision making occurs within the context of romantic relationships, none of the longitudinal data sets included an assessment and analysis of these important relational variables. Moreover, the studies reviewed continue the tradition of exclusively focusing on sexual intercourse while neglecting a wide range of sexual behaviors that adolescents may use ... Future studies should address these gaps, given the importance of these contexts and behavioral strategies to adolescent sexual health and psychosocial development" (Rostosky et al., 2004: 692).

The following analysis has investigated the impact of social change on the life course transition to first romantic relationships in case of three religious groups in two different social contexts with varying speed of experienced social change. The two contexts were Israel and Germany, the three religious groups were Christians, Jews, and Muslims, and the varying speed of social change was captured by migration: in Germany, besides the group of native Germans, a group of German repatriates from Russia, a group of work migrants from Turkey, and a group of Jewish migrants from Russia were included; in Israel, besides the group of native Jewish Israelis, a group of Jewish repatriates from Russia and a group of Israeli Arabs were included.

The general research question was in which way the belonging to a specific religious group influenced the life course transition to a first romantic relationship in early adolescence. The theoretical mechanisms, which may explain this relationship, are rather unclear, however. Because the belonging to a religious group is normally not a matter of choice and thus of selectivity according to personal traits or individual preferences, two main arguments remain. Either specific forms of spirituality, related to the respective religion, may covary with specific habits, frames, and especially scripts of life, which, in turn, result in preferences for the individual choices for romantic relationships; in this case, differences between outcomes for religious groups would be first of all driven by individual religiosity. Or, different forms of social control, related to the respective religion, may covary with different outcomes in romantic relationships; in this case, individual religiosity would be of minor importance, but the differences would be mainly explained by the social and institutional structure, in which the adolescent is embedded.

It is also unclear which influence the status of belonging to a (migrant) minority has on the development of spirituality on the one hand and the development of romantic relationships on the other hand. Two counterbalancing theoretical mechanisms are here in force. On the one hand, minority membership increases efforts of structure maintenance, which may result in increased symbolic adherence to cultural roots, within which membership to a religious group is of strategic importance. On the other hand, migration implies increased exposure to social change, non-redundant information and alternative options, as well as loose-knit social networks, which may result in rapid behavioral changes within the life course and across generations. Moreover, exposure to migration itself may be seen as a critical life event, which may accelerate sexual behavior (South, Haynie & Bose, 2005) and thus has a direct effect on early romantic relationships.

The analysis empirically explored how these theoretical mechanisms are related to possible differences between the three religious groups with regard to first romantic relationships. After the description of the design of the study and the obtained data set, the first part of the empirical analysis describes the level differences between the religious groups with regard to the involvement in romantic relationships of male and female adolescents. The second part of the analysis investigates the effects of religiosity and social control on this involvement.

Data for the analysis was gathered in a research project on "Regulation of Developmental Transitions in Second Generation Immigrants in Germany and Israel." Among the studied transitions, the involvement of adolescents in first romantic relationships was seen as a significant non-normative transition in the life course, and significant differences between the studied groups were expected. The data collection took place between fall 2007 and summer 2008 and comprised dyads of mothers and their children between 15–17 years of age from Germany and Israel. Seven culturally different social groups were included, namely native Germans, German repatriates, Turkish immigrants, and Russian Jewish immigrants in Germany, and native Israelis, Russian Jewish immigrants, and Israeli Arabs in Israel.

Thus, the study comprised groups of three religions (Christians, Jews, Muslims), from four regions of origin (Germany, Russia, Turkey, Israel) in two national contexts (Germany, Israel). The data was obtained by standardized, language-equivalent personal interviews with interviewers from the respective ethnic group. Members of the language minorities had the individual choice whether the interview was conducted in the minority language (Turkish, Russian, Arabic) or in the majority language (German, Hebrew).

In order to analyze intergenerational transmission and parental social control, variables from both the interviews with the mothers and their adolescent children were included in the analysis. Mothers from the religious groups showed considerable differences:

– The differences for the *educational level*, classified according to the international ISCED-scheme (UNESCO, 2006), were extreme between the groups. Whereas 52 percent of the Turkish mothers and 21 percent of the Israeli Arab mothers had no or only elementary schooling, the share for the other groups was less than 5 percent. Tertiary education had 70 percent of the German Jewish mothers, 50 percent of the Jewish repatriate mothers to Israel, 35 percent of the German repatriates, 30 percent of the native German mothers and 18 percent of the native Israelis, but only 5 percent of the Israeli Arab and 1 percent of the Turkish mothers.

– Differences for the *mother's self-perceived religiosity* was also significant (Eta = .54***), with the Israeli Arab mothers and the Turkish mothers being the most religious and the German Jews and the Israeli repatriate mothers being the least religious.

For the adolescents, *age* and *gender* was controlled for because the age distribution within the several groups differed significantly (Eta = .45***) and because involvement in romantic relationships is strongly age-dependent, and because *gender* and religiosity within the respective religious group may interact. Besides belonging to one of the seven groups with their inherent dimension of *religious group*, *country of origin*, and *country of residence*, the following predictors were included: *Self-esteem* was included as a shortened 4-item scale (α = .80) of Rosenberg (1965) and used as a proxy for the level of individuation of the adolescent, making him independent from the direct influences of the parents. *Self-efficacy* was included as a 5-item scale (α = .79) of Jerusalem and Schwarzer (1992), capturing the development of own attitudes and behaviors despite possible social control. Perceived *self-disclosure* was measured with a shortened 3-item scale (α = .65) of Kerr and Stattin (2000). Perceived *parental control* was measured with a shortened

4-item scale (α = .70) of Kerr and Stattin (2000). The *adolescent's religiosity* was measured with a single item ("How religious are you?") ranging from (1) "not religious at all" to (5) "very religious." Whereas no significant differences between the religious groups were observed for self-esteem and self-disclosure, moderate differences existed for self-efficacy of the adolescents, with the second generation of Russian Jewish immigrants to Israel showing the highest and the Russian Jewish immigrants to Germany showing the lowest. The perceived social control of the parents was lowest for the native German adolescents and highest for the Israeli Arabs. The variability of religiosity between the seven groups was almost as high for the adolescents (Eta = .52) as for the mothers (Eta = .54), with the Turkish adolescents having the highest level of religiosity, followed by the native Israelis and the Israeli Arabs, and with the Jewish immigrants both to Germany and Israel showing the lowest level. Thus, whereas the religiosity level of Israeli Arab adolescents, the native German adolescents, and the Jewish immigrant adolescents in Germany was markedly decreased in comparison to their mother, it was slightly increased for the native Israeli and the Turkish migrant adolescents.

Romantic Relationships

Two main areas within the domain of romantic relationships of adolescents were studied: Partner preferences and the involvement in romantic relationships. Descriptive results showed the differences between male and female adolescents of the religious groups within their respective social setting and controlling for their age.

Partner preferences: A multidimensional set of 11 characteristics that a potential partner to the adolescent should possess, was provided, to which the respondents were supposed to evaluate the "importance" of these characteristics. An oblique factor analysis revealed three factors, explaining 56 percent of the variance. These findings can easily be interpreted in terms of utility expectations toward potential partners within the theory of social production functions (Lindenberg, 1990; Ormel et al., 1999; Nauck, 2001b; 2007b); that is, the specifically expected gratifications from romantic relationships. Therefore, the first factor was labeled "*status* expectations," the second factor was labeled "expectations of *social approval*," and the third factor was labeled "*stimulation* expectations." These three factors were used as factor scores in subsequent analyses.

When looking at the gender differences alone, the empirical analysis revealed expected results: female adolescents had a higher preference for a romantic partner, who meets their status expectations (Beta = .20***), whereas this dimension was the most unimportant for male adolescents. The same difference occurred for expectations of social approval in a partnership, which was again significantly more important for female adolescents (Beta = .15***). In reverse, stimulation expectations were slightly higher for males, but the differences were far less marked (Beta = .07).

If the religious groups together with gender are compared, the smallest, insignificant differences were obtained for the stimulation expectation, which was always somewhat higher for males in all three religions, with the Jews having the highest expectations in this regard, followed by the Christians, whereas for the Muslim adolescents, this expectation was comparably unimportant. In all three religions, expectations of social approval within a romantic relationship were more important for female adolescents than for male adolescents, which was the predominant effect, but also with a significantly different rank order between religions. It was most important for the (female) Christian adolescents, followed by the Muslims, whereas it was least important for the (male) Jewish adolescents. The most extreme differences were found for status expectations toward a romantic partner. These expectations were highest for the (female) Muslim adolescents and lowest for the (male) Christian adolescents. Here, the predominant effect resulted from the belonging to the respective religious group (Beta = .47), but with an also relatively strong effect resulting from gender (Beta = .20). To put results on religious differences into a nutshell, Christian adolescents sought communication and behavioral confirmation in romantic relationships, Jews sought leisure sensation and physical attraction, whereas Muslim adolescents were very much status seekers and looked for someone who would be well-respected in their social environment.

Involvement in romantic relationships: With regard to the involvement of the young adolescents in romantic relationships, they were asked whether they ever had a romantic relationship and which kind of sexual activity was ever involved in one of these relationships. Table 13.1 displays the respective adjusted proportions for the males and females of the three religious groups, controlled for the age of the respondents by means of a multiple classification analysis (MCA). Additionally, it displays the results for an index of the sexual intensity of the romantic relationship (cumulative for the first six columns) in column 7 and for the satisfaction with the current partnership situation in column 8. Moreover, it displays the Beta-coefficients for MCA's for gender and age alone, and for religion and age alone, respectively.

As a general result, there was monotonous decrease in the percentages for all six categories from the experience of a romantic relationship over

Table 13.1. Adjusted Proportions of Male (m) and Female (f) Adolescents with a Christian, Moslem and Jewish Background with Partnership Experience (MCA)

Religion		Partnership Experience (percent)	Holding Hands (percent)	Kissing (percent)	French Kissing (percent)	Petting (percent)	Intercourse (percent)	Sexual Intensity (mean)	Partnership Satisfaction (mean)
Christian	m	73.8	71.1	70.2	66.7	50.1	29.6	3,5	4,4
	f	70.8	68.6	69.5	68.8	40.6	24.7	3,4	4,4
Muslim	m	76.8	52.9	43.9	36.0	19.3	11.1	2,4	4,5
	f	50.9	20.0	16.9	9.1	1.0	–	0,9	4,3
Jewish	m	54.7	53.6	51.2	40.8	40.4	15.9	2,6	3,6
	f	64.1	63.6	60.8	47.9	37.6	13.5	2,9	3,9
Beta[1]		.20***	.33***	.35***	.37***	.33***	.27***	.35***	.24***
Beta[2]		.06	.06	.04	.05	.09*	.08	.07	.01
Beta[3]		.11***	.26***	.31***	.33***	.31***	.24***	.30***	.22***

[1] Results for religion and gender, controlled for age;

[2] Results for gender, controlled for age;

[3] Results for religion, controlled for age

"holding hands" to "petting" and "sexual intercourse" (exception: Christian girls report slightly higher "kissing" frequencies than "holding hands"). However, the level differences between these six groups were very significant and to a large extent owing to the religious affiliation and to its interaction with gender effects, whereas gender itself had a negligible effect, as the comparison of the respective Beta-values revealed. This result justified the construction of a cumulative index (column 7 in Table 13.1), showing that the highest level of sexual intensity was to be observed for the Christian religion, followed by the Jewish adolescents. Gender differences were rather small for the Christian adolescents, with a majority having experience with French kissing and petting in this age group and a quarter with sexual intercourse. Gender differences were higher for the Jewish adolescents, with the females showing more activity in romantic relationships than the males, however, mostly in those with less sexual involvement. These differences were accompanied by the lowest level of satisfaction with the partnership situation for the Jewish male adolescents, followed by the female Jews.

Although the level of sexual intensity in romantic relationships between the Christian adolescents and the Muslim adolescents differed most, their level of satisfaction with this situation did not. In fact, the involvement in romantic relationships of the Muslim youth showed a distinct pattern, which was characterized by the following: strong differences between males and females with regard to sexual activity in this age group, however, little difference with regard to involvement in romantic relationships (77 percent of the Muslim boys and 51 percent of the Muslim girls reported to have or have had a romantic relationship, of which for them only a small fraction was ever accompanied by the mildest form of body contact). Accordingly, the "partnership experience" as such (Beta = .20) and the "satisfaction with the partnership situation" (Beta = .24) showed the smallest differences between the groups. Whether the reported plus on sexual activity on the Muslim males side despite the general higher age of males in a romantic relationship was because of the fact that the studied Muslim groups were in a minority situation with partnership opportunities outside the own religious group (unlikely) or whether they result from experiences with sexually hyperactive girls (unlikely), or whether they were owing to a gender specific under- and/or over-reporting, could not be tested in this study.

The general pattern of differences with regard to sexual involvement in romantic relationships between the Muslim group and the two others was consistent with the findings on partner preferences: if status seeking and acceptance of relationships by significant others was the predominant utility expectation, then an early screening of the partnership market for suitable partners was an efficient, satisfying strategy; however, sexual commitment was delayed to an institutionalized relationship (marriage), which assures the status gain. If, however, the search for communication and behavioral confirmation in romantic relationships or the search for leisure sensation and physical attraction was the predominant utility expectation toward romantic partnerships, then higher levels of early sexual involvement was an efficient strategy. However, as the level differences on satisfaction with the partnership situation showed, this strategy seemed to be easier realized for the Christian than for the (male) Jewish adolescents.

Religious Affiliation and Involvement in Romantic Relationships

Multivariate analyses revealed that the religious affiliation had a strong effect on the sexual involvement of adolescents in romantic relationships, with the Christian reference population showing the highest level. The respective affiliation interacted with the gender of the respondent. For the Muslim adolescents, a low level of sexual involvement in romantic relationships referred only to the Muslim girls, but not to the Muslim boys. For the Jewish adolescents, the reverse was true: within the same age bracket, Jewish boys showed a rather low sexual involvement as compared to their female counterparts. The individual level of religiosity had a significant negative effect on the sexual involvement of adolescents in romantic relationships, which seems to be a rather independent additive effect to religious affiliation, as an interaction term between religiosity and religious affiliation showed no effect.

The respective country of origin and the country of residence had comparatively small effects on the involvement of adolescents in early romantic relationships. Jewish immigrant adolescents showed a higher degree of sexual involvement in romantic relationships than the native Jewish population in Israel. Stronger effects of the respective country of origin were revealed for the Muslim adolescents. Muslims from Turkey in Germany were significantly more sexually involved in romantic relationships than the Arabic adolescents in Israel – whether this was because of the migrant situation with its extended opportunities both for the provision of alternative scripts of the life course or for an extended partnership market, could not be tested in this study. This finding is an indication that the culture of the respective religious ethnic group operates to a large extent independently from the respective location. Instead, it has to be noted that the effect of individual religiosity on lowered sexual involvement in romantic relationships remained stable when religious affiliation, country of origin and

Table 13.2. Religious Affiliation, Partner Preferences, Intergenerational Relationships and Involvement in Romantic Relationships of Adolescents

	(1)	(2)	(3)	Zero Order Correlation
Female	.01	.03	.05	−.06
Muslim[1]	−.07	−.06	−.12*	−.24**
Jewish[1]	−.20***	−.20***	−.15**	−.04
Muslim * female	−.16**	−.17**	−.14*	
Jewish * female	.07	.06	.07	
Adolescent's religiosity	.07	−.07*	−.02	−.18**
Partner: Status	−.32***	−.33***	−.32***	−.37**
Partner: Social approval	.20***	.18***	.18***	.18**
Partner: Stimulation	.07*	.07*	.04	.05
Self-esteem		.06	.09*	.08*
Self-efficacy		.01	.02	.03
Self-disclosure			−.21***	−.18**
Parental control			−.08*	−.14**
Mother's education			−.14***	.08*
Mother's religiosity			−.08	−.20**
Adol. * Mother's religiosity			−.09**	
R^2	.23	.23	.29	

[1] Religious affiliation, reference: Christian

country of residence were controlled. This independent effect of religiosity made a more complex analysis necessary, which also included mechanisms related to individual competencies and preferences.

Thus, the main theoretically interesting question was whether the sexual involvement in romantic relationship of adolescents is primarily driven by individual religiosity and related scripts of life, or driven by religious affiliation and the respective institutional structure of the social context and its enforced social control. Table 13.2 introduces in three steps the partner preferences of the adolescents: (1) some general personal traits, which may be related to success in romantic partnerships, such as self-esteem and self-efficacy, (2) several characteristics of the relationship of the adolescent to his or her family, such as self-disclosure, perceived parental control, the educational level of the mother, her religiosity, and an interaction term of her and the adolescent's religiosity, indicating a strongly religious family climate, and (3) in the fourth column, zero order correlations of the respective variable with involvement in romantic relationships are displayed.

The main result of the first model was that the significant effect of individual religiosity from the models in Table 4 vanished if the partnership preferences of the adolescent were added, whereas the strong effect of religious affiliation remained stable and high, including the strong interaction effect for Muslim females. This indicates that the observed additive effect of religiosity on (reduced or delayed) sexual involvement in romantic relationships was mainly a matter of distinct expectations toward such a partnership, following the rationale that stimulation, social approval, and communication feedback favored early involvement, whereas status attainment favored deferred involvement. Model two shows additionally that personal traits such as self-esteem and self-efficacy had no direct effect on the involvement of adolescents in romantic relationships.

The effects of social control on involvement in romantic relationships of adolescents with different religious affiliation can be assessed in model three. The main result of this model was that the strong effects of religious affiliation and of partner preferences remained stable when the relationship with the parents of the adolescents was controlled. However, this relationship had a significant additional effect on the involvement. This is already shown by the independent effect of a strong religious climate in the homes of the adolescents on reduced or delayed involvement in romantic relationships, independent of the respective religious affiliation and only becoming significant if the interaction effect of the adolescent's and the mother's religiosity was introduced.

Obviously, early sexual involvement of adolescents was strongly connected with their self-disclosure to their parents and with lower perceived parental control. The causal direction of this connection may be both ways: on the one hand, adolescents with a less harmonious, sharing relationship with their parents or with less controlling parents are more likely to engage early in romantic relationships; on the other hand, the involvement in a romantic relationship may result in keeping it secret to their parents because of anticipated sanctions.

Complicated is the relationship between the mother's educational level and the involvement of their adolescent children in romantic relationships. Whereas the zero order correlation was moderately positive, the effect became significantly negative when all the other considered variables were controlled. This indicates at first hand that the proportion of better educated mothers was higher in the Christian and Jewish population than in the Muslim population. If religious affiliation and religiosity as well as partner preferences were controlled, the multivariate model then revealed the suppressed effect of the mother's education on the *delay* of romantic relationships.

Summary and Conclusion

The empirical findings of this comparative study on the relationship between religious affiliation and involvement in romantic relationships of young adolescents from different residential populations in Germany and Israel may be summarized as follows.

First, the Christian, Jewish, and Muslim adolescents vary significantly with regard to their levels of religiosity, with the Jewish adolescents having the most heterogeneous composition with their low levels of religiosity among the immigrant youth from Russia and high levels among the native Israeli youth. Considerable differences also exist among the Muslim adolescents, where the Israeli Arabs have a lower level of religiosity than the Turkish migrants in Germany, but more religious mothers, which is accompanied by high parental control.

Second, the respective religious affiliation is related to marked differences in expectations toward romantic relationships. A clear divide is between the Muslim adolescents on the one hand, being primarily status oriented (especially the female Muslims) and expecting increased respect from their social environment by having an appropriate partner. On the other hand, Christian and Jewish adolescents primarily expect communication feedback and behavioral confirmation (especially the Christians) and leisure sensation and physical attraction (especially the Jews). These utility expectations toward romantic relationships steer involvement in romantic relationship to a large extent, with status expectations being related to delayed or lower levels of sexually intense romantic relationships, and with stimulation and communication expectations being related to early and higher levels of sexually intense romantic relationships.

Third, with regard to the level of involvement in romantic relationships of adolescents, religious affiliation interacts with gender, but not with religiosity. Whereas levels of religiosity seem to have the same impact on delayed or decreased involvement in romantic relationships irrespective of the religious affiliation, gender differences are observed for the Jewish and especially the Muslim religion. Whereas the level of sexual involvement is somewhat higher for the Jewish females than for Jewish males, the involvement for the Muslim males is much higher than that of the Muslim females. These effects of religious affiliation and religiosity seem to be to a large extent independent of the larger social context within the respective society of origin and the society of residence.

Fourth, parental control is related to the involvement in early romantic relationships in several ways. On the one hand, the religious groups differ significantly with regard to parental control, with relatively low levels among the Christians and the highest levels among the Muslims. On the other hand, early involvement in romantic relationships is a cause or consequence of the adolescent's disclosure from his/her family and/or lacking parental control. Higher resources of parents, as indicated by the educational level, and a strong religious climate of the parental home reduces or delays the involvement of adolescents in romantic relationships.

Fifth, only minor differences exist between adolescents of different religious affiliation and levels of religiosity with regard to their satisfaction with their current partnership situation. That is, the adolescents seem to follow their distinct strategies of partnership selection based on different utility expectations, with similar confidence and satisfaction. Accordingly, when these related factors are controlled, most adolescents are satisfied with their relationship situation when the involvement has become more intense and is accompanied by high self-esteem and a sharing-feelings relationship with their parents. The most dissatisfied adolescents with their current partnership situation are the Jewish males and the Muslim females.

Although the comparative design of the study was able to shed light on some of the mechanisms, which may explain religious-based differences in early involvement of adolescents in intimate relationships, it has several limitations with regard to its conclusiveness. One very specific shortcoming is that the information on the involvement in romantic relationships did not include event-based data. As this involvement in adolescence is very much age related, this shortcoming did not allow for the separation of the level differences and the timing differences; an event history-based data set would also have allowed for the inclusion of time dependent covariates, such as time of migration, school and occupational career, or marriage. For theoretical reasons, such a separation would have been very important, as it would have helped to separate migration effects of adaptation from cultural effects of conformity with religious-based habits, frames, and scripts. Instead, the analysis tried to keep the age factor constant in even controlling for age variations within the age bracket of the sample, thus making as sure as possible that the empirical findings are not owing to possible age variations between the studied groups.

In a more general sense, the design of the study, comprising groups of three religions (Christians, Jews, Muslims), from four regions (Germany, Russia, Turkey, Israel) in two national contexts (Germany, Israel), is not balanced and thus not able to strictly separate the effects of migration and religious affiliation. Moreover, more direct indicators of social control are missing, which did not allow for a more satisfactory separation of factors related to individual spirituality from those related to the control structure of the respective religious institutions. Finally, the religious affiliation was inevitably confounded with the societal welfare situation, placing the Muslim population in a distinctively disadvantaged position in comparison to the two other religious groups. It may well be – and cannot be tested, unless these two explanatory mechanisms can be empirically clearly separated – that the found differences among the Muslim groups are much more related to efficient (and therefore, intergenerationally transmitted) strategies of partner selection under conditions of very scarce resources and thus may be found also among populations with a different religious background, but similar living conditions.

NOTES

1. This paper reports results from the project "Regulation of Developmental Transitions in Second Generation Immigrants in Germany and Israel" (Principal Investigators: Yoav Lavee, Bernhard Nauck, Avi Sagi-Schwartz, Rainer K. Silbereisen, Anja Steinbach), funded by the German Federal Ministry of Education and Research (BMBF). We thank our collaborators from the Universities of Chemnitz, Jena, and Haifa: Susanne Clauß, Falk Gruner, Mohini Lokhande, David Mehlhausen-Hassoen, Andrea Michel, Katharina Stößel, and Peter Titzmann.

REFERENCES

Baykara-Krumme, H., & Fuß, D. (2009). Heiratsmigration nach Deutschland: Determinanten der transnationalen Partnerwahl türkeistämmiger Migranten [Marriage migration to Germany: Determinants of transnational partner choice of migrants with Turkish origin)]. *Zeitschrift für Bevölkerungswissenschaft*, **34**, 135–163.

Bengtson, V. L., Copen, C., Putney, N., & Silverstein, M. (2009). A longitudinal study of the intergenerational transmission of religion. *International Sociology*, **24**, 325–345.

Berry, J. W. (1997). Immigration, acculturation, and adaptation. *Applied Psychology: An International Review*, **46**, 5–34.

Bjorck, J. P., Braese, R. W., Tadie, J. T., & Gililland, D. D. (2010). The adolescent religious coping scale: Development, validation, and cross-validation. *Journal of Child and Family Studies*, **19**, 343–359.

Diehl, C., & Koenig, M. (2009). Religiosität türkischer Migranten im Generationsverlauf. Ein Befund und einige Erklärungsversuche [Intergenerational changes in religiosity of Turkish migrants. A finding and some explanational attempts]. *Zeitschrift für Soziologie*, **38**, 300–319.

Fowler, J. W., & Dell, M. L. (2006). Stages of faith from infancy through adolescence: Reflections on three decades of faith development theory. In E. C. Roehlkepartain,

P. E. King, L. M. Wagener, & P. L. Benson (Eds.), *The handbook of spiritual develop-ment in childhood and adolescence* (pp. 34–45). Thousand Oaks, CA: Sage.

French, D. C., Eisenberg, N., Sallquist, J., & Purwono, U. (2012). The social context of religion in Indonesian Muslim adolescents. In G. Trommsdorff & X. Chen (Eds.), *Values, religion, and culture in adolescent development* (pp. 146–163). New York: Cambridge University Press.

French, D. C., Eisenberg, N., Vaughan, J., Purwono, U., & Suryanti, T. A. (2008). Religious involvement and the social competence and adjustment of Indonesian Muslim adolescents. *Developmental Psychology, 44*, 597–611.

Gans, D., Silverstein, M., & Lowenstein, A. (2009). Do religious children care more and provide more care for older parents? A study of filial norms and behaviors across five nations. *Journal of Comparative Family Studies, 40*, 187–201.

Güngör, D., Bornstein, M. H., & Phalet, K. (2011). Cultural patterns and acculturation of religiosity: A study of Turkish, Turkish Belgian, and Belgian adolescents. *Journal for Cross-Cultural Psychology, 42*, 1356–1374.

Güngör, D., Fleischmann, F., & Phalet, K. (in press). Religious identification, beliefs, and practices among Turkish Belgian and Moroccan Belgian Muslims: Intergenerational continuity and acculturative change. *Child Development*.

Jerusalem, M., & Schwarzer, R. (1992). Self-efficacy as a resource factor in stress appraisal processes. In R. Schwarzer (Ed.), *Self-efficacy: Thought control of action* (pp. 195–213). Washington, DC: Hemisphere.

Kerr, M., & Stattin, H. (2000). What parents know, how they know it, and several forms of adolescent adjustment: further support for a reinterpretation of monitoring. *Developmental Psychology, 36*, 366–380.

King, P. E., & Furrow, J. L. (2004). Religion as a resource for positive youth develop-ment: Religion, social capital, and moral outcomes. *Developmental Psychology, 40*, 703–713.

Knafo, A., Assor, A., Schwartz, S., & David, L. (2009). Culture, migration, and fam-ily-value socialization: A theoretical model and empirical investigation with Russian immigrant youth in Israel. In U. Schönpflug (Ed.), *Cultural transmission. Developmental, psychological, social and methodological aspects* (pp. 269–296). New York: Cambridge University Press.

Knafo, A., & Schwartz, S. (2009). Accounting for parent–child value congruence: Theoretical considerations and empirical evidence. In U. Schönpflug (Ed.), *Cultural transmission. Developmental, psychological, social and methodological aspects* (pp. 240–268). New York: Cambridge University Press.

Laflin, M. T., Wang, J., & Barry, M. (2008). A longitudinal study of adolescent transition from virgin to nonvirgin status. *Journal of Adolescent Health, 42*, 228–236.

Lim, C., & Putnam, R. D. (2010). Religion, social networks, and life satisfaction. *American Sociological Review, 75*, 914–933.

Lindenberg, S. (1990). Rationalität und Kultur. Die verhaltenstheoretische Basis des Einflusses von Kultur auf Transaktionen [Rationality and culture. The behav-ioral base of the influence of culture on transactions]. In H. Haferkamp (Ed.), *Sozialstruktur und Kultur* (pp. 249–287). Frankfurt: Suhrkamp.

Manlove, J., Logan, C., Moore, K. A., & Ikramullah, E. (2008). Pathways from family reli-giosity to adolescent sexual activity and contraceptive use. *Perspectives on Sexual and Reproductive Health, 40*, 105–117.

Myers, S. M. (1999). Childhood migration and social integration in adulthood. *Journal of Marriage and the Family*, **61**, 774–789.

Nauck, B. (1989). Intergenerational relationships in families from Turkey and Germany. An extension of the "value of children" approach to educational attitudes and socialization practices. *European Sociological Review*, **5**, 251–274.

(1995). Educational climate and intergenerative transmission in Turkish families: A comparison of migrants in Germany and non-migrants. In P. Noack, M. Hofer, & J. Youniss (Eds.), *Psychological responses to social change. Human development in changing environment* (pp. 67–85). Berlin: de Gruyter.

(1997). Migration and intergenerational relations: Turkish families at home and abroad. In W. W. Isajiw (Ed.), *Multiculturalism in North America and Europe: Comparative perspectives on interethnic relations and social incorporation* (pp. 435–465). Toronto: Canadian Scholar's Press.

(2001a). Intercultural contact and intergenerational transmission in immigrant families. *Journal of Cross-Cultural Psychology*, **32**, 159–173.

(2001b). Der Wert von Kindern für ihre Eltern. "Value of Children" als spezielle Handlungstheorie des generativen Verhaltens und von Generationenbeziehungen im interkulturellen Vergleich [The value of children for their parents. "Value of children" as a special action theory of generative behavior and intergenerational relationships in cross-cultural comparison]. *Kölner Zeitschrift für Soziologie und Sozialpsychologie*, **53**, 407–435.

(2007a). Immigrant families in Germany. Family change between situational adaptation, acculturation, segregation and remigration. *Zeitschrift für Familienforschung*, **19**, 34–54.

(2007b). Value of children and the framing of fertility: Results from a cross-cultural comparative survey in 10 societies. *European Sociological Review*, **23**, 615–629.

(2008). Acculturation. In F. J. R. van de Vijver, D. A. van Hemert, & Y. Poortinga (Eds.), *Multilevel analysis of individuals and cultures* (pp. 379–409). New York: Erlbaum.

Ormel, J., Lindenberg, S., Steverink, N., & Verbrugge, L. M. (1999). Subjective well-being and social production functions. *Social Indicators Research*, **46**, 61–90.

Oser, F. K., Scarlett, W. G., & Bucher, A. (2006). Religious and spiritual development throughout the life span. In R. M. Lerner (Ed.), *Handbook of child psychology* (6th ed., Vol. 1: Theoretical models of human development, pp. 942–996). Hoboken, NJ: Wiley & Sons.

Roehlkepartain, E. C., Benson, P. L., King, P. E., & Wagener, L. M. (2006). Spiritual development in childhood and adolescence: Moving to the scientific mainstream. In E. C. Roehlkepartain, P. E. King, L. M. Wagener, & P. L. Benson (Eds.), *The handbook of spiritual development in childhood and adolescence* (pp. 1–15). Thousand Oaks, CA: Sage.

Rosenberg, M. J. (1965). *Society and the adolescent self-image*. Princeton: Princeton University Press.

Rostosky, S. S., Wilcox, B. L., Wright, M. L., & Randall, B. A. (2004). The impact of religiosity on adolescent sexual behavior: A review of evidence. *Journal of Adolescent Research*, **19**, 677–697.

South, S. J., Haynie, D. L., & Bose, S. (2005). Residential mobility and the onset of adolescent sexual activity. *Journal of Marriage and Family*, **67**, 499–514.

Trommsdorff, G. (2009). Intergenerational relations and cultural transmission. In U. Schönpflug (Ed.), *Cultural transmission. Developmental, psychological, social and methodological aspects* (pp. 126–160). New York: Cambridge University Press.

UNESCO (2006). *International standard classification of education – ISCED 1997* (2nd ed.): UNESCO Institute for Statistics.

Part Four

SOCIALIZATION PROCESSES OF VALUES AND
RELIGION IN ADOLESCENT DEVELOPMENT

14 Attachment and Religious Development in Adolescence

The Implications of Culture

Pehr Granqvist

Abstract

In this attachment-theoretical chapter, I highlight relations between attachment and religious development in adolescence, while taking cultural implications into account. I argue that adolescence is a sensitive phase of development related to both attachment and religiosity. This period is often associated with transfer of attachment functions from parents to age-mates. In the religious realm, this period may be linked to either increased religiosity (e.g., conversion) or to disengagement from religion. During adolescence, an attachment-like relationship with God may also develop. Furthermore, on the basis of empirical studies, I discuss the implications of individual differences in attachment security for religious development in adolescence. I distinguish between two notable developmental pathways: secure attachment to religious caregivers as a basis for religious stability ("correspondence pathway") and insecure attachment to caregivers as a basis of distress regulation through religion ("compensation pathway"). In the first case, believers are more likely to experience well-being; in the latter case, religion may serve as a protective factor in development. I also take into account possible negative effects of religion on adjustment. Finally, I discuss the cultural generalizability versus specificity of each of the central arguments in the chapter.

In this chapter, I argue that attachment theory is a viable framework for understanding certain aspects of religious development, values, and adjustment in adolescence. Adolescence is a key period of development both for attachment and religion. Regarding attachment, adolescence signifies an important transitional period when attachment functions are transferred from parents to others, typically love partners and close friends. Not coincidentally, a century of research indicates that adolescence also represents an age of religious awakening, during which an attachment-like relationship with God may be especially likely to develop. However, adolescence is also known as the age of apostasy, marked by disengagement from the faith one was brought up in. Besides highlighting a connection between normative aspects of attachment and religious development, I review findings of individual differences that suggest two attachment-related pathways in relation to adolescent religious development. The first goes via secure attachment to religious caregivers ("correspondence" pathway) and is typically associated with religious stability or reaffirmation in adolescence. The second goes via distress regulation in the context of insecure attachment ("compensation" pathway). Adolescence in general and attachment transfer in particular are associated with emotional turbulence, not least for adolescents with a history of insecure attachment, who may find in God an appealing attachment surrogate. In that context, I highlight the possibility that religion in general, and religion-as-compensation in particular, may serve as a protective factor on youth adjustment and values, for example, against the adverse effects that are otherwise typically associated with insecure attachment.

The first three main sections of the chapter largely take a "Western perspective" in that they describe research and theorizing that have mostly been undertaken in the Western world. Whereas there is a dearth of systematic research on most of these matters in other parts of the world, an additional main section on cultural considerations (vis-à-vis attachment theory and research, the notion of attachment transfer, and the religion-as-attachment idea) is offered before concluding the chapter.

Brief Overview of Attachment Theory and Research

John Bowlby (1969–1980), the originator of attachment theory, defined attachment as a strong disposition on the part of offspring in many mammalian species to seek proximity to and contact with a specific figure. During the first year of life, human infants typically develop one or a few attachment relationships, typically with their primary caregiver(s). Bowlby (1969–1980) described attachment relationships as strong and enduring affectional bonds characterized by the attached person (i.e., the offspring) selectively maintaining proximity to the caregiver, using the caregiver as a safe haven during distress, and as a secure base when exploring the environment. Finally, in using the caregiver (or attachment figure) in these ways, this figure is implicitly perceived as stronger and wiser by the attached person.

According to Bowlby (1969–1980), attachment behaviors (e.g., crying, locomotion) are governed by an attachment behavioral system, held to have been naturally selected over the course of evolution because it potentiated gene survival in our evolutionary environment(s) by protecting mammalian offspring from natural dangers via keeping them in proximity to their attachment figures. The attachment system is held to be universal and to be activated by natural clues to danger, which can have both external (e.g., physical separation, predators approaching) and internal (e.g., fear, illness) sources. The system is held to be deactivated by natural clues to safety, most notably physical contact with the attachment figure.

Bowlby (1969–1980) also argued that early interactions with the attachment figure lay the foundation for what he termed "internal working models" (IWMs) of Self and Others in relationships. Such working models are believed to serve as generalizing templates from early experience that guide our perceptions, expectations, and behaviors in future close relationships. Although these working models are held to be continually updated, principles of cognitive assimilation and behavioral automatization make a complete transformation of IWMs based on later experiences less likely. Therefore, Bowlby (1969–1980) expected general continuity of IWMs across maturation and relationships, while acknowledging that in the wake of marked, lingering shifts in experience, lawful discontinuity was expected. Such IWMs are described as partially unconscious, due at least in part to the immaturity of the brain's memory systems at early ages of development (Bowlby, 1969–1980).

Finally, Bowlby (e.g., 1969–1980) argued that the attachment system is active from cradle to grave, for example, in long-term adult pair-bonds. However, physical proximity gradually becomes a less important component of attachment. A psychological sense of "felt security" has therefore been suggested as a more viable aspect of attachment in older individuals (Sroufe & Waters, 1977). Felt security may be achieved by purely non-physical means, such as thinking about or looking at a picture of the attachment figure.

Ainsworth and colleagues observed that a substantial minority of children did not behave as expected based on Bowlby's normative model (Ainsworth, Blehar, Waters, & Wall, 1978), which set the stage for a focus on individual differences in attachment patterns. At the core of secure attachment (B; ca 60–70 percent in normal samples; van IJzendoorn, Schuengel, & Bakermans-Kranenburg, 1999) is the assumption of a positive and coherent set of IWMs. This is manifested in a behavioral balance between attachment and exploration in infants and in linguistic coherence in discussions of attachment-related memories in adolescents and adults (Main, Goldwyn, & Hesse, 2003). Throughout development, secure attachment is marked by a view of the self as worthy of care and an expectation of others as able and likely to provide care.

Insecure attachment (ca 30–40 percent in normal samples; van IJzendoorn et al., 1999) is often subdivided to three categories, avoidant (A), resistant (C), and disorganized/ disoriented (D; Main & Solomon, 1990). Avoidant children engage in (defensive) exploration at the expense of attachment. In contrast, C children engage in attachment at the expense of exploration. Finally, D children display various forms of behavioral breakdowns in the presence of the attachment figure (e.g., opposing behaviors, such as moving away from parent while crying; Main & Solomon, 1990). Across different types of insecurity, IWMs are supposedly negative and incoherent (see Cassidy & Shaver, 2008).

Research has shown aspects of caregiving, especially during the individual's first year of life, to be the most consistent predictors of attachment quality, while the direct role of genetic heritability has typically been found negligible (for a review, see Cassidy & Shaver, 2008). More specifically, the following aspects of caregiving have been associated with the different qualities of attachment: sensitivity (i.e., responding promptly and appropriately) with B; rejection with A; markedly inconsistent responsiveness with C; and abusive, frightening, or dissociative caregiving with D (ibid.).

Individual differences in attachment organization have been established as important predictors of socioemotional development (ibid.). For example, B has predicted prosocial behaviors and a low degree of behavioral problems in childhood and adolescence. In contrast, D has foreshadowed later behavioral problems (e.g., aggression), dissociative inclinations, and psychopathology (van IJzendoorn et al., 1999).

Much of the early attachment research also suggested that secure children are more successfully socialized than other children (e.g., Stayton, Hogan, & Ainsworth, 1971; see also Richters & Waters, 1991). The conclusion from these studies was that socialization does not require special techniques of discipline but that it is a natural consequence of the child obtaining sensitive caregiving, where the child's signals and needs are given high priority.

Normative Aspects of Adolescent Development

The Transfer of Attachment
A key task for the adolescent is to develop a certain measure of autonomy vis-à-vis parents. Initially, pubertal changes tend to initiate some distancing from

parents (e.g., Steinberg & Morris, 2001), which is further strengthened by the adolescent's increasing capacity to think about relationships, including a ripening ability to evaluate the internal consistency (or lack thereof) between what parents say and do (often associated with deidealization of parents). Thus, autonomy strivings tend to take place most often at the instigation of the adolescent, who typically wants to take it faster and farther than his/her parents are often willing to allow (e.g., Smetana, 2002). For example, the adolescent may not only accept to be in charge of what clothes to wear, but may now also expect to have a certain say on how much to study, what friends to hang out with, what partners to date, what to *do* with the partners, what drugs to take, and what hours to be home in bed.

Besides behavioral autonomy strivings, adolescents often question parental values or the values of the older generation (e.g., conservation values), and instead express values of their own (e.g., openness values; e.g., Knafo & Schwartz, 2001). Such a generational chasm in value endorsement (e.g., religious values) between youth and their parents is especially pronounced among immigrant youth facing the dual task of balancing the values of their parents' home cultures with those of their current host countries (cf. the notion of "acculturation gaps;" e.g., Birman & Poff, 2010). Thus, parents only rarely go along for the full "autonomy" ride, presumably because of lingering perceptions of immaturity in the offspring on part of the parents (e.g., Allen, 2008). Hence, some turbulence tends to surround the adolescent's autonomy strivings.

Moreover, adolescents' growing push for autonomy (Steinberg, 1990) typically coincides with their increasing (and perhaps seemingly inappropriate) dependence on peers, typically romantic partners and friends (Allen, 2008). This means that attachment functions can be met through peers while adolescents establish some autonomy in relation to parents.

Zeifman and Hazan (e.g., 2008) have suggested that attachment formation with peers may unfold in steps analogous to attachment formation with caregivers in infancy. In other words, the transfer of attachment may begin with the transfer of the proximity-seeking component, via the safe haven function, and end with the transfer of the secure base component in a step-by-step process. This process is typically initiated already in middle childhood (transfer of the proximity component), intensified in adolescence (the safe haven function), and concluded in early adulthood (the secure base component). Empirical research in the United States, Germany, Sweden, and mainland China has tended to support this stepwise model (e.g., Fraley & Davis, 1997; Friedlmeier & Granqvist, 2006; Zeifman & Hazan, 2008; Zhang, Chan, & Teng, 2011).

Long-term romantic partners are most often ultimately selected out as the principal attachment figures of adulthood (Bowlby, 1969–1980; Zeifman & Hazan, 2008). From an evolutionary perspective, it is not difficult to imagine that this developmental transformation from a principal attachment to protective parents in childhood to a principal attachment to reproductive partners following pubertal maturation has been selected (i.e., adaptive). Besides surviving until adolescence, the offspring may now also pass their parents' genes on to the next generation. Moreover, in a species such as *Homo sapiens*, where offspring are immature and dependent on high parental investment for a long period of their lives, genetic reproduction does not suffice, but the parents have also had to stick together for mutual investment in the next generation. Attachment may serve here as an emotional "glue" that binds prospective parents together. Thus, evolution may have co-opted the attachment system and put it to use also in the context of adult pair-bonds (e.g., Zeifman & Hazan, 2008).

The Age of Religious Awakening and Apostasy: God as a Symbolic Attachment Figure

This period of attachment transition coincides with one of the major periods of religious and spiritual transformations in many peoples' lives. Adolescence and young adulthood have been noted as major religious transitional periods since the infancy days of the psychology of religion (e.g., Hall, 1904; James, 1902; Starbuck, 1899). Almost a century later, Argyle and Beit-Hallahmi (1975, p. 59) still referred to adolescence as "the age of religious awakening." One important reason for this is that adolescence and early adulthood are the life periods most intimately associated with sudden religious conversions and other significant changes in one's relationship with God. Moreover, it is well known that cult recruiters make teenagers and young adults primary targets of their proselytizing and recruitment activities. However, besides being linked to increased religiousness, as in the experience of religious conversion, adolescence and early adulthood are associated with apostasy, that is, the disengagement from religion among those raised in a religious home (e.g., Roof & McKinney, 1987; Tamminen, 1994).

The reason that adolescence and early adulthood are religious transitional periods has, however, remained unclear. Naturally, researchers of very different theoretical persuasions have struggled with this question based on, for example, Piaget's theory of the development of formal operational thinking, ideas about increased libidinal energy within classical psychoanalysis, the search for an identity (including a religious identity) within psychosocial theory, and a focus on re-socialization processes within socialization theories (for a review, see Hood, Hill, & Spilka, 2009).Without denying that these other processes may be involved as well, I suggest that one important reason may be because attachment transfer is co-occurring (see also Granqvist & Kirkpatrick, 2008). According to Weiss (1982, p. 178), relinquishing one's parents as attachment figures has a number of predictable consequences, including vulnerability to emotional loneliness, which he defines as "the absence from one's internal world of an attachment figure." At such a time, adolescents may turn to God (or perhaps a charismatic religious leader) as a substitute attachment-like figure. That is to say, attachment components may not only be transferred to peers, but also, in some cases, to God, and in other cases away from God. In line with this reasoning, Kupky (1928, p. 70) made a poignant observation more than 80 years ago, in saying that "True love and religious experience are nearly impossible before adolescence."

This naturally leads to the question why the believer-God relationship should be conceptualized as an attachment relationship in the first place. Here, I will give a few examples of past findings from the psychology of religion that illustrate how the believer-God relationship comes to function as an attachment-like relationship (or a symbolic attachment; for more comprehensive reviews, see Granqvist & Kirkpatrick, 2008; Kirkpatrick, 2005).

First, regarding proximity/closeness maintenance, prayer may function as a religious analogue of attachment behaviors (Kirkpatrick, 2005). Although there are many kinds of prayers, one of the most frequently endorsed reasons for praying is to experience a sense of closeness to God (Hood et al., 2009). The importance of proximity or closeness to God is also highlighted by what it means to be separated from God; in much Christian theology, this is the very essence of Hell, the worst case scenario.

Second, concerning God as a safe haven, people are particularly likely to turn to God during stress, and the more stressful a situation is, the more likely people are to do so (e.g., Pargament, 1997). Research also suggests that an overwhelming majority of sudden religious conversions occur during emotional turmoil (e.g., Ullman, 1982).

Third, with respect to the secure base component, believers maintain that God is loving, supportive, guiding, and protective (Kirkpatrick, 2005), qualities that are important for any secure base to possess in order to promote well-being and exploration in the attached person. Also, experiencing a personal relationship with such a God predicts aspects of well-being (e.g., freedom from worry and remission from depression) over and above conceivable covariates (Granqvist & Kirkpatrick, 2008; Smith, McCullough, & Poll., 2003).

Finally, that believers perceive God as stronger and wiser really goes without saying. In fact, at least within Christianity, God is typically even perceived as omnipotent, omniscient, and omnipresent, representing qualities that are difficult for any other attachment figure to outdo, as sensitive as he or she might be.

To summarize, many aspects of religious beliefs and experiences, particularly those related to perceived relationships with God, reflect the operation of attachment processes. Although God and other divine figures are typically unseen as interaction partners, religions thus likely capitalize on the operation of the attachment system. Hence, believers' perceived relationships with God can profitably be characterized as symbolic attachment relationships.

Individual Differences in Adolescent Development

Attachment Security and its Socioemotional Correlates

There are important individual differences to consider in relation to the turbulence surrounding adolescent development in general and attachment transfer in particular. Security of attachment, unlike insecurity, is associated with generally favorable developmental outcomes, such as constructiveness of conflict resolution with parents, social competence with peers, and a relative absence of externalizing (e.g., aggression and risk behaviors, such as heavy drug and alcohol consumption, sexual promiscuity) and internalizing (e.g., anxiety, depression) behavior problems (Allen, 2008; Kobak, Cole, Ferenz-Gillies, & Fleming, 1993; Kobak & Ferenz-Gillies, 1995; Kobak, Ferenz-Gillies, Everhart & Seabrook, 1994). Hence, security of attachment fosters continuity of adaptation throughout adolescence (e.g., Armsden & Greenberg, 1987; Lapsley, Rice, & Fitzgerald, 1990; Rice, 1990).

In addition to its association with adjustment problems, insecurity of attachment is linked to making a premature transfer of attachment in adolescence (Friedlmeier & Granqvist, 2006). Moreover, adolescents with an insecure attachment history are less likely to build close, trusting, and satisfactory peer relations (Allen, 2008). Thus, insecurely attached adolescents may be left in a state wherein felt security cannot be derived either by turning to parents or to peers for support. In sum, attachment turbulence is likely to be especially pronounced for adolescents with insecure attachment characteristics.

Based on these developmental profiles, it is common to think about secure attachment as a protective factor for adolescents' adjustment, whereas insecure (particularly disorganized) attachment is held as a vulnerability factor in development (see Cassidy & Shaver, 2008). When combined with other vulnerability and risk factors, insecure attachment may pave the way for serious adjustment problems.

Two Developmental Pathways to Religion

What implications do these individual differences in attachment security have for religious development in adolescence? Two general hypotheses have been derived from attachment theory about how individual differences in attachment security relate to religion.

The Correspondence Pathway. First, with the correspondence hypothesis, we (e.g., Granqvist & Kirkpatrick, 2008) have suggested that religion in the case of secure attachment develops from (1) generalized, positive representations of self and other (IWM aspect), and (2) partial adoption of a sensitive caregiver's religion (social aspect). Hence, insofar as the caregivers have been actively religious, the secure offspring is expected to become likewise, and in which case his or her beliefs in and perceptions of the divine will mirror that of a sensitive attachment figure.

This hypothesis has received considerable empirical support in studies across the lifespan (for a review, see Granqvist & Kirkpatrick, 2008), including two prospective longitudinal studies of adolescents. The first of these adolescent studies contained Swedish 15 to 17-year-olds drawn from both secular schools and religious youth groups. As in adult studies, estimates of parental sensitivity in childhood and a current secure peer attachment orientation were linked to a comparatively high degree of parent–adolescent similarity in religiousness (Granqvist, 2002). In other words, these adolescents tended to affirm (and possibly reaffirm) the faith or lack of faith of their parents. Moreover, in the same study, security was associated with religious stability (Granqvist, 2002); the religiosity of these adolescents did not characteristically wax and wane over time.

However, religiosity is under dynamic development throughout life, and especially in adolescence, implying that absolute religious stability should not be expected even for securely attached adolescents. Thus, when these adolescents experienced a prospective increase in religiousness, this increase tended to be gradual and to occur in the context of a positive influence from others (Granqvist, 2002). To give a more specific example, in follow-up analyses we found that secure attachment prospectively predicted increased religiousness over the 15-month time span studied, but only when the participants had experienced the formation of a romantic relationship between assessments (Granqvist & Hagekull, 2003).

Some of these results were conceptually replicated in the second study, which was conducted in the United States on mid-adolescents who had signed up for a Young Life evangelical summer camp. Secure attachment with parents prospectively predicted a reaffirmation of the faith one had been brought up with (i.e., a recommitment to God during the camp; Schnitker, Porter, Emmons, & Barrett, 2012).

In addition, several studies that were not explicitly informed by attachment theory have shown that parental religiousness is the best predictor of offspring religiousness and that this extends to adolescence, especially when the parent–adolescent relationship is marked by warmth and closeness (for a review, see Hood et al., 2009). Thus, there is substantial support for the social aspect of the correspondence hypothesis.

In contrast, researchers have been less devoted to studying the content aspects (as opposed to the presumed roots) of adolescent religiousness. Therefore, at this point, no conclusion can be drawn with regard to the IWM aspect of the correspondence hypothesis for adolescents. It is notable, however, that both child and adult studies have found, in line with the idea of generalizing IWMs, that securely attached individuals tend to view God as a reliable safe haven and secure base, as evident in loving God imagery and implicit usage of God as a "functional" attachment figure (for a review, see Granqvist & Kirkpatrick, 2008). In principle, there is no reason to assume that adolescent studies would yield a different conclusion.

The Compensation Pathway. Bowlby (1969–1980) speculated that certain conditions may lead people to seek out surrogate attachment figures. Insecure attachment in the principal attachment relationships may be one of these conditions. Accordingly, with the second hypothesis, labeled the compensation hypothesis, we (e.g., Granqvist & Kirkpatrick, 2008) have suggested that religiosity in the case of insecure attachment develops from attachment-related distress regulation strategies, where God functions as a surrogate attachment figure. This hypothesis has also received empirical support in several studies across the lifespan, including the two adolescent studies previously described. In the Swedish study, we found positive relations between insecure peer attachment and estimates of parental insensitivity on the one hand and scores on an "emotionally based" religiousness scale on the other, referring to the extent to which God is used to regulate attachment-related distress (Granqvist, 2002; Granqvist & Hagekull, 1999).

In particular, insecurity and parental insensitivity were linked to religious instability; religiosity did characteristically wax and wane over time for these adolescents. Also, their religiousness tended to increase specifically during stress. This conclusion was later corroborated in a meta-analysis of sudden religious conversions, which included nearly 1,500 participants, some of whom were adolescents. In the meta-analysis, insecurity as compared to security with parents was overrepresented among the sudden converts (9 percent vs. 5 percent, respectively) but not among gradual converts or non-converts (Granqvist & Kirkpatrick, 2004). In follow-up analyses of the adolescent sample, we found that the religiosity of insecure adolescents prospectively increased, but only when the participants had experienced a romantic relationship break up between assessments (Granqvist & Hagekull, 2003). Notably, religion also decreased for some of the insecure adolescents, which tended to happen following the formation of other close relationships (ibid.).

Some of these findings were also conceptually replicated in the U.S. Young Life summer camp study (Schnitker et al., 2012). For example, late adolescent summer camp staff members whose relationship narratives suggested insecure parental attachment were significantly more likely (38 percent) to have experienced a sudden religious conversion when they attended camp themselves, compared to those whose relationship narratives suggested secure parental attachment (10 percent).

As the findings from the meta-analysis of sudden conversions indicate, sudden religious conversion experiences are typically rare even among insecure adolescents. Indeed, since the infancy days of the psychology of religion at the turn of the 19th century, parts of the world – and especially the European "Welfare states" (of which Sweden is a prime example) – have seen traditional, institutionalized religion take on an increasingly marginalized role in society (e.g., Gill & Lundsgaarde, 2004). At the same time, more privatized and self-centering forms of spirituality have increased, especially among younger segments of the population (e.g., Houtman & Aupers, 2007). This change in the religious and spiritual landscape prompted us to ask whether some of the insecure adolescents who might have sought out religion as compensation a century or so ago would be especially inclined to adopt these "New Age" forms of spirituality. Our findings confirmed an association between maternal insensitivity and a particular form of insecure peer attachment orientation known as fearful avoidant attachment (cf. disorganized attachment; Mikulincer & Shaver, 2007) on the one hand and

New Age spirituality on the other (Granqvist & Hagekull, 2001). As New Age spirituality typically does not contain the postulate of a metaphysical attachment-like figure, these findings were initially somewhat puzzling on theoretical grounds. However, follow-up analyses on adults clarified that a relation between disorganized attachment and New Age spirituality was indirect, mediated by a general propensity to experience dissociative alterations in consciousness (Granqvist, Fransson, & Hagekull, 2009).

Religion as a Protective Factor in Adolescent Development

Although the compensation hypothesis may seem to represent a "deficiency" approach to religion, it is likely that religion in general and religion as compensation in particular fills a protective factor in development, for example, against the adverse effects on adolescent adjustment that are otherwise often associated with insecure attachment. There are three strands of empirical evidence, some of which is inferential, suggesting that this may indeed be the case.

First, religion is connected to adjustment-promoting values and behaviors (e.g., Hood et al., 2009; Resnick et al., 1997), such as prosociality. For example, adolescents who say that religion is important in their lives are more likely to do volunteer work in the community than adolescents who say that religion is not important (e.g., Youniss, McLellan, & Yates, 1999). By the same token, religions often preach the abstinence from maladaptive distress regulation behaviors, such as drug consumption and binge drinking. Consequently, perhaps, religiousness is related to decreased externalizing behavior problems, such as delinquent behaviors, lower rates of drug and alcohol use, less sexual activity, and delayed onset of sexual activity (for a review, see Hood et al., 2009). In addition, according to the same review, religiousness is related to decreased internalizing behavior problems, such as anxiety and depression. Moreover, religiousness is associated with positive indicators of adjustment, such as well-being, particularly among adolescents in at-risk populations (e.g., Moore & Glei, 1995). It is notable in this literature that although the causality question remains far from settled, most researchers tackle it in terms of the adjustment promoting effects of religious socialization processes (Hood et al., 2009).

Second, whether occurring in adolescence or adulthood, conversions and other profound religious experiences tend to be associated with substantial attenuations in the distress that typically preceded those experiences (e.g., Ullman, 1982; Zinnbauer & Pargament, 1998; see also reviews by Hood et al., 2009; Pargament, 1997). In other words, "personal problems may set the stage for conversion, and it can be a constructive solution to those difficulties" (Hood et al., 2009, p. 447). However, research about the long-term "effects" of such experiences has yielded mixed conclusions. Some studies suggest that sudden converts, while initially experiencing dramatic levels of decline in suffering and an increase in states of joy and bliss, may eventually relapse into experiences of sin, guilt, and suffering (e.g., Kildahl, 1965; Spellman, Baskett, & Byrne, 1971). By comparison, the "therapeutic effect" of gradual conversions seems more reliable (ibid.). In either case, however, Hill (2002) notes how such spiritually transformative experiences may create changes in meaning systems that yield a positive affective state through a new (or renewed) sense of purpose, value, and self-worth.

Finally, attachment to God and other aspects of religion may also, in some cases, ultimately promote some degree of "earned attachment security" (Main et al., 2003) in the secular domain. This speculation has been spurred by two sets of findings in the adult literature on attachment and religion. First, self-reported insecure attachment history and romantic attachment (in the latter case, particularly a negative self-model or a high degree of attachment anxiety) have been linked to increasing religiousness and spirituality over time, and yet secure attachment has been linked to higher religiousness and spirituality at a given point in time (see Kirkpatrick, 2005). One interpretation of this pattern is that increasing religiousness somehow helps the individual to gain attachment security. Second, independent Adult Attachment Interview (AAI; Main et al. 2003) coders' estimates of parental insensitivity in study participants' pasts have predicted a history of using religion as compensation for inadequate attachments, but current AAI-assessed insecurity (incoherent attachment discourse) has been unrelated to religion as compensation (Cassibba et al., 2008; Granqvist, Ivarsson, Broberg, & Hagekull, 2007). Thus, similarly, religion as compensation may lead to an increase in attachment security.

Hence, it is possible that a process of positive change in IWMs of relatively insecure individuals might be initiated by experiencing God's love and forgiveness, which would be comparable to the idea of reparative effects from other relationship experiences, such as with a good therapist or a secure romantic partner (e.g., Bowlby, 1988; Main et al., 2003). Although speculative at this point, this interpretation would make theoretical sense if the individual's perceived relationship with God actually functions as a compensatory attachment relationship. It would also be theologically plausible, given the portrayal of God as a sensitive secure base and haven of safety that has been described in this chapter.

In particular, repair of a negative self-model might be one avenue through which earned security via religion/spirituality plays itself out. After all, God supposedly loves everyone, despite their "unworthiness." Notably, such an earned security effect may require religious practice for many years and would probably not play itself out until adulthood.

In summary, religions generally encourage behaviors that counteract a developmental path to maladjustment and promote a path to adjustment. Religious experiences also serve to attenuate distress and shift the mind's focus to a new (or renewed) meaning system, including prosocial values. Finally, by offering a compensatory attachment-like figure, religion may ultimately promote some degree of earned attachment security, which in turn would aid in offsetting the deleterious effects that are otherwise often associated with adverse experiences in past attachment relationships.

Of course, elaborating on these promises is in no way to deny that religions may also have what most would view as negative effects on adjustment. At the individual or micro level, for example, the blooming sexual urges of adolescents, often expressed in masturbation, consumption of pornography, and trembling sexual encounters, may be experienced as sinful and hence become a source of guilt. As another example, at the societal or macro level, disagreements over religious contents may become the source of intergroup conflicts, with potentially explosive consequences for the surrounding. In particular, I speculate that religion, in any of its authoritarian forms, may have its most deleterious effects when harshly imposed by insensitive caregivers on offspring who find themselves in a homogenous cultural (or subcultural) situation that gives them limited opportunity to distance themselves from the preaching of such a religion.

Cultural Considerations

In the previous review, I have almost exclusively focused on research pertaining to attachment, adolescent development, religion, and values of the contemporary Western world. Therefore, it is an open question whether the conclusions drawn are generalizable to other parts of the world, let alone earlier historical periods in the West. Some may be, whereas others may not. In this section, I will discuss cross-cultural considerations pertaining to the central proposals of this chapter.

Attachment Theory and Research

Cross-cultural considerations regarding attachment theory and research do not inevitably lead to any marked changes in the conclusions of this chapter, although the cross-cultural validity of attachment theory and research have been challenged (e.g., Rothbaum, Weisz, Pott, Miyake, & Morelli,

2000). Rothbaum and colleagues (2000) argued, for example, that attachment theory is culturally biased in emphasizing exploration and autonomy as hallmarks of security, and that Western-based assessments of security such as the strange situation (Ainsworth et al., 1978) give misleading results when utilized in cultures with other values and practices surrounding relationships (i.e., customs of caregiving). In my view, critical cross-cultural considerations are a most welcome contribution to the attachment literature – issues pertaining to universality versus cultural embeddedness are important for theoretical as well as practical reasons. For illustrational purposes, Rothbaum and colleagues (2000) focused their critique exclusively on differences between Japan and the United States. They reviewed evidence showing that Japanese mothers value and foster more dependency (or *amae* – but see Behrens, 2004, for an alternate, multifaceted view of this construct) in their children, whereas U.S. mothers value and foster more independence. The implication of this review is, in part, that what would be regarded as signs of insecurity in the United States (dependency) is understood very differently in Japan.

However, Rothbaum and colleagues' (2000) conclusions are not without problems. First, the values of attachment theory should not necessarily be viewed as an expression of United States' values, or values of the Western world for that matter. For example, attachment is not about individualism or independence, but about relatedness and willingness to allow oneself to depend on others. Indeed, one of Bowlby's (e.g., 1969–1980) major points as far as values are concerned is that healthy development in all phases of life is characterized by one's willingness to develop close relationships with others, and the ability to use them as safe havens and secure bases. To put matters simply, and as noted previously in this chapter, attachment security is characterized by a *balance* between attachment and exploration. Second, and relatedly, although cultures may differ somewhat in their emphases on attachment versus exploration, perhaps with the United States and Japan as two good examples of differential emphases, Rothbaum and colleagues (2000) most likely exaggerated the implications of such differences. In fact, the hallmarks of security (i.e., a balance between the two) are positively valued in both countries (e.g., Posada et al., 1995). Hence, just as the willingness to use the caregiver as a safe haven in distress is a desideratum in U.S. infants, the ability to use the caregiver as a secure base for exploration is a desideratum in Japanese infants.

The only unequivocal universality assumption within attachment theory of which I am aware is the proposal that mammalian offspring possess an attachment-behavioral system and develop selective attachments to their caregivers (Bowlby, 1969–1980). This assumption is uncontroversial and has a strong standing in psychology, anthropology, and ethology alike. Tellingly, Bowlby's original ideas on these matters were developed largely based on observations of other mammals. Also, it is worth noting that the first systematic observations of human infants based on attachment theory were conducted not in the West but in Uganda, Africa (Ainsworth, 1967). These observations ultimately paved the way for the development of the strange situation procedure (Ainsworth et al., 1978) in the West. As it turned out, U.S. infants displayed fewer attachment behaviors than Ugandan infants. Studying U.S. infants' attachment behaviors was therefore accomplished by placing them in a novel environment and separating them from their caregivers (i.e., stronger measures were required to activate their attachment systems).

In addition to the universality assumption, cross-cultural research has been evaluated in relation to assumptions regarding individual differences in attachment, such as the normativity assumption (i.e., secure attachment is the predominant pattern of attachment across cultures), the sensitivity assumption (i.e., caregiver sensitivity is related to child attachment security), and the competence assumption (i.e., secure attachment is related to various competencies in socioemotional aspects of development) (see van IJzendoorn & Sagi-Schwartz, 2008). Regarding the normativity assumption, it is founded on the implicit premise that most caregivers and caregiving arrangements across cultures are "good enough" to foster secure attachment. Thus, the normativity assumption is predicated on the sensitivity assumption. In principle, however, there could be cultures where malevolent caregiving practices are normative, marked by, for example, harsh physical discipline and consistent rejection of the children's attachment behaviors. If so, secure attachment would not be expected as the modal outcome. Luckily, however, in the studies reviewed by van IJzendoorn and Sagi-Schwartz (2008), across a wide array of cultures from the West, Asia (including Japan and China), Israel, and Africa (including the Dogon of Mali, the Gusii of Kenya, and impoverished Khayelishta of South Africa), secure attachment was the norm. Thus, to date, the cross-cultural database has supported the normativity assumption.

However, the prevalence of different kinds of insecure attachment has been found to differ somewhat across cultures and, perhaps more notably, across samples within the same cultures. Japanese studies are again a good case in point. One Japanese study (Takahashi, 1986; see also Miyake, Chen, & Campos, 1985) showed an unexpectedly high proportion (32 percent) of insecure/resistant (C) attachment and an absence of avoidant (A) attachment. Drawing in part on that study, Rothbaum and colleagues (2000) suggested that C attachment does not contain the same insecurity connotation within Japan as in the West, presumably because of *amae*/dependency being a desideratum in Japan. However, at least two other Japanese studies have shown a distribution of attachment that is more comparable to the Western world (Behrens, Hesse, & Main, 2007; Durrett, Otaki, & Richards, 1984; see van IJzendoorn & Sagi-Schwartz, 2008, for additional Q-sort based studies). Considering cultural variations in caregiving and the difficulty of administering a complex procedure such as the strange situation in a culturally sensitive way, such mixed findings are not unexpected. In line with the positive valence of *amae* in Japan, for example, Japanese infants are carried more and separated less than infants in the West (Behrens, 2004). Consequently, Japanese infants probably find the usual three-minute separations of the strange situation more stressful and may find it more difficult to settle following reunion with the caregiver. As the strange situation should be no more than mildly to moderately stressful (Ainsworth et al., 1978), a (culturally) sensitive administration necessitates briefer separations for infants (whether Japanese or not) who show strong and persistent separation protest. It is notable, in this regard, that Takahashi (1986) allowed up to a full two minutes of continuous crying during separations before the reunions took place, whereas other studies tend to allow only 20–30 seconds (van IJzendoorn & Sagi-Schwartz, 2008).

Takahashi (1986) herself acknowledged this possible role of excessive stress in producing "false Cs." Looking more carefully at the distribution, she found that roughly half of the C infants (or 15 percent of the full sample) were made C ("inconsistent C") only after potentially excessive stress exposure in the second separation episode, leaving only 17 percent of "consistent C" in the sample. When part of this sample was later re-analyzed by Grossmann and Grossmann (1989), several of the overstressed infants (whether originally assigned C or B classifications) were found to display odd and opposing behaviors, suggesting that the excessive stress may also have produced behavioral breakdowns that would have warranted (false) D classifications if the D system (Main & Solmon, 1990) had been in use at the time.

It is notable that although most of the cross-cultural discussions of attachment distributions have focused on Japan, C attachment has been found more consistently overrepresented in Israel, possibly owing to hypervigilance and "overprotection" on the part of Israeli mothers who face the constant threat of terror (van IJzendoorn & Sagi-Schartz, 2008). Unless parts of the Western world had dominated this area of studies, we would probably have asked why A attachment is overrepresented (compared with C) in many Western nations (see in particular Grossmann, Grossmann, Spangler, Suess, & Unzner, 1985). Rather than viewing such findings as a challenge to the cross-cultural validity of attachment theory, however, we may view them as indicating a need for research on the contextual variations (e.g., caregiving arrangements) that conceivably produce those differences. Such findings should also provoke a potentially fruitful methodological discussion vis-à-vis cultural considerations.

In their review, van IJzendoorn and Sagi-Schwartz (2008) conclude that, as compared with the normativity assumption, the sensitivity and competence assumptions have received less extensive support in the cross-cultural attachment database. The most important reasons for this may be that relevant aspects pertaining to these assumptions have been insufficiently researched outside of the West and that the studies that have been conducted have employed insufficient sample sizes. For example, the meta-analytic link between maternal sensitivity and attachment security uncovered on largely Western samples is but $r = .24$ (DeWolff & van IJzendoorn, 1997). Many studies conducted outside of the West have not used large enough samples to uncover effects of such a modest to moderate magnitude.

Adolescent Development and Attachment Transfer

Likewise, cross-cultural considerations regarding adolescent development and attachment transfer do not inevitably lead to any marked changes in the conclusions of this chapter. Initially, the idea of a strong push for autonomy from parents in order to develop a family constellation separate from that of the original family might seem like a case in point of a 20th century ethnocentric psychology of the West. After all, in many non-Western cultures – as well as in past historical periods of the West – people live(d) in extended family networks that include(d) members of at least one spouse's original family. Thus, continued codependence on the original family would seem like a more pronounced theme in such cultures and historical periods than the "autonomy" (or even "separation") theme that is currently characteristic of the Western world. As a simple illustration of the differing roles of family and peers among cultures, Western youth spend much more time with peers and leisure activities outside of the family context than do adolescents from nonindustrial and Asian populations (Larson & Verma, 1999). On the basis of such findings, Larson and Verma hypothesized that, "the substantial amount of time that youth in nonindustrial and Asian populations spend with their families is related to experience of greater family support and to greater socialization into family and cultural norms " (p. 724). One implication of such findings is that Western youth may make a comparatively early (perhaps premature) transfer of attachment from parents to peers (cf. Zhang et al., 2011).

Nevertheless, even in non-Western cultures, child–parent conflict tends to increase following puberty (e.g., Steinberg & Morris, 2001). Indeed, in some non-industrialized parts of the world, as among non-human primates, adolescence (i.e., post puberty) is associated with leaving the family group to seek a new family, although non-married daughters are a notable exception to this conclusion (e.g., Schlegel & Barry, 1991). In general, Western youths may be unusual in their delay of moving out (ibid.), which may also be why they are so inclined to *psychologically* distance themselves from their parents and instead spend time with their peers. Also, even if the timeline for attachment transfer differs somewhat across cultures, most individuals within most cultures do conceivably ultimately transfer their principal attachments from parents to peers (cf. Zhang et al., 2011).

Religion as Attachment
Naturally, the cross-cultural variations in attachment, as previously reviewed, does not provide a particularly solid basis for speculating about their effects on religion. One reason for this is that the normativity assumption has been supported across cultures. We are left with mostly minor and occasionally inconsistent variations in proportions of A versus C attachment across cultures. However, in principle, one might expect that cultures with a large proportion of C attachment would foster clingy, all-consuming, and strongly emotional forms of religiosity, where deities would be viewed as inconsistently responsive. In contrast, cultures with a large proportion of A attachment might foster authoritarian forms of religiosity, marked by fundamentalism and hostility to members of out-groups, and where deities would be perceived as distant and inaccessible. Finally, cultures with a large proportion of D attachment might foster religions, or perhaps expressions of spirituality, that sanctify various dissociation-related altered states of consciousness, such as trance, mystical experiences, and spirit possession (cf. Granqvist, Hagekull, & Ivarsson, 2012). It is conceivable that the deities (or spirits) of such cultures would be viewed as punitive, aberrant, and frightening. Whereas these speculations stray quite a bit from what is available in the empirical literature, extant cross-cultural research has shown, in line with the idea of generalizing working models, that deities are construed as more loving in cultures where parenting is warm and accepting and as more distant in cultures marked by harsh, rejecting parenting (Lambert, Triandis, & Wolf, 1959; Rohner, 1986).

However, it is largely an open question whether attachment theory really is applicable to religion outside of the Judeo-Christian faith traditions. Very few explicit attachment and religion studies have been conducted outside of the Western world and, to the best of my knowledge, none outside of the major monotheistic traditions (other than the "New Age"-related beliefs and activities discussed previously). Of course, the theistic idea of a personal God who is involved in peoples' everyday affairs fits especially well to an attachment theory conceptualization. However, even in countries dominated by Eastern religions such as Hinduism and Buddhism, which Westerners tend to think of as abstract, godless philosophies, believers often focus on the more theistic components of the belief system and on personal gods imported from ancient folk religions (see Kirkpatrick, 2005, for a discussion). For example, although Buddhism is supposedly non-theistic as far as metaphysical beliefs are concerned, it is very common for everyday Buddhists to pray and sacrifice to Buddha (or perhaps a boddhisattva), suggesting that Buddha may function as a symbolic attachment figure after all (see also Granqvist, Mikulincer, & Shaver, 2010). However, unless one is willing to semantically dilute the attachment construct, the same can probably not be said for philosophies such as Confucianism, Communism, and Daoism that are dominating peoples' worldviews in parts of the world, such as China, in spite of not being associated with any particular symbolic attachment figure. These latter examples illustrate that the religion as attachment idea should not be couched in universalist parlance. I hasten to add in this context that a view of religion as an evolutionary by-product (not an adaptation) (e.g., Granqvist, 2006; Kirkpatrick, 2005), which *capitalizes* on the operation of other evolved systems (such as attachment), does not necessitate universality for religion, let alone its "hijacking" of the attachment system.

A more specific generalizability concern relating to the attachment-religion connection stems from the importance assigned in this literature to radical religious changes, including sudden religious conversions. Modeled on Saul's/Paul's conversion on the road to Damascus, such experiences could be construed as unique to Christianity, and particularly to Protestantism (see Hood et al., 2009). In other words, it should be questioned whether insecure attachment would express itself in a propensity for such experiences in other faith traditions. Nevertheless, a recent study of orthodox and non-orthodox Jewish converts (compared with non-converts) replicated a connection with an insecure attachment history with parents for those raised unorthodoxly who converted to orthodox Judaism as well as for those raised orthodox who converted to unorthodox Judaism (Pirutinsky,

2009). Future studies should address whether these findings replicate outside of the monotheistic faith traditions. Studies addressing the possible transfer of attachment components from parents to multiple deities, such as are available within Hinduism, would also make a welcome contribution to the literature.

Conclusions

In this chapter, I have argued that attachment theory is a viable framework for understanding religious development and values in adolescence. Adolescence was portrayed as a key period of developmental transitions both for attachment and religion. In their growing push for autonomy from parents, adolescents with an insecure attachment history are especially likely to develop a surrogate attachment to God, via religious conversion experiences and the like, and typically during a period of emotional turmoil. Other insecure adolescents actively distance themselves from the religion of their parents or come to embrace the diverse tenets of New Age spirituality, or engage in "sex, drugs and rock 'n' roll" at levels that may pave the way for serious adjustment problems. Most adolescents, however, and especially those with a secure attachment history, go about their religious and spiritual business without any notable fluctuations. They typically affirm the religious or non-religious standards of their parents, while remaining emotionally close with them. They may also experience gradual changes in religiousness, typically a reaffirmation of the faith they grew up in, which tends to occur following the formation of other important relationships in their lives, such as a romantic relationship. Moreover, I noted that although there are notable exceptions, religion in general, and religion as compensation in particular, may serve as a protective factor on youth adjustment and values. Finally, although cross-cultural considerations do not inevitably lead to marked changes in the substantive conclusions of this chapter, they do suggest that some forms of insecure attachment may be somewhat more common in some cultures than in others, that cultures may differ somewhat in the timing of attachment transfer from parents to peers, and that the religion as attachment idea may be more applicable in some cultures than in others.

In closing, while many questions remain unanswered, especially concerning cross-cultural generalizability of the connections proposed in this chapter, I maintain that attachment theory offers a viable framework for understanding the development of certain aspects of religion, adjustment, and values among youth. I encourage other researchers to further explore such links outside of the monotheistic faith traditions.

REFERENCES

Ainsworth, M. D. S. (1967). *Infancy in Uganda*. Baltimore: John Hopkins University Press.

Ainsworth, M. D. S., Blehar, M. C., Waters, E., & Wall, S. (1978) *Patterns of attachment: A psychological study of the strange situation*. Hillsdale, NJ: Erlbaum.

Allen, J. P. (2008). The attachment system in adolescence. In J. Cassidy & P. R. Shaver (Eds.), *Handbook of attachment: Theory, research, and clinical applications* (2nd Ed.) (pp. 419–435). New York: Guilford.

Argyle, M., & Beit-Hallahmi, B. (1975). *The social psychology of religion*. London: Routledge & Kegan Paul.

Armsden, G. C., & Greenberg, M. T. (1987). The inventory of parent and peer attachment: Individual differences and their relationship to psychological well-being. *Journal of Youth and Adolescence*, 16, 427–453.

Behrens, K. Y. (2004). A multifaceted view of the concept of amae: Reconsidering the indigenous Japanese concept of relatedness. *Human Development*, 47, 1–27.

Behrens, K. Y., Hesse, E., & Main, M. (2007). Mothers' attachment status as determined by the Adult Attachment Interview predicts their 6-year-olds' reunion responses: A study conducted in Japan. *Developmental Psychology*, 43, 1553–1567.

Birman, D., & Poff, M. (2010). Acculturation gaps and family adjustment. *International Society for the Study of Behavioural Development Bulletin*, Number 2 (Serial no. 58), 29–33.

Bowlby, J. (1969–1980) *Attachment and loss: Vols. 1–3*. New York: Basic Books.

(1988). *A secure base: Parent–child attachment and healthy human development*. New York: Basic Books.

Cassibba, R., Granqvist, P., Costantini, A., & Gatto, S. (2008). Attachment and God representations among lay Catholics, priests, and religious: A matched comparison study based on the Adult Attachment Interview. *Developmental Psychology*, 44, 1753–1763.

Cassidy, J., & Shaver, P. R. (Eds.). (2008). *Handbook of attachment: Theory, research, and clinical applications* (2nd Ed.). New York: Guilford.

DeWolff, M. S., & van IJzendoorn, M. H. (1997). Sensitivity and attachment: A meta-analysis on parental antecedents of infant attachment. *Child Development*, 68, 571–591.

Durrett, M. E., Otaki, M., & Richards, P. (1984). Attachment and the mother's perception of support from the father. *International Journal of Behavioural Development*, 7, 167–176.

Fraley, R. C., & Davis, K. E. (1997). Attachment formation and transfer in young adults' close friendships and romantic relationships. *Personal Relationships*, 4, 131–144.

Friedlmeier, W., & Granqvist, P. (2006). Attachment transfer among German and Swedish adolescents: A prospective longitudinal study. *Personal Relationships*, 13, 261–279.

Gill, A., & Lundsgaarde, E. (2004). State welfare spending and religiosity: A cross-national analysis. *Rationality and Society*, 16, 399–436.

Granqvist, P. (2002). Attachment and religiosity in adolescence: Cross-sectional and longitudinal evaluations. *Personality and Social Psychology Bulletin*, 28, 260–270.

(2003). Attachment theory and religious conversions: A review and a resolution of the classic and contemporary paradigm chasm. *Review of Religious Research*, 45, 172–187.

(2006). On the relation between secular and divine relationships: An emerging attachment perspective and a critique of the depth approaches. *The International Journal for the Psychology of Religion*, 16, 1–18.

Granqvist, P., Fransson, M., & Hagekull, B. (2009). Disorganized attachment, absorption, and New Age spirituality – A mediational model. *Attachment and Human Development*, 11, 385–403.

Granqvist, P., & Hagekull, B. (1999). Religiousness and perceived childhood attachment: Profiling socialized correspondence and emotional compensation. *Journal for the Scientific Study of Religion*, 38, 254–273.

(2001). Seeking security in the new age: On attachment and emotional compensation. *Journal for the Scientific Study of Religion*, 40, 529–547.

(2003). Longitudinal predictions of religious change in adolescence: Contributions from the interaction of attachment and relationship status. *Journal of Social and Personal Relationships*, 20, 793–817.

Granqvist, P., Hagekull, B., & Ivarsson, T. (2012). Disorganized attachment promotes mystical experiences via a propensity for alterations in consciousness (Absorption). *The International Journal for the Psychology of Religion*, 22, 180–197.

Granqvist, P., Ivarsson, T., Broberg, A. G., & Hagekull, B. (2007). Examining relations between attachment, religiosity, and New Age spirituality using the Adult Attachment Interview. *Developmental Psychology*, 43, 590–601.

Granqvist, P., & Kirkpatrick, L. A. (2004). Religious conversion and perceived childhood attachment: A meta-analysis. *The International Journal for the Psychology of Religion*, 14, 223–250.

(2008). Attachment and religious representations and behavior. In J. Cassidy & P. R. Shaver (Eds.), *Handbook of attachment: Theory, research, and clinical applications* (2nd Ed.) (pp. 906–933). New York: Guilford.

Granqvist, P., Mikulincer, M., & Shaver, P. R. (2010). Religion as attachment: Normative processes and individual differences. *Personality and Social Psychology Review*, 14, 49–59.

Grossmann, K., Grossmann, K. E., Spangler, K. Suess, G., & Unzner, L. (1985). Maternal sensitivity and newborns' orientation responses as related to quality of attachment in northern Germany. *Monographs of the Society of Research in Child Development*, 50 (1–2, Serial No. 209), 231–233.

Grossmann, K. E., & Grossmann, K. (1989). Preliminary observations on Japanese infants' behavior in Ainsworth's Strange Situation. *Annual Report of the Research and Clinical Center for Child Development*, no. 13, 1–12.

Hall, G. S. (1904). *Adolescence: Its psychology and relations to physiology, anthropology, sociology, sex, crime, religion and education (2 Vols.)*. New York: Appleton.

Hill, P. C. (2002). Spiritual transformation: Forming the habitual center of personal energy. *Research in the Social Scientific Study of Religion*, 13, 87–108.

Hood, R. W., Jr., Hill, P. C., & Spilka, B. (2009). *The psychology of religion: An empirical approach* (4th Ed.). New York: Guilford.

Houtman, D., & Aupers, S. (2007). The spiritual turn and the decline of tradition: The spread of post-Christian spirituality in 14 western countries, 1981–2000. *Journal for the Scientific Study of Religion*, 46, 305–320.

James, W. (1902). *The varieties of religious experience*. New York: Longmans, Green.

Kildahl, J. P. (1965). The personalities of sudden religious converts. *Pastoral Psychology*, **16**, 37–44.

Kirkpatrick, L. A. (2005). *Attachment, evolution, and the psychology of religion*. New York: Guilford.

Knafo, A., & Schwartz, S. H. (2001). Value socialization in families of Israeli-born and Soviet-born adolescents in Israel. *Journal of Cross-Cultural Psychology*, **32**, 213–228.

Kobak, R., & Ferenz-Gillies, R. (1995). Emotion regulation and depressive symptoms during adolescence: A functionalist perspective. *Development and Psychopathology*, **7**, 183–192.

Kobak, R., Ferenz-Gillies, R., Everhart, E., & Seabrook, L. (1994). Maternal attachment strategies and emotion regulation with adolescent offspring. *Journal of Research on Adolescence*, **4**, 553–566.

Kobak, R. R., Cole, H. E., Ferenz-Gillies, R., & Fleming, W. S. (1993). Attachment and emotion regulation during mother-teen problem solving: A control theory analysis. *Child Development*, **64**, 231–245.

Kupky, O. (1928). *The religious development of adolescents*. New York: MacMillan.

Lambert, W. W., Triandis, L. M., & Wolf, M. (1959). Some correlates of beliefs in the malevolence and benevolence of supernatural beings: A cross-societal study. *Journal of Abnormal and Social Psychology*, **58**, 162–169.

Lapsley, D. K., Rice, K. G., & Fitzgerald, D. P. (1990). Adolescent attachment, identity, and adjustment to college: Implications for the continuity of adaptation hypothesis. *Journal of Counseling and Development*, **68**, 561–565.

Larson, R. W., & Verma, S. (1999). How children and adolescents spend time across the world: Work, play, and developmental opportunities. *Psychological Bulletin*, **125**, 701–736.

Main, M., Goldwyn, R., & Hesse, E. (2003). *Adult attachment scoring and classification systems*. Unpublished manuscript, University of California at Berkeley.

Main, M., & Solomon, J. (1990) Procedures for identifying infants as disorganized/disoriented during the Ainsworth Strange Situation. In M. T. Greenberg, D. Cicchetti, & E. M. Cummings (Eds.), *Attachment in preschool years: Theory, research, and intervention* (pp. 121–160). Chicago: University of Chicago.

Mikulincer, M., & Shaver, P. R. (2007) *Attachment patterns in adulthood: Structure, dynamics, and change*. New York: Guilford.

Miyake, K., Chen, S., & Campos, J. (1985). Infant temperament, mother's mode of interaction, and attachment in Japan: An interim report. *Monographs of the Society of Research in Child Development*, **50** (1–2, Serial No. 209), 276–297.

Moore, K. A., & Glei, D. (1995). Taking the plunge: An examination of positive youth development. *Journal of Adolescent Research*, **10**, 15–40.

Pargament, K. (1997). *The psychology of religion and coping*. New York: Guilford.

Pirutinsky, S. (2009). Conversion and attachment insecurity among Orthodox Jews. *The International Journal for the Psychology of Religion*, **19**, 200–206.

Posada, G., Gao, Y., Wu, F., Posada, R., Tascon, M., Schoelmerich, A., … Lynnevaag, B. (1995). The secure-base phenomenon across cultures: Children's behavior, mothers' preferences and experts concepts. In E. Waters, B. E. Vaughan, G. Posada, & K. Kondo-Ikemura (Eds.), *Caregiving, cultural, and cognitive perspectives on secure-base behavior and working models* (pp. 27–48). Chicago: Chicago University of Chicago Press.

Resnick, M. D., Bearman, P. S., Blum, R. W., Bauman, K. E., Harris, K. M., Jones, J., ... Udry, J. R. (1997). Protecting adolescents from harm: Findings from the national longitudinal study on adolescent health. *Journal of the American Medical Association*, **278**, 823–832.

Rice, K. G. (1990). Attachment and adolescence: A narrative and meta-analytic review. *Journal of Youth and Adolescence*, **19**, 511–538.

Richters, J. E., & Waters, E. (1991). Attachment and socialization: The positive side of social influence. In M. Lewis & S. Feinman (Eds.), *Social influences and socialization in infancy* (Genesis of Behavior Series, Vol. 6, pp. 185–213). New York: Plenum.

Rohner, R. P. (1986). *The warmth dimension: Foundations of parental acceptance-rejection theory*. Newbury Park, CA: Sage.

Roof, W. C., & McKinney, W. (1987). *American mainline religion: Its changing shape and future*. New Brunswick, NJ: Rutgers University Press.

Rothbaum, F., Weisz, J., Pott, M., Miyake, K., & Morelli, G. (2000). Attachment and culture: Security in the United States and Japan. *American Psychologist*, **55**, 1093–1104.

Schlegel, A., & Barry, H., III. (1991). *Adolescence: An anthropological inquiry*. New York: Free Press.

Schnitker, S. A., Porter, T. J., Emmons, R. A., & Barrett, J. L. (2012). Attachment predicts adolescent conversions at Young Life religious summer camps. *The International Journal for the Psychology of Religion*, **22**, 198–215.

Smetana, J. G. (2002). Culture, autonomy, and personal jurisdiction in adolescent–parent relationships. In R. V. Kail & H. W. Reese (Eds.), *Advances in child development and behavior* (Vol. 29, pp. 51–87). San Diego, CA: Academic Press.

Smith, T. B., McCullough, M. E., & Poll, J. (2003). Religiousness and depression: Evidence for a main-effect and the moderating influence of stressful life-events. *Psychological Bulletin*, **129**, 614–636.

Spellman, C. M., Baskett, G. D., & Byrne, D. (1971). Manifest anxiety as a contributing factor in religious conversion. *Journal of Consulting and Clinical Psychology*, **36**, 245–247.

Sroufe, L. A., & Waters, E. (1977). Attachment as an organizational construct. *Child Development*, **48**, 1184–1199.

Starbuck, E. D. (1899). *The psychology of religion*. New York: Scribner.

Stayton, D., Hogan, R., & Ainsworth, M. D. S. (1971). Infant obedience and maternal behavior: The origins of socialization reconsidered. *Child Development*, **42**, 1057–1069.

Steinberg, L. (1990). Interdependency in the family: Autonomy, conflict, and harmony in the parent–adolescent relationship. In S. Feldman & G. Elliott (Eds.), *At the threshold: The developing adolescent* (pp. 225–276). Cambridge, MA: Harvard University Press.

Steinberg, L. D., & Morris, A. S. (2001). Adolescent development. *Annual Review of Psychology*, **52**, 83–110.

Takahashi, K. (1986). Examining the strange-situation procedure with Japanese mothers and 12-month-old infants. *Developmental Psychology*, **22**, 265–270.

Tamminen, K. (1994). Religious experiences in childhood and adolescence: A viewpoint of religious development between the ages of 7 and 20. *The International Journal for the Psychology of Religion*, **4**, 61–85.

Ullman, C. (1982). Change of mind, change of heart: Some cognitive and emotional antecedents of religious conversion. *Journal of Personality and Social Psychology*, **42**, 183–192.

van IJzendoorn, M. H., & Sagi-Schwartz, A. (2008). Cross-cultural patterns of attachment: Universal and contextual dimensions. In J. Cassidy & P. R. Shaver (Eds.), *Handbook of attachment: Theory, research, and clinical applications* (2nd Ed.) (pp. 880–905). New York: Guilford.

van IJzendoorn, M. H., Schuengel, C., & Bakermans-Kranenburg, M. J. (1999). Disorganized attachment in early childhood: Meta-analysis of precursors, concomitants, and sequelae. *Development and Psychopathology*, **11**, 225–250.

Weiss, R. S. (1982). Attachment in adult life. In C. M. Parkes & J. Stevenson-Hinde (Eds.), *The place of attachment in human behavior* (pp. 171–184). New York: Basic Books.

Youniss, J., McLelan, J. A., & Yates, M. (1999). Religion, community service, and identity in American youth. *Journal of Adolescence*, **22**, 243–253.

Zeifman, D., & Hazan, C. (2008). Pair bonds as attachments: Evaluating the evidence. In J. Cassidy & P. R. Shaver (Eds.), *Handbook of attachment: Theory, research, and clinical applications* (2nd Ed.) (pp. 906–933). New York: Guilford.

Zhang, H., Chan, D. K. S., & Teng, F. (2011). Transfer of attachment functions and adjustment among young adults in China. *The Journal of Social Psychology*, **151**, 257–273.

Zinnbauer, B. J., & Pargament, K. I. (1998). Spiritual conversion: A study of religious change among college students. *Journal for the Scientific Study of Religion*, **37**, 161–180.

15 Cross-Cultural Perspectives on Adolescents' Religiosity and Family Orientation

Boris Mayer and Gisela Trommsdorff

Abstract

This chapter explores cultural and individual religious roots of adolescents' family orientation on the basis of multilevel analyses with data from 17 cultural groups. Religion and the family are seen as intertwined social institutions. The family as a source of social support has been identified as an important mediator of the effects of religiosity on adolescent developmental outcomes. The results of the current study show that religiosity was related to different aspects of adolescents' family orientation (traditional family values, value of children, and family future orientation), and that the culture-level effects of religiosity on family orientation were stronger than the individual-level effects. At the cultural level, socioeconomic development added to the effect of religiosity, indicating that societal affluence combined with nonreligious secular orientations is linked to a lower family orientation, especially with regard to traditional family values. The authors suggest that individual religiosity may be of special importance for adolescents' family orientation in contexts where religiosity has lost some significance but religious traditions are still alive and can be (re-)connected to.

Religion and the family represent closely linked social institutions. Both function through psychological processes that may vary during development and across cultures. Religious socialization takes place in families, and religions in turn can influence family life. The focus of the current chapter is on the relation between adolescents' religiosity and their family orientation. Taking a cross-cultural and multilevel perspective, we will both theoretically and empirically explore three major questions: How are adolescents similar or different across cultures with respect to the importance of religious beliefs and family orientation? How are adolescents' religiosity and family orientation related in different cultures? And, how is nation-level religiosity as well as nation-level socioeconomic development related to adolescents' family orientation? We deal with these questions on the basis of data from the cross-cultural research project "Value of Children and Intergenerational Relations" (Trommsdorff & Nauck, 2005).

Adolescence is a sensitive period for religious and spiritual development. Because of the intermediate position between childhood and adulthood and the related insecurities, adolescents' identity development comes with an intense striving for meaning and a need for autonomy and relatedness (Erikson, 1968; Youniss & Smollar, 1985). Therefore, adolescents often engage in religious and spiritual exploration (Elkind, 1964; Good & Willoughby, 2008; Oser, Scarlett, & Bucher, 2006). According to Elkind (1999), adolescents (especially those in Western societies) prefer an intense personal religiosity and consider the formal aspects of religiousness (e.g., regular church attendance) to be less important (see also Lopez, Huynh, & Fuligni, 2011). Therefore, our focus here is on adolescents' subjective importance subscribed to religious beliefs.

Numerous cross-sectional and longitudinal studies have shown that religiosity is associated with better physical and mental health (George, Ellison, & Larson, 2002; Hackney & Sanders, 2003). For adolescents, Wagener, Furrow, King, Leffert, and Benson (2003) showed that religiosity was related to lower risk-taking, successful coping, and higher prosocial values and behavior (see also French, Eisenberg, Sallquist, & Purwono, Chapter 6 in this volume). Similar results with respect to moral outcomes (e.g., empathic concern and altruism) were reported by King and Furrow (2004) and Youniss, McLellan, and Yates (1999).

As mechanisms or mediators of these effects, some studies have identified religion's positive influences on social support, community inclusion, and on a stable sense of identity (Cohen, 2002; George et al., 2002; Steger & Frazier, 2005; Wagener et al., 2003). Critical voices argue that religion is not the only source of these (secular) mediators and suggest that researchers focus on the mediators themselves rather than on religion per se (Funder, 2002). On the contrary, Pargament (2002b) points to the unique effects of religion emphasizing the "sacred" as a powerful defining feature of religion. Furthermore, the kind of religious practice and religiosity also play a role: whereas an intrinsically motivated religiosity has been positively linked to well-being, an imposed and unexamined religiosity has been negatively linked (Pargament, 2002a) (see also Kornadt, Chapter 2 in this volume;

Saroglou, Chapter 17 in this volume). Whether religion's effects on adolescent development are unique or mediated, there is no doubt that the *family* as an essential source of social support plays an important role for the link between religiosity and adolescent developmental outcomes (Regnerus & Burdette, 2006; Sabatier, Mayer, Friedlmeier, Lubiewska, & Trommsdorff, 2011). Therefore, the focus of the current chapter is to understand the relations between adolescent religiosity and their family orientation. Before dealing more closely with this issue, the necessity of a cross-cultural perspective will be emphasized.

Most studies on psychological functions of religiosity are based on Western, educated, industrialized, rich, and democratic (WEIRD, see Henrich, Heine, & Norenzayan, 2010) samples. The question arises as to what extent (if at all) results based on these samples can be generalized to adolescents from different cultural contexts. In spite of growing global connections through the Internet along with the dissemination of mainstream (North American) pop music and movies that have arguably led to a universal popular youth culture (Dasen, 2000; Jensen, 2003; Schlegel, 2000), cross-cultural and cross-ethnic studies on several aspects of adolescents' lives show that large cultural differences still prevail (Brown, Larson, & Saraswathi, 2002; Fuligni, Tseng, & Lam, 1999; Mayer & Trommsdorff, 2010). Furthermore, a globalized youth culture in modernizing, but in large part still traditional, cultural contexts like India or China may be restricted to adolescents from urban areas and a Western-oriented middle-class youth. Even the concept of "emerging adulthood" may only hold for Western developmental contexts (Arnett, 2010).

Few studies shed light on the function of religiosity for adolescent development across cultures. In samples of African American and European-American 11th graders, Markstrom (1999) found that various forms of religious involvement were associated with indicators of ego strength and psychosocial maturity. In a recent study comparing the mediating role of adolescents' family orientation in the relation between religiosity and life satisfaction across four Christian cultures, Sabatier et al. (2011) found that religiosity was indirectly related to adolescent life satisfaction via family orientation across all four cultures (France, Germany, Poland, and the United States). In a study of U.S. adolescents with Latin American, Asian, and European backgrounds, Lopez, Huynh, and Fuligni (2011) showed that regardless of religious and cultural background, changes in adolescents' religious identity were closely related to changes in their family identity.

Researchers have also taken cross-cultural perspectives on the role of religion for the study of *value orientations* (see Bond, Lun, & Li, Chapter 5 in this volume; Schwartz, Chapter 4 in this volume). Values represent standards of behavior ("oughts" and "shoulds") that are transmitted by various social institutions, such as religion. Early studies on the relation between religiosity and values found that religious participants reported a higher importance of values like salvation, forgiveness, and obedience than did nonreligious participants, who reported a higher importance of independence, pleasure, and intellectualism (Rokeach, 1969). Later studies using the Schwartz' circumplex model of values tended to find similar associations (e.g., Schwartz & Huismans, 1995). In a meta-analysis, Saroglou, Delpierre, and Dernelle (2004) corroborated these findings across 21 samples from 15 countries and three denominations (Christians, Jews, and Muslims): higher religiosity was positively related to values supporting the preservation of the social order and to prosocial values whereas it was negatively related to values promoting openness to change and autonomy as well as to hedonistic values. These cross-cultural relations between religiosity and prosocial, as well as socially conservative values, are related to the main question of this chapter: what is the relation between adolescents' religiosity and their family orientation? Religion has been identified as a "propagator" of family ideologies (Pearce & Thornton, 2007, p. 1227) which are in turn related to family-relevant behaviors like the decision to have children (Barber, 2000). The link between religiosity and family orientation is an understudied field (Pankhurst & Houseknecht, 2000) and is especially important during the transition to adulthood (Pearce & Thornton, 2007). We understand family orientation as a construct encompassing traditional family values, values of children, and the importance of a future family. This broad definition allows us to study the effects of religiosity on several aspects of family orientation including normative and subjective emotional aspects, and general as well as personal future-oriented aspects.

The following empirical portion of this chapter consists of three sections. First, we analyze cross-cultural similarities and differences in adolescents' religiosity and their family orientation. Second, we focus on the relation between religiosity and family orientation within different cultures and on a potentially moderating role of culture-level religiosity for this relation. The third section is concerned with culture-level effects of religiosity and of a nation's socioeconomic development on adolescents' family orientation. In all three sections we introduce the respective topic theoretically and subsequently present results of cross-cultural and multilevel analyses from the Value of Children Study.

Adolescents' Religiosity and Family Orientation across Cultures: The Roles of Secularization and Modernization

The cross-cultural study of the psychology of religion is an understudied field (Tarakeshwar, Stanton, & Pargament, 2003). In this section, we will first discuss the phenomenon of secularization and the related topic of the transmission of religiosity in different cultural contexts. Then we will discuss to what degree modernization processes affect the significance of the family across cultural contexts. Subsequently, we will introduce the sample of the Value of Children Study and present cross-cultural empirical findings on adolescents' religiosity and family orientation.

Decline of Religiosity: The Secularization Thesis

The question of a decline of religiosity and a rise of secular orientations is quite controversial (e.g., see Halman & Pettersson, 2006). In a large-scale longitudinal study of religion and its intergenerational transmission, Bengtson and colleagues analyzed the changes of religious beliefs, values, and practices across three decades and three connected generations in the United States (Bengtson, Copen, Putney, & Silverstein, 2009). From 1971 to 2000 there was a considerable decline of reported religious affiliation for all three generations. This result is in line with the phenomenon of secularization, reflecting a continuous decline of religiosity in Western Europe and the English-speaking world during the second half of the 20th century (Inglehart & Baker, 2000). Secularization has been described as resulting from modernization, economic development, and individualization. Though it is acknowledged that traditional religious values can persist to some degree (Inglehart & Baker, 2000; Inkeles, 1998), some authors assume that sooner or later all cultures will overcome traditional religious values and come to prefer secular–rational and autonomous self-expressive values ("human development sequence," see Inglehart & Welzel, 2005).

This view has not been unchallenged. Georgas (2006) argues that the thrust of modernization itself is based on religious and cultural values that developed out of Calvinist Protestantism. In a similar vein, Eisenstadt (1973) postulates that the development of transcendental religions during the axial age (Confucianism, Buddhism, Hinduism, Judaism, Christianity, and later Islam) are the basis of later modernization processes. According to this view, axial civilizations are characterized by a tension between transcendental and worldly orientations. This tension leads to the conception of the world and human beings as in need of redemption and correction or improvement. Instead of a single modernity as implicated by Inglehart's model, Eisenstadt (2006) suggests the presence of multiple modernities based on each culture's unique way of dealing with this tension.

In a study of Christian societies with data from the International Social Survey Programme, Höllinger and Haller (2009) conclude that although traditional forms of religion have declined considerably in some cultures, religion continues to play an important role in the public sphere as well as in private life in other cultures. They argue that the worldviews and doctrines of Protestantism have led to a greater "disenchantment of the world" (p. 281) and to a subsequent decline of religiosity as compared to Catholicism and Orthodoxy (see also Georgas, 2006). Furthermore, bureaucratic state churches (as in some Western European countries) and Communism in Eastern Europe were related to lower religiosity. The historical significance of religion in the United States owing to an emphasis on religious freedom (in contrast with Europe) has possibly contributed to the relatively small decline in the importance of religion in this country. A declining importance of religion has also been accorded to socioeconomic development: economic prosperity and the rise of welfare state provisions can buffer existential risks related to religious needs. However, there is no direct link: in a cross-cultural study, Georgas, van de Vijver, and Berry (2004) showed that religion and economic prosperity (at the cultural level) were related to psychological variables in different and partly contrasting ways.

Transmission of Religiosity: Family and Society
Closely related to the issue of religious decline or persistence is the question of how religiosity and related value orientations are transmitted from generation to generation within a specific cultural context (see also Knafo, Daniel, Gabay, Zilber, & Shir, Chapter 16 in this volume). This question has been studied from a socialization theoretical perspective focusing on transmission processes between generations from the same family (vertical transmission) and from a cohort approach focusing on the influence of peers, culture, and the *zeitgeist* (i.e., the general intellectual and political climate within a nation or cultural group) (horizontal and oblique transmission). How do these transmission processes contribute to the decline versus stability of religion in different cultural contexts?

According to Boyatzis, Dollahite, and Marks (2006) the factor with the greatest impact on children's religious development is the socialization experience within the family. In their three-generation longitudinal study, Bengtson et al. (2009) found that parents as well as grandparents substantially influenced several aspects of their offspring's religiosity. Thus, for most adolescents, the importance of a specific religious belief is strongly influenced by their family's religious beliefs (see also Regnerus, Smith, & Smith, 2004; Trommsdorff, 2009a). Kelley and De Graaf (1997) analyzed the transmission of religious beliefs by way of parental socialization in 15 nations in the International Social Survey Programme (ISSP). The focus was on the moderating influence of the cultural religious environment on how religious beliefs are transmitted across generations. The results showed that after controlling for a nation's level of economic development and for exposure to Communism, "people living in religious nations will, in proportion to the religiosity of their fellow-citizens, acquire more orthodox beliefs than otherwise similar people living in secular nations" (p. 639). Furthermore, in more secular nations, parents' religiosity had a greater impact on children's religiosity, and the national religious context had a smaller impact than in more religious nations. In turn, parents' religiosity was less related to child religiosity in cultures with a high normativity of religion whereas the national context had a greater effect in these cultures. Thus, the relative importance of vertical and horizontal/oblique transmission processes depends on the cultural context. In cultures where most people are religious and where one specific religion prevails, the family is only one among many socialization agents for religious beliefs. In these societies, peers, schools, the media, and religious institutions contribute to religious socialization and enculturation, building on the highly normative and shared collective notion of religious truth. As Baumeister (2002) notes,

It is easier for an individual to maintain religious faith if he or she lives in a community where everyone else holds that same faith [and] it is far more difficult to maintain one's own faith while living amid people who do not share your faith and who instead either subscribe to other, alternative religious beliefs or reject religious belief altogether (p. 166).

Differential transmission processes depending on the nation-level religious context thus may reinforce a culture's tendency to either change to more secular values (as in the case of a plurality of religious beliefs and/or an already lowered normativity of religion) or to keep religious values at a constantly high level (as in the case of a high normativity and exclusivity of one specific religion). Taken together, the above theorizing lets us expect substantial cross-cultural differences in the religiosity of adolescents from cultures that differ with regard to the normativity of religion, economic development, and basic value orientations.

Because values regarding the family are deeply rooted in many religious traditions, a parallel decline of family orientation can be expected for cultures where religious beliefs are on the decline. Indeed, modernization theoretical approaches support this argument, but they are not uncontended, as will be shown in the next section.

Modernization and Family Change

Discussion about the decline of the family can be traced back to the French Revolution, which disturbed the equilibrium of the traditional extended family system and patriarchal authority (according to Auguste Comte, as cited in Georgas, 2006). Similarly, Parsons (1949) argued that the industrial revolution required the formation of a nuclear family that became more and more alienated from its extended kin network. There are manifold indicators of this decline continuing today: an increasing number of single-parent families; an increasing divorce rate; an increase of step-families and patchwork families; and, most of all, a declining birth rate (Georgas, 2006; Goode, 1963). The post-nuclear family (Popenoe, 1988) is characterized by a further decreasing family size, fewer joint activities and less quality contact between parents and children, and reduced contact with collateral kin (e.g., aunts, nephews, etc.), but more contact with grandparents. According to Bengtson (2001), this increasing importance of multigenerational bonds may signify a qualitative change in family solidarity structures rather than a decline of the family. Pankhurst and Houseknecht (2000) argue that in spite of the manifold changes that religion and the family undergo in the modern era, both institutions are not on the decline but still vital and important in most societies, raising doubts with regard to the general validity of the secularization thesis and the thesis of family decline.

Whereas it is commonly agreed that the above-mentioned indicators reflect a weakening of familial bonds in modernized Western cultures, the implications for modernizing non-Western cultures remain unclear. In many modernizing societies, a trend toward a separate residence for the nuclear conjugal family can be observed. However, can we also observe a functional nucleation, or do the relationships to the extended kin network stay intact (Inkeles, 1998)? In India, for example, the extended family members are still psychologically and normatively connected to each other despite being separated by large distances (Mishra, Mayer, Trommsdorff, Albert, & Schwarz, 2005; Sinha, 1991).

Yang (1996) suggests that psychological change in modernization is restricted to those cultural and psychological characteristics that are incompatible with a modern way of life. The question is here whether these characteristics include a decline in personal closeness between family members and kin as proposed by classical modernization theory (Inkeles & Smith, 1974). Kagitcibasi (2007) contends that despite socioeconomic development, a shift towards lower emotional closeness among family members is not taking place in modernizing cultures. Rather, she postulates a shift toward a *family model of emotional interdependence* in these cultures, characterized by continuing emotional interdependence but declining material interdependence (and rising personal autonomy). Studies directly testing these assumptions are rare. In a large study of families in 30 cultures, Georgas, Berry, van de Vijver, Kagitcibasi, and Poortinga (2006) examined cross-cultural differences on a number of measures (family values, family roles, etc.) both from the perspective of the ecocultural framework (e.g., Georgas et al., 2004) and from Kagitcibasi's theory of family change. Results showed that with socioeconomic development of a culture, family values became less traditional, family networks and emotional cohesion less strong, and family roles less expressive, in line with the expectations of the ecocultural framework. The expectations with regard to Kagitcibasi's model were also partly confirmed: nuclear family relationships were close in modernizing cultures and even in Western individualistic cultures, suggesting a trend to the emotionally interdependent family model. Thus, modernization in terms of socioeconomic development does have a weakening effect on the significance of the family in society, but more traditional (hierarchical and patriarchal) aspects of the family seem to be more affected than the importance of the family in general (see also Trommsdorff, 2009b). A more direct test of the theory of family change was carried out recently by Mayer, Trommsdorff, Kagitcibasi, and Mishra (2012). Using mothers' and adolescents' data from three cultures in the Value of Children Study (Germany, Turkey, and India), the authors identified three patterns of family values that could be related to the three ideal-typical family models suggested by Kagitcibasi (2007). Furthermore, the cross-cultural and cross-generational differences with regard to these family value patterns were in line with predictions based on the theory of family change.

To conclude, both socioeconomic development and the role of religion have important implications for the role of the family in a culture. As previously discussed, however, socioeconomic development cannot be equated with religious decline/secularization. In this sense, religious traditions may be an important factor for canalizing changes brought about by modernization processes. Consequently, both phenomena (socioeconomic development and religion) are assumed to have unique effects on the significance of the family in a society.

The Value of Children (VOC) Study

The data presented here is part of the cross-cultural and international research project "Value of Children and Intergenerational Relations" (Trommsdorff & Nauck, 2005), which studied family-related values, intergenerational relations and support, as well as family-related future orientation of adolescents in connected samples of families (grandmothers, mothers, and adolescents). The data for the current chapter includes the adolescent samples from 17 cultural groups (see Table 15.1). In all cultures, participants were surveyed by members of the local collaborating team, completing a questionnaire either at home or in school. In cultures where strong urban–rural differences continue to exist (i.e., China, India, Indonesia, Poland, South Africa, and Turkey), samples from both rural and urban areas were included. In all other cultures, adolescents from suburban or urban regions were considered typical for the cultures. The participants were between 12 and 23 years old, with 98 percent of the sample being between 13 and 19 years old ("teenagers"); the overall mean age was 15.6 years (SD = 1.65 years). All adolescents over the age of 20 came from Switzerland (M age: 19.8 years). Because participants' ages differed significantly across cultural groups, age was included as a covariate in all cross-cultural comparisons. Participants from Israel were all Jewish, partly from secular and partly from Orthodox Jewish contexts. Participants from South Africa were recruited from the Northern Sotho cultural group (Limpopo Province), whose standard of living is considerably below the South African average (Sam, Peltzer, & Mayer, 2005). There were two Indian samples: one from Northern India (Varanasi area), and one from Southern India (Puducherry area). Because the two Indian samples are culturally diverse and speak different languages (Hindi in the North, Tamil in the South) we consider them as separate cultural groups for our analyses.

The cultures represent a wide range of economic development, considerable differences in exposure to Communism, and in secular–rational value orientations, all of which should be related to lower religiosity and to a lower family orientation. To assess adolescents' religiosity, we asked for their religious belief/affiliation and for the importance of these religious beliefs. The latter was a one-item measure, with ratings ranging from 1 (*not important at all*) to 5 (*very important*); it was only to be answered if a specific religious belief was indicated before. If participants indicated that they were not religious/had no religious affiliation, a value of 1 (*not important at all*) was set a posteriori in the importance measure. Of the overall sample, 22 percent were Roman Catholic Christians, 9 percent were Protestant Christians, 7 percent were Orthodox Christians, and 4 percent were of other Christian denominations. Thirteen percent were affiliated to Islam; 12 percent to Hinduism; 4 percent to Judaism; 2 percent to Buddhism, Shintoism, Taoism or Confucianism; and 1 percent believed in Animism, Paganism or reported a personal religious belief. The largest group of 26 percent reported no religious belief (see Table 15.1 for further information).

Table 15.1. Cultures, Sample Composition, and Religious Affiliation

Region/Country	n	% Female	% Non-religious	Highest Religious Affiliation (%)[1]
North America				
United States	337	64	12	Protestantism (58 %)
Europe				
France	200	55	35	Roman Catholicism (58 %)
Germany	311	56	44	Roman Catholicism (26 %)
Switzerland	131	58	26	Roman Catholicism (28 %)
Italy	381	54	15	Roman Catholicism (84 %)
Poland	327	60	2	Roman Catholicism (94 %)
Czech Republic	260	100	79	Roman Catholicism (17 %)
Estonia	300	51	84	Protestantism (6 %)
Russia	334	54	12	Orthodox Christian Church (86 %)
Middle East				
Turkey	308	53	3	Islam (93 %)
Israel	194	63	9	Judaism (90 %)
Africa				
South Africa	317	62	1	Protestantism (incl. Zion Christian Church) (48 %)
Southeast Asia				
India (North)	300	51	1	Hinduism (94%)
India (South)	300	50	2	Hinduism (98%)
Indonesia	300	50	0	Islam (98 %)
East Asia				
China	306	58	83	Confucianism (7%)
Japan	208	63	66	Buddhism (15 %)

Note: [1] Religious denomination indicated by the highest percentage of adolescents in the respective culture (and its proportion in the full cultural sample), regardless of whether "No religion" was the dominant category or not.

Adolescents' Religiosity across Cultures. A comparison of the importance of adolescents' religious beliefs yielded large cross-cultural differences with culture explaining half of the variance in adolescents' religiosity, $F(16, 4610) = 285.30$, $p < .001$, $\eta^2 = .50$. Figure 15.1 shows that adolescents from Indonesia reported the highest importance of religion, followed by Northern Indian, South African, Polish, Turkish, and Southern Indian adolescents. An importance of religion at or slightly below the midpoint of the scale was reported by U.S., Israeli, Russian, and Italian adolescents. Swiss, French, and German adolescents reported a low importance of religion and Japanese, Czech, Chinese, and Estonian adolescents reported a very low importance of

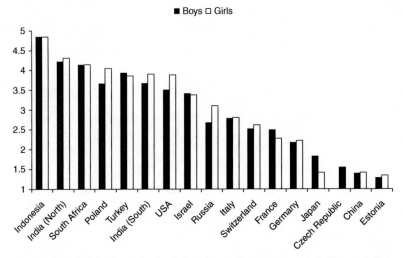

Figure 15.1. Cultural and gender differences in the importance of religious beliefs.

religion. Gender and its interaction with culture each explained ≤ 1 percent of the overall variance and are not considered in detail here.

Overall, adolescents from more prosperous nations reported to be less religious than adolescents from less well-off nations. However, the considerable differences between Western European and U.S. adolescents indicate that economic development cannot be equaled with religious decline. German adolescents' low level of religiosity was additionally influenced by the sample composition: one third of the German sample came from East Germany, where the exposure to Communistic ideology resulted in a very low level of religious affiliation. This can also be observed in two Eastern European nations – Estonia and the Czech Republic – where an extremely low level of religiosity was reported. Despite a similar Communist experience in Poland and Russia, a high level of religiosity was reported there. In Poland, Catholicism helped to preserve the Polish national identity during the Communist era, and in Russia, a revival of traditional values has been observed during the last two decades (Höllinger & Haller, 2009; Mayer, Kuramschew, & Trommsdorff, 2009; Stetsenko, 2002). Communism has also had a diminishing effect on Chinese adolescents' religiosity, but here additional factors come into play. Many Chinese (still, and despite Communism) adhere strongly to Confucian philosophy but do not regard themselves as religious. A similar phenomenon with respect to Shintoist or Daoist beliefs may be responsible for the very low level of Japanese adolescents' self-reported religiosity. Here, cultural differences in the *meaning* of religion are relevant (see Trommsdorff, 2012).

Adolescents' Family Orientation across Cultures. As indicated above, adolescents' family orientation is operationalized here as entailing adolescents' values with respect to (traditional) family relations, their value of children, and their future orientation with regard to having their own family (Mayer & Trommsdorff, 2010; Seginer, 2009). In the following sections, we introduce the instruments measuring adolescents' family orientation and present the results of cross-cultural comparisons. The effects of gender and its interaction with culture will not be reported in detail because of negligible effect sizes ($\eta^2 \leq .01$).

- *Family Values* are assessed using a 5-item scale that measures a traditional view on the family and family relationships based on Georgas' (1991) scale. Sample items include: "We should honor and protect our family's reputation" and "Children should obey their parents." With the exception of South Africa ($\alpha = .45$), the internal consistencies (Cronbach's alpha) were between .57 and .81 for the 17 cultures in the study. The ANOVA showed that culture explained a substantial amount of the variance of family values, $F(16, 4695) = 84.53$, $p < .001$, $\eta^2 = .22$. The highest importance of family values was reported by South African adolescents; the lowest by Japanese adolescents (see Figure 15.2).
- *Emotional Values of Children* represent emotional reasons for having children. Sample items include "Because it is a joy to have a small baby" and "Because of the special feeling of love that develops between a parent and a child." The scale was developed for the Value of Children Study (e.g., Arnold et al., 1975; Kagitcibasi, 1982; Schwarz, Chakkarath, Trommsdorff, Schwenk, & Nauck, 2001). The cross-cultural construct equivalence of the value of children dimensions has been demonstrated (Mayer & Trommsdorff, 2010). Cronbach's alphas of this 7-item scale were between .72 and .89. The culture effect was relatively weak, $F(16, 4692) = 23.44$, $p < .001$, $\eta^2 = .07$. The highest importance of emotional values of children was reported by Southern Indian adolescents, and the lowest by Israeli adolescents (see Figure 15.2).
- *Utilitarian–normative Values of Children* combine economic–utilitarian and social–normative reasons for having children (Kagitcibasi, 1982). Example items include "To have one more person to help your family economically" and "Because some of your older relatives feel that you

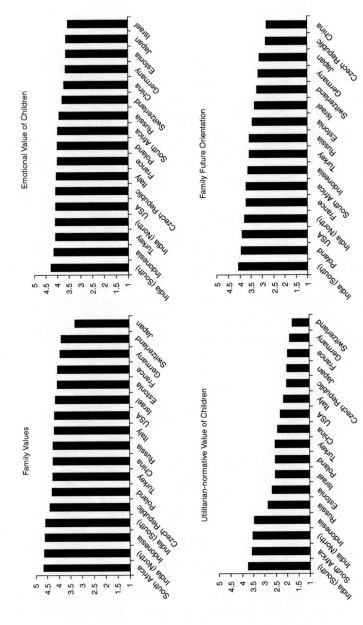

Figure 15.2. Cultural differences in family orientation: Family Values, Emotional VOC, Utilitarian-normative VOC, and Family Future Orientation.

should have more children." With the exception of Southern Indian adolescents ($\alpha = .55$) Cronbach's alphas for this 8-item scale were between .68 and .86. There was a strong culture effect, $F(16, 4692) = 180.88$, $p < .001$, $\eta^2 = .38$. Southern Indian adolescents reported the highest importance of these values, and Swiss adolescents reported the lowest importance (see Figure 15.2).

- *Family Future Orientation* indicates to what extent the statement "Family will be the most important thing in my life; everything else will be less important" corresponds with adolescents' personal way of thinking on a scale ranging from 1 (*Not at all*) to 5 (*Quite a lot*). Data from Italy was not available for this variable. Cultural differences were substantial, $F(15, 4306) = 27.73$, $p < .001$, $\eta^2 = .15$, with adolescents from Southern India reporting the highest importance and adolescents from China reporting the lowest importance of a future family.

Overall, the results indicate strong cultural differences for *Family Values* and *Utilitarian-normative Values of Children*. As shown in Figure 15.2, these differences are also substantially related to a culture's level of religiosity and economic prosperity, as cultures that were both highly religious and relatively poor (Indonesia, South Africa, and the two Indian samples) reported the highest family values and utilitarian–normative VOCs, whereas the rather secular and wealthy Western European and East Asian cultures (Japan) reported the lowest level of these values. Weaker differences were found for *Family Future Orientation* and *Emotional Values of Children*. Here, no relations with culture-level religiosity or economic prosperity are obvious from Figure 15.2. Thus, we may preliminarily conclude that a decreased importance of the family as a consequence of modernization processes can be observed with regard to the two more traditional and conservative–normative aspects of family orientation (family values and utilitarian–normative VOC), but not for the two aspects related to emotional closeness and more personal issues (emotional VOC and family future orientation). In the remainder of this chapter, we will examine and present concrete empirical evidence for this preliminary observation.

In the next section we turn to our main objective: analyzing the effect of adolescents' religiosity on their family orientation both within and across cultures. Within cultures, we will explore how individual religiosity affects the four aspects of family orientation (and how the religious context moderates this influence); across cultures, we will analyze how the religious context and other cultural characteristics are related to adolescents' family orientation at the cultural level.

Relations between Religiosity and Family Orientation: Multilevel Perspectives

The family may be the most important source of social capital for adolescents and functions as an important mediator for the relation between religiosity and well-being. Furthermore, the family plays an important role in religious worldviews and religious moral doctrines (Dollahite, Marks, & Goodman, 2004; Pankhurst & Houseknecht, 2000). Thus, as a cultural system, religion shapes family values and can instill an "ethos" of the family (Chatters & Taylor, 2005). Many religions (e.g., Islam, Judaism, most traditions in Christianity) pronounce family relations and specific family roles and hierarchies as sacred. Moral directives derived from religious doctrines (e.g., that children are advised to honor their parents) "can constitute a key form of religious influence among youth" and can offer "purposes and processes that have no direct equivalent within secular systems of meaning and motivation" (Regnerus & Burdette, 2006, p. 178). The sanctification of family relationships can have desirable implications for family life (Mahoney, Pargament, Murray-Swank, & Murray-Swank, 2003). Taking the Christian tradition as an example, many scriptures in the Bible (especially in the Old Testament) affirm and authorize positive norms of filial obligations and assistance to family members. The milestones of family life, such as birth and marriage, are celebrated through religious rituals and ceremonies.

Most of the literature in the field is concerned with (1) possible links between religion and parents' marital and parental functioning and with (2) the role of religion for the formation of family bonds. In these studies, religion is often not only seen as a promoting factor for family cohesion, but also as a potentially problematic authority legitimizing abusive forms of parental discipline and domestic violence, especially in very traditional families (see the review by Mahoney, 2010, based on studies with mainly Christian denominations and U.S. samples). With regard to the perspective of adolescents, Agate, Zabriskie, and Eggett (2007) reported a positive effect of family religiosity for family functioning (cohesion and adaptability) in a U.S. sample with a diverse religious background. Using data from the American National Longitudinal Study of Adolescent Health, Regnerus and Burdette (2006) found that a growing religious salience over time was consistently related to better family relations. Gamoran (1992) found that U.S. Jewish adolescents' synagogue attendance and their family orientation were positively related. In a 31-year longitudinal study, Pearce and Thornton (2007) found that mothers' religious affiliation and religious service attendance at the time when the child was born was significantly positively related to various indicators of the child's family ideology when the child was 23 and 31 years old, respectively. Furthermore, they found that the child's own religiosity at age 18 was substantially related to his/her family ideology at later ages.

Sabatier et al. (2011) found a weaker positive relation between adolescent religiosity and family orientation in low-religiosity cultures as compared to high-religiosity cultures. A similar moderating effect of the religious context has been found for the link between religiosity and psychological well-being (e.g., Lavric & Flere, 2008). As Okulicz-Kozaryn (2010) summarizes, "religiosity makes people happier in religious nations" (p. 166). However, only forms of religiosity that promote social capital were related to higher life satisfaction in this study (Okulicz-Kozaryn, 2010). Thus, sharing religious norms to a substantial degree within a cultural context seems to have a positive effect on the links between individual religiosity, well-being, and family orientation. With regard to the latter, the impact of personal religiosity on one's views about the family may be stronger in highly religious contexts than in contexts where religious norms are not as widely shared. This does not mean that in more secular contexts religious adolescents may not have strong family commitments, but rather that other (nonreligious) pathways to valuing familial bonds may be more important in these contexts. In secular cultures, scientific (psychological and educational) theories such as attachment theory as well as political ideologies emphasize the importance of family life. These provide messages regarding how to maintain and enhance good parental and marital relationships as well as how to create a sense of connectedness in the family (see Agate et al., 2007; Mahoney, 2005).

Individual-Level Relations between Religiosity and Family Orientation and the Moderating Role of Religious Context

Based on the theorizing presented above, we expected that religiosity would be related to our measures of family orientation in all cultures, but that the relation may be stronger for cultures with a high normativity of religious beliefs.

In 13 of the 17 cultures studied, a significant positive correlation was observed between adolescents' religiosity and their *family values* (see Table 15.2). With one exception, the nonsignificant correlations occurred in the cultures with the lowest average importance of religion. For the *emotional value of children*, significant positive correlations with adolescents' religiosity were found in six cultures. The relations were rather weak with the exception of the United States ($r = .33$). Even weaker relations were found

Table 15.2. Relationships between Religiosity and Different Measures of Family Orientation in Different Cultures

Culture	Family Values	Emotional VOC	Utilitarian–normative VOC	Family Future Orientation
Indonesia	.17**	.06	.10+	.04
India (North)	.16**	.15*	.22***	.20***
South Africa	.29***	.09	.11+	.03
Poland	.40***	.07	.08	.29***
Turkey	.18**	.17**	.13*	.16**
India (South)	.06	.05	.09	.05
United States	.29***	.33***	.04	.24***
Israel	.23**	.09	−.13+	.03
Russia	.28***	.22***	.25***	.17**
Italy	.27***	.12*	.21***	na
Switzerland	.25**	.22*	.16+	.21*
France	.30***	.07	.12	.15*
Germany	.20***	.08	−.04	.24***
Japan	.15*	.10	.12+	.10
Czech Republic	.08	−.05	−.03	−.02
China	.03	.01	.08	.04
Estonia	.04	.02	.01	.04

Note: Pearson correlations. Cultures ordered according to average importance of religion in descending order from top to bottom. na: not available.
$+ p < .10.$ $* p < .05.$ $** p < .01.$ $*** p < .001.$

between the *utilitarian–normative value of children* and adolescents' religiosity. Here, only 4 out of 17 correlations were positively significant. In eight cultures, adolescents reporting higher religiosity also reported a higher *family future orientation* than did adolescents reporting a lower religiosity.

Thus, highly religious adolescents were overall more family-oriented than were less religious or nonreligious adolescents, although the relations were not very strong. For cultures with a very low average level of religiosity (Japan, China, Czech Republic, and Estonia), hardly any significant relations resulted. Also, it seems that in cultures with a medium level of religiosity (Switzerland, Italy, Russia, Israel, and the United States) adolescents' religiosity was more positively related to their family orientation than it was in cultures with a very low or a very high level of religiosity. Therefore, we may hypothesize that in addition to a linear relationship between culture-level religiosity and the size of the individual-level effect of religiosity on adolescents' family orientation, there may be a negative quadratic effect signifying an attenuation of the (linear) moderating function for highly religious cultures. In other words, the individual-level effect of religiosity on family orientation may be especially relevant in cultures with a moderate level of religiosity. In secular, low-religiosity cultures, adolescents' family orientation may be fueled by other cultural institutions (including the family), as previously suggested. In cultures with a very high normativity of religious beliefs, the relationship between personal levels of religiosity and family orientation may be weaker than in moderately religious cultures. In this case, personal religiosity may play only a minor role for adolescents' family orientation because the latter is strongly influenced by highly normative cultural expectations. The more various socialization agents (e.g., family, school, church, media) simultaneously favor religion *and* traditional family views, the less relevant individual differences in religiosity may be for family-related values and attitudes.

To test these assumptions, we computed random coefficient multilevel analyses with linear and quadratic cross-level interactions. Adolescents' religiosity was included group-centered (per culture) to separate individual-level and culture-level variation. The covariates gender and age were included in all models but their effects will not be presented since they were small for all variables. The program HLM 6.08 was used employing full maximum likelihood estimation. We omit technical information regarding the denotation of coefficients in multilevel models (for more information on multilevel models in cross-cultural psychology, see Nezlek, 2010).

The average within-culture effect of adolescents' religiosity on their family orientation was significantly positive for all four aspects of family orientation and the cross-cultural variations of this effect (variance component or random effect of slope) were also all significant.[1] In these models, adolescents' religiosity explained relatively small amounts of the level-1 variance of the different aspects of family orientation (5.4 percent for family values, 1.5 percent for emotional VOC, 1.5 percent for utilitarian–normative VOC, and 1.9 percent for family future orientation). To test the moderation hypotheses, we included linear and quadratic cross-level interactions of culture-level religiosity with the individual-level effect of religiosity in all models (slope-as-outcome models). Results showed positive linear cross-level interactions for *family values* (*Coeff.* = 0.03, SE = 0.01, $p < .05$) and for the *emotional VOC* (*Coeff.* = 0.03, SE = 0.01, $p = .05$), indicating stronger individual-level relations between religiosity and family orientation in cultures with higher average religiosity. A trend-level negative quadratic cross-level interaction resulted for *family values* (*Coeff.* = -0.02, SE = 0.01, $p = .08$), indicating that the linear moderation may be attenuated with high culture-level religiosity for this variable. All further cross-level interactions were nonsignificant.

To summarize, adolescents' religiosity was significantly related to all four aspects of their family orientation. For family values and emotional VOC, this relation was weaker for cultures with a low level of religiosity; for family values, highly religious cultures may exhibit slightly lower relations than moderately religious cultures.

In addition to a moderating effect of the cultural normativity of religion on the relevance of adolescents' religiosity for their family orientation, culture-level religiosity may also be directly linked to adolescents' family orientation. This is the topic of the following section.

Culture-Level Relations between Religiosity, Socioeconomic Development, and Adolescents' Family Orientation

In this section, we take up our earlier reasoning regarding the interrelations among secularization, economic development, and family change. How are the culture-level importance of religion and the importance of the family related across cultures? To what degree can economic development add uniquely to the explanation of family orientation?

In the random coefficient multilevel analyses, the primary predictor variable at the cultural level is adolescents' religiosity aggregated from individual scores. Thus, the same variable was used at the individual and at the cultural level (Fontaine, 2008; van de Vijver, van Hemert, & Poortinga, 2008). In addition to religiosity, the Human Development Index (HDI, see United Nations Development Programme, 2010) was included as a culture-level predictor.[2] The HDI is a good proxy for a culture's level of socioeconomic development.

In the following, the focus is on a summary of the culture-level fixed effects (intercept-as-outcome models) and their explanatory power (see Table 15.3). The results showed significant culture-level effects of the HDI and of Religiosity on adolescents' family values (see Table 15.3, Model 1). The higher the HDI, the *lower* were adolescents' family values; and the higher the culture-level religiosity, the *higher* were the family values. Together, HDI and religiosity explained 66 percent of the cross-cultural differences in adolescents' family values. For the emotional VOC, culture-level religiosity was related to higher emotional VOC, explaining 46 percent of the cross-cultural differences in emotional VOC, whereas the HDI had no significant effect. For the utilitarian–normative VOC, a significant negative effect resulted for the HDI and a significant positive effect resulted for religiosity, indicating a higher importance of the utilitarian–normative VOC for

Table 15.3. Culture-Level Effects in Multilevel Analyses with HDI and Religiosity Predicting Different Aspects of Adolescents' Family Orientation

	Coeff.	*SE*	*T*	*df*
Family Values				
HDI	−1.18	.44	−2.71*	14
Religiosity	0.12	.05	3.09**	14
Emotional VOC				
HDI	−0.42	.38	−1.11	14
Religiosity	0.10	.04	2.40*	14
Utilitarian–normative VOC				
HDI	−3.77	.51	−7.36***	14
Religiosity	0.16	.06	2.92*	14
Family Future Orientation				
HDI	−0.24	.56	−0.42	13
Religiosity	0.21	.06	3.53**	13

adolescents from religious cultures and a lower importance of this measure for adolescents from affluent cultures. Together, the HDI and culture-level religiosity explained 88 percent of the cross-cultural differences in adolescents' utilitarian–normative VOC.

Last, for family future orientation, whereas the HDI was unrelated to this outcome variable, a significant positive effect of religiosity resulted that explained 57 percent of the cultural differences in family future orientation. Thus, adolescents from religious cultures had a higher family future orientation.

To summarize the culture-level effects, whereas culture-level religiosity was positively related to all aspects of family orientation, the level of socioeconomic development (HDI) of a culture was negatively related (only) to adolescents' traditional family values and to their utilitarian–normative VOC. Thus, overall, adolescents from more religious and less economically developed cultures were more family-oriented than were adolescents from less religious and richer cultures. However, although religiosity seems to be strongly related to *all* aspects of adolescents' family orientation, economic development seems to affect only the conservative aspects of family orientation as reflected in traditional family values and utilitarian–normative reasons for having children. Thus, religiosity is strongly related to an overall importance of the family independent of economic development, and economic development seems to weaken only traditional aspects of family orientation whereas other aspects like the wish to have an own family in the future and the importance of emotional bonds parents have with their children remain stable.

Conclusions

The family as a potential source of social and cultural capital, as a safe haven, and as the central place to satisfy basic needs of human dependency represents an important mediating link in the relation between religiosity and well-being. The results presented here indicate that living in a religious culture and personally being religious are both related to a higher family orientation for adolescents. Religiosity may be especially beneficial for adolescents' family orientation in moderately religious cultures where a plurality of worldviews exist, ranging from secular to very religious beliefs. In this sense, individual religiosity may act as a buffer for a decreasing significance of the family. However, the effects of individual religiosity on family orientation were rather weak when compared to the culture-level effects of religiosity. The results also showed that the presence of economic development and secularization in a culture have to be considered independently for predicting adolescents' family orientation: Economic development is clearly linked to processes that release or disconnect adolescents from traditional, hierarchical, and obedience-related views on the family, but it does not contribute to a loss of significance of the family per se. When a high level of societal affluence is combined with a low level of societal religiosity, however, all aspects of adolescents' family orientation seem to suffer.

Limitations in the present study include the sole reliance on adolescents' reported importance of religion, not distinguishing between religious denominations. Also, our results from cross-sectional studies cannot indicate cultural change (Thornton, 2005). Further research has to look deeper into the culture-specific aspects of religiosity and its role in adolescent development (Belzen, 2010). Nevertheless, religions share features of spirituality and normativity, rendering religiosity a unique aspect of the adolescent experience across cultures. Although we emphasize the family-consolidating effects of religion, this does not mean that religiosity (or specific kinds of religiosity) cannot also have negative impacts on adolescents' family life, such as when adolescents convert to fundamentalist forms of religiosity that are not in line with the religious beliefs emphasized in their family of origin; nor do we contend that being nonreligious is necessarily related to a low family orientation.

Providing adolescents with opportunities to (re-)discover religiosity for their personal lives may be especially relevant in cultural contexts where religion has lost some of its significance but individuals can relatively easily reconnect to resources from religious traditions. In these cultures, religion is only one of many possible life orientations, but it may be a powerful one that can satisfy basic needs for relatedness and agency (Baumeister & Leary, 1995; Rothbaum & Trommsdorff, 2007) and fill a void of meaning. In this sense, the cultural and religious context and the fit of developmental pathways within these contexts have to be taken into account in research and interventions with regard to adolescent religiosity and family orientation.

AUTHORS' NOTE

This study is part of the of the cross-cultural and interdisciplinary research project "Value of Children and Intergenerational Relations." Principal investigators: Gisela Trommsdorff, University of Konstanz, Germany, and Bernhard Nauck, Chemnitz University of Technology, Germany. For seven countries (People's Republic of China, Germany, Indonesia, Israel and the Palestinian Authority, Poland, Turkey, United States), the study was funded by the German Research Foundation (TR 169/9–1, -2, -3 and NA 164/9–1, -3, -4). In Northern India (Varanasi), the study was co-funded by the University of Konstanz and the German Research Foundation. In Southern India (Puducherry), the study was funded by the Chemnitz University of Technology; in the Czech Republic by the Masaryk University, Brno; in Estonia by the European Social Fund Measure 1.4 "Enhancing Administrative Capacity"; in France by the University Victor Segalen, Bordeaux; in Russia by the Lobatchevskij State University, Nizhnij Novgorod; and in South Africa by the University of Limpopo. We would like to thank the collaborators who carried out the study in the respective countries: Gang Zheng, Shaohua Shi, and Hong Tang, People's Republic of China; Ivo Mozny and Petr Pakosta, Czech Republic; Kairi Kasearu, Estonia; Colette Sabatier and Lyda Lannegrand-Willems, France; Bernhard Nauck, Beate Schwarz, Daniela Klaus, Jana Suckow, and Isabelle Albert, Germany; Ramesh Mishra, Northern India; Arun Tipandjan, Southern India; Lieke Wisnubrata, Samsunuwijati Marat, Kusdwiratri Setiono, and Peter R. Nelwan, Indonesia; Asher Ben-Arieh and Muhammad M. Haj-Yahia, Israel and the Palestinian Authority; Katarzyna Lubiewska, Poland; Zaretkhan Kh. M. Saralieva, Vladimir A. Blonin, and Alexandre A. Iudin, Russia; Karl Peltzer, South Africa; Cigdem Kagitcibasi and Bilge Ataca, Turkey; Wolfgang Friedlmeier and Mihaela Friedlmeier, United States. Data from Italy was collected by Daniela Barni as part of her doctoral dissertation supervised by Eugenia Scabini, Catholic University of Milan, Italy. Data from Japan was collected by Chiaki Yamada as part of her master's thesis supervised by Collette Sabatier, University Victor Segalen, France. Data from Switzerland was collected by Karen Fux as part of her diploma thesis supervised by Gisela Trommsdorff, University of Konstanz, Germany. The authors would like to thank Tobias Heikamp for valuable comments on an earlier version of the manuscript and Holly Bunje for her assistance in language editing.

Correspondence concerning this article should be addressed to Boris Mayer, Department of Psychology, P.O. Box 31, University of Konstanz, D-78457 Konstanz, Germany. E-mail: boris.mayer@uni-konstanz.de

NOTES

1. Family Values (*Coeff.* = 0.10, *SE* = 0.01, *p* < .001; *Var. Comp.* χ^2 = 53.69, *p* < .001); Emotional VOC (*Coeff.* = 0.06, *SE* = 0.01, *p* < .001; *Var. Comp.* χ^2 = 33.56, *p* < .001); Utilitarian–normative VOC (*Coeff.* = 0.07, *SE* = 0.02, *p* < .001; *Var. Comp.* χ^2 = 44.70, *p* < .001); Family Future Orientation (*Coeff.* = 0.12, *SE* = 0.02, *p* < .001; *Var. Comp.* χ^2 = 34.79, *p* < .01).
2. Culture-Level Religiosity and the HDI were substantially correlated (*r* = −.53) but are far from representing collinear variables.

REFERENCES

Agate, S. T., Zabriskie, R. B., & Eggett, D. L. (2007). Praying, playing and successful families: An examination of family religiosity, family leisure, and family functioning. *Marriage & Family Review, 42,* 51–75.
Arnett, J. J. (2010). Emerging adulthood(s): The cultural psychology of a new life stage. In L. A. Jensen (Ed.), *Bridging cultural and developmental approaches to psychology: New syntheses in theory, research, and policy* (pp. 255–275). New York: Oxford University Press.
Arnold, F., Bulatao, R. A., Buripakdi, C., Chung, B. J., Fawcett, J. T., Iritani, T., ... Wu, T. S. (1975). *The value of children. A cross-national study* (Vol. 1). Honolulu, HI: East-West Population Institute.
Barber, J. S. (2000). Ideational influences on the entry into parenthood: Mothers' preferences for family and nonfamily behaviors. *Social Forces, 79,* 319–348.
Baumeister, R. F. (2002). Religion and psychology: Introduction to the special issue. *Psychological Inquiry, 13,* 165–167.
Baumeister, R. F., & Leary, M. R. (1995). The need to belong – desire for interpersonal attachments as a fundamental human motivation. *Psychological Bulletin, 117,* 497–529.
Belzen, J. A. (2010). Psychology of religion: Perspectives from cultural psychology. *Mental Health, Religion & Culture, 13,* 329–347.
Bengtson, V. L. (2001). Beyond the nuclear family: The increasing importance of multigenerational bonds. *Journal of Marriage and the Family, 63,* 1–16.
Bengtson, V. L., Copen, C. E., Putney, N. M., & Silverstein, M. (2009). A longitudinal study of the intergenerational transmission of religion. *International Sociology, 24,* 325–345.

Boyatzis, C. J., Dollahite, D. C., & Marks, L. D. (2006). The family as a context for religious and spiritual development in children and youth. In E. C. Roehlkepartain, P. E. King, L. Wagener, & P. L. Benson (Eds.), *The handbook of spiritual development in childhood and adolescence* (pp. 297–309). Thousand Oaks, CA: Sage.

Brown, B. B., Larson, R. W., & Saraswathi, T. S. (Eds.). (2002). *The world's youth: Adolescence in eight regions of the globe.* Cambridge: Cambridge University Press.

Chatters, L. M., & Taylor, R. J. (2005). Religion and families. In V. L. Bengtson, A. C. Acock, K. R. Allen, P. Dilworth-Anderson, & D. M. Klein (Eds.), *Sourcebook of family theory & research* (pp. 517–541). Thousand Oaks, CA: Sage.

Cohen, A. B. (2002). The importance of spirituality in well-being for Jews and Christians. *Journal of Happiness Studies, 3,* 287–310.

Dasen, P. (2000). Rapid social change and the turmoil of adolescence: A cross-cultural perspective. *International Journal of Group Tensions, 29,* 17–49.

Dollahite, D. C., Marks, L. D., & Goodman, M. (2004). Family and religious beliefs, practices, and communities: Linkages in a diverse and dynamic cultural context. In M. J. Coleman & L. H. Ganong (Eds.), *Handbook of contemporary families: Considering the past, contemplating the future* (pp. 411–431). Thousand Oaks, CA: Sage.

Eisenstadt, S. N. (Ed.). (1973). *Post-traditional societies.* New York: Norton.

Eisenstadt, S. N. (2006). *The great revolutions and the civilizations of modernity.* Leiden, The Netherlands: Brill.

Elkind, D. (1964). Age-changes in the meaning of religious identity. *Review of Religious Research, 6,* 36–40.

(1999). Religious development in adolescence. *Journal of Adolescence, 22,* 291–295.

Erikson, E. H. (1968). *Identity, youth, and crisis.* New York: Norton.

Fontaine, J. R. J. (2008). Traditional and multilevel approaches in cross-cultural research: An integration of methodological frameworks. In F. J. R. van de Vijver, D. A. van Hemert, & Y. H. Poortinga (Eds.), *Multilevel analysis of individuals and cultures* (pp. 65–92). New York: Erlbaum.

Fuligni, A. J., Tseng, V., & Lam, M. (1999). Attitudes toward family obligations among American adolescents with Asian, Latin American, and European backgrounds. *Child Development, 70,* 1030–1044.

Funder, D. C. (2002). Why study religion? *Psychological Inquiry, 13,* 213–214.

Gamoran, A. (1992). Religious participation and family values among American Jewish youth. *Contemporary Jewry, 13,* 44–59.

Georgas, J. (1991). Intrafamily acculturation of values in Greece. *Journal of Cross-Cultural Psychology, 22,* 445–457.

(2006). Families and family change. In J. Georgas, J. W. Berry, F. J. R. van de Vijver, C. Kagitcibasi, & Y. H. Poortinga (Eds.), *Families across cultures* (pp. 3–50). Cambridge: Cambridge University Press.

Georgas, J., Berry, J. W., van de Vijver, F. J. R., Kagitcibasi, C., & Poortinga, Y. H. (Eds.). (2006). *Families across cultures.* Cambridge: Cambridge University Press.

Georgas, J., van de Vijver, F. J. R., & Berry, J. W. (2004). The eco-cultural framework, ecosocial indicators and psychological variables in cross-cultural research. *Journal of Cross-Cultural Psychology, 35,* 74–96.

George, L. K., Ellison, C. G., & Larson, D. B. (2002). Explaining the relationships between religious involvement and health. *Psychological Inquiry, 13,* 190–200.

Good, M., & Willoughby, T. (2008). Adolescence as a sensitive period for spiritual development. *Child Development Perspectives*, **2**, 32–37.

Goode, W. J. (1963). *World revolution and family patterns*. Glencoe, IL: Free Press.

Hackney, C., & Sanders, G. S. (2003). Religiosity and mental health: A meta analysis of recent studies. *Journal for the Scientific Study of Religion*, **42**, 43–55.

Halman, L. C. J. M., & Pettersson, T. (2006). A decline of religious values? In P. Ester, M. Braun, & P. Mohler (Eds.), *Globalization, value change, and generations* (pp. 31–59). Leiden, The Netherlands: Brill.

Henrich, J., Heine, S. J., & Norenzayan, A. (2010). The weirdest people in the world? *Behavioral and Brain Sciences*, **33**, 61–135.

Höllinger, F., & Haller, M. (2009). Decline or persistence of religion? Trends in religiosity among Christian societies around the world. In M. Haller, R. Jowell, & T. W. Smith (Eds.), *The International Social Survey Programme 1984–2009: Charting the globe* (pp. 281–301). London: Routledge.

Inglehart, R., & Baker, W. E. (2000). Modernization, cultural change, and the persistence of traditional values. *American Sociological Review*, **65**, 19–51.

Inglehart, R., & Welzel, C. (2005). *Modernization, cultural change, and democracy: The human development sequence*. Cambridge: Cambridge University Press.

Inkeles, A. (1998). *One world emerging. Convergence and divergence in industrial societies*. Boulder, CO: Westview Press.

Inkeles, A., & Smith, D. H. (1974). *Becoming modern: Individual change in six developing countries*. London: Heinemann.

Jensen, L. A. (2003). Coming of age in a multicultural world: Globalization and adolescent cultural identity formation. *Applied Developmental Science*, **7**, 189–196.

Kagitcibasi, C. (1982). Old-age security value of children: Cross-national socioeconomic evidence. *Journal of Cross-Cultural Psychology*, **13**, 29–42.

(2007). *Family, self, and human development across cultures: Theory and applications* (2nd ed.). Hillsdale, NJ: Erlbaum.

Kelley, J., & De Graaf, N. D. (1997). National context, parental socialization, and religious belief: Results from 15 nations. *American Sociological Review*, **62**, 639–659.

King, P. E., & Furrow, J. L. (2004). Religion as a resource for positive youth development: Religion, social capital, and moral outcomes. *Developmental Psychology*, **40**, 703–713.

Lavric, M., & Flere, S. (2008). The role of culture in the relationship between religiosity and psychological well-being. *Journal of Religion & Health*, **47**, 164–175.

Lopez, A. B., Huynh, V. W., & Fuligni, A. J. (2011). A longitudinal study of religious identity and participation during adolescence. *Child Development*, **82**, 1297–1309.

Mahoney, A. (2005). Religion and conflict in marital and parent–child relationships. *Journal of Social Issues*, **61**, 689–706.

(2010). Religion in families, 1999–2009: A relational spirituality framework. *Journal of Marriage and the Family*, **72**, 805–827.

Mahoney, A., Pargament, K. I., Murray-Swank, A., & Murray-Swank, N. (2003). Religion and the sanctification of family relationships. *Review of Religious Research*, **44**, 220–236.

Markstrom, C. A. (1999). Religious involvement and adolescent psychosocial development. *Journal of Adolescence*, **22**, 205–221.

Mayer, B., Kuramschew, A., & Trommsdorff, G. (2009). Familienbezogene Werte und Zukunftsvorstellungen in der Adoleszenz: Ein deutsch-russischer Vergleich [Family-related values and future orientation in adolescence: A German-Russian comparison]. *Zeitschrift für Soziologie der Erziehung und Sozialisation, 29*, 29–44.

Mayer, B., & Trommsdorff, G. (2010). Adolescents' value of children and their intentions to have children: A cross-cultural and multilevel analysis. *Journal of Cross-Cultural Psychology, 41*, 671–689.

Mayer, B., Trommsdorff, G., Kagitcibasi, C., & Mishra, R. C. (2012, April 5). Family models of independence/interdependence and their intergenerational similarity in Germany, Turkey, and India. *Family Science.* Advance online publication. doi: 10.1080/19424620.2011.671503.

Mishra, R. C., Mayer, B., Trommsdorff, G., Albert, I., & Schwarz, B. (2005). The value of children in urban and rural India: Cultural background and empirical results. In G. Trommsdorff & B. Nauck (Eds.), *The value of children in cross-cultural perspective: Case studies from eight societies* (pp. 143–170). Lengerich: Pabst Science.

Nezlek, J. B. (2010). Multilevel modeling and cross-cultural research. In D. Matsumoto & F. J. R. van de Vijver (Eds.), *Cross-cultural research methods in psychology* (pp. 299–347). Oxford: Oxford University Press.

Okulicz-Kozaryn, A. (2010). Religiosity and life satisfaction across nations. *Mental Health, Religion & Culture, 13*, 155–169.

Oser, F. K., Scarlett, W. G., & Bucher, A. (2006). Religious and spiritual development throughout the lifespan. In R. M. Lerner (Ed.), *Handbook of child psychology: Vol. 1. Theoretical models of human development* (6th ed., pp. 942–998). Hoboken, NJ: Wiley.

Pankhurst, J. G., & Houseknecht, S. K. (2000). Introduction: The religion-family linkage and social change – a neglected area of study. In S. K. Houseknecht & J. G. Pankhurst (Eds.), *Family, religion, and social change in diverse societies* (pp. 1–40). Oxford: Oxford University Press.

Pargament, K. I. (2002a). The bitter and the sweet: An evaluation of the costs and benefits of religiousness. *Psychological Inquiry, 13*, 168–181.

(2002b). Is religion nothing but …? – Explaining religion versus explaining religion away. *Psychological Inquiry, 13*, 239–244.

Parsons, T. (1949). The social structure of the family. In R. N. Anshen (Ed.), *The family: Its functions and destiny* (pp. 33–58). New York: Harper.

Pearce, L. D., & Thornton, A. (2007). Religious identity and family ideologies in the transition to adulthood. *Journal of Marriage and the Family, 69*, 1227–1243.

Popenoe, D. (1988). *Disturbing the nest: Family change and decline in modern societies.* Chicago: Aldine.

Regnerus, M. D., & Burdette, A. (2006). Religious change and adolescent family dynamics. *Sociological Quarterly, 47*, 175–194.

Regnerus, M. D., Smith, C., & Smith, B. (2004). Social context in the development of adolescent religiosity. *Applied Developmental Science, 8*, 27–38.

Rokeach, M. (1969). Value systems and religion. *Review of Religious Research, 11*, 2–23.

Rothbaum, F., & Trommsdorff, G. (2007). Do roots and wings complement or oppose one another? The socialization of relatedness and autonomy in cultural context. In

J. E. Grusec & P. Hastings (Eds.), *The handbook of socialization* (pp. 461–489). New York: Guilford.

Sabatier, C., Mayer, B., Friedlmeier, M., Lubiewska, K., & Trommsdorff, G. (2011). Religiosity, family orientation, and life satisfaction of adolescents in four countries. *Journal of Cross-Cultural Psychology*, 42, 1375–1393.

Sam, D. L., Peltzer, K., & Mayer, B. (2005). The changing values of children and preferences regarding family size in South Africa. *Applied Psychology: An International Review*, 54, 355–377.

Saroglou, V., Delpierre, V., & Dernelle, R. (2004). Values and religiosity: A meta-analysis of studies using Schwartz's model. *Personality and Individual Differences*, 37, 721–734.

Schlegel, A. (2000). The global spread of adolescent culture. In L. Crockett & R. K. Silbereisen (Eds.), *Negotiating adolescence in times of social change* (pp. 71–88). Cambridge: Cambridge University Press.

Schwartz, S. H., & Huismans, S. (1995). Value priorities and religiosity in four Western religions. *Social Psychology Quarterly*, 58, 88–107.

Schwarz, B., Chakkarath, P., Trommsdorff, G., Schwenk, O., & Nauck, B. (2001). *Report on selected instruments of the Value of Children main study*. Unpublished manuscript. University of Konstanz, Germany.

Seginer, R. (2009). *Future orientation: Developmental and ecological perspectives*. New York: Springer.

Sinha, D. (1991). Rise in the population of the elderly, familial changes and their psychosocial implications: The scenario of the developing countries. *International Journal of Psychology*, 26, 633–647.

Steger, M. F., & Frazier, P. (2005). Meaning in life: One link in the chain from religiousness to well-being. *Journal of Counseling Psychology*, 52, 574–582.

Stetsenko, A. (2002). Adolescents in Russia: Surviving the turmoil and creating a brighter future. In B. B. Brown, D. B. Larson, & T. S. Saraswathi (Eds.), *The world's youth: Adolescence in eight regions of the globe* (pp. 243–275). Cambridge: Cambridge University Press.

Tarakeshwar, N., Stanton, J., & Pargament, K. I. (2003). Religion – An overlooked dimension in cross-cultural psychology. *Journal of Cross-Cultural Psychology*, 34, 377–394.

Thornton, A. (2005). *Reading history sideways. The fallacy and enduring impact of the developmental paradigm on family life*. Chicago: University of Chicago Press.

Trommsdorff, G. (2009a). Intergenerational relations and cultural transmission. In U. Schönpflug (Ed.), *Cultural transmission: Psychological, developmental, social, and methodological aspects* (pp. 126–160). Cambridge: Cambridge University Press.

(2009b). A social change and a human development perspective on the value of children. In S. Bekman & A. Aksu-Koc (Eds.), *Perspectives on human development, family and culture* (pp. 86–107). Cambridge: Cambridge University Press.

(2012). Development of "agentic" regulation in cultural context: The role of self and world views. *Child Development Perspectives*, 6, 19–26.

Trommsdorff, G., & Nauck, B. (Eds.). (2005). *The value of children in cross-cultural perspective: Case studies from eight societies*. Lengerich: Pabst Science.

United Nations Development Programme (2010). *Human Development Report 2010– 20th anniversary edition. The real wealth of nations: Pathways to human development*. New York: Palgrave Macmillan.

van de Vijver, F. J. R., van Hemert, D. A., & Poortinga, Y. H. (2008). Conceptual issues in multilevel models. In F. J. R. van de Vijver, D. A. van Hemert, & Y. H. Poortinga (Eds.), *Multilevel analysis of individuals and cultures* (pp. 3–26). New York: Erlbaum.

Wagener, L. M., Furrow, J. L., King, P. E., Leffert, N., & Benson, P. (2003). Religious involvement and developmental resources in youth. *Review of Religious Research*, **44**, 271–284.

Yang, K. S. (1996). The psychological transformation of the Chinese people as a result of societal modernization. In M. H. Bond (Ed.), *Handbook of Chinese psychology* (pp. 479–498). Hong Kong: Oxford University Press.

Youniss, J., McLellan, J. A., & Yates, M. (1999). Religion, community service, and identity in American youth. *Journal of Adolescence*, **22**, 243–253.

Youniss, J., & Smollar, J. (1985). *Adolescent relations with mothers, fathers, and friends*. Chicago: The University of Chicago Press.

16 Religion and the Intergenerational Continuity of Values

Ariel Knafo, Ella Daniel, Sigal Gabay,
Ran Zilber, and Rivka Shir

Abstract

Adolescence is an important period for the development of values and identity. As relationships with parents are negotiated and convictions are questioned, it is an especially intriguing time to study the interface of religion with processes leading to the intergenerational continuity of values. Religion can provide the content of values, as well as the context of intergenerational value continuity, by developing appropriate establishments, and by enabling (or not) disengagement from parental values. In addition, individuals' religiosity is reflected in their values and in family processes of value negotiation, influence, and modification.

Two Israeli case studies illustrate these processes. Study 1 studied 107 parent–adolescent dyads from three religious minorities in Israel: Muslim Arabs, Christian Arabs, and Jerusalem Armenian Christians. Muslims ascribed less importance than Christians to hedonism and power, exemplifying the content process. Armenians, a very small and secluded minority, were the only group in which adolescents ascribed lower importance for openness than their parents, exemplifying the role of context with a cocooning process, in which socialization shields children from competing messages (Goodnow, 1997).

Study 2 involved 36 non-religious Jewish youth whose parents were either religious or not. The average value profile parent–child correlation was .50 in non-religious families, much higher than in families who had been religious but decided to become non-religious (.18), exemplifying the importance of religion.

Future directions include the need for studying non-Western religions and family processes in religious as compared to ethnic minorities.

For thousands of years, religion has provided the human species with a sense of meaning. All major religions have a say about the way individuals and groups should behave, and sometimes even think and feel. In that sense, religions are involved in prescribing the values of individuals and groups (Fontaine, Duriez, Luyten, Corveleyn, & Hutsebaut, 2005; Pepper, Uzzell, & Jackson, 2010, Roccas, 2005; Saroglou, Delpierre, & Dernelle, 2004). Values are abstract, transsituational goals serving as guides for behavior and evaluation of other individuals and the self (Schwartz, 1992). Across many cultural and religious groups, 10 values are typically found:

Benevolence: caring for others who are closely related to the self
Universalism: understanding, appreciation, and protection for all people and of nature
Self-direction: independent thought and action
Stimulation: diversity, change, and excitement
Hedonism: pleasure and sensual satisfaction
Achievement: personal success through competence according to social standards
Power: social status, control, and dominance
Security: safety, harmony, and stability of the social structure and of the self
Conformity: limiting violation of social expectations and norms
Tradition: respect, commitment, and acceptance of the costumes and ideas imposed by one's culture or religion

See Schwartz (Chapter 4 in this volume), for a description of the values theory.

A key factor in the transmission of cultural ideas from one generation to the other is the family context. Parents are often expected to "transmit" their values to their children. The processes in which values are negotiated, transmitted, and modified across generations often occur in the context of specific religions and religious practices and establishments. Going beyond the family level, religions and religious institutions have a stated goal – to influence the individuals affiliated with the religious group. Here we describe some of the processes in which religion impacts the intergenerational continuity of values, and we exemplify them with data from parents and their children.

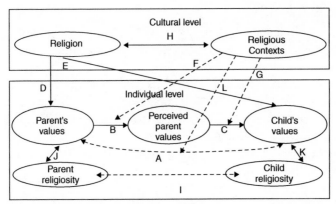

Figure 16.1. A schematic representation of the role of religion and religiosity in intergenerational value continuity.

Intergenerational Continuity of Values

The family is an open system in which parents and children influence each other with input from the environment influencing family members (e.g., Whitchurch & Constantine, 1993). The impact of each member is a function of the larger network of family relationships, and of the contexts within which the family is nested (Hinde, 1989; O'Connor, et al., 1997). For example, parents' influence varies depending on the family's ecological context (e.g., culture or neighborhood) (Bronfenbrenner, 1986). Thus, Figure 16.1 distinguishes between cultural level factors and individual/family level factors.

Figure 16.1 schematically presents the values of the parent–child dyad as interrelating within a family system; the family exists within a broader cultural context that may include the community, the religious denomination, and the religion with which families are affiliated. In addition to these cultural-level factors, parents and children appear as individuals, each with his or her own values as well as religiosity levels. This schematic representation of a very complex process leading to intergenerational (dis)continuity in values shows several broad processes that exemplify the role of religion and religiosity.

Grusec and Goodnow (1994) suggested that parent–child value continuity results from a two-step process of internalization. In the first step (perception), children perceive parents' values with varying degrees of accuracy (Knafo & Schwartz, 2003). In the second step (acceptance), children choose to what extent to accept or reject the values they perceive. To the extent that children perceive accurately and accept their parents' values, parent–child value congruence should be high (e.g., Barni, Ranieri, Scabini, & Rosnati, 2011; Okagaki & Bevis, 1999). Figure 16.1 includes the values children perceive their parents to hold as mediating links between parents' actual values and children's own values (Paths B and C).

Knafo and Schwartz (2008) showed that the combination of high accuracy of perception of parental values and high acceptance of these perceived values is associated with the highest degree of parent–adolescent value congruence. Interestingly, tradition, the value most strongly associated with religiosity (Saroglou et al., 2004), showed the highest accuracy, acceptance and congruence, of the 10 Schwartz (1992) values (Knafo & Schwartz, 2008). This is congruent with other findings of higher parent–child congruence in values and attitudes related to religiosity (Acock & Bengtson, 1978; Cavalli-Sforza, Feldman, Chen, & Dornbusch, 1982; Troll & Bengtson, 1979).

It is important to note that not all parent–child congruence is accounted for by the two steps (Path A). This is true for also for tradition values, which were the ones most strongly predicted by demographic variables, as both accuracy of perception and acceptance were higher for values that were predictable by parents' socio-demographic characteristics (Knafo & Schwartz, 2008). Because parents and children share in part the same background, the values and cultural practices of the social context in which these families operate may cause part of similarity between parents and children (Roest, Dubas, Gerris, & Engels, 2009), regardless of the intra-familial socialization processes.

Another factor that may account for parent–child congruence beyond socialization processes is shared genetic heritage (Knafo & Spinath, 2011). Genetic influence has been shown for religion-related values and behaviors (e.g., Waller, Kojetin, Bouchard, Lykken, & Tellegen, 1990), with evidence for increase in heritability from adolescence to adulthood (Koenig, McGue, Krueger, & Bouchard, 2005). To the extent that parents and children share their genetic heritage and that values are heritable, parent–child value congruence can reflect the shared genetic relatedness rather than direct transmission from parent to child. Nevertheless, there is evidence for the importance of accurate perception and acceptance for at least some of the congruence between parents and children; it is therefore important to consider these processes when studying the continuity of values in the family.

The Role of Religion
Religion and religiosity may be meaningful to intergenerational value continuity for several reasons. First, religion can provide the *content* of

values. Second, individuals' *religiosity* is reflected in their values and possibly in how parents and children behave to each other. Third, religion provides the *context* of intergenerational value continuity, by developing appropriate establishments, and by enabling (or not) disengagement from parental values. Following a review of the literature discussing each of these processes, we use two case studies from four religious groups in Israel to illustrate the roles of religion and religiosity in intergenerational value continuity.

Content. First, religion can provide the content of values that are carried on from one generation to the next, as indicated by value differences between religions. These could reflect either the different teachings of the religions, or the practices and traditions associated with each religion. Theorizing by Weber, Huntington, and others (see Inglehart & Baker, 2000) suggests that the religious tradition of a society has a long-term impact on the values of the individuals within the society. A telling case concerns the differences across European countries, which largely share a Christian heritage. Looking at the value dimension of survival versus self-expression, predominantly Protestant countries show high importance to self-expression, while Orthodox countries show higher importance to survival. Catholic (European and Latin American) countries rank in the middle of the dimension (Inglehart & Baker, 2000). However, as Inglehart and Baker (2000) note, a society's culture reflects additional aspects of its historical and economic heritage. Going back to the European example, the religious distinctions parallel a wide range of other variables, such as economic development, the influence of different European superpowers at different times, and perhaps even linguistic differences.

Another complication is that the same religion can have different meanings in different cultural contexts (e.g. Catholicism in the Philippines and in Italy). It would also be telling to compare different religious groups nested within the same geographical and political context. Although we are not aware of systematic evidence comparing different religions within the same sociopolitical niche, there is some evidence that members of different religions differ in their values. For example, differences were found in the values of individuals believing in two different religions (Buddhist and Christian) within the same cultural environment (Saroglou & Dupuis, 2006). In contrast, Inglehart and Baker (2000) found that different religions within the same country show smaller differences than those found in cross-national comparisons.

As individual parents and children are typically nested within the same cultural context, the religion they are affiliated with may exert influence on both of them (Paths D and E in Figure 16.1). The implication is that by virtue of belonging to the same religious group, parents and children share some of their values, and the parent–child value similarity (Path A) may reflect in part their shared religious belonging. To test the *content* process, we studied adolescents and their parents with both Christian and Muslim backgrounds, within the same (Israeli) sociopolitical context (Study 1).

Religiosity, the degree of personal ascription to religion, is reflected in the values of individuals and in the processes in which values are negotiated in the family. It should be noted that across several religious groups, religiosity has been found to relate consistently to the importance of several values. Specifically, religiosity is associated positively with values reflecting conservation (such as tradition and conformity) and benevolence (focusing on the welfare of others close to the individual) as well as associated negatively with values indicating openness to change and self-enhancement (self-direction, hedonism, stimulation, and less systematically, power and achievement) (Saroglou, et al., 2004; Schwartz & Huismans, 1995). Most of these findings were replicated in a study with Muslim participants (Kusdil & Kagitcibasi, 2000 in Saroglou & Galand, 2004). Recently, Schwartz (Chapter 4 in this volume) extended the findings to adolescents. With data from 30 countries he found that even for adolescents, religiosity relates most positively to tradition values and most negatively to hedonism values.

The implication of the relationship between values and religiosity to the issue of intergenerational continuity is that some of the parent–child similarity in values may reflect commonality in religiosity between family members. As parents' religiosity is associated with their values (Path J), so is the case for children (Path K). Because these relationships are similar for adults and adolescents (Saroglou, et al., 2004; Schwartz, Chapter 4 in this volume), and because parents' religiosity correlates positively with that of their children (Path I) (Cavalli-Sforza et al., 1982; Troll & Bengtson, 1979), similarity in values is likely to be associated with parent–child similarity in religiosity.

To exemplify this point, we draw on data from 352 father–adolescent and 519 mother–adolescent dyads (Knafo & Schwartz, 2008). These family members were all Israeli Jews, with varied levels of religiosity (Knafo, 2003). Adolescents' religiosity correlated highly with that of fathers and mothers (respectively, $r=.63$, $r=.62$, both $p < .001$). Nevertheless, there were intergenerational differences, with parents slightly more religious than adolescents (fathers, $t(351) = 5.94$. $p < .001$, $D = 0.27$; mothers, $t(518) = 7.34$. $p < .001$, $D = 0.28$).

More interestingly, there were individual differences, with some families showing higher and other families showing lower parent–adolescent differences in religiosity. Figure 16.2 shows that in parent–adolescent dyads in which religiosity similarity was high, adolescents were more accurate in how they perceived their parents' values, and were more likely to accept the values of the mother, as compared to dyads showing low similarity in religiosity. As would be expected by the two-step process (Grusec & Goodnow, 1994; Knafo & Schwartz, 2008), this higher accuracy and acceptance was manifest also in higher similarity of adolescents' values to their parents' values (Figure 16.2).

It is difficult to establish the direction of causality accounting for the values–religiosity relationship. It is possible that some values promote the adoption of religion to a larger extent. Another possibility is that being highly religious (or not) promotes the adoption of a certain set of values. Schwartz (Chapter 4 in this volume) suggests that the similarity of the pattern of correlations between values and religiosity across different religions is indicative more of a value-based choice for level of religiosity than of a process in which all religions socialize to the same values. In most likelihood, the relationship may involve a complex cycle of influence, in which being involved in religious practice and the development of faith may contribute to change in values, and vice versa.

Research has pointed out several pathways through which parental factors contribute, directly or indirectly, to the continuity of religion in the family. Although this is beyond the scope of this paper, aspects of the family structure, such as living with two biological parents, predict religious behavior in the offspring generation (Desmond, Morgan & Kikuchi, 2010). Factors like parental religiosity behavior, parental desire for children to be religious, and dyadic discussion of faith all relate to religious intergenerational continuity (Flor & Knapp, 2001). Moreover, parental generative concern (Erikson 1968) is related to offspring's absence of religious repudiation (Peterson, 2006), and offspring's religiousness during early, middle, and late adulthood (Dillon, Wink, & Fay, 2003).

Religiosity is also relevant to parenting style, although the evidence is not always consistent and may depend on the religion involved (Duriez, Soenens, Neyrinck, & Vansteenkiste, 2009; Knafo & Schwartz, 2004; Mahoney, Pargament, Tarakeshwar, & Swank, 2001). Thus, religiosity may have a role in the intergenerational continuity of values through affecting the parenting behavior toward children and adolescents and through it the family processes of value negotiation, influence, and modification. For example, research on parents' responses to their children's values suggests that

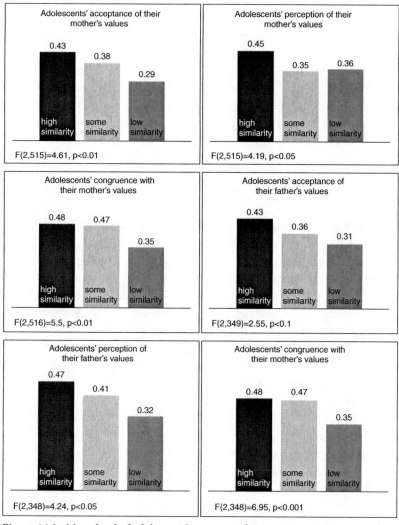

Figure 16.2. Mean level of adolescents' accuracy of perception, acceptance, and congruence with parents' values by parent–adolescent similarity in subjective religiosity.

Note: Based on a study of Israeli Jewish families (described in detail by Knafo, 2003). Parents and adolescents (57 percent female, mean age = 17.1) rated their subjective religiosity on a 0–6 scale ("How religious, if at all, do you consider yourself to be?" 0= "not at all religious," 6="very religious;" Schwartz & Huismans, 1995). Parent–adolescent dyads were classified as showing high similarity in religiosity if the absolute difference in their religiosity scores was 0 or 1 (64 percent), showing moderate similarity if it was 2 (20 percent), and showing low similarity if the difference was 3 or higher (16 percent). Parent–Child Value Congruence was assessed by computing a within-dyad Pearson correlation between parents' socialization value ratings and their own child's value ratings across the value system. Accuracy of perception was measured by correlating parents' socialization value ratings with their own child's rating of the values he or she perceived them as wanting him/her to endorse. Acceptance was measured by correlating the child's own values with the values the child perceived his or her parents wanting for him or her.

parents who were higher in self-reported religiosity tended to report that values were more important to them, which, in turn, predicted their degree of desired control over their children (Padilla-Walker & Thompson, 2005).

Context. The values and cultural practices of the social context in which families operate affect the processes leading to value continuity across generations. In addition, technical factors such as the availability of religiously oriented schooling in the neighborhood (or even the absence of competing agents of socialization in the religious area), as suggested by Glass and Bengtson (1986) may contribute to parents' ability to influence the values and attitudes of their children. We refer to this set of factors as "contexts," which can have an impact on family value continuity (Path L in Figure 16.1), possibly through accuracy of perception and acceptance (Paths F and G). Families are nested in a multitude of contexts (e.g., neighborhood, ethnic group, religious group, social class), and it would be impossible to review all of these contextual influences here; instead, we will discuss some key issues and provide some examples that will be detailed in Study 1. Particularly, one should consider how such contexts can constrain the breadth of values to which family members are exposed and can choose from, the degree to which cultures allow for child influence, and the degree to which embedding religion into the identity of group members affects family members' values.

Cultures (Arnett, 1995) and individual parents (Padilla-Walker & Thompson, 2005) differ in the importance they ascribe to continuity in values across generations. Homogenous cultures tend to transmit specific values according to their original narrow set of values and tend to emphasize conformity and obedience (Arnett, 1995; Welch, 1984). One way this is achieved is through providing family members with daily routines, religious ceremonies, and cultural practices. These habitual patterns facilitate the acceptance of certain values by making associated behaviors appear so "natural" they require no explanation or justification (Goodnow, 1997; Grusec, et al., 2000).

Religious establishments, such as schools, churches, and charities, are often built to promote the continuation of certain values across generations. When choosing to send their children to a religious school, parents, in a way, rely on these establishments to promote the values they believe in. In contrast, sometimes parents choose environments for their children that are inconsistent with their own values (Kuczynski, et al., 1997). For example, Muslim immigrant parents inevitably expose their children to value systems different from their own by moving to a historically Christian country.

In such cases, parents may find themselves in a need to protect the values in the face of conflicting value messages. A study of Jewish families in Israel looked at another source of conflicting messages. Knafo (2003) focused on a small proportion of parents who sent their children to schools that had a different religious ideology than that prevalent in the family (e.g., non-religious parents and a religious school). In such low-fit families, adolescents' accurate perception, acceptance of parental values, and congruence with parents' values, tended to be lower than in high-fit families. The relationship with the father was warmer and closer in high-fit contexts, and perceived value conflicts with both parents were less frequent (Knafo, 2003).

Some cultures may prevent children from exposure to competing value messages, a strategy called *cocooning* (Goodnow, 1997). Such processes may enhance the continuity of values in the family as parents and children are exposed to similar value messages. Thus, a limited set of options may reduce the need to accurately perceive parents' values and enhance acceptance of the perceived values by virtue of having a lower number of conflicting messages. In one study, parents who preferred cocooning over *pre-arming* (anticipatory preparation of adolescents with counter-arguments and other ways of dealing with conflicting values in their encounters with the broader world; Goodnow, 1997), tended to be more religious than other parents (see Padilla-Walker & Thompson, 2005). Applied to the group level, some secluded religious contexts such as the Amish communities may perpetuate selected values from one generation to the next through cocooning. For example, television, most newspapers, and most of the Internet websites are banned by ultra-Orthodox Jews. In Study 1, we examine the possibility of cocooning in a highly secluded ethnic group, namely Jerusalem Armenians.

Intergenerational Value Continuity in Three Religious Minorities in Israel: Study 1

Our first case study looked at intergenerational value continuities in dyads of adolescent (aged 13–18, $M=15.97$, $SD=1.34$) and parents in three religious minorities in Israel: Muslim Arabs ($N=63$), Christian Arabs ($N=24$), and Jerusalem Armenian Christians ($N=20$). These three groups have partially overlapping but sometimes dramatically different ethnic, historical, and religious backgrounds. Our purpose is to demonstrate the role of different religious affiliations in adolescents' and their parents' values.

The two Arab groups (recruited as part of a larger study, Knafo, Daniel, & Khoury-Kassabri, 2008) include Palestinians with Israeli citizenship. This minority group, forming 20.2 percent of the Israeli population, lives mostly in homogenous Arab villages or in their own neighborhoods in mixed cities, such as Jerusalem (Rabinowitz, 2001).

The Armenian community includes 2,000 members living in the Old City of Jerusalem. The Armenian heritage emphasizes the devotion to the family (Phinney, Ong, & Madden, 2000). This and their historical background (moving to a predominantly Arab part of the world from Armenia) might underlie their specific identity, which is based on nation, church, and family (O'Grady, 1981). Although this community maintains relationships with the larger ethnic communities of Jews and Arabs in Israel, it lives in a segregated society (e.g., the Armenian Quarter within the Old City walls is surrounded by a second wall.) Importantly, the size and seclusion of this cultural group are reflected in the fact that parents typically send their children to a single school, limited only to children of this group and run by church personnel.

We conducted a two-way ANOVA (two generations x three religious groups) for each of the 10 values, measured with the Portrait Values Questionnaire (PVQ; Schwartz & Rubel, 2005), and computed as residual scores controlling for adolescent age and the gender of the parent and the adolescent.[1]

Generation effects are not central to this investigation, but worth mentioning nevertheless. Parents gave higher importance to the conservation values of security and tradition, and lower importance to stimulation, as would be expected from past research (e.g., Knafo & Schwartz, 2001). In addition, they showed higher importance to universalism values than adolescents did.

Religious group differences were also found, as Muslims were lower than Christians in hedonism, power, and security, and gave higher importance to self-direction values in comparison to their Christian counterparts. Taken together, the religious differences provide support for the *content* process, in which different religions provide group members with different values.

Intergenerational Differences Contingent on Religious Group. Three significant interactions (Figure 16.3) emerged between generations and religious groups. These were found in three values of openness to change: self-direction, stimulation, and hedonism. The pattern of generational differences in the two Arab groups was similar across values, as adolescents gave higher importance than parents to openness (Knafo & Schwartz, 2001). A very different finding was found in Armenian families, in which

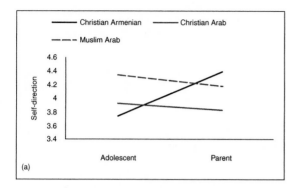

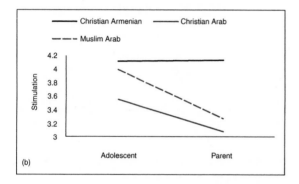

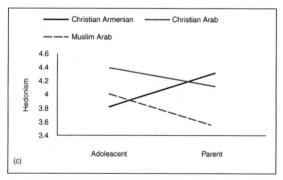

Figure 16.3. Interactions between generation and religious group in the importance of openness to change values (Study 1) (a) self-direction; (b) stimulation; (c) Hedonism.

adolescents ascribed *lower* importance than their parents (in stimulation, similar importance), to openness. The result is consistent with Armenian obligations to nation, church, and family (O'Grady, 1981; Phinney et al., 2000). The unique results in this very small and highly secluded minority may be interpreted as evidence for a cocooning process (Goodnow, 1997) as socialization promotes children's adoption of relatively conservative values.

In sum, the results of Study 1 exemplify the *context* process, in which religious establishments affect the formation of values and parents' ability to transmit their values from one generation to the next.

Value Continuity Processes when Adolescents Reject their Parents' Religiosity: Study 2

Earlier we presented data showing that similarity in religiosity levels was associated with higher accuracy of perception, acceptance, and congruence between the values of parents and adolescents. Differences in religiosity imply a move away from parents' affiliation to a different stance on religiosity. This secondary analysis did not directly investigate the direction of change in religiosity (e.g., a religious parent could have a non-religious child if either the parent became more religious or the child left the religion). We are not aware of a previous study that directly addressed value continuity processes in families in which adolescents openly rejected their parents' religiosity.

Our second case study, therefore, compared two groups of parent–youth dyads. Youth could come either from religious or non-religious families, but were all self-defined non-religious Israeli Jews. Our first goal was to examine parent–youth value similarity, comparing non-religious families with those of religion leavers. On the one hand, one could expect to see some parent–youth value similarity in both groups, owing to shared genetic heritage and socialization influences. On the other hand, religion leavers may come to adopt values negatively related to religiosity (e.g., hedonism), and reduce the importance of values such as tradition. By leaving religion, youth are making a strong value-relevant decision, possibly rejecting some or much of their parents' values. We therefore expected lower value congruence in parent–child dyads of religion leavers.

The second goal of Study 2 was to address the specific value characteristic of religion leavers. Religion leavers can distance themselves from their religious heritage either because of theoretical/moral reasons (e.g., not believing in humans' subjection to a supreme, divine force) or by rejecting the regulations and behavioral prescriptions of religion, which, in most Western religions, limit individuals' ability to pursue many bodily or sensual desires. The first process will entail mainly a rejection of conformity values (and possibly a strong belief in self-direction) because these values prescribe preservation of the status quo, acceptance of a higher authority over one's life, and subjection to social norms. The second process would mean an especially high preference for hedonism (possibly also stimulation) values.

Participants were 36 non-religious Jewish Israeli university students (39 percent male, Mean age=26.06, SD=2.06) and one of their parents. Seventeen dyads included a religious parent and a non-religious child, while the other group consisted of 19 dyads of predominantly non-religious youth and their parents. We compared the parent–child correlation value profile across the 10 Schwartz values (Rohan & Zanna, 1996) in the two groups. Whereas the average correlation was .50 in non-religious families (SD=.31), in families of religion leavers it was .18 (SD=.30), $t(df$=34$) = 3.19$, $p <.01$. Thus, religion leaving involves a large (D=1.09) difference in parent–child value congruence, exemplifying the importance of religion in family value continuity, and the religiosity process (Figure 16.1).

Intergenerational Differences Contingent on Religiosity Status. As in Study 1, we ran for each value a two-way ANOVA (two generations x two religious groups); main results are available upon request. In this chapter, we focus on the interaction results. Four significant interactions were found between generation and religiosity status in the importance of values. First, as would be expected, religious parents were much higher than either their non-religious offspring or the parents and youth in the non-religious group in tradition values (the *content* process). Second, a weaker difference was found in benevolence values, for which youth who came from non-religious families showed slightly higher importance than other study participants.

Two interaction effects (Figure 16.4) are particularly worth mentioning. As noted above, hedonism is usually negatively associated with religiosity. However, although both groups of youth were non-religious, hedonism was especially high among religion leavers as compared to their religious parents, more than the parallel difference for non-religious parents. Possibly, leaving religion is motivated by high hedonism (rejecting the constraints and regulations associated with religion). Second, conformity values were especially low among religion leavers, perhaps reflecting low importance to the norms and rules associated with religion. Possibly, low conformity may provide a motivational impetus to breaking social constraints, such as the one needed for leaving religion.

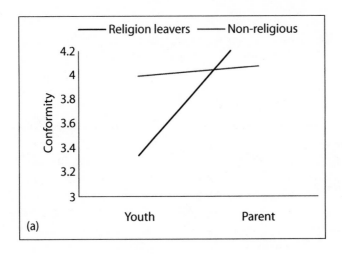

(a)

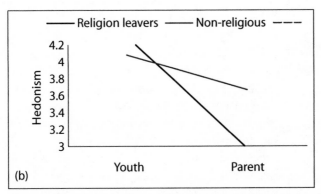

(b)

Figure 16.4. Interactions between generation and religiosity group in the importance of conformity and hedonism values (Study 2) (a) Conformity; (b) Hedonism.

Interestingly, computing the value profile parent–child correlation without conformity and hedonism still showed higher similarity across the eight remaining values in non-religious families ($M= .55$, $SD =.31$) than in families of religion leavers ($M=.24$, $SD=.33$, $t[df=34] = 2.96$, $p <.01$). Thus, conformity and hedonism cannot fully account for the reduction in parent–child congruence among religion leavers.

The unique results in religion leavers suggest several intriguing possibilities. First, we found support for the possibility that rejection of parents' religion is grounded in both the lack of importance to social norms and the desire to engage in pleasurable activities not espoused by religion.

Second, religion leaving was associated with lower parent–child congruence even for the other eight values, indicating a nonspecific distancing from parental values. Third, despite the generally low parent–child value congruence among religious leavers, they still shared their values to some extent with their parents, as indicated in a positive value congruence score, $t(df=16) = 2.60$, $p <.02$. Genetic relatedness between parents and children, shared social environments, or perhaps a successful influence process in values less relevant to religiosity may account for the remaining similarity.

Conclusions

In a meta-analysis, every single one of Schwartz's (1992) 10 values was associated to some extent with within-culture religiosity differences (Saroglou et al., 2004). In our Study 1, six of these values varied significantly across religious groups. Thus, religion is not only relevant to how people behave, but also to their values across many cultures. Religiosity relates to individuals' identity (Paryente & Orr, 2010) and to how individuals socialize their children (Padilla-Walker & Thompson, 2005). Even in contexts in which the political system was opposed to religion, religiosity (or the lack thereof) played a role in individuals' values (Roccas & Schwartz, 1997), and as our Study 2 shows, religion is relevant even to the lives of people who decide to leave it, as apparent from value differences between non-religious youth and religion leavers.

Our analysis points to the importance of religion and religiosity to processes of value influences in the family. The role of culture as the context in which these influences take place has also been exemplified. The position of cultures on the cultural dimensions of power-distance or hierarchy (Hofstede, 1980; Schwartz, 1999) may affect, for instance, tolerance and legitimacy for child influence. Similarly, accuracy of perception of the parent's value may be less relevant to the development of values in narrow-socialization cultures (Arnett, 1995) in which the range of values is limited, possibly enabling children to infer parents' values from many sources other than their own parents. The potential for competing value messages in a culture is also important (Goodnow, 1997). For example, Cavalli-Sforza (1993) described one African context with no schools and only few age peers, where parental influence was the major cultural process. The cultural context can operate through the societal establishments it uses for monitoring the values of future generations. We briefly mentioned two examples (religious and non-religious Jewish Israeli schools, and the secluded

Jerusalem Armenian school), but our findings call for the investigation of additional contextual factors.

As we noted in the introduction to this chapter, one of the complications in the study of religion is its overlap with other factors, in both the cultural level and the individual level (Inglehart & Baker, 2000; Saroglou & Dupuis, 2006). This was the case in the current investigation, too. For example, the two Arab groups differ not only in their religion, but also in their socioeconomic background, as the Arab Christians tend to be more affluent than the Muslims, and have substantially lower birth rates. We thus cannot fully disentangle the effect of religion from that of other variables. Similarly, it is difficult to generalize from the differences between Muslims and Christians in this sociopolitical context to other contexts. Muslim-Christian differences are likely to depend on whether they are both ethnic political minorities (the Israeli case), whether one religious group is dominant and affluent and the other is an immigrant minority (the Dutch case), or whether they are two historically neighboring groups competing for dominance within the same political entity (the Lebanese case, Shiite and Sunni distinctions notwithstanding).

The samples we reached were quite small, which is another limitation. Larger samples with longitudinal designs will provide more power for addressing complex patterns of influence and more validity to causal claims. Nevertheless, the unique findings, especially with regard to the Armenian families, show a promising direction for future research on the role of religion and ethnicity in family value continuity.

We view the set of findings merely as appetizers for future research. Despite its complexity, Figure 16.1 only presents a simplified schematic depiction of processes that are each complicated by the content of values at hand and by the cultural, religious, and perhaps also political context. For example, we focused our review of values on major world religions such as Christianity, Judaism, and Islam. The role of religion in non-Western religions should be addressed. Are some religions more tolerant of change and deviation from tradition, for example? Are there religions whose teachings are less lined up with the conservation side of the openness–conservation dimension? In Study 2 we showed the richness of family processes involving values and religion while focusing on a single ethnic-religious group. A follow-up, hopefully using a longitudinal design, of religion leavers in a multitude of comparable religions and social contexts may not only teach us about religion leavers, but also about religious experience itself.

NOTES

1. The means, standard deviations, and the results of the ANOVAs are available from the authors.

REFERENCES

Acock, A. C., & Bengtson, V. L. (1978). On the relative importance of mothers and fathers: A covariance analysis of political and religious socialization. *Journal of Marriage and the Family*, **40**, 519–530.

Arnett, J. J. (1995). Broad and narrow socialization: The family in the context of a cultural theory. *Journal of Marriage and the Family*, **57**, 615–628.

Barni, D., Ranieri, S., Scabini, E., & Rosnati, R. (2011). Value transmission in the family: Do adolescents accept the values their parents want to transmit? *Journal of Moral Education*, **40**, 105–121. doi: 10.1080/03057240.2011.553797

Bronfenbrenner, U. (1986). Ecology of the family as a context for human development: Research perspectives. *Developmental Psychology*, **22**, 723–742. doi: 10.1037/0012-1649.22.6.723

Cavalli-Sforza, L. L. (1993). How are values transmitted? In M. Hechter, L. Nadel, & R. E. Michod (Eds.), *The origin of values* (pp. 305–317). New York: Aldine de Gruyter.

Cavalli-Sforza, L. L., Feldman, M.W., Chen, K. H., & Dornbusch, S. M. (1982). Theory and observation cultural transmission. *Science*, **218**(4567), 19–27. doi: 10.1126/science.7123211.

Desmond, S. A., Morgan, K. H., & Kikuchi, G. (2010). Religious development: How (and why) does religiosity change from adolescence to young adulthood? *Sociological Perspectives*, **53**, 247–270. doi: 10.1525/sop.2010.53.2.247

Dillon, M., Wink, P., & Fay, K. (2003). Is spirituality detrimental to generativity? *Journal for the Scientific Study of Religion*, **42**, 427–442. doi: 10.1111/1468-5906.00192

Duriez, B., Soenens, B., Neyrinck, B., & Vansteenkiste, M. (2009) Is religiosity related to better parenting?. *Journal of Family Issues*, **30**, 1287–1307. doi: 10.1177/0192513X09334168

Ellison, C. G., & Sherkat, D. E. (1993). Obedience and autonomy: Religion and parental values reconsidered. *Journal for the Scientific Study of Religion*, **32**, 313–329.

Erikson, E. H. (1968). *Identity: Youth and crisis*. New York: Norton.

Flor, D. L., & Knapp, N. F. (2001). Transmission and transaction: Predicting adolescents' internalization of parental religious values. *Journal of Family Psychology*, **15**, 627–645. doi: 10.1037/0893-3200.15.4.627

Fontaine, J. R. J., Duriez, B., Luyten, P., Corveleyn, J., & Hutsebaut, D. (2005). Research: "Consequences of a multidimensional approach to religion for the relationship between religiosity and value priorities." *International Journal for the Psychology of Religion*, **15**, 123–143. Doi: 10.1207/s15327582ijpr1502_2

Glass, J., Bengtson, V. L., & Dunham, C.C. (1986). Attitude similarity in three-generation families: Socialization, status inheritance, or reciprocal influence? *American Sociological Review*, **51**, 685–698.

Goodnow, J. J. (1997). Parenting and the "transmission" and "internalization" of values: From social-cultural perspectives to within-family analyses. In J. E. Grusec

& L. Kuczynski (Eds.), *Handbook of parenting and the transmission of values* (pp. 333–361). New York: Wiley.

Grusec, J. E., & Goodnow, J. J. (1994). Impact of parental discipline methods on the child's internalization of values: A reconceptualization of current points of view. *Developmental Psychology, 30,* 4–19. doi: 10.1037/0012-1649.30.1.4 .

Grusec, J. E., Goodnow, J. J., & Kuczynski, L. (2000). New directions in analyses of parenting contributions to children's acquisition of values. *Child Development, 71,* 205–211. doi: 10.1111/1467-8624.00135.

Hinde, R. (1989). Reconciling the family systems approach and the relationships approach to child development. In K. Kreppner & R. Lerner (eds.), *Family systems and life-span development* (pp. 149–163). Hillsdale, NJ: Erlbaum.

Hofstede, G. (1980). *Culture's consequences: International differences in work-related values.* Beverly Hills, CA: Sage.

Inglehart, R., & Baker, W. E. (2000). Modernization, cultural change, and the persistence of traditional values. *American Sociological Review, 65,* 19–51.

Knafo, A. (2003). Contexts, relationship quality, and family value socialization: The case of parent-school ideological fit in Israel. *Personal Relationships, 10,* 373–390. doi: 10.1111/1475-6811.00055.

Knafo, A., Daniel, E., & Khoury-Kassabri, M. (2008).Values as protective factors against violent behavior in Jewish and Arab high schools in Israel. *Child Development, 79,* 652–667. doi: 10.1111/j.1467-8624.2008.01149.x

Knafo, A., & Schwartz, S. H. (2001). Value socialization in families of Israeli-born and Soviet-born adolescents in Israel. *Journal of Cross-Cultural Psychology, 32,* 213–228. doi: 10.1177/0022022101032002008

(2003). Parenting and adolescents' accuracy in perceiving parental values. *Child Development, 74,* 595–611. doi: 10.1111/1467-8624.7402018

(2004). *Value transmission in the family: Effects of family background and implications for educational achievement.* Jerusalem, IL: NCJW Research Institute for Innovation in Education (Hebrew).

(2008). Accounting for parent–child value congruence: Theoretical considerations and empirical evidence. In U. Schönpflug (Ed.), *Cultural transmission: Developmental, psychological, social, and methodological perspectives* (pp. 240–268). Cambridge: Cambridge University Press.

Knafo, A., & Spinath, F. M. (2011). Genetic and environmental influences on girls' and boys' gender-typed and gender-neutral values. *Developmental Psychology, 47,* 726–731. doi: 10.1037/a0021910

Koenig, L. B., McGue, M., Krueger, R. F., & Bouchard, T. J. (2005). Genetic and environmental influences on religiousness: Findings for retrospective and current religiousness ratings. *Journal of Personality, 73,* 471–488. doi: 10.1111/j.1467-6494.2005.00316.x

Kuczynski, L., Marshall, S., & Schell, K. (1997). Value socialization in a bidirectional context. In J. E. Grusec & L. Kuczynski (Eds.), *Parenting and the internalization of values: A handbook of contemporary theory* (pp. 23–50). New York: Wiley.

Kusdil, M. E., & Kagitcibasi, C. (2000). Tuerk oegretmenlerin deger yoenelimleri ve Schwartz deger kurami [Value orientations of Turkish teachers and Schwartz's theory of values]. In V. Saroglou and P. Galand (Eds.), Identities, values, and religion:

A study among Muslim, other immigrant, and native Belgian young adults after the 9/11 attacks. *Identity*, 4, 97–132. doi: 10.1207/s1532706xid0402_1

Mahoney, A., Pargament, K. I., Tarakeshwar, N., & Swank, A. B. (2001). Religion in the home in the 1980s and 1990s: A meta-analytic review and conceptual analysis of links between religion, marriage, and parenting. *Journal of Family Psychology*, 15, 559–596. doi: 10.1037/1941–1022.S.1.63

Maio, G. R., & Olson, J. M. (1998). Values as truisms: Evidence and implications. *Journal of Personality and Social Psychology*, 74, 294–311. doi: 10.1037/0022–3514.74.2.294

O'Connor, T. G., Hetherington, E. M., & Clingempeel, W. G. (1997). Systems and bidirectional influences in families. *Journal of Social and Personal Relationships*, 14, 491–504. doi: 10.1177/0265407597144005

O'Grady, I. P. (1981). Shared meaning and choice as components of Armenian immigrant adaptation. *Anthropological Quarterly*, 54, 76–81.

Okagaki, L., & Bevis, C. (1999). Transmission of religious values: Relations between parents' and daughters' beliefs. *Journal of Genetic Psychology*, 160, 303–318. doi: 10.1080/00221329909595401

Padilla-Walker, L. M., & Thompson, R. A. (2005). Combating conflicting messages of values: A closer look at parental strategies. *Social Development*, 14, 305–323. doi: 10.1111/j.1467–9507.2005.00303.x

Paryente, B., & Orr, E. (2010). Identity representations and intergenerational transmission of values: The case of a religious minority in Israel. *Papers on Social Representations*, 19, 1–36.

Pepper, M., Uzzell, D., Jackson, T. (2010). A study of multidimensional religion constructs and value in the United Kingdom. *Journal for the Scientific Study of Religion*, 49, 127–146. doi: 10.1111/j.1468–5906.2009.01496.x

Peterson, B. E. (2006). Generativity and successful parenting: An analysis of young adult outcomes. *Journal of Personality*, 74, 847–869. doi: 10.1111/j.1467–6494.2006.00394.x.

Phinney, J. S., Ong, A., & Madden, T. (2000). Cultural values and intergenerational value discrepancies in immigrant and non-immigrant families. *Child Development*, 71, 528–539. doi: 10.1111/1467–8624.00162.

Rabinowitz, D. (2001). The Palestinian citizens of Israel, the concept of trapped minority and the discourse of transnationalism in anthropology. *Ethnic and Racial Studies*, 24, 64–85. doi: 10.1080/01419870150052505

Roccas, S. (2005) Religion and value systems. *Journal of Social Issues*, 61, 747–759. doi: 10.1111/j.1540–4560.2005.00430.x.

Roccas, S., & Schwartz, S. H. (1997). Church-state relations and the association of religiosity with values: A study of Catholics in six countries. *Cross-Cultural Research*, 31, 356–375. doi: 10.1177/106939719703100404

Roest, A. M. C., Dubas, J. S., Gerris, J. R. M., & Engels, C. M. E. (2009). Value similarities among fathers, mothers and adolescents and the role of a cultural stereotype: Different measurement strategies reconsidered. *Journal of Research on Adolescence*, 19, 812–833. doi: 10.1111/j.1532–7795.2009.00621.x

Rohan, M. J., & Zanna, M. P. (1996). Value transmission in families. In C. Seligman, J. M. Olson, & M. P. Zanna (Eds.), *The psychology of values: The Ontario Symposium, Vol. 8* (pp. 253–276). Hillsdale, NJ: Erlbaum.

Saroglou, V., Delpierre, V., & Dernelle, R. (2004). Value and religiosity: A meta-analysis of studies using Schwartz's model. *Personality and Individual Differences*, **37**, 721–734.

Saroglou, V., & Dupuis, J. (2006). Being Buddhist in Western Europe: Cognitive needs, prosocial character, and values. *The International Journal for the Psychology of Religion*, **16**, 163–179. doi: 10.1207/s15327582ijpr1603_2

Schwartz, S. H. (1992). Universals in the content and structure of values: Theoretical advances and empirical tests in 20 countries. *Advances in Experimental Social Psychology*, **25**, 1–65.

    (1999). A theory of cultural values and some implications for work. *Applied Psychology: An International Review*, **48**, 23–47. doi: 10.1111/j.1464–0597.1999.tb00047.x

Schwartz, S. H., & Huismans, S. (1995). Value priorities and religiosity in four western religions. *Social Psychology Quarterly*, **58**, 88–107.

Schwartz, S. H., & Rubel, T. (2005). Sex differences in value priorities: Cross-cultural and multi-method studies. *Journal of Personality and Social Psychology*, **89**, 1010–1028. doi:10.1037/0022–3514.89.6.1010

Troll, L., & Bengtson, V. (1979). Generations and the family. In W. R. Burr, R. Hill, F. I. Nye, & I. L. Reiss (Eds.), *Contemporary theories about the family*, Vol. 1 (pp. 127–161). New York: The Free Press.

Waller, N. G., Kojetin, B. A., Bouchard, T. J., Lykken, D. T., & Tellegen, A. (1990). Genetic and environmental influences on religious interests, attitudes, and values: A study of twins reared apart and together. *Psychological Science*, **1**, 138–142.

Welch, M. R. (1984). Social structural expansion, economic diversification, and concentration of emphases in childhood socialization. *Ethos*, **12**, 363–382. doi: 10.1525/eth.1984.12.4.02a00040

Whitchurch, G. G., & Constantine, L. I. (1993). System theory. In P. Boss (Ed.), *Sourcebook of family theory and methods* (pp. 325–353). New York: Plenum Press.

17 Adolescents' Social Development and the Role of Religion

Coherence at the Detriment of Openness

Vassilis Saroglou

Abstract

Previous reviews of research conclude that, overall, adolescents' religiosity is linked with many positive individual and social outcomes. Only negative forms of religion would imply negative outcomes. In the present chapter, such a conclusion is importantly nuanced. I systematically review here previous studies and present new data on the relation between religiosity (major forms of it) and key aspects of adolescents' social development: personality, values, identity status, and collective (ethnic and immigrants' new) identities. Attention is paid to provide cross-cultural information, when available. In addition, I present a new study integrating the cognitive, emotional, personality, and moral factors involved with religious doubting in adolescence. Consistently across studies and domains of social development, the findings are in favor of the "coherence at the detriment of openness" hypothesis. Adolescent religion seems to reflect stability, conservation, engagement, and cohesion, but potentially somehow at the detriment of plasticity, openness, exploration, and autonomy – all important for optimal development. Complementing others' argument that adolescence is a "sensitive" period for spiritual development, I argue that adolescence is also a "sensitive" period for religious doubting and agnosticism.

What role does religion play in adolescents' social development? More specifically, how does individual religiousness relate to or influence adolescents' personality, values, personal and collective identities, and social relationships? In recent years, several overviews of studies on the role of religion and spirituality on child, adolescent, and youth development in general have been published (for major overviews, see Lerner, Roeser, & Phelps, 2008; Oser, Scarlett, & Bucher, 2006; Roehlkepartain, King, Wagener, & Benson,

2006; see also Boyatzis, 2009; Holden & Vittrup, 2010; King & Roeser, 2009; Scarlett & Alberts, 2010; Warren, Lerner, & Phelps, 2011). The major conclusion consistently observed from these reviews is that, overall, religion/ spirituality has a positive impact on many aspects of adolescent and youth development including meaning, identity, values, prosocial attitudes and behavior, social responsibility, life goals, adjustment, coping with adversity, emotion- and self-regulation, and healthy behaviors (low risk-taking and impulsivity-related behaviors). A very recent meta-analysis of 40 studies confirmed that the religious involvement of adolescents is positively associated with various constructive behaviors and negatively associated with various destructive behaviors (respective average effect sizes, $Zs = .20$ and $-.17$; Cheung & Yeung, 2011). Although most of these reviews are, by the nature of the existing literature, heavily based on cross-sectional and correlational studies, when longitudinal studies are available, they tend to confirm the trends in the findings (see, for instance, French, Eisenberg, Purwomo, & Sallquist, Chapter 6 in this volume).

In the present chapter, the conclusion regarding the positive role of religion/spirituality in the life of adolescents will be nuanced and, in a way, challenged. The argument that will be developed is that the positive outcomes or correlates of religiousness in adolescents' social development are limited. They point to a sense of coherence and stability, but constitute only part of the picture. In fact, adolescents' religiousness does not seem to reflect or contribute to the major trends of optimal development such as openness, autonomy, critical thinking, flexibility, and pluralism.

To support this argument, I will review the empirical research on the role religion plays with regard to four specific domains, each important for adolescent social development: (1) personality (integrative framework of the Five-Factor Model), (2) values (Schwartz's 1992 circumplex model of values), (3) personal identity (Marcia's 1980 model of identity statuses), and (4) collective identities (ethnic and transnational identities, and, for immigrant adolescents, origin and new identities). This review will be importantly, but not exclusively, based on studies (primary studies and meta-analyses) carried out in recent years in our laboratory. The review of domains (1) and (2) will be partly based on existing meta-analyses (Saroglou, 2010; Saroglou, Delpierre, & Dermelle, 2004), but new data will also be presented (e.g., from the European Social Survey and a study on children's values and religion). The review of domains (3) and (4) is totally new. Moreover, a new study will be presented that explores an additional domain, that is (5) religious doubt and the way it can be understood with respect to optimal adolescent development. Finally, in the conclusion, the major findings and the global argument from this review chapter will allow us to revisit the issue of positive versus negative effects of religion in adolescent social development. Suggestions for directions of future research will also be made.

Religion, Spirituality, and Universal Existential and Moral Issues: Clarifications

Before examining the main issues of the present chapter, it is important to define and clarify the constructs of religion and spirituality and their connection with, and distinction from, the universal human tendencies to deal with existential and moral issues.

There exists today some consensus among researchers that religion (or religiosity) and spirituality are overlapping but distinct constructs (Zinnbauer & Pargament, 2005; see also Flanagan, & Jupp, 2007). Empirical research has shown that religiosity and spirituality, despite several commonalities, differ in many psychological characteristics, predictors, and outcomes (Saroglou & Muñoz-García, 2008; Saucier & Skrzypińska, 2006). Religiosity is individuals' reference to (what they consider to be a) transcendence through beliefs, rituals, moral norms, and/or community, somehow regulated by an institutionalized authority. Spirituality is individuals' reference to (what they consider to be a) transcendence through personal beliefs, experiences, and/or moral attitudes that may be independent from any authority or organized group (Saroglou, 2011). However, within the context of organized religions, spirituality has been considered a part of religion (in addition to other aspects such as theology, rituals, and ethics). This is why the two constructs are still treated sometimes as interchangeable. Nevertheless, for the sake of scientific rigor and clarity of communication, it is important to keep the distinction between (traditional) religiosity and (modern) spirituality, at least when referring to modern societies that encourage sacred experiences that are autonomous from religious institutions. Indeed, although many people define themselves as "religious and spiritual," an increasing part of Western populations define themselves as "spiritual, not religious."

In the present chapter, the emphasis will be on the roles of religion and religiosity rather than on the role of (new forms of) spirituality in adolescent development. This is for two reasons. First, in the domain of adolescent development, most research has been carried out in religious contexts, on adolescents who have most often received religious socialization in their family or community in connection with some kind of religious institution and tradition. "Spiritual but not religious" adolescents constitute an emerging reality that will very likely be increasingly present. Studies on the role of (nonreligious) spirituality among these adolescents will soon constitute an important body of research to be reviewed. Second, and in line with the first, using the two terms as interchangeable or using a combined term such as "religion/spirituality" may lead to erroneous conclusions. It could, for instance, be suspected that some of the many positive effects of religion on adolescent development concluded by various studies and reviews previously cited may have been overestimated: spirituality's effects are overall more positive than those of religiosity, and thus "religion" may benefit undeservedly from being combined with "spirituality."

Finally, it is of interest to clarify another distinction. Religiosity and spirituality imply, but are not equivalent to, dealing with existential and moral issues and looking for self-transcendence. The latter are universal human dimensions, whereas being religious or spiritual is less universal. Indeed, religiosity and spirituality imply specific ways of dealing with universal existential and moral issues (e.g., affirmation that one's own life and the world are meaningful; emphasis on specific moral standards and norms; believing in an external, personal or impersonal, transcendence) (Saroglou, 2011). Other people, nonreligious and/or non-spiritual, may deny one or all of the above. The non-distinction between these constructs may contaminate results and inflate the positive effects of religion and spirituality. If, for instance, one conceptualizes and measures spirituality as including compassion for all beings, no doubt positive associations will be found between this construct and prosocial attitudes, values, emotions, and behavior.

Personality and Religiousness: Stability but not (Necessarily) Plasticity

High versus low interest and investment in religious attitudes, beliefs, and practices has traditionally been suspected to reflect, among other factors, individual differences in personality dispositions and traits. Using the terminology of the dominant model of the five basic personality factors, Saroglou and Muñoz-García (2008) stated:

A religious person may think, feel, and behave – personality traits by definition imply some consistency across these three activities – in a somewhat different way than a nonreligious person when facing stress and emotions ('*neuroticism*'), novelty ('*openness to experience*'), challenges from the internal and external world that ask for self-control, orderliness, and responsibility ('*conscientiousness*'), when s/he is invested in interpersonal relationships ('*agreeableness*'), or is in contact and functions with others in general and in groups ('*extraversion*'). (p. 84)

Several dozen studies have investigated how religiousness, and its different forms, is associated with broad personality traits. Using the framework of the Five-Factor Model, a recent meta-analysis of studies with 71 samples from 19 countries (total $N = 21,715$) showed that religiousness (but also fundamentalism and spirituality) is common among people who tend to be high in the dimensions of agreeableness and conscientiousness (Saroglou, 2010). These findings are consistent with those of dozens of other studies using Eysenck's model of personality, where religiousness has typically been found to relate to low psychoticism (Francis, 2009; Lodi-Smith & Roberts, 2007). The studies included in the recent meta-analysis come mostly from Western samples of Christian background, but a few existing studies in other religious and cultural contexts suggest the generalizability of the findings, at least among the three monotheistic religions and Buddhism. Closed-minded (e.g., fundamentalism) versus open-minded (e.g., spirituality) orientations are characterized by, respectively, low and high openness to experience. The other two personality dimensions, that is, extraversion and neuroticism, are either unrelated to religiousness in general or related to it only in very specific contexts (Saroglou, 2010).

Only three studies in that meta-analysis provided data on adolescents. These studies were carried out in Australia (Heaven & Ciarrocchi, 2007), Belgium (Duriez & Soenens, 2006), and Poland (Kosek, 1999). Interestingly, the mean effect sizes of the religiosity–personality associations in these three studies with adolescents parallel those found with young adults and adults (see Table 17.1). In other words, adolescents who are religious tend to be agreeable and conscientious, but not necessarily high or low on extraversion or neuroticism. Moreover, they tend to be slightly low in openness to experience. Several studies on adolescents, using the Eysenck's model, suggest similar personality tendencies toward prosociality, order, and responsibility (i.e., low psychoticism) (Francis, 2009).

Moreover, three longitudinal studies provided information on the causal direction suggesting that child and adolescent personality influences later attitudes toward religion. Religiousness in late adolescence, adulthood, and late adulthood was predicted by conscientiousness or low psychoticism, measured when the participants were children or adolescents (Heaven & Ciarrocchi, 2007; McCullough, Enders, Brion, & Jain, 2005; McCullough, Tsang, & Brion, 2003; Wink, Ciciolla, Dillon, & Tracy, 2007). In addition, adolescents who were open to experience tended to invest more in spirituality

Table 17.1. Mean Effect Sizes (r) of the Personality Correlates of Religiousness

Age Group	k (N)	Extraversion	Agreeableness	Conscientiousness	Neuroticism	Openness to Experience
Adolescents	3 (990)	–.05	**.22**	**.20**	.01	–.13
Young adults	31 (9,433)	.06	**.17**	**.16**	–.02	–.03
Adults	8 (2,281)	**.12**	**.25**	**.14**	–.01	–.09

Note: Results are taken from the meta-analysis by Saroglou (2010). *k* = number of studies. Mean effects are bold when > .10.

in late adulthood (Wink et al., 2007). Of course, the other causal direction, that is, influences of religiousness on adolescents' personality, cannot be excluded. However, the existing evidence is in favor of the idea that adolescents who are agreeable and conscientious tend to embrace – look for or maintain, depending on family's religious socialization – ideologies, practices, and groups (religion) that correspond to these personality tendencies by proclaiming and enforcing social harmony, quality in interpersonal relations, investment in life goals, personal order, and moral self-transcendence in general (Saroglou, 2010).

Agreeableness and conscientiousness are often considered to be the two "moral character" personality traits, since they imply social and personal responsibility (Cawley, Martin, & Johnson, 2000). These two broad personality traits are often found to point to a higher order personality dimension denoting *stability* and *regulation*. In contrast, openness to experience and extraversion – being more heavily "temperamental" factors – are often found to constitute a higher order dimension denoting *plasticity* and *growth* (Digman, 1997; Markon, Krueger, & Watson, 2005; but see Ashton, Lee, Goldberg, & de Vries, 2009). Thus, adolescent religiousness does not seem to necessarily reflect, or result from, personality dispositions for curiosity; experiential openness; alternative ways of thinking, feeling, and acting (openness to experience); or gregariousness, playfulness, and energy (extraversion).

There are a variety of possible trajectories in religiousness during adolescence and early adulthood. However, some decrease in religious practice, identification, and beliefs is a common trend in adolescent development and emerging adulthood (Dillon, 2007; Hood, Hill, & Spilka, 2009). Interestingly, this decrease seems to parallel, or better follow, the developmental changes of personality. Series of studies on the developmental changes of personality attest that, during adolescence, the mean level of agreeableness and conscientiousness decrease, whereas the mean level of openness to experience increases (Roberts, Wood, & Caspi, 2008). It is very likely that the biological, cognitive, relational, and social changes that are concomitant to these personality changes lead to the questioning, doubting, reconsideration, and decrease of religiousness in adolescence (see more in a later section). Thus, the decrease of religiousness in adolescence may result from the same adaptive functions of these personality changes, that is, to distance oneself from what is known and familiar and to explore new and challenging alternatives.

Values and Religiousness: In-Group Conservation but not (Necessarily) Openness

Value hierarchies can be observed universally but differ across groups depending, for instance, on culture, age, and gender, or across individuals as a function of individual differences (Schwartz, 2007). Religiosity of adults, but also adolescents and possibly children, may be more present among people with specific value hierarchies – or, taking the other causal direction, may have an influence on people's value hierarchies. Interestingly, both conceptually and empirically, religiosity is closer to values than to basic personality traits (Roccas, Sagiv, Schwartz, & Knafo, 2002; Saroglou & Muñoz-García, 2008).

Schwartz's (1992) model has been the dominant model of values in the last 20 years. This model includes 10 major values (more precisely, sets of several lower level-specific values) organized under two bipolar, almost orthogonal axes. The first axis opposes values denoting conservation (*tradition, conformity*, and *security*) against values denoting openness to change (*self-direction, stimulation*, and partly *hedonism*). The second axis contrasts self-transcendence (*benevolence* and *universalism*) to self-enhancement (*power, achievement*, and partly *hedonism*).

Another meta-analysis clarified the mean effect sizes of the associations between religiosity and value hierarchies using Scwhartz's model of values (Saroglou et al., 2004). This meta-analysis included 21 samples from studies in 15 different countries (total $N = 8,551$). In that meta-analysis, no distinct analyses were made by age group and there was no study on adolescents. Nevertheless, the majority of the samples consisted of young students (from 18 to 30 years old). The results confirmed earlier theorization and findings by Schwartz and Huismans (1995). Overall (see Table 17.2, first block), religiousness primarily implies valuing conservation (in particular, tradition and conformity) at the detriment of openness to change (self-direction,

Table 17.2. Correlations between Religiousness and Values

	TR	CO	SE	PO	AC	ST	HE	SD	UN	BE
Saroglou et al. (2004) ($k = 21, N =$ 8,551)	.45	.23	.07	−.09	−.11	−.26	−.30	−.24	−.09	.14
ESS 2 (25 countries)										
Adults (41,318)	.34	.16	.13	−.03	−.06	−.20	−.23	−.17	.03	.05
Adolescents (2,323)	.32	.15	.07	−.07	−.01	−.14	−.24	−.13	.04	−.04
ESS 3 (23 countries)										
Adults (38,042)	.32	.16	.14	−.04	−.10	−.18	−.23	−.13	.03	.04
Adolescents (2,055)	.29	.14	.09	−.09	−.03	−.11	−.23	−.13	.03	−.03
Boseret (2009) ($N = 200$ children)	.28	.08	.03	−.03	−.08	.00	−.15	−.19	−.03	.02

Note: For Saroglou et al. (2004), the reported results are weighted mean effect sizes of the meta-analysis (young adults and adults). For ESS2, ESS3, and Boseret (2009), simple coefficient correlations are reported. Adults = ≥ 19 yrs old; adolescents = 13–18 years old; children = 9–12 years old. Correlations are bold when ≥ .10. TR = Tradition; CO = Conformity; SE = Security; PO = Power; AC = Achievement; ST = Stimulation; HE = Hedonism; SD = Self-direction; UN = Universalism; BE = Benevolence.

hedonism, and stimulation). Additionally, religiosity implies valuing limited self-transcendence: benevolence toward in-group members, but not universalism; that is, broad concern for the welfare of all people and the world. Depending on the country's context, the association between religiosity and security may shift from positive (in traditionally religious countries) to negative (when the State is against religion, as in the ex-communist Eastern European countries; Roccas & Schwartz, 1997). The association of religiosity with universalism may turn out to be negative in countries with a dominant mono-religious tradition (e.g., Mediterranean countries of Catholic, Jewish, Muslim, and Orthodox tradition; Saroglou et al., 2004). In sum, general religious attitudes, beliefs, and practices imply valuing conservation and in-group care at the detriment of openness to personal and societal change and hedonism in life.

Very specific open-minded forms of religiousness such as symbolic religious thinking, religious quest (being open to doubting or questioning one's own beliefs), and spirituality may still be concerned with valuing tradition and demonstrating low consideration for hedonism. However, these forms put the emphasis on the axis of self-transcendence (valuing both universalism and benevolence) versus self-enhancement (not valuing power and achievement) (Fontaine, Duriez, Luyten, Corveleyn, & Hutsebaut, 2005; Saroglou, 2008, for review). Nevertheless, it remains unclear whether these results are because of the specific religious forms under study or totally attributable to deeper social cognitive structures denoting flexibility, which in turn are translated, in the religious domain, into symbolic and relativistic religious thinking.

In order to examine whether adolescents' religiosity implies value hierarchies that may or may not be similar to those held by young adults or adults, I carried out, for the purposes of the present chapter, correlational analyses on the data of the European Social Survey (ESS), Waves 2 and 3 (http://www.europeansocialsurvey.org). This data (as in 2008) comes from, respectively, 25 and 23 countries (if combined, this makes 28 countries) and includes a total of, respectively, 45,175 and 40,757 participants.[1] Among these participants, there are 2,323 adolescents (13 to 18-year-olds) in ESS2 and 2,055 adolescents (14 to 18-year-olds) in ESS 3. Values in the ESS are measured through Schwartz's (2003) 21-item Portrait Value Questionnaire (also called Human Values Scale). I computed a global score of religiousness (Cronbach's alphas were .81 in both waves) by averaging the scores participants gave on three items measuring (1) personal religiousness ("Regardless of whether you belong to a particular religion, how religious would you say you are?"), (2) religious public practice ("Apart from special occasions such as weddings and funerals, about how often do you attend religious services?"), and (3) religious private practice ("Apart from when you are at religious services, how often, if at all, do you pray?").

The results from the correlational analyses are presented separately for adolescents and adults (all the non-adolescent participants) in Table 17.2 (second and third blocks). They replicate the results of the 2004 meta-analysis.[2] Moreover, religious adolescents hold value hierarchies that are similar to religious adults' ones, and the similarity in many cases is also reflected in the size of the effects. The only notable difference in effect size seems to be the fact that the modest association between religiousness and security among adults is even weaker in adolescents. Similarly, the negative association between religiousness and stimulation also seems to be attenuated when one shifts from adults to adolescents. These two differences may be because of age and/or cohort. Religiosity of contemporary adolescents, compared to older adults, expresses, to a lesser degree, strong conservatism (security concerns) and discomfort with excitement and challenges in life (stimulation). However, it still reflects, globally across countries, social conformity and attachment to tradition (tradition, conformity, and low self-direction; in other terms, collectivist values) as well as anti-materialism and discomfort with sensuous gratification (low hedonism).

The major trends of adolescents' value hierarchies as a function of religiosity can be observed in an even earlier age, that is, among children of 9 to 12 years old. In the possibly only, to my knowledge, (unpublished) study on religion and Schwartz's values among children, Boseret (2009) distributed questionnaires on different aspects of beliefs and values to 200 Belgian children between the 4th and the 6th grades (mean age = 11.02, SD = 0.9; 40% boys). Values were measured by adapting for children the 21 items of Schwartz's (2003) Human Values Scale used for the European Social Survey. Religiosity was measured through three items referring to the importance of God in one's life, frequency of individual prayer, and frequency of prayer in the family (4-point scales; $\alpha = .72$). As shown in Table 17.2 (last block), children's religiosity was associated with high importance attributed to tradition, and low importance attributed to hedonism and self-direction.

There is thus some lifespan continuity from childhood to adulthood through adolescence in that individual religiosity parallels the preference of conservation values and the low consideration of values denoting autonomy change and hedonism. Taking into account the relative stability of personality throughout the lifespan, one can suspect the underlying personality traits (agreeableness and conscientiousness, but not necessarily openness) and corresponding values (conservation versus openness to change and hedonism) to be partly responsible for the overall relative stability of religiosity throughout the lifespan. Changes in religiosity (Hood et al., 2009), as well as changes in personality (Roberts et al., 2008) and values (Bardi & Goodwin, 2011), throughout the lifespan exist, but they are quantitatively less considerable than stability.

Beyond stability, developmental changes in values exist and seem to parallel changes of personality. More precisely, cross-sectional correlations between age and values in 20 countries (data from the ESS) show that hedonistic values (hedonism and stimulation) are of higher importance among people of younger ages compared to people of older ages, whereas the opposite is true for all three conservation values (Schwartz, 2007). Such developmental trends again parallel those of religiosity, which is lower in late adolescence and emerging adulthood but may increase in adulthood (Dillon, 2007).

Identity Status and Religiousness: Engagement but not (Necessarily) Exploration

In people's lives, and possibly more importantly in adolescent development, religion is often involved with identity processes and outcomes. Religion is indeed concerned, among other things, with providing answers to, and ways of dealing with, existential questions typically involved in personal identity (who I am, where do I come from, what is the goal of my life, and whether the world is meaningful). Having said this, it is more intriguing to examine which kind of identity is facilitated within a religious context, especially among adolescents.

Erikson (1968) distinguished between two key dimensions involved in the adolescent identity crisis, that is, exploration and commitment. Exploration involves testing out possible identity alternatives, whereas commitment entails choosing and investing in a given identity. Crossing these two dimensions, Marcia (1980) conceived four identity statuses: diffusion, foreclosure, moratorium, and achievement. The identity status of *diffusion* is characterized by a lack of both exploration and commitment. In *foreclosure*, people have made identity commitments but have not gone through a process of exploration. *Moratorium* is the process of identity exploration and may or may not lead to commitments. Finally, individuals in identity *achievement* have gone through a process of exploration and made identity commitments. On the basis of existing evidence, a likely normative developmental process seems to be the transition from diffusion, as a starting point, to achievement, as an end point, with foreclosure and moratorium being somewhere in between, depending on many personal and situational factors (Meeus, Iedema, Helsen, & Vollebergh, 1999).

For the purposes of this chapter, I carried out a search for published studies on religion and identity status through PsycINFO (as of August 2011). In total, 19 published studies among adolescents and late adolescents were identified, presenting results from 24 samples (see Table 17.3). The studies were carried out mostly in the United States and Belgium, but also in Canada and Israel. Participants were mostly of mainstream Christian traditions (Protestantism and Catholicism), but there were also studies on Jewish (Markstrom-Adams & Smith, 1996; Tzuriel, 1984), Muslim (Saroglou & Galand, 2004), and Mormon adolescents (Markstrom-Adams, Hofstra, & Dougher, 1994). The findings, beyond minor divergences, converge to demonstrate a clear pattern of how religiousness in general, and specific religious orientations in particular, are interconnected with identity status. General religiousness and indicators of religious involvement and practice are positively

Table 17.3. Studies on Religion and Identity Status in Adolescence and Late Adolescence

Study	Sample (N)	Country	Rel. Dimensions	Major Findings
Duriez, Smits, and Goossens (2008)	Flemish (Catholic) adol. (724; longitudinal)	Belgium	R. Transcendence Symbolic R. style	+Normative ident. +Informational, -Diffuse/avoidant
Duriez and Soennes (2006)	1. Flemish late adol. (332) 2. Flemish middle adol. (323)	Belgium	R. Transcendence Symbolic R. style	+Normative (1) +Infor., -Diff. (1, 2)
Duriez, Soenens, and Beyers (2004)	Flemish (Catholic) l. adol. (335)	Belgium	R. Transcendence Symbolic R. style	+Normative ident. +Inform., -Diff.
Fulton (1997)	White students in Christian college (176)	United States	Intrinsic R. Extrinsic R. Quest R.	+ACH, -DIFF +MOR, DIFF, FOR +MOR
Hardy, Pratt, Pancer, Olsen, and Lawford (2011)	Late adol. (418; longitudinal)	Canada	Religious change	-DIFF; -MOR, +FOR (changes)
Hunsberger, Pratt, and Pancer (2001)	University (132) and high school (937) students	Canada	R. commitment R. doubt Managing doubt	+FOR +MOR, +DIFF +ACH
Hutsebaut (1997)	Students (539)	Belgium	Orthodoxy Against religion	+FOR +DIFF
Klaassen and McDonald (2002)	Students in Christian university(160)	Canada	Quest R.	+MOR, -DIFF
Leak (2009)	Students (228)	United States	R. commitment Faith develop. R. fundamental.	+ACH +MOR -MOR

Study	Sample	Country	Measure	Findings
Lee, Miller, and Chang (2006)	Christian Korean-American adol. (49)	United States	Intrinsic R.	+ACH, +FOR, -MOR, -DIFF.
Markstrom (1999)	Afrian- (62) and European- (63) American adol.	United States	R. practice	No findings
Markstrom-Adams and Smith (1996)	1. Mormon & non-M. adol. (85) 2. Jewish adol. (102)	United States Canada	Extrinsic R. Indiscriminate R.	+DIFF (1, 2) +FOR (1), ACH (2)
Markstrom-Adams, Hofstra, and Dougher (1994)	1. Mormon adol. (36) 2. Christian adol. (47)	United States	Church attend.	+FOR, -DIFF (1,2); +ACH(1), -ACH(2)
McKinney and McKinney (1999)	Students, mostly Christian (77)	United States	R. practice and commitment	-MOR, -DIFF
Padilla-Walker, McNamara Barry, Carroll, Madsen, and Nelson (2008)	Students (491), mostly Christian and European-American	United States	Religiosity	+FOR
Puffer, Pence, Graverson, Wolfe, Pate, & Clegg (2008)	Religious adol. (600)	United States	Religious doubt Quest R Intrinsic R.	+MOR, +DIFF +ACH, +MOR -MOR, -DIFF
Saroglou and Galand (2004)	1. Native late adol. (81) 2. Muslim immigrant late adol. (72) 3. Other immigrant l. adol. (86)	Belgium	Religiosity (R) Spirituality (S)	+ACH, +FOR (1,2,3), +MOR (1); -DIFF (1,3)
Tzuriel (1984)	Israeli students (1129)	Israel	Religiousness	+ Commitment and Purposefulness
Verhoeven and Hutsebaut (1995)	Students (1,438)	Belgium	R. practice Personal religion Irreligion	+FOR +ACH +DIFF

Note: R. = religious; ACH = achievement; DIFF = diffusion; FOR = foreclosure; MOR = moratorium.

associated with commitment in identity; that is, positively with achievement and/or foreclosure, and negatively with moratorium and/or diffusion. Finer distinctions are obtained when focusing on specific religious dimensions. Intrinsic religion or symbolic religious thinking predicts high achievement, whereas extrinsic religiosity or orthodoxy predicts high foreclosure. People high in moratorium tend to present many doubts about religion; they may also be high in quest religiosity or high in faith development.

The general trend, consistent across studies, countries, and religious traditions, is that religion in adolescence and youth implies, or at least is associated with, commitment but not necessarily exploration. Exploration in personal identity seems to be typical of a quest-religious orientation or faith development. Irreligiosity and religious doubts may also be characterized by exploration, but they may also reflect the presence of a diffused identity status.

Three studies in Belgium (Flanders) by Duriez and collaborators (see also Table 17.3) used Berzonsky's (1990) more recent model of three identity styles. This model distinguishes between informational, normative, and diffuse/avoidant styles.

Information oriented individuals deal with identity issues by actively seeking out and evaluating relevant information before making commitments. When confronted with information that is dissonant with their self-conceptions, they will revise these self-perceptions. *Normative oriented* individuals rely on the norms and expectations of significant others (e.g., parents or authority figures) when confronted with identity-relevant issues. They rigidly adhere to their existing identity structure, into which they assimilate all identity-relevant information. *Diffuse/avoidant oriented* individuals avoid personal issues and procrastinate decisions until situational demands dictate their behavior, resulting in a fragmented identity structure. (Duriez et al., 2008, p. 1024)

Consistently across the three studies, being a believer – a dimension these authors called Inclusion versus Exclusion of Transcendence – implied a normative identity style. Approaching the religious ideas in a symbolic rather than literal way implied an informative identity style and low diffuse/avoidant style.

Studies on religion and identity formation most often provide cross-sectional data and focus on patterns of individual differences. They are thus insufficient to inform us on the role of religion regarding the underlying processes and patterns of identity changes. Nevertheless, two recent longitudinal studies among Belgian (Duriez et al., 2008) and Canadian (Hardy et al., 2011) adolescents provide interesting initial evidence in favor of bidirectional links between religion and identity formation. First, the maintenance of, or an increase in, religious involvement (attendance to religious service) across late adolescence and emerging adulthood predicts an increase in foreclosure and a decrease in diffusion and moratorium, that is, commitment but no exploration (Hardy et al., 2011). (An increase of commitment together with exploration, i.e., achievement, was present among adolescents with community involvement but not religious involvement). The opposite process also exists: once identity commitments are made, they facilitate religious involvement (Hardy et al., 2011). In addition, identity styles may or may not have real impact on being globally religious, but high versus low exploration in identity later influences the way one approaches religious ideas, symbolically versus literally, respectively (Duriez et al., 2008).

In sum, religion, compared to irreligion, follows and contributes to commitment in identity, often by adopting that which has been transmitted by authority figures and parents. A foreclosed identity is clearly present in traditional and orthodox religious environments. Irreligion is more often present among adolescents with low commitment but possibly also among those with high identity exploration. Only symbolic religious approaches and quest-religious orientation seem to result from a process of actively seeking, testing, and revising information during identity formation.

Collective Identities and Religiousness: Ethnic but not (Necessarily) New and Transnational Identities

Beyond personal identity, children, adolescents, and adults deal with (re-) elaboration of their collective, social identities. This includes ethnic (and race) identity (Quintana & McKown, 2008), but also new (for those born of immigration), multiple, and transnational identities (e.g., European or citizen of the world). The focus of this section will be on the role of religion with regard to ethnic (for natives and immigrants), new/adoptive (for immigrants, in the process of acculturation), and transnational identities of adolescents and young adults.

As argued elsewhere (Saroglou & Cohen, in press), there are several reasons to favor the hypothesis that religiosity should relate positively to ethnic identity. The two share common collectivist needs and values, concerns for self-enhancement and collective self-esteem, as well as the need for self-transcendence. In addition, historically, religions and nations or ethnic groups have incarnated entities that seem to meet, through symbols,

rituals, and ideas, the human search for unity, continuity, and even whole-
ness (Saroglou, 2006). Sociological work has even established a typology of
the relations between ethnicity and religion (see Kivisto, 2007). In few cases,
the two may be independent (e.g., American Indians, Romania). However,
in most cases, either (1) ethnicity reinforces religion (e.g., Serbian or Greek
Orthodox, Church of England), or (2) religion is a major foundation of ethnicity (e.g., Amish, Jews), or shapes, colors ethnicity (e.g., Irish, Italian, or
Polish Catholics).

Several studies suggest that adolescents' and young adults' religiosity positively relates to ethnic identity and pride, but not broader identities. As multi-country data from the European Values Study shows, young
Europeans (18–29 years old) who identify strongly with their religion
(Catholics and Protestants) exhibit a stronger national pride (Campiche,
1997), stronger feelings of belonging to their region and country, and
weaker feelings of belonging to Europe and the world, compared to their
nonreligious peers (Belot, 2005; Bréchon, 2003).

Other recent studies confirm the positive association between religiosity and ethnic (origin) identity among adolescents and young adults who
live in Western countries and belong to ethno-religious minorities and/or
are born of immigrants. However, these studies also show that religiosity
within these ethnic minorities is either unrelated or negatively related to
identification with the new, adoptive country and culture. This was found
to be the case in European countries (Belgium and/or the Netherlands) for
Jews (Saroglou & Hanique, 2006), Muslims of North African and Turkish
descent (Friedman & Saroglou, 2010; Güngör, Fleischmann, & Phalet, 2011;
Saroglou & Galand, 2004; Saroglou & Mathijsen, 2007; Verkuyten & Yildiz,
2007), and other (Christian) adolescents born of immigrants from different countries (Friedman & Saroglou, 2010; Saroglou & Galand, 2004). The
same was the case in the United States with Asian-Americans and African
Americans (but not Latinos; Ghorpade, Lackritz, & Singh, 2006), and
Muslims from various countries (Sirin et al., 2008).

The relation of immigrants' religiosity with only strong ethnic/origin
identity and, possibly, even weak identity with the new/adoptive culture
seems to be rather consistent across studies. Note, however, that most
often these studies include samples from ex-immigrant populations of low
or medium socioeconomic status. An exploratory study on adult expatriates in Brussels, originating from other Western countries and working in
European institutions or having good jobs in companies, suggested that the
picture may be more complex, depending on the specific religious denomination. Indeed, among Protestants from North European countries and

Christians from the United States, religiosity was related to high identification with the host country, that is, Belgium, whereas the opposite was
the case with Orthodox Christians coming from the Balkan countries;
Catholics from other European countries were in the between (Rangel &
Saroglou, 2010).

Is such a pattern of results positive or negative for adolescent and youth
development? Some scholars have argued that religion's role in the development of a strong ethnic identity is part of positive youth development
since it allows for integration into a community, a sense of belonging, pride
that contributes to positive mental health, and the development of a sense
of responsibility, especially for ethnic minorities and immigrants (e.g.,
Juang & Syed, 2008; King & Roeser, 2009). This may be true, especially as
far as the mental health of immigrant and minority groups is concerned.
Religious institutions, beliefs, and practices, as well as individual religiosity of the members of these groups are reasonably considered, both in
sociological and psychological research, to positively contribute to several
aspects of mental health, integration to a community, and social support
(Cadge & Ecklund, 2007; Viladrich & Abraído-Lanza, 2009). Studies on
African Americans confirm this idea (e.g., Bierman, 2006; Ellison, Musick,
& Henderson, 2008).

Nevertheless, this is just part of a bigger picture. As the above mentioned studies in ethno-religious minorities suggest, strong identification
with the culture of origin among religious adolescents and young adults
born of immigrants does not seem to be paralleled by strong identification with, and acculturation into, the new, adoptive country; the two may
even be in conflict. Thus, religiosity may contribute to adolescent immigrants' integration into their ethno-religious community (which in turn is
beneficial when facing mental health risks and when needing a minimal
insertion into a local community), but not to the broader multiethnic and
multireligious national community (which supposedly contributes to optimal well-being and full and deep acculturation). Given the importance of
developing a double positive identification with respect to both original
and adoptive cultures (i.e., the optimal acculturation strategy of "integration"), doubts may occur as to how helpful religion may be for immigrants'
full acculturation. This is what initial evidence suggests: religiosity predicts not only low identification with the adoptive country, but also low
acculturation attitudes and practices (Ghorpade et al., 2006; Saroglou &
Mathijsen, 2007). Moreover, there is some evidence that, under specific
contextual influences (e.g., perceived discrimination, large cultural distance), religiosity of early adolescents from an ethno-religious minority

predicts prejudice toward other ethno-religious and convictional groups (Verkuyten & Thijs, 2010).

In the context of perceived discrimination and/or relations of conflict between the majority and the minority, it may be that religiosity directly or indirectly predicts low well-being among minority members. For instance, rather than buffering, religiousness was found to exacerbate the deleterious effects of discrimination and acculturative stress on depressive symptoms among Mexican-Americans (Ellison, Finch, Ryan, & Salinas, 2009). In another study on Belgian Muslim late adolescents and young adults born of immigrants, religiosity was found to indirectly relate to decreased self-esteem and increased depressive symptoms through perceived religious intolerance from the majority and feelings of anger toward the majority (Friedman & Saroglou, 2010).

Attachment to family and thus intergenerational transmission may be a key mediator of the preferential relation between religion and ethnic/origin identity rather than new, adoptive country identity and full acculturation. Research shows that family plays an important role in transmitting values, religion, and ethnic identities, especially among immigrants (Güngör et al., 2011; Knafo, Daniel, Gabay, Zilber, & Shir, Chapter 16 in this volume); and that family-related processes may be partially responsible for religious young people's well-being (Sabatier, Mayer, Friedlmeier, Lubiewska, & Trommsdorff, 2011) as well as heritage culture maintenance and weak acculturative change (Güngör et al., 2011).

Finally, note that the synthesis of recent research focused on the role of religion in collective identities for natives and immigrants. Interestingly, in contrast to religiosity, spirituality of adolescents and young adults implies high importance attributed to the value of universalism (Spain; Saroglou & Muñoz-García, 2008) and strong identification as a citizen of the world among adolescents of various cultural backgrounds: natives of Christian tradition, Muslims and Christians born of immigrants, all living in the same country (Belgium: Saroglou & Galand, 2004; Saroglou & Mathijsen, 2007). These studies suggest that a shift from traditional, in-group religiosity, to more open-to-the-world spirituality may be responsible for, or at least reflect, a valorization of universalistic ideals. However, prudence is needed. It may be that spiritual and religious adolescents and young adults, particularly those born of immigrants, who strongly identify with the citizen-of-the-world identity indeed point to a faith that transcends ethnic and national barriers (e.g., Universal Church for Christians, Ummah for Muslims, spiritual universe for non-atheists), but not necessarily a faith that supports multiple collective identities, multiculturalism, and a universe fully tolerant of all convictions (see Saroglou & Galand, 2004).

Religious Doubt: Relational Insecurity but also Optimal Social Development

Doubting religious beliefs, and religion per se, is a process that typically emerges in adolescence (Hood et al., 2009). For instance, doubt may arise regarding religious beliefs' logical pertinence and relation to truth and regarding religion's social usefulness and moral quality. In psychology of religion, there has been some ambivalence regarding religious doubt. Initially, religious doubt was perceived to constitute a maturational process inherent to religious faith. In the conceptualization of religious quest as a specific reflective and mature religious orientation, valuing doubt is an important component that coexists with self-criticism and openness to the possibility of changing one's own beliefs (Batson, Schoenrade, & Ventis, 1993).

However, the empirical evidence suggests that, overall, religious doubt in adolescence is more often a precursor to "losing" religion than to a maturation of one's faith (Hood et al., 2009). Religious doubts are not exclusively focused on one or a few specific aspects of religion, but quickly become numerous and lead to more global negative attitudes toward religion, thus facilitating the decrease and abandon of religious practice, group identification, and beliefs (Altemeyer, 2004).

In addition, as far as psychological well-being is concerned, religious doubt is typically found to relate to psychological distress, anxiety, and low quality parent–child relationships, particularly among adolescents and young adults (Hunsberger, Pratt, & Pancer, 2002; Kézdy, Martos, Boland, & Horváth-Szabó, 2011). The causal direction may be double-sided. On one hand, adolescents who tend to be emotionally unstable and, in particular, insecure in their attachment to parents, may more easily fall into a state of turmoil with regard to religion as a way to express their discomfort and opposition to religious parents or to the environment of socialization in general. On the other hand, distancing oneself from one's parents and their religion may create a source of conflict and contribute to emotional instability and relational anxiety. In contrast with religious doubt, religious continuity in adolescence is facilitated in the context of emotional stability and positive quality relationships with one's parents. In turn, religious continuity may contribute to and enhance emotional and relational stability and positivity.

The argument that will be presented here is that, beyond its disadvantages in terms of emotional instability and relational insecurity, religious doubt may be a sign of, or contributor to, positive social development of adolescents in many other respects. Integrating fragmented evidence from previous research and theory, Scardigno and Saroglou (2009b) hypothesized that adolescent religious doubt points to many positive aspects of social development: personality (in particular, openness to experience), self- and relational development (individuation-autonomy with respect to parents and openness to peer influences), increased interest in sexuality (resulting in some disinhibition), moral development (in particular, high sensitivity to moral hypocrisy), and cognitive development (decreased magical thinking and increased rational thinking).

Scardigno and Saroglou (2009b) integrated each of these factors into the same study as correlates and predictors of adolescents' religious doubts. They administered questionnaires to 307 Belgian adolescents (12 to 20 years old; mean age = 15.37, SD = 1.75; boys = 44%) that measured attachment to parents (Hazan & Shaver, 1987), individuation with respect to parents (12 items from the Emotional Autonomy Scale; Schmitz & Baer, 2001), peer influence (ad hoc measure of seven items), disinhibition (i.e., the seeking of intense experiences in parties, social drinking, and sex – a subscale of the Sensation Seeking Scale; Zuckerman, 1971), sensitivity to moral hypocrisy (ad hoc measure of 11 items), magical thinking (subscale of the Disgust scale; Olatunji et al., 2007), abstract/rational thinking (20 items from the R80 and R85 intelligence tests that focus on logical results in resolving various kinds of problems), and openness to experience (from the Big Five Inventory; John, Donahue, & Kentle, 1991). In addition, they investigated the intensity of religious doubt through a measure of 11 items that, after an exploratory factor analysis, was found to tap three interrelated but distinct types of doubt. These were (1) cognitive doubts (religious beliefs do not seem to be true and logical), (2) social doubts (religion seems to be outdated with respect to the needs and challenges of contemporary society), and (3) moral doubts (human suffering and injustice raise doubt in religion) (Scardigno & Saroglou, 2009a).

The results on the associations between religious doubts and the hypothesized correlates are detailed in Table 17.4 (partial correlations controlling for gender and age did not change the results). With the exception of peer influences, all other hypothesized factors turned out to be significant. Religious doubts, most clearly the cognitive and social doubts, but occasionally also the moral doubts, were more present among adolescents with

Table 17.4. Types of Religious Doubt and Correlations with Aspects of Social Development

Aspects of Social Development	Cognitive Doubts	Social Doubts	Moral Doubts
Relational factors			
Insecure attachment (father)	.11*	.15**	.07
Insecure attachment (mother)	.07	.12*	.11*
Self-development			
Individuation	.22***	.21***	.07
Peer influences	−.07	.04	.04
Moral factors			
Sensitivity to hypocrisy	.20***	.24***	.11*
Biological changes-based factors			
Disinhibition	.24***	.20**	.08
Cognitive factors			
Intelligence (abstract)	.20***	.11*	.06
Magical thinking	−.16**	−.19***	−.08
Personality			
Openness to experience	.15**	.15*	.04

Note: N = 307. Results are taken from Scardigno and Saroglou (2009b). Copyright © 2009 by Rosa Scardigno and Vassilis Saroglou.
* $p < .05$. ** $p < .01$. *** $p < .001$.

insecure attachment (to both father and mother), high openness to experience, need for individuation, sensitivity to moral hypocrisy, rational thinking, and, finally, low magical thinking. Distinct correlations by age group (three age groups were created) suggest that factors related to cognitive development (abstract thinking, low magical thinking), sexual development (disinhibition), and self-development (individuation) play a role in religious doubt from early adolescence (12–14 years old). From the age of 15–16 years, moral and personality factors (sensitivity to moral hypocrisy, openness to experience) also start to play a role in religious doubt.

Given some possible overlap between these various constructs associated with high religious doubt, a multiple regression analysis was also conducted. As shown in Table 17.5, it turned out that many dimensions involved in adolescent development uniquely and additively predict high religious doubt. This was the case with moral (sensitivity to hypocrisy), cognitive (low magical thinking), social-relational (individuation and insecure attachment), and sexuality-based (disinhibition) factors.

It seems reasonable to conclude from the results of that study that typical processes inherent to adolescent social development are responsible for

Table 17.5. Multiple Regression of Religious Doubt (Cognitive and Social) on the Significant Predictors

	b	t-test
Insecure attachment (parents)	.10	1.66†
Individuation	.12	1.97*
Disinhibition	.16	2.74**
Sensitivity to hypocrisy	.17	3.10**
Magical thinking	−.16	−2.86**
$R^2 = .15$		

Note: N = 307. Results are taken from Scardigno and Saroglou (2009b). Copyright © 2009 by Rosa Scardigno and Vassilis Saroglou.
* $p < .05$. ** $p < .01$. † $p < .10$.

religious doubt in adolescence. Abandoning magical thinking and developing rational, abstract thinking can call into question religious beliefs and practices that may appear to be incompatible with truth and rationality (see also Nybord, 2009). Openness to experience and disinhibition place the priority of attention and interests on sexuality, gender relations, dating, and new, alternative, and sensation-seeking based experiences. Religion, with which the above constructs may be in conflict, is thus put in the margin. There is considerable evidence on religion's effect in adolescence and youth on inhibiting behaviors such as risk-taking activities, smoking, sexual behavior (Cheung & Yeung, 2011), and even humor (Saroglou, 2002). Aversion toward moral hypocrisy, alone or in combination with rational thinking, can lead to criticism of religious hypocrisy, especially in reference to institutions and important figures (see also Altemeyer, 2004). Finally, individuation can lead to reflection on and distance-taking from everything that represents the parental world, societal norms, and culture's established traditions. From this perspective, religion seems to be a susceptible target since it often represents an ancestral past and a component of the "establishment."

Therefore, one can wonder whether it is not more reasonable, instead of seeing adolescent religious doubt as a problem inducing potential risks for optimal development, to consider it as being in line with the adaptive functions of the many changes in adolescence. Integrating what was reviewed in the previous sections, one cannot neglect the fact that biological and social changes in adolescence result in personality, values, and identity changes that have obvious adaptive functions for growth, exploration, plasticity, and thus both personal and societal transformations. Distancing oneself from religion may thus be natural in light of these adaptive functions, whereas religious continuity without questioning may, from this perspective, be mal-adaptive. Thus, in comparison to childhood, where it seems to be somehow natural to hold (1) religious beliefs in counter-intuitive, mostly benevolent but surely omnipotent agents, (2) wishful thinking transformed in prayer, and (3) belief in intentionality and order in the world (Boyer, 2001; Keleman, 2004; Woolley & Phelps, 2001), religion in adolescence may be less natural.

Such a concluding argument may be seen to be in total contrast with the idea that adolescence is a "sensitive" period for spiritual development (Good & Willoughby, 2008). The authors define a sensitive period as "a span of time that is optimal for developing a certain skill, capacity, or behavior" (p. 32). They argue that normative developmental characteristics of ado-lescence may make teenagers more responsive to spiritual overtures. These characteristics are abstract thinking, metacognition, conversion and com-mitment experiences based on strong emotions, and the need to cope with adversity, as well as endurance of commitments throughout the lifespan. My argument is not really in contrast with this, but importantly complements it. First, Good and Willoughby (2008) maintain an ambiguity by using in their review "spirituality" and "religiosity" interchangeably. No doubt, nor-mative developmental changes may push adolescents to orient themselves, through religious doubting, toward reflective and autonomous spirituality and mature forms of religion and faith (Oser et al., 2006; Scarlett & Albert, 2010). The question – at the center of the adaptive functions issue – is whether this process represents a major pathway or concerns a minority of adolescents. Evidence is in favor of the idea that in adolescence, at least in Western countries, religious doubting and apostasy is much more com-mon than religious and spiritual conversions (Hood et al., 2009). Second, no doubt, adolescence may be a more sensitive, more efficient period for religious and spiritual conversions and commitments than later age peri-ods; this may be interesting (in terms of applications) for those who value religion and/or spirituality. However, the same is true for alternative forms of worldviews and ideologies: adolescence, for reasons that are probably similar to those as for spirituality and religiosity, may be a "sensitive period" for agnosticism, irreligion, and atheism, too.

Conclusion: Positive or Negative Role of Religion?

The concluding argument of the present review will differ from conclu-sions of recent review books and chapters on religious and spiritual devel-opment in general or among adolescents in particular. In these reviews, as mentioned earlier in the introduction, the conclusions focus on the positive role of religion (and/or spirituality), although the authors also acknowledge some negative aspects of religion. For instance, "involvement with religion can promote many aspects of adolescent wellbeing and identity and enhance one's sense of purpose and meaning in life and thus service towards others" (Boyatzis, 2009, p. 61); and "increased understanding will elucidate how spirituality may serve as a potentially potent aspect of the developmental system, through which young people can gain a greater understanding of themselves and their connections to the greater world in ways that fosters a sense of responsibility and compassion to the greater good" (King & Roeser, 2009, p. 471). More nuanced conclusions put the emphasis on some forms of religion: "*higher stages* of positive religious and spiritual development provide adaptive functions" (Oser et al., 2006, p. 991; my italics).

In those reviews, the negative aspects of religion are not totally neglected, but only briefly presented. Moreover, these aspects are located in negative forms of institutional and/or individual religion, such as belonging to cults, authoritarian religious groups, and terrorist organizations; having occultist practices, being extrinsic in religious orientation, having negative images of God, experiencing negative religious emotions, or having "pathological spiritual development;" and they are diagnosed by their negative effects especially in terms of prejudice, violence, and risks for mental disorder (Holden & Vittrup, 2010; King & Roeser, 2009; Oser et al., 2006; Scarlett & Albert, 2010; Wagener & Mlony, 2006).

I contest neither the positive role of religion (although some prudence is needed in light of the fact that most research is based on correlational data and paper-and-pencil measures) nor the negative effects of problematic religious expressions. However, it seems somehow easy to locate the negative effects on adolescents' development in only problematic religious forms. Additionally, it is easily acceptable that religious and spiritual expressions characterized by flexibility, questioning, symbolic thinking, and maturity lead to positive outcomes whereas authoritarian, dogmatic, or neurotic religious forms contribute to negative outcomes. It may also be that the real cause is not "religion" per se or its specific forms, but underlying social cognitive structures typical of closed-mindedness or neuroticism-related dispositions and traits.

What, on the contrary, is at the heart of the argument in the present chapter is that personal, general, common religiousness (positive attitudes toward religion, common religious beliefs, investment, practice, and/or identification) among adolescents sampled from the general population of average religiosity reflect, or contribute to, *limited* positive outcomes in relation to social development. Moreover, it is the same underlying processes that explain both the positivity and its limitations. As the research reviewed in this chapter shows, adolescents' religion overall reflects, results from, or influences:

(1) stability in personality (in relation with the self and the others) but not necessarily growth and plasticity;

(2) in-group social responsibility and conservation of social order instead of individualism–hedonism in values but not necessarily universalistic concerns and autonomy, thus openness to change;

(3) coherence, meaning, and goals that allow for a sense of engagement in personal identity, but not necessarily exploration of the alternatives and re-elaboration of this identity;

(4) attachment to the ethnic identity – and thus the origin identity for adolescents born of immigration – but not necessarily attachment and acculturation to the new/adoptive culture, and endorsement of trans-national, frontier-breaking identities; and

(5) relational security in attachment but low need for individuation and dis-inhibition as well as a tendency for magical thinking and low abstract, rational thinking.

In sum, adolescent religion seems to lead to or consolidate social stability and personal coherence at the cognitive, moral, emotional, and social levels, but somehow at the detriment of openness, autonomy, flexibility, critical thinking, and pluralism, all important for optimal development. This concerns domains of major importance for adolescent social development such as personality, values, personal and collective identities, attachment to parents, individuation, sexuality, and cognition.

In a way, this double-sided role of religion in adolescence parallels what research has shown regarding religion's role in mental health and optimal well-being in general. On the basis of studies among members of new religious movements, Buxant and Saroglou (2008) concluded that belonging to these groups helps members feel good, since it provides structure and personal strength, especially in the context of previous vulnerability. However, this is at the detriment of optimal development and well-being, which include autonomy, flexibility, and critical thinking. Similarly, Gartner, Larson, and Allen (1991), reviewing research on religion and mental health in general, concluded that religion may be an efficient means to maintain or restore control in situations implying under-control, but nevertheless includes potential risks for over-control. Adolescent religiosity seems to function in a similar way: it fosters coherence, but one may need to look to other resources to enhance openness.

At least two issues seem to be key for future research. As mentioned earlier, an emerging part of Westerners, certainly adults but also adolescents, define themselves as no longer religious, but spiritual. The contrast between religion and spirituality seems stronger among adolescents than adults (Saroglou, 2003). To the extent that there is some shift from traditional religion to more autonomous and reflective forms of spirituality, it may be that some of the conclusions of the present review need to be re-examined. For instance, modern spirituality and symbolic forms of faith seem to be less characterized by discomfort with novelty and concerns for conservation of social order, family, and national security and instead reflects, more clearly than religiosity, ethical concerns of interpersonal care and self-transcendence (Fontaine et al., 2005; Saroglou & Muñoz-García, 2008).

Another important issue is how culture influences the religion's role with regard to adolescent social development (see, for instance, Bond, Lun, and Li, Chapter 5 in this volume; and Trommsdorff, Chapter 1 in this volume). Throughout different sections of the present chapter, the emphasis was in showing how the major lines of existing research seem to apply across various religious and cultural contexts. However, there is a tremendous need for more nuanced approaches that allow for detecting cultural specifics. Emerging research in psychology of religion and culture (Saroglou & Cohen, in press, for review) as well as in psychology of human development and culture (Bornstein, 2010, for review) confirms the importance of a culturally sensitive perspective on our psychological understanding of how religion works in people's, including adolescents', lives.

NOTES

1. These countries are: Austria, Belgium, Denmark, Estonia, Finland, France, Germany, Hungary, Ireland, Norway, Poland, Portugal, Spain, Slovakia, Slovenia, Sweden, Switzerland, the Netherlands, United Kingdom, Ukraine (both waves), Czech Republic, Greece, Iceland, Luxembourg, Turkey (2nd wave), Bulgaria, Cyprus, and Russia (3rd wave).
2. When computing the average of the distinct-by-country correlations, the associations of religiousness with benevolence and universalism (positive) as well as power and achievement (negative) become slightly stronger (e.g., for ESS3, respectively, .09, .07, -.08, and -.13). Note also that Schwartz (Chapter 4 in this volume) presents results distinct by religious group.

REFERENCES

Altemeyer, B. (2004). The decline of organized religion in Western civilization. *International Journal for the Psychology of Religion*, **14**, 77–89.

Ashton, M. C., Lee, K., Goldberg, L. R., & de Vries, R. E. (2009). Higher order factors of personality: Do they exist? *Personality and Social Psychology Review*, 13, 79–91.

Bardi, A., & Goodwin, R. (2011). The dual route to value change: Individual processes and cultural moderators. *Journal of Cross-Cultural Psychology*, 42, 271–287.

Batson, C. D., Schoenrade, P., & Ventis, W. L. (1993). *Religion and the individual: A social-psychological perspective*. New York: Oxford University Press.

Belot, C. (2005). Du local au mondial: Les espaces d'appartenance des jeunes Européens [From the local to the world: Belonging spaces among young Europeans]. In O. Galand & B. Roudet (Eds.), *Les jeunes Européens et leurs valeurs* [Young Europeans and their values] (pp. 177–203). Paris: La Découverte.

Berzonsky, M. D. (1990). Self-construction over the life-span: A process perspective on identity formation. *Advances in Personal Construct Psychology*, 1, 155–186.

Bierman, A. (2006). Does religion buffer the effects of discrimination on mental health? Differing effects by race. *Journal for the Scientific Study of Religion*, 45, 551–566.

Bornstein, M. H. (Ed.). (2010). *Handbook of cultural developmental science*. New York: Psychology Press.

Boseret, L. (2009). *Développement philosophique, spirituel et religieux: Impact du système éducatif* [Philosophical, spiritual and religious development: Impact of the educational system]. Unpublished Master's thesis, Université catholique de Louvain, Louvain-la-Neuve.

Boyatzis, C. J. (2009). Examining religious and spiritual development during childhood and adolescence. In M. de Souza, L. J. Francis, J. O'Higgins-Norman, & D. G. Scott (Eds.), *International handbook of education for spirituality, care and wellbeing* (pp. 51–68). Dordrecht, Netherlands: Springer.

Boyer, P. (2001). *Religion explained*. New York: Basic Books.

Bréchon, P. (2003). Integration into Catholicism and Protestantism in Europe: The impact on moral and political values. In L. Halman & O. Riis (Eds.), *Religion and secularizing society: The Europeans'religion at the end of the 20th century* (pp. 114–161). Leiden, Netherlands: Brill.

Buxant, C., & Saroglou, V. (2008). Feeling good, but lacking autonomy: Closed-mindedness on social and moral issues in new religious movements. *Journal of Religion and Health*, 47, 17–31.

Cadge, W., & Ecklund, E. H. (2007). Immigration and religion. *Annual Review of Sociology*, 33, 359–379.

Campiche, R. J. (Ed.). (1997). *Cultures jeunes et religions en Europe* [Youth cultures and religions in Europe]. Paris: Cerf.

Cawley, M. J., III, Martin, J. E., & Johnson, J. A. (2000). A virtue approach to personality. *Personality and Individual Differences*, 28, 997–1013.

Cheung, C. K., & Yeung, J. W. K. (2011). Meta-analysis of relationships between religiosity and constructive and destructive behaviors among adolescents. *Children and Youth Services Review*, 33, 376–385.

Digman, J. M. (1997). Higher-order factors of the Big Five. *Journal of Personality and Social Psychology*, 73, 1246–1256.

Dillon, M. (2007). Age, generation, and cohort in American religion and spirituality. In J. A. Beckford & N. J. Demerath, III (Eds.), *The Sage handbook of the sociology of religion* (pp. 526–546). London: Sage.

Duriez, B., Smits, I., & Goossens, L. (2008). The relation between identity styles and religiosity in adolescence: Evidence from a longitudinal perspective. *Personality and
Individual Differences, 44*, 1022–1031.

Duriez, B., & Soenens, B. (2006). Personality, identity styles, and religiosity: An integrative study among late and middle adolescents. *Journal of Adolescence, 29*,
119–135.

Duriez, B., Soenens, B., & Beyers, W. (2004). Personality, identity styles, and religiosity: An integrative study among late adolescents in Flanders (Belgium). *Journal of
Personality, 72*, 877–908.

Ellison, C. G., Finch, B. K., Ryan, D. N., & Salinas, J. J. (2009). Religious involvement
and depressive symptoms among Mexican-origin adults in California. *Journal of
Community Psychology, 37*, 171–193.

Ellison, C. G., Musick, M. A., & Henderson, A. K. (2008). Balm in Gilead: Racism, religious involvement, and psychological distress among African American adults.
Journal for the Scientific Study of Religion, 47, 291–309.

Erikson, E. H. (1968). *Identity: Youth and crisis*. Oxford: Norton.

Flanagan, K., & Jupp, P. C. (Eds.). (2007). *A sociology of spirituality*. Burlington, VT:
Ashgate.

Fontaine, J. R. J., Duriez, B., Luyten, P., Corveleyn, J., & Hutsebaut, D. (2005).
Consequences of a multi-dimensional approach to religion for the relationship
between religiosity and value priorities. *International Journal for the Psychology of
Religion, 15*, 123–143.

Francis, L. J. (2009). Comparative empirical research in religion: Conceptual and operational
challenges within empirical theology. In L. J. Francis, M. Robbins, & J. Astley (Eds.),
Empirical theology in texts and tables (pp. 127–152). Leiden, Netherlands: Brill.

Friedman, M., & Saroglou, V. (2010). Religiosity, psychological acculturation to the host
culture, self-esteem and depressive symptoms among stigmatized and nonstig-
matized religious immigrant groups in Western Europe. *Basic and Applied Social
Psychology, 32*, 185–195.

Fulton, A. S. (1997). Identity status, religious orientation, and prejudice. *Journal of Youth
and Adolescence, 26*, 1–11.

Gartner, J., Larson, D. B., & Allen, G. D. (1991). Religious commitment and mental
health: A review of the empirical literature. *Journal of Psychology and Theology,
19*, 6–25.

Ghorpade, J., Lackritz, J. R., & Singh, G. (2006). Intrinsic religious orientation among
minorities in the United States: A research note. *International Journal for the
Psychology of Religion, 16*, 51–62.

Good, M., & Willoughby, T. (2008). Adolescence as a sensitive period for spiritual development. *Child Development Perspectives, 2*, 32–37.

Güngör, D., Fleischmann, F., & Phalet, K. (2011). Religious identification, beliefs, and
practices among Turkish Belgian and Moroccan Belgian Muslims: Intergenerational
continuity and acculturative change. *Journal of Cross-Cultural Psychology, 42*,
1356–1374.

Hardy, S. A., Pratt, M. W., Pancer, S. M., Olsen, J. A., & Lawford, H. L. (2011). Community
and religious involvement as contexts of identity change across late adolescence
and emerging adulthood. *International Journal of Behavioral Development, 35*,
125–135.

Hazan, C., & Shaver, P. R. (1987). Romantic love conceptualized as an attachment process. *Journal of Personality and Social Psychology*, **52**, 511–524.

Heaven, P. C. L., & Ciarrocchi, J. (2007). Personality and religious values among adolescents: A three-wave longitudinal analysis. *British Journal of Psychology*, **98**, 681–694.

Holden, G. W., & Vittrup, B. (2010). Religion. In M. H. Bornstein (Ed.), *Handbook of cultural developmental science* (pp. 279–295). New York: Psychology Press.

Hood, R. W., Jr., Hill, P. C., & Spilka, B. (2009). *The psychology of religion: An empirical approach* (4th ed.). New York: Guilford.

Hunsberger, B., Pratt, M., & Pancer, S. M. (2001). Adolescent identity formation: Religious exploration and commitment. *Identity: An International Journal of Theory and Research*, **1**, 365–386.

(2002). A longitudinal study of religious doubts in high school and beyond: Relationships, stability, and searching for answers. *Journal for the Scientific Study of Religion*, **41**, 255–266.

Hutsebaut, D. (1997). Identity statuses, ego-integration, God representation and religious cognitive styles. *Journal of Empirical Theology*, **10**, 39–54.

John, O. P., Donahue, E. M., & Kentle, R. L. (1991). *The Big Five Inventory: Versions 4a and 54*. Berkeley, CA: University of California, Berkeley, Institute of Personality and Social Research.

Juang, L., & Syed, L. M. (2008). Ethnic identity and spirituality. In R. M. Lerner, R. W. Roeser, & E. Phelps (Eds.), *Positive youth development and spirituality: From theory to research* (pp. 262–284). West Conshohocken, PA: Templeton Foundation Press.

Kelemen, D. (2004). Are children 'intuitive theists'? *Psychological Science*, **15**, 295–301.

Kézdy, A., Martos, T., Boland, V., & Horváth-Szabó, K. (2011). Religious doubts and mental health in adolescence and young adulthood: The association with religious attitudes. *Journal of Adolescence*, **34**, 39–47.

King, P. E., & Roeser, R. W. (2009). Religion and spirituality in adolescent development. In R. M. Lerner & L. Steinberg (Eds.), *Handbook of adolescent psychology* (3rd ed., pp. 435–478). Hoboken, NJ: Wiley.

Kivisto, P. (2007). Rethinking the relationship between ethnicity and religion. In J. A. Beckford & N. J. Demerath, III (Eds.), *The SAGE Handbook of the sociology of religion* (pp. 490–510). London: Sage.

Klaassen, D. W., & McDonald, M. J. (2002). Quest and identity development: Re-examining pathways for existential search. *International Journal for the Psychology of Religion*, **12**, 189–200.

Kosek, R. B. (1999). Adaptation of the Big Five as a hermeneutic instrument for religious constructs. *Personality and Individual Differences*, **27**, 229–237.

Leak, G. K. (2009). An assessment of the relationship between identity development, faith development, and religious commitment. *Identity: An International Journal of Theory and Research*, **9**, 201–218.

Lee, J., Miller, L., & Chang, E. S. (2006). Religious identity among Christian Korean-American adolescents. *Psychological Reports*, **98**, 43–56.

Lerner, R. M., Roeser, R. W., & Phelps, E. (Eds.). (2008). *Positive youth development and spirituality: From theory to research*. West Conshohocken, PA: Templeton Foundation Press.

Lodi-Smith, J., & Roberts, B. W. (2007). Social investment and personality: A meta-analysis of the relationships of personality traits to investment in work, family, religion, and volunteerism. *Personality and Social Psychology Review*, **11**, 68–86.

Marcia, J. E. (1980). Identity in adolescence. In J. Andelson (Ed.), *Handbook of adolescent psychology* (pp. 159–187). New York: Wiley.

Markon, K. E., Krueger, R. F., & Watson, D. (2005). Delineating the structure of normal and abnormal personality: An integrative hierarchical approach. *Journal of Personality and Social Psychology*, **88**, 139–157.

Markstrom-Adams, C., Hofstra, G., & Dougher, K. (1994). The ego-virtue of fidelity: A case for the study of religion and identity formation in adolescence. *Journal of Youth and Adolescence*, **23**, 453–469.

Markstrom-Adams, C., & Smith, M. (1996). Identity formation and religious orientation among high school students from the United States and Canada. *Journal of Adolescence*, **19**, 247–261.

Markstrom, C. A. (1999). Religious involvement and adolescent psychosocial development. *Journal of Adolescence*, **22**, 205–221.

McCullough, M. E., Enders, C. K., Brion, S. L., & Jain, A. R. (2005). The varieties of religious development in adulthood: A longitudinal investigation of religion and rational choice. *Journal of Personality and Social Psychology*, **89**, 78–89.

McCullough, M. E., Tsang, J. A., & Brion, S. (2003). Personality traits in adolescence as predictors of religiousness in early adulthood: Findings from the Terman Longitudinal Study. *Personality and Social Psychology Bulletin*, **29**, 980–991.

McKinney, J. P., & McKinney, K. G. (1999). Prayer in the lives of late adolescents. *Journal of Adolescence*, **22**, 279–290.

Meeus, W., Iedema, J., Helsen, M., & Vollebergh, W. (1999). Patterns of adolescent identity development: Review of literature and longitudinal analysis. *Developmental Review*, **19**, 419–461.

Nyborg, H. (2009). The intelligence-religiosity nexus: A representative study of white adolescent Americans. *Intelligence*, **37**, 81–93.

Olatunji, B. O., Williams, N. L., Tolin, D. F., Sawchuck, C. N., Abramowitz, J. S., Lohr, J. M., & Elwood, L. S. (2007). The disgust scale: Item analysis, factor structure, and suggestions for refinement. *Psychological Assessment*, **19**, 281–317.

Oser, F. K., Scarlett, W. G., & Bucher, A. (2006). Religious and spiritual development throughout the lifespan. In W. Damon & R. M. Lerner (Eds.), *Handbook of child psychology: Vol. 1. Theoretical models of human development* (6th ed., pp. 942–998). Hoboken, NJ: Wiley.

Padilla-Walker, L. M., McNamara Barry, C., Carroll, J. S., Madsen, S., & Nelson, L. J. (2008). Looking on the bright side: The role of identity status and gender on positive orientations during emerging adulthood. *Journal of Adolescence*, **31**, 451–467.

Puffer, K. A., Pence, K. G., Graverson, T. M., Wolfe, M., Pate, E., & Clegg, S. (2008). Religious doubt and identity formation: Salient predictors of adolescent religious doubt. *Journal of Psychology and Theology*, **36**, 270–284.

Quintana, S. M., & McKown, C. (Eds.). (2008). *Handbook of race, racism, and the developing child*. New York: Wiley.

Rangel, U., & Saroglou, V. (2010). Religiosity and acculturation among expatriates of high socio-economic status: An exploratory study. Unpublished raw data.

Roberts, B. W., Wood, D., & Caspi, A. (2008). The development of personality traits in adulthood. In O. P. John, R. W. Robins, & L. A. Pervin (Eds.), *Handbook of personality: Theory and research* (3rd ed., pp. 375–398). New York: Guilford.

Roccas, S., Sagiv, L., Schwartz, S. H., & Knafo, A. (2002). The Big Five personality factors and personal values. *Personality and Social Psychology Bulletin*, **28**, 789–801.

Roccas, S., & Schwartz, S. H. (1997). Church-state relations and the association of religiosity with values: A study of Catholics in six countries. *Cross-Cultural Research*, **31**, 356–375.

Roehlkepartain, E. C., King, P. E., Wagener, L., & Benson, P. L. (Eds.). (2006). *The handbook of spiritual development in childhood and adolescence*. Thousand Oaks, CA: Sage.

Sabatier, C., Mayer, B., Friedlmeier, M., Lubiewska, K., & Trommsdorff, G. (2011). Religiosity, family orientation, and life satisfaction of adolescents in four countries. *Journal of Cross-Cultural Psychology*, **42**, 1375–1393.

Saroglou, V. (2002). Religion and sense of humor: An a priori incompatibility? Theoretical considerations from a psychological perspective. *Humor: International Journal of Humor Research*, **15**, 191–214.

(2003). Spiritualité moderne: Un regard de psychologie de la religion [Modern spirituality: A psychology of religion perspective]. *Revue Théologique de Louvain*, **34**, 473–504.

(2006). Quête d'unité: Spécificité religieuse d'une fonction non nécessairement religieuse [Quest for unity: Religious specifics of a non-necessarily religious function]. *Archives de Psychologie*, **72**, 161–181. English version retrieved from http://www.uclouvain.be/cps/ucl/doc/psyreli/documents/QuestForUnity.pdf

(2008). Religion and psychology of values: "Universals" and changes. In E. Agazzi & F. Minazzi (Eds.), *Science and ethics: The axiological contexts of science* (pp. 247–272). Brussels: Peter Lang.

(2010). Religiousness as a cultural adaptation of basic traits: A Five Factor Model perspective. *Personality and Social Psychology Review*, **14**, 108–125.

(2011). Believing, bonding, behaving, and belonging: The big four religious dimensions and cultural variation. *Journal of Cross-Cultural Psychology*, **42**, 1320–1340.

Saroglou, V., & Cohen, A. B. (in press). Cultural and cross-cultural psychology of religion. In R. F. Paloutzian & C. L. Park (Eds.), *Handbook of the psychology of religion and spirituality* (2nd ed.). New York: Guilford.

Saroglou, V., Delpierre, V., & Dernelle, R. (2004). Values and religiosity: A meta-analysis of studies using Schwartz's model. *Personality and Individual Differences*, **37**, 721–734.

Saroglou, V., & Galand, P. (2004). Identities, values, and religion: A study among Muslim, other immigrant, and native Belgian young adults after the 9/11 attacks. *Identity: An International Journal of Theory and Research*, **4**, 97–132.

Saroglou, V., & Hanique, B. (2006). Jewish identity, values, and religion in a globalized world: A study of late adolescents. *Identity: An International Journal of Theory and Research*, **6**, 231–249.

Saroglou, V., & Mathijsen, F. (2007). Religion, multiple identities, and acculturation: A study of Muslim immigrants in Belgium. *Archive for the Psychology of Religion*, **29**, 177–198.

Saroglou, V., & Muñoz-García, A. (2008). Individual differences in religion and spirituality: An issue of personality traits and/or values. *Journal for the Scientific Study of Religion*, **47**, 83–101.

Saucier, G., & Skrzypińska, K. (2006). Spiritual but not religious? Evidence for two independent dispositions. *Journal of Personality*, **74**, 1257–1292.

Scardigno, R., & Saroglou, V. (2009a, April). *Religious doubt in adolescence: Types of doubts and the role of sensitivity to moral hypocrisy.* Paper presented at the 7th Annual Mid-Year Conference on Religion and Spirituality, Columbia, Maryland, USA.

(2009b, August). *Religious doubts in adolescence: Integrating the many dimensions of adolescents' development.* Paper presented at the International Association for Psychology of Religion Conference, Vienna, Austria.

Scarlett, W. G., & Alberts, A. (2010). Religious and spiritual development across the lifespan. In R. M. Lerner (Series Ed.), M. Lamb, & A. Freund (Vol. Eds.), *The handbook of lifespan development: Vol. 2. Social and emotional development* (pp. 631–682). Hoboken, NJ: Wiley.

Schmitz, M. F., & Baer, J. C. (2001). The vicissitudes of measurement: A confirmatory factor analysis of the Emotional Autonomy Scale. *Child Development*, **72**, 207–219.

Schwartz, S. H. (1992). Universals in the content and structure of values: Theoretical advances and empirical tests in 20 countries. In M. Zanna (Ed.), *Advances in experimental social psychology* (Vol. 25, pp.1–65). Orlando, FL: Academic Press.

(2003). A proposal for measuring value orientations across nations. In *European Social Study Questionnaire development report* (Chapter 7). Retrieved from http://www.europeansocialsurvey.org/

(2007). Value orientations: Measurement, antecedents and consequences across nations. In R. Jowell, C. Roberts, R. Fitzgerald, & G. Eva (Eds.), *Measuring attitudes cross-nationally: Lessons from the European Social Survey* (pp. 169–204). London: Sage.

Schwartz, S. H., & Huismans, S. (1995). Value priorities and religiosity in four western religions. *Social Psychology Quarterly*, **58**, 88–107.

Sirin, S. R., Bikmen, N., Mir, M., Fine, M., Zaal, M., & Katsiaficas, D. (2008). Exploring dual identification among Muslim-American emerging adults: A mixed methods study. *Journal of Adolescence*, **31**, 259–279.

Tzuriel, D. (1984). Sex role typing and ego identity in Israeli, Oriental, and Western adolescents. *Journal of Personality and Social Psychology*, **46**, 440–457.

Verhoeven, D., & Hutsebaut, D. (1995). Identity status and religiosity. *Journal of Empirical Theology*, **8**, 46–64.

Verkuyten, M., & Thijs, J. (2010). Religious group relations among Christian, Muslim and nonreligious early adolescents in the Netherlands. *The Journal of Early Adolescence*, **30**, 27–49.

Verkuyten, M., & Yildiz, A. A. (2007). National (dis)identification, and ethnic and religious identity: A study among Turkish-Dutch Muslims. *Personality and Social Psychology Bulletin*, **33**, 1448–1462.

Viladrich, A., & Abraído-Lanza, A. F. (2009). Religion and mental health among minorities and immigrants in the U.S. In S. Loue & M. Sajatovic (Eds.), *Determinants of minority mental health and wellness* (pp. 149–174). New York: Springer.

Wagener, L. M., & Malony, H. N. (2006). Spiritual and religious pathology in childhood and adolescence. In E. C. Roehlkepartain, P. E. King, L. Wagener, & P. L. Benson (Eds.), *The handbook of spiritual development in childhood and adolescence* (pp. 137–139). Thousand Oaks, CA: Sage.

Warren, A. E. A., Lerner, R. M., & Phelps, E. (Eds.). (2011). *Thriving and spirituality among youth: Research perspectives and future possibilities*. New York: Wiley.

Wink, P., Ciciolla, L., Dillon, M., & Tracy, A. (2007). Religiousness, spiritual seeking, and personality: Findings from a longitudinal study. *Journal of Personality*, 75, 1051–1070.

Woolley, J. D., & Phelps, K. E. (2001). The development of children's beliefs about prayer. *Journal of Cognition and Culture*, 1, 139–166.

Zinnbauer, B. J., & Pargament, K. I. (2005). Religiousness and spirituality. In R. F. Paloutzian & C. L. Park (Eds.), *Handbook of the psychology of religion and spirituality* (pp. 21–42). New York: Guilford.

Zuckerman, M. (1971). Dimensions of sensation seeking. *Journal of Consulting and Clinical Psychology*, 36, 45–52.

18 Hindu Religious Values and Their Influence on Youths in India

Ramesh Chandra Mishra

Abstract

This chapter explores Hindu religious values and their influence on adolescent development in India. The position adopted in the chapter is that peoples' values and beliefs are influenced by the respective religious features of the groups embedded in the wider cultural context. Guided by this assumption, the chapter describes the contextual features of youth development in India, the values exemplified in traditional Hindu religious texts, and the process of transmission of those values among adolescents. As an illustration of the socialization process, empirical studies on children and adolescents from traditional and modern schools are described. Some details of adolescents' daily activities are presented and their effects on the development of adolescents' values are analyzed. The evidence suggests that among Indian youths, traditional collectivistic values coexist with modern individualistic values, which are considered necessary for societal development in the present-day world. It is argued that traditional Hindu values can be seen as universally human values, and they can be meaningfully used for promoting positive and healthy youth development in the Indian context. The chapter contributes to the existing knowledge about youth development by its focus on different types of schools that provide very different kind of socialization experiences.

This chapter presents a brief account of Hindu religious values and their influence on youths in India. The chapter is organized in three sections. The first section describes the contextual features of youth development in India, the traditional Hindu religious values, and the processes of their transmission among youths using the Indian theoretical perspectives. The next section presents some research studies carried out with children and adolescents of traditional and modern schools; it also describes a study that analyzes daily activities of adolescents in traditional and modern schools and examines their consequences for the development of values. The last section contains concluding comments to argue that Hindu religious values are basically human values, and they can be fruitfully utilized for healthy youth development in India.

Cultural Background and Theoretical Perspectives

Adolescence in Cultural Context

In today's world, India stands as the second most populous country in which adolescents constitute about 22.8 percent of the total population (Registrar General & Census Commissioner, India, 2001). Until a decade ago, the adolescents of India did not draw the attention of researchers or policy planners. In the year 2000, the U.N. Agency Working Group on Population and Development prepared a document, "Adolescents in India: A Profile," which suddenly drew people's attention to adolescents. Standing at the threshold of adulthood and "at risk" of physical, psychological, and social health problems (e.g., HIV, stress, crime), this population needs opportunities to develop necessary psychological and social competencies and skills.

In developmental psychology, adolescence is viewed as a period of transition from the stage of childhood to adulthood. Adolescents have to deal with several rapidly concurrent biological, hormonal, physical, and behavioral changes in their lives. They also have to master several tasks for functioning effectively in psycho-social domains. Hence, some researchers consider adolescence as a phase of life that has a biological beginning and a social end (Sharma, 1996). The nature of adolescence is still a globally debated issue. Apart from the age range, which constitutes the period of "adolescence," people in different cultures also hold different notions of adolescence. Brown, Larson, and Saraswathi (2002) have presented an account of youths growing in eight different regions of the world. The picture of adolescents' lives drawn in this volume is very different from the accounts presented by Western psychologists. The evidence Brown et al. (2002) present challenges the universal hypothesis that adolescence is a period of "stress and storm."

Socialization plays an important role in determining how the changes taking place among adolescents are viewed and handled. Whereas the diversity of youths' experiences in different parts of the world is fairly well-known (Verma & Saraswathi, 2002), there is also evidence for the emergence of a "world youth community," which exhibits several commonalities such as the style of dressing, habits of eating, preference for music and dance, and so on. These commonalities do mold or enfold across cultures in ways that help people ascribe specific meaning to them in each culture. Brown and Larson (2002) argue that understanding adolescents requires a thorough analysis of the historical and cultural contexts in which their lives are nested.

In the Indian cultural context, the word "adolescent" is used less commonly in day-to-day interactions and more at the level of program development (Singh, 1997). In *Srimadbhagavadgita* (a traditional Indian scripture), "*kaumaarya*" (puberty), "*yauvan*" (adulthood) and "*jaraa*" (old age) are regarded as the periods of life associated with significantly distinguishable physical and psychological changes (Section 2, Verse 13). Because *kaumaarya* marks the transition to a stage of life where children have to accept responsibility for everything they do, the ancient texts prescribe very specific duties and codes of conduct. These are deeply rooted in the peoples' psyche and influence the cultural practices directed toward adolescents (Verma & Saraswathi, 2002).

Research indicates that boys and girls undergo very different experiences during adolescence in India. A girl child in India is considered to have low status in the family and society, and is exposed to several discriminatory practices (Anandalakshmi, 1994). This observation does not hold true everywhere (Singh & Mishra, 1999); however, for girls, the beginning of puberty means greater participation in household activities and restrictions on movement. Factors like urban or rural residence, tribal or non-tribal setting, and religious group affiliation also characterize differences in adolescence. For example, in rural settings, both boys and girls share responsibilities and participate in adult activities at an early age. Boys help parents in agricultural and other economic activities, whereas girls share household activities (e.g., cleaning house, cooking, fetching water, child care). In the tribal groups, economic pressures on the lives of boys and girls are almost of the same level, which result in low enrollment and high dropout of both genders from school during the primary years of education (Mishra, 2008).

Despite these differences, some features are common to all adolescents in India. For example, "traditionalism" and "family orientation" are fairly strong in both rural and urban settings (Mishra, Mayer, Trommsdorff, Albert, & Schwarz, 2005: Mishra & Tiwari, 1980). Parental involvement in and behavioral control of children is high in both groups (S. Sinha, 2009; S. Sinha & Mishra, 2009). Emotional interdependence among family members, respect for and obedience to elders, care of the young, and support to the weak stand as cardinal values; they are considered as *dharma* (sacred duties) of adolescents in the majority of Indian families.

Religion as a Context for Human Development

Religion represents an important component of the overall context within which human development takes place (Dasen, 2003). An interesting feature of religion is its resistance to change in cultural contact situations (Camilleri & Malewska-Peyre, 1997). Ethnographic accounts document considerable differences in religious beliefs and practices across cultures, but their consequences for human development still remain largely speculative (Dasen, 2003).

Religion performs many functions in personal and social lives of individuals and groups. It influences the ways in which people see the world and organize their lives (Nsamenang, 2002). That is how it becomes an important source of values and beliefs. Osho (2006) points out that religious value makes society a better place of living for human beings. In the Western world, people who hold religious values and beliefs experience greater happiness and positive affect than those who do not (Heaven et al, 2010). Tripathi (2009) indicates religion as a major aspiration for the advancement of values. Religion also dictates ethical and moral principles and codes of conduct for individual as well as social living (Emmons, 2005). The quest of all religions for the search of "truth" engages them with an "other worldly reality" (D. Sinha, 1988) or power that is often labeled as "God."

For many religious persons in India, God is the deepest experiential reality that can be achieved intuitively through engagement in processes like disengaged action, devotion, and meditation – not something to be understood through the use of intellectual capacities. The lives and teachings of the founders of all great religions present us with numerous examples of value-based living to experience that reality.

The search for values is a common theme in all religious and philosophical traditions. In the ancient inquiries, the focus was on the ultimate, absolute, or terminal values. In the Greek tradition, Truth, Goodness, and Beauty were recognized as the ultimate values. In India these values are labeled as *"satyam, shivam, sundaram,"* all of which find an important place in the Hindu system of thought. In the *vedant* philosophical tradition, *sat, chit,* and *anand* (existence, consciousness, and bliss) are regarded as absolute values; they represent the characteristic features of the universal Self, called *paramatman.* In the Buddhist tradition, liberation from the bondage of *dukha* (sorrow) is held as the terminal value.

Whereas people do have faith in one religion or another, there are variations within every religious tradition. It is also evident that people's values and beliefs do not simply depend on the religious group they belong to; the wider cultural context in which individuals negotiate their daily lives and their experiences in other cultural contexts play important roles in the organization of beliefs and values, including the understanding of their meaning in a given culture. Hence, the understanding of religious values and their influence on youths require analyses not only in the context of traditional religion, but also in the context of the long history of people's contact with the members of other religious groups. For example, in India, this could be the contact with Muslims or Christians who came from outside and ruled the country for centuries.

The effect of religion today is not confined to people's attitudes, beliefs, values, and practices; it is a critical factor governing political activities at the global level. History tells us that during the last 2,000 years, the world has witnessed almost 14,000 wars. Why should there be so many wars if people were truly religious in the strict sense of the term? Intergroup conflicts and episodes of violence currently evident in different parts of the world suggest that religion is not simply a matter of individuals' faith, and its practice is also not restricted to the attainment of peace, happiness, positive states of mind and other healthy conditions of human existence. Although religion cannot be isolated from the overall sociocultural context, many believe that religion provides people with an ideal kind of social frame to assess the conditions of their lives relative to those of others (Nsamenang, 2002). R.C. Tripathi (1988) has argued that religious values, if properly aligned with individual and social development, can help people pursue their aspirations and live a life filled with dignity and hope.

Hindu Religious Traditions and Values

As indicated earlier, religion is always contained in a set of beliefs and values that people hold and practice in their lives. Some researchers (Saraswathi & Ganapathy, 2002; Shweder, 2008) have discussed the dominant Hindu religious belief systems and the way they shape psychological dispositions and behavior of Indians. However, a distinction between religious beliefs and values needs to be maintained. Rakodi (2010) indicates that religious beliefs may be considered as the cosmological lenses through which people make sense of the world they live in, whereas religious values refer to the moral or ethical principles that people use (or tend to use) for making crucial decisions in their lives. These principles are derived from the religious tradition to which one feels a sense of belonging.

Hindu religion (also called Hinduism) refers to the faith systems of a group of people who live mainly in India (about 900 million), but also now in many other countries. Sanskrit or Hindi language has no word that can convey the exact meaning of the word "religion" the way it is interpreted today. Its literal translation is "*dharma*," which broadly connotes a sense of "duty" (Prabhupad, 2006). This could be toward oneself, the family, the community, the nation, and all of humanity. Thus, Hinduism is regarded as "a way of life," not a compartmentalized belief system or religion like Christianity or Islam (Radhakrishnan & Moore, 1957). In the long history of its evolution, Hinduism has developed through several stages and taken several forms (Reat, 1990), which also presents great difficulty in accepting it as one particular religion.

The difficulty is further complicated by the coexistence of polytheistic (faith in many gods and goddesses), monotheistic, and atheistic elements in Hindu religion. However, the dominant Hindu belief system is that there is just one God, the Supreme Being. Several gods and goddesses mentioned in Hindu religious scriptures are only the diverse expressions of a single Almighty God. The presence of many gods essentially provides people with several ways to fulfill their psychological needs. The scholars of religious studies find this idea a bit difficult to digest; for them Hindu religion is extremely complex and not easily reconcilable, since one can make anything out of this faith system.

Traditional scriptures regard nonviolence (in thought, speech and action) as the highest religion for mankind (*ahimsa paramo dharmah*). According to Mahabharat (an old religious scripture of the Hindus), "*prbhavarthaya bhutanam dharmapravachanm kritam, yah syat prabhava sanyuktah sa dharma iti nishchayah*" (Shantiparva, Chapter 109, Verse 10); that is, "preventing violence against organisms is the main purpose and the chief characteristic of *dharma*." This value (of nonviolence), which distinguishes human beings from animals, is reflected in many different ways, called the indicators of *dharma*. The 10 salient indicators include: endurance or fortitude, forgiveness, self-control, non-theft (i.e., respect for other's possessions), internal and external purity (not causing harm to anyone physically or mentally), restraint of sensuous desires, wisdom, learning-based knowledge, truthfulness, and absence of anger or patience (*dhritih kshama damosteyam shauchmindriya nigrahah, dheeh vidya satyamakrodho dashakam dharma lakshanam*). As elements of *samanya dharma* (general duties), they make one's life virtuous. In extraordinary situations, one is recommended to pursue *vishisht dharma* (specific duties).

On the practical side, all Hindu systems of thought agree that there are four main values to be acquired and brought to perfection in the course of one's life. Two of them are *artha* (wealth) and *kama* (sensuality). They signify material prosperity, good health, and long life, which are desired by most Indians. As worldly values, these are considered legitimate as long as they are kept in their places, their limits are recognized, and they are not suppressive of other values. The third value, called *dharma*, includes all roles and obligations that characterize individual and social duties as well as ethical responsibilities. The fourth value is *moksha* (release from the cycle of birth and rebirth), which is a supreme spiritual ideal, but not achievable without proper experience and resolution of the former three values.

According to Hindu religious tradition, soul is eternal, immutable, and everlasting (Srimadbhavadgita, Section, 2, Verse, 24). What we do in this life determines the form the soul will take in each new life. This is known as the law of *karma* (action), which simply means "as you sow, so shall you reap." Performing one's duties in righteous ways constitutes good *karma* (called *dharma)*, whereas violating one's duties constitutes bad *karma* (called *adharma*). Thus, the doctrine of *karma* permits freedom in the sense that it is under our control, and not determined by cosmic or environmental forces. Shweder (2008) illustrates how this principle is used in the explanation of sufferings in India.

There is further division of *karma* according to an individual's stages of life, which is contained in the concept of *ashram* (stations of life). One's duties are set by the stage of life in which (s)he has arrived at a particular point of time. Conduct according to the prescribed roles or duties for each stage of life is called "*ashram dharma*," which is very close to the notion of "stage-specific developmental tasks." The four stages are: (1) *brahmacharya* – the period of childhood and youth in which relevant knowledge and life skills need to be acquired, (2) *grihastha* – the long period of a household characterized by the acceptance of personal, familial, and social responsibilities, (3) *vaanaprastha* – the period of disengagement from worldly affairs through the practice of meditation and reflection, and (4) *sanyaas* – the period of complete renunciation of worldly things, self-control, and realization of *Brahman* (the True Self). Successful passage through these stations leads to fulfillment of life and attainment of liberation, the final destination in the journey of human life. There is also a division of *karma* according to time, place, and person. The same action (*karma*) cannot be desirable all the time, at all places, and with all persons. Knowledge of these subtle delicacies of *karma* can make all actions religious and life dedicated to the pursuit of *dharma*.

Associated with the belief in "many lives" is the notion of *sanchit karma* (accumulated deeds) from the previous lives. Just as some trees produce fruits after many years, so do many of our deeds. Some effects observed in one's present life might be the outcome of actions performed in the previous lives. Thus, the theory of *karma* largely serves as a guiding principle for Hindus' behavior.

This discussion indicates that Hinduism is neither a philosophical enterprise, nor a religion that provides individuals with opportunity for the outlet of emotions, called the "religion instinct." It is a meaningful science of life and an art of practical living. It simply means the organization of life according to certain principles that ensure well-being.

Transmission of Hindu Religious Values

The admission that Hinduism is a "way of life" does away with the distinction among personal, social, religious, ethical, and moral values. If the well-being of "self" and "others" is the prime goal of all academic discourse and practical concerns about values, then all values may be labeled as "human values." In fact, the discussion of values revolves around "human beings," who themselves are not independent entities according to Hindu tradition. They are part of a "textured" eco-cultural system (Berry, 1983), which is shared by other individuals, human groups, and many creatures of nature. Realization of the fact that everything in this universe is interconnected and innervated by a common energy (called God) is the first step in being religious, since it generates respect for all around us, be it human beings, animals, plants, rivers, or mountains.

In the agrarian Hindu society, these values were informally transmitted to children in the course of their development. Parents and others present in the children's environment served as models. Many rituals were organized to signify respect for nature (e.g., trees, rivers, animals). They inscribed in children's minds the idea of humans' "coexistence" with nature. Family was the main institution of children's education, except for a few privileged ones who could go to traditional Sanskrit schools (Mishra & Vajpayee, 2008). During the 19th century, the British opened schools (called "modern schools"; Mishra, 1988), which introduced new syllabi, new methods of education, and a new set of values into the Indian society.

Technological advancements and changing socioeconomic conditions in India over the last decades have generated some threats to the continuity of traditional values. Exposure to the larger world and life patterns of other cultural groups, competitive demands of the consumer economy, and high parental expectations from children have considerably changed Indian family dynamics (Mishra & Sinha, 2010). Differential skills, abilities, values, and coping styles required for effective functioning in the present context are stressful for adolescents and parents (Verma & Saraswathi, 2002). Having grown up in fairly stable and tightly knit social groups (D. Sinha, 1988), many parents find difficulty in dealing with the pressures of social and cultural change. The suspected utility of traditional values for success in the present scenario often puts them in states of conflict. Parents feel helpless in presenting adolescents with a "successful" role model. Saraswathi and Pai (1997) indicate that even highly modern parents exhibit a tendency of falling back on traditions when they find adolescents violating traditionally established social norms with respect to marriage, career choice, or general living. A "swing back reaction" (Mishra, Sinha, & Berry, 1996) in the course of social and cultural change is not a new phenomenon.

Despite these changes witnessed in many Indian families, several traditional values are still observed; in crisis situations, they function as a guide. Indian adolescents still have a family to return to; this serves as a "cushion" against many adversities during adolescents' transition to adulthood.

Empirical Studies

We now turn to examine the relationship between religion, schooling, and development in India by citing some empirical studies. As indicated earlier, cosmology and religion form an important component of a child's overall cultural context. Silberman (2005, p. 645) shows that religion has the "…function as a lens through which reality is perceived and interpreted." Emmons (2005) believes that religion provides meaning to an individual's life. However, because of its focus on the sacred, this meaning system is very different from other meaning systems (Silberman, 2005).

Considering religion as an important factor in human behavior, many studies in other parts of the world have examined the relationship of religiousness with personality characteristics of individuals (Emmons & Paloutzian, 2003; Heaven & Ciarrochi, 2007), but the focus is mainly on adults. Given that adolescents face a variety of other challenges (Smetana, Campione-Barr, & Metzger, 2006), especially in developing countries, the role of religious values in their psychological functioning needs serious research.

In comprehending adolescent development studies, researchers have relied mainly on data obtained from adolescents who attend Western- or modern-type schools. These schools lay emphasis on "progressive" or "secular" values. In culturally plural societies, pursuit of these values as "ideals" is considered essential for individual and social development. The common assumption is that "religious values" are inimical to healthy human and social development, although some empirical studies also suggest that they can promote social and emotional well-being (see Heaven et al., 2010).

India provides an interesting site for studying adolescents in traditional schools (often called "religious schools"). These schools have existed for centuries; even today they exist in large numbers in many old cities (e.g., Varanasi) as an alternative to modern schools. Mishra and Vajpayee (2008) present a detailed account of Sanskrit schooling in India and its effects on cognitive and social development of children. How the routines of life and values nurtured in these schools influence adolescents' development are not much known.

Some research related to intergroup relations (Berry & Kalin, 1995) indicates that respect for and confidence in one's own cultural identity and values generates respect and tolerance for other groups. However, it greatly depends on how one defines confidence. If it is taken in the sense of "security," then respect and tolerance for other groups are the likely outcomes. If it is defined in terms of "own group glorification," the likely outcomes are intolerance and prejudiced behavior for other groups.

Bano and Mishra (2005) examined the perception and evaluation of Hindu and Muslim children (aged 3–12 years) in India. Using a *Model Identification Task* and a *Projective Prejudice Task* they found that, irrespective of age, both Hindu and Muslim children generally preferred their own group members and expressed a slightly negative attitude toward other group members. They also evaluated their own group's performance positively and attributed negative outcomes to the out-group. In another study with Hindu and Muslim adolescent girls (aged 14–20 years), Bano and Mishra (2009) reported almost similar results, that is, positive rating of own group model, negative rating of other group model, positive evaluation of own group's performance, attribution of negative outcomes to the out-group, and greater in-group bias on the part of Muslim as compared to Hindu girls.

Using the same tasks, Bano and Mishra (2006) compared children (3–12 years of age) within traditional Sanskrit schools (called *pathshala*), traditional Muslim schools (called *madarsa*) and modern schools with respect to the awareness of their ethnic identity (i.e., Hindu and Muslim) and prejudice against other group members. Findings revealed no significant difference between traditional and modern school children with respect to the *awareness* of their own and the other group. With respect to *preference* for own and the other group, significant differences were noted between the school groups in terms of children's overall liking of other group members (modern>traditional) and choice of own group members for interpersonal activities (traditional>modern). Hindu children, either of traditional or modern school, did not show any significant evidence of in-group bias, whereas Muslim children of modern schools displayed greater in-group bias than those of the traditional schools.

In another study with the same three school groups, but this time with adolescent boys and girls, Bano and Mishra (in press) examined their relational orientations toward each other. The findings indicated a stronger "separation" orientation (i.e., positive evaluation of own culture and identity, and desire to keep away from participation in the life of the other cultural group) among traditional Sanskrit than traditional Muslim school pupils. These findings give the impression that Hindu adolescents attending Sanskrit schools maintain greater psychological distance from Muslim adolescents than do traditional Muslim school adolescents from Hindus. Gender difference in this respect was negligible.

These studies illustrate what may happen to children in different schools in a multicultural society. The lack of significant correlation noted between prejudice scores of mothers and their children (Bano & Mishra, 2006) suggests that school may be a potential influence on children's development, at least in the social domain of functioning. Segregation of children from those of other groups, as it happens in traditional schools, may generate different beliefs, values, and dynamics of relationship when they grow up as adolescents.

Adolescents in Traditional and Modern Schools at Varanasi

In the preceding section we have seen that Sanskrit schools are an important source of transmission of Hindu religious values among pupils. In the following pages, we will look at a study carried out with adolescent pupils attending traditional Sanskrit (n = 125) and modern (n = 132) schools at Varanasi. The ancient city at the bank of the holy river Ganges has witnessed a continuous history of human population for the last 3,500 years. A strong Hindu belief is that anyone graced to die in Varanasi attains liberation from the cycle of birth and rebirth. The belief is so strongly shared that even today several thousand old people stay in the city awaiting their death.

For centuries, Varanasi has been regarded as the "cultural capital of India" (Kumar, 2000). Knowledge in fields like philosophy, yoga, music, dance, and other art forms was developed and disseminated in commune-like organizations, called "*math*" and "*ashram.*" Many of them also operated a Sanskrit school on their premises; these schools have played a major role in preserving traditional Indian knowledge and culture (Mishra & Vajpayee, 2008). Some educational traditions (e.g., oral tradition), which run the risk of extinction in modern times, are still preserved in Sanskrit schools at Varanasi. During the last decades, several Hindi- and English-medium schools have also come up in the city. The *math, ashram,* and Sanskrit schools organize education for Hindu children in traditional ways, whereas other schools promise education in ways that can link children to the upcoming market economy.

Daily Activities and the Values of Adolescents

The specific influences Sanskrit schools provide on adolescent pupils are: (1) regulation of life by prescribing highly fixed and timed routines, (2) practice of moral values in daily life, (3) exposure to different sets of experiences, (4) placing different demands on life, (5) encouraging different activities, and (6) emphasizing different sets of values (Mishra & Vajpayee, 2008). Some of these influences do not operate on adolescents in other schools, whereas others operate in very different ways.

In this study, a home questionnaire (Dasen & Mishra, 2010) was used to assess the level of *affluence* of pupils' families, but no significant difference between the two school groups was found. Spot observations and semi-structured interviews were focused on *activities* the pupils generally engaged in. The *religious beliefs* were assessed with the help of a scale, which contained five extrinsic (e.g., visiting temples) and five intrinsic (e.g., faith in God) aspects of religion. Each participant also rated on a 5-point scale the importance of values like altruism, helping, obedience, responsibility, nurturance, tolerance, sharing, and compassion.

The percentage of the time Sanskrit and Hindi school pupils spent on different activities was calculated. The main activities of Sanskrit school pupils along with the percentage of the time spent on each were: bathing in the Holy Ganges (20 percent), visiting temples (20 percent), morning prayers (15 percent), evening prayers (10 percent), praying with meals (5 percent), religious activities (10 percent), studies (15 percent) and cleaning of room or clothes (5 percent). Taken together, the Sanskrit school pupils spent almost 80 percent of their active time (out of 16 hours) on activities, which may be characterized either as religious or religion-related. Play and other leisure-time activities did not form part of the life of Sanskrit school adolescents.

Pupils of the Hindi school stood almost in sharp contrast to those of the Sanskrit school. Main activities of Hindi school pupils and the percentage of the time spent on each activity were: study and homework (30 percent), watching television (25 percent), playing (20 percent), tutoring (10 percent), visiting friends (5 percent), shopping (5 percent), and household activities

(5 percent). These pupils were engaged in diverse activities (e.g., playing, watching TV), and they also spent considerable time on study and homework, but religious activities were altogether absent from their life.

With respect to the importance of Hindu values, the analysis revealed that, in comparison to Hindi school, pupils of the Sanskrit school generally gave greater importance to all values, but significantly more so to obedience, responsibility, tolerance, sharing, and compassion.

Do these values have any effect on the day-to-day life of Sanskrit school pupils? The observational data suggest some general and some specific effects. The general effects include polite and highly respectful behavior with teachers, elders, or visitors. The specific effects include maintenance of cultural heritage (e.g., language, dressing) and less participation in social and recreational activities (e.g., visiting friends, going to the cinema). These features of Sanskrit school pupils give the impression that they are traditional, away from acculturative influences, cut off from the mainstream society, and less susceptible to change.

Observational and interview data provide evidence for many behavioral qualities to be more strongly placed among Sanskrit than Hindi school adolescents. For example, these adolescents show great flexibility between independent and interdependent modes of functioning according to the demands of the situation. Commitment to ethical and moral values in daily life, strong sense of cultural identity, non-selfish orientation, satisfaction with minimal resources, effort oriented philosophy of life, happiness, optimism, and overall satisfaction are some distinctive qualities that can distinguish Sanskrit school adolescents from those in Hindi schools.

These observations suggest that culture-level generalizations about adolescents' behaviors are not appropriate. Hindu religious values do not influence all adolescents in similar ways. The nature of schooling engages adolescents in different sets of activities and emphasizes some values more than others. These experiences can produce different hierarchies of values or transform the relative importance of some values for adolescents. The values Sanskrit school adolescents strongly endorsed characterize "human values," which are concerned with distribution of human welfare. Hindu religious values thus cannot be blamed to be inimical to individual or social development. Competition is not the only method of promoting human and social development (Krishnamurti, 1998; Osho, 2005). In the absence of appropriate resource structures in India, enhanced aspirations of individuals resulting from competition have led to corrupt practices that destroy the spirit of development (J.B.P. Sinha, 1968).

Evaluation of the influence of Hindu religious values on youth development in India requires focus on factors that produce individual variations within the same group. The variability displayed by the school effect in our study warns against advancing group-level generalizations. In studies of youth development in the "majority world" (Kagitcibasi, 1998), the effects of type and quality of schooling need to be examined more seriously.

The model of development based on technological and economic advancement of societies has been under attack for the last few decades. It involves severe human and social costs and makes life occupied with endless meaningless routines (R.C. Tripathi, 1988). Social scientists (e.g., Capra, 1982) have argued in favor of an ecological model that focuses on the "capacity building" of individuals and societies so that they can organize their life around their own values and objectives. The values need to be channeled for creating a society that is "meaningful" (Krishnamurti, 2001), that is, a society that prevents youths from being thrown into conflict with their own cultural traditions and utilizes the cultural strengths in harnessing their activities toward productive ends.

Concluding Comments

In spite of infinite variety and diversity present in people's social and cultural backgrounds in India, there is a common outlook based on human values that constitutes the Indian psyche (Sinha, 1988). The relevance of many traditional Hindu religious values in the present-day context is not only questioned, but some of them are also viewed as obstacles to economic development (Singh, 1975).

Before judging the utility of religious values, however, we need to know more about the religious values that are strongly held by Indians today. We also need to examine the extent to which they regulate people's behavior in diverse settings (e.g., personal life, family, workplace). Values inferred on the basis of Hindu religious scriptures are not enough to appreciate youth development in India. Although religious values do have potential to shape the outlook of youths, paucity of empirical studies will not permit to claim that the same has actually happened there. As D. Sinha (1988, p. 48) points out, "There is always a gap between the expected or the ideal and the actual. From the ancient texts and scriptures to contemporary attitudes and behaviour of Indians is a big leap fraught with dangers of erroneous overgeneralizations."

Some research (Mishra, 1994, D. Sinha & Tripathi, 1994) indicates that among Indian youths, traditional collectivistic values may stay in a state of coexistence with modern individualist values. Such findings suggest that Indian youths can deal with traditional and modern values at the same time. Strong representation of religious values among the youths of both Sanskrit and Hindi schools provides support for this contention. In the multicultural context of India, values like tolerance, sharing, and compassion are extremely important for promoting positive intergroup relationships.

There is a need for serious research on both traditional religious and progressive modern values by using samples from the diverse cultural and social settings of India. The contexts in which religious values tend to work toward destructive ends, instead of playing constructive roles, need to be examined using innovative methods of study and analysis.

Inculcation of values among youths is an issue of national concern. The youth who have fallen prey to drug abuse, crime, delinquency, violence, and other social problems have become the main focus; prevention for those "at risk" of these problems is a major challenge. In schools, colleges, and universities, "value studies" are now offered as small but compulsory courses (Tripathi, 2009). We may hope that in the upcoming years, these efforts will be intensive and widespread. We may also hope that value education programs will be carried out in real field settings with a focus on value-related conflicts confronting youths in their day-to-day lives. Theory without a sound empirical research base is blind. Hindu religious values derived from traditional scriptures require serious research to discover their structural and functional patterns across different population groups.

REFERENCES

Anandalakshmi, S. (1994). *The girl child and the family: An action research study*. New Delhi: Ministry of Human Resource Development.
Bano, S., & Mishra, R. C. (2005). Intergroup perception and evaluation among Hindu and Muslim children. *Psychological Studies*, **50**, 144–149.
(2006). Effect of schooling on the development of social identity and prejudice in Hindu and Muslim children. *Indian Journal of Community Psychology*, **2**, 168–182.
(2009). Social identity and inter-group perception of Hindu and Muslim adolescents. *Journal of Psychosocial Research*, **4**, 417–425.
(in press). Relational orientations of Muslim and Hindu adolescents in traditional and modern schools. In P. Singh, P. Bain, L. Chan-Hoong, G. Misra, & Y. Ohtsubo (Eds.), *Identity, multiculturalism and changing societies: Psychological, group and cultural processes*. Australia: MacMillan.
Berry, J. W. (1983). Textured contexts: Systems and situations in cross-cultural psychology. In S. H. Irvine & J. W. Berry (Eds.), *Human assessment and cultural factors* (pp. 117–126). New York: Plenum.

Berry, J. W., & Kalin, R. (1995). Multicultural and ethnic attitudes in Canada: An overview of the 1991 national survey. *Canadian Journal of Behavioural Science, 27,* 301–320.

Brown, B. B., & Larson, R. W. (2002). The kaleidoscope of adolescence: Experience of the world's youth at the beginning of the 21st century. In B.B. Brown, R.W. Larson, & T. S. Saraswathi (Eds.), *The world's youth: Adolescence in eight regions of the globe* (pp. 1–20). Cambridge: Cambridge University Press.

Brown, B. B., Larson, R. W., & Saraswathi, T. S. (2002). *The world's youth: Adolescence in eight regions of the globe.* Cambridge: Cambridge University Press.

Camilleri, C, & Malewska-Peyre, H. (1997). Socialization and identity strategies. In J. W. Berry, P. R. Dasen, & T. S. Saraswathi (Eds.), *Handbook of cross-cultural psychology, Vol. 2* (pp. 41–68). Boston: Allyn & Bacon.

Capra, F. (1982). *The turning point.* New York: Simon & Schuster.

Dasen, P. R. (2003). Theoretical frameworks in cross-cultural developmental psychology: An attempt at integration. In T. S. Saraswathi (Ed.), *Cross-cultural perspectives in human development* (pp. 128–165). New Delhi: Sage.

Dasen, P. R., & Mishra, R. C. (2010). *Development of geocentric spatial language and cognition: An eco-cultural perspective.* Oxford: Cambridge University Press.

Emmons, R. A. (2005). Striving for the sacred: Personal goals, life meaning, and religion. *Journal of Social Issues, 61,* 731–745.

Emmons, R. A., & Paloutzian, R. F. (2003). The psychology of religion. *Annual Review of Psychology, 54,* 377–402.

Heaven, P. C. L., & Ciarrochi, J. (2007). Personality and religious values among adolescents: A three-wave longitudinal analysis. *British Journal of Psychology, 98,* 681–694.

Heaven, P. C. L., Ciarrochi, J., & Leeson, P. (2010). Parental style and religious values among teenagers: A 3-year prospective analysis. *The Journal of Genetic Psychology, 171,* 93–99.

Kagitcibasi, C. (1998). *Family, self and human development across cultures: Theory and applications.* Hillsdale, NJ: Erlbaum.

Krishnamurti, J. (1998). *Education and the significance of life.* Varanasi: Krishnamurti Foundation India.

(2001). *The matter of culture.* Chennai: Krishnamurti Foundation India.

Kumar, N. (2000*). Lessons from schools: The history of education in Banaras.* New Delhi: Sage.

Mishra, R. C. (1988). Learning strategies among children in modern and traditional schools. *Indian Psychologist, 5,* 21–26.

(1994). Individualist–collectivist orientations across generations. In U. Kim, H. C. Triandis, C. Kagitcibasi, S. Choi, & G. Yoon (Eds.), *Individualism and collectivism: Theory, method, and practice* (pp. 225–238). Thousand Oaks, CA: Sage.

(2008). Education of tribal children in India. In P. R. Dasen & A. Akkari (Eds.), *Educational theories and practices from the majority world* (pp. 145–167). New Delhi: Sage.

Mishra, R. C., Mayer, B., Trommsdorff, G., Albert, I., & Schwarz, B. (2005). *The value of children in urban and rural India: Cultural background and empirical findings* (pp. 143–170). Berlin: Pabst.

Mishra, R. C., Sinha, D., & Berry, J. W. (1996). *Ecology, acculturation and psychological adaptation: A study of Adivasis in Bihar.* New Delhi: Sage.

Mishra, R. C., & Sinha, S. (2010). Intergenerational differences in values in rural and urban settings of India. *Asian Journal of Social Psychology* (communicated).

Mishra, R. C., & Tiwari, B. B. (1980). Intergenerational attitudes: A psychological analysis. *Psychologia*, **23**, 160–166.

Mishra, R. C., & Vajpayee, A. (2008). Sanskrit schools in India. In P. R. Dasen & A. Akkari (Eds.), *Educational theories and practices from the majority world* (pp. 245–267). New Delhi: Sage.

Nsamenang, A. B. (2002). Adolescence in sub-Saharan Africa: An image constructed from Africa's triple inheritance. In B. B., Brown, R. W. Larson, & T. S. Saraswathi (Eds.), *The world's youth: Adolescence in eight regions of the globe* (pp. 61–104). Cambridge: Cambridge University Press.

Osho (2005). *Jeevan kya hai* (What is life). Delhi: Hind Pocket Books.

(2006). *Krishna: The man and his philosophy*. Mumbai: Jaico Publishing House.

Prabhupad, A. C. B. S. (2006). *Dharma: The way of transcendence*. Mumbai: The Bhaktivedant Book Trust.

Radhakrishnan, S., & Moore, C. A. (1957). *A source book in Indian Philosophy*. Princeton, NJ: Princeton University Press.

Reat, N. R. (1990). *Origins of Indian psychology*. Berkeley, CA: Asian Humanities Press.

Registrar General & Census Commissioner, India (2001). *Census of India 2001. Provisional population totals*. Paper 1 of 2001, Series 1. New Delhi: Government of India.

Rakodi, C. (2010). *Lived religion: Religious values and beliefs in developing countries and their implications for development thinking, policy and practice*. Proceedings of the Development Studies Association Conference, 5th November, London.

Saraswathi, T. S., & Ganapathy, H. (2002). Indian parents' ethnotheories as reflections of Hindu scheme of child and human development. In H. Keller, Y. H. Poortinga, & A. Scholmerich (Eds.) *Between culture and biology: Perspectives on ontogenetic development* (pp. 80–88). Cambridge: Cambridge University Press.

Saraswathi, T. S., & Pai, S. (1997). Socialisation in the Indian context. In D. Sinha & H. S. R. Kao (Eds.), *Asian perspectives in psychology* (pp. 74–92). New Delhi: Sage.

Sharma, N. (1996). *Identity of the adolescent girl*. New Delhi: Discovery Publishing.

Shweder, R. A. (2008). The cultural psychology of suffering: The many meanings of health in Orissa, India (and elsewhere). *Ethos*, **3**, 60–77.

Silberman, I. (2005). Religion as a meaning system: Implications for the new millennium. *Journal of Social Issues*, **61**, 641–663.

Singh, A. K. (1975). Hindu culture and economic development in India. *Indian Social and Psychological Publication*, **1**, 89–108.

Singh, D. V., & Mishra, R. C. (1999). Parent–child interaction in rural and urban settings. *Social Science International*, **15**, 67–74.

Singh, S. (1997). *Adolescent reproductive and sexual health needs in India*. Paper presented at the Workshop on Youth Across Asia, Kathmandu, Nepal

Sinha, D. (1988). Basic Indian values and behavior dispositions in the context of national development: An appraisal. In D. Sinha & H. S. R. Kao (Eds.), *Social values and development: Asian perspectives* (pp. 31–55). New Delhi: Sage.

Sinha, D., & Tripathi, R. C. (1994). Individualism in a collectivist culture: A case of coexistence of opposites. In U. Kim, H. C. Triandis, C. Kagitcibasi, S. Choi, & G. Yoon

(Eds.), *Individualism and collectivism: Theory, method, and practice* (pp. 123–136). Thousand Oaks, CA: Sage.

Sinha, J. B. P. (1968). The n-Ach and n-cooperation under limited/unlimited resource condition. *Journal of Experimental Social Psychology*, **4**, 233–246.

Sinha, S. (2009). *Gender differences in intergenerational relationships in the context of socialization.* Unpublished doctoral thesis, Banaras Hindu University.

Sinha, S., & Mishra, R. C. (2009). Role of value of children, parenting style and attachment pattern in intergenerational relationship. In A. K. Tiwari (Ed.), *Psychological perspectives on social issues and human development* (pp. 167–178). New Delhi: Concept.

Smetana, J. G., Campione-Barr, N., & Metzger, A. (2006). Adolescent development in interpersonal and societal contexts. *Annual Review of Psychology*, **57**, 255–284.

Tripathi, A. N. (2009). *Human values.* New Delhi: New Age International.

Tripathi, R. C. (1988). Aligning values to development in India. In D. Sinha & H. S. R. Kao (Eds.), *Social values and development: Asian perspectives* (pp. 315–333). New Delhi: Sage.

Verma, S., & Saraswathi, T. S. (2002). Adolescence in India: Street urchins or Silicon Valley. In B. B. Brown, R. W. Larson, & T. S. Saraswathi (Eds.), *The world's youth: Adolescence in eight regions of the globe* (pp. 105–140). Cambridge: Cambridge University Press.

Index